Windows 3 SECRETS Testimonials

"Windows 3 SECRETS includes more undocumented features, tips, and
techniques than any other Windows book."
— David Angell & Brent Heslop, *Computer Currents*

"It's a fantastic book. No serious Windows consultant
can do without it. It's invaluable."
— John Schmitt, Managing Editor, *Windows Shopper's Guide*

"Windows 3 SECRETS is a storehouse of facts and figures that will help
anyone to get more out of Windows . . . . Get Brian Livingston's book."
— Tom Swan, *PC Techniques*

"There is just too much great stuff here . . .
Simply stated, this book is a must for serious programmers."
— Mitchell Waite, *BasicPro* Magazine

"This is the most thorough, well-researched, and in-depth computer book
I've ever seen. It solved every nightmarish problem I had with Windows."
— Wes Thomas, Contributing Editor, *Windows Journal*

"Windows 3 SECRETS is full of juicy tidbits for real Windows users. I use it myself!"
— Stewart Alsop, Editor-in-Chief, *InfoWorld*

"Readable, friendly, and packed with information; every regular
Windows user will find at least one nifty fix between these covers."
— Tim Phillips, *Personal Computer Magazine,* UK

"Inside are literally thousands of little-known tidbits. . . ."
— Gordon McComb, *Computer Buyer's Guide & Handbook*

"Windows 3 SECRETS is packed with information you can't get anywhere else."
— Daniel J. Willis, Senior Analyst, 3M Corporation

Windows 3.1 SECRETS, 2nd Edition Testimonials

"Livingston is a Windows consultant, and it is hard to imagine
any tricks or tips he has omitted from these 990 pages.
True to the name, there are lots of undocumented hints
that can make life easier for the intermediate and advanced user."
— Peter H. Lewis, *New York Times*

"Brian Livingston's ability to reveal powerful undocumented features in Windows
is astounding. His tips, descriptions of undocumented features and advice
are a must-read for any power Windows user."
— Michael Elgan, *Windows Magazine*

"I think just about every conceivable chapter/topic is covered.
As with all IDG publications, this one is a real value."
— Frank H. Thomas, Narberth, Great Britain

"Brian Livingston has brought Windows 3.1 to newer and greater heights
by covering everything and putting it into one complete, easy to read book."
— Ryan Pellicano, Sacramento, CA

"This book is well written. I enjoyed reading it, as well as
using the 'SECRETS' to optimize Windows' performance."
— Betty Hsia, Westford, MA

"Nice job of anticipating user confusions — and setting them right
in diverse hardware and software configurations."
— C.O. McGorkey, San Diego, CA

"I feel fortunate to have 'stumbled' onto this book.
I'm telling all my friends about it!"
— Virgil Poe, Katy, TX

The IDG Books SECRETS Advantage

Windows 95 SECRETS, 3rd Edition, is part of the SECRETS series of books brought to you by IDG Books Worldwide. We designed the SECRETS series because we know how much you appreciate insightful and comprehensive works from computer experts. Authorities in their respective areas, the authors of the SECRETS books have been selected for their ability to enrich your daily computing tasks.

The formula for a book in the SECRETS series is simple: Give an expert a forum to pass on his or her knowledge to readers. A SECRETS author, rather than the publishing company, directs the organization, pace, and treatment of the subject matter. SECRETS authors maintain close contact with end users through feedback from articles, training sessions, e-mail exchanges, user group participation, and consulting work. Because our authors know the realities of daily computer use and are directly tied to the reader, our SECRETS books have a strategic advantage.

SECRETS authors have the experience to approach a topic in the most efficient manner, and we know that you, the reader, will benefit from a "one-on-one" relationship with the author. Our research shows that readers make computer book purchases because they want expert advice on a product. Readers want to benefit from the author's experience, so the author's voice is always present in a SECRETS series book.

In addition, the author is free to include or recommend useful software in a SECRETS book. The software that accompanies a SECRETS book is not intended to be casual filler but is linked to the content, theme, or procedures of the book. We know that you will benefit from the included software.

You will find what you need in this book whether you read it from cover to cover, section by section, or simply one topic at a time. As a computer user, you deserve a comprehensive resource of answers. We at IDG Books Worldwide are proud to deliver that resource with *Windows 95 SECRETS,* 3rd Edition.

Brenda McLaughlin
Vice President and Group Publisher
Internet: YouTellUs@IDGBooks.com

Windows® 95 SECRETS™
3rd Edition

by Brian Livingston and Davis Straub

IDG Books Worldwide, Inc.
An International Data Group Company

Foster City, CA ♦ Chicago, IL ♦ Indianapolis, IN ♦ Southlake, TX

Windows® 95 SECRETS™, 3rd Edition

Published by
IDG Books Worldwide, Inc.
An International Data Group Company
919 E. Hillsdale Blvd., Suite 400
Foster City, CA 94404
http://www.idgbooks.com (IDG Books Worldwide Web site)

Library of Congress Catalog Card No.: 95-78408

ISBN: 1-56884-453-0

Printed in the United States of America

10 9 8 7 6 5

3B/RX/RS/ZW/IN

Distributed in the United States by IDG Books Worldwide, Inc.

Distributed by Macmillan Canada for Canada; by Transworld Publishers Limited in the United Kingdom and Europe; by WoodsLane Pty. Ltd. for Australia; by WoodsLane Enterprises Ltd. for New Zealand; by Longman Singapore Publishers Ltd. for Singapore, Malaysia, Thailand, and Indonesia; by Simron Pty. Ltd. for South Africa; by Toppan Company Ltd. for Japan; by Distribuidora Cuspide for Argentina; by Livraria Cultura for Brazil; by Ediciencia S.A. for Ecuador; by Addison-Wesley Publishing Company for Korea; by Ediciones ZETA S.C.R. Ltda. for Peru; by WS Computer Publishing Company, Inc., for the Philippines; by Unalis Corporation for Taiwan; by Contemporanea de Ediciones for Venezuela. Authorized Sales Agent: Anthony Rudkin Associates for the Middle East and North Africa.

For general information on IDG Books Worldwide's books in the U.S., please call our Consumer Customer Service department at 800-762-2974. For reseller information, including discounts and premium sales, please call our Reseller Customer Service department at 800-434-3422.

For information on where to purchase IDG Books Worldwide's books outside the U.S., please contact our International Sales department at 415-655-3172 or fax 415-655-3295.

For information on foreign language translations, please contact our Foreign & Subsidiary Rights department at 415-655-3021 or fax 415-655-3281.

For sales inquiries and special prices for bulk quantities, please contact our Sales department at 415-655-3200 or write to the address above.

For information on using IDG Books Worldwide's books in the classroom or for ordering examination copies, please contact our Educational Sales department at 800-434-2086 or fax 817-251-8174.

For press review copies, author interviews, or other publicity information, please contact our Public Relations department at 415-655-3000 or fax 415-655-3299.

For authorization to photocopy items for corporate, personal, or educational use, please contact Copyright Clearance Center, 222 Rosewood Drive, Danvers, MA 01923, or fax 508-750-4470.

is a trademark under exclusive license to IDG Books Worldwide, Inc., from International Data Group, Inc.

SECRETS™ is a trademark under exclusive license to IDG Books Worldwide, Inc., from International Data Group, Inc.

About the Authors

Brian Livingston is the author of IDG Books' bestselling *Windows 3 Secrets*; *Windows 3.1 Secrets,* 2nd Edition; *More Windows 3.1 Secrets;* and coauthor of *Windows Gizmos,* a collection of shareware and freeware tools and games. His books are printed in more than 20 languages. In addition to writing books, Mr. Livingston is a contributing editor of *InfoWorld* and *Windows Sources* magazines, and has been a contributing editor of *PC Computing, PC World,* and other magazines. He was a recipient of the 1991 Award for Technical Excellence from the National Microcomputer Managers Association.

Davis Straub is a Windows multimedia software developer. He is the former president of Generic Software, developer of Generic CADD, the first successful affordable CADD program. Author of more than 200 articles, Mr. Straub first wrote for *PC World* magazine in 1983.

Publishing History

Windows 3 Secrets	Published 1991
Windows 3.1 Secrets, 2nd Edition	Published 1992
Windows 95 Secrets, 3rd Edition	Published 1995

ABOUT IDG BOOKS WORLDWIDE

Welcome to the world of IDG Books Worldwide.

IDG Books Worldwide, Inc., is a subsidiary of International Data Group, the world's largest publisher of computer-related information and the leading global provider of information services on information technology. IDG was founded more than 25 years ago and now employs more than 8,500 people worldwide. IDG publishes more than 275 computer publications in over 75 countries (see listing below). More than 60 million people read one or more IDG publications each month.

Launched in 1990, IDG Books Worldwide is today the #1 publisher of best-selling computer books in the United States. We are proud to have received eight awards from the Computer Press Association in recognition of editorial excellence and three from *Computer Currents'* First Annual Readers' Choice Awards. Our best-selling *...For Dummies®* series has more than 30 million copies in print with translations in 30 languages. IDG Books Worldwide, through a joint venture with IDG's Hi-Tech Beijing, became the first U.S. publisher to publish a computer book in the People's Republic of China. In record time, IDG Books Worldwide has become the first choice for millions of readers around the world who want to learn how to better manage their businesses.

Our mission is simple: Every one of our books is designed to bring extra value and skill-building instructions to the reader. Our books are written by experts who understand and care about our readers. The knowledge base of our editorial staff comes from years of experience in publishing, education, and journalism — experience we use to produce books for the '90s. In short, we care about books, so we attract the best people. We devote special attention to details such as audience, interior design, use of icons, and illustrations. And because we use an efficient process of authoring, editing, and desktop publishing our books electronically, we can spend more time ensuring superior content and spend less time on the technicalities of making books.

You can count on our commitment to deliver high-quality books at competitive prices on topics you want to read about. At IDG Books Worldwide, we continue in the IDG tradition of delivering quality for more than 25 years. You'll find no better book on a subject than one from IDG Books Worldwide.

John J. Kilcullen

John Kilcullen
President and CEO
IDG Books Worldwide, Inc.

**Eighth Annual
Computer Press
Awards ≥1992**

**Ninth Annual
Computer Press
Awards ≥1993**

**Tenth Annual
Computer Press
Awards ≥1994**

**Eleventh Annual
Computer Press
Awards ≥1995**

IDG Books Worldwide, Inc., is a subsidiary of International Data Group, the world's largest publisher of computer-related information and the leading global provider of information services on information technology. International Data Group publishes over 275 computer publications in over 75 countries. Sixty million people read one or more International Data Group publications each month. International Data Group's publications include: **ARGENTINA:** Buyer's Guide, Computerworld Argentina, PC World Argentina; **AUSTRALIA:** Australian Macworld, Australian PC World, Australian Reseller News, Computerworld, IT Casebook, Network World, Publish, Webmaster; **AUSTRIA:** Computerwelt Osterreich, Networks Austria, PC Tip Austria; **BANGLADESH:** PC World Bangladesh; **BELARUS:** PC World Belarus; **BELGIUM:** Data News; **BRAZIL:** Annuário de Informática, Computerworld, Connections, Macworld, PC Player, PC World, Publish, Reseller News, Supergamepower; **BULGARIA:** Computerworld Bulgaria, Network World Bulgaria, PC & MacWorld Bulgaria; **CANADA:** CIO Canada, Client/Server World, ComputerWorld Canada, InfoWorld Canada, NetworkWorld Canada, WebWorld; **CHILE:** Computerworld Chile, PC World Chile; **COLOMBIA:** Computerworld Colombia, PC World Colombia; **COSTA RICA:** PC World Centro America; **THE CZECH AND SLOVAK REPUBLICS:** Computerworld Czechoslovakia, Macworld Czech Republic, PC World Czechoslovakia; **DENMARK:** Communications World Danmark, Computerworld Danmark, Macworld Danmark, PC World Danmark, Techworld Denmark; **DOMINICAN REPUBLIC:** PC World Republica Dominicana; **ECUADOR:** PC World Ecuador; **EGYPT:** Computerworld Middle East, PC World Middle East; **EL SALVADOR:** PC World Centro America; **FINLAND:** MikroPC, Tietoverkko, Tietoviikko; **FRANCE:** Distributique, Hebdo, Info PC, Le Monde Informatique, Macworld, Reseaux & Telecoms, WebMaster France; **GERMANY:** Computer Partner, Computerwoche, Computerwoche Extra, Computerwoche FOCUS, Global Online, Macwelt, PC Welt; **GREECE:** Amiga Computing, GamePro Greece, Multimedia World; **GUATEMALA:** PC World Centro America; **HONDURAS:** PC World Centro America; **HONG KONG:** Computerworld Hong Kong, PC World Hong Kong, Publish in Asia; **HUNGARY:** ABCD CD-ROM, Computerworld Szamitastechnika, Internetto online Magazine, PC World Hungary, PC-X Magazin Hungary; **ICELAND:** Tolvuheimur PC World Island; **INDIA:** Information Communications World, Information Systems Computerworld, PC World India, Publish in Asia; **INDONESIA:** InfoKomputer PC World, Komputek Computerworld, Publish in Asia; **IRELAND:** ComputerScope, PC Live!; **ISRAEL:** Macworld Israel, People & Computers/Computerworld; **ITALY:** Computerworld Italia, Macworld Italia, Networking Italia, PC World Italia; **JAPAN:** DTP World, Macworld Japan, Nikkei Personal Computing, OS/2 World Japan, SunWorld Japan, Windows NT World, Windows World Japan; **KENYA:** PC World East African; **KOREA:** Hi-Tech Information, Macworld Korea, PC World Korea; **MACEDONIA:** PC World Macedonia; **MALAYSIA:** Computerworld Malaysia, PC World Malaysia, Publish in Asia; **MALTA:** PC World Malta; **MEXICO:** Computerworld Mexico, PC World Mexico; **MYANMAR:** PC World Myanmar; **NETHERLANDS:** Computer! Totaal, LAN Internetworking Magazine, LAN World Buyers Guide, Macworld Netherlands, Net, WebWereld; **NEW ZEALAND:** Absolute Beginners Guide and Plain & Simple Series, Computer Buyer, Computer Industry Directory, Computerworld New Zealand, MTB, Network World, PC World New Zealand; **NICARAGUA:** PC World Centro America; **NORWAY:** Computerworld Norge, CW Rapport, Datamagasinet, Financial Rapport, Kursguide Norge, Macworld Norge, Multimediaworld Norge, PC World Ekspress Norge, PC World Nettverk, PC World Norge, PC World ProduktGuide Norge; **PAKISTAN:** Computerworld Pakistan; **PANAMA:** PC World Panama; **PEOPLE'S REPUBLIC OF CHINA:** China Computer Users, China Computerworld, China InfoWorld, China Telecom World Weekly, Computer & Communication, Electronic Design China, Electronics Today, Electronics Weekly, Game Software, PC World China, Popular Computer Week, Software Weekly, Software World, Telecom World; **PERU:** Computerworld Peru, PC World Profesional Peru, PC World SoHo Peru; **PHILIPPINES:** Click!, Computerworld Philippines, PC World Philippines, Publish in Asia; **POLAND:** Computerworld Poland, Computerworld Special Report Poland, Cyber, Macworld Poland, Networld Poland, PC World Komputer; **PORTUGAL:** Cerebro/PC World, Computerworld/Correio Informático, Dealer World Portugal, Mac*In/PC*In Portugal, Multimedia World; **PUERTO RICO:** PC World Puerto Rico; **ROMANIA:** Computerworld Romania, PC World Romania, Telecom Romania; **RUSSIA:** Computerworld Russia, Mir PK, Publish, Seti; **SINGAPORE:** Computerworld Singapore, PC World Singapore, Publish in Asia; **SLOVENIA:** Monitor; **SOUTH AFRICA:** Computing SA, Network World SA, Software World SA; **SPAIN:** Communicaciones World España, Computerworld España, Dealer World España, Macworld España, PC World España; **SRI LANKA:** Infolink PC World; **SWEDEN:** CAP&Design, Computer Sweden, Corporate Computing Sweden, Internetworld Sweden, it.branschen, Macworld Sweden, MaxiData Sweden, MikroDatorn, Nätverk & Kommunikation, PC World Sweden, PCaktiv, Windows World Sweden; **SWITZERLAND:** Computerworld Schweiz, Macworld Schweiz, PCtip; **TAIWAN:** Computerworld Taiwan, Macworld Taiwan, NEW ViSiON/Publish, PC World Taiwan, Windows World Taiwan; **THAILAND:** Publish in Asia, Thai Computerworld; **TURKEY:** Computerworld Turkiye, Macworld Turkiye, Network World Turkiye, PC World Turkiye; **UKRAINE:** Computerworld Kiev, Multimedia World Ukraine, PC World Ukraine; **UNITED KINGDOM:** Acorn User UK, Amiga Action UK, Amiga Computing UK, Apple Talk UK, Computing, Macworld, Parents and Computers UK, PC Advisor, PC Home, PSX Pro, The WEB; **UNITED STATES:** Cable in the Classroom, CIO Magazine, Computerworld, DOS World, Federal Computer Week, GamePro Magazine, InfoWorld, I-Way, Macworld, Network World, PC Games, PC World, Publish, Video Event, THE WEB Magazine, and WebMaster; online webzines: JavaWorld, NetscapeWorld, and SunWorld Online; **URUGUAY:** InfoWorld Uruguay; **VENEZUELA:** Computerworld Venezuela, PC World Venezuela; and **VIETNAM:** PC World Vietnam.   10/22/96

Dedication

This book is dedicated to Margie Livingston and Belinda Boulter.

Credits

Senior Vice President and Group Publisher
Brenda McLaughlin

Acquisitions Manager
Gregory S. Croy

Acquisitions Editor
Ellen L. Camm

Software Acquisitions Editor
Tracy Lehman Cramer

Marketing Manager
Melisa M. Duffy

Managing Editor
Andy Cummings

Administrative Assistant
Laura J. Moss

Editorial Assistant
Timothy J. Borek

Production Director
Beth Jenkins

Supervisor of Project Coordination
Cindy L. Phipps

Supervisor of Page Layout
Kathie S. Schutte

Supervisor of Graphics and Design
Shelley Lea

Production Systems Specialist
Debbie J. Gates

Project Editors
Sandy Reed
Mary Bednarek
Mary C. Corder

Editors
Jim Grey
Pat O'Brien

Technical Editors
Brian Moura
Beth Slick
Pat O'Brien
Jim Grey

Project Coordinator
Valery Bourke

Layout and Graphics
Cameron Booker
Linda M. Boyer
Elizabeth Cárdenas-Nelson
Jae J. Cho
Dominique DeFelice
Maridee V. Ennis
Angela F. Hunckler
Mark C. Owens
Carla C. Radzikinas
Gina Scott

Proofreaders
Jennifer Kaufeld
Melissa D. Buddendeck
Rachel Garvey
Dwight Ramsey
Robert Springer

Indexer
Sherry Massey

Production Administration
Tony Augsburger
Todd Klemme
Jason Marcuson
Jacalyn L. Pennywell
Leslie Popplewell
Patricia R. Reynolds
Theresa Sánchez-Baker
Melissa Stauffer
Bryan Stephenson

Acknowledgments

No book is the sole work of its authors. While our efforts were focused on writing this work, many others provided the help we needed to complete it. Our editor, Sandy Reed, turned our best efforts into much more readable text. Brian Moura, Beth Slick, Jim Grey, and Pat O'Brien, our technical reviewers, checked our findings to make sure they weren't idiosyncratic.

We spent a considerable amount of time on the Windows 95 beta forum on CompuServe and in working over the phone with Microsoft Personal Systems support personnel. Our fellow Windows 95 beta testers provided us with crucial assistance and guidance. The Windows 95 beta support people at Microsoft were top notch and deserve great praise from everyone in the industry for their commitment to quality and their willingness to help make Windows 95 a better product.

Throughout this book we have mentioned various beta testers and support personnel who were especially helpful and insightful. Without their assistance *Windows 95 Secrets,* 3rd Edition, would not be nearly as useful.

(The publisher would like to give special thanks to Patrick J. McGovern, without whom this book would not have been possible.)

Contents at a Glance

Table of Contents

Chapter 24: The Mighty Mouse (Other Pointing Devices, Too) 605

Chapter 1

Read This First

Why Windows 95 Secrets

Windows 95 is a large and complicated piece — actually many pieces — of software with thousands of features and capabilities. Microsoft focused on writing the code for the operating system as its primary task. Documentation is a secondary consideration.

Microsoft has decided that the Windows 95 operating system should be "discoverable" without a manual. Company officials contend that no one reads the manual anyway, so they left you, the user, to figure out how to use Windows 95 on your own. That's where we come in. *Windows 95 Secrets* is a detailed map of the Windows 95 territory. While the *Microsoft Windows 95 User's Guide* delivers only a jumping off point, we give you guidance at (almost) every turn in the road.

We give you access to all those helpful features and capabilities that Microsoft didn't take the time or effort to document — or documented in a manner not accessible to mere mortals. *Windows 95 Secrets* exists because there is much that is not obvious in Windows 95 and much that must be coaxed to the surface.

How to Use This Book

If you want an overview of Windows 95 and a summary of its features, check out the next chapter. It is written both for users who are new to Windows and for those familiar with previous versions of Windows.

If you haven't yet installed Windows 95 or need to install additional portions of the operating system to support a network, modem, or printer, turn to Chapter 3 in Part I.

If you want to get a feel for Windows 95 (assuming that it is already installed) turn to Chapters 4 and 5. These chapters provide a quick look at, a basic tutorial on, and an overview of the Windows 95 desktop.

More detailed information on aspects of the Windows 95 user interface is provided in Part II. Go to the chapter that addresses the aspect you are most interested in.

If you have DOS programs that you continue to use, you will be happy to know that Windows 95 provides a robust DOS environment and lots of services to help you better use these older applications. Turn to the two chapters in Part III to learn (among other secrets) how to customize the DOS environment for each of your DOS applications.

Windows 95 comes with routines to automatically detect the hardware in your computer. This doesn't mean that you won't need to or want to make some changes in how that hardware is configured. Part IV covers virtually all the hardware types that are found in computers today. Turn to the chapter in Part IV that covers the hardware that interests you.

Windows 95 provides many tools to facilitate communication through dial-in remote network access, faxes, e-mail, connections to online services, local area networking, and direct access to the network of networks — the Internet. Turn to the chapters in Part V for details on how to configure and use these communications options.

Finally, Part VI provides you with some software help and fun to go with your new operating system. We provide the best shareware selected by the coauthors and by other expert Windows 95 users.

This Book's Overall Structure

Windows 95 Secrets is organized into six sections:

Part I: Introduction and Installation

This section summarizes the features of Windows 95 and how it differs from previous versions of Windows. It also details the installation procedures required to get Windows 95 up and working on your computer. If you already have Windows 95 installed, but need to provide additional software drivers for new hardware or a network connection, this is where you will find out how to do so.

In addition, two chapters will familiarize you with the underlying logic of the Windows 95 user interface. If you read and carry out the procedures in chapters 4 and 5, it will be that much easier to become proficient at using Windows 95.

Part II: The Windows 95 User Interface

Most of us think of the user interface as Windows 95, forgetting all that is going on in the background. This section goes into detail about every aspect of the Windows 95 user interface, providing you with the knowledge you need to use and control Windows 95 and its applications.

Part III: DOS Secrets

This section gives you the complete story on how to continue running DOS applications and take advantage of the DOS services provided by Windows 95. You can run DOS programs in a sizable window using TrueType fonts, or you can run them full screen. Each DOS virtual machine (the environment surrounding your DOS application) can be tailored to provide just the right amount of memory and other resources.

Part IV: Plug and Play

This section tells you how to make changes in the Windows 95 configuration of your hardware. We introduce you to the Device Manager, the new Fonts and Printers folders, new characters sets, and tell you how to set up your display and change your desktop. Windows 95 comes with some powerful disk and file management tools you'll want be familiar with so you can protect your data.

Modems, ports, and the operating system's new phone management capabilities are all covered in this section.

Part V: Communications

Computers are becoming more and more like communications tools. Windows 95 provides a wealth of new tools to facilitate communication. Dial-Up Networking gives you a way to hook your portable computer to your desktop computer, whether your portable is in the office, at home, or on the road. The Windows 95 Briefcase helps you make sure that both your computers have the latest copies of your files and documents.

You can connect to bulletin boards using HyperTerminal, connect your portable to your office networking using Direct Cable Connection, and send e-mail through your local area network or over the Internet. With tools from Microsoft you can surf the Internet and connect your computer to any of the popular local area networks.

Part VI: Windows 95 Shareware

Shareware authors have been busy creating Windows 95-specific software to give you added features, more functionality, and more control. We provide you with the best shareware available.

Getting Commands Right the First Time

You'll be able to use the secrets in this book faster if you know exactly how to type the many Windows commands shown in the text.

Throughout this book, we've indicated many commands like this:

```
WORDPAD {/P} filename
```

or

Wordpad {/p} *filename*

In this command, *filename* is shown in *italics* to indicate that you should change *filename* to the actual name of the file you want to open in the WordPad text editor. The command /P is shown in curly braces {like this} to indicate that this *command-line switch* is optional. You should *not* type the curly braces if you decide to add /P to this command. Since Windows often uses square brackets [like this] to indicate the beginning of sections in initialization *(.ini)* files and the text version of the Registry, we do not use square brackets to indicate optional switches. If you see a line that contains square brackets, you must type the square brackets along with the rest of the line.

If you want to print the Readme.txt file using WordPad, for example, you could click the Start button on the Taskbar, click Run, and then type this line followed by Enter.

Wordpad /p Readme.txt

or

```
WORDPAD /P README.TXT
```

When such a command is within the text of a paragraph, it usually appears in regular type, like the rest of the paragraph, because Windows itself is far more flexible than DOS in the formats it allows and we want this book to reflect what you see when you use Windows. (At times, for clarity, the commands you are to type are shown in **boldface type**.) Generally, filenames are capitalized, but commands can be entered any way you'd like — in small letters, ALL CAPITALS, or A mixture Of both. In Chapter 17, which focuses on DOS, we use SMALL CAPITAL LETTERS to indicate DOS commands, but elsewhere in the book we use both small letters and Mixed Small And Capital Letters for both Windows commands and what you type in windowed DOS sessions.

Whenever you see the term *filename* in italics, you can change it to any form of a valid file name that DOS or Windows will recognize, including drive letters and directory names. For example, if C:\Windows\Command is your current folder, any of the following names for the README.TXT file are valid in this WordPad command:

```
WORDPAD README.TXT
Wordpad Readme.txt
WORDPAD C:\WINDOWS\COMMAND\README.TXT
WORDPAD \WINDOWS\COMMAND\README.TXT
```

We denote special keys on your keyboard with an initial capital letter, like this: Enter, Tab, Backspace, Shift, Alt (alternate), Ctrl (control), and Esc (escape). When you see a phrase such as *press Enter*, you know not to type the keys *e, n, t, e,* and *r,* but to press the Enter key.

If one of the shift keys (Shift, Alt, or Ctrl) should be *held down* at the same time that you also press another key, the two keys are written with a plus sign between them. For example, *press Ctrl+A* means *hold down the Ctrl key, then press the A key, then release both.*

If you are supposed to *let up* on a key *before* pressing another one, those keys are separated by commas. If we say, *press Alt, F, O,* this means *press and release Alt, then F, then O.* This sequence activates the main menu of a Windows application, then pulls down the File menu, then executes the Open menu item. This is the same as saying *click File, Open.*

In this book, we usually do not indicate a keyboard-only procedure every time we describe how to do something with your mouse. The phrase *click File, Open* always means *click the File and Open menu items with your mouse,* but also can mean *press the keys on your keyboard that represent the File and Open menu items.*

Finding the Good Parts

At the beginning of each chapter you will find an introduction where you can very quickly get an idea of the neat tricks in store in that chapter. The summary at the end of each chapter provides a little more detailed look at what you can expect from that chapter.

When we discuss a secret, an undocumented feature, a tip, or a set of steps to carry out a specific task, you'll see an icon in the margin of the page. If you want to just hit the high points of this book, you can go from icon to icon, reading the surrounding paragraphs for helpful supporting material.

Secret

The secret icon indicates some useful information that Microsoft would rather that the end user not be aware of. Microsoft feels that the rest of us need to be protected from ourselves, so it would rather that you didn't mess with the Registry, for example.

Undocumented

An undocumented feature is an aspect of Windows 95 that really should be explained but for some reason got left out of the manual. Windows 95 is filled with helpful features that the programmers put in but the documenters didn't have an opportunity to tell you about.

Tip

Tips are just that— little explanations about how to do a certain task in a particularly nifty manner. Windows 95 gives you lots of ways to do various things and the documentation from Microsoft misses quite a few of them.

STEPS

We often will give you step-by-step instructions on how to carry out a specific task. One of our goals in creating these steps is to make sure that nobody gets lost. So even if you're unfamiliar with the theory, we include enough details in the steps for you to do complete specific tasks. You can breeze through some of the steps as you learn more about Windows 95.

Getting Technical Support for Windows 95

All Windows programs have bugs. This includes all retail Windows software and all shareware featured in *Windows 95 Secrets*. Every program, no matter how simple, has some unexpected behavior. This is the nature of software and is usually fixed with the release of a newer version.

It is not possible for the coauthors or IDG Books to provide technical support for Windows 95 or the many DOS and Windows applications that may cause conflicts within your system. For technical support for the shareware on the CD-ROM, see the section *Technical Support for the CD-ROM* later in this chapter, and the discussion of this topic in Chapter 35.

For technical support for Windows 95, you will be better off contacting Microsoft directly—or using electronic support (which we describe in a moment).

Microsoft provides telephone technical support for its DOS and Windows products through these numbers:

Type of Support	*Number to Call at Microsoft*

Microsoft Windows 95 support
    90 days of free support starting with your
    first phone call
	206-637-7098

Microsoft Pay-Per-Call Support ($2 per minute to a maximum of $25)	900-555-2000 (U.S.) or 800-936-5700 (U.S.)

Microsoft Foreign Pay-Per-Call Support	206-635-3909
Microsoft International Support (for referral to a non-U.S. office)	206-882-8080
Microsoft General Support	206-454-2030
Microsoft Windows Environment	206-637-7098
Microsoft Windows Applications	206-637-7099
Microsoft Download Service (BBS)	206-936-6735
Microsoft Fast Tips - automated touch tone	800-936-4200 (U.S.)

Secret

The best technical support, however, has *never* been provided on phone lines — instead, the best help has always been provided (this is the secret) through electronic BBSes and online services such as the CompuServe Information Service, which is described later in this chapter, and the Microsoft Network.

Online News about Windows 95

Here's where to seek technical support for Windows 95 and where to go specifically on each service.

Where to Get Help	*How to Get There*
CompuServe	Type **Go Winnews**
AOL	**Winnews**
Prodigy	Type **Jump Winnews**
WWW	**http:\\www.microsoft.com**
FTP	**ftp://ftp.microsoft.com/PerOpSys/Win_News**
MSN	Click Microsoft icon, click Windows 95, and then click WinNews

Accessing Technical Support on CompuServe

The CompuServe Information Service (CIS) is a worldwide computer service (one of many) that, among other things, allows you to exchange messages with almost every other electronic mail address in existence. Many vendors of Windows products maintain forums on CompuServe. A *forum* is a message area that technical support people monitor on a daily basis, answering questions and comments left by users of each vendor's products. Telephone support is considered expensive and boring to provide. But a company's top programmers often look in on its CompuServe forum, which is more convenient since questions can be answered at night or any time.

To get electronic technical support from Microsoft on CompuServe, for example, you call a CompuServe local number with your modem, then type **GO MICROSOFT** at any CompuServe prompt. You will see a list of services, including several Microsoft forums supported in different languages and countries of the world. After choosing your language group, you then choose the forum for the product you need technical support for: DOS or Windows, Word for Windows, Excel, and so on.

If you need support from a vendor other than Microsoft, type **GO SOFTWARE** or **GO HARDWARE**. You will see a listing of scores of companies, each with its own forum or forums filled with technical messages between company technicians and users.

Once you're in the forum for your particular vendor, choose the menu option Announcements from Sysop. This displays a listing of system operators (sysops), along with the latest news about the forum: new program enhancement files you can copy (download) to your computer, for example. Write down the name and CompuServe number that corresponds to the sysop in your particular area of interest. Then switch to the Messages section of the forum, compose a detailed message about your problem, and address it to the number of the sysop you wrote down.

When you *post* a message in this way, it is seen not only by the sysop you addressed it to, but also by anyone else who reads the messages for that forum. Check the Messages section 24 to 48 hours later, and you'll probably find several responses. Some of them will likely be from people who are not employees of the vendor, but are more expert users of the company's products than many employees!

At this writing, CompuServe charges a basic fee of $9.95 a month and a forum fee of $9.60/hour for 9600 bps service and above. This can add up, but expert users of CompuServe have found many ways to reduce these fees to the bare minimum. The primary means of doing this is to run a program that takes your outgoing messages, dials CompuServe, spurts your messages into the appropriate forums, and retrieves any messages addressed to you — all within a fraction of the time that you could do this manually.

To gain access to CompuServe, call the Customer Service Dept. at 800-848-8990 in the U.S. or 614-457-8650 outside the U.S. Customer service is available 8 a.m. to 12 midnight, Eastern Time, Monday through Friday, and 12 noon to 10 p.m. Saturday and Sunday (except on U.S. holidays). CIS will send you a packet of information on how to find the closest local number in your area, and how to use the service.

Many Windows programs now include a coupon good for a free trial membership on CompuServe as well as information on how to reach that vendor's forum. You should look for these valuable free offers when you open the box of software.

If you don't already have a modem, we encourage you to buy the fastest modem that is available — 14,400 bps (14.4Kbps) or higher — and start taking advantage of BBSes and online services such as CompuServe for the excellent technical support and services they provide.

On CompuServe you can type **GO WINNEWS** to go to the WinNews forum and get the latest information about Windows 95. Type **GO MSNWRKGRP** to interact with Microsoft support engineers. The Microsoft Knowledge base is available at **GO MSKB**. For Windows 95 shareware, type **GO WINSHARE** or **GO WUGNET**.

Microsoft Network Windows 95 Support

Microsoft now has its own online network. You can sign up for it as soon as you have installed Windows 95. The user interface for the Microsoft Network is the same as the Windows 95 user interface, so you will be able to use MSN as soon as you can use Windows 95.

On the Microsoft Network, forums are called *bulletin boards*. You can read messages posted to any of the bulletin boards and post your own. You can also enter chat areas and type messages to other MSN users while online.

There are support bulletin boards for Windows 95 on the Microsoft Network and you can get help from Microsoft support engineers and other Windows 95 users. To get the Windows 95 support areas after you dial into MSN, click on the Computers and Software icon in the Categories area, click the Microsoft icon, and then the Windows 95 icon.

Windows 95 shareware is available on the Shareware bulletin board. Help regarding how to use the Microsoft Network is also available online by clicking the Microsoft Network icon.

Technical Support for the CD-ROM

If the CD-ROM disc that comes with this book is damaged, you should of course contact IDG Books, which is committed to providing you with a CD-ROM disc in perfect condition.

However, the coauthors of this book, and IDG Books Worldwide Inc., are not familiar with the details of every program on the CD-ROM and do not provide any technical support for the programs on the CD-ROM. The programs are supplied as-is. Most shareware authors, but not all, provide technical support to users after they register. Some shareware authors provide limited technical support to unregistered users if they have problems installing the software. In either case, the best way to get technical support is to look in the text file or help file that accompanies each program and send electronic mail to the e-mail address listed there. Some shareware authors also provide technical support by fax or by U.S. mail.

Shareware authors do not usually have a technical support telephone line, although some do for registered users. If a program is freeware, it probably has no technical support. In this case, if a program does not work on your particular PC configuration, you probably will not be able to obtain technical support for it. See Chapter 35 for further information on the CD-ROM and its contents, and see the complete text of the IDG Books Worldwide License Agreement at the back of this book for a complete discussion of the uses and limitations of the CD-ROM and its contents.

What Are Windows 95 Secrets?

Where do secrets come from? And what makes something a secret or an undocumented feature?

Windows 95 is the first operating system written with the reasonable expectation that it would sell more than 100 million copies. It is vastly more complex and feature-rich than its predecessor, Windows for Workgroups 3.11. While Brad Silverberg at Microsoft has overall responsibility for Windows 95, no one person knows everything about it. In fact, all the people presently working at Microsoft who have worked on Windows 95 taken together do not know everything about Windows 95. Windows 95 is too complex to be completely understood.

Windows 95 is a very big piece of software. In fact, there is no way you can really call it a piece of software. A typical setup includes more than 1,000 files — and many more that are on the Windows 95 source diskettes or CD-ROM are not copied to your hard disk.

Many different programmers have worked to create Windows 95 — an evolving operating system. Much of its core functionality is found in Windows 386 Version 2.0 and later versions of Windows. Because it has been created over time, because so many have been involved in it, and because it is so multifaceted, no one person can document or even be aware of it all.

Windows 95 resembles an organism in its complexity. In the same manner that there isn't a book that completely describes a dog, there isn't a manual that completely describes Windows 95. We have to make do with books that help us understand dogs and operating systems. (No implication here that this operating system is a dog.)

We have been participants in the Windows 95 (and previously Chicago) beta forums on CompuServe since December 1993. We have been running various versions of Chicago and then Windows 95 since Alpha version milestone 5. We collectively discovered and submitted over 570 bug reports to Microsoft, many of which resulted in improvements to the beta code.

Some of the secrets and undocumented features we discuss in this book were first discovered by other beta participants and shared freely on the beta forum.

By the time this book went to the printer, we had spent 18 months using Windows 95 every day, as our one and only operating system. We looked at and used almost every user-accessible aspect of it. It is this experience with the actual thing itself that formed the basis of most of our secrets and undocumented features.

We had hoped that the Windows 95 beta forum (WINBTU) on CompuServe would be a rich source of beta testers' "secrets." As the number of beta testers grew, the message traffic on the forum became a roaring river of more than 1,000 messages a day. We hoped to find little nuggets of wisdom in the flow.

We did find some gems and have included them in this book, with the proper credit where applicable. We (and in turn, you) are indebted to the hardy adventurers who, without a map, braved the wilds of the Registry database to show us how to change the basic Windows 95 configuration.

But most of the messages on the forum were about problems that beta testers were having — problems that were often fixed by Microsoft. Some beta testers shared their discoveries, but most were looking for help from others who were more knowledgeable. We helped where we could and appreciated the help that others gave us.

As we wrote this book, we had to rely on our own experience of Windows 95 to be the rock bottom guide to what Windows 95 truly was. It didn't matter to us what was written about how it was supposed to work. What mattered was how it in fact did work. It is our experience that we have written about in this book.

The people responsible for the documentation of Windows 95 at Microsoft are under the impression that you don't read the documentation. Maybe you just don't read *their* documentation. We feel that Microsoft is justified in their cynicism, whatever the cause, and it really makes little sense for them to write something that you won't read.

The documentation writers at Microsoft can't write a book about Windows 95 secrets, because they are obliged to maintain that there aren't any. They can't poke at the rough edges of the operating system and give you workarounds, because they need to put the operating system in the best light. Some areas just don't get mentioned.

We are not so constrained. So when we see something that definitely shows that an operating system is the handiwork of human beings, we point out how to get around its shortcomings.

The "secrets" and "undocumented features" were there waiting for us and others to find and document. The official documenters had their hands full with other issues. All of us taken together still haven't gotten it all down on paper.

Something is a "secret" or an "undocumented feature" if it is useful and isn't found in the documentation that you get when you purchase Windows.

This book is meant to be a reference work. It doesn't read like a novel. If you want to know more about an area, you should follow along on the computer as you read through the steps that we detail.

We feel that if you find just one really clever trick that helps you use Windows 95, then your purchase of this book will be worth it. We have striven to provide you many more than one really neat insight into how to effectively master this operating system

Because the world of computers is increasingly online and wired together, this book is just one way of obtaining the information that you can use to better use Windows 95.

We hope you enjoy this book.

Summary

▶ Because plenty is missing from Microsoft's documentation of Windows 95, it's difficult to find how to access all its power.

▶ If you have a question about Windows 95, use this chapter to find out where you can turn in this book to find the answer.

▶ We tell you how to recognize commands that you will need to type in from your keyboard.

▶ We describe icons, step-by-step lists, and other shortcuts that will help you find the best parts of the book.

▶ We tell you how to get the best technical support for Windows 95, by phone from Microsoft and electronically through the real experts on services such as CompuServe.

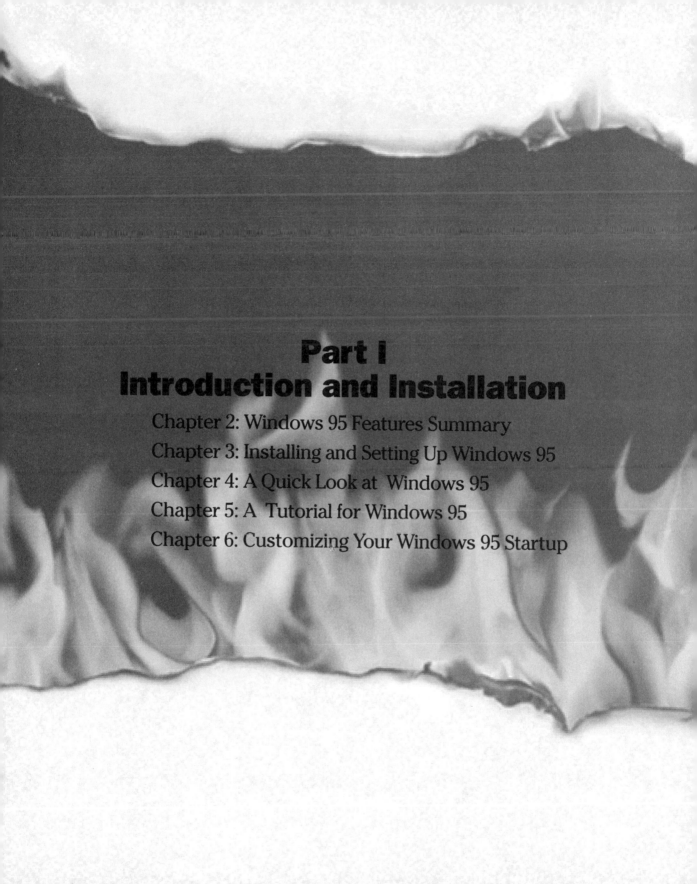

Part I
Introduction and Installation

Windows 95 Features Summary

Find a Feature and Get More Information

What's the point of writing a whole chapter summarizing the features of Windows 95? This chapter gives you another entry point into Windows 95. After skimming this list and finding features that interest you, you can turn to the associated chapter for details on how to implement or use those features.

Microsoft wants Windows 95 to be "discoverable." A novice user should be able to figure out how to do something useful by working with Windows 95. This is a great feature (details later in this chapter), but it is also nice to have an overview, a map that shows all the features in the territory. You could wander around "discovering" things for quite a while, but it sure is nice to have a map to help you through the jungle.

Here's an overview of the major features and guidance about which chapters contain more information.

The User Interface

Simple user interface. What you see on your video monitor is the Windows 95 desktop. The desktop is simple and has an obvious entry point — The Start button on the Taskbar at the bottom, top, or one side of your screen. This desktop is a radical departure from the Windows 3.*x* desktop with its Program Manager and File Manager "shells." (See Chapter 7.)

When you start Windows 95, before you start changing things to suit you, there are only three or four things on the desktop — the Taskbar with its Start button, plus icons for My Computer, Network Neighborhood, the Recycle Bin and, optionally, Microsoft Exchange, Microsoft Network, and the Internet. (See Chapter 7.)

Discoverability. This starts with the Start button. New Windows users can click the Start button — click, not double-click — and then follow the cascading menus to find out what is available. (See Chapter 11.)

The Start button. Clicking it once lets you find and start an installed application. One drawback is that the icons shown in the Start button menus are only a quarter as large as they were in the Windows 3.x Program Manager. They are therefore significantly more difficult to identify. You exit Windows 95 (and prepare to turn off your computer) by clicking Shut Down at the bottom of the menu that pops up when you click the Start button. (See Chapter 7.)

Taskbar. The Taskbar contains the Start button and icons of all the active programs — programs that you have already started. Only one click of an icon in the Taskbar is required to bring a program to the top of the desktop. Because all active applications (whether or not they have been minimized) show up on the Taskbar, it is easy to switch between active applications.

The icons in the Taskbar are a quarter as large as they were on the Windows 3.x desktop — so they take up less room but are harder to recognize.

The Taskbar can be moved from the bottom to the right, top, or left side of the desktop and increased in size to half of the desktop. It can be forced to always be on top and/or hidden so it only pops up when you move your mouse pointer to it. (See Chapter 7.)

Clock. You don't have to go searching for the time because the Taskbar contains a clock. Double-click (or right-click) it; you will see the date, and you can change the time. Park your mouse pointer over the clock and the date pops up. (See Chapter 7.)

My Computer. Double-click this icon on the desktop to view the contents of your disk drives, folders (directories), files, and programs stored on your computer. This feature is something of a combined Program Manager and File Manager. (See Chapter 8.)

Network Neighborhood. Same as My Computer, but for all the computers connected to yours. You see the shared resources — disk drives, printers, and other resources available to you on the network. (See Chapter 34.)

Microsoft Exchange. A unified e-mail and fax front end (user interface). All your electronic mail communications, whether they be just across your local network, through information providers such as CompuServe or the Microsoft Network, or across the Internet, can be routed through Microsoft Exchange. (See Chapter 32.)

The desktop. You can put icons representing applications — and documents — right on the desktop. Better still, put "shortcuts," which are links to applications or documents, on the desktop — somewhat like the Program Manager. (See Chapter 7.)

Folders. Directories have been renamed "folders." When you double-click a folder icon, you get a folder window — a window displaying the contents of the folder. This is a very visual way of browsing through My Computer or Network Neighborhood to find the application or file you want. (See Chapter 8.)

Big icons in folder windows. You can browse through your local disks or those on the network, and all files can have large icons above their names. The icons are big, like they were in the Windows 3.x Program Manager. You can start an application by double-clicking its icon in the folder window. (See Chapter 8.)

New. You can create a new document of any particular type in any folder — even on the desktop — by right-clicking the folder window client area (or desktop) and choosing the New menu item. Windows 95 knows about all the software you have installed and prompts you for what type of document (bitmap, word processor, etc.) to create. You can then double-click the new document and launch the application associated with it. (See Chapter 13.)

The Explorer. Right-click the My Computer Icon and choose Explore. Up pops an Explorer window with a two-pane window "client" area. The left pane contains an outline, or *hierarchical,* view of the contents of your computer and the network connected to it. The right pane has a view of all the disk drives, folders, and/or files contained within the folder or disk drive highlighted in the left pane. The Explorer is especially useful when copying and moving files and folders. While the File Manager in Windows 3.x often required that you open two separate windows in order to copy or move files, this is not necessary with the Explorer. (See Chapter 9.)

Help. Help is well organized, with a hypertext table of contents and index. Each topic is covered with several explanations and, often, shortcut buttons that take you to the area you are searching for. There was no overall unified help in Windows 3.x. (See Chapter 11.)

Program Manager and File Manager. These applications are still there and provide for a transition to the new user interface for people familiar with Windows 3.x. You no longer exit Windows by exiting the Program Manager, as you did in Windows 3.x. (See Chapter 12.)

Right-click. Both buttons on two-button mice — and two out of three on three-button mice — do something useful now. When the mouse pointer is over a file or folder icon, clicking the right button — or left button for left-handed mousers — pops up a menu. Right-clicking gives you many shortcuts to useful file or folder operations. It also lets you investigate and change the properties of the object you clicked. (See Chapter 24.)

Properties. There are "properties" associated with just about everything in Windows 95. This includes all the applications and files on your disk drives. For example, right-clicking the desktop and choosing Properties from the popup menu lets you change the desktop and display Properties sheets about display resolution, or which wallpaper or screen saver to use. (See Chapter 16.)

Find. You want to find a file and you don't know where you put it. Or you want to find a file that contains some known text. Find can do both of these tasks and much more. For example, it can find all the files with "Seed" in their filename, having the words "Cantaloupe and Pineapple" in their contents, and modified in the last three days. Searches can be saved and modified — oh, thank you, Microsoft (the Windows 3.x version of this was lame, at best). Windows Grep (a shareware application for searching for text strings) is our favorite tool for finding text within any group of files. (See Chapter 11.)

Shortcuts. You can place a "shortcut," or a link, on the desktop or in a folder — somewhat in the manner of the Program Manager. You can gather all references to your applications in one or a few places, and launch them from there. This works without actually having to move the applications around. All the application icons shown on the Start button menus are shortcuts. Shortcuts can also be placed in documents created by WordPad or Word for Windows — any OLE 2-compliant application client. (See Chapter 10.)

QuickView. Microsoft supplies more than 30 file viewers and expects application developers to provide more with their applications. A viewer lets you look at the contents of a file, most likely a document of some kind, without having to open the application that created it — presumably a quicker operation. Viewers exist for Quattro Pro, Excel, Word for Windows, WordPerfect 5 and 6, Word, Ami Pro, executable files (files with *exe* extensions), ASCII text files, and GIF, BMP, and TIFF graphics files.

These viewers are scaled-down versions of viewers found in the Windows utility Outside In, developed by System Compatibility Corporation. QuickView Plus, which contains many more viewers and additional features, is scheduled to be available when Windows 95 is. (See Chapter 13.)

Control Panel folder. Configuration information is consolidated in the Control Panel folder. Click the Start button, click Settings, and then Control Panel. If you want to configure anything about a network, double-click the Network icon in the Control Panel folder. We know this seems obvious, but previously it wasn't. (See Chapter 16.)

Themes. Microsoft Plus! comes with 16 themes that integrate desktop icons, screen savers, wallpaper, sounds, mouse pointers, colors, and fonts. (See Chapter 22.)

Alt+Tab+Tab. Task switching is accessible from the keyboard. Instead of going to the Taskbar, you can quickly choose between active applications with this key combination. Hold down the Alt key and continue to press the Tab key to cycle through active applications. (See Chapter 21.)

Ctrl+Esc. Pressing Ctrl+Esc is just like pushing the Start button, except that the Start menu doesn't obscure the application icons on the Taskbar. (See Chapter 21.)

Communications

Microsoft Exchange, a universal mail client for all e-mail or fax communications. The Exchange provides a single user interface to connect with a myriad of electronic-mail providers. You can send and receive e-mail across your local network; over the phone lines from your mobile computer to your office network; through information service providers like CompuServe, the Microsoft Network, and others; or through an Internet service provider (ISP) using a SLIP (Serial Line Internet Protocol) or PPP (Point to Point) account — all integrated through the Exchange front-end and back-end message store. You can send and receive faxes using the same user interface. Microsoft Plus! includes the Internet Exchange client. (See Chapter 32.)

Dial-Up Networking. Connect to your office computer or office network from home or your hotel room as though it were a local resource. Get your e-mail, copy files, and run programs on the distant computer as though you were directly networked to it. Dial into your Windows 95 desktop computer, a Windows NT server, a NetWare server, or a Unix-based server through Microsoft's 32-bit TCP/IP stack. Create a "connectoid" to connect to your Internet service provider. (See Chapter 28.)

Wizard helps set up Dial-Up Networking. Using a Wizard is like having some-one lead you by the hand during the setup process. (See Chapter 28.)

Maintain the latest version of all your files on both your portable and desktop computers. Use the Windows 95 Briefcase to update the files that you are working on so both of your computers have the latest versions. (See Chapter 31.)

Access all Internet services. Connect to the Internet either through your local network or a dial-in Internet service provider with a SLIP or PPP account. Because Windows 95 comes with a high speed 32-bit TCP/IP networking stack, you are ready to connect to the net of nets. (See Chapter 33.)

World Wide Web browser. Microsoft Plus! includes the Internet Explorer. The Explorer is integrated with the Windows 95 shell, Dial-Up Networking, and the Microsoft TCP/IP stack. You can dial out to the Internet and surf the Web by double-clicking the Internet icon on your desktop. (See Chapter 33.)

High-speed communications, both foreground and background. Previous versions of Windows did not provide reliable background communications at high speeds. Certain tasks — like formatting a diskette — would cause commu-nications programs running in the background to drop transmitted characters. Windows 95 has been rewritten to significantly improve this situation, essen-tially through the use of 32-bit protected-mode code in file management and network system software, and hand optimization of time-critical code.

When new 32-bit protected-mode communications applications become available — not counting the excellent HyperTerminal, which comes with Windows 95 — there will be even better communications possibilities. (See Chapter 25.)

HyperTerminal. A 32-bit protected-mode terminal emulator, HyperTerminal provides easy access to bulletin boards and includes numerous file transfer protocols. It gives you a feel for how the new capabilities underlying the Windows 95 communications architecture can ease communications and improve reliability and speed. Of course, this is still the old communications model in which, like a carriage turned into a pumpkin, your smart, fast com-puter becomes a semi-smart terminal connected to some "big" computer elsewhere. (See Chapter 29.)

TAPI. TAPI stands for Telephony Application Programming Interface. End users don't get to see this, but TAPI provides the basis for software developers to create new communications applications. TAPI shields end users from the arcana of modem AT commands. Developers of communications software can count on Windows 95 to recognize the installed modem. (See Chapter 26.)

Applications share the modem. No longer do you have to quit one communications application to use another — if these applications are TAPI-aware. Right now you can have Microsoft at Work Fax monitoring the phone line for incoming faxes while you are using HyperTerminal to call an information service. You still have only one phone line, and your line is busy while you are using HyperTerminal, but fax monitoring restarts automatically when you finish communicating with the information service. (See Chapter 26.)

Single address book. Windows 95 maintains an address book that can be used by all TAPI-aware communication applications. In the future, you will no longer need one book for faxes, another for e-mail, and a third for snail mail and voice communications. (See Chapter 32.)

File Management

Long filenames. You can give your files names up to 255 characters — assuming your application software supports these long names. The applications that come with Windows 95 do (except Program Manager and File Manager). (See Chapter 27.)

VFAT. The Virtual File Allocation Table is an extension of the existing file format for the DOS and Windows 3.*x* File Allocation Table (FAT). This means that you don't need to reformat your hard disk when you install Windows 95. You get access to long filenames without changing how files are stored. (See Chapter 27.)

Fast hard disk access with protected-mode disk drivers. Windows 95 doesn't have to switch your processor to real mode just to access your hard disks. This dramatically speeds up reading and writing to the disk. Windows 95 doesn't go through DOS or through your computer's BIOS to get to the hard disk, thereby saving lots of time. (See Chapter 27.)

A faster 32-bit CD-ROM file system. A major limitation in presenting video images on a computer display is the speed of reading the video frames off the CD-ROM. The new 32-bit protected-mode CD-ROM drivers replace the real mode MSCDEX driver and implement protected-mode caching for the CD-ROM drive. With your CD-ROM cached in RAM, you will be able to access its files and images much quicker. (See Chapter 27.)

Dynamic caching in protected memory. Windows 95 provides faster caching. There's no need to allocate a fixed amount of hard disk space for swapping; it's all handled without any end user input. You don't need to use the SmartDrive disk cache, and you don't need to set a swap file size in the Control Panel. Setting up Windows to use virtual memory (swapping code and data out of RAM to the hard disk as necessary) no longer requires a permanent swap file. The swap file is automatically sized and resized as you run Windows 95. (See Chapter 27.)

Universal naming convention. Files and folders on network servers can be accessed without resorting to mapping the server name to a drive letter. The path name for the file is now prefaced with the server name and two back slashes: \\server-name\folder-name\filename. This makes it as easy to access files and folders on servers as on your computer. (See Chapter 34.)

Ability to handle multiple file systems. Network servers don't necessarily use the FAT file system used by DOS and previous versions of Windows. With the Installable File System Manager, Windows 95 can speak to different types of network servers simultaneously, including Novell NetWare and Windows NT servers. (See Chapter 34.)

DOS

Virtual machines for each DOS application. Each DOS application thinks that it has all the hardware to itself. Windows virtualizes the hardware, so while the DOS application thinks it's talking to the hardware, it's really talking to software. DOS virtual machines are preemptively multitasked so one application doesn't hog all the resources. If things get out of hand, you can kill a DOS virtual machine without having to end the DOS application first. (See Chapter 17.)

More memory for DOS applications. Because Windows 95 uses protected-mode components and drivers, conventional memory — that memory below the 640K boundary that DOS applications need — is not used up. Your computer may have hardware that requires a real-mode driver because Microsoft or the hardware manufacturer didn't write a 32-bit protected-mode driver to replace it. The Windows Setup program checks for this and if there isn't a protected-mode driver you will find the real-mode drivers in Config.sys. (See Chapter 18.)

Greater compatibility between DOS and Windows. DOS programs often take over hardware resources, causing conflicts. Because Windows 95 lets the DOS program think it has control of the hardware while continuing to control it itself, it is much easier for Windows and DOS programs to work together. (See Chapter 17.)

Run any DOS program "under" Windows. Almost all DOS applications will be able to run in the DOS virtual machine provided by Windows 95. This was not true of previous Windows versions. For those few DOS programs that have a difficult time getting along with Windows 95, a special MS-DOS mode unloads Windows 95 and gives the finicky application access to 100 percent of the system resources. (See Chapter 17.)

DOS programs that run in VGA graphics mode can run in a window. Windows 3.*x* required that DOS VGA graphics applications switch to full-screen mode. Now you can more easily multitask DOS programs with Windows. (See Chapter 17.)

Toolbar for a DOS window. Just like a real Windows 95 window, the DOS window has a Toolbar that makes it easier to carry out such tasks as: cut and paste, switch to full-screen mode, change the properties of the DOS virtual machine, and change the font and size of the DOS window. (See Chapter 17.)

TrueType for DOS applications. You are not stuck with one font to display DOS text. Bitmapped and TrueType fonts are available and can be changed quickly. Font size can automatically change to match DOS window size. (See Chapter 20.)

25-, 43-, or 50-line DOS screens. You can set the number of lines in your DOS window — or full screen — and have that setting be specific to each of your DOS applications. (See Chapter 17.)

Separate Autoexec.bat for each DOS virtual machine. Each of your DOS applications can have a separate batch file that runs before the application begins. This is just like an Autoexec.bat file that sets up the DOS virtual machine environment just the way the application likes it. (See Chapter 17.)

Clean killing of errant DOS applications. Any DOS virtual machine can be killed, either with a simple close command or with Ctrl+Alt+Delete, without bringing down the Windows 95 operating system. This was not always the case with Windows 3.x. All memory allocated to the DOS session is freed. (See Chapter 17.)

Start command. An extension to the existing DOS commands, Start lets you launch a DOS application in a new DOS virtual machine, start an application by naming its associated document, or start a Windows application. (See Chapter 17.)

Printing

Quick return to your application after initiating a print job. Windows 95 quickly puts the printing of your document into the background, releasing the application that initiated the printing to go on to other things. Windows 95 sends your documents to the print spooler using the compact Enhanced Metafile Format (EMF). EMF is a new version of the Windows Metafile Format (WMF), an application-independent file type that includes graphical and formatted text information. The print spooler translates the EMF files — in the background and without stopping you from carrying out other work — into printer commands that are sent directly to your printer. (See Chapter 23.)

DOS file print spooling. Files sent to the printer from DOS and Windows applications now go to the same print spooler — there is no conflict about which has control of the printer. (See Chapter 23.)

Print later. If you are not currently connected to a printer, you can queue up a batch of print jobs that can be printed the next time you reconnect to your printer. This is very handy if you are on the road with your portable computer. (See Chapter 23.)

Printers folder. All print-related tasks are handled through one place — the Printers folder. Installation, configuration, and spooler management are accessed here. You can place printer icons on your desktop and drag and drop documents to any of the printers connected to your computer, either directly or through the network. (See Chapter 23.)

A Wizard to help install your printers. A Wizard can guide you through printer installation. If your printer supports bidirectional communication, Windows 95 will query the printer for configuration information. (See Chapter 23.)

Bidirectional communication. Windows 95 supports bidirectional communication, which allows the printer to report on its current state, such as out of paper. This enables an application to take some appropriate measure — like notifying you to get more paper, perhaps through a message on the sound board. (See Chapter 23.)

Support for Plug and Play printers. These printers support bidirectional communications and help in the installation process. If you change printers, you can force Windows 95 to query the new printer and switch to the other printer driver or install a new printer driver. (See Chapter 23.)

Remote print management. The print queue on another printer is available to you if you have administrator access. This allows you to manage it without having to physically be at the computer the printer is hooked up to. You can cancel or pause pending print jobs. (See Chapter 23.)

Print to a networked printer without the drivers for that printer having been installed on your computer. Using Windows 3.x you had to install drivers for each kind of printer before you could use them. With all kinds of printers spread throughout the network, this was a hassle. With Windows 95, the drivers are automatically downloaded to your computer when you print to a shared printer if you don't have that printer configured on your computer. (See Chapter 23.)

No need for LPT port redirection. You can print to a printer with a universal convention name (such as \\SERVER\LASER) without having to associate it with a logical port. (See Chapter 23.)

Hardware

Plug and Play. Installing a new piece of hardware will no longer be such a painful process. If you install Plug and Play-enabled hardware, configuration and conflict avoidance is automatic. Windows 95 knows what resources (one of 16 hardware interrupts, various DMA channels, and memory I/O addresses) are available and can assign them to the new device without user input. (See Chapter 19.)

Support for existing, pre-Plug and Play hardware. Much of the hardware currently in your computer is automatically detected upon installation of Windows 95. Any conflicts — say, between interrupts, ports, or addresses — are highlighted to help you resolve them. Windows 95 Setup has a database of non-Plug and Play hardware and does a reasonable job of detecting such hardware. (See Chapter 19.)

Hot docking and hot swapping. Portable computers can connect — while running — to a network through a docking station. PC cards can be pulled from or inserted into their sockets without crashing the computer. Windows 95 tracks these events and notifies all applications regarding the new hardware configuration. Plug and Play-aware applications can use this notification to take appropriate actions. How can this help? Microsoft Exchange can check for your e-mail when you come into the office in the morning, so when you plug your portable into its docking station, the messages will be waiting for you. (See Chapter 19.)

New device wizards. A helping hand is provided when you install new hardware. (See Chapter 19.)

Mice

One protected-mode mouse driver for DOS and Windows. There is no need to reduce the amount of memory available for DOS programs by loading a 16-bit mouse driver. If a DOS program is started in a DOS Window, Windows 95 automatically activates the DOS mouse pointer. (See Chapter 24.)

Set multiple mouse features. The Mouse Control Panel gives you the power to change the mouse pointer size and color (great for LCD screens on portables), add mouse trails (again good for LCD screens), switch to a left-handed mouse, and change the mouse tracking speed. You can change the mouse pointer to an animated pointer. One thing that Microsoft still doesn't offer is support for the middle mouse button. Logitech provides software that lets you program the middle mouse button. Making it send a double-click is often very handy. (See Chapter 24.)

Support for serial ports 1 through 4. Windows 3.x didn't support COM3 and COM4. For example, serial mice could not use either. Windows 95 supports all four serial ports equally. This reduces the potential for conflict between other devices that want the first two serial ports. (See Chapter 25.)

Keyboard

Multi-language keyboard support. Easily switch between languages in one document with multiple-language keyboard layouts. If you have specified multiple-language and keyboard-layout options in the Keyboard Control Panel or in Windows 95 Setup, you can switch between keyboard layouts by pressing Alt+Shift. (See Chapter 21.)

Change the keyboard character repeat speed. The keyboard can never be fast enough for us. We want the arrow keys to move that cursor right along. Use the Keyboard Control Panel to set a fast (or slow) repeat rate and delay period for repeating the pressed key. (See Chapter 21.)

Use the cursor control keys or number pad to control the mouse pointer. If you don't like the mouse or can't use it, use your keyboard to provide mouse pointer control. Use the Accessibility Options Control Panel to configure the speed and acceleration of the mouse keys. (See Chapter 21.)

Hard disks and floppy drives

Enhanced IDE support. With new IDE hard disks becoming available at sizes greater than half a gigabyte, Microsoft has added protected-mode support for these bigger drives. (See Chapter 27.)

Protected-mode drivers for IDE based CD-ROM drives. There aren't many of these on the market yet, but given the fact that they can be hooked to the IDE hard disk controller in many computers, there may be more soon. (See Chapter 27.)

SCSI support. No SCSI device drivers shipped with Windows 3.1, so SCSI hardware manufacturers had to write their own drivers. Windows 95 support is built-in. (See Chapter 27.)

Fast 32-bit floppy disk driver. No longer will formatting a floppy disk stop all other tasks under Windows. The routine responsible for formatting diskettes is now a protected-mode application. When a diskette is being formatted, a preemptively multitasked thread is created that can run in the background and won't hog your computer. The new driver also brings increased reliability and speed. (See Chapter 27.)

Display

Protected-mode display drivers. Microsoft is providing a broad range of video drivers for many popular display cards on the market. Video card manufacturers can use Microsoft's new display software technology to create additional protected-mode drivers that feature greater reliability and speed. (See Chapter 22.)

Safe mode to fix bad display drivers. If a display driver fails to work correctly, Windows 95 can always be brought up automatically in Safe mode with the standard VGA display driver. This allows you to make the changes necessary to get Windows running properly. (See Chapter 22.)

The Display Properties Control Panel. Right-click the desktop and choose Properties from the popup menu to change any of the characteristics of the display. This includes wallpaper, screen savers, fonts used to display text on the display, desktop and window colors, the magnification factor for your display, and so on. The Display Properties dialog box is also available from the Control Panel folder. (See Chapter 22.)

Smooth fonts. Microsoft Plus! enables font smoothing to anti-alias TrueType fonts. This adds one of four shades around some of the edges of each letter to make them appear smoother. (See Chapter 22.)

Energy Star support. If your display adapter and monitor meet the Energy Star and VESA specifications, Windows 95 lets you control how long after keyboard inactivity the low-power standby mode of the monitor occurs. The display driver must support this feature. (See Chapter 22.)

Changing screen resolutions. There is no longer any need to restart Windows 95 when you change video resolutions. (See Chapter 22.)

Modems

Unimodem. Centralized modem configuration is available to all Windows communications applications that are designed to take advantage of it. Windows 95 detects which modem you have and properly sets the modem initialization string. No longer will you have to configure each communications application for your modem — if you use only TAPI-aware or 32-bit communications applications. (See Chapter 25.)

16550A UART support. The 16550A is an advanced chip that handles serial communications in your modem or serial port — if you have a computer with this chip in it. Windows 3.x didn't make use of all its advanced features. Windows 95 support for the 16550A makes communications more reliable as well as faster. (See Chapter 25.)

128 serial ports and 127 parallel ports. You probably won't need this many ports on your personal computer, but they are supported for those people who pack their computers with special serial port boards. Modems that operate off the parallel port are now available. (See Chapter 25.)

Installation

Hardware detection. You might have some existing hardware conflicts that have gone unnoticed but will cause problems in the future. Windows 95 Setup thoroughly searches your computer and creates a database of hardware to identify all your components as well as conflicts. (See Chapter 3.)

Recovery of setup failures. If setup of Windows 95 fails — due to incorrect hardware detection, for example — you can start the Setup program again without having to worry about knowing where the failure occurred. Setup keeps track of the failure and skips over the area where it happened. (See Chapter 3.)

Multiboot (allows you to boot older versions of DOS, Windows NT, OS/2, and Windows 3.x). You can keep your previous version of Windows — and Windows NT — and set up a new Windows 95 directory when you load Windows 95 for the first time. That way you can go back to the old version — or run Windows NT. Windows 95 has a multiboot capability that lets you choose between a number of operating systems previously stored on your hard disk. (See Chapter 3.)

Support for batch file control of Setup. The Windows 95 Setup program requires that you answer a series of configuration questions. With a batch file working with Windows 95 Setup, the answers can be automatically provided without user input. (See Chapter 3.)

Installation from a network administrator's workstation. Windows 95 can be installed on a local computer (or on a network server) from the workstation of a network administrator. It can be configured to be used by either a local computer with a hard disk, a local computer with just a floppy disk, or a diskless computer with a RIPL boot PROM (programmable read only memory) chip and disk storage on a network server. (See Chapter 3.)

Verification of Windows 95 installation. What if you accidentally delete a file that is vital to the operation of Windows 95 or a file gets corrupted by some means? Rerunning Windows 95 Setup lets you verify your existing Windows 95 software. If there are problems, Windows 95 will reinstall the bad or missing files from the original diskettes or CD-ROM. (See Chapter 3.)

Fonts

New font installer/viewer. Click the Start button, then Settings, then Fonts to invoke the new Font installer/viewer. You can copy fonts from fonts diskettes to the \Windows\Fonts folder, or leave them in separate folders on your hard disk. You can use it to uninstall fonts and/or delete font files from your hard disk. (See Chapter 20.)

32-bit TrueType rasterization. The TrueType rasterizer takes the TrueType font descriptions and turns them into the dots that are displayed on the computer screen. The new rasterizer does a better job of being faithful to the outline and hints of the TrueType fonts. (See Chapter 20.)

Font smoothing. Anti-aliasing improves the appearance of fonts on your display. It requires that the video driver be in at least the 256-color mode, and that you have Microsoft Plus! and a 486 processor. (See Chapter 22.)

Error Handling and Reliability

Local reboot. DOS and Windows applications that become "hung" — quit responding — can be closed without also hanging Windows 95.

Safe mode. If Windows 95 can't start normally for any reason, it starts in Safe mode. This allows you to make changes to the configuration if necessary to solve the problem.

Better cleanup of resources. Windows 3.x applications often forgot to return memory resources that they borrowed from the operating system while running. This eventually caused Windows to run out of resources and stop running. Windows 95 cleans up after Windows 3.x applications.

Basic Structure

DOS and Windows combined. DOS functionality is now provided by 32-bit components. A portion of real-mode DOS is started when Windows boots in order to read and process real-mode drivers in Autoexec.bat and Config.sys. Windows is then automatically loaded and some of real-mode DOS unloaded from memory. (See Chapter 17.)

32-bit preemptive multitasking and multithreading. Much of the benefit of this new underlying structure for Windows 95 won't become apparent until you use 32-bit protected-mode Windows applications. The Windows 95 printing subsystem, HyperTerminal, and other applets are 32-bit applications that provide some of the benefits now. For example, the printing subsystem provides faster printing and releases the computer to other tasks by doing most of its work in the background.

32-bit protected-mode software drivers everywhere. Windows interacts with hardware devices through software components commonly called drivers. These drivers have been rewritten to place themselves above the 1MB memory boundary. Therefore, they take up no conventional memory — freeing up more for DOS applications — and reduce many memory conflicts. Protected-mode drivers mean that Windows doesn't have to take time to switch the processor to real-mode whenever it interacts with hardware other than the processor and memory. (See Chapter 19.)

Rapid performance increases as you add more memory. Windows 95 runs at about the same speed as Windows 3.1 in 4MB of memory — very slowly. Add more memory and Windows 95 starts to run faster than its predecessor.

Compatibility with existing hardware and software. Microsoft would have been foolish not to make Windows 95 compatible with Windows 3.x. Upgrading everything would have been a major hassle. While some software utilities created for Windows 3.1 will not be needed under Windows 95, most utility vendors are planning new Windows 95 versions of their products. These Windows 95 versions are expected to take advantage of the advanced features of Windows 95.

More resources. Windows 3.x would run out of system "resources" long before it ran out of memory. This is due to the structure of the lists — the various memory "heaps" — of resources available to Windows 3.x applications. Microsoft has redesigned the resource allocation scheme in Windows 95 to make sure it is less likely to run out of resources before you actually run out of memory. (See Chapter 18.)

Networking

Built for networking. While much work has gone into updating virtually every area of the Windows operating system, the area that has received the most attention is networking. Much has been done to make networking easier, more reliable, faster, more security conscious, and more compatible with the leading networking operating systems, including Novell NetWare, Windows NT, and Banyan Vines. (See Chapter 34.)

Protected-mode networks. No more using up all that precious memory below 640K (or in the upper memory blocks) with network drivers. Windows 95 network components (drivers, clients, and so on) have no conventional memory footprints — they get loaded above the 1MB boundary. Accessing networked hard disks is much faster and your DOS applications have memory enough to breathe. The drawback is that many third-party networks don't yet provide protected-mode network components. Microsoft provides 32-bit protected-mode network components for Microsoft Windows Network, Novell NetWare, and TCP/IP. (See Chapter 34.)

Reduced conflict between applications and networking components. Real-mode networking drivers compete with Windows for the same resources. They conflict in memory and attempt to exclusively control response to hardware and software interrupts. Windows 95 eliminates these conflicts. Again, this is true only with networks that provide protected-mode support — Microsoft Windows Network, Novell NetWare, Windows NT, and TCP/IP at this writing. (See Chapter 34.)

Multiple simultaneous network support. Your computer can be hooked up to completely different kinds of networks at the same time using the same network card. You get the protocol associated with Internet and Unix — TCP/IP, NetWare's IPX/SPX, and Microsoft's NetBEUI (pronounced *net buoy*). Windows works with other protocols provided by other vendors. From your workstation you can "see" Unix servers, Windows NT servers, and Novell NetWare servers simultaneously. (See Chapter 34.)

One password for all logins. One network logon password can be the master key password for resources that you have previously logged onto. Enter your logon password once. When you access other password-protected resources (for example, a hard disk on a network server), the correct password is sent from your encrypted store of passwords. (See Chapter 34.)

Protected-mode client for NetWare. This 32-bit protected-mode network component replaces the real-mode network drivers provided by Novell. You can still connect to NetWare servers, browse their file systems, use NetWare command line utilities and logon scripts — as long as they don't have calls to TSRs. If you want to use Novell's real-mode components, you are still free to do so — but beware of conflicts. (See Chapter 34.)

File and printer services for NetWare. Disk drives, files and folders, and printers on local computers — not just NetWare servers—can be shared on the network. (See Chapter 23.)

Support for workstations with no local hard disks. Windows 95 can be installed on a network server, allowing computers with no local storage (or floppy drives only) to run Windows from the server. (See Chapter 34.)

Network Administration and Security

Standard network system management protocols are supported. Windows 95 provides a Simple Network Management Protocol (SNMP) agent, allowing a network administrator to monitor and manage a local computer. Third-party network management tools can use these agents to provide the network administrator with system information and management functions. (See Chapter 34.)

Registry-base systems management. The Windows 95 Registry replaces Win.ini, System.ini, and other *ini* files with a unified approach to the storage of system configuration information. This Registry information is available to the network system administrator. Microsoft provides the Registry editor. (See Chapter 34.)

System Policy editor. The systems administrator can set a number of configuration parameters with the administration configuration application — the System Policy editor. These policies — rules — determine if local workstations can share their files or printers, whether users can change their desktop configurations, and so on. The editor provides network administrators with an easy to use point-and-click check box approach to network security. (See Chapter 12.)

Unified logon. A single logon dialog box can connect you to your workgroup or to multiple network servers. Password-protected resources — such as files and printers — are available to you after you have entered their passwords once. These passwords are stored with your master logon password. (See Chapter 34.)

Performance monitoring. From a single workstation, a network administrator can monitor the I/O performance of any or all local computers on the network. (See Chapter 34.)

Net Watcher. The network administrator can see who is currently logged onto various servers on the network and what resources they are accessing. Administrators can also add shared folders and files, and disconnect users from a server or from specific files. (See Chapter 34.)

Different users with different settings on the same local computer. Different users can use the same computer — at different times — and have it configured just for them. User data is stored in a Registry file separate from the computer configuration data. Users can have different desktops and different privileges on the same computer. (See Chapter 12.)

User settings follow them around to different computers. Users can "roam" around the corporate network, logging on to different computers, and have their settings/configurations/permissions follow them around. The user portion of the Registry can be stored on a network server to allow this "roaming." (See Chapter 12.)

Summary

▶ Windows 95 is a vast and complex software system. We review the main elements of the territory without overwhelming you with details.

Chapter 3

Installing and Setting Up Windows 95

In This Chapter

We discuss how to install and set up Windows 95 on your hard disk on a single computer.

▶ The minimum requirements for installing and running Windows 95

▶ How to get enough free hard disk space to install Windows 95

▶ Microsoft's big mistake that lets your Windows directory just keep on growing

▶ Protecting your DOS files from being erased by Windows 95 Setup

▶ Stopping Windows 95 Setup from erasing Windows Write

▶ Applets that Windows 95 forgot

▶ How to run Setup the fast way

▶ Problems setting up Windows 95 from a network server or CD-ROM drive

▶ A guided tour through the setup process

▶ Fixing a sick Windows 95

▶ Installing Windows 95 on Windows NT and OS/2 computers

▶ Uninstalling Windows 95

Take a Moment to Reflect

In this chapter we discuss how to install and set up Windows 95 on a single standalone computer. By *standalone* we mean the computer can (and will) boot Windows 95 from its local hard disk without requiring any connection to a network. The standalone computer can be attached to a network and operate as a server on a peer-to-peer network. A standalone computer can stand alone but is not necessarily unconnected.

Windows 95 can be installed on a network server. Network client computers can use and share this single copy of Windows 95. While we don't discuss this type of installation here, you can turn to Chapter 34 for a discussion of networking.

Requirements

Before you install Windows 95, you'll want to take stock of your situation. If you are going to install it on a new computer, the odds are very good that this computer meets the minimal requirements necessary to run Windows 95. If you are installing it on an older computer, you'll want to be sure that it meets the requirements shown in Table 3-1.

Table 3-1 Hardware Requirements for Installing and Running Windows 95

Component	Requirements
Processor	386 or greater. Windows 95, because of its 32-bit code, runs slower (when compared with Windows 3.x) on a 386SX processor, which has a 16-bit external data path. 386DX or 386 processors with 32-bit external data paths will run Windows 95 as fast as they did Windows 3.1 (which is relatively slow) — the faster the processor, the happier the user. If you have a B-step 386 processor (one marked ID 0303), you can't install Windows 95.
Memory	4MB of RAM is required for Windows 95 to work as well as Windows 3.x did with 4MB of RAM (marginally). Some Windows programs won't run in 4MB of RAM even with virtual memory (swapping to hard disk) turned on. And 8MB is recommended by Microsoft. More is better if you want to cut down on the virtual memory manager's swapping to the hard disk as you open multiple applications or use OLE objects in compound documents. We recommend at least 16MB.
Video	VGA is the minimum, with SVGA recommended by Microsoft. Larger monitors and higher resolution give you more real estate for multiple applications or larger areas for more text, numbers, and so on. Accelerated display cards make a real difference.
Disks	Windows 95 comes on high-density diskettes or a CD-ROM. It takes a large number of high-density diskettes, so the higher capacity $3\frac{1}{2}$-inch diskette drive is best. Getting Windows 95 in the CD-ROM format is vastly superior, just from the standpoint of ease of installation.
	You need between 24MB and 70MB of free hard disk space just for the Windows 95 files. You'll need the hard disk space for your Windows 95 files as well as for dynamically sized swap space. For your Windows 95 installation, you'll want to free up as much hard disk space as possible so as to not run into conflicts during installation.
	If you are installing Windows 95 into a directory containing Windows 3.x, you can subtract the size of the Windows 3.x files from this requirement. See *Hard Disk Space Requirements* later in this chapter.
	Depending on choices that you make during installation, the amount of hard disk space required can increase significantly. During the installation process, the amount of hard disk space required will be indicated on screen.

Component	Requirements
	If you are installing on a computer with compressed drives, you'll need at least 3MB of free uncompressed hard disk space during installation. This uncompressed disk space must be on your host drive (the physical drive or partition that "hosts" the compressed logical drive), such as C:.
	You must have a File Allocation Table (FAT) disk partition (required if you are running DOS and/or Windows 3.x). Computers that run Windows NT or OS/2 do not necessarily have FAT partitions on their hard disks.
Others	Windows 95 takes advantage of modems, CD-ROM drives, sound cards, midi add-on cards, accelerated video, network cards, joy sticks, and so on.

Starting with DOS

You may have heard that Windows 95 does away with DOS. It turns out that Microsoft got carried away with this claim and now many people wonder if they can put Windows 95 on their DOS and Windows 3.x computers.

You need to have at least DOS running on your computer in order to install the upgrade version of Windows 95. Your hard disk must contain a DOS FAT partition big enough to contain the Windows 95 files (greater than 32MB).

The non-upgrade version of Windows 95 comes with a bootable DOS diskette that allows you to partition your hard disk, format the hard disk partitions for DOS, and install the necessary files to boot the computer from the hard disk into DOS 7.0.

Windows 95 requires that the partition size for the volume on the hard disk where you install Windows 95 be greater then 32MB. You need to be running DOS 3.2 or greater on a computer that you want to upgrade to Window 95, and you will need to repartition the hard disk if the volume on which you will install Windows 95 is less than 32MB.

Windows 95 stores its files on a DOS-formatted hard disk just like DOS and Windows 3.x do. Windows 95 isn't some foreign invader that requires that you wipe out everything first and restructure it to work with Windows 95. You start with what you've got and make a few changes to get to Windows 95.

Making room for Windows 95

Before you install Windows 95, carefully consider its hard disk space requirements. If you have a 386 computer with a 40MB hard drive, Windows 95 is going to eat up a big chunk of your hard disk space. You might want to consider using disk compression software (built into Windows 95), a new hard disk, or a new computer.

No matter what computer you have, make sure there is plenty of room for Windows 95. The trends over the last few years with respect to the hard disk requirements of Windows programs should have prepared you for the demands that Windows 95 will make on your equipment and wallet. Windows 95 is no shrinking violet when it comes to using hard disk resources.

Windows 95 is not just one program, but a whole series of programs that provide a vastly greater amount of functionality than in Windows 3.x. This translates into enough hard disk space to store these programs. Not only that, it gets worse as you install other Windows programs.

Hard disk space requirements

You can install Windows 95 into a new folder or over your existing Windows directory. Table 3-2 provides a rough approximation of the free additional disk space required to install and run Windows 95. These are rough estimates and don't include additional requirements for fonts, application programs, DLLs, and so on.

Table 3-2	Free Disk Space Requirements	
New or Upgrade	**Installation Type**	
	Typical	**Compact**
New	56MB	49MB
Over Windows 3.1	41MB	34MB
Over Windows for Workgroups	41MB	34MB

Make sure you have plenty of room to install Windows 95. If you can move some directories to other hard disk volumes or off onto diskettes, you should consider doing so. After the installation is complete, you may be able to move some of these back.

The actual amount of hard disk space used will depend on which options you choose when installing Windows 95. If you take the route of a custom installation, you will have the opportunity to tailor your hard disk space usage.

We recommend that you choose the Custom Installation option when you install Windows 95, unless you have a reason to use a different option.

If you are installing Windows 95 on a compressed volume, you will need a great deal more space than is shown in Table 3-2. The executable files that come with Windows 95 aren't very compressible. Expect to need at least double the amount of hard disk space required for Windows 95 on a compressed drive

Not only will you find the programs that come with Windows 95 stored in the Windows 95 folder (and subfolders), but other programs want to store pieces of themselves there. Your C:\Windows or C:\Win95 folder will grow and grow and grow. This is actually a disaster.

The DLL mistake

Microsoft made a huge mistake that it has never fessed up to. It encouraged application software developers (including ones at Microsoft) to put parts of their programs into the \Windows or \Windows\System directories. This causes these folders to grow to an unmanageable size.

Most of these portions of programs are in the form of dynamic link libraries (DLLs). DLLs are both a curse and a blessing. Actually, they'd be just a blessing if they stayed in each application's folder or subfolders.

DLLs are loaded into memory by an application when you run it. They allow a programmer to create a file (library) of functions that can be called by the program's executable file. They are a neat way to package usable functions without having to put them all together in one huge executable file. They also can be called by other programs and shared by different programs while stored in memory.

Microsoft ships some DLLs that can (and are) used by application developers. These include the common dialog boxes (both 16-bit and 32-bit) that allow users to open and save files in applications. Microsoft put these DLLs in the \Windows\System folder. Because many programs can and do use these DLLs, it is appropriate that they be stored in a commonly accessible folder.

However, most DLLs are used by only one program. They do not need to be in a common location. They should be stored in their application's folder. Because application setup procedures store them in the \Windows or \Windows\System folders, these folders continue to grow in size. After a while they become unmanageable.

While uninstall programs allow you to track down these DLLs, they do nothing to solve the problem of bloated Windows folders if you want to keep these programs installed. In addition, programs like Microsoft Office and LapLink for \Windows add more folders that are by default attached to the Windows folder, increasing the space requirements of the Windows folder and subfolders.

This problem is not solved by Windows 95. Programs can still put their DLLs in the Windows folders and subfolders. In addition, all the fonts that you add to Windows are stored in the \Windows\Fonts folder. Windows just gets bigger and bigger.

Because of this problem, you must be sure that you have enough space for Windows 95 and for all the files that get attached to it. If you have divided your hard disk(s) up into a number of smaller volumes, you may not have enough space on a given volume to store the ever-expanding Windows folders.

New or used?

All this adds up to a number of considerations:

1. Should you install Windows 95 over (and in) your existing Windows 3.1 directory? There is so much stuff in this directory and its subdirectories, stuff that you might not be using any more, that you might want to start fresh.

2. How much room do you need to set aside for the Windows folder and its subfolders as it continues to grow? If you install Windows in its own volume (say an uncompressed drive) and everything else on other volumes, how big should the Windows volume be?

3. How can you maintain some semblance of order so you are able to manage the growth of these folders?

If you are using a permanent swap file with Windows 3.x, you might want to get rid of that file, at least during Windows 95 installation. This will give the Windows 95 Setup program more free hard disk space. Some Windows 3.x programs, such as Photoshop, however, require that you have a permanent swap file.

To get rid of the Windows 3.x permanent swap file, at least temporarily, take the following steps:

STEPS

Getting Rid of the Windows 3.x Permanent Swap File

Step 1.   Run Windows 3.x.

Step 2.   Double-click the Control Panel icon in your Program Manager. Double-click the Enhanced icon in the Control Panel.

Step 3.   Click the Virtual Memory button and then Change.

Step 4.   From the drop-down list in the Type field, choose Temporary. Click the OK buttons to exit from the Control Panel.

Step 5.   Exit Windows 3.x to DOS.

Step 6.   At the DOS command prompt, change directories to the root directory of the boot drive **(cd \).**

Step 7.   Type **attrib 386spart.par** and press Enter.

Step 8.   If the result of Step 7 is a listing for this file, type **del 386spart.par** and press Enter.

You have now freed up the hard disk space that was taken up by this file. You do not need a permanent swap file to run Windows 95. (It automatically creates a *dynamic* swap file as described.) If you need a permanent swap file to continue running programs under Windows 3.x, you can re-create it using the Windows 3.x Control Panel.

Where to put the Windows folder

The Windows 95 folder (and its subfolders) can be installed on any hard drives (or drive partitions or volumes) as long as the disk partition is a FAT partition. Some Windows 95 files will be installed on your boot drive (most likely C:).

The boot drive must have at least 3MB of uncompressed hard disk space. If your boot drive is completely compressed, you must uncompress enough of it to get 3MB of uncompressed space on the host drive. This may require you to move some files off your hard disk.

Windows 95 installs files on the boot drive. One of those files, Io.sys, will reside in the boot tracks. It takes over the startup process for your computer. In addition, Windows 95 has its own Command.com file and can have Autoexec.bat and Config.sys files that reside in the root directory of the boot drive. Windows 95 keeps other files on the boot drive as well. These are detailed in Chapter 6.

The total size of the files on the boot drive attributable to Windows 95 is less than 1MB. The rest of Windows 95 can be placed in another volume. If your hard disk is partitioned into multiple volumes (each with a letter name), Windows 95 can be placed into a non-bootable volume. If you have multiple physical hard drives, Windows 95 can be placed on a non-bootable hard drive.

Compressed drives

Compressed drives are actually large files, compressed volume files (CVFs), on a physical drive (the host drive) that are treated as (and named as) separate drives. Windows 95 can be installed on a compressed drive.

Secret

The estimates of the amount of space on a compressed drive that will store Windows 95 files are wildly inaccurate. This is because the Windows files can't be compressed as much as the estimated compression ratio that is used to report the amount of free space on compressed drives assumes they can be. If you are going to install Windows 95 on a compressed drive, you will have to have a lot more space than shown in Table 3-2.

Windows 95 manages a dynamically sized swap file. This swap file can be on the compressed drive that stores the bulk of the Windows 95 files or it can be on an uncompressed drive. Windows 95 handles the swap file so it is not slowed by file compression by placing it at the end of the CVF and not compressing it. The issues of file compression and the swap file are discussed in detail in Chapter 27.

Upgrade Windows 3.*x* or start anew

If you install Windows 95 in your existing Windows directory, you carry the past forward with you — all of the past. You don't have to reconfigure or reinstall any of your applications. Your Registry (a database that stores information about Windows and your Windows applications) is automatically updated to reflect your installed applications (as it reads your Windows 3.*x* Win.ini, System.ini, and Protocol.ini files) during the setup process.

In short, here are the advantages of installing Windows 95 in your existing Windows 3.*x* directory:

- The values stored in System.ini, Win.ini, and Protocol.ini are now stored in your Windows 95 Registry.

- Values stored in these files that refer to other applications are stored in the Registry, maintaining existing file/application associations and fonts.

- Existing network client software is automatically updated for a number of networks including those from Microsoft, Novell, Digital Equipment Corporation, Sun, and Banyan, among others.

- Existing Windows 3.x Program Manager groups are converted to menus on your Start button.

If you install to a new folder or delete your old Windows 3.1 directory and install to an empty Windows folder, you will need to reinstall some of your Windows applications. This is required because many Windows applications:

- Installed portions of themselves in the Windows folder and that folder is either wiped out or no longer on the path (the DLLs won't be found when the executable is called).

- Need to be registered in the Registry if they use OLE or create file associations.

- Installed configuration files (*ini* files) in the Windows directory that need to be moved to the new Windows folders and, perhaps, re-edited.

Installing Windows 95 in a new folder makes a clean break with the past. You have to deliberately reinstall those applications that you use. You have to configure all the settings to match your preferences. You have to remember (or relearn) where all those settings were hidden. You have to go find all the diskettes for the applications that you now have to reinstall. All this because Windows 3.x got out of control.

If you install over Windows 3.x, you might first want to use an uninstall program and get rid of these unused files. You can manually edit Win.ini and System.ini (using Sysedit.exe in the \Windows\System directory) to clean up references to the unused past. If you have a lot of fonts that you don't use, you can uninstall and delete them from your hard disk.

Another route to take is to install Windows 95 over a *copy* of your Windows 3.x directory. The Windows 95 Registry would be updated with all the information about your installed Windows applications, your Program Groups, etc. But you would still have an intact installation of Windows 3.x to go back to if need be.

We give a complete step-by-step method of installing over a copy of your existing Windows directory, while keeping your Windows 3.x directory intact so that you can dual-boot back to Windows 3.x during the transition period. See the section later in this chapter entitled *Installing Windows 95 Safely Over Windows 3.x*.

If you choose to install over Windows 3.1, you do have the option of saving enough information to uninstall Windows 95 and to get back to Windows 3.1. We'll show you when to do that in the *Setup Process* section later in this chapter.

Alternatively, you can keep your Windows 3.x directory intact and install Windows 95 in its own folder. This will allow you to dual-boot between these two operating systems. You just want to make sure you have enough disk space for both. Of course, you'll still have to reinstall some of your applications after you boot up Windows 95. Their DLLs will then be installed in both the Windows 3.x directory and the Windows 95 folder.

Secret

If you install Windows 95 in its own folder, a temporary way to get around reinstalling all these Windows 3.x programs is to include references in your path statement to the old Windows directory and System directory at the *end* of your Path *after* all other directories. This may let your old Windows applications find their DLLs. It doesn't update their file associations or register them for OLE.

Protecting your DOS files

Windows 95 installs its own DOS files in its Command folder (\Windows\Command). These files are updated versions of some of the DOS files that are installed in your DOS (version 5.x or 6.x) directory. Not all files that come with DOS 6.2x come with Windows 95.

Some of the files that came with earlier versions of DOS will cause problems if they are run after you install Windows 95. DOS 6.x versions of Scandisk.exe and Defrag.exe are disk utilities that break the link between short filenames and long filenames maintained by Windows 95. You should not run these versions of these programs after you install Windows 95.

Some newer DOS programs that come with Windows 95 are really no different than the older DOS versions; they are just given a new file creation date and placed in the new Command folder upon installation.

When you install Windows 95, the setup procedures rename the older DOS programs that cause problems with long filenames. For example, Scandisk.exe becomes Scandisk.ex~. In addition, a batch file is created, Scandisk.bat, which is invoked when you type Scandisk at the DOS prompt (if you boot to the old operating system). This batch file essentially tells you to use the ScanDisk program in Windows 95 (found in the Command folder or by using the Explorer and right-clicking a hard disk icon).

Secret

If you install Windows 95 in an existing Windows 3.1 directory, about 2MB worth of DOS files will be deleted from your existing DOS directory, including the DOS 6.x version of Scandisk.exe. These files are either not needed (as far as Microsoft is concerned), replaced by files installed in the Command folder, or too dangerous to use with Windows 95.

If you install Windows 95 to a new folder, the DOS files are not deleted. This allows you to have full DOS functionality when you dual-boot to the previous DOS version instead of into Windows 95. Even if you boot to the previous DOS version, you don't want to use previous versions' DOS disk tools that cause problems with long filenames. That is why, no matter where you put Windows 95, these previous disk utilities are renamed.

Microsoft decided to delete these older DOS programs because it replaced them in the new Command folder and saw a way to reclaim 2MB of disk space for you automatically. As long as you were overwriting Windows 3.1 and changing your path to include the Command folder, Microsoft felt that the right thing to do was to get rid of replicated DOS programs.

Tip

If you want to make sure that the Windows 95 installation procedures don't change or delete any existing DOS programs, copy them to another directory that is not on your path, or compress a copy of all of them. Changing their attribute to read-only won't do any good. Check the section entitled *BootMulti* in Chapter 6 for more details.

After Windows 95 is installed, you can copy the files back from the other folder, or unzip the zipped files. Just be sure not to use the older disk utilities, such as ScanDisk and Defrag.

Saving some Windows 3.x applets

Some applets that Microsoft included with Windows 3.x have not been upgraded or even made available with Windows 95. If you like using these applets, you'll need to make them available under Windows 95. If you installed Windows 95 in a new folder, you can create shortcut icons on the desktop of Start menus that refer to these applets in the Windows 3.x directory.

Windows Write

Windows Write is not saved. If you install Windows 95 in your Windows 3.x directory, then the Write executable file (Write.exe) is written over by an executable stub (Write.exe) that merely calls WordPad.exe. If you install Windows 95 to a new folder, this same stub executable is installed. All your Windows Write files will now be opened by WordPad.

Secret

To keep this from happening, make sure you save a copy of the original Write.exe and Write.hlp files. If you are going to install Windows 95 in the Windows 3.x directory, copy these files to a temporary directory before you install Windows 95. After installing Windows 95, you can copy these files back into the Windows 95 folder.

Secret

It does no good to write-protect Write.exe because Windows 95 Setup ignores the read-only attribute and writes right over it.

Microsoft wants you to use WordPad, its new 32-bit less-than-word-processor. Windows Write is now an out-of-date, 16-bit, half-text-editor, half-word-processor. But Write has the benefit of being smaller, faster, and more powerful than the newly updated Notepad.

Even after you restore Windows Write, you won't be able to engage it by double-clicking on files with the *wri* extension. You'll need to change the file extension association in the file type dialog box. For step-by-step instructions on how to do this, turn to Chapter 13.

The Recorder

The least-appreciated of Windows tools, the macro recorder, is not included with Windows 95 and doesn't work well with the new 32-bit applets. If you install Windows 95 over Windows 3.1, however, the Recorder is still there and isn't overwritten like Windows Write.

While many of the sophisticated Windows applications have their own macro recorders, it would be great to have a general purpose version that could help automate your repetitive tasks. If you purchased Windows 95 without ever installing Windows 3.x, your system doesn't have a copy of Recorder.exe. We have featured some shareware on the CD-ROM that gives you some general macro capabilities with Windows 95.

However, *bat* files are a major exception to this rule. If you drag a *bat* file to the desktop, it is *moved* — a shortcut is *not* created.

Clipbook

Clipbook (which comes with Windows for Workgroups 3.11) doesn't come with Windows 95. Clipboard, however, does. If you installed over Windows for Workgroups 3.11, you still have Clipbook. Both Clipbook and Clipboard work the same way in Windows 95 as they did in Windows 3.x.

Secret

If you have any problems using the sharing facilities of Clipbook, put NetDDE.exe in your Startup folder (and start it up). Windows for Workgroups 3.11 automatically starts NetDDE. Windows 95 doesn't.

Other applets

Cardfile is also gone. During the beta cycle, Cardfile was replaced by WinPad, Microsoft's Personal Digital Assistant software. WinPad was subsequently dropped, but nothing replaced it.

Schedule+ 1.0 is gone, but you should be able to get an update to Schedule+ 2.0 from Microsoft soon after Windows 95 is released.

Dual-booting

Before you install Windows 95, you'll need to decide whether you want to keep the capability to start your computer using your old version of DOS and/or Windows. Windows 95 is no mere upgrade and it is with some trepidation that you install it without a safety net.

If you are unsure whether some of your Windows applications will work with Windows 95 and you have the hard disk space, you should install Windows 95 in a separate folder. You can then migrate your Windows applications over one at a time and be sure that everything is working.

If Windows 95 doesn't work out, you can then uninstall it and go back to your previous version of Windows. You'll need to be sure that you have protected your DOS files as per the instructions in the section earlier in this chapter entitled *Protecting your DOS files*.

In order to easily install later, you must also answer Yes to the question "Save system files?" when you install Windows 95.

Still, Windows 95 is an upgrade, even if it is no mere upgrade, and the point is to move from your previous version of Windows into the future.

A new face

Windows 95 has a completely new user interface, and this is going to take a little getting used to. It is possible to run slightly revised Windows 95 versions of the Windows 3.x Program Manager and File Manager. If you choose the Custom setup, you are presented (if you dig a little) with the option of starting the Program Manager when you boot Windows 95.

The Program Manager is just not up to the task of handling the new capabilities of Windows 95. If you have to have it to provide a reassuring look to your users (perhaps including yourself), you can install it during setup, but it is not a long-term solution.

We recommend you make a clean break with the past and take the time to learn the new user interface. Throughout this book, we provide plenty of guidance for dealing with the many user interface issues.

Clean up your Startup folder

If you install Windows 95 over your existing Windows directory, the applications in your Startup group will migrate to your new Startup folder. When you start Windows 95, these programs will also be started.

Some of these programs may not be applicable to Windows 95. For example, the Windows 3.1 version of Plug-In, a wonderful add-on to the Program Manager, will not work with Windows 95. Windows 95 Setup should find Plug-In and take references to it out of Win.ini.

You will want to remove this type of offending programs from your Startup group before you install Windows 95.

CD-ROM or diskette version?

If there is any way that you can swing it, get the CD-ROM version of Windows 95. It saves a tremendous amount of diskette-swapping aggravation. Windows 95 is just too big to fit on a convenient number of diskettes.

Microsoft ships Windows 95 on special extra high density (1.7MB) diskettes that can be read but not written to (without special formatting and diskette writing software, which you will find on the shareware CD-ROM accompanying this book). This was to cut down on the materials cost and give you the benefit of fewer diskettes to swap.

Even if you are installing Windows 95 on a computer without a CD-ROM, you should still think about getting the CD-ROM version. Do this if you can copy the Windows 95 source files off the CD-ROM onto your computer's hard disk by connecting to a computer with a CD-ROM over a network, or through a serial or parallel cable to a PC with a CD-ROM. (See Chapter 30, "Laptop to Desktop," for information on computer connection.)

Loading the source files

Installing Windows 95 from diskettes or a single or dual-speed CD-ROM can be quite slow. Loading from diskettes is the worst. If you have a quad-speed CD-ROM, things are quite a bit brighter.

Tip

If you have the spare hard disk space to copy the CD-ROM or the diskettes to a temporary hard disk directory, you should consider this option. Copying the diskettes takes a while but Windows 95 installation goes much faster after all the installation files are on the hard disk.

You'll need about 33MB of free hard disk space to copy the CD-ROM files to your hard disk. Most of the files are in a compressed format and are stored in files that end in the extension *cab*, which stands for cabinet. The setup routines will extract the files from the file cabinets.

The nice thing about this method is that the original source files are always available locally off a high speed device (your hard disk). If you make changes to your Windows setup, the reconfiguration routines point back to the source files on your hard disk and quickly allow you to update Windows 95. You don't have to go searching for your Windows 95 diskettes or CD-ROM.

The problem is, of course, that you just used up 33MB of hard disk space ($9.90 worth at 30 cents a megabyte) that you might actually need. You can erase these source files after you have successfully installed Windows 95, but another problem arises. Any subsequent updates will point back to the now-erased source files, expecting to find them on your hard disk.

You will need to point the update routines in the direction of your CD-ROM or diskettes when prompted to do so.

To copy the cabinet files from the diskettes you use the Extract command, which is on the first diskette. You won't be able to use the copy command or drop and drag them with the File Manager from the special diskettes.

Use the extract command (in DOS or a DOS window at the c:\win95scr prompt) as follows:

```
extract /c a:\precopy2.cab c:\win95src
```

Replace *precopy2.cab* with the name of each cabinet file. Use the DOS DIR command to display the names of the files on the DMF diskettes. You can type **extract /?** to view the online documentation for the Extract command.

Tip

You can get a listing of all the files in the Windows 95 source cabinets (starting with Win95_02.cab) by using a variation of the Extract command and piping the results to a file. At the DOS prompt (while in the Windows 95 source directory) issue the command:

```
extract /d /a win95_02.cab > List95.txt
```

Installing over a network or from a CD-ROM

If your computer is connected to a network and the source files are stored on a server, either on a hard disk or a CD-ROM, you can install Windows 95 from the server. Unless you have a system administrator who has custom-designed the installation procedures, it is no different than installing Windows 95 from a local diskette drive, CD-ROM, or hard disk — with one exception.

Secret

Near the end of the Windows 95 installation, Windows 95 reboots your computer and grabs further files from the source cabinets. It reboots your computer under Windows 95. If, using the Windows 95 network or CD-ROM drivers, it is unable to make the connection to your network server or to your local CD-ROM drive, Windows 95 can't continue configuring itself.

If you're upgrading over a previous Windows directory, it may be difficult to get back to your previous connections to the server or the CD-ROM. There is obviously a bug if Windows 95 can't access your network or CD-ROM. But the bug shows up at an inopportune time.

While you won't be able to completely install Windows 95 because you don't have access to some files, in particular the printer files, you will have a semi-working version of Windows 95 at the end of your setup process. You will need to make some changes in your configuration to regain access to the network or your CD-ROM, perhaps using your previously working 16-bit drivers.

Getting Ready to Start Windows 95 Setup

Your installation of Windows 95 may choke if you have loaded DOS TSRs into memory or are running Windows utilities or add-ons. Microsoft provides a list of TSRs known to cause problems in the file Setup.txt, which you will find on the Windows 95 CD-ROM or diskettes. Setup also searches through one of its files, Setupc.inf, to see if there are conflicts.

So many combinations of TSRs and Windows utilities could cause problems that Microsoft would prefer you eliminate as many variables as possible. Already, most support calls are regarding setup issues.

Just before you install Windows 95 you should remark out as many of the calls to TSRs in Config.sys and Autoexec.bat as you can live without during the installation. You should also close any programs that are started by your Windows Startup group and eliminate unnecessary programs from the Startup group before installing Windows 95.

Back up some files

Changes are going to be made to a number of your existing files. If you want to play it safe, you can back them up and edit the newer versions later.

If you are updating your Windows 3.1 directory, you'll want to back up all configuration *(ini)* files, Registry *(dat)* files, and password *(pwl)* files. No matter how you install Windows 95, you'll want to back up Autoexec.bat and Config.sys and any network configuration files and logon scripts.

Changes will be made

You don't want to remark out the real-mode drivers in Autoexec.bat and Config.sys before you start installation. Hardware detection procedures in Windows 95 Setup use these calls to help configure Windows 95.

Changes will be made to your Autoexec.bat and Config.sys files. Lines will be remarked out that are no longer needed. You will undoubtedly want to edit Autoexec.bat and Config.sys further or even remove these files.

If you have a Config.sys file with different sections for multi-configuration, only the currently active portion of the Config.sys file is used by Windows 95 Setup when configuring Windows 95. All other sections of Config.sys (and Autoexec.bat) are remarked out. If you want to use a multi-configuration version of Config.sys and Autoexec.bat with Windows 95, you will need to edit these files after the Windows 95 installation is complete.

A new file, Dosstart.bat, is created by Setup. You'll find it in the Windows 95 folder. Lines remarked out of your Autoexec.bat file are placed in this file. Dosstart is run when you start an MS-DOS mode session under Windows 95 (under some circumstances). Check out Chapter 17 for more details.

Running Setup from DOS or Windows 3.1*x*

Windows 95 Setup can be run from either your previous version of DOS (version 3.2 or higher) or from Windows 3.1*x* (not Windows 3.0). If you have only DOS on your computer, you can run Setup from DOS.

When you start Windows 95 Setup from DOS, it loads a mini version of Windows 3.1 from your Windows 95 source files and then runs Setup from this version of Windows. It will run a DOS 7.0 version of ScanDisk before it loads this mini version of Windows. If you start from Windows 3.*x*, the DOS 7.0 version of ScanDisk will be run behind the scenes.

If a previous version of Windows 3.1*x* is loaded on your computer when you run Windows 95 Setup from DOS, Setup will find it and ask you if you want use this version of Windows to run Setup. There's no reason not to.

Setup switches

The easiest way to run the Windows 95 setup/installation is to double-click, in your Windows 3.1*x* File Manager, Setup.exe in the Windows 95 source directory. However, if you run Setup from the DOS prompt or by choosing File, Run in the Windows 3.1*x* File Manager, you can add some command line parameters. They are shown in Table 3-3.

Table 3-3	Command Line Parameters for Setup
Switch	*Resulting Action*
Setup /?	Lists some of the Setup switches.
Setup /d	Don't use the existing version of Windows to run Windows 95 Setup.
Setup /id	Don't check for minimum hard disk space requirements.
Setup /is	Run Setup without first running ScanDisk. It is recommended that you run ScanDisk first. If you get a message that there is not enough free conventional memory to run ScanDisk, and you have freed up as much conventional memory as possible, you can run Setup with this switch.
Setup /iq	This is the same as Setup /is except that you use it if you are running Setup from DOS. Use this switch or /is if you are using compression software other than DriveSpace or DoubleSpace.
Setup /nostart	Copy from the Windows 95 source files the minimum Windows 3.*x* DLLs required to run the Windows 95 Setup and then exit to DOS.
Setup *script-file*	If you have a script file that automates the setup process, this is how you run it. Often the script file will be on a network server, which you will need to log into before you begin setting up.

The Setup Process

You might be getting the idea that setting up Windows 95 is no simple matter. The setup procedures have to check for thousands of different hardware and software combinations. Developing the setup software was almost as complicated for Microsoft as creating the core of Windows 95 itself.

Running Windows 95 Setup is not that difficult because Microsoft has done so much work to make it do the work for you. While we can't cover every step, we do point out some key areas and give you extra guidance about how to proceed.

Most of the dialog boxes that you'll see while Setup runs have Next and Back buttons. You get to choose when you go forward. If you want to go back and make a choice over again, you often have that option.

Starting Sotup

You can start Windows 95 Setup using any one of the three methods described previously in this chapter in the section entitled *Setup switches*. If you are running Setup from Windows, it will display the dialog box shown in Figure 3-1. Click OK to continue.

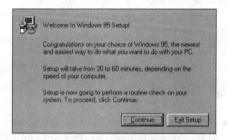

Figure 3-1: The Windows 95 Setup opening dialog box. If you decide that you really weren't ready to start, you can exit Setup now. There will be other opportunities to quit or go back without consequences later during Setup.

If you are running Setup from the DOS prompt, you won't see this screen, but rather, you see the DOS 7.0 version of ScanDisk (found with the Windows 95 source files) running first.

Running ScanDisk

As soon as Setup starts, the ScanDisk program from the Windows 95 source files is called to check your hard disk.

If you start Windows 95 Setup from the DOS prompt, a DOS 7.0 version of ScanDisk will run in the foreground. If you start it from Windows, the DOS 7.0 version of ScanDisk runs in background while Setup tells you in a Windows message box that it is performing a routine check of your system, as shown in Figure 3-2.

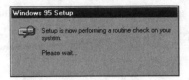

Figure 3-2: If you start Windows 95 Setup from Windows 3.1*x*, this message box appears while the DOS 7.0 version of ScanDisk (not the Windows 95 version) is running in background.

If, while running Windows 95 Setup, ScanDisk reports a lack of conventional memory, quit Setup. You can then edit your existing Autoexec.bat and Config.sys files and restart your computer to get more conventional memory. This may allow the DOS 7.0 ScanDisk program to work correctly.

Undocumented

If Windows 95 Setup has trouble running the DOS 7.0 version of ScanDisk, you can run an earlier version of ScanDisk before you run Setup again. You'll need to be running DOS 6.2 or later to have ScanDisk. You can also run Defrag if you have DOS 6.0 or later. *Don't run the old versions of ScanDisk or Defrag after you have installed Windows 95.*

You can, alternately, run the DOS 7.0 version of ScanDisk that comes on the Windows 95 diskettes or CD-ROM (even though you are running an earlier version of DOS). You can run this version of ScanDisk from the DOS prompt before you start Windows 95 Setup again.

If you get an error message that you that must run ScanDisk to fix some problems encountered on your hard disk, you'll want to run the DOS 7.0 version of ScanDisk. To do so, take the following steps:

STEPS

Running DOS 7.0 ScanDisk to Correct Hard Disk Problems

Step 1.   Quit Windows 95 Setup (and Windows 3.1*x*).

Step 2.   Make sure that the first diskette in the Windows 95 set of diskettes is in your diskette drive, that your Windows 95 CD-ROM is in its drive, or that the Windows 95 source files are on your hard disk (should be already there).

Step 3.   At the DOS command prompt type:

   *a***:Scandisk.exe /all**

   Where *a* is the drive (and directory) designator for the location of the Windows 95 source files.

Step 4. Follow the directions on the screen.

Step 5. Start your earlier version of Windows again and run Windows 95 Setup again.

If you were originally running Windows 95 Setup from DOS, the DOS 7.0 ScanDisk will run and you'll be able to fix most disk problems without having to get out of Setup.

After ScanDisk runs under Setup, you are asked if you wish to continue running Setup. You can exit without any consequences at this point.

Warning about open programs

If Setup detects that some Windows 3.x programs are running, you will get the error message shown in Figure 3-3. Press Alt+Tab to switch to those programs, close them, and then continue Setup by clicking OK.

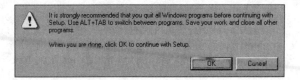

Figure 3-3: Windows 95 Setup detects running Windows programs. Click OK to continue Setup, Alt+Tab to close the programs, or Cancel to stop Setup.

Windows 95 Setup detects all running Windows programs, the vast majority of which will cause no problems. Microsoft just doesn't want any problems here, so it asks you to close all Windows programs. We have never had a problem with just proceeding, but for safety's sake, you might want to take the time to close your apps at this point.

Collecting information

You'll know that the next phase of setting up Windows 95 has begun once the dialog box shown in Figure 3-4 is displayed. Setup is ready to get some information from you and from your computer. You can quit Setup by clicking Cancel or continue by clicking Next. As this is the start of a new phase, you can't go back. You can, however, cancel and run the startup phase again.

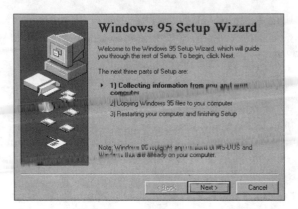

Figure 3-4: The Windows 95 Setup Wizard dialog box. You can quit Setup by clicking Cancel, or proceed to the fact-finding portion of Setup. The Back button is grayed out because the first phase has been completed and you can go back only by clicking Cancel and starting again.

The Windows 95 directory

Windows 95 Setup will, by default, attempt to install Windows 95 in your existing Windows 3.x directory. You have to tell it *twice* if you want to install Windows 95 in a new directory. You are presented with the dialog box shown in Figure 3-5. You can choose between the current Windows 3.x directory or another directory.

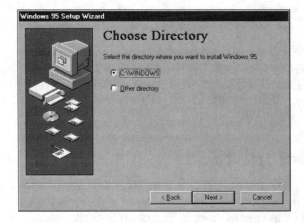

Figure 3-5: The Choose Directory dialog box. Windows 95 calls directories *folders*. Windows 95 Setup is the transition phase to Windows 95. Therefore the Windows 95 folder is called a *directory* in this dialog box. The default choice is to upgrade your existing Windows 3.x directory with Windows 95. Click Other to put Windows 95 in a new directory.

If you choose to install Windows 95 into your existing Windows 3.x directory, you do have the option of saving crucial parts of your Windows 3.x directory so that you can uninstall Windows 95 and go back to Windows 3.x.

If you choose Other directory and click Next, you get the dialog box shown in Figure 3-6. Again, Setup wants to put Windows 95 into your current Windows 3.x directory. You will have to type in the volume, path, and directory name of your new Windows 95 directory if you want to install it in a directory other than your existing Windows 3.x directory.

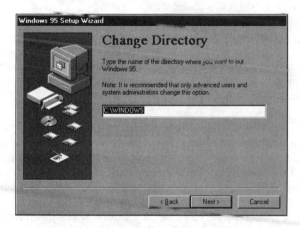

Figure 3-6: The Change Directory dialog box. The default is the current Windows 3.x directory — not much of a change. Type in the name of a new directory if you want to install Windows 95 in a new separate directory.

Checking for free hard disk space

Windows 95 Setup now checks whether your computer meets the minimum requirements, including sufficient available disk space. If it determined that there is not enough free hard disk space for a Typical installation, it warns you with the dialog box shown in Figure 3-7. If you use the Compact or Custom install options, you may be able to get in under the limit.

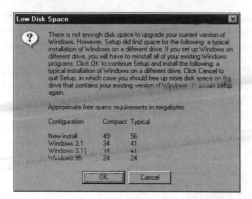

Figure 3-7: The Not enough disk space warning. If you feel that there is in fact enough free hard disk space to install Windows 95, click OK. If you are unsure, quit Setup by clicking Cancel and free up as much hard disk space as you can.

This dialog box can be quite confusing. You have told Setup where Windows 95 should be installed so you would think it should know if it it's updating an existing Windows 3.x directory or being installed in a new one. In addition, between the Choose or Change Directory dialog boxes and this "not enough disk space" dialog box, if you were updating Windows 3.x, Setup presented you with a Preparing Directory screen that indicated it was searching the current Windows 3.x directory for installed Windows components. Again, you would think that Setup would be smart enough to know which setup you're performing.

Instead, this dialog box presents you with a chart with four rows, each representing a different upgrade or setup option. Since Setup doesn't appear to be smart enough to know whether it is upgrading or installing to a new Windows 95 directory, you have to know which one you want and which one Setup should have found, in order to read this chart correctly.

Finally, since Windows 95 Setup doesn't yet know just what parts of Windows 95 you are going to install, it can't be sure that you don't have enough room to install Windows 95. It assumes you are going to choose the Typical option later on. Since you haven't made that choice yet, you might not have thought about it. You also don't know just what Typical means.

Did you check your hard disk space before you started? If not, click Cancel and do so before you begin Setup again.

Read the chart in this dialog box using the row that corresponds to the kind of upgrade or new setup that you want to perform. Combine that row with the column for the type of setup you will choose in a minute. We recommend that you do a custom installation for the greatest flexibility, but make your best guess from the "columnar" options now.

If you feel you have enough free hard disk space, click OK and go to the next dialog box, which lets you choose from among four Setup options. If you are unsure about how much hard disk space you have, click Cancel and check things out before you begin Setup again.

If it turns out that you do not have enough free hard disk space, Setup will quit prematurely. You can recover from this and run Setup again from DOS if you have overwritten crucial parts of Windows 3.1*x* and Windows 3.1*x* doesn't run anymore.

Get connected

Microsoft wants to highlight the fact that Windows 95 is a very communicative operating system. Microsoft Exchange, its universal e-mail and fax client, gets installed if you install any of the options in the dialog box shown in Figure 3-8.

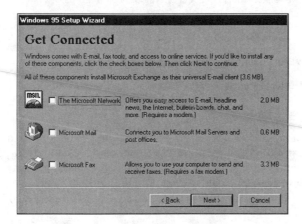

Figure 3-8: The Get Connected dialog box.

Don't install Microsoft Mail unless your computer is connected to a local area network and your co-workers are using Microsoft Mail. Though you can install the Microsoft Network now, that doesn't mean you've signed up for it. You do that later. Microsoft Fax is integrated with Microsoft Exchange so you can keep your e-mail and faxes in one unified message store, with one user interface.

Setup Options

After you choose a directory for Windows 95, you are given four options: Typical, Portable, Compact, and Custom. The dialog box that presents these choices is shown in Figure 3-9. You are not given enough information to intelligently decide what these choices mean—that is, what features of Windows 95 will be installed with each choice.

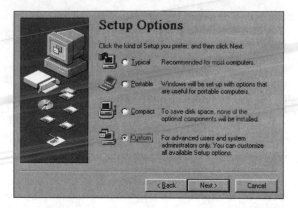

Figure 3-9: The Setup Options dialog box. We suggest choosing Custom so you can have the option of making a more refined choice of specific Windows 95 features.

We suggest you take the Custom option. Later during the setup process you'll get to define just what features you want to install.

Click Next to continue. If you want to go back, click Back at any time.

User Information

After you choose a type of setup, you are asked to supply user information. This information isn't particularly important for the successful operation of Windows 95. It will show up in About Boxes, and in your Fax configuration dialog box. Both authors put their name on the first field and underscores in the second field, as shown in Figure 3-10.

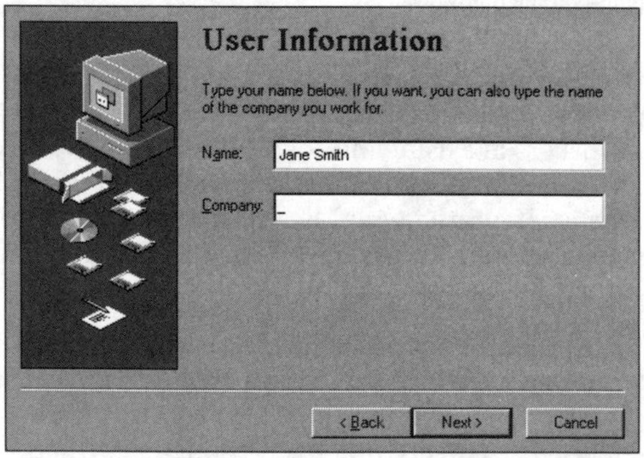

Figure 3-10: The User Information dialog box. The user name and company name shows up in the Help About dialog box and as the default when setting up Microsoft Fax.

Hardware Detection

Setup next probes your computer for information about the hardware installed in it. It has previously checked to make sure your computer met the minimum hardware requirements for a Windows 95 computer and that it had enough free hard disk space to install Windows 95. Now Setup looks at each piece of hardware and builds a list in your Registry of what it finds.

You will see the Analyzing Your Computer dialog box shown in Figure 3-11. Let Setup automatically detect your hardware unless you have a very good reason to specify it yourself. Knowing that you have some hardware that crashes Setup would qualify as a "very good reason."

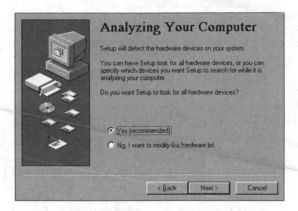

Figure 3-11: The Analyzing Your Computer dialog box.

Hardware detection may need some extra encouragement to look for certain pieces of hardware if it doesn't find references to them in Config.sys or Autoexec.bat and wonders if they are really there. After you click the Next button in the Analyzing Your Computer dialog box, you may get another Analyzing Your Computer dialog box like that shown in Figure 3-12. You can tell Setup to look for these additional pieces of hardware.

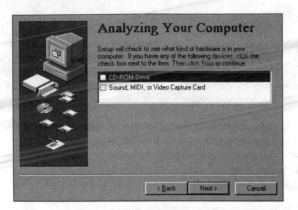

Figure 3-12: The second Analyzing Your Computer dialog box. Click the check boxes for those pieces of hardware you know you have installed in your computer.

After you click Next on this second Analyzing Your Computer dialog box, Setup performs hardware detection. This takes a while and you'll hear a lot of accesses to the hard disk.

Hardware detection may fail. If so, all is not lost. You can run Setup again and it will pass over the area where hardware detection failed. If hardware detection fails, you most likely will have to press Ctrl+Alt+Del or even the reset button on your computer.

Unless you have a computer that has a plug and play BIOS and is populated with plug and play cards, much of hardware detection will consist of the hardware detection routines probing hardware and testing what it finds against a database of known hardware. On older hardware it won't find ROM chips that contain properly formatted identifiers. The Setup hardware detection routines have to perform a lot of different little tricks to detect what is there.

The great thing about this is that you don't have to have plug and play hardware to be up to date with Windows 95. Microsoft has made the effort to bring along existing hardware and let it use the new operating system — a wise choice.

The hardware detection process also determines which resources (interrupts, memory addresses, memory ranges, and DMA channels) are used by the hardware. If conflicts over the use of these resources exist, hardware detection will note them for your later resolution.

Safe Recovery

If hardware detection crashes, you can start again. Setup will notice the fact that it had a problem because it left a trail behind it. The trail consists of four log files: Bootlog.txt, Detlog.txt, Setuplog.txt, and Detcrash.log.

- If Setup fails *before* hardware detection begins, Setup uses Setuplog.txt to determine where it went wrong when you restart it.

- If Setup fails *during* hardware detection, Detcrash.log is created. Rerunning Setup finds this file and uses it to determine which detection module was running. Setup goes into Safe Recovery mode, reading the Registry to determine what hardware has been found and not using any failed detection modules.

- If Setup fails *after* hardware detection, Smart Recovery skips the hardware detection process.

The Safe Recovery dialog box shown in Figure 3-13 will appear when you restart Setup. Choose Use Safe Recovery if there was a problem with your last attempt to run Setup and you want to skip over that problem.

Figure 3-13: The Safe Recovery dialog box. The Use Safe Recovery option is the default. Click Next to use this option if there was a problem with your last attempt to run Setup.

Select Components

If you have chosen the Custom setup option, you will get to choose just what add-on Windows 95 features you want installed using the Select Components dialog box, which is shown in Figure 3-14. *Read the text in this dialog box carefully.*

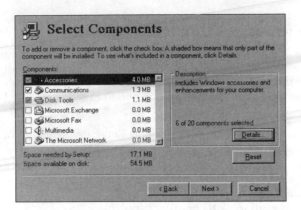

Figure 3-14: The Select Components dialog box. Use it to determine what features you want installed with Windows 95. Double-clicking items in the list box opens another dialog box with more choices.

The Select Components dialog box is the top of a hierarchy. Each element displayed in the list in the center of the dialog box leads to a further list of individual components that you can have installed. Double-clicking any item in the list (or highlighting an item and clicking Details) brings up an additional dialog box listing these individual components.

The Select Components dialog box also displays the amount of free hard disk space and the amount that will be consumed by installing Windows 95 and whatever components you choose. As you select each component for installation, the amount of hard disk space required to install Windows 95 increases and this increase is displayed in this dialog box right under the component list box. Notice that there is a certain amount of hard disk space used to install basic Windows 95 and the default components.

In order to make wise choices about what components to install you need to know:

■ What benefits/features the component offers

■ How much hard disk space it costs

If you are not familiar with the features offered, you may want to skim Chapter 2 or other chapters in this book that relate to these components as you install Windows 95.

The Custom setup option provides you with the most choice (after all, you get this Select Components dialog box), but it also asks you to make decisions that you may not be ready to make. You can easily add or delete any of these components anytime after you have installed Windows 95, so you can wait to make choices later if you so desire. See the section later in this chapter entitled *Adding and removing parts of Windows 95* or turn to Chapter 16 for more details.

Accessories

Highlight Accessories in the Select Components dialog box and click the Details button. You will see a dialog box that lists the individual accessories you can install with Windows 95, as shown in Figure 3-15.

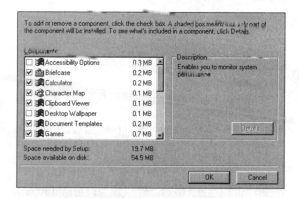

Figure 3-15: Accessories components dialog box. Scroll through this list to see all the possible accessory choices that you have.

When you highlight an individual accessory in this list, details about that accessory are shown in the description portion of the dialog box. The hard disk size requirements are shown to the right of each accessory named in the list box. To add an accessory to the list of components to be installed, click the check box to the left of the accessory name in the list. When you are finished choosing accessories, click OK.

The Online Users Guide and the Windows 95 Tour include help files about Startup for the new Windows 95 user. Some of these files are in the form of rather large video files, which you can tell from the 8.2MB size of the Online Users Guide. These help files are very basic. If you need very basic help and have the space, install them. You can always remove the video files (those with *avi* extensions) later.

Communications

If you want to connect two computers together using a parallel or serial cable to easily transfer files, select Dial-Up Networking and Direct Cable Connection from the Communications components dialog box shown in Figure 3-16.

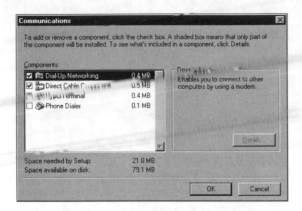

Figure 3-16: The Communications components dialog box. The first two choices allow you to connect two computers.

If you have a modem, you might want to choose HyperTerminal to dial into bulletin boards or the applet Dialer, which remembers a few phone numbers and can dial your phone for you.

Disk Tools

The Disk Tools component includes hard disk backup, defragmentation, and compression. Backup is not chosen by default. You might want it if you have a device that works with it (some tape drives). You need compression only if you have compressed hard drives and want to add compressed volumes later.

Microsoft Exchange

Microsoft Exchange is a complete electronic mail and fax management system. It allows you to send and receive mail through the Internet (if you also purchase Windows 95 Plus!), over local and wide area networks, through CompuServe, or the Microsoft Network. You'll need a network connection (either through a network card, Dial-Up Networking or Direct Cable Connection) or a modem.

Microsoft Fax

Install Microsoft Exchange if you want to install Microsoft Fax. Your faxes get managed like e-mail. You'll need access to a fax/modem, either locally or over a LAN.

Multimedia

You need a sound card if you want to take advantage of any of the accessories offered in the Multimedia components list.

The Microsoft Network

To access the Microsoft Network (MSN), you'll need a modem or network connection to a modem (at least until Microsoft provides direct Internet access). The Microsoft Network is an online service you can access if you have installed Windows 95. If you install MSN, you'll have to install Microsoft Exchange.

Network connection

Windows 95 Setup configures a network connection for you if you have a network card installed, or you chose to install Dial-Up Networking. You get complete access to all the network configuration dialog boxes. The top-level network configuration dialog box is shown in Figure 3-17.

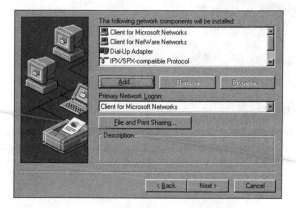

Figure 3-17: The network configuration dialog box. Components that will be installed are shown in the components list box in the upper right.

Numerous network configurations and settings can be determined with this dialog box. You can set up your network now or you can wait and do it after Windows 95 is installed. We discuss the intricacies of network setup in Chapter 34.

If your computer will be connected to a Windows NT computer, you will want to make a change in the properties of the Client for Microsoft Network. Double-click Client for Microsoft Network in the Network Configuration dialog box and check the Log on to Windows NT domain check box, as shown in Figure 3-18.

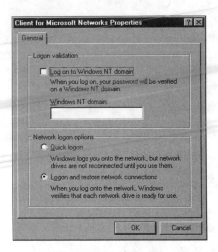

Figure 3-18: The Client for Microsoft Windows Properties sheet.

Identification

In order to keep track of who is who on a network, Windows 95 needs a unique identifier for your computer. You enter this information, plus the name of your workgroup if you are on a Microsoft Windows network, in the dialog box shown in Figure 3-19.

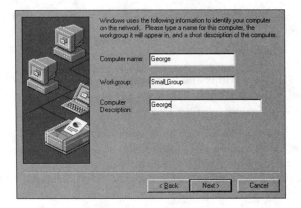

Figure 3-19: The identification dialog box. Enter a unique computer name, the name of the workgroup to which you wish to be attached, and, if you like, a description to help others identify your computer.

The computer must be unique on your network. The name connot be longer than 15 characters and may not contain spaces. The name should contain alphanumeric characters and may include the following special characters:

$$! @ \# \$ \% \wedge \& (\,) - \_ \, ' \{ \, \} . \sim$$

Your workgroup name uses these same naming conventions (remember, no spaces). A workgroup name is shared between members of the workgroup. If you are connecting to an existing one, get the name from a network administrator or your fellow networkees.

The description field will be displayed as a comment to the right of your computer name when other users on the Microsoft Windows network search for your computer.

This computer name is used only if you are using NetBIOS. If you are using TCP/IP or IPX/SPX without NetBIOS, you won't need to worry about it.

Network Information Required

Unless your network card is plug and play compatible, Setup may not be able to correctly configure its driver to match the card's setup. If this is the case, you will see the dialog box shown in Figure 3-20. If you know the network card's settings you can enter them. If you want to wait until later to correctly configure this card, choose the first option in this dialog box.

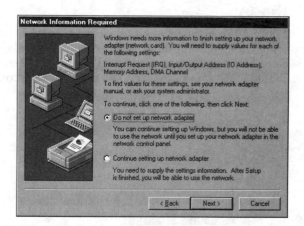

Figure 3-20: The Network Information Required dialog box. You'll need to know how your network card is configured to use it with Windows 95. With non-plug and play cards, this is set by hardware jumpers on the board or through the use of a DOS or Windows 3.x program. You may have to take your computer apart to find the values or run the program that came with the card.

If you are able to remember or find the values for your network card, click the second radio button in the Network Information Required dialog box and click Next. You can set these values in the Network Resources dialog box shown in Figure 3-21.

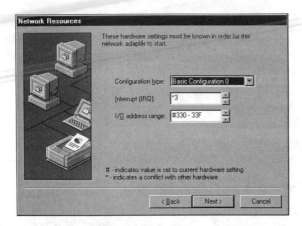

Figure 3-21: The Network Resources dialog box. Enter Interrupt and I/O address range for your network card.

Computer Settings

Remember way back during this setup process when Setup went out and detected your hardware? Some of the results of that search are displayed in the Computer Settings dialog box, as shown in Figure 3-22. You get to change these settings if they don't actually match what you know your hardware configuration to be.

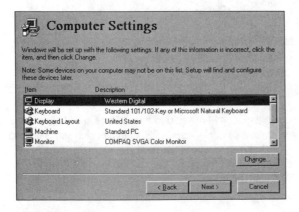

Figure 3-22: The Computer Settings dialog box. Scroll through this description of your hardware. If anything needs to be changed, double-click it.

Scroll down the list of Computer Settings. If you find an item you want to change, highlight it and click Change.

Tip

Windows 95 Setup may not have been able to correctly identify your video card. If so, it may show your display as VGA. You can change this later. You should wait to do this as Setup sometimes has difficulties if you make that change now.

Keyboard Layout is used by Windows to correctly identify the layout of keys on your keyboard. Setup will also modify Autoexec.bat and Config.sys to match that layout when you are in a Windows DOS session. If you change keyboard layout later using the Keyboard icon in the Control Panel, you will need to edit Autoexec.bat and Config.sys.

Setup looks for some odd computers that Windows 95 treats a little differently. If you double-click the Machine item in the list you can see this list of computers. If you have one of these computers and it has not been correctly identified by Setup, choose it now.

Most likely, Setup will not correctly identify your monitor unless you have a plug and play version. You can double-click Monitor and choose from the list.

You can change almost all of these settings later using icons in the Control Panel (other than Machine, User Interface, and Power Manager, if you don't have any power management features in your computer). You can change User Interface using other methods.

Tip

The last item in the Computer Settings list box is User Interface (use the scrollbar to get down to it), which defaults to Windows 95. The other option is Windows 3.1. If you choose Windows 3.1, you actually get both interfaces. A shortcut to the Windows 95 version of the Windows 3.x Program Manager is placed in the Startup folder and Program Manager is started up when you start Windows 95.

Startup Disk

If there is a problem with booting your computer under Windows 95 from the hard disk, you will want to be able to boot from a floppy diskette. Setup gives you the opportunity to create such a diskette. You can choose to do so when prompted by the Startup Disk dialog box, as shown in Figure 3-23.

You can always create a bootable startup diskette later using the Add/Remove program icon in your Control Panel. The startup diskette will not be able to connect you to your network. It will contain the files listed in Table 3-4.

Table 3-4	Files on Startup Diskette
Files	*Function*
Io.sys	Boot DOS
Msdos.sys	Startup configuration
Command.com	DOS Prompt
Attrib.exe	Change file attributes
Chkdsk.exe	Disk status
Edit.com	DOS-based editor
Edit.hlp	Help for same
Fc.exe	File Compare utility
Fdisk.exe	Low-level disk partition utility
Format.exe	Disk format utility
Mem.exe	Display memory status
More.com	Display one page at a time
Mscdex.exe	CD-ROM driver
Msd.exe	System diagnostics
Scandisk.exe	Utility to check and repair disk drives
Scandisk.ini	Configuration file for above
Setver.exe	Utility to set DOS versions for some programs
Sys.com	Utility to allow creation of bootable drive
Xcopy.exe	Extended copy utility

Figure 3-23: The Startup Disk dialog box. Choose whether you want to create a startup diskette or not. If you have a bad floppy drive and it may have trouble creating such a diskette, wait until later.

You might want to add a few files to the startup diskette, such as appropriate Autoexec.bat and Config.sys files as well as copies of System.dat, Win.ini, System.ini, and User.dat.

Copy files

Once Setup has gathered the information it needs from you and your computer to successfully configure and install Windows 95, it copies files that it needs from the Windows 95 cabinet source files. You initiate this process by clicking Next in the Start Copying Files dialog box, which is shown in Figure 3-24.

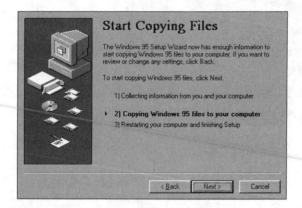

Figure 3-24: The Start Copying Files dialog box. You can go back, Cancel Setup, or go forward with Setup by clicking Next.

Setup takes a while to copy the files that it needs to install Windows 95. If you are installing over an existing Windows 3.*x* directory, most of the files will be copied to that directory over some previous versions of these files. The previous versions will no longer exist unless you have stored copies of them in some other directory.

If you have the hard disk space, it is possible to make a complete copy of your Windows 3.*x* directory and store it on another volume. You can then install Windows 95 over Windows 3.*x,* secure in the knowledge that you have the option of restoring your Windows 3.*x* directory if things go very wrong.

You can also back up your hard disk or just your Windows 3.*x* directory and restore it later if there is a problem. Of course, you'll want to do this before you start Setup, or at least before you take this somewhat irreversible step.

Finishing Setup

Copying files precedes automatically and at the end (if you didn't run out of hard disk space), Setup takes you to the Finishing Setup dialog box shown in Figure 3-25. You're not really finished with Setup, but Setup is now going to force your computer to reboot and start up in Windows 95. It configures a number of files before it starts Windows 95.

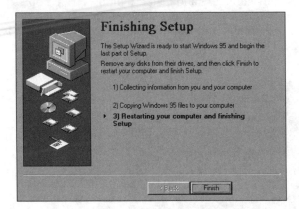

Figure 3-25: The Finish Setup dialog box. If you get this far, click Finish.

After you click Finish, Setup reboots your computer. It takes a while for the Windows 95 files to be configured and Windows 95 to start. If you didn't correctly configure your network card, you will receive a message to that effect and be told you can make the required changes later.

Next, your Control Panel will be set up, your Startup menus configured, your help files set up, and you will be asked to choose your time zone setting. You will also be prompted to set up your printer, your modem if you have one, and Microsoft Exchange if you installed it.

You can ignore these Setup dialog boxes now, if you like clicking the Cancel button, and can set up your time zone and other devices later through the Control Panel.

If VGA was chosen for your display during Setup, you can change it after Windows 95 starts by right-clicking the desktop, clicking Properties, and clicking the Settings Tab. Click the Change Display Type button and choose a new video adapter. See Chapter 22 for more details.

Installing Windows 95 Safely Over Windows 3.x

The Windows 95 Setup offers two options: install Windows 95 in its own directory or install it in the same directory as your Windows 3.x files. However, if you install Windows 95 into your Windows 3.x directory it'll be impossible to dual-boot between the two versions of Windows. Installing Windows 95 in its own directory also has drawbacks: Windows 95 won't inherit your Win 3.x preferences. Nor will it inherit your application settings in Win.ini and System.ini (to re-establish these settings, you'll have to painstakingly reinstall your applications).

Windows 95 also offers you the option during Setup to "save your System files." This helps if you need to uninstall Windows 95, but doesn't help you preserve both Windows 3.x and Windows 95 so you can dual-boot between them.

Secret

For the best of both worlds, we recommend *copying* your Windows 3.x directory and installing Windows 95 there. This not only saves your Windows 3.x settings, but it lets you dual-boot. Here's how to do it.

STEPS

Installing Windows 95 in a copy of the Windows 3.x directory

Step 1. Exit Windows 3.x and return to the C: prompt.

Step 2. At the C:\ prompt, type **Xcopy C:\Windows*.* C:\Win95*.* /s /e.**

This command duplicates your Windows 3.x files. Substitute the name of the directory in which your Windows 3.x files reside (*.*). Then name the directory where you want to place your Win95 files (*.*). The /e switch copies all subdirectories, including empty ones (handy when programs create directories that aren't used initially, such as Tmp directories). When you install Windows 95 in its new directory, it replaces most of the files there but still needs an extra 20MB to fully install. If the Setup routine issues a message that there's not enough disk space, it may not be considering the space it recovers by overwriting files. So if Setup complains you don't have the space available when in fact you do, you can ignore the message.

Step 3. You should still be at the C:\ prompt. Type **Xcopy C:\DOS*.* C:\DOSSave*.*. /s /e.**

This command saves your DOS files. When you install Windows 95 into a directory containing Windows 3.x, Windows 95 deletes older DOS files that aren't compatible with such Windows 95 features as long filenames. But you'll need these files later to dual-boot.

(continued)

STEPS *(continued)*

Installing Windows 95 in a copy of the Windows 3.x directory

Step 4.   At the C: prompt, type **Edit C:\Autoexec.bat**. In your Autoexec file, replace references to C:\Windows with C:\Win95. Save the file and exit. Also change Config.sys in the same way.

Next, type **Edit C:\Win95\Progman.ini** and change references to C:\Windows to C:\Win95. Unfortunately, some Windows applications (including Word) reference C:\Windows in their *ini* files. To ensure that these apps work in Windows 95, you'll have to edit every single *ini* file in the C:\Win95 directory. The best command to do this is:

```
For %f in (C:\Win95\*.ini) Do Edit %f
```

This loads, in turn, each *ini* file. Save each file and exit. Now reboot. Windows 3.x should start normally in the renamed directory (C:\Win95).

Edit any Program Manager icons that mention C:\Windows and change them to C:\Win95.

Step 5.   Now you're in Windows 3.x. Click File Run and then type **REGEDIT/v.** In the Registration Editor that appears, search for all instances of C:\Windows and change them to C:\Win95. Exit Reg Edit. Now run Windows 95 Setup.

Setup will see a copy of Windows 3.x in C:\Win95 and install there by default. (You've not preserved your Windows 3.x preferences under Windows 95, and you still have a stored copy of your Windows 3.x configuration.)

Step 6.   Delete your old C:\DOS directory using the Windows 95 Explorer.

Then rename C:\DOSSave to C:\DOS. (You've just restored your old DOS utilities.)

Remember: when running Windows 95 your new DOS 7.0 utilities will be in C:\Win95\Command. But when you dual-boot to Windows 3.x, your DOS 5 or 6 files are in C:\DOS. Either way, Windows 95 automatically switches between two sets of Autoexec.bat files to set the correct path statement.

Step 7.   When you boot to Windows 95, your old Config.sys and Autoexec.bat files for Windows 3.x are renamed Config.dos and Autoexec.dos. Open these files with a text editor and change the references to C:\Win95 back to C:\Windows (or whatever directory holds your original Windows 3.x installation).

Step 8.   Exit to MS-DOS and change the properties of Msdos.sys (a hidden file in the root directory) so it is not read-only, hidden, or system. Do this by changing to the C:\Windows\Command directory, then typing **Attrib -r -h -s C:\Msdos.sys.** Now, open Msdos.sys with a text editor.

In the [Options] section, add this line, then save the file:
```
BootMulti=1
```

Step 9   Reboot your PC. When you see the message that Windows 95 is starting, press F8 to intercept the boot process. You'll be presented with a series of options, the last one of which is Previous version of MS DOS. Choose this option and your system will boot to Windows 3.*x*. If you don't press F8 you boot to Windows 95.

Is Your Windows 95 Sick?

What happens if you accidentally delete a file that is needed to run Windows 95? What if a spot on your hard disk goes bad? Have you ever copied over a system file with a file of the same name but an earlier date?

You can rerun Windows 95 Setup in file-verification mode to fix problems that might be due to corrupted or missing Windows 95 files. Double-click Setup.exe and Setup knows (by looking at Setuplog.txt) that you have already installed Windows 95 and asks you if you want to verify your copy of Windows 95.

Using Setuplog.txt, Setup checks your files. If it finds one that fails its integrity check, it copies a new copy from the source files onto your hard disk.

Adding and Removing Parts of Windows 95

The list of Windows 95 components that you last saw in the Select Components dialog box during Setup can be revisited. You'll once again have the opportunity to add or remove parts of Windows 95. This makes decision-making less difficult when you originally install Windows 95. Here's how to make changes:

STEPS

Adding or Removing Parts of Windows 95

Step 1.   Click the Start button. Click Settings and then Control Panel.

Step 2.   Double-click the Add/Remove Programs icon.

Step 3.   Click the Windows Setup tab. Highlight a category of components and click Details.

Step 4.   You can uncheck installed components that you want removed, and check uninstalled components that you want installed.

This can get quite confusing because you can quickly forget which components you are installing and uninstalling and there is no way to see which is which. You'll have to click Cancel and start again if you get confused. Too bad the check marks don't have different colors.

Secret

A subfolder of Windows 95 contains the files that guide the installation and removal of Windows 95 components (as well as Windows 95 Setup). This folder, the Inf folder, contains setup information files; files with the *inf* extension.

You can view and edit these files by double-clicking them. They are all short enough to be edited by Notepad. The *Windows 95 Resource Kit* from Microsoft provides some documentation on the structure of these files, but they are somewhat self-explanatory if you open them in Notepad.

If you want to do away with your (or someone else's) ability to easily add or remove Windows 95 components, and save about $1.50 worth of hard disk space, you can delete this folder.

Installing Windows 95 With Other Operating Systems

If your computer has OS/2, Windows NT, or DR DOS installed as its operating system, it is still possible to install Windows 95 on it and have both operating system live in harmony. There are a few basic requirements.

MS-DOS

This whole chapter, up to now, has been about installing Windows 95 using a previous version of MS-DOS. So why go over it again? Here are the high points.

You can install Windows 95 using MS-DOS versions 3.2, 4.*x*, 5.*x*, and 6.*x*.

You can install Windows 95 on a computer that doesn't have Windows 3.*x* installed and dual-boot between your previous version of DOS and Windows 95. You will need to be sure that the following line is in the Msdos.sys file in your boot directory (turn to Chapter 8 for more details about Bootmulti):

```
BootMulti=1
```

About 2MB of your DOS 6.*x* files will be deleted unless you protect them as detailed earlier in this chapter in the section entitled *Protecting your DOS files*.

DR DOS

Installing Windows 95 on a computer with DR DOS version 3.*x* through 7.*x* is similar to installing it on a computer with MS-DOS. None of the DR DOS files are erased. Certain DR DOS programs will cause a conflict with Setup. Setup checks to see if these programs are running. Remark them out of Autoexec.bat and Config.sys if there is a problem with Setup.

When Setup creates new Autoexec.bat and Config.sys files, at the end of Setup, command lines that start DR DOS utilities that cause problems for Io.sys are commented out.

Remove password protection for your volumes before you start Windows 95 Setup.

Windows NT

Windows NT has its own multi-boot capability, the Windows NT Boot Loader. This is not true of MS-DOS, DR DOS, or Windows 3.x.

On a computer that will have both Windows NT and Windows 95 installed, you want the Windows NT Boot Loader to be in charge. The Windows NT Boot Loader will be in the boot tracks of the boot device, your bootable hard disk.

When you boot your computer, the Windows NT Boot Loader will appear first and let you choose between NT and DOS. Windows 95 Setup doesn't change this arrangement. To run Setup, you need to choose MS-DOS.

Once Setup has run and rebooted your computer, you must choose DOS again to let Windows 95 Setup configure all the files that it needs to continue successfully. Choosing MS-DOS from the Windows NT Boot Loader will allow your computer to load Windows 95.

It is possible that the copy of Windows NT on your computer, was installed in your Windows 3.x directory. Both Windows NT and Windows 3.x can successfully run from the same directory. This is not true of Windows NT and Windows 95. You will need to install Windows 95 in a different directory than your Windows NT directory.

After installing Windows 95 on a Windows NT computer, you can boot to Windows 95 by choosing to boot to MS-DOS at the Windows NT Boot Loader. The Windows 95 file Io.sys will actually be started if you make this choice at boot time. Io.sys reads a file, Msdos.sys, that determines whether it will automatically boot into Windows 95, DOS 7.0, or your previous version of DOS, or Windows 3.x, if Windows 3.x, is installed on your computer.

You can edit Msdos.sys to determine which way your Windows NT computer will boot if you choose MS-DOS. See Chapter 6 for guidelines on editing this file. The same guidelines apply whether you have a Windows NT or a Windows 95 computer.

Windows 95 can be set up only on a disk partition that is formatted for the FAT file system. This is the file system that works with DOS. Windows NT can manage this kind of disk partition as well as NTFS driver partitions. Windows 95 won't even see these NTFS partitions.

Secret

You can install Windows NT on a Windows 95 computer. Io.sys will be moved out of the boot tracks by the Windows NT setup, just as though it were the DOS version of Io.sys. The Windows NT Boot Loader will be placed there instead.

You'll want to install Windows NT from the DOS 7.0 prompt.

OS/2

Like Windows NT, you let the OS/2 Boot Manager have the first crack at deciding which operating system is going to be loaded. Like Windows NT, OS/2 has its own file system (HPFS) that it manages along with any FAT drive partitions on your computer. Windows 95 must be installed in a FAT partition. It cannot see the HPFS partitions.

Windows 95 Setup needs to run from MS-DOS. Be sure that your OS/2 system is configured to dual-boot to MS-DOS. You may need to reconfigure OS/2 before you run Windows 95 Setup.

The OS/2 Boot Manager is disabled by Windows 95 Setup. You'll want to re-enable it by running the OS/2 Fdisk utility from your OS/2 boot diskette after Windows 95 is completely installed.

An OS/2 computer will most likely have Windows 3.x installed also. You will need to install Windows 95 in a new directory. This will give you the option of booting to OS/2, DOS, Windows 3.x, or Windows 95.

You can install OS/2 after you have installed Windows 95. Like Windows NT, the OS/2 installation thinks that the Windows 95 Io.sys file in the boot tracks is the DOS version.

Secret

Uninstalling Windows 95

You can uninstall Windows 95, and there are various levels of uninstall.

You can uninstall just the Windows portion of Windows 95 and keep the DOS 7.0 portions. You can remove the DOS 7.0 portions and go back to booting your computer to an earlier version of DOS. It helps if you have protected your previous DOS files, although you can also restore them from your DOS diskettes.

If you have installed Windows 95 to a directory other than your Windows 3.x directory, you can go back to your earlier version of Windows. If you installed Windows 95 in your Windows 3.x directory and didn't choose to save the information necessary to uninstall Windows 95, you'll need to reinstall Windows 3.x (as well as nearly all of your Windows programs).

Most of Windows 95 is installed in the Windows 95 folder. This may be named Windows or Win95, or whatever you called it when you installed Windows 95.

Back to DOS 7.0

You can remove Windows 95 and still boot to its DOS 7.0 portions. You can run Windows 3.x from DOS 7.0 (although you may have to reinstall Windows 3.x if you installed Windows 95 over it). You can use the DOS 7.0 that comes with Windows 95 just like an upgraded version of DOS, which it is (although not completely).

Secret

STEPS

Deleting Windows 95 Back to DOS 7.0

Step 1.   Turn on your computer. When you see the message on your screen that Windows 95 is starting, press F8. Choose Command prompt only.

Step 2.   Create a DOS 7.0 folder and copy over the DOS 7.0 files. At the DOS 7.0 command prompt, type:

```
c:
cd\
md\DOS70
cd\DOS70
xcopy \Win95\Command\*.*
xcopy \Win95\Emm386.exe
xcopy \Win95\Smartdrv.exe
xcopy \Win95\Command.com
xcopy \Win95\Msd.exe
xcopy \Win95\Setver.exe
```

\Win95 is your Windows 95 folder.

Step 3.   Delete most of the Windows 95 files. At the DOS 7.0 command prompt type:

```
path c:\DOS70
deltree c:\WIN95
```

Step 4.   Edit your Autoexec.bat and Config.sys files to refer to the DOS70 directory instead of the \Win95 or \Win95\Command directory. You may want to put Smartdrv back into your Autoexec.bat file to get disk caching. You can add Emm386.exe to Config.sys to get memory management. Turn to Chapter 17 for more details on DOS.

Step 5.   Edit Msdos.sys to start at the DOS 7.0 command prompt. At the DOS 7.0 command prompt type:

```
attrib -r -h -s Msdos.sys
edit Msdos.sys
```

Add the following lines to the [options] section of Msdos.sys:

```
BootGUI=0
BootWin=1
```

When you are finished editing Msdos.sys, save it and type the following at the command prompt:

```
attrib +r +h +s Msdos.sys
```

(continued)

Deleting Windows 95 Back to DOS 7.0

Step 6.   You can delete some extraneous files. At the DOS 7.0 command prompt, type:

```
del Setuplog.*
del Bootlog.*
del Setlog.*
del Suanlog.*
del Netlog.*
del System.1st
```

Back to an earlier version of MS-DOS

You can remove Windows 95 completely and revert to your earlier DOS and perhaps Windows 3.x operating system.

You remove Windows 95 from the command line prompt (as only seems fitting). You can do this from either the DOS 7.0 command line prompt or the command prompt of your earlier version of DOS (if you have dual-boot capability).

Removing Windows 95 Completely

Step 1.   Make sure you have a DOS diskette that will boot your computer to your previous version of DOS. This diskette must contain the file Sys.com. If you have deleted your earlier version of DOS from your hard disk, you will also want diskettes containing all your earlier DOS files. The number 1 diskette in the DOS 6.x set is bootable. This is not true of earlier versions of MS-DOS and you may need to create such a bootable diskette, perhaps using another DOS computer.

Step 2.   Turn on your computer. When you see the message "Starting Windows 95," press F8. Choose Command prompt only, or Previous version of MS-DOS. Choosing Command prompt only boots your computer to DOS 7.0. Choosing Previous version of MS-DOS boots it to your older DOS (if you have dual-boot capability).

Step 3.   Copy the Windows 95 versions of Deltree.exe and Scandisk.exe to the root directory. At the command prompt type:

```
c:
cd\
copy \Win95\Command\Deltree.exe
copy \Win95\Scandisk.*
```

It is assumed that \Win95 is your Windows 95 folder.

Step 4.   Edit your Scandisk.ini file so ScanDisk can clean up your long filenames. At the command prompt type:

```
edit scandisk.ini
```

Set labelcheck=on and spacecheck=on so ScanDisk will check for invalid characters and spaces in volume labels and filenames.

Step 5.   Run ScanDisk to remove these bad filenames (long names that are proper under Windows 95). At the command prompt type:

```
Scandisk c:
```

You can scan all your volumes from inside ScanDisk.

Step 6.   Delete most of your Windows 95 files. At the command prompt type:

```
deltree c:\Win95
```

Step 7.   You can now delete files in the root directory that are associated with Windows 95. If you chose menu item 6 in Step 2, at the command prompt type:

```
del Autoexec.bat
del Config.sys
ren Autoexec.w40 Autoexec.bat
ren Config.w40 Config.sys
```

If you chose menu item 8 in Step 2, at the command prompt type:

```
del Autoexec.w40
del Config.w40
del Winboot.sys
```

Step 8.   Delete additional files in the root directory associated with Windows 95. At the command prompt type:

```
del Setlog.*
del Detlog.*
del Bootlog.*
del Sudhlog.*
del netlog.*
del System.1st
del *.---
```

(continued)

STEPS *(continued)*

Removing Windows 95 Completely

Step 9. Delete the real-mode DOS files associated with Windows 95. If you chose menu item 6 in Step 2, at the command prompt type:

```
del Io.sys
del Msdos.sys
del Command.com
```

If you chose menu item 8 in Step 2, at the command prompt type:

```
del Winboot.sys
del Msdos.w40
del Command.w40
```

If your boot drive is compressed, you will need to erase these files from the root directory of your host drive.

Step 10. If you were using DoubleSpace or DriveSpace compression under Windows 95 you can also delete the compression drivers. Don't do this if you are using Stacker version 3.1. At the command prompt type:

```
del D??space.*
```

If your boot drive is compressed, you will need to erase these files from the root directory of your host drive.

Step 11. Put your bootable DOS diskette into drive A and reboot your computer.

Step 12. Place the boot portion of your earlier version of DOS in the boot tracks of your bootable hard disk by typing at the command prompt (after your computer starts):

```
sys c:
```

Step 13. You may need to copy Command.com from your boot diskette to the root directory of your hard disk. Also, you may need to edit Autoexec.bat and Config.sys.

Step 14. If you have MS-DOS version 6.*x* and you are using disk compression, you'll want to place the real-mode DOS 6.*x* version of the Double-spaced or DriveSpace compression driver in the root directory.

Step 15. Remove the bootable floppy from drive A and restart your computer.

Back to Windows NT

If you have installed Windows 95 on a computer that has Windows NT with its Boot Loader managing the bootup process, you can erase Windows 95 and restore your computer to its previous configuration.

STEPS

Removing Windows 95 from a Computer with Windows NT

Step 1.   Follow all the steps used above to get back to your previous version of MS-DOS.

Step 2.   Reboot your computer with the Windows NT #1 Setup diskette in drive A.

Step 3.   Choose the Repair option after you boot off this diskette.

Step 4.   When you are prompted to do so, put your Windows NT emergency repair diskette in drive A and choose the option to repair the boot files.

Step 5.   You may need to edit your MS-DOS Autoexec.bat and Config.sys files and reinstall Windows 3.x if it is in a separate directory from Windows NT and you installed Windows 95 in that directory.

Summary

Lots of little wrinkles come with installing and setting up Windows 95.

▶ Follow our guidelines to determine if your computer can run Windows 95.

▶ We show you how to free hard disk space so that you can have enough room to install Windows 95.

▶ Microsoft made a big mistake when it encouraged developers to put parts of their applications in the Windows directory, which is now growing out of control.

▶ If you want to maintain your old DOS setup, we show you how to protect your existing DOS files.

▶ Did you like Windows Write? We get it back for you.

▶ The Windows 95 Setup is slow. We show you how to speed it up.

▶ You can run into problems setting up Windows 95 from a CD-ROM or a network server. We show you now to avoid these problems.

▶ Windows 95 Setup goes on and on. We help you each step of the way.

▶ If your Windows 95 has gone bad, we give you a method to get it straightened out.

▶ Want to inhabit a multi-operating system environment? We show you how Windows 95 can co-exist with OS/2 and Windows NT.

▶ If you want to revert to an earlier operating system, Windows 95 can be uninstalled.

Chapter 4

A Quick Look at Windows 95

In This Chapter

This chapter is an introduction to the workings of Windows 95. Follow along and in a few minutes you will have grasped the basic notions that underlie everything about Windows 95.

▶ What are those icons doing on my Desktop?

▶ Where do I start?

▶ How do I run a program?

▶ Where do I find help?

▶ What is the My Computer icon?

▶ What happens when I double-click a computer icon, a hard disk icon, a folder icon?

▶ How do I find what is on My Computer?

▶ How do I quit Windows 95?

The Desktop

We're going to assume that you have been able to install and set up Windows 95 correctly (or that it was already installed on your computer), and the Windows 95 desktop is now displayed on your computer screen. Your screen should look something like Figure 4-1. If this is not the case, then you will need to go back one chapter.

On the left side of the desktop you'll find three or more icons, depending on the options you chose during installation. You are going to use these icons to find and view the files and folders that are stored on your computer (and, if you are connected to other computers, on the network of computers).

At the bottom of the desktop is the Taskbar with its Start button and clock. The Taskbar is a switcher — it lets you easily move between open documents and applications. If it's on the Taskbar, you need to click it only once.

Figure 4-1: The Windows 95 desktop. Single-click the Start button, but double-click the icons on the desktop.

For a little fun, try moving the Taskbar around the edges of the desktop. Take the following steps:

STEPS

Moving the Taskbar

Step 1.   Position your mouse pointer over the Taskbar, but not over the clock or the Start button.

Step 2.   Press and hold the left mouse button.

Step 3.   Holding the left mouse button down, move the mouse pointer to a side or the top of the desktop.

Step 4.   When an outline of the Taskbar appears on the side or top of the desktop, release the mouse button.

Step 5.   Repeat Steps 1 through 4 to move the Taskbar around the desktop.

The Start button

Click the Start button. Among the items on the menu is Help. This is general help for Windows 95; you can click it (once) and find out a lot. If something is on a menu, you need to click it only once.

Click Programs on the Start menu, then Accessories, then Games (if you installed Games during the setup process) and then FreeCell. This is how you run Programs from the Start button in Windows 95.

What's on the Desktop?

There are at least three icons on the desktop. These icons do not represent running or active programs or "tasks." The Windows 3.1 icons on the desktop did, which is why we are emphasizing this point.

The icons represent *capabilities* sitting there waiting for you to do something. Nothing happens or is happening until you double-click one of these Desktop icons. When you double-click one of these icons, you open a *window*.

The My Computer icon looks like a computer and it represents your computer. Double click this icon and see what you get. (See Figure 4-2.)

Figure 4-2: The My Computer window. Your computer is displayed in the My Computer window. This computer has two hard disks, two floppy diskette drives, a CD-ROM drive, a network drive, and three folders — Control Panel, Printers, and Dial-Up Networking. You can double-click any of them.

What's in the My Computer Window?

What you get in the My Computer window are icons that look like disk drives and represent the disk drives connected to your computer. These disk drive icons in the My Computer window act just like icons on the desktop. That is, they can be double-clicked.

You also see three manila folder icons labeled Control Panel, Printers, and Dial-Up Networking. These can be double-clicked also.

Double-click the C: hard disk icon in the My Computer window and the C: window appears on your desktop, as shown in Figure 4-3.

Figure 4-3: The C: window. The hard disk window has folder and file icons in it.

The My Computer icon on the desktop and the disk drive icons in a My Computer window act just the same. Double-click them and a window opens on your desktop.

My Computer, Disk Drives, and Folders

The C: window contains icons that look like little yellow manila folders with tabs on the left side. These manila folder icons represent folders. Folders contain files and other folders.

The other icons in the C: folder window represent different kinds of files. On the desktop is an icon that looks like the Recycle Bin.

You started with the My Computer icon, which looks like a computer. When you opened My Computer, you found that it contained disk drive icons and some folder icons. When you opened a hard disk icon, it contained folders, files, and a Recycle Bin.

Disk drives are connected to computers, either your computer or another computer on the network. Folders and files are stored on disk drives. Folders are stored within folders. Files are stored within folders.

All the icons that are on your desktop the first time that you start Windows 95 represent containers. They contain disk drives, folders, and/or files. When you double-click them, you can see what they contain. The window that appears when you double-click them is referred to as a *folder window* or *folder view*, even if it appeared after you double-click a hard disk icon or the My Computer icon.

The Folder Windows

It is this container or folder mentality that we want you to grasp in this first look. Everything can be found within the folder windows. You open a window by double-clicking an icon that represents a computer, a network, a hard disk, or a folder. Even the Recycle Bin and the My Briefcase icons (if you installed the Briefcase) are special kinds of folders.

Special folders, like the Recycle Bin and My Briefcase, are an improvement on the old concept of "directories" in DOS. Like a directory, a folder can contain files and other folders (subdirectories). But special folders are "objects" that can have properties beyond merely containing files and folders.

For example, the Recycle Bin has the property that files within it can be "restored" until you click Empty the Recycle Bin on the Recycle Bin's main menu. My Briefcase has the special property that files you copy into this folder can be changed and then used to "update" the original files on your hard disk.

When files are within these special "object" folders, Windows knows the properties that those folders support and automatically takes advantage of them.

Quitting

If this is enough and you want to quit now — after all, this is just a first look — click the Start button on the left end of the Taskbar, then click Shut Down and select the menu choice, Shut down the computer, on the Start menu that appears.

You will find a great deal of discussion about the desktop, the Start button, folders, and windows in *Part II: The Windows 95 User Interface*.

Summary

We provide a quick look at Windows and its desktop metaphor. If you follow the steps in this chapter you can very quickly grasp the most basic structure of Windows 95.

▶ What's on the desktop.

▶ How to move the Taskbar around the desktop.

▶ How to use the Start button to start a program and find help.

▶ What is in the My Computer window.

▶ How to open a window on your hard disk.

▶ How to quit Windows 95.

Chapter 5

A Tutorial for Windows 95

In This Chapter

We provide a step-by step tutorial that introduces the basic features of the Windows 95 user interface. You will learn about:

▶ Creating files and folders

▶ Moving a file between folders

▶ Creating a shortcut to the file and putting it on the desktop

▶ Deleting the shortcut and the file

▶ Restoring the file and shortcut

Starting

Complete this tutorial and within a few minutes you'll be familiar with the main concepts underlying Windows 95. Grasp these concepts and the logic of Windows 95 is revealed. Using this logic, you can explore on your own.

Before continuing here, be sure to go over the steps in Chapter 4 so you are familiar with the concepts we use in this chapter.

Windows 95 comes with its own guided tour (if you installed it). Before you start this tutorial, you should take the guided tour. Take the following steps to take the tour:

STEPS

Starting the Windows 95 Guided Tour

Step 1. Click the Start button.

Step 2. Click Help on the Start menu.

Step 3. Highlight "Tour: Ten minutes to using Windows" in the Help Contents window.

Step 4. If you get an error message that Windows 95 can't run the tour because you are using Large Fonts, right-click the desktop, click Properties in the right mouse button menu, click the Settings tab, click the down arrow in the Font Size drop-down list, click Small Fonts, click OK, and then click OK again to restart Windows.

(continued)

Starting the Windows 95 Guided Tour

Step 5.   Click the Display button.

After you finish with the guided tour, you're ready for the following tutorial.

Creating a Folder or Two

The first thing you need to do is create some folders you will use to store files. These folders can be easily deleted later.

STEPS

Creating a Folder

Step 1.   Double-click My Computer (the My Computer icon on the Desktop).

Step 2.   Double-click the C: disk drive icon in the My Computer window.

Step 3.   Right-click in the empty area of the C: window, away from any of the icons that populate this "client" area.

Step 4.   Click New in the pop-up right mouse button menu.

Step 5.   Click Folder in the tear-off menu that appears next to the New menu item. A folder icon will appear in the client area of the C: window. The name of the folder will be highlighted.

Step 6.   Type in **Temporary** as the name of the folder and press Enter.

Step 7.   Right-click the client area of the C: window (away from any icons), and this time in the right mouse button menu, click Arrange Icons, and then Auto Arrange.

Step 8.   Repeat Steps 3 through 6, but this time type in **Temporary 2** as the folder name.

You have just created two folders in the root directory of the C: drive. They are named Temporary and Temporary 2 so you'll know you can delete them later with no consequences.

Creating a File

Now, you are going to create a file and edit it a bit.

STEPS

Creating a File

Step 1.   Double-click the Temporary folder in the C: window.

Step 2.   Right-click the client area of the Temporary window. There are no icons in this folder so you don't have to worry about staying away from them when you right-click the client area.

Step 3.   Click New in the right mouse button menu.

Step 4.   Click Text Document in the tear off menu. A file icon with the name New Text Document.txt appears in the Temporary folder. The name is highlighted.

Step 5.   Type **Temporary File.txt** as the new name for the document and press Enter.

Step 6.   Double-click the Temporary File.txt icon. The Notepad application will start and give you a blank client area in which to type some text. When you have a bit of text in the file, click File and then Save on the Notepad menu.

Step 7.   Click the "x" box in the upper right side of the Notepad window in the caption area. This will quit the Notepad application.

You have now created a new file, added some text to it, and saved the edited file in the Temporary folder.

Moving a File

Next, you will move the Temporary File.txt from the Temporary folder to the Temporary 2 folder.

STEPS

Moving a File

Step 1.   Right-click the Temporary File.txt icon in the Temporary window.

Step 2.   Click Cut in the right mouse button menu. The document icon for the Temporary File.txt is now grayed out to show the file is being cut.

Step 3.   On the Taskbar, click the button with the hard disk icon, which should be the button that represents your C: hard disk.

Step 4.   Right-click the Temporary 2 folder icon in the C: window. You may have to scroll the client area of the window by clicking the scrollbars (if any) on the right side and bottom of the C: window.

(continued)

STEPS *(continued)*

Moving a File

Step 5. Click Paste in the right mouse button menu. You'll notice that the Temporary File.txt document disappears from the Temporary window. If you can't see the Temporary window, click its button in the Taskbar.

Step 6. Double-click the Temporary 2 folder icon in the C: window. If this folder icon is obscured by the Temporary window, click the caption area of the C: window to bring it to the top of the desktop.

Step 7. Notice that Temporary File.txt is now in the Temporary 2 folder.

You have just moved a file from one folder to another. You could have used the drop and drag technique, which entails dragging the Temporary File icon over to the Temporary 2 folder and dropping it. There are more details about this technique in Chapter 7.

Creating a Shortcut

The Temporary File.txt is now in the Temporary 2 folder. If you are going to work on this file a bit, it is not a bad idea to put a shortcut on your desktop for ready access. Here's how you do that (without actually putting it on your desktop):

STEPS

Creating a Shortcut to a File

Step 1. Double-click the Temporary 2 folder icon in the C: window.

Step 2. Locate the mouse pointer over the Temporary File icon and press and hold the right mouse button.

Step 3. Move the mouse pointer until it is over a clear space on your desktop.

Step 4. Release the right mouse button.

Step 5. Click Create Shortcut.

Step 6. Type in a new name for the shortcut, something like **Temporary File.**

Step 7. Notice the little curved arrow that has been added to the lower left corner of the file icon. This indicates that this icon represents a shortcut and not the file itself.

Step 8. Click the Temporary 2 button on the Taskbar and notice that the Temporary File icon is still there. Putting a shortcut to a file onto the desktop (or anywhere else) doesn't move the file.

Step 9. Double-click the Temporary File shortcut icon on the desktop. The Notepad application appears and the Temporary File text is in its client area.

Step 10. Click the "x" button in the upper-right hand corner of the Notepad application to close it.

Deleting a Shortcut

You can delete a shortcut to a file or application without affecting the file or application itself. Here's how:

STEPS

Deleting a Shortcut

Step 1. Right-click the Temporary File icon on the desktop.

Step 2. Click Delete on the right mouse button menu.

Step 3. A message box appears asking if you are sure that you want to delete the Shortcut to Temporary File.txt.

Step 4. Click Yes.

Step 5. Click the Temporary 2 folder button on the Taskbar. Notice that the Temporary File is still there.

Deleting a File

Deleting a shortcut didn't affect the file. Now you can delete (and restore) the file.

STEPS

Deleting a File

Step 1. Right-click the Temporary File icon in the Temporary 2 folder.

Step 2. Press the Delete key on your keyboard. You will be asked if you want to delete the Temporary File.txt file.

Step 3. Click Yes.

Step 4. Notice that the Temporary File icon has disappeared from the Temporary 2 window.

Deleting a File

Step 5. Double-click the Recycle Bin icon on the desktop. Notice that both Temporary File and the Temporary File shortcut are stored in the Recycle Bin.

Step 6. To restore the Temporary File to the Temporary 2 folder, right-click Temporary File in the Recycle Bin window and click Restore.

Step 7. Notice that the Temporary File is back in the Temporary 2 folder's window.

You can also restore the Temporary File shortcut to the desktop. It doesn't do much good to restore the shortcut and not restore the file. Try it and see what happens when you double-click the shortcut.

So What Was the Point?

Using the windows that started with My Computer, you can graphically see that My Computer contains a hard disk drive, C:, which in turn contains folders, including two that you just created. These folders in turn contain folders and files.

A folder can contain other folders and files as well as links to other folders and/or files stored in other folders.

The desktop is a folder. You can learn more about this in Chapter 7.

Starting with a file, you can get to an application just by double-clicking the file's icon.

Shortcuts to files (or folders) don't move the file or folder, they just present another view.

Deleting a shortcut doesn't delete a file or application. Deleted shortcuts and files reside in the Recycle Bin until you empty it.

Summary

In this chapter we provide a hands-on, step-by-step tutorial to familiarize you with some of the basic concepts of working with the Windows 95 user interface.

▶ You learn how to create folders and create and store files in those folders.

▶ You move a file between folders.

▶ You create a shortcut to the file on the desktop.

▶ You delete a shortcut and a file.

Chapter 6

Customizing Your Windows 95 Startup

In This Chapter

Your computer can start up in all sorts of different configurations. We show you how to set the options for how Windows 95 starts up. We discuss:

▶ Getting rid of the Windows 95 startup logo

▶ Booting your computer to a DOS 7.0 prompt instead of the Windows 95 graphical user interface

▶ Using a hotkey to start Windows in Safe mode if there is a problem with your hardware

▶ Booting to your previous version of DOS or Windows

▶ Choosing a startup hardware profile depending on your computer's hardware configuration

▶ Using multiconfiguration Config.sys and Autoexec.bat files to control startup

Do I Need to Do This?

Do you need to customize your Windows 95 startup? No. Not if all the defaults are just right for you. The Windows 95 Setup program creates all the necessary files and sets up everything invisibly and automatically so you may not need to worry about anything.

But if you installed Windows 95 in a separate directory from your Windows 3.*x* directory and you want to be able to switch back and forth between operating systems, you will want to know some of the tricks provided here to make that easier. If you want to know the sequence of commands and actions that are taken when your computer starts up, you'll find them here.

If you want to know what basic changes to make in your Autoexec.bat and Config.sys files for Windows 95, you'll find that information here. If you are curious about the files in your root directory, see the sections later in this chapter.

How Windows 95 Starts Up

A lot happens between the time you turn on your computer and when the Windows 95 desktop appears on your screen.

First, the BIOS

First, the commands stored in your computer's BIOS (and video card's ROM) chips are carried out. These commands provide low-level drivers for some of your basic hardware (disk drives, ports, video cards, and so on). The last command of the BIOS is to execute the program that resides in the boot tracks of the boot device (most likely your hard disk).

The BIOS will find Io.sys in the boot tracks unless you have Windows NT or OS/2 installed. In those cases, their boot program will be found in the boot tracks. These operating systems will allow you to start Io.sys, if you desire, instead of their boot programs.

Often the BIOS settings will be displayed on your screen as your computer goes through the startup process. Right under the BIOS settings you may see on the left side of your text screen a message that Windows 95 is starting. This is your clue that you can now press one of the startup keys to alter the startup process. For more information, see the section later in this chapter entitled *Startup Keys*.

Then, DOS

Io.sys is DOS. Just as in DOS 4, 5, and so on, Io.sys is a hidden file in the root directory of your boot drive. Io.sys starts your processor in real mode, sets up the DOS data structures in conventional memory, and initializes the low-level DOS functions. DOS starts before Windows 95 starts. DOS starts Windows 95. Your processor is set to real mode and runs DOS before Windows 95 gets going.

Io.sys also calls some DOS real-mode programs, carries out the commands in Config.sys, and loads the command interpreter for Autoexec.bat, if these files exist. Depending on what it finds in Config.sys and Autoexec.bat, it may carry out a number of DOS real-mode commands.

Before Io.sys reads Config.sys and Autoexec.bat, it reads Msdos.sys, which is a text file that determines the startup configuration for Windows 95. Msdos.sys may tell Io.sys to ignore your Config.sys and Autoexec.bat files.

Finally, Windows 95

Config.sys and Autoexec.bat are read next, in that order, unless you have asked (perhaps through pressing a startup key or through the parameters of Msdos.sys) that they be ignored. (If you hold down the Shift key during startup, Config.sys and Autoexec.bat are ignored.) If Msdos.sys is configured so Windows is set to start, Windows 95 is loaded and Winstart.bat, if it exists, is read and acted upon. Your computer is now under the control of the Windows 95 operating system.

Msdos.sys

Undocumented

Msdos.sys is a very important configuration file. It is read early on by Io.sys. It can be used to determine whether you will start in DOS 7.0 or Windows 95, whether you will boot to a previous version of DOS or not, whether you see the Windows 95 startup logo or not, and whether you can use the startup function keys.

You will find Msdos.sys in the root directory (folder) of your boot hard disk, most likely the C: drive. In spite of its *sys* extension, it is a text file like Config.sys. You can edit it with Notepad or Microsoft Edit (Edit.com in the \Windows\Command folder).

Msdos.sys is a hidden, read-only system file. To find and check out the attributes of this file, take the following steps:

STEPS

Viewing the Attributes of Msdos.sys

Step 1.   Right-click My Computer on your desktop and then click Explore.

Step 2.   Click the hard disk icon in the left pane of the Explorer that represents your boot drive, most likely C:. Scroll the right pane until you see Msdos.sys.

Step 3.   Right-click Msdos.sys and then Properties.

You can change the attributes of Msdos.sys by unchecking the boxes on its General Properties sheet. The System property is not available to be changed. To be able to edit this file, uncheck the Read-Only box.

Editing Msdos.sys

We have created a batch file that can be used to help edit Msdos.sys. The batch file changes the attributes of Msdos.sys, opens Microsoft Edit, allows you to make changes to the files, and then resets the attributes of the file back to their original values.

To use this batch file to edit your Msdos.sys file, take the following steps:

STEPS

Using a Batch File to Edit Msdos.sys

Step 1. Using the Explorer, copy the file Msdossys.bat from the Registry folder of the shareware CD-ROM accompanying this book to an appropriate folder on your hard disk. You might have a folder where you store batch files, but it cxan be any folder.

Step 2. Right-drag Msdossys.bat from this folder to the desktop. Click Create Shortcut on the right mouse button menu. Press F2 and edit the shortcut's name to **Edit Msdos.sys.**

Step 3. Right-click the Edit Msdos icon on your desktop and choose Properties. Click the Program tab. Click Change Icon.

Step 4. You will be presented with icons from the Pifmgr.dll file. Pick one that reminds you that you are editing the Msdos.sys file.

Step 5. Click OK in the Change Icon dialog box, and OK on the Edit Msdos.sys Properties sheet.

Step 6. Double-click the Edit Msdos.sys icon on your desktop to begin editing Msdos.sys.

Msdos.sys file contents

Your Msdos.sys file may look something like this:

```
[Paths]
WinDir=C:\WINDOWS
WinBootDir=C:\WINDOWS
HostWinBootDrv=C

[Options]
BootGUI=1
Network=1
;
;The following lines are required for compatibility with other programs.
;Do not remove them (MSDOS.SYS needs to be >1024 bytes).
;xxxxxxxxxxxxxxxxxxxxxxxxxxxxxxxxxxxxxxxxxxxxxxxxxxxxxxxxxxxxxxxxxxa
;xxxxxxxxxxxxxxxxxxxxxxxxxxxxxxxxxxxxxxxxxxxxxxxxxxxxxxxxxxxxxxxxxxb
;xxxxxxxxxxxxxxxxxxxxxxxxxxxxxxxxxxxxxxxxxxxxxxxxxxxxxxxxxxxxxxxxxxc
;xxxxxxxxxxxxxxxxxxxxxxxxxxxxxxxxxxxxxxxxxxxxxxxxxxxxxxxxxxxxxxxxxxd
;xxxxxxxxxxxxxxxxxxxxxxxxxxxxxxxxxxxxxxxxxxxxxxxxxxxxxxxxxxxxxxxxxxe
;xxxxxxxxxxxxxxxxxxxxxxxxxxxxxxxxxxxxxxxxxxxxxxxxxxxxxxxxxxxxxxxxxxf
;xxxxxxxxxxxxxxxxxxxxxxxxxxxxxxxxxxxxxxxxxxxxxxxxxxxxxxxxxxxxxxxxxxg
```

```
;xxxxxxxxxxxxxxxxxxxxxxxxxxxxxxxxxxxxxxxxxxxxxxxxxxxxxxxxxxxxxxxxxxxxh
;xxxxxxxxxxxxxxxxxxxxxxxxxxxxxxxxxxxxxxxxxxxxxxxxxxxxxxxxxxxxxxxxxxxxi
;xxxxxxxxxxxxxxxxxxxxxxxxxxxxxxxxxxxxxxxxxxxxxxxxxxxxxxxxxxxxxxxxxxxxj
;xxxxxxxxxxxxxxxxxxxxxxxxxxxxxxxxxxxxxxxxxxxxxxxxxxxxxxxxxxxxxxxxxxxxk
;xxxxxxxxxxxxxxxxxxxxxxxxxxxxxxxxxxxxxxxxxxxxxxxxxxxxxxxxxxxxxxxxxxxxl
;xxxxxxxxxxxxxxxxxxxxxxxxxxxxxxxxxxxxxxxxxxxxxxxxxxxxxxxxxxxxxxxxxxxxm
;xxxxxxxxxxxxxxxxxxxxxxxxxxxxxxxxxxxxxxxxxxxxxxxxxxxxxxxxxxxxxxxxxxxxn
;xxxxxxxxxxxxxxxxxxxxxxxxxxxxxxxxxxxxxxxxxxxxxxxxxxxxxxxxxxxxxxxxxxxxo
;xxxxxxxxxxxxxxxxxxxxxxxxxxxxxxxxxxxxxxxxxxxxxxxxxxxxxxxxxxxxxxxxxxxxp
;xxxxxxxxxxxxxxxxxxxxxxxxxxxxxxxxxxxxxxxxxxxxxxxxxxxxxxxxxxxxxxxxxxxxq
;yyyyyyyxxxxxxxxxxxxxxxxxxxxxxxxxxxxxAAAAAAAAAAUUUUUUUUUMMMMyyyyyyyyyyyyxxxxr
;xxxxxxxxxxxxxxxxxxxxxxxxxxxxxxxxxxxxxxxxxxxxxxxxxxxxxxxxxxxxxxxxxxxxs
```

While only two options are listed in this sample file, numerous options can be added to change how your computer starts up. The WinDir folder may in fact be named something other than C:\Windows if you have installed Windows 95 onto another hard drive volume or in a different directory.

Msdos.sys options

The options you can specify in Msdos.sys are listed in table 6-1. If an option is not listed in the Msdos.sys file, its default value is used. The default value depends on the option. Most of the options' default values are 1. The default value for each option is the first value listed after the equal sign.

Table 6-1	Options for Msdos.sys
BootMulti=0 or 1	
BootWin=1 or 0	
BootGUI=1 or 0	
BootMenu=0 or 1	
BootMenuDefault=n (default is either 1 or 3)	
BootMenuDelay=n (default is 30 seconds)	
BootKeys=1 or 0	
BootDelay=n (default is 2 seconds)	
Logo=1 or 0	
DrvSpace=1 or 0	
DblSpace=1 or 0	
DoubleBuffer=1 or 0	
Network=1 or 0	
BootFailSafe=1 or 0	
BootWarn=1 or 0	
LoadTop=1 or 0	

BootMulti

BootMulti=1: You can boot to a previous version of DOS and/or Windows.

BootMulti=0: This is the default. You can start only Windows 95 (or DOS 7.0). If no reference to BootMulti is found in Msdos.sys, you will not be able to boot to your previous version of DOS or Windows.

If you do not have this option in Msdos.sys and if Io.sys is in the boot tracks of your hard disk, you will not be able to start previous versions of DOS or Windows. If either the Boot Manager for OS/2 or the Windows NT multi-boot program is in the boot tracks, then these programs control whether you are able to multi-boot or not.

DOS by itself doesn't have a multi-boot capability. You will not have a multi-boot capability if you set up Windows 95 over your existing Windows 3.x directory, i.e. you updated Windows 3.x. If you installed Windows 95 in a separate directory (folder), you will have the ability to start your previous version of DOS.

Undocumented

You must be careful when setting up Windows 95 because the setup routines automatically delete a number of DOS files without telling you. These DOS files have almost exact DOS 7.0 equivalents, but these new files will be stored in the C:\Win95\Command directory and not in your old DOS directory. If your path statements vary depending on which operating system you start up (very likely), you may not have access to your previous DOS functions.

If you want to save existing DOS programs that would otherwise be erased, you need to take some steps before you set up Windows 95.

Copy all your DOS files to a separate directory that is not found in your path statement. The Windows 95 Setup program looks for a set of files and uses the path statement to help it find them. Once it finds them it erases them. For an extra margin of comfort you might compress this backup copy of your DOS directory.

After Windows 95 is set up, you can copy all your DOS files back to your regular DOS directory and erase the temporary directory.

If Windows NT or OS/2 controls the boot tracks, and you indicate when prompted by one of their multi-boot dialog boxes that you want to boot to DOS and BootMulti=1, you will then have the option of booting to your previous version of DOS or Windows 95 (or DOS 7.0).

If BootMulti=0 or 1 is not found in Msdos.sys, the function key F4 will not do anything at startup.

The program System Commander from V Communications can allow you to boot to any operating system set up on your computer and works great with Win95. You can also boot any other PC compatible OS. Call V Communications for more information at 408-296-4224 or 800-648-8266.

BootWin

BootWin=1: The default value. Boot to Windows 95 (or DOS 7.0). BootWin means to boot to Windows 95, which includes DOS 7.0.

BootWin=0: Without any intervention by the user, boot automatically to the previous DOS version. BootWin=0 means to boot to DOS 5 or 6, or Windows 3.x, instead of Windows 95.

If the value is 1, then Windows 95 (or DOS 7.0) is started by default — without any action required by you.

If the value is 0, then your previous version of DOS is started by default. Autoexec.dos and Config.dos are renamed Autoexec.bat and Config.sys and the commands in them are executed.

This setting determines the effect of the F4 startup key. After Msdos.sys is read, a startup message appears. If BootWin=1, then this message will say that Windows 95 is starting. If you press F4 at this point, a new message appears, saying that MS-DOS is starting.

If BOOTWIN=0, then the initial message states that MS-DOS is starting. You'll need to press F4 before this message appears to get the message that Windows 95 is starting.

If the boot programs for OS/2 or Windows NT are in the boot sectors of your boot device (your hard disk), they will determine first if you can boot to another operating system. If you choose to boot to DOS from their boot programs, you then have the choice of booting to Windows 95 or your previous version of DOS.

If BootWin=0, using MS-DOS mode will automatically restart your computer using your previous version of DOS. You must press F4 to avoid this. See Chapter 17 for details on MS-DOS mode.

BootGUI

BootGUI=1: The default value. If BootWin=1 (or BootWin is not in the Msdos.sys file), start Windows 95.

BootGUI=0: If BootWin=1, don't start Windows 95 after starting DOS 7.0.

If BootWin=0, and you do not press F4, the value of BootGUI is ignored.

If BootWin=1 and BootGUI=1, the WIN command is issued automatically after your Autoexec.bat file (if any) is processed. If BootWin=1 and BootGUI=0, no WIN command is given and you will be presented with the DOS 7.0 prompt after the Autoexec.bat file is processed.

Whether BootGUI=1 or BootGUI=0, all the commands in Config.sys and Autoexec.bat will be carried out. All the default commands, including the loading of Himem.sys, will also occur.

If BootGUI=0, your computer starts up DOS 7.0 and you are presented with the DOS prompt. Your computer is now running real-mode DOS. You can run Windows 95 by typing **win** at the command prompt and pressing Enter.

Tip

You can also create a Win.bat file in the root directory. If this file is empty, Windows 95 boots to the Command prompt. This is the same as setting BootGUI=0 in the Msdos.sys file.

Undocumented

If you boot to the command prompt instead of to the Windows 95 desktop, you can get to the desktop by typing **win** and pressing Enter. If you start Windows 95 in this manner, when you shut down Windows 95, you can get back to the DOS 7.0 command prompt when you see the message "You can now safely turn off your computer." Simply type **mode co80** and press Enter. You won't see the keystrokes you're typing (because the graphical screen covers them up), but when you press Enter, you will be back at a C:\ prompt.

BootMenu

BootMenu=1: Display the Startup menu.

BootMenu=0: The default value. Don't display the Startup menu.

The default is to require that F8 be pressed in order for the Startup menu to appear. Setting BootMenu=1 forces the menu to appear each time you start up or reboot your computer.

The Startup menu as shown in Figure 6-1 obviously provides you with a number of different ways to start up your computer. Some of these mirror the values that you can set in the Msdos.sys file.

```
Microsoft Windows 95 Startup menu
=============================
    1.      Normal
    2.      Logged (\BOOTLOG.TXT)
    3.      Safe mode
    4.      Safe mode with network support
    5.      Step-by-Step confirmation
    6.      Command prompt only
    7.      Safe mode command prompt only
    8.      Previous version of MS-DOS
Enter a Choice: 1              Time Remaining: 30

F5=Safe mode Shift+F5=Command Prompt Shift+F8=Step-byStep Confirmation [N]
```

Figure 6-1: The Startup menu. Interactively make a choice about whether your computer starts in Windows 95 or your previous version of DOS, whether in Safe mode, and whether Autoexec.bat and Config.sys are read.

BootMenuDefault

BootMenuDefault=*n*: The default value is 1 or 3 as appropriate. Set the value you wish the BootMenu to use without user input.

The Startup menu is not fixed. Whether certain values appear in this menu will depend on the values you set in Msdos.sys and Config.sys. You may want to choose which value in your menu is the default choice.

BootMenuDelay

BootMenuDelay=*n*: The default value is 30 seconds. Set the number of seconds the Startup menu is displayed before the default menu item is acted upon.

BootKeys

BootKeys=1: This is the default. The function keys that work during the boot process (F4, F5, F6, F8, Shift+F5, Ctrl+F5, Shift+F8) are enabled.

BootKeys=0: These function keys don't work.

If you, as a system administrator, want to disallow certain actions, you can disable the actions taken by these function keys. These function keys are described in detail in the section later in this chapter entitled *Startup Keys*. This does nothing to make a PC "more secure," because anyone can change Msdos.sys from within Windows or DOS.

BootDelay

BootDelay=*n*: The default is 2 seconds. The time in seconds the bootup process will wait for you to press a BootKey after the message that Windows 95 is starting is displayed.

If you want to have enough time to press a BootKey, you should put in a value greater than 2 seconds. If BootKeys=0, there is no delay.

Logo

Logo=1: The default value. Display the Windows 95 logo screen as Windows 95 boots up.

Logo=0: Leave the screen in text mode.

Some third-party memory managers have trouble when this logo is displayed. Also, it can be annoying in general and prevent you from seeing important messages from real-mode drivers. You can replace Logo.sys with another *bmp* file. See the section below entitled *Changing the Startup Graphic.*

Drvspace

Drvspace=1: The default value. Load Drvspace.bin if it is there.

Drvspace=0: Don't load Drvspace.bin even if it is there.

If you have a drive that is compressed with Drvspace, you most likely will want to have it mounted and available. If not, you can disable this action.

Dblspace

Same as Drvspace, except for the spelling. DoubleSpace and DriveSpace drives are now handled by one 32-bit driver, Drvspace.bin.

DoubleBuffer

DoubleBuffer=1: The default value. This is used only if you have a SCSI drive that requires double buffering.

DoubleBuffer=0: If you don't think that your SCSI driver requires this, then set it equal to 0.

Network

Network=1: The default value if network components are installed. Enables the Startup menu option, Safe mode with network support.

Network=0: Either the network isn't installed or you don't want the option of booting in Safe mode with network support. If Network=0, then item 4 will not appear in the boot menu and the items below it will be renumbered.

BootFailSafe

BootFailSafe=0: The default value. Windows 95 doesn't boot into Safe mode automatically.

BootFailSafe=1: Forces your computer to start in the safe mode.

BootWarn

BootWarn=1: The default value. There is a warning message box that comes up when you boot in Safe mode. The default is for this message box to appear.

BootWarn=0: Don't show the Safe warning message box.

LoadTop

LoadTop=1: The default value. Command.com and/or Drvspace.bin can be loaded at the top of conventional memory. This is standard.

LoadTop=0: If there is a problem with NetWare or other software, then force these programs to not load at the top of conventional memory.

The Windows 95 Startup Menu

The Windows 95 Startup menu, which was shown in Figure 6-1, gives you a set of choices regarding how your computer starts before Io.sys carries out its default commands and before Autoexec.bat and Config.sys are read. Msdos.sys is read by Io.sys before the Startup menu appears.

Normal

If BootGUI=1, start Windows 95; otherwise goes to DOS 7.0 prompt. Carry out the commands in the Autoexec.bat and Config.sys files. Hangs if BootWin=0.

Logged

Same as Normal but writes out the file Bootlog.txt, which tracks the load and startup sequence. Hangs if BootWin=0.

Safe mode

If BootGUI=1 and BootWin=1, start Windows 95 in Safe mode. Safe mode is a generic Windows 95 startup with VGA graphics, no networking. It doesn't read or carry out the commands in Config.sys or Autoexec.bat, and boots to DOS 7.0 or Windows 95 (depending on BootGUI) even if BootWin=0.

Safe mode with network support

Same as Safe mode but also loads the network drivers. You would want to do this if you are loading Windows 95 off the network or need network resources when trying to change your incorrect drivers.

Step-by-step confirmation

Same as Shift+F8. Ask for confirmation before each command from Io.sys, Config.sys, and Autoexec.bat is carried out. Helps to isolate trouble. Boots to DOS 7.0 or Windows 95 (depending on BootGUI) even if BootWin=0.

Command prompt only

Carry out a normal boot sequence but don't start Windows 95. If BootWin=0, starts previous DOS version.

Safe mode command prompt only

Same as Safe mode but don't start Windows 95. Autoexec.bat and Config.sys are not read; nor are their commands carried out.

Previous version of MS-DOS

Same as F4. Load the previous version of DOS. If BootWin=0, restarts Windows 95 Startup menu, and if chosen again loads previous version of DOS.

Startup Keys

Table 6-2 shows which keys are read before the Windows 95 graphic appears on your screen, and right after the text message that Windows 95 is starting appears. The keys are used to modify how Windows 95 starts. If BootKeys=0 in Msdos.sys, the keys won't work.

Table 6-2	Keys That Modify How Windows 95 Starts
Key	**Result**
F4	If BootWin=1, starts the previous version of DOS. If Windows 95 has been installed in its own directory on the computer that has MS-DOS 6.x or previous DOS operating system, then this key will start that version of DOS instead of Windows 95. This also works if Windows 95 has been installed on a computer that already has OS/2 and Windows NT installed after you use their multi-boot menus.
	If BootWin=0, pressing F4 boots up Windows 95.
	Only works if BootMulti=1. Same as menu choice 8 on the Windows 95 Startup menu.
F5	Safe startup of Windows 95. This allows Windows 95 to start with its most basic configuration, bypassing your Autoexec.bat and Config.sys files, using the VGA driver for video, and not loading any networking drivers. Safe startup is used if there are any problems starting Windows 95.
	Same as menu choice 3 on the Windows 95 Startup menu.
Shift+F5	Command line start. Boots to real-mode DOS 7.0. MS-DOS, Command.com, and Dblspace.bin (or Drvspace.bin) are loaded in low memory, taking up valuable conventional memory space. Bypasses Config.sys and Autoexec.bat.
	Same as menu choice 7 on the Windows 95 Startup menu.
Ctrl+F5	Command line start without compressed drives. The Dblspace.bin and Drvspace.bin files are ignored and DoubleSpace and DriveSpace drives are not mounted.
F6	Safe startup (like F5) but with the addition of the network. Same as menu choice 4 on the Windows 95 Startup menu.
F8	Starts the Windows 95 Startup menu.
Shift+F8	Interactive start that goes through Config.sys and Autoexec.bat one line at a time and lets you decide if you want that line read and acted upon. Also goes through each command that Io.sys initiates before it carries out the commands in Config.sys. (This is interesting to watch in itself.)
	Same as menu choice 5 on the Windows 95 Startup menu.

What Gets Loaded When

Undocumented

Io.sys carries out a default sequence of commands. These commands can be overridden or modified by entries in Config.sys. You can easily see just what commands Io.sys carries out if you don't have a Config.sys or an Autoexec.bat file (rename your existing files) or if these files are empty. You can also just instruct your interactive startup (Shift+F8) to ignore these files.

When you see the message that Windows 95 is starting, press Shift+F8 to start interactive startup. You will be asked to confirm if you want various actions to be carried out. Here's how to interpret the questions:

> Load DoubleSpace driver [Enter=Y, Esc=N]?

> Process the system registry [Enter=Y, Esc=N]?

If you are actually going to start Windows 95 you will want the Registry to be processed.

> Create a startup log file (BOOTLOG.TXT) [Enter=Y, Esc=N]?

The file Bootlog.txt is created and a backup of the previous Bootlog.txt is written to Bootlog.prv.

> Process your startup device drivers (CONFIG.SYS) [Enter=Y, Esc=N]?

If you have a Config.sys file, Io.sys will read and carry out the commands within it. Answer **N** to this question to see the bare commands that Io.sys carries out.

> DEVICE=C:\WINDOWS\HIMEM.SYS [Enter=Y, Esc=N]?

Windows can't start unless Himem.sys is loaded first. Your Windows directory may be C:\Win95, or some other name and drive letter.

> DEVICEHIGH=C:\WINDOWS\IFSHLP.SYS [Enter=Y, Esc=N]?

This is the helper file for the installable file system. This is needed for the Virtual File Allocation Table (VFAT) file system that Windows 95 uses to imitate the standard DOS and Windows FAT file system and still store long filenames.

> DEVICEHIGH=C:\WINDOWS\SETVER.EXE [Enter=Y, Esc=N]?

This command reads in a table of program names and values that fools these named programs into thinking that an earlier version of DOS is running. Notice that the last two commands asked to be loaded high. They are in fact loaded in conventional memory as long as you haven't loaded Emm386.exe.

Process your startup command file (AUTOEXEC.BAT) [Enter=Y, Esc=N]?

Answer **N** to this request.

AUTOEXEC [Enter=Y, Esc=N]?

Answer **N** again

WIN [Enter=Y, Esc=N]?

If you say no to the last question, you are left at a command line prompt with the Windows 95 version of DOS loaded. Windows hasn't been loaded because you answered no to that command. This is the same as choosing Shift+F5 or putting the line BootGUI=0 in Msdos.sys.

This default load sequence gives you an idea why Config.sys and Autoexec.bat are not needed. Many of the functions that would be carried out by Config.sys are carried out by Io.sys, if you let it. In the next sections, you will see that Io.sys sets values that are normally set in Config.sys. You also will see that Io.sys sets parameter values normally set in Autoexec.bat.

Undocumented

You can suppress the commands loaded by Io.sys by putting the following line in your Config.sys file:

```
DOS=NOAUTO
```

Config.sys

There is a great deal more, hardware-wise, to the standard personal computer than was the case when MS-DOS was designed. Your Config.sys file has undoubtedly reflected that growth. This file on most modern computers is filled with calls to software drivers that support additional hardware.

Mice, sound cards, CD-ROM drives, and network cards are among the hardware that didn't have built-in support in the original MS-DOS operating system. Memory management, including the ability to load programs in high memory and provide expanded memory for DOS programs that required it, also necessitated software drivers that were called by references to them in Config.sys.

These software drivers are now (with the advent of a mostly 32-bit operating system, Windows 95) referred to as real-mode or 16-bit drivers. Under MS-DOS or Windows 3.x these drivers were required to be loaded either in conventional memory (below the 640K line) or in upper memory between the 640K line and the 1MB line.

Windows 95 incorporates most of these drivers into the operating system, i.e., they are part of Windows 95. No longer are these drivers stored in conventional or upper memory blocks. This frees up a significant amount of conventional memory that can be used for DOS programs that require it.

The new drivers are referred to as 32-bit or protected-mode drivers. They are loaded above the 1MB boundary. Information about them is stored in the Registry. When Windows 95 starts, it reads the Registry files and loads the appropriate protected-mode drivers.

You do not need a Config.sys file unless you have to use real-mode drivers for a piece of hardware that is not supported by 32-bit drivers. Rather than using a 16-bit mouse driver, full mouse functionality is provided to DOS programs in a Windows DOS session by 32-bit mouse drivers built into Windows 95.

Config.sys variables

Various values that were previously set in Config.sys, like files=, or fcbs=, are now set at values higher than the previous defaults. You may still need to set higher values for some of these variables, but that may not be necessary.

The new default values:

```
files=30
fcbs=4
buffers=22
stacks=9,256
lastdrive='
```

Memory management

If you have real-mode drivers (say you have a CD-ROM drive that isn't supported with 32-bit drivers) and want to load them in upper memory, you will want to use the expanded memory manager (with perhaps the expanded memory option turned off) to access the memory between 640K and 1MB. Loading these drivers into upper memory gives you more conventional memory for DOS programs. If you are not running DOS programs that require much memory, then there is no point in doing this.

You would put the following lines in Config.sys:

```
DEVICE=C:\WINDOWS\HIMEM.SYS /TESTMEM:OFF
DEVICE=C:\WINDOWS\EMM386.EXE NOEMS
DOS=HIGH,UMB
```

Calls to the real-mode drivers would follow the preceding lines and be preceded by DEVICEHIGH=.

For a more thorough discussion of memory management, see Chapter 18.

Autoexec.bat

Much of the functionality that was found in Autoexec.bat and Config.sys is now incorporated into the Registry or into Windows 95 defaults, so these files can be much shorter or even eliminated altogether.

Tip

For example, the default DOS prompt is now the equivalent to that created by the PROMPT pg line in Autoexec.bat. This prompt command creates a DOS command prompt that includes the volume and directory name and the greater than symbol (C:\Windows>), If you want a different DOS prompt, you will still need to create an Autoexec.bat file and put in your own prompt statement.

The Windows 95 default path is C:\Windows;C:\Windows\Command. If your programs require additional directories in the path, you will need to create a path statement in your Autoexec.bat. There is no reason why a Windows program should require a path value, but a lot do. DOS programs use them extensively.

DOS programs that require a path can start a batch file that sets the path for them in a Windows DOS session. You don't have to mangle the global path statement to accommodate these DOS programs. By creating a specific short-cut (actually a *pif*) to the DOS program, you can name the batch file that is run before your DOS program starts. More details are found in Chapter 17.

It is a good idea not to store the temporary files that are created by Windows 95 and various application programs in the extensive Windows directory. Windows 95 automatically sets the environment variables TMP and TEMP to C:\Windows\Temp. This makes it convenient to browse this folder and erase old temporary files.

You will want your Autoexec.bat file to load any program whose capabilities you will need when you open any DOS window on the Windows 95 desktop. For example, if you want to keep a history of DOS commands in your DOS window so you can easily go back to previous ones and edit or run them again, you will want to put the statement Doskey in Autoexec.bat.

Multiple Configurations

Using previous versions of DOS, you could create a menu of configuration choices to be displayed when you first started your computer. Special commands in Config.sys and Autoexec.bat were used to create the menus and respond to your choices.

Windows 95 also accommodates multiple configurations. The menu of configuration choices will be displayed after a normal startup (Config.sys and Autoexec.bat files are read) but before Windows 95 itself is started. (See Figure 6-2.)

```
Microsoft Windows 95 Startup menu
===========================
    1.        Normal
    2.        Logged (\BOOTLOG.TXT)
    3.        Safe mode
    4.        Safe mode with network support
    5.        Step-by-Step confirmation
    6.        Command prompt only
    7.        Safe mode command prompt only
    8.        Previous version of MS-DOS
Enter a Choice: 1              Time Remaining: 30

F5=Safe mode Shift+F5=Command Prompt Shift+F8=Step-byStep Confirmation [N]
```

Figure 6-2: If you have BootMenu=1 in your Msdos.sys file or press F8 during Windows 95 startup, this Startup menu is displayed.

Here are example Config.sys and Autoexec.bat files illustrating the creation of a multiple configuration menu.

Config.sys

```
;config.sys, Config.w40 when booted to DOS 6.2x
[menu]
Menuitem=windows,Load Windows for Workgroups 3.11
Menuitem=win95,Load Windows 95
Menudefault=win95,7
[global]
DEVICE=C:\WIN95\himem.sys /testmem:off /v
DEVICE=C:\WIN95\EMM386.EXE NOEMS /V
dos=UMB,High
[windows]
include=global
BUFFERS=20,0
FILES=99
LASTDRIVE=H
FCBS=16,0
BREAK=ON
STACKS=9,256
DEVICEHIGH=C:\WIN95\SETVER.EXE
DEVICEHIGH=C:\UTIL\SFXCD\DEV\MTMCDE.SYS /D:MSCD001 /P:310 /A:0 M:64 /T:S /I:5 /X
DEVICEHIGH=c:\windows\IFSHLP.SYS
DEVICEHIGH=C:\WIN95\COMMAND\DRVSPACE.SYS /MOVE
shell=C:\WIN95\COMMAND.COM c:\WIN95 /e:512 /p
[win95]
include=global
shell=C:\WIN95\COMMAND.COM c:\WIN95 /e:512 /p
```

Autoexec.bat

```
@rem autoexec.bat, autoexec.w40 when booted to DOS 6.2x
@echo off
goto %config%
:windows
PROMPT $P$G
PATH;
PATH C:\WINDOWS;C:\WIN95\COMMAND;C:\UTIL\BATCH
SET TEMP=C:\UTIL\TEMP
SET LMOUSE=C:\UTIL\LOGITECH
LH C:\UTIL\LOGITECH\MOUSE
LH C:\WINDOWS\SMARTDRV.EXE /X 2048 128
LH C:\WINDOWS\MSCDEX.EXE /S /D:MSCD001 /M:10
LH C:\WIN95\COMMAND\doskey
WIN
GOTO END
:win95
PATH;
PATH C:\WIN95;C:\WIN95\COMMAND;C:\UTIL\BATCH
LH C:\WIN95\COMMAND\doskey
:END
```

These files both start DOS 7.0 and allow you to choose between running Windows for Workgroups 3.11 or Windows 95.

These two files will allow you to choose between Windows for Workgroups 3.11 or Windows 95. They both assume that you want to startup DOS 7.0. BootGUI should be set to **1** in Msdos.sys if you want to boot to Windows 95 and not DOS 7.0. If BootWin=0, these files will not be read and their associated configuration menu will not be displayed.

These files will create the Startup menu shown in Figure 6-3.

```
Microsoft Windows 95 Startup menu
==============================
     1.      Load Windows for Workgroups 3.11
     2.      Load Windows 95

Enter a Choice: 2          Time Remaining: 07


F5=Safe mode Shift+F5=Command Prompt Shift+F8=Step-byStep Confirmation [N]
```

Figure 6-3: The Multiple Configuration menu. In spite of the heading for this menu, it is not the same as the Windows 95 Startup menu. That menu can be displayed before this menu is shown. Shift+F8 won't work. Shift+F5 will.

Multiple Hardware Configurations

You can create multiple hardware configurations for one computer. For example, if you have a non-plug and play portable computer that sometimes is connected to a docking station, you will want to create a hardware configuration that includes the cards in the docking station and perhaps the network connected to the docking station.

The startup sequence for a computer with multiple hardware configurations includes a menu that allows you to choose which hardware configuration you wish to use. An example hardware configuration startup menu is shown in Figure 6-4.

Windows cannot determine what configuration your computer is in:
Select one of the following:

1.   Docking Station with Network
2.   Disconnected Portable
3.   None of the Above

Enter your choice:

Figure 6-4: The multiple hardware configuration menu. This text menu will appear after the Windows 95 logo is displayed.

To create multiple hardware configurations, take the following steps:

STEPS

Creating Multiple Hardware Configurations

Step 1. Click the Start button, then Settings, and then the Control Panel.

Step 2. Double-click the System icon, and then the Hardware Profiles tab. The Hardware Profiles list, as shown in Figure 6-5, will be displayed on your desktop.

Step 3. Click the Rename button to rename your current profile to something that appropriately describes your current hardware configuration.

Step 4. Click the Copy button, highlight the new hardware profile, and click Rename to rename the new hardware profile.

Step 5. Click the Device Manager tab. Click the plus sign next to the device types that will vary between hardware profiles.

(continued)

STEPS *(continued)*

Creating Multiple Hardware Configurations

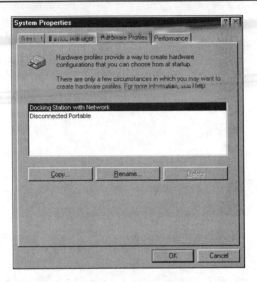

Figure 6-5: The Hardware Profiles list. You can copy, remove, and rename hardware profiles. You define hardware profiles in the Device Manager.

Step 6.   Click a device that will be found in one hardware profile but not in the other. Uncheck the box next to the name of the hardware profile that will not use this device, as shown in Figure 6-6.

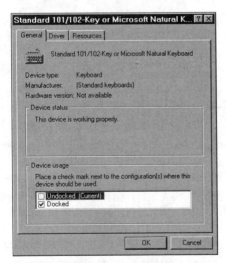

Figure 6-6: Choosing which devices go with which hardware configuration.

Your Device Manager may not list all the devices that are available among your various hardware configurations. You will have to install device drivers for these devices before you can assign them to your different hardware profiles.

To learn how to add hardware device drivers, turn to Chapter 19.

QEMM and F4

Tip

If you are using QEMM 7.*x*, and it loads a file called Dosdata.sys in Config.sys, this file will reboot to optimize memory.

When you press the F4 key to boot your previous operating system, Dosdata.sys reboots the machine to re-optimize the memory, and then you see the message that Windows 95 is starting. Pressing F4 again should boot the previous operating system.

The only resolution to this problem is to remark out the QEMM lines in Config.sys and Autoexec.bat or to remember to press F4 two times. You want to be very careful remarking the QEMM lines, since QEMM may be loading some important 16-bit device drivers in real mode.

Changing the Startup Graphic

Undocumented

When Windows 95 starts, a graphic is displayed. If you have installed Microsoft Plus! this graphic is found in the file Logo.sys in the root directory. In spite of its sys extension, it is a bmp file and can be edited by MS Paint.

If you haven't installed Microsoft Plus! a very similar graphic is displayed. This graphic is found in the Io.sys file.

Logo.sys is an animated bitmapped file so if you edit it with MS Paint, you'll lose the animation. You can substitute any other bitmapped file. You might want to save Logo.sys as Logo.bmp and then rename your new graphics file Logo.sys.

We have placed BMP Wizard on the shareware CD-ROM; you can use it to create another animated logo.

Secret

If you delete Logo.sys, the version in Io.sys will be used instead. Getting rid of Logo.sys doesn't make the graphic go away.

There are two files in your \Windows folder, Logos.sys and Logow.sys. These are the two screens that you see when you shut down Windows 95. You can back up these files and create new shut down screens.

Dual-Boot Configuration

You can have multiple operating systems running on your computer. DOS 6.2*x* combined with Windows 3.1*x*, Windows 95, OS/2, and Windows NT can all coexist on the C: drive (or on multiple drives) of your computer as long as you have the room for them (and the FAT file system is used).

You can put almost all of DOS 6.2*x* and Windows 3.1*x* and Windows 95 on a non-bootable hard disk, even a compressed hard disk. You just need to leave the boot up files (Io.sys, Msdos.sys, Config.sys, and Autoexec.bat) as well as the files that work with a compressed drive on the boot drive.

When you first install Windows 95 over an existing DOS/Windows system, you have the option of installing over an existing Windows 3.1*x* directory or in a new directory. Windows 95 uses the existing DOS file structure, so there is no need to start by reformatting your hard disk. If you install Windows 95 to a new directory then you have the option of booting either DOS (which can get you to Windows 3.*x*) or Windows 95.

If you have a computer that dual-boots between DOS and Windows 95, the files in the root directory will be renamed depending on whether you have booted into DOS or booted into Windows 95. Assuming that you previously booted into Windows 95, the renaming shown in Table 6-4 will take place if you boot into DOS:

Table 6-4	Files Renamed in Dual Boots from Windows 95 to DOS
From	**To**
Io.sys	Winboot.sys
Msdos.sys	Msdos.w40
Command.com	Command.w40
Autoexec.bat	Autoexec.w40
Config.sys	Config.w40
Io.dos	Io.sys
Msdos.dos	Msdos.sys
Command.dos	Command.com
Config.dos	Config.sys
Autoexec.dos	Autoexec.bat

The Startup Folder

When Windows 95 starts, it runs the programs in the \Windows\Startup folder. Windows 95 knows which folder is the Startup folder because there is an entry in the Registry specifying a particular folder, usually \Windows\Startup. You can change which folder is used as the Startup folder, as well as the characteristics of other folders, by editing the following entry in the Registry:

HKEY_CURRENT_USER\Software\Microsoft\Windows\CurrentVersion\Explorer\shellfolders

For details on editing your Registry, turn to chapter 15.

Windows 95 Troubleshooting

If you press F8 at startup and go to the command prompt, you can start Windows 95 with the debug switch. Here's the debug syntax:

WIN {/D:{F}{M}{N}{S}{V}{X}}

/D:	Used for troubleshooting when Windows does not start correctly.
F	Turns off 32-bit disk access. Equivalont to SYSTEM.INI file setting: 32BitDiskAccess=FALSE.
M	Enables Safe mode. This is automatically enabled during Safe start (function key F5).
N	Enables Safe mode with networking. This is automatically enabled during Safe start (function key F6).
S	Specifies that Windows should not use ROM address space betweenF000:0000 and 1 MB for a break point. Equivalent to SYSTEM.INI file setting: SystemROMBreakPoint=FALSE.
V	Specifies that the ROM routine will handle interrupts from the hard disk controller. Equivalont to SYSTEM.INI file setting: VirtualHDIRQ=FALSE.
X	Excludes all of the adapter area from the range of memory that Windows scans to find unused space. Equivalent to SYSTEM.INI file setting: EMMExclude=A000-FFFF

Summary

Windows 95 gives you a great deal of control over how your computer starts up. By editing a few files you can control the startup process.

▶ Boot your computer to a DOS 7.0 prompt either by creating an empty Win.bat file or editing Msdos.sys.

▶ Start up in your previous version of DOS or Windows either by pressing a function key or by default.

▶ Edit Msdos.sys in order to get rid of the Windows 95 logo.

▶ Use function keys to go step-by-step through the startup process, start Windows 95 in Safe mode if there is a problem with your hardware, or bring up the Startup menu.

▶ Create different hardware profiles and choose between them at startup time depending on your current hardware setup.

▶ Develop multiconfiguration Config.sys and Autocxec.bat files to design your own Windows 95 Startup menu.

Part II
The Windows 95 User Interface

Chapter 7

The Desktop and the Taskbar

In This Chapter

Windows 95 presents itself to you as a graphical user interface — pretty pictures on your display. The desktop is represented by a graphical background. The Taskbar sits on top of the desktop and is attached to an edge. In this chapter, we discuss:

▶ Arranging the icons on your desktop the way you want them

▶ Changing the invisible grid that determines icon spacing

▶ Changing the font and font sizes used for icon titles

▶ Placing new blank documents on your desktop ready to be opened by an application with a double-click

▶ Putting the Taskbar where it will do you the most good

▶ Getting rid of "sliding" windows

▶ Task switching between applications and folders using the keyboard

▶ Using the Task Manager as a floating task switcher

What You See Is What You Get

The Windows 95 "user interface" is a desktop with stuff on it. The background graphic represents the desktop. The icons on your desktop represent all kinds of different applications and documents, sort of like a regular desktop. The Taskbar keeps track of whatever you are currently working on. The Start button helps you start something new. The clock ... well, you can figure that out for yourself.

We discuss the desktop and the Taskbar in this chapter. We discuss some aspects of the Start button, but leave deeper details to *The Start Button and Finding* chapter, (Chapter 11). Each of the icons on the desktop has its own chapter — see below for where to find each.

First, Your Password

Before you can use Windows 95 the first time, you are asked to enter your name and password. You may choose to configure the computer differently from other users. Type in your name and password, and your configuration is used. If you are on a network, your name and password let you log on to other servers.

When you type in your name and password a dialog box appears. You can make this password dialog box go away and not reappear the next time you start your computer by typing in your name and then clicking the OK button. You will be asked to confirm that you want a blank password.

Passwords, multiple users, and multiple Windows 95 configurations are discussed in Chapter 12.

Once past the logon dialog box, Windows 95 displays some graphics on your screen, as shown in Figure 7-1. You see a background that can vary (based on how you set it up later) from one plain color to a photographic image. There are three (but maybe four, five, or six) icons — 32-by-32-pixel pictures — in the upper left corner on your display. On the bottom edge is the Taskbar, a rectangular bar with a button labeled Start on the left hand side and a digital clock on the right.

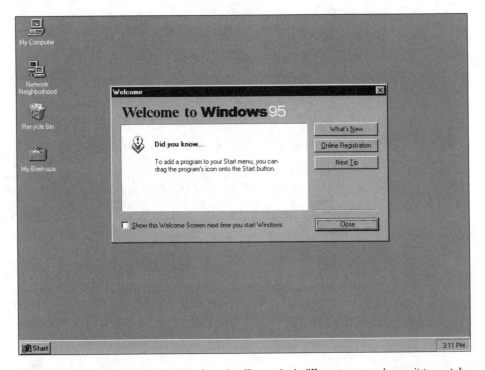

Figure 7-1: The Windows 95 user interface. It will soon look different as you change it to match the way you use Windows.

In the middle of the screen, Windows 95 announces the fact that you are new to it and may need a few hints. You can have this reminder of your neophyte-hood come up everytime you start Windows 95 or you can ask it to quiet down. Just click the "Show this Welcome screen next time you start Windows" box to uncheck it, and then click Close button. It's easy to get this welcome screen back any time you want — double-click the Welcome.exe file in your Windows 95 folder.

The Desktop

Windows 95 uses a desktop metaphor that originated at Xerox's Palo Alto Research Center in the 1970s. (You must have heard this story by now.) Your screen is turned into a graphical desktop with lots of little items on the desktop for you to work with.

It doesn't look much like a desktop and it really doesn't matter if you consider it as such or not. The point is that Windows 95 uses a graphical display to place icons and windows on your screen.

Your Windows applications and documents will be displayed on the desktop within their own windows. The desktop and the Taskbar can be used to determine how those windows are displayed.

If you right-click anywhere on the desktop (where there is not an icon, a window, or the Taskbar), a menu appears. This menu is your control point for the desktop. The basic desktop menu — it does change — is shown in Figure 7-2.

Figure 7-2: The desktop menu. Right-click anywhere on the desktop to bring up this menu. Click Properties to change much of the desktop. Move the icons around with Arrange Icons and Line up Icons.

Undocumented

When you right-click the desktop, the desktop menu appears. When the desktop menu is showing, you will be able to carry out only the actions listed on that menu until you left-click on the desktop or click (either left or right) in a window or someplace other than the desktop. If you have a hidden Taskbar, it will not pop up as long as the desktop menu appears on the desktop.

The invisible grid

There is an invisible grid on your desktop. The icons on the desktop are centered in the cells defined by this grid and placed on the left side of the desktop starting at the top. It is possible to place the icons in other locations, although most are not as convenient as this default top/left positioning. You can determine the size of the grid cells.

Arranging the icons

To align icons in the center of the grid cells, right-click the Desktop and then click Line up Icons. This enables you to place the icons in different parts of the desktop and still have them look orderly when you are finished.

To arrange the icons in one of four predefined orders, click Arrange Icons and then choose: by Name, by Type, by Size, or by Date. The icons will arrange themselves starting in the upper left corner and proceeding down to the next cell in the sort order specified. A second and further columns of icons will be added to the right if there are more icons than can fit in the first column.

To have the icons always place themselves in columns starting at the left-hand side of the desktop, right-click the desktop, and then click Arrange Icons and then Auto Arrange. Auto Arrange is a toggle switch with a check mark next to it if it is active. If Auto Arrange is checked, the icons will always move back into the columnar arrangement no matter where you move them or where they are initially placed.

Undocumented

Auto Arrange does not sort the icons. With Auto Arrange checked, you can move any icon to a new location and it will be inserted in the columns in the order you indicate by where you drop the icon. Move the icon to the right of the column(s) of icons and it will be placed at the bottom of the right most column.

Turn Auto Arrange off (uncheck it) and you can place icons wherever you like and in any order. Click Line up Icons and they will snap to (move to) the nearest cell center.

Click Arrange Icons, then any of the sort choices, and the icons will move back to the left side of the desktop and arrange themselves in columns in the order specified.

To place your icons elsewhere on the desktop — not in the order and locations prescribed by Auto Arrange and Arrange Icons — then don't click these menu items. Place the icons by dragging and dropping them where you like and as close or as far from each other as you like. Don't use Line up Icons, Arrange Icons, or Auto Arrange.

Changing the size of the grid

The grid starts in the upper left corner of the desktop. The vertical line that marks the right hand edge of the first cell is so many pixels to the right of the left edge of the desktop. The horizontal line that marks the bottom edge of the first cell is so many pixels below the top edge of the desktop. The invisible grid is revealed in Figure 7-3.

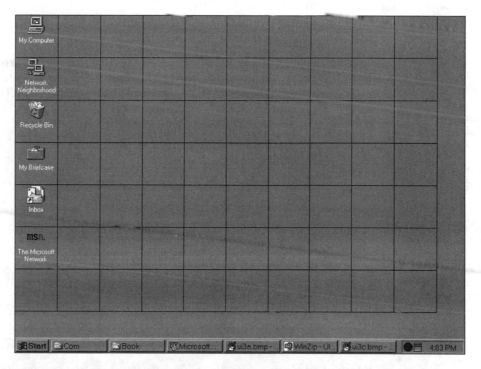

Figure 7-3: A faux icon spacing grid. The size of each cell in the default grid spacing in pixels (assuming a display magnification set at small fonts) is 75 pixels high and 75 pixels wide.

Secret

The size of the cells depends on the icon pixel size, icon spacing (both horizontal and vertical), and display magnification (small, large, or custom font size) , as discussed in Chapter 22. The default cell size (for small fonts) is 75 x 75 pixels with a default icon size of 32 pixels and default icon spacing of 43 pixels (32+43 = 75). The grid in Figure 7-3 is set at 75 pixels high by 75 pixels wide.

You can change the size of the icon spacing grid by editing the vertical and horizontal icon spacing values. To do this, take the following steps:

STEPS

Editing Icon Spacing

Step 1. Right-click the desktop, Set Auto Arrange to on. Right-click the desktop, Click Properties. Click the Appearance tab.

Step 2. Click the drop-down arrow in the Item field to open up the drop-down list of desktop items.

Step 3. Click, one at a time, Vertical Icon Spacing and Horizontal Icon Spacing.

Step 4. Adjust the size of each — in pixels — using the spin controls in the Size field to the right of the Item field. (Click on the up and down arrows or enter a new number value to change the size). The total vertical size of the cell will be the sum of the icon size plus the vertical spacing. Horizontal size is calculated similarly.

Step 5. To see what the effect is on icon spacing, click the Apply button when both sizes are adjusted. Keep adjusting icon spacing until you are pleased with the results.

Step 6. Click OK.

The icon title text will be shortened and ellipses added to the end of the text if it doesn't fit within the boundaries of the cell. If you make the vertical or horizontal spacing too small, the icons will overlap — not a good idea.

Changing the icon title text font and size

By default, the icon titles use the MS Sans Serif 8-point font (at 800 x 600 display resolution, higher resolution displays will default to 10-point fonts). You have the option of changing the font used to display the icon titles. You can also change the font's point size and whether it is bold and/or italic. You can't change its color from black unless you set your Desktop to a dark color, in which case the icon font title color is set to white automatically.

Tip

MS Sans Serif is a *screen font*, which means that it has been designed to be readable on standard monitors that display pixels at 96 or 120 pixels per logical inch. You can use any font that you want, including Arial, which looks a lot like MS Sans Serif, but is a TrueType font. Check out the various fonts and choose one that you find easy to read.

If you increase the font point size, you are going to have to deal with whether the icon titles fit in the grid cells.

To change the font used for the icon titles, take the following steps:

STEPS

Changing Icon Title Fonts

Step 1.   Right-click the desktop. Check Auto Arrange on. Right-click the desktop. Click Properties. Click the Appearance tab.

Step 2.   Click the drop down arrow in the Item field to open the drop-down list of desktop items.

Step 3.   Click Icon Titles. The Font and Size fields can be changed. So can the Bold and Italic buttons. Figure 7-4 shows both.

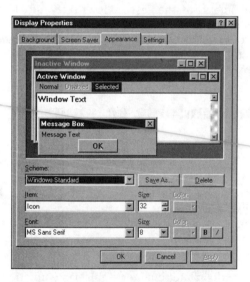

Figure 7-4: The Display Appearance Properties sheet. Click the drop-down arrow in the Item field and then choose Icon Title. Pick a font style from the Font drop-down list and a font point size from the Size field. The B and / buttons stand for bold and italics, respectively.

Step 4.   Click the Apply button when you have chosen a font, point size, and so on, to see the effect of the choices. Keep adjusting these values until you are pleased with the results.

Step 5.   When you are done, click OK.

Changing other properties of the desktop

You can change the background graphics, the colors used on the desktop, as well as many other properties of the desktop. All these changes are described in Chapter 22.

Putting new items on the desktop

It is easy to put new items, represented by icons, on the desktop. You have the option of placing new folders, shortcuts, or any one of five (or more) document types on the desktop. The five default document types are Text, Microsoft Word 6.0, Rich Text Format, Bitmap Image, or Wave Sound. Additional document types can be added to the list (how to do so is discussed in Chapter 13).

Tip

Placing new documents on the desktop is a pretty nifty feature and contributes to the document-centric character of Windows 95. You can put a new blank document on your desktop and then double-click to bring up the application that can open and edit it. To add new documents to the desktop, right-click the desktop. Click New and then click the document type that you want to add.

Pasting and undoing actions

The desktop menu gives you the option of copying (or moving) a file (or application, folder, or shortcut) to the desktop. The applicable menu item is Paste.

You can select a file in a folder window or in the Explorer. Right-click the file and choose Copy, which means "copy this file to someplace as soon as I tell you where." By clicking Paste in the desktop menu you are saying, "this is where I want you to copy the file."

We haven't really gone into folder windows, the Explorer, shortcuts, and other topics yet, but we do in later chapters. This paste function is also found on menus used in these other, yet to be investigated, desktop items. The idea of the terminology is like cutting and pasting text in a word processor.

You may find other menu options below the Paste command. They appear depending on other actions that you have taken in other folder windows. If you happened to have renamed a file, you will see the Undo rename command. If you deleted a file, you will see the Undo delete command.

The Undo command shows up in this menu (and most right mouse button menus) whenever you have taken an action that can be undone. If you remember what it was that you did and you want to undo (as long as you haven't quit and restarted Windows 95), here's your chance. For additional details, see the *Undo* section in Chapter 8.

The Icons on the Desktop

The icons that originally appear on the desktop stand for powerful Windows functions. They are discussed in later chapters. The My Computer icon is discussed in Chapter 8. The Recycle Bin is covered in Chapter 14. The My Briefcase icon is discussed in Chapter 31 and the Inbox icon in Chapter 32.

The great part about the desktop is that there are icons on it. The desktop takes over much of the function of the Windows 3.x Program Manager. Put up a digitized photograph as your background and the icons hang there in space on your desktop. Unless you had a specialized wallpaper application, the Windows 3.x Program Manager presented a rather boring background for your program groups.

You can put any icon on the desktop that you want. It is so much more natural to have the stuff you are working on there on your desktop and not constrained to the confines of the Program Manager. We go into this a lot more in Chapter 10.

You can use the System Policy Editor to get rid of all the icons on your desktop, or just get rid of the Network Neighborhood icon. You'll need to turn to Chapter 34 to see how to install the System Policy Editor. To use it to deal with desktop icons, take the following steps:

STEPS

Getting Rid of Icons on the Desktop

Step 1.   Install the System Policy Editor.

Step 2.   Click the Start button, then Programs, Accessories, System Tools, and then System Policy Editor.

Step 3.   Double-click the Local User icon in the System Policy Editor's client window.

Step 4.   Click the plus sign next to the word Shell and then the plus sign next to the word Restrictions.

Step 5.   Click the check box next to "Hide all items on Desktop" or "Hide Network Neighborhood."

Step 6.   Click OK. Click File, Save on the System Policy Editor's menu bar. Click File, Exit.

Step 7.   Restart Windows 95.

Scraps

Some Windows 95-aware applications can place "scraps" on the desktop (or in any folder window). You can try this out using WordPad. Open up a WordPad document. Select some of the text in the document. Drag and drop it onto the desktop.

An icon with the name Scrap will appear on the desktop. This is a document that can be read by WordPad. It is made up solely of the text that you dropped on the desktop. Double-click its icon on the desktop, and WordPad launches.

This is an easy way to pile up a bunch of scrap paper on your desktop (or any other folder) and then make something of them later. Scraps give you an alternative to the Clipboard with the advantage of allowing multiple pieces to be quickly available at one time.

The Taskbar

The Taskbar has the Start button and a digital clock. It is the home of the *active* applications — those applications that you started by double-clicking a file or an application icon. There is a button on the Taskbar for every active application. Maybe this is a good time to step back and examine just what Windows 95 means by an active application.

When you first turn on your computer, it is just Windows 95 (and whatever applications are in the Startup folder) that get read off the hard disk and loaded into your RAM. An application or a document needs to be read into memory from the hard disk before it can act or be acted upon.

We refer to an application that has been loaded into memory as an *active* application. Applications that are stored on your computer's hard disk but haven't been loading into memory are *inactive*. A document is loaded into memory with its application. There aren't any stray documents out there in memory without their associated applications.

Some documents are *compound documents* — they were created using multiple applications. Not all applications that were used to create such a document will be loaded into memory when such a document is.

The Taskbar buttons

The icons that represent the active applications and their names are placed on buttons on the Taskbar. If there is an associated document or file with the application, it also gets named on the application's button on the Taskbar. The icons on the Taskbar button are shrunken versions of the icons that you see on the desktop. They are 16 x 16 pixels instead of 32 x 32 pixels.

Windows 3.*x* applications place their name on the Taskbar buttons. Windows 95 applications are supposed to place their opened document's name on the Taskbar button if this is appropriate. For example, open the Windows 95 NotePad without a document and Untitled will appear on the Taskbar button.

Open a couple of copies of Windows 3.*x* version of Word for Windows 6.0 and you'll see buttons labeled Microsoft Word ....

Tip

Every active application is on the Taskbar. *This means that the Taskbar is a task switcher.* No matter if the active application has been minimized or is now buried under the windows of other applications on the desktop, it can be brought to the top of the desktop by clicking its icon or button (a single click at that) on the Taskbar. This is one of the fundamental improvements in ease of use in Windows 95 over Windows 3.*x*. It is also an advantage that Windows 95 has over the user interface found on the Apple Macintosh. This new feature makes it almost impossible to lose track of which documents and programs are open when they are on top of each other.

The Taskbar takes the place of the minimized active application icons that by default were displayed on the bottom of your Windows 3.*x* desktop. Because it also has a button for every active application whether minimized or not, it has much of the task-switching functionality of the Windows 3.*x* Task Manager.

Tip

The single-click operation of the Taskbar makes it easy to switch between *tasks* — which are simply active applications. Combine this with Windows 95's enhanced resource management and it is easy to find yourself with multiple active applications. Windows 95 makes multitasking (defined from the users' perspective as quickly jumping between active applications) easy enough to be useful.

Drag and wait to a Taskbar button

You can *drag and hold* a file (continue to hold down the mouse button as you drag) over to a button on the Taskbar. As you hold the file over the Taskbar button, the application associated with that button will spring to life. If it is minimized, it will expand and display itself on the desktop. If it is buried on the desktop, it will come to the top.

Tip

Once the application window has appeared, you can drop the file icon on it. The application determines what happens next. If the application is a Windows editor or word processor, it will open or insert the dropped file, depending on where you drop it. If the program is a DOS editor, it will put the name of the dropped file at the insertion point in a DOS file.

Windows 3.*x* applications that work as icons and don't expand into windows will not work with Windows 95.

Hiding the Taskbar

The Taskbar has two mode switches:

> Always on top or not

> Auto hide or not

Always on top means always on top of other windows on the desktop. Not exactly *always*, but often enough anyway. Turn on this feature and other windows will do their best to stay out of the way of the Taskbar. Turn off this feature and other windows don't know that the Taskbar is there.

Turn on Auto hide and the Taskbar disappears unless it is the last thing to have been clicked. An Auto-hidden Taskbar doesn't take up desktop real estate except when you want to do something with it — like switch to another task.

The Taskbar isn't shown when Auto hide is on if you have clicked another application. To get the Taskbar to display itself you need to bring the mouse pointer to the edge of the screen. You will be able to see on the bottom (side or top) of your desktop a 2-pixel wide line that is a remnant of the Taskbar. When your mouse pointer hot spot gets within 2 pixels of the edge of the desktop it will change into a resize arrow and the Taskbar will pop up. The mouse pointer will then change back to a normal selection arrow.

Undocumented

If you move your mouse pointer more than 10 pixels away from the Taskbar without clicking it (and not one of the buttons on the Taskbar) first, the Taskbar will disappear. It doesn't disappear instantly. Depending on what is beneath the Taskbar, the screen usually takes longer to repaint the desktop to show what was obscured by the Taskbar than it took to pop up the Taskbar in the first place. This can be quite a bother.

If you click the Taskbar after it pops up, it gains the focus. You can then move the mouse pointer around the desktop and the Taskbar doesn't disappear until you click another window or the desktop. You have to click the Taskbar and not on any of the buttons. Sometimes this is a little difficult as much of the Taskbar itself can be taken up with buttons.

If Auto hide is on and Always on top is off, when the Taskbar pops up it will pop up behind any window that it might have otherwise obscured. You may still be able to have a partial view of the Taskbar and be able to switch tasks, and so on.

If Auto hide is off and Always on top is on, the Taskbar sits on top of your desktop and other windows try to get out of its way. When you maximize a window, it will not cover up the Taskbar. The application calculates the maximum window size as the actual screen resolution minus the number of pixels in the Taskbar.

If Always on top is on, this doesn't mean necessarily that the Taskbar will always be on top. Other windows can have this same property. If two windows have this "always on top" property, whichever window has the focus will be on top.

To change the Auto hide and Always on top modes take the following steps:

STEPS

Changing Taskbar Modes

Step 1.   Right-click the Taskbar. Click Properties. The Taskbar Properties sheet will be displayed on the desktop, as shown in Figure 7-5. (You can also get to this dialog box by selecting Start button, Settings, Taskbar).

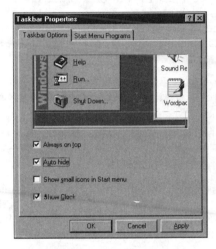

Figure 7-5: The Taskbar Properties sheet. Check the Auto hide and/or Always on top boxes to change these Taskbar modes.

Step 2.   Click Auto hide and/or Always on top to change the Taskbar modes. Click the Apply button to see the effect of these modes.

Step 3.   When you are done, click OK.

Sizing the Taskbar

The Taskbar starts out thin but it can be made bigger. It can be as large as one-half of the desktop.

Move your mouse pointer to the top edge of the Taskbar so that the mouse pointer turns into a resize arrow. Hold down the left mouse button and drag the Taskbar upper edge up. The Taskbar will increase in height in button-height increments.

The buttons on the Taskbar are sized automatically. All the buttons are the same size no matter how long the name of the application and its associated document. The names are cut off within the button if they don't fit and ellipses placed at the end of the name if there is room for them.

You can see the full name of the application and document associated with a given button by placing your mouse pointer over the button and waiting for less than a second. A Tooltip (a small pop-up box with text) appears next to your mouse pointer. This happens only if the full name of the application and its associated document can't be shown on the button face.

Undocumented

As you add active applications, the buttons shrink, unless you increase the size of the Taskbar. When the buttons become so small that they are just big enough to contain the 16 x 16 pixel icons within them, they get no smaller. If you add more active applications, all the icons will not be displayed at the same time on the Taskbar.

In that case, a *spin control* is displayed in the Taskbar. This gives you the option of spinning the control to see icons that are not currently shown on the Taskbar.

The Taskbar is attached to the edges of the desktop. If it is on the bottom, you can't make it smaller by detaching it from the right or left side. The resize arrow appears only when the mouse pointer is near the top of the Taskbar.

Tip

The icons on the desktop will move to avoid the Taskbar as you resize the Taskbar (as long as it isn't in Auto hide mode, as explained in the *Which desktop edge is best for the Taskbar?* section that follows). You will have to have a few more than three icons on the desktop to see this effect.

Moving the Taskbar

The Taskbar doesn't have to be on the bottom of your desktop. You can move it to any other edge (top, bottom, left, or right side of screen).

To move the Taskbar, position the mouse pointer over it, but not over any of the buttons on the Taskbar. Press down the left mouse button and drag the mouse pointer toward one of the other desktop edges. As you begin moving the mouse, an outline of the Taskbar will appear. Release the mouse button when the outline of the Taskbar is positioned on the edge that you prefer.

Which desktop edge is best for the Taskbar?

At the top of an application's window you'll find the menu bar. No doubt you use the menu quite often. You will be used to moving your mouse to the right, to the top, and to the bottom of a Windows application client area, in that order of frequency. The desktop left and bottom edges are the least "natural" areas for Windows users to move their mouse pointers toward.

Tip

If you have your Taskbar as a column on the right side, it will be an easy mouse movement to get to the buttons on the Taskbar. If the Taskbar is hidden it may be too easy and quite a bother. Move the mouse quickly to the right to scroll a document and you are likely to overshoot the scroll bar on the right edge of your client window and go to the desktop edge if your document is anywhere near the right edge of your desktop. Up pops the Taskbar, which you didn't want. Now you have to move the mouse at least 10 pixels to the left of the Taskbar to get it to disappear — a waste of time.

Placing the Taskbar to the right means that it is easy and natural for you to get to it. If Autohide is off then it won't pop up. If you are accurate with your mouse pointing it won't pop up, but this is constraining. A vertical Taskbar with horizontal buttons is most likely fatter than a horizontal Taskbar with horizontal buttons. You need the extra real estate to see the names on the buttons. This is only an issue if Auto hide is off.

Put the Taskbar on the top, turn on Auto hide, and you'll again have the problem of mouse overshoot, although not nearly as bad, when you go to pick a menu item. If Auto hide is on, the Taskbar pops up when you don't want it to, and it takes a long time to disappear.

Placing the Taskbar on the top edge of the desktop is a lot like making it a menu or a Toolbar. Again this is a learned "natural" movement for Windows users. The Start button menu drops down in a familiar manner. If you have the real estate, put the Taskbar on the top edge and keep it Always on top with Auto Hide off, and it will feel comfortable.

Leaving the Taskbar on the bottom or moving it to the left means that you can have Auto hide on, and still not accidentally pop up the Taskbar so often that it becomes annoying. The left side is a difficult adjustment. If placed on the bottom, the menus on the Taskbar pop up instead of drop down. Still, both these placements can work for you.

Test out different locations for a couple of days each to test your reactions over a reasonable amount of time. If you are left handed, attaching the Taskbar to the left edge of the desktop may feel more natural.

Secret

Windows 3.x applications may be partially covered by the Taskbar if they are at their restored size and the Taskbar is set as Always on Top, Auto hide off, and attached to the top edge of the desktop. When these applications are maximized they are not obscured by the Taskbar.

The fact that Windows 3.x applications can't seem to find the Taskbar when they are at their restored size can be quite annoying. To be able to see an application's caption area you are required to press Alt+Spacebar, M and then move the application's window down.

Resizing and moving windows on the desktop

Using the Taskbar, you can cascade, tile, or minimize all the sizable windows on the desktop. Right-click the Taskbar and choose one of these sizing options.

Minimize all is a very powerful function, because it is paired with Undo minimize all. (Right-click the Taskbar again, and this time an Undo Minimize All item will be available.) You can clear your desktop in one command and then place everything back where it came from with the opposite command. This is a very handy feature if you want to get to some icons on your desktop that are covered up by your application windows.

The Start button

We discuss many of the Start button's interesting secrets in Chapter 11, but here are a few of the high points.

The Start button contains the Stop button in the form of the Shut Down command. Click the Start button and then Shut Down to get out of Windows 95.

Clicking the Start button displays the Start button menu. This provides a series of cascading menu choices that give you access to much of the functionality of Windows 95. All of the menus that are attached to the Programs menu item can be easily changed to display the menus, folders, files, and applications that you want displayed.

Right-clicking the Start button lets you open and explore your computer and easily change items in the Start menus.

You can add items to the Start button menu by dragging them over and dropping them on the Start button.

Ctrl+Esc gets you to the Start button.

The Clock

The Taskbar has a digital clock. You can set the date and time. Place your mouse pointer over the time and you'll see the date in a Tooltip. Right-click the time and you can adjust the date and time. The Date/Time Properties sheet, as shown in Figure 7-6, will be displayed.

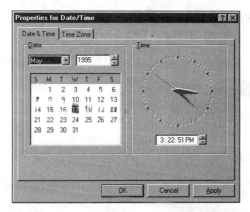

Figure 7-6: The Date/Time Properties sheet. You can set the date and time by typing in new values or spinning the spin control in the date and time fields.

You can change the date by spinning the month and year fields and clicking on a day. You can change the time by typing in a new time or using the spin control. To change the clock to a 24 hour display (instead of AM and PM) you'll need to take the following steps:

STEPS

Changing the Time Format Display

Step 1. Click the Start button, Settings, and then Control Panel.

Step 2. Double-click the Regional Settings icon.

Step 3. Click the Time tab.

Step 4. Click the down arrow in the Time style field and choose a style with an upper-case H.

Step 5. Click the OK button in the Regional Settings properties sheet.

If you want to change the date format, click the Date tab in Step 3 instead of the Time tab. You can also set your time zone. Check out the nifty world map with the highlighted time zone, as shown in Figure 7-7. Even if this function didn't do anything useful, it would be worth it just to have this graphic.

Figure 7-7: The Time Zone map. Click the drop-down box above the map to pick a time zone. Watch the map move from side to side as you pick out different ones. Or drag the "sun" until it's over your time zone — cooler still. You can also use your arrow keys to move the time zone around.

You can tell your computer what time zone it is in by dragging the "sun" in the map until it is over your time zone. There is also a drop down box for a more conventional method. You can also use the arrow keys to move the sun around.

Undocumented

There are 51 separate entries in the list of time zones even though you might assume that there are only 24 unique time zones. Windows 95 keeps track of the daylight savings time rules for various locations, so, for example, there is a unique entry for Arizona (USA) that doesn't honor daylight saving time. There are also separate entries for Darwin and Adelaide (Australia), both of which are plus $9^1/2$ hours from Greenwich Mean Time.

Using your arrow keys (and not your mouse) you can move the time zone map to each of these different locations. Some odd time zones in the southwestern Pacific are not accounted for.

When the first day of daylight savings time arrives, you get a message asking you if you want to have your computer's clock moved an hour ahead.

The time zone value does have something of a practical value. If you are on a network that crosses time zones, say, your own company's WAN, or Microsoft Network, this time zone value can be used to get everyone's time synched to a universal standard like Zulu, Greenwich Mean Time, or whatever arbitrary one you choose. Files that are time-stamped on the west coast can be compared correctly with files that are time-stamped on the east coast.

Sliding windows

You'll notice as you click application buttons on the Taskbar that the window caption area of the application is displayed first in a shrunken form and then expanded until the complete application is displayed in a window on the desktop. This is called *sliding* or *zooming* windows, and occurs only if the application has been minimized first.

If you minimize an application on the desktop, the opposite effect occurs as the window's caption bar is shrunk and then the application's window disappears. Windows 95 is trying to show you that your application has now gone to the Taskbar and to get it back you need to click its button there.

Secret

If you don't like this effect you can turn if off. Here's how:

STEPS

Turning Off Sliding Windows

Step 1. Double-click on Regedit.exe, the Registry editor in the \Windows folder. See later chapters on viewing the \Windows folder in the Explorer or a folder window.

Step 2. Click the plus sign to the left of HKEY_CURRENT_USER. (This will make the change for the current user only. Often the current user will be the only user.)

Step 3. Click the plus sign to the left of Control Panel and then Desktop. Highlight WindowMetrics.

Step 4. Click Edit, New, String Value in the Registry editor menu bar. Type in **MinAnimate** as the new name for the string value.

Step 5. Double-click MinAnimate in the right pane. Type in the value 0. Click OK.

Step 6. Restart Windows 95.

If you want the sliding windows effect to reappear, you can always change this value back to 1. If you find that MinAnimate has already been created, you can change its value by double-clicking MinAnimate.

Task Switching with the Keyboard

Three keyboard combinations let you switch between active applications and folders.

Hold down Alt and press the Tab key. A window that contains the icons of the active applications and folders appears on the desktop. By pressing and releasing the Tab key you can switch between the active applications and folder windows.

If you want to get back to the Start button, press Ctrl+Esc. This will bring up the Taskbar and the Start button menu. You can get to the menu items on the Start menu by using the down arrow or the key corresponding to the letter underlined in the menu. Press the Enter key to choose the menu item. Menu items in the other menus (that cascade off the Start button menu) don't have assigned letters. You can still use the up and down arrows to get to them and Enter to choose them.

Undocumented

You can get to the icons on the Taskbar or the icons on the desktop with the keyboard. Press Ctrl+Esc to get to the Start button. Press Esc to put the focus on the Start button and remove the Start button menu. Press Tab to put the focus on the Taskbar. You can now use the arrows keys to move among the Taskbar icons.

Press a second Tab after the first to shift the focus to the icons on the desktop. You can then use the arrow keys to highlight one after another. The Tab keeps toggling the focus between the Start button, the Taskbar, and the icons on the desktop. If the focus is on the Start button, press Enter to display the Start button menu.

You can switch to the desktop by placing the desktop (actually a folder that contains the icons on the desktop) on the Taskbar. To see how to do this, check out the *Putting the Desktop on the Taskbar* section of the next chapter. You can also place the desktop on the Start button. For details, see the *Start Button and Finding* chapter.

Undocumented

If you are in a DOS Windows session, but in full-screen mode, you can return to the desktop by holding down Alt, pressing the Tab key, and clicking the pop-up window that is displayed when you press Alt+Tab.

You can also switch between tasks by holding down Alt and pressing the Esc key. If the task switched to is minimized, the only action you will notice is that the task's button is depressed on the Taskbar and the caption bar of the previously active application changes to its inactive color.

The Task Manager

The Windows Task Manager is still here, although in a new suit of clothes. Many of its functions have been taken over by the Taskbar, but the doesn't mean it isn't useful. Some may find it just the tool for them.

The nice thing about the Windows 3.x Task Manager was that it was always right there, a double-click on the desktop away. You always had the option of bringing up the Task Manager and using it to switch to another task no matter how deeply it was buried in the pile on your desktop. Short of minimizing all the covering windows, this was often the only way to switch to a non-minimized task.

Third-party vendors had a field day with the Windows 3.x Task Manager, finding lots of ways that they could improve upon it. They turned their Task Manager replacements into shells that replaced the Windows 3.x Program Manager.

The Task Manager in Windows 95 is a floating Taskbar without the Start button or the clock.

The Task Manager is Taskman.exe in the \Windows folder. You can always double-click it in a folder window or the Explorer. Bring it up and you get a button for every active task, as shown in Figure 7-8.

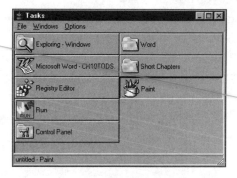

Figure 7-8: The Task Manager. Click a button to switch to that task.

You can change the size of the buttons and whether or not they have text in them by clicking Options on the menu bar. One nice thing about the Task Manager is that it has buttons that display the big icons.

Unfortunately, the Windows 95 Task Manager does not appear when you double-click the desktop, like the Windows 3.x Task Manager did. If you'd like to use the Task Manager, you'll want to create a shortcut for it and assign a hot key to it so that you get to it when you need it. To do this follow the steps detailed in Chapter 10. You can put a shortcut to the Task Manager in your Startup folder so that is available to you when you start Windows.

The Windows 95 Task Manager does get activated when there is a problem with the normal Windows 95 shell program, Explorer.exe — suddenly there it is on your desktop. You can switch tasks or shut down Windows.

Summary

The desktop and the Taskbar form the core of the Windows 95 user interface. In this chapter (and Chapter 22) we show you how to set them up your way.

▶ We show you how to arrange the icons on your desktop and change the underlying invisible grid that determines their placement.

▶ It is easy to place empty documents on the desktop and then double-click them to bring up applications to edit these documents.

▶ The Taskbar can be transformed into a useful tool if you take the time to move and size it for your needs. We show you what kind of problems you will run into using it in certain configurations and how to find the right edge of the desktop to use.

▶ If you don't like that "sliding windows" effect when you minimize and restore application windows, we show you how to get rid of it.

▶ You can use Alt+Tab, Alt+Esc, and Ctrl+Esc to choose between active applications and folders.

▶ The Task Manager is still with us. You can use it as a floating task switcher.

Chapter 8

My Computer — Folders and Windows

In This Chapter

We discuss the Windows 95 file management system including:

▶ Turning My Computer into Your Computer

▶ Quickly viewing the disk drives, folders, and files on your computer

▶ Tricking Windows 95 into showing you an extra copy of a folder window

▶ Ordering and placing your icons in a folder window just the way you want them

▶ Closing multiple folder windows with one click

▶ Navigating with the keyboard through multiple folder windows

▶ Quickly moving, copying, renaming, or deleting folders and files

▶ Using special key and mouse-click combinations to speed the selection of files and folders

▶ Hot-keying to the desktop

▶ Treating your folder windows as though they were Program Managers

Viewing Your Computer

You need a window, or several windows, on your computer in order to see what is there. This chapter focuses on how to use folder windows for file management. In the next chapter, we discuss the Explorer, a different kind of window. Much of what you learn in this chapter can be applied to both folder windows and the Explorer. Anything you try here will also work with an Explorer window.

My Computer, Your Computer

There it is in the upper left corner of your display — My Computer. Wait a minute, it's *your* computer. *My* computer is here. As far as you are concerned it's *your* computer, but then you would tell us that "It's *My* Computer."

Microsoft was well aware of this "Who's on first, What's on second, and I don't know who's on third" problem but went ahead and called it My Computer anyway. You can imagine some computer instructor saying to his or her students, "Double-click My Computer," and then having to say, "No, I mean double-click the My Computer icon on the screen of *your* computer."

Not only that, My computer is just an icon on your computer's screen. It's not your computer. It's a computer within a computer. Microsoft hopes that this doesn't confuse you.

As you shall see, this is not just a semantic issue. When something has a representation of itself within itself, the representation has to be distorted so as not to go on endlessly. After all, My Computer is on the desktop, but the desktop is both in My Computer and is displayed on your computer. For an example, see the section later in this chapter entitled *Put the Desktop on the Taskbar.*

Changing My Computer to Fred

Tip

Fortunately, you can change the My Computer icon to something else, like Your Computer. Highlight the My Computer icon, press F2 and type in a new name.

You can also change the Network Neighborhood to something like Network Neighbourhood if you are in England. You can change the name of the Recycle Bin, if you use the Registry editor (see Chapter 14.)

The My Computer Window

When you first set up Windows 95, you will see three to six icons on the left side of your desktop. The number depends on which options you chose during the Windows 95 setup process.

The My Computer icon (and a rather generic-looking computer icon it is) is the first icon on the desktop — an indication of its importance in the hierarchy of items on the desktop. You can place it somewhere else, if you want, but if you arrange the desktop icons in any of the predetermined sort orders (by right-clicking the desktop, clicking Arrange Icons, and choosing any of the sort orders), it will again appear in the upper left corner.

Double-click My Computer, and a window much like that shown in Figure 8-1 will appear on your desktop. The window displays within its client area the contents of My Computer.

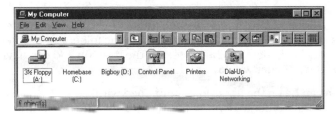

Figure 8-1: My Computer window. Double-click the My Computer icon on the desktop to open it.

Tip

You don't have to double-click the My Computer icon to open it. You can just right-click it and then click Open from the menu that appears on the desktop to the right of the My Computer icon. The Open command is at the top of this menu. You can left- or right-click the menu item — the menu item doesn't care which button you use.

Double-clicking My Computer "opens" a window that displays the contents of My Computer. *Open* means to display in a window. If you open an application, it will be displayed in a window. If you open a document, it also will be displayed in a window. Opening an icon like the My Computer icon means to display its contents within a window.

You don't find windows on real-world desktops — so much for metaphors. You might think of a window as the thing itself plus its edges. A window displays a document on the desktop, and the edges of the document contain commands that determine how the document is displayed.

The contents to be displayed are not the physical contents of the computer — what you would normally expect to see when you "opened" up your computer — but its logical contents. The My Computer window contains icons that look like physical items: your floppy drive(s) (and diskette(s)) and your hard disk(s). The window also has some manila folder icons with graphics on them.

The diskette and hard disk drive icons represent the logical contents of these devices — the files, folders, documents, and applications that are stored on these devices. The folder icons stand for directories or folders that are stored on the hard disk(s). While most folders can contain any types of files, the folders shown in the My Computer window contain specific types of files. For example, the Printers folder contains the printer driver files. We discuss these particular folders in much more detail in other chapters.

Folders

Microsoft has built on a metaphor used in the Windows 3.*x* File Manager. In the File Manager, each directory on your disk drive has a little manila folder icon to the left of its name. The File Manager icon is a file cabinet. The idea is that all the folders are stored in the file cabinet.

Windows 95 has replaced the terminology *directory* with *folder* — a more office-oriented terminology. Also, folders can do much more than directories. Specialized folders have additional capabilities, such as the folders seen in the My Computer window. Folders can be placed on the desktop and can have windows of their own (folder windows).

A folder icon can be on the desktop or contained within a folder window. Folders can contain other folders, just as directories can be subdirectories of other directories. Because they are not stuck in the File Manager, the Windows 95 folders are more accessible. Instead of using the File Manager to organize and locate your files, you double-click any folder icon to bring up a folder window.

In the Windows 3.*x* File Manager, the hard disk and floppy disk drive icons used to sit on a special bar or ribbon above the client area window. With Windows 95, they have come down to join the folders and files in the folder window client area.

The special folders in the My Computer folder window

The three folders shown in the My Computer window (the three folders on the right-hand side in Figure 8-1) are stored on one of the hard disks. It is an arbitrary design decision that their folder icons should be displayed in the My Computer folder window and that these icons should have little graphics on them. These folder icons are there because this provides an easy way to get to the folders that contain useful Windows 95 functions. We have devoted a chapter to each of these folders.

The Printers folder is covered in Chapter 23, the Control Panel folder in Chapter 16, and the Dial-Up Networking folder in Chapter 28.

My Computer window properties

If you right-click in the client area of the My Computer folder window, but not near one of the icons, a menu like the one shown in Figure 8-2 is displayed. This menu is similar to the one you get when you right-click the desktop. It has the addition of the View menu item, which lets you change how the icons in the folder window are displayed: large icon, small icon, and so on.

Figure 8-2: The right mouse button menu for the My Computer folder window with the four views showing.

Click Properties and you get the System Properties sheets. This gets you into the guts of the Windows 95 hardware interface. Turn to Chapter 19 for details on setting systemwide properties on these sheets.

Hard disk properties

Click a hard disk icon in the My Computer folder window and you get a report of its free space and disk capacity in the status bar. Right-click a hard disk icon (the second and third icons from the left in Figure 8-1) and click Properties. You can change the hard disk's volume label, as shown in Figure 8-3. You can also check it for errors, back it up, or defragment it by clicking the Tools tab on the Properties sheet. Check out Chapter 27 for details.

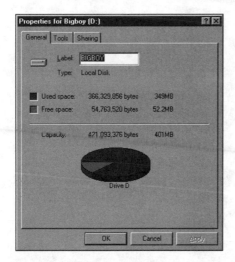

Figure 8-3: The Disk Drive General Properties sheet. Type in a new volume label for your drive. If you want to check for errors, click the Tools tab. You can share your drive with others on your network by clicking the Sharing tab and setting your share configuration.

Opening a new folder window

If you double-click a hard disk icon in the My Computer window, a new window that contains the contents of the hard disk is opened. The contents will consist of folder and file icons (and a Recycle Bin). You won't see any file icons if you don't have any files in the root directory of your hard disk.

Each icon has an associated window. You double-click an icon in one of these windows and open another window. While My Computer has a window and each of your disk drives can have a window, we refer to these windows generically as *folder* windows.

You can continue to double-click folder icons to move through the folders stored on your hard disk. You can find subfolders of folders and subfolders of subfolders. You can move sideways by returning to a parent folder and then moving to a subfolder.

One folder window or many?

Click View, Options from the menu bar of a folder window. You get a tabbed set of Options dialog boxes, as shown in Figure 8-4. In the Options, Folder dialog box you can choose whether to open a separate window each time that you double-click an icon within the My Computer and subsequent folder windows. The other option is to re-use and rename the My Computer folder window as you double-click icons within the folder window.

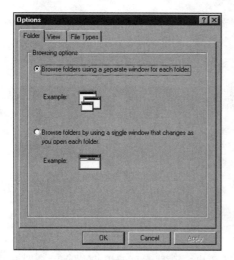

Figure 8-4: The Options dialog box for a folder window.

These are two different metaphors. You can take your pick between one window that shows all views of your computer and a new window for each hard disk or folder that you double-click, between one folder window within which to view each folder, and letting each folder have its own folder window.

Your desktop can fill up pretty quickly if you choose to open a new folder window every time you double-click a folder icon (see below regarding closing folder windows). This does give you the option of seeing everything as you move about your computer. It is also easier to move items from one window to another. As you open each folder window, an associated button is placed on the Taskbar.

Switch to a single window view on the fly

Secret

If you are opening multiple windows as you go from folder to folder, you can open the next folder in the last window instead of opening a new window. The last folder window will display the contents of the new folder.

Instead of double-clicking a folder icon in a folder window to display the new folder in its own folder window, hold down the Ctrl key and double-click the folder icon. The existing folder window will now display the contents of the folder whose icon you just double-clicked.

By the way, this trick doesn't work with the middle mouse button if you have defined the button to be a double-click. You actually have to double-click with the left mouse button. The Ctrl key appears to mess up the mouse communications. See Chapter 24 for details on how to define the middle mouse button as a double-click.

Open an Explorer window from a folder window

Secret

If you hold down the shift key and double-click a folder icon in a folder window, the new folder window opens as an Explorer window. Be careful, though, because the shift key is also used with the mouse to pick multiple items. You may find yourself opening a few more Explorer windows than you had planned. Be sure that the focus is on the folder icon that you want to open before you hold down the Shift key.

This option, unlike the one described in *Switch to a single window view on the fly*, does work with the middle mouse button defined as a double-click.

Two copies of the My Computer folder window

You get only one copy of the My Computer folder window no matter how many times you double-click the My Computer icon. This is not true of the Explorer, which we discuss in the next chapter.

Secret

If you have set the View, Options, Folder property to a single window, it is difficult to get two copies of any folder window. There is a tricky way you can get an extra copy (or as many as you want) of the folder window, even if you have chosen a single window.

STEPS

Getting Two Folder Windows of the Same Folder

Step 1.   Double-click the My Computer icon. Click View, Options, Folder and choose separate folder windows.

Step 2.   Double-click a hard disk icon in the My Computer folder window.

Step 3.   In the hard disk's folder window, click View, Options, Folder and choose single window.

Step 4.   Click the "up one level" icon in the Toolbar of the hard disk's folder window.

You now have two My Computer folder windows. You can do this same trick to get an extra copy of a folder window by making a child window into a parent window for any folder window. Of course, if you have separate windows as your settings for folder windows, you can use a variation on this theme to create multiple copies of a given folder window.

Change Your Folder Window View

You can choose how the hard disk icons, folder icons, and all other icons are displayed in a folder window. You can also choose whether a folder window like the My Computer window displays a Toolbar and/or a status bar.

The Toolbar and status bar are options in the View menu. You can also choose how to display files and folders icons and names in a folder window. You can use a large icon, small icon (rows), list (columns), or details view. You can use the four buttons on the right end of the Toolbar to change these four views.

You can order the icons by type, name, size and date, in ascending or descending order. This is all pretty straightforward. Just use the View menu or the Toolbar, and click the column title buttons in the details view to toggle between ascending and descending order.

Undocumented

It is possible to globally set some of these display preferences so they will apply to any folder window that hasn't been opened and hasn't yet had its preferences set individually. Each folder window that you have already opened once has its own settings for these variables. To change these settings, you must change them individually for each folder window.

The global setting for all folder windows is large icons, don't show the Toolbar, show the status bar, and order icons by name. When a folder window is opened for the first time, it uses these global settings to determine how to display itself. Once you change these settings within a folder window, the new settings are used the next time that particular folder window is opened. The global settings apply to folder windows not yet opened.

You can't go back and globally change the settings for all the folder windows. There is also no way for you to change all the default global settings for displaying a new (as yet undisplayed) folder view. There is no way to choose a subset of folders and set their view properties.

Secret

It is possible to set some of the view parameters for as yet unopened folder windows. To do this, open a folder window and arrange it using the View menu. Choose to turn on or off Toolbar and Status bar. Choose from the following views: Large Icons, small icons, List, or Details.

When you are finished, hold down the Ctrl key and click the Close caption button. Your changes are now used as the new defaults when you open as yet unopened folder windows. Auto Arrange and Icon sort order is not set in this manner and will not be used in the new folder windows.

You might find that some folder windows are slightly smaller the next time you start Windows 95. They seem to have shrunk vertically. The scroll bar may appear on the right side of the window client area as some of the icons in the last row aren't fully visible.

The whole issue of folder window view properties is dealt with poorly by Windows 95. This is something that many users are interested in getting a handle on, and Microsoft hasn't been able to program a decent way to do it.

Many users want to be able to make their folder windows look "just so" and to be placed in a certain spot and don't appreciate it when they keep changing (even a little bit). A global or semi-global way to change folder window view properties would be greatly appreciated (and we can expect third-party shareware or retail software to offer that capability soon after Windows 95 is released).

The bugs that we (and many others) have found in retaining individual folder window view properties need to be fixed by Microsoft.

Other View options

The tabs for two other dialog boxes are displayed on your desktop when you click View, Options on the My Computer folder window menu bar. The View dialog box is discussed in Chapter 9. The File Types dialog box is discussed in Chapter 13.

Order the icons

You can specify in what order your icons are displayed in a folder window. They can be sorted by name, date, size, and file type. They can be ordered either ascending or descending, if they are displayed in details view.

The sort order is provided as a menu choice in View menu. Click View, Arrange Icons, and then take your pick. If you select the details view, you have additional heading buttons (Name, Size, Type, and Modified) that let you choose the variable to sort on, as well as whether the order is ascending or descending. A folder window with the details view and the sort order buttons is shown in Figure 8-5.

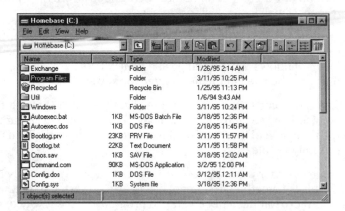

Figure 8-5: A folder window in details view. Click one of the title buttons (Name, Size, Type, and Modified) at the top of the columns to order the icons and file/folder names by that variable.

The sort order buttons are just above the columns in the folder window client area. Click these buttons to sort the file/folder names and their associated icons by the variable clicked. To change between ascending and descending order, click the title button again.

Line up your icons

Secret

If you use the large or small icon view of a folder window, you can place the icons where you like. They will stay where you place them, even if you switch views, resize the folder window, exit the folder window, and go back to it. The large icon view will mirror the small icon view and vice versa.

As on the desktop, there is an invisible grid in every folder window. It comes into play only in the small and large icon views. The size of the grid depends on the size of the icons, the font size or magnification, and the display resolution. You can snap your icons to the center of the cells in the grid by clicking Line up icons in the View menu of the folder window. There is a similar command for the desktop that is accessed from the right-mouse menu.

Changing the column widths in details view

When you choose the details view of a folder window, little column title buttons appear above each column. At the edge of each of these buttons is a black vertical spacer line. Put your mouse cursor over the vertical line and the mouse pointer becomes a black cursor with a vertical line and two horizontal arrows.

You can change the width of the columns by dragging the vertical spacer line between the column buttons to the left or right. Drag on the line on the right edge of the name button and all the columns to the right are moved.

Tip

If you want to get rid of a column in details view for a given folder window, drag the right edge of the column all the way to the left of the column. You can get it back — even though you can't see it — by dragging the now-invisible column edge to the right.

The changes in column width stay with the folder window. Each folder has its own properties, and before you move the columns, they have the default properties. Change the column widths, and the next time you open that particular folder window, your changes will still be there. This is true even if you make changes in the folder window view and open it in the Explorer view.

Freshening up the folder window

Tip

It may be the case that your folder window doesn't represent the latest state of the folder. Files may have been copied in and out of the folder without the folder window noticing and updating itself. Files may have been changed in size, content, or name. You can update a folder window's display by pressing the F5 key.

You can also use View, Refresh on the folder window menu bar to update your folder window view.

Checking the status bar

The status bar at the bottom of your folder window can provide some useful information, as you may have seen earlier if you opened a hard disk drive folder window. Open a folder window full of files; on the status bars you will see how much disk space they use, how many files there are, and the amount of free disk space.

Closing a folder window

The three buttons in the upper right side of a folder window in the caption area allow you to minimize, maximize, and close a folder window, respectively from left to right. The close button, the "x", is new to Windows 95.

Hold down the Shift key and click Close to close not only the folder window with the focus but all its parent folder windows. If you have opened a number of folder windows to get to the current one, this method gives you an easy way to get rid of all the preceding windows. Just Shift+click the close button of the current folder window.

Creating a New File, Folder, or Shortcut

As was true of the desktop, you can create a new file, folder, or shortcut in a folder window. Right-click the folder window client area, or choose File, New from the menu bar to get a choice of file types, folder, or shortcut.

Once you have created a folder or file, you can open it by double-clicking it. We discuss creating new folders in more detail later in this chapter.

Folder Window Properties

Previously in this chapter, we mentioned the properties sheets of My Computer and of a hard disk. An ordinary folder also has properties. To see them, right-click the client area of a folder window (or right-click a folder icon) and choose Properties from the right mouse button menu.

The first tabbed sheet is the General Properties sheet, as shown in Figure 8-6. You can set the folder attributes (Read-only, Archive, Hidden) by clicking the check boxes. This Properties sheet also displays the total size and number of the files stored in the folder. In addition, it tells you the number of subfolders and includes the files in these subfolders (and further sub-subfolders) in its total file size and number count. This information is not shown on the status bar of the folder window.

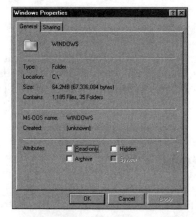

Figure 8-6: The General Properties sheet for a folder. While not too exciting, this properties sheet does give you some very useful information about the size and number of files (and subfolders) within the folder and subfolders.

You can choose to share your folder with others on the network by choosing the Sharing Properties sheet. This gives other network users the ability to read-only or read-write to this folder. You can ask for a password or leave this option blank. If the Share tab on the Properties sheet is not visible, you will have to go to the Network icon in the Control Panel and activate file and print sharing for this feature to be available.

There isn't a Properties sheet that displays the folder window's view properties. This is unfortunate. While these properties can be changed by using the folder window's menu bar, it would be convenient to have a Properties sheet to allow another way to get at them.

Moving Forward and Back Using a Folder Window

Double-click the My Computer icon on the desktop. In the My Computer folder window, make sure that you are showing the Toolbar. Click the drop-down arrow in the combo box on the left side of the Toolbar. An indented list of icons is displayed in the drop-down list.

Click the up arrow on the right side of the combo box. The Desktop icon is displayed along with the other icons, as shown in Figure 8-7.

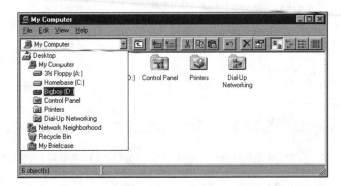

Figure 8-7: The My Computer folder window with its drop-down list. You can display any of the items in the list by clicking once on it. The My Computer folder window is changed to the folder window of the item you pick.

Notice that the items in the drop-down list are indented. The indents indicate which icons belong to which other icons. The icons that are two indents to the right of My Computer are displayed in the My Computer folder window. The icons that are one indent (and one indent only) to the right of the Desktop icon are displayed on the desktop.

If you click the Desktop icon, the My Computer folder window changes to the Desktop folder window. The icons on the desktop are now also displayed in the Desktop folder window.

You can move from icon to icon using this drop-down box and have the contents of the folder, disk drive, desktop, or whatever displayed in the transformed My Computer folder window.

Only certain items are displayed in the drop-down list: Desktop, My Computer, Network Neighborhood, Recycle Bin, My Briefcase, special folders, and the items contained within My Computer, but only at the first level. If, starting in the My Computer folder window, you double-click on a hard disk icon and progress through different folders, the current folder and all its parents will be displayed in this drop-down list. The current folder's siblings will not be displayed in this list.

You can transform the folder window into either a parent's folder window, or a folder window for any one of the icons in the combo box, just by clicking that icon. As you saw earlier in this chapter in the section entitled *Opening a new folder window*, you move forward through child windows by double-clicking folder icons within the client areas of a folder window.

Secret

You can move up through a thread of parent folders using the backspace key. This works even if you are using only a single window to display folder windows. If your current folder window is showing a folder or a subfolder, etc., you can backspace all the way back to My Computer if you like.

If you are displaying separate folder windows, you can use Alt+Tab+Tab to go either direction. Hold down Alt and press the Tab key until you get to the folder window you want.

To display the combo box you can also use the F4 key.

New, Copy, Cut, Paste, Rename, and Delete

Folder windows can be used for file maintenance. You can create, copy, move (cut and paste), rename, and delete files and folders. You can drag and drop files or folders from one folder window to another.

Creating a folder

It's easy to create a new folder. All you have to do is right-click in the folder window of the folder where you want to place your new folder. Follow these steps:

STEPS

Creating a New Folder

Step 1.   Double-click the My Computer icon on the desktop.

Step 2.   Decide on which disk drive you want to store your folder. Double-click the disk icon for that disk drive. This will open the disk drive's folder window.

Step 3.   If you want your folder to be stored in the root, i.e. at the top of the hierarchy of folders on that disk drive, then go to Step 5. If you want your folder to be stored within another folder on the hard disk, then double-click that folder's icon in the disk drive's folder window.

Step 4.   Continue double-clicking folder icons until you get to the folder window of the folder that you want to contain your new folder.

Step 5.   Right-click the client area of the current (on top) folder window. Click New, Folder on the popup menu. A new folder icon will appear in the folder window.

Step 6.   You can name the folder by typing a new name in the highlighted area.

Instead of right-clicking in the client area of the folder window in Step 5, you could have clicked File, New, Folder on the current folder window's menu bar.

Moving a file or folder

There are numerous ways to move a file or folder from one folder to another. If you have both the "from" folder window and the "to" folder window on your desktop and fully visible at the same time, it is easier to accomplish this task and to see how it is done.

Move with Cut and Paste

Follow these steps to move a file or folder with Cut and Paste.

STEPS

Moving a File or Folder with Cut and Paste

Step 1.   Double-click the My Computer icon. Click View, Options, Folder and separate windows if you have not already chosen this mode.

Step 2.   Double-click the disk icon that contains the folder that contains the file or folder that you want to move. Continue double-clicking folder icons until you open a window that contains the icon of the file or folder that you want to move.

(continued)

STEPS *(continued)*

Moving a File or Folder with Cut and Paste

Step 3.   Click the folder window of the parent folder of the folder that you wish to move the file or folder to. If the parent folder window is not available, find an ancestor folder window and click it. Open folder windows by double-clicking folder icons in this folder window until you open the window of the folder to which you will move the file or folder.

Step 4.   Make sure that you can see both the "from" and the "to" folder windows. They don't have to be fully visible.

Step 5.   Right-click the "from" folder or file. Click Cut. Or click the file or folder to highlight it and then click Edit, Cut in the menu bar.

Step 6.   Right-click the client area of the "to" folder window. Click Paste.

Yes, a move is, in this case, referred to as a cut and paste. It Makes you think you are in a word processor.

Move with right drag and drop

You can also drag and drop the file or folder to the "to" folder window. As you drag the file or folder icon, it will appear to be semi-transparent.

STEPS

Moving a File or Folder with Right Drag and Drop

Step 1.   Carry out the first four steps in the *Move with Cut and Paste* section above.

Step 2.   Position the mouse pointer over the file or folder to be moved. Press the right mouse button and, while holding it, pull the file or folder over to the "to" folder window.

Step 3.   Release the right mouse button when the mouse pointer is over the "to" folder window but not over an icon in the folder window. You can drop it in the caption area, the menu area, the Toolbar, or the client area.

Step 4.   Click Move to on the right mouse menu that is displayed when you release the right mouse button. The file or folder is moved to the "to" folder window.

Move with left drag and drop

You can also use the left mouse button to drag and drop and you don't have to worry about the popup menu. But it helps to know what kind of file you are moving and where you are moving it to.

STEPS

Moving a File or Folder with Left Drag and Drop

Step 1. Carry out the first four steps shown in the *Move with Cut and Paste* section earlier in this chapter.

Step 2. Position the mouse pointer over the file or folder to be moved. Press the left mouse button and, while holding it, drag the file or folder over to the "to" folder window.

Step 3. Release the left mouse button when the mouse pointer is over the "to" folder window but not over an icon in the folder window. You can drop it in the caption area, the menu area, the Toolbar, or the client area.

Secret

If you have followed the steps in this section, you've taken the steps required to open two folder windows. You therefore know where — that is on which disk drives (or volumes) — the "to" and "from" folders reside. When you drag and drop a file or folder, it is moved out of the "from" folder and into the "to" folder *only if both folders are on the same drive.*

If you are dragging and dropping a file or folder from a folder on one disk drive to a folder on another disk drive, then it is *copied*.

In both cases, this is *not* true if you are dragging a file that isn't a document or a data file, but rather an application. Instead, a *shortcut* to the application is created in the "to" folder. What is an *application file*? You can identify application files by their extension (if you have unchecked the box that says Hide MS-DOS file extensions; see Chapter 9). Application files have extensions like *exe*, *com*, or *bat*. There is an even easier way to tell, as you'll see if you keep reading.

You can force a *move* by holding down the Shift key after you have selected the file or folder to move. Don't press Shift until you have selected the file or folder to move. If you do, you may instead change which icons were selected because the Shift key is also used to select icons.

Tip

If you drag an executable file (an application file), a shortcut will be created. You can see this as you drag the file over the "to" folder window. A black curved arrow in a white box appears in the lower right corner of the semi-transparent file icon. Press and hold the Shift key and the arrow disappears, indicating that a *move* will take place. This is one way to know that Windows 95 thinks you are dragging an application file.

The desktop is treated just like a folder window. Like all folders, it is located on a disk drive, most likely your C drive. If you try to *move* something to the desktop (most often you will want to create only shortcuts on the desktop), and it is on a drive other than the one that contains the file or folder you are dragging, it will, by default, be *copied* (unless you hold down the Shift key).

Tip

You can tell if a file or folder is going to be copied because a plus sign will appear in the lower right corner of the semi-transparent icon representing the file or folder icon as you drag it over the "to" folder window (or desktop). If you see this black plus sign in a white box, you know a *copy* will occur if you release the left mouse button. Press and hold the Shift key to force a *move*.

If you decide not to move the icon, just put it back where you got it — in the same folder window. If you were using a left drag and drop, then nothing will happen. If you were using a right drag and drop, the right drag and drop menu will appear. Click Cancel.

Secret

If you don't want to continue with your drag and drop, press Esc while holding down the mouse button. We love this secret because it makes Windows 95 just that much more user friendly. You don't have to worry that you will do something wrong. If it looks wrong, just press Esc. Later, you will see how you can undo by releasing the mouse button.

There is an even trickier way to cancel a drag and drop. Click the other mouse button before you release the primary mouse button.

Tip

You can drop your file or folder icon on a folder icon to move it into that folder. You don't have to open up a "to" folder window. If the "to" folder icon is visible in its parent folder window, you can drop the file or folder icon on it to move it to that folder.

You can't move a disk icon. The disk is fixed in place. You can't move the total contents of the disk by selecting the disk icon. You have to select the contents of the disk if you wish to move them. If you try to move the disk drive, you will be given the option of creating a shortcut to the drive.

You can't move any of the icons in the My Computer folder window. You can only create shortcuts to them.

Secret

If you select a file or folder icon in a folder window that has the focus (its title caption is highlighted), the name of the selected icon is highlighted. If you place the mouse pointer over an icon in a folder window that does not have the focus and then press the left or right mouse button, the icon is not highlighted although it is selected and ready to be moved. In addition, the folder window without the focus does not gain the focus.

It is possible to place the "to" folder window over and partially obscuring the "from" folder window, as shown in Figure 8-8. The "to" folder window is highlighted and has the focus so it can be on top. You can left or right drag a file or folder icon from the "from" folder window without this folder window gaining the focus and thereby covering up the "to" folder window.

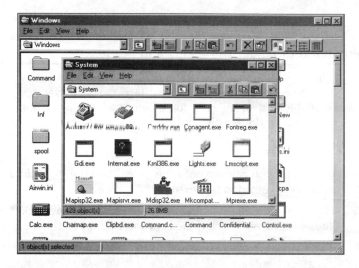

Figure 8-8: The "to" folder window is over and partially obscuring the "from" folder window. You can move a file or folder icon from the "from" folder window by dragging it from the folder window into the "to" folder window. The "from" window does not obscure the "to" window.

Copying a file or folder

You copy a file or folder to a new folder or disk drive using pretty much the same methods that you use to move a file or folder, but with a slight variation — just enough of a variation to make a copy rather than a move. Therefore, much of the previous sections regarding moving applies to the copy command. This is your clue to look there for further help with the copy methods, especially to the previous tips and secrets.

Copy with Copy and Paste

Follow these steps to copy a file or folder with Copy and Paste:

STEPS

Copying a File or Folder with Copy and Paste

Step 1. Double-click the My Computer icon. Click View, Options, Folder, and separate windows if you have not already chosen this mode.

Step 2. Double-click the disk icon that contains the folder that contains the file or folder that you want to copy. Continue double-clicking folder icons until you open a folder window that contains the icon of the file or folder that you want to copy.

(continued)

STEPS *(continued)*

Copying a File or Folder with Copy and Paste

Step 3.   Click the folder window of the parent folder of the folder that you wish to copy the file or folder to. If the parent folder window is not available, find an ancestor folder window and click it. Open folder windows by double-clicking folder icons in this folder window until you open the folder window of the folder to which you will copy the file or folder.

Step 4.   Make sure you can see both the "from" and the "to" folder windows. They don't have to be fully visible.

Step 5.   Right-click the "from" folder or file. Click Copy. Or, click the file or folder to highlight it and then click Edit, Copy in the menu bar.

Step 6.   Right-click the client area of the "to" folder window. Click Paste.

Yes, a copy is, in this case, referred to as a *Copy and Paste*. Makes you think you are in a word processor. Yes, we know that we just copied and pasted the *Move with Cut and Paste* section and edited it slightly to create this section. Pretty cheap.

Copy with right drag and drop

Follow the instructions above in the *Moving with right drag and drop* steps, but with the following exception: Click Copy instead of move. Is that better?

Copy with left drag and drop

Follow these steps to copy with left drag and drop:

STEPS

Copying a File or Folder with Left Drag and Drop

Step 1.   Carry out the first four steps in the *Copy with Copy and Paste* section.

Step 2.   Position the mouse pointer over the file or folder to be copied. Press the left mouse button and, holding the left mouse button, pull the file or folder over to the "to" folder window.

Step 3.   Press and hold the Ctrl key.

Step 4.   Release the left mouse button when the mouse pointer is over the "to" folder window but not over an icon in the folder window. You can drop it in the caption area, the menu area, the Toolbar, or the client area.

Notice that to force a copy, Step 3 says to press the Ctrl key. If you are copying from a folder on one disk drive to a folder on another disk drive, you don't have to do this. Dragging and dropping between volumes (between local disk drives or over the network) automatically means copying.

A little black plus sign in a small white box will appear on the icon as it is being dragged over the "to" folder window if the action is to *copy* this file or folder. If you don't see the plus sign, press and hold the Ctrl key.

Tip

You won't be able to copy a disk icon. Double-click on the disk icon and view its contents in a folder window. You can copy the contents of a disk. You won't be able to copy any of the icons in the My Computer folder window.

If you drag and drop a file onto an icon that represents an executable file, the application will be started. If it can read and use the file dropped on to it, it will do so. For example, dropping icons for a file with a *doc, rtf,* or *txt* extension onto the WordPad icon will start WordPad and open the file.

Cut or Copy now, Paste later

While you can see what you're doing if you have both the "from" and the "to" folder windows on the desktop, you don't have to do it that way. You can cut or copy a file or folder and paste it to its new location when you get to it later. If you prefer using the File Manager from Windows 3.x, that is also available. You can double-click the icon Winfile.exe in your Windows 95 subdirectory. From File Manager, you can create two window panes and drag and drop between them instead of opening two copies of the Windows 95 Explorer.

The Paste option will be on the right mouse button menu. Right-click in the folder window (or on the folder icon) of the "to" folder and choose Paste.

Renaming file and folders

You can rename a file or folder in a folder window by slowly clicking the name twice and then typing in a new name. The clicks have to be far enough apart that they qualify as separate clicks and not a double-click. It's easier to highlight the file or folder with a single click and then press the F2 key.

You can also right-click an icon, click Rename on the right mouse button menu, and then edit the name. Finally (actually, not quite finally, as you will see), you can click an icon in a folder window, click File, Rename in the menu bar of the folder window, and then edit the name.

Tip

A little dotted window appears around the name to be edited. The name is highlighted, ready to be wiped out if you type a letter. If you instead press an arrow key, the highlighting goes away and you can move to a spot in the name to begin your editing. Press the Home or End key instead of the arrow keys to get to the beginning or end of the name to be edited.

If you are displaying extensions of filenames (check out Chapter 9) and you change an extension, a message box appears when you finish editing the name asking if you are sure you want to change the name. In the few hundred times we have done this, neither of us has said no. It is easier and more reliable to change filename extensions with the display extensions feature "on" in Windows 95 than it is if the feature is "off."

This renaming process can get quite tedious if you are renaming a lot of files, for example, all your *.in4w files to *.doc files. If you want to do group renames, you must use the File Manager or the DOS command line. Folder window commands aren't quite strong enough. Turn to Chapter 9 to learn more about the File Manager or to Chapter 17 to learn more about DOS.

Microsoft would rather that we not discuss file extensions. They want file extensions to go away and for Windows users to quit seeing them in their folder windows. For now, we feel it is a much better idea to display file extensions because they are used so heavily by Windows (and DOS). Check out Chapter 13 for more details.

Valid file and folder names are discussed in the *Valid Filenames* section of Chapter 27.

Deleting files and folders

To get rid of a file or folder, highlight its icon and press the Delete key. You can also right-click an icon and click Delete on the right mouse button menu or highlight an icon and click File, Delete in the folder window menu bar.

Dragging and dropping an icon from a folder window to the Recycle Bin on the desktop also works. The benefit of this method is that you are not asked to confirm the delete. (You can configure the Recycle Bin to not require a confirmation for a file delete.)

Your files and folders aren't necessarily deleted just yet. The Recycle Bin provides a safety net for us careless users. We tell you more about deleting in Chapter 14.

Tip

To delete a file or folder without recourse to the Recycle Bin, hold down the Shift key while you press the Delete key. The highlighted file or folder will be deleted and not found in the Recycle Bin.

The Undo Command

Undocumented

Every time you take an action like renaming, copying (in the same Windows 95 session), moving, or deleting, you get a chance to undo it. Not just now, but later also. An undo stack is built as you do things. One action is stacked on top of another. You can undo a list of actions only in the reverse order that you did them.

The Undo command and its associated action verb — Rename, Copy, Move, or Delete — will appear on the right mouse button menu when you right-click a folder window or the desktop (but only if you have taken some action first). If you renamed something, Undo Rename will appear on the menu when you right-click the folder window

This undo business is global. It doesn't matter if you renamed a file in one folder window and deleted a file in another folder window, they both show up (actually you see only the last action) on the right mouse button menu in any folder window. Choose that Undo and the previous action pops up and now shows on the menu. And so forth.

This can get kind of confusing. You may not remember in which folder window you renamed or deleted or copied a file or folder. But when you right-click a folder window, the reference to that previous action shows up.

It's best to undo something in the folder window that you did it in. That way you can see the action take place — for example, the file takes back its old name. If the action is a few actions down the stack, that may be a problem as you try to remember which folder windows you did what in. Unless you are working in just one or two folder windows, it's all too complicated.

Undo is a great confidence builder. You just can't mess up too badly, as you can undo the damage that you did. This gives you a little leeway to experiment with Windows 95.

Tip

To undo the last action, press Ctrl+Z.

Selecting Items in a Folder Window

You can click an icon in a folder window to select it. (This is an illustration of the Windows syntax — first a noun, then a verb.) Select an object (an object is a noun as it has a name), then choose an action like Move, Copy, Delete, Rename, and so on.

Undocumented

If you click an icon in a folder window, the folder window is automatically highlighted and given the focus. If you simply drag an icon from a folder window, the folder window doesn't get the focus. The icon isn't highlighted either. This comes in quite handy when copying or moving files or folders between folder windows.

Click a file or folder icon to select it. You can also right-click on an icon or file or folder name in a folder window to select and highlight it. A convenient right mouse button menu appears next to the highlighted icon with a series of verbs — actions — you can take.

Selecting multiple files and folders

If you want to move, copy, or delete (but not rename) more than one file or folder, you can select an icon with a click of the left mouse button and then click another icon while holding down the Ctrl key. Both icons are highlighted. You can continue this until you have highlighted all the files or folders that you are going to act upon. The Ctrl key is just a continue selection key.

Tip

You can't do this with Rename. It just won't work. When you click Rename, only one icon is highlighted.

Selecting a group of files and/or folders

You can also choose a group of icons with the Shift key. To choose a group of icons in between two icons, click (or right-click if you like) an icon. Hold the Shift key and click the second icon. All the icons in between will be selected.

When the icons are displayed in details view, it is pretty clear what *in between* means. You click one file or folder and then you Shift+click the second one either above or below the first selection. All the icons in between these two are chosen.

Undocumented

In other views, *in between* means different things. In the large icon view, *in between* means all the icons that fit in a rectangle formed when you take the corners of the rectangle as the two selected icons. To use it, select the icon in the upper left corner of the client area of the folder window and the second icon in the second column and third row; then all icons in the first two columns; and rows one through three are selected, as shown in Figure 8-9.

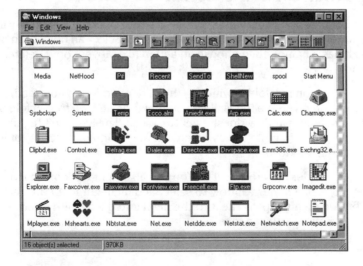

Figure 8-9: The large icon view of a folder window. The icons were chosen by clicking an icon in one corner of a rectangle and then Shift+clicking an icon in the opposite corner.

In the large icon view, select both icons in the same row or column, and all the icons between the two selected icons in the same row or column are chosen.

The small icon view works the same as the large icon view. You form rectangles to select icons. The small icon (and large icon) view orders icons by rows.

Undocumented

The list view orders icons by columns — sort of like wrapping columns of text in a word processor. There is no rectangle of selection in the list view. Click an icon in the first column and Shift+click another icon in the second column, and all the icons below the selected icon in the first column are chosen, along with all the icons above the Shift-selected icon in the second column, as shown in Figure 8-10.

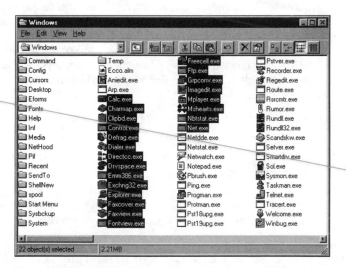

Figure 8-10: Selecting icons in the list view. The list view lists icons by column. Click an icon in the first column and then Shift+click an icon in the second column. All the icons below the selected icon in the first column are selected, and all icons above the Shift+clicked icon in the second column are chosen, including, of course, the icons that were clicked.

Lasso those icons, cowboys and cowgirls

You can draw your own rectangle (or lasso) around or through the icons that you want to select. You don't have to completely enclose the icon to get it lassoed.

Undocumented

To drag a rectangle around the icons that you want to select, move the mouse pointer to an area near the icons that you wish to select. Press and hold down the left mouse button. Drag the mouse pointer over the additional icons that you want to select. They are highlighted as you lasso them. Release the mouse button when you have highlighted all the icons that you want selected. A group of icons selected with a lasso is shown in Figure 8-11.

Figure 8-11: Lassoing the icons. Drag a rectangle around a group of icons to select them. Use either the left or right mouse button.

Secret

You can also do this with the right mouse button. When you release the right button, a menu will appear. You can then select an action off the right mouse button menu to apply to all the icons that you have rounded up. Exactly which right mouse button menu appears depends on what kind of icons you have rounded up. The menu will be the one whose proffered actions can be used on almost all the files and folders chosen. Some of the actions may not be applicable to some of the icons.

You can use the lasso on the desktop just like you use it in a folder window.

Select everything

There is a Select All menu item in the menu bar of a folder window. Click Edit, Select All and you highlight everything in the folder window, just like you select all the text in a document. See, you already knew how to do this.

Tip

To select all the icons in a folder window, highlight the window (make sure the window's caption area shows that it has the focus) and press Ctrl+A.

Select everything but

Select, by whatever means you want (except, of course, Select all), everything that you *don't* want to select. Then click Edit, Invert Selection. This selects everything in the folder window that you didn't select the first time. This is great for selecting everything but a few things.

De-select with Ctrl+click

Select everything, or select a bunch of icons with the lasso or with Shift+click. De-select a few of the icons with Ctrl+click. That is, hold down the Ctrl key and click the icons that you don't want selected. This is an easy way to select a bunch of icons, but pull out a few that you don't want selected. You can then use right-click if you want an action menu to pop up.

Select a few bunches of icons

Combine click and Ctrl+click with Shift+click and Ctrl+Shift+click to select bunches of icons. Ctrl+Shift+click (that is holding down Ctrl and Shift while clicking) works the same as Shift+click, but it doesn't wipe out previous selections. The Ctrl key continues to be the continue key.

Choose some icons with click, Ctrl+click, and/or Shift+click. Chose another bunch of icons with a Ctrl+click and then a Ctrl+Shift+click. This way you can grab little grouplets of icons in the folder window. There are many variations on how this works (we'll let you experiment rather than go through them all) but it is consistent — trust us on that.

Grabbing the icon group

If you have selected a group of icons and want to move or copy them with drag and drop, you need a way to grab all of them. You need to left or right drag them by placing the mouse pointer over one of the items in the group and dragging the whole group with you. If you press the mouse button while the mouse pointer is, say, between the icons in a group, all the highlighting goes out of your selected icons. You get the whole group to go along only by dragging from a highlighted icon.

Dragging multiple icons

Here is where it gets ugly, literally. When you drag a single icon (and its name), you get an aesthetically-pleasing transparent version of the icon with its name in black. You can tell right away what you're dragging around. When you drag a group of icons you get a group of box outlines that stand for the icons and lines that stand for the icon names, as shown in Figure 8-12.

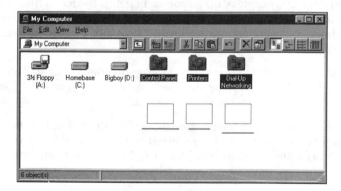

Figure 8-12: Dragging multiple files and folders in a folder window. The icons in this large icon view are portrayed as box outlines and the icon names are portrayed as lines.

We find these icon ghosts quite displeasing; Microsoft can't be too happy about them either. The Windows 3.x File Manager didn't use such ugly icon stand-ins. We assume that users just didn't get the stacked-documents icon that the File Manager uses to represent multiple icons.

Why didn't Microsoft just make all the icons in the group transparent like when you choose one icon? Because on slower computers with unaccelerated video cards, the repaint time is too slow.

Not only are the ghosted icons ugly, but they are hard to manage because they are so spread out. You still have your mouse pointer to tell you where the hot spot is, but visually you can get confused as to where the icons are as you drag them to another folder window or to the desktop. It feels like you're dragging around this big blob of stuff, which is no fun at all.

Undocumented

Normally, when you select and then drag an executable file, a shortcut is created to the "to" folder and the executable is left in its original folder. If you select a group of files that includes executable files (but not exclusively), *all* the files will be moved (or copied) instead. This is dangerous, because it can make some programs cease to work.

Press Esc to cancel

We mentioned this earlier in the *Moving a file or folder* section, but we want to emphasize it again here. If there is a problem while you're dragging an icon or group of icons around, just press Esc. This aborts the drag, but leaves the icons selected.

You can also just click the other mouse button.

Put the Desktop on the Taskbar

It is easy to cover up your desktop so you can't get to the icons that are on your desktop. In the preceding chapter, we showed you how to use the Minimize All and Undo Minimize All commands to solve this problem. There is a way to deal with this problem that is even more powerful.

Secret

Put a copy of most of the icons on your desktop on your Taskbar. That way you can always get to your desktop because you can always get to your Taskbar (if you have it set for Always on top).

Unfortunately, you can't put the desktop in the Startup folder, but then it doesn't really matter. Just leave it minimized on the Taskbar when you shut down Windows 95 and it will be there the next time you start up. Here's how you do it:

STEPS

Putting Your Desktop on Your Taskbar

Step 1.   Double-click the My Computer icon. Make sure that the Toolbar is displayed.

Step 2.   Click the down arrow on the drop-down list. Click the up arrow on the scrollbar bar in the drop-down list.

Step 3.   Click the Desktop icon. Size and format the resultant Desktop folder window the way you want it.

Step 4.   Minimize the Desktop folder window.

The Desktop folder window is now on your Taskbar. You can use Alt+Tab to task switch to the desktop. You can do this even if you are running a DOS program in a full-screen DOS box. Hold down the Alt key and press and release the Tab key until you highlight the Desktop icon.

If your computer crashes or does not close down in a normal fashion, you may have to open this Desktop folder window again.

Folder Windows Are Like the Program Manager

Putting the desktop on the Taskbar is sort of like turning the desktop folder window into the Program Manager. All the icons on the desktop are now in a folder window. If the folder window is in the large icon view, it looks like the Windows 3.x Program Manager. If you have folders (or shortcuts to folders) on your desktop they can act like Program Manager's program groups. We discuss these issues further in Chapter 7.

Folder windows in general are a lot like the Windows 3.x Program Manager, especially when the icons are displayed in large format. Any folder window is a great deal more useful and powerful than the Program Manager, and you can have multiple folder windows, but some of that old look and feel is still there.

The Explorer is the complement of the File Manager, the hierarchical view of your computer. We discuss the Explorer in the next chapter. We discuss the Program Manager and the File Manager, which are included in Windows 95 to provide a transition to the new user interface, in Chapter 12. But you don't really need a transition, do you, if you're reading this book?

Summary

If you want to know how to most efficiently manage your computer, this chapter and the next chapter are the places to look.

▶ We show you how to change the name of My Computer.

▶ We provide you with a score of secrets and tips on how to speed your way through the maze of files and folders on your computer. Get these tips down and your computer is a delight.

▶ We show you how to get multiple copies of any folder window.

▶ The folder window views afford you a method of looking at your computer in many different ways, and we show you how to change those views to match your needs.

▶ We provide a number of ways that you can use to quickly select files and folders you want in a folder window.

▶ Afraid of drag and drop? Don't be. We show you how to use this powerful process with all the safety built in.

▶ Want to have a copy of the desktop on the Taskbar so you can hotkey to it from a full-screen DOS session? We show you how.

Chapter 9

The Explorer — Displaying the Hierarchy

In This Chapter

We show you how to use the Explorer to really grab hold of your computer and wrestle it into shape. We discuss:

▶ Modifying the Explorer on the Start button to act the way you want it to

▶ Putting the Explorer on the desktop

▶ Launching the Explorer with one mouse click

▶ Using the Explorer to quickly copy and move files and folders

▶ Using keyboard shortcuts to reduce mouse clicking in the Explorer and My Computer windows

▶ Controlling multiple Explorer windows on your desktop

▶ Making sure that you can see all the files on your computer

▶ Learning to use the Explorer for just about everything you did with the File Manager, and much more

What Is This Explorer Thing?

The Windows 95 Explorer is the hierarchical file cabinet or outline view of My Computer — actually *your* computer. It is a tool for more easily understanding the file and folder structure of your computer. It is a replacement for the Windows 3.*x* File Manager. It can be used to move, copy, rename, compress, view, and delete files and folders on your computer and on the network. It is a two-paned view of a folder window.

Files and folders get stored on your disk drives in a hierarchical structure before you ever get a chance to get in there and muck it up. You'll find folders dividing up a hard drive, subfolders dividing up folders, and sub-subfolders dividing up subfolders. This natural organization of your drives is shown in Figure 9-1. The Explorer makes this more evident to you.

Figure 9-1: An Explorer view of the organization of My Computer. Notice that the hard disk (Homebase C:) is connected to and to the right of My Computer. This indicates that it is a part of My Computer. The folder labeled Windows is a part of Homebase, and Command is a subfolder of the Windows folder.

Like the File Manager, the Explorer shows both a tree view and a folder (directory) view. In the left window pane you get to see the outline, the tree, the hierarchical view of the computer, disk drives, and folders. In the right pane is a view of the contents of a given folder, disk drive, computer, or networked server computer.

Unlike the File Manager, each branch of the tree can be viewed by single-clicking the plus sign in a box to the left of the folder and disk icons. Gone is the need to double-click the icon to expand the branch. A click on the plus sign does not highlight the folder, nor display its contents in the right pane. This ability to navigate the tree independent of the contents of the folders makes the Explorer easier to use and more versatile than the File Manager.

Tip

You can quickly navigate through your folders and subfolders by clicking the plus sign next to the folder's name. The Explorer won't try to read the filenames in a folder until you highlight a folder name; therefore, it is much faster.

The Explorer displays the file cabinet, the storage space of the files, all tucked in their folders. The file cabinet is a metaphor for the disk storage in your computer. If you want to see what is inside your computer, you go to the file cabinet. The files are stored there hierarchically.

Almost everything that we said in Chapter 8 regarding My Computer is applicable to the Explorer window. All the various ways of copying, moving, renaming, and deleting work are exactly the same for the Explorer.

But Where Is the Explorer?

There is a file named Explorer.exe in your \Windows folder, and if you double-click it, you will find the Explorer displayed on your desktop. But surely this isn't how it is meant to be. After all, My Computer sits there in all its glory as the first among icons on the desktop. Doesn't the Explorer rate something better than a convoluted pathway to Explorer.exe? (Remember you can change the name of the My Computer icon on your desktop to, say, Steve's Computer by right-clicking the icon and selecting Rename.)

If you right-click My Computer, the right mouse-button menu invites you to Explore. Click Explore and My Computer turns into a two-pane window view of your computer. The caption bar says it all: Exploring - My Computer.

Tip

You can also explore by holding down the Shift key and double-clicking the My Computer icon. Just be sure that My Computer is the only icon on your desktop that is highlighted. Otherwise you will inadvertently open all the highlighted applications on your desktop because the Shift key will be interpreted by Windows 95 to mean "select all the icons between the last one highlighted and the My Computer icon."

The Explorer is masquerading as a version of a folder window: the Explorer as My Computer transformed. The Explore menu option is available when you right-click the Network Neighborhood icon, the Recycle Bin, the Microsoft Network icon, the Start button, or any folder or disk drive icon. You can explore any of these items. You can view any of the contents of these items in the Explorer view.

The Windows Explorer and the Start button

The Explorer (actually a shortcut to Explorer.exe) has its own icon on the Start button menu.

Click the Start button, and then click the Programs item. The Windows Explorer is on the Programs menu. Click it and the Explorer is displayed on your desktop. You can determine just how the Explorer starts up by editing the properties of this menu item. See the section later in this chapter entitled *Explorer Command Line Parameters*.

Putting the Explorer on the desktop

My Computer is on the desktop. You can put the Explorer on the desktop, too. By doing this you are saying that the Explorer view is just as important as the My Computer view of your computer. The best way to do this is put a shortcut to the Explorer on the desktop. To do this, take the following steps:

STEPS

Putting the Explorer on the Desktop

Step 1.   Click the Start, Programs, Windows Explorer menu item.

Step 2.   Click the Windows folder icon in the left pane of the Explorer. Scroll down the right pane until Explorer.exe is showing.

Step 3.   Drag Explorer.exe to the desktop and drop it. There's no need to click Create Shortcut since dragging the icon from Explorer to the desktop already does that. (Dragging an executable file like Explorer.exe to the desktop always creates a shortcut, rather than moving the file itself. Dragging other file types, however, actually moves them into the \Desktop folder.)

Step 4.   Edit the Explorer icon's name to be **Explorer** or whatever else you want.

Putting the Explorer on a launching pad

You may use the Explorer so often that you'll want to have it only one click away, even if you haven't started it yet. Of course, once you have activated the Explorer, it is on the Taskbar, only a mouse move and a click away. But before that, you had to right-click My Computer and then click Explore, or you clicked the Start button, Programs, and Windows Explorer.

You can put the Explorer on a launchpad and have it just one click away. We feature Russell Holcomb's Run program on the CD-ROM included with this book. Run is a launchpad that requires only one click to start a program. Run also doesn't cost you anything because it is freeware.

To use the program you need to create a folder to store it in. Copy it into its folder on your hard disk and unzip it there. Create a shortcut to Run in the Startup folder. The first time, double-click Run.exe in a folder window or Explorer view of its folder. Drag Explorer.exe from a folder view of the \Windows folder and drop it on one of the Run buttons. The Run buttons are like shortcuts — you can edit their properties by right-clicking them.

Now you've got a launchpad that allows you to get to the Explorer view with one click. We just outlined the steps you need to take to make this actually work. Check out Chapters 10 and 11 for further details on putting a shortcut to Run in the Startup folder.

Turning My Computer into the Explorer

It would be neat if you could change the My Computer Icon into the Explorer. We wish we knew a way to do it. If you double-click My Computer it opens up a single-pane folder window view of your computer. Open is the default action and the first action listed on the right mouse button menu when you right-click My Computer. Explore is the second available action.

It is possible in some cases to swap Open for Explore. For example, you can change the meaning of double-clicking a folder icon from Open to Explore. We don't know a way to do this for My Computer, Network Neighborhood, or Recycle Bin.

Getting an Overview of Your Computer

The Explorer displays eight different icons arranged hierarchically in its left pane, as shown in Figure 9-2. The eight are the Desktop icon, My Computer icon, floppy disk icon, hard disk icon, manila folder icons (some with little graphics on them), Network Neighborhood icon, Recycle Bin icon, and My Briefcase icon.

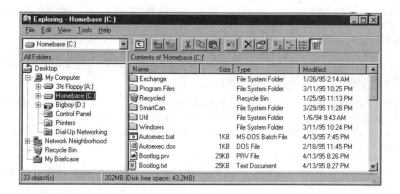

Figure 9-2: The Explorer view. The left pane shows the desktop and those items that are attached to it.

The Explorer's left pane view of your computer is strange. It displays the Desktop, which in turn contains My Computer, which in turn contains the Explorer. In addition, you have to mentally block out the fact that your Explorer window is currently on your desktop

So making a conceptual leap, you see that My Computer is connected to the desktop, and that the disk drives, hard and floppy (or diskette), are connected to My Computer.

The dotted lines are your guides. If a vertical dotted line comes out of the bottom of an icon, the icons connected to that line by horizontal dotted lines are contained within the thing that is the top icon. My Computer, Network Neighborhood, and Recycle Bin are all contained within the desktop. The disk drives are contained within My Computer.

The Network Neighborhood icon represents all the computers connected to yours over a LAN. You won't have a Network Neighborhood icon on your desktop unless you have installed a network, or set up Dial-Up Networking or Direct Cable Connection.

Network Neighborhood and Recycle Bin are displayed on the same level as My Computer. Microsoft wants you to think of the network the same way you think of your computer.

The Recycle Bin spans computers and hard disk drives (but not diskette drives). In this way, it is equal to My Computer. Also, Microsoft wanted the Recycle Bin on the desktop permanently.

Shortcuts that appear on the desktop don't appear in the left pane of the Explorer — too much clutter. They will appear in the right pane if you highlight the desktop icon in the left pane. Microsoft Exchange and the Microsoft Network icons, even though they are on the desktop, don't show in the left pane. File icons on the desktop also don't show.

If you place folders on the desktop, they show up in the left pane. Shortcuts to folders do not.

Some special folders, such as Control Panel and Printers, are displayed on the same level as the disk drives. Microsoft doesn't want you to have to go searching for them through the hierarchy of folders. Like cream, they have risen to the top.

Ordinary folders are stored on the disk drives, and the manila folder icons are connected to the disk drive icons. Figure 9-2 doesn't show any folder icons attached to the hard disk icons because the outline view in the left pane hasn't been expanded to include them. They are shown in Figure 9-1. File icons never show up in the left pane of the Explorer window.

Two panes — connected and yet independent

The two parts of the Explorer window, the two views of your computer, are connected. You click on an icon in the left pane and the contents of that folder are shown in the right pane. If you have the Explorer description bar turned on (click View, Options in the Explorer Menu Bar and then check "Include description bar for right and left panes"), the right pane will be labeled Contents of *xxx* where *xxx* is the name of the highlighted folder in the left pane.

Much of the power of the Explorer comes from the fact that the two panes are independent of each other. You can view the contents of one folder in the right pane and, without disturbing that view, expand the folder tree in the left pane to find another folder. This makes it easy to copy or move files and folders from one folder to another.

Think of the right pane of the Explorer window as the folder window view. It acts just like a folder window, except that its default action when double-clicking a folder icon displayed within it is to open in the existing Explorer window, not to open another folder window.

Navigating with the Explorer

The Explorer is your navigator. It guides you to the files and folders on your computer's disk drives or, if you are connected to a network, on other computers. The Explorer displays, in an expandable outline, your computer's drives and the drives of other computers to which you are networked. You search through the computer drives by clicking the Explorer outline to expand it. The Explorer also gives you an easy way to copy, move, and link files or folders across disk drives, folders, or the network.

Because the Explorer gives you an overview and a roadmap of your computer and the server computers that you are connected to, you can use it to find your way around computer space. The key to navigating is using the little plus signs to the left of the icons in the folder tree. Clicking on a plus sign expands that branch of the tree. For example, clicking the plus sign next to your Homebase (C:) icon expands the folder tree to allow you to see all the folders attached to the root directory of the C drive.

Click the plus sign next to any of the folders on the C drive, and you'll see the folders contained within that folder. Each branch of the folder tree gets expanded as you climb out the branches.

To collapse a branch, click the minus sign to the left of a folder icon. The minus sign appeared when you first clicked the plus sign.

Highlighting a folder icon

If you click an icon in the left pane, you see the contents of that folder in the right pane. If the contents of the right pane include folder icons, you can expand a branch by double-clicking one of these folder icons in the right pane. The folder tree in the left pane of the Explorer also expands when you do this.

The default action of clicking a folder icon in the left pane is to display the contents of the folder in the right pane. If you right-click it and click Open on the right mouse button, a new folder window is displayed on the desktop with the contents of the folder. The same is true if you right-click a folder icon in the left pane.

Tip

If you double-click a folder icon in the folder tree, you both expand the branch at that node and display the contents of the folder in the right pane.

Making the left pane bigger

The two panes of the Explorer window are divided by a vertical bar. To increase the size of the left pane, as you expand branches of the folder tree, move the bar to the right. Do this by placing your mouse pointer over the bar. The mouse cursor turns into a vertical line with two arrows. Drag the bar.

The Network Neighborhood

The Network Neighborhood icon contains the shared resources of the computers that you are connected to. Double-click this icon to see the disk drives, folders, and printers that are available (shared) to you.

You can expand branches of the folder trees found on other computers just as easily as you can on your computer. The networked computers are treated just like My Computer. Windows 95 treats them the same, so that you will be encouraged to do likewise. You can browse the networked computers just like you do your computer using the Explorer window. If you want to map a shared folder or disk drive to a drive letter, thereby making it appear as though it is part of My Computer, you can certainly do that.

Just click the Map Network Drive icon in the Explorer Toolbar and choose which shared disk to map to which drive letter. You can connect to shared printers using the Printers folder.

Using the keyboard with the folder tree

Secret

It is possible to expand all the branches of the folder tree at once. This is not really recommended as it can take a long time. If you hold down the ALT key and press the asterisk next to the number pad, all the branches of the folder tree will be expanded.

To collapse a branch, click the minus sign next to it. To collapse all the branches, click the minus signs at the highest level. To collapse all the branches underneath the highest branches once you have collapsed them, press F5. If you don't press F5, the next time you click the plus sign next to a high branch, all the branches underneath will be displayed.

You can also expand the branch of a highlighted node or folder icon by pressing the plus key on the keypad. Collapse an expanded node by pressing the minus key on the keypad.

Creating New Folders

You'll see that folders make up the bulk of the hierarchical structure displayed by the Explorer. The Explorer displays a folder tree.

You need to create these folders if there are to be any other than those created by Windows 95 when you set it up, and those created by your applications when you installed them. To create folders using the Explorer, take the following steps:

STEPS

Creating a Folder

Step 1. Right-click the My Computer icon on the desktop. Click Explore.

Step 2. Expand the folder tree in the left pane of the Explorer window until you see the folder icon where you will place your new folder. Click this folder's name. Make sure that the folder name is highlighted and that its name is in the Explorer window caption area.

Step 3. Right-click the client area of the Explorer window in the right pane. Click New and then click Folder.

Step 4. A new folder icon appears in the right pane. Its name is highlighted. Type in an appropriate name for the folder and press Enter.

It would seem natural to be able to right-click a folder or disk icon in the left pane of the Explorer and choose New as a menu option to create a new whatever within the folder or root directory. Unfortunately, you can't, as there is no New option on this menu.

Copying and Moving Files and Folders

You can move and copy files a lot easier with the Explorer window than with a regular folder window. You just have to be willing to put up with this hierarchical view of your computer (and the attached network).

You can view the contents of the source folder in the right pane and independently find the destination folder in the left pane. Once you see both source and destination in your Explorer window, you can copy or move the files and/or folders from the right pane to the left.

All the copying and moving techniques detailed in Chapter 8 work the same with the Explorer. Instead of dragging and dropping from and to folder windows, you select icons in the Explorer window's right pane and drop them on folder icons in the left pane.

You can select icons in the right pane with any of the techniques detailed in the previous chapter. If you choose to copy or cut those icons, then when you display the contents of another folder in the right pane, the Paste command is available to you to copy or move the selected files and/or folders to the new folder.

Creating Two Explorer Windows

File management was greatly facilitated when using the Windows 3.*x* File Manager if you had two child windows open at the same time. Each window had two panes (the directory tree and the contents of a directory pane), so with two child windows, four panes show in the File Manager.

In one of the child windows you could display the source directory and in the other the destination. This made it much easier to copy and move files, or to simply compare the contents of two directories side-by-side.

The Explorer makes file management possible with just two panes. It does this by making each pane more independent of the other than they were in the File Manager. Using the File Manager, you couldn't expand the directory tree while maintaining the same contents in the right pane.

Still, to reduce the amount of scrolling that one has to do to find the source and then go to the destination folder, it can be easier to have two Explorer windows open at the same time on the desktop. Here is where the File Manager has an advantage. The File Manager has a multi-document interface. It can contain two child windows within its window border. Microsoft decided to drop this multi-document interface and have the operating system, not the applications, control the window borders.

Therefore, the Explorer does not have a multi-document interface. If you want to have two views of your computer to ease copying and moving, you need to bring up two Explorer windows. This is quite easy, as a new copy of the

Explorer is created by default each time that you right-click My Computer and click Explore or when you double-click the Explorer shortcut that you created on the desktop earlier in this chapter.

Undocumented

You can open another copy of the Explorer focused on a particular folder by taking the following steps:

STEPS

Opening a Second Copy of the Explorer

Step 1.   In the left pane of an Explorer window, right-click the folder icon that you want to Explore. This could be either the source or destination folder.

Step 2.   Click Open on the right mouse button menu.

Step 3.   Right-click the system menu icon (at the left end of the title bar) of the newly opened folder window.

Step 4.   Select Explore from the right mouse button menu.

Step 5.   Click the close button on the folder window that you created in Step 2.

This will open a new copy of the Explorer with the focus on the selected folder. Once you have two Explorer windows, you can have one focus on your destination folder and the other on your source folder.

Tip

You can line up the Explorer windows like the child windows in the File Manager by right-clicking the Taskbar and choosing Cascade, Tile Horizontally, or Tile Vertically. When tiled, the two Explorer windows cover your desktop completely and appear similar to two child windows in the Windows 3.*x* File Manager in maximize mode.

Undocumented

If you leave open two tiled Explorer windows when you shut down your computer, they will be ready to go when you start it again. Unfortunately, they won't be side by side, but on top of one another. (This is because Window 95 erroneously saves the position of any one Explorer Window.) You'll need to right-click the Taskbar and choose Tile to separate them again.

Explorer (and My Computer) Keyboard Shortcuts

The Explorer and the folder windows share a common set of keyboard shortcuts. They are listed in Table 9-1. A couple of the shortcuts listed in the table don't have any equivalent menu choices.

Table 9-1	Explorer and Folder Window Keyboard Shortcuts
Key	*Action*
F1	Help
F2	Rename the highlighted file or folder.
F3	Bring up the Find dialog box.
F4	Drop down the drop-down list in the Toolbar. This is a toggle switch.
F5	Refresh the windows. You saw one use for this command in the section earlier in this chapter entitled *Using the keyboard with the folder tree*. If the files or folders in a window have changed and not been updated, this will update the window display.
F6	Move the focus from left pane to drop-down box in Toolbar to the right pane and back. In a folder window there is only one pane.
F10	Put the focus in the menu bar on the File menu.
ALT+*	Expand all the branches in the folder tree.
*	Expand all branches below the focused node (or folder or disk icon).
Backspace	Move up one level in the folder hierarchy.
Tab	Same as F6; shift the focus between the two panes and the Toolbar. This is very useful in navigating the folder tree or picking out files and folders in the right window pane.
Arrow keys	Move up and down the folder tree in the left pane or the list of files and folders in the right pane. If you move quickly enough, moving from icon to icon in the left pane the highlighted folder's content does not show in the right pane. Leave the focus on one icon for more than a second and its contents are displayed in the right pane.
Right arrow	Expand the highlighted folder if it isn't expanded already. If it is, go to the subfolder.
Left arrow	Collapse the current highlighted folder if is it expanded. If not, go to the parent folder.
Ctrl+Arrow keys	Scroll either the left or right pane depending on which pane has the focus. You can use PgUp and PgDn keys also. The focus isn't changed.
Enter	Does nothing in the folder tree. It will run the file or open the folder in the right pane. Same as double-click.
Shift+F10	Same as right-click. Display the right mouse button menu. Shift+F10 is always the right mouse button throughout the Windows interface.
+	The keypad plus sign: +. When a folder name is highlighted, and the branch below it is collapsed, expand the branch.

Key	Action
–	The keypad minus sign, "–". When a folder name is highlighted, and the branch below it expanded, collapse the branch. When combined with F5, collapse all the branches below.
Alt+Space	Open the system menu. This menu allows you to move, minimize, maximize, size, or close the folder or Explorer window.
Alt + Enter	Display the folder's Properties sheets.
Ctrl+G	Open the Go To dialog box. This allows you to enter the name of a folder or computer to go to.
Alt+F4	Close window. Alt + F4 closes all applications throughout the Windows interface.

Seeing All the Files on Your Computer

Microsoft is somewhat ashamed of the three-letter file extensions used to define file types. It is also a bit embarrassed by its 8- followed by 3-character filenames. It has created a way of doing long filenames (255 characters long) without upsetting its existing file structure (FAT, for file allocation table) and now wants Windows 95 users to forget about file extensions.

When you first install Windows 95, files with certain extensions are not shown in folder windows or in Explorer windows. The three-letter extensions on all filenames of registered file types are not shown. You can turn the ability to see these missing files and missing file extensions back on. Here's how:

STEPS

Viewing All Files and File Extensions

Step 1. Open a folder or Explorer window. One way to do this is by right-clicking My Computer and choosing either Open or Explore.

Step 2. Click View, Options in the window's menu bar. The View Options dialog box sheet, as shown in Figure 9-3, is displayed.

Step 3. Check "Show all files" and uncheck "Hide MS-DOS file extensions for file types that are registered."

Step 4. Click OK.

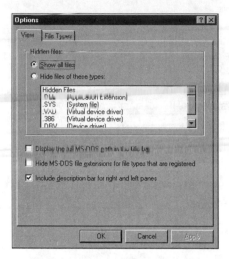

Figure 9-3: The View Options dialog box. Some of the extensions of the files that will be hidden are shown in the Hidden files window at the top of this dialog box. Check the appropriate boxes to unhide these files.

Notice that you can make these changes in either a folder window or an Explorer window. We chose to write about this capability in this chapter only because Microsoft views the Explorer window as an advanced interface, and sees this capability as an advanced feature. Of course, the whole point of this book is to make every advanced feature visible to anyone who wants to take advantage of it.

Seeing Hidden Folders

Secret

If you check Show all files, you also get to see more folders contained in the Windows folder. Microsoft appears to think that less "advanced" users will have a problem with these folders showing up in their folder windows, so it hides them from the view of those users who don't want to see all the files regardless of file extension.

You can see which folders get hidden by opening an Explorer window and expanding the branch connected to your Windows folder icon in the folder tree. Watch the list of folders change as you switch back and forth between Show all files and Hide files of these types.

Explorer Command Line Parameters

Take a moment to look at how the Explorer command line parameters work by taking the following steps:

STEPS
Viewing the Windows Explorer Command Line Parameters

Step 1. Right-click the Start button and then click Explore.

Step 2. Click Programs in the left pane of the Explorer.

Step 3. Right-click Windows Explorer in the right pane and then click Properties.

Step 4. Click the Shortcut tab and then look at the Target field.

When you click the shortcut tab, you will notice that the target for the Windows Explorer shortcut is:

```
c:\Windows\Explorer.EXE /n,/e,C:\
```

With the command line parameters /n,/e,C:\, an Explorer window opened by clicking the Windows Explorer in the Start menu will look like Figure 9-4.

Figure 9-4: An Explorer window focused on the C drive.

The syntax for the Explorer command line is:

```
c:\Windows\Explorer.exe {/n},{/e},{options},{folder}
```

The parameters have the following meanings:

/n,   Opens a *new* Explorer window

/e,   Opens an *expanded* folder with its contents displayed

{*options*} may be either one of the following:

/root,   Selects a folder as the *root* of a folder tree

or

/select   Highlights a folder and displays the folder's parent

{*folder*} may be any folder name or path, such as:

C:\

or

C:\Windows

Note that commas are required between switches on the Explorer.exe command line.

Undocumented

If there were no command line parameters after Explorer.exe, clicking Windows Explorer in the Start button menu would bring up an Explorer window focused on the C drive.

If you add **C:\Windows** or any other folder name, clicking Windows Explorer in the Start menu displays a folder window view of that folder. The Explorer has turned into My Computer. You can put in any folder name, such as **C:\Windows\System** if you like, to get a folder window view focused on that folder.

Undocumented

If you put **/e,** (the comma is required) in front of the folder name, clicking Windows Explorer in the Start menu will display an Explorer window focused on that folder with the folder *expanded* and with the contents of the folder (or other object) displayed in the right pane. Putting a folder name in the Target field (command line) takes Explorer out of its default behavior. Using **/e,** restores some of that default; **/e,** means *Explorer View*.

If instead of clicking Windows Explorer in the Start menu, you open an Explorer window and double-click the shortcut to Windows Explorer found in the C:\Windows\Start Menu\Program folder, it will not display another Explorer window. Instead it will refocus your existing Explorer window on the folder in the Target field. To force the creation of a new Explorer window, you need **/n,** as a command line parameter. Adding **/n,** restores the rest of the Explorer's default behavior (except for its focus); **/n,** means *new*.

You can click Windows Explorer in the Start, Programs menu and get another Explorer window without having the /n, command parameter. It is only the case of double-clicking the Windows Explorer shortcut within an Explorer window that fails without the /n, parameter.

You can't replace **C:\Windows** with **My Computer** or **Network Neighborhood**. **Desktop** will work, but it doesn't get you to the top of the hierarchical view of your computer. You might try it to see what we mean.

The normal top-most icon in the Explorer is the Desktop. This is referred to as the root of the folder tree. You can specify a different root if you want. Add **/root,** to the command line and follow it with your new root. The new root could be My Computer, or C:\Windows, or whatever you like. Here's an example:

```
C:\WINDOWS\EXPLORER.EXE /n,/e,/root,C:\
```

This example produces an Explorer window that looks like Figure 9-5.

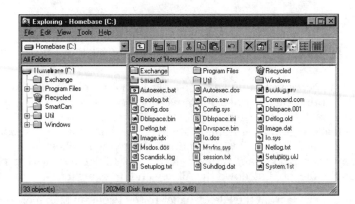

Figure 9-5: An Explorer window with the C drive as its root (/root,).

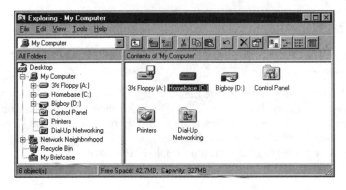

Figure 9-6: An Explorer window focused on the C drive with its parent, My Computer, open (/ select,).

You can use the, **/select,** parameter to highlight a given folder and open the folder's parent. Here's an example (see Figure 9-6):

```
C:\WINDOWS\EXPLORER.EXE /n,/e,/select,C:\
```

Notice the differences that these command line parameters produce by comparing Figure 9-6 with Figure 9-4.

From the File Manager to the Explorer

How do you go from using the File Manager to using the Explorer? In this section, we review almost all the things you can do with the File Manager and show you how to do them better with the Explorer or another part of the Windows 95 interface. Much of what we say here about the Explorer is also true of the My Computer folder windows. Where it isn't true, and isn't obviously *not* true, we point it out.

Open, Copy, Move, Delete

From the File menu, File Manager offers these choices: Open, Copy, Move, and Delete.

The Explorer accomplishes those same tasks with the right mouse button menu, substituting Cut and Paste for Move, and Copy and Paste for Copy. Because the Explorer can use the right mouse button, it can use right drag and drop, which allows for easier-to-understand copies and moves. The Explorer also supports the Windows 3.*x* conventions of copying by clicking on a file, holding down the Ctrl key and dragging it to a new folder and moving a file by clicking on the file, holding down the Alt key and dragging it to a new folder.

You could drag a file from the File Manager to the Program Manager to create a shortcut. This ability to create shortcuts has been greatly enhanced in the Explorer with both drag and drop and the right mouse button menu.

Rename

File Manager lets you do wild card file renames. This makes it easy to rename a group of files, or change a bunch of file extensions.

Explorer lets you only rename one file at a time. You can also rename files in the common file dialog box. Just click a filename twice slowly (but don't double-click it). You can also click a file to highlight it; then press F2 to rename it. Right-clicking a file icon or name allows you to select Rename. There is no way to rename multiple files simultaneously in the Explorer.

Run

File Manager lets you run an executable file by clicking the File menu in its menu bar, then choosing Run, typing in the filename, and adding command line parameters. If you are focused in the File Manager on a particular directory It puts the directory's path name in the command line.

In Windows 95, Run is on the Start button on the Taskbar. It doesn't know which folder you have highlighted, so it doesn't put your current path in the Run dialog box's command line. (The Run dialog box does use an open folder window, if any, as the current directory.) Run keeps a history of past command lines from session to session.

File association

File Manager can create an *association* with an application to open and print associated documents.

The Explorer has a similar easy-to-use file association, but one that is much more powerful. You can create many more commands than opening and printing. Just double-click an unregistered file type, enter an optional name for the file type, and pick an application to open it.

The Print command is on the right mouse button for files of registered types. The File Manager's print command is not grayed out in its File menu even when you highlight a file that it doesn't know how to print.

With the Explorer, you can add other commands or change an existing association by using View, Option, File Type. Check out Chapter 13 for details.

Open an unassociated file

With the File Manager you can drag a file to an open application or a minimized icon on the desktop to view or open it.

With the Explorer, you can put a shortcut in the Send To folder to a default file opener (or two), right-click a file in the Explorer and send it to the default file opener. (See Chapter 13 for details.) You can also drag a file to a minimized application button, the Taskbar, or an application window that is open on the desktop.

Create directory

A frequent use of the File Manager is to create new directories or, in the case of Windows 95, new folders. This is the main mechanism for building a hierarchical folder structure.

In the Explorer, highlight the folder icon in the left pane that will contain the new folder. Right-click the right pane, Click New and Folder. Rename the folder from "New Folder" to whatever you like.

Create file

You can't create a new, empty file in the File Manager.

You can in the Explorer. Right-click in the right pane and choose New.

Search or File Find

You could use the File Manager to find a file using wild cards, telling it in what directory (and its subdirectories) to look for the missing files.

The Explorer has a much more powerful Find capability. It remembers its searches so they can be edited and searched again, has a greater number of search criteria, can search for files by looking for text within them, and on and on. There is no comparison. Check out Chapter 11 for details.

You initiate a Find with the Explorer by clicking Tools, Find in the menu bar or by pressing F3 if your focus is on the desktop, a folder, or an Explorer window. You can also search for computers on your local network or for documents on the Microsoft Network with Find.

File view filters

By clicking View, By File Type and typing in an extension or filename you can restrict the File Manager so it will display only the files with that extension or filename.

The Explorer lets you do this with Find. You display in the Find window only those files with a given name or extension. This is slower than the File Manager's way of doing it, but less prone to error and what is going on is much more obvious.

Copy, Label, Format, make a system disk

The File Manager lets you do a disk copy. You can change the label of a disk drive, including a hard disk drive. You can format a diskette (or hard drive) and create a system diskette.

To disk-copy a diskette in the Explorer, right-click the diskette icon and select Copy Disk from the right mouse button menu.

To label a drive or diskette, right-click the drive icon, click Properties, and then type in the new label.

To format a drive, right-click the drive icon, and click Format.

To make a system disk or diskette, right click the drive icon and click "Format." If you want to format the diskette and make it bootable, click "Full" and "Copy system files" in the Other Options box (see Figure 9-7). If the disk is already formatted, click "Copy system files only" and click Start.

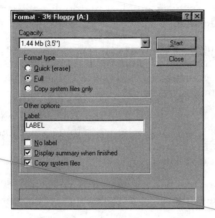

Figure 9-7: The Format dialog box. Check "Copy system files only" to make a system diskette of a formatted diskette. Click "Full" and "Copy system files" to format a bootable diskette.

To create an emergency boot diskette, click the Control Panel icon in the left pane of the Explorer window, double-click the Add/Remove Programs icon, click the Startup Disk tab, and then click the Create Disk button.

Change the font used

In the File Manager you can decide on what font to use to display files, etc.

The font used by the Explorer is determined by the Icon font setting in Display, Appearances. Right-click the desktop and click Properties. Click the Appearances tab and then the Item drop-down list. Highlight Icon and then choose font and size.

Print a directory listing

Tip

You can't print a directory listing in either the File Manager or the Explorer. You need to click File Run and then type:

```
COMMAND/c DIR *.* >LPT1
```

This command a file listing. Even then, you need to manually eject the last page on a laser printer.

Put two directory listings side-by-side

The File Manager has a multiple-document interface so you can compare two directories side-by-side, or show a source and destination directory all within one window controlled by the File Manager.

The Explorer has a single-document interface. To get two copies of a folder or two different folders on the desktop, you need to open two Explorers. If you want to have them side-by-side, you need to minimize all other applications, and then click Tile "Vertically on the Taskbar."

The Explorer has a stronger mechanism for expanding the folder tree that allows you to copy and move files and folders between folders without requiring the use of dual windows as the File Manager does. This significantly reduces the requirements for a dual-window Explorer.

Click the [+] and [–] signs next to the folder names to expand and collapse branches of the folder tree in the Explorer. This doesn't affect the contents of the right pane.

All the disk drives are shown in one folder tree. You don't need to have two windows in order to see more than one disk drive's folders.

Sort files by name, date, file type, size

The File Manager lets you click a Toolbar icon or choose a menu item to sort your files. The order is fixed for each variable: ascending for name, descending for date, and so on.

The Explorer will sort on name, date, file type, or size in all four icon views (the File Manager has only two icon views). It will order your files and folders either by ascending or descending order. The Explorer sorts on the file type name, while the File Manager will sort alphabetically on the extension.

Tip

To sort a detailed view of an Explorer window, click any of the column header buttons in the right pane. Click twice to reverse the order.

View file contents

The File Manager doesn't have a set of file viewers that let you see the file without launching the program that created the file.

The Explorer comes with a raft of file viewers that Microsoft calls *Quick Viewers*. They are accessed by right-clicking a file. You can put the Quick Viewer manager in the Send To folder. (Quick Viewers are actually a stripped-down version of the popular Outside In program for Windows from Systems Compatibility, which also markets additional Quick Viewers.)

Undo and Delete

Undo is not available in the File Manager. The Explorer has undo on the right mouse button menu for rename, copy, move, and delete. You can recover a previously deleted file from the Recycle Bin.

When you delete a file using the File Manager you are asked to give a confirmation. If you confirm that you wanted it deleted, it's gone (unless you use Unerase). If you delete a file using the Explorer, it goes to the Recycle Bin (unless you turned this capability off) and you can recover it later if you realize you were too hasty when you deleted it.

Share a disk drive or folder

In the Explorer, right-click on the folder or disk icon and choose Sharing. This isn't available in the File Manager.

Customize the Toolbar

The File Manager lets you customize the Toolbar. Just double-click it.

You can't do this with the Explorer. You can customize the right mouse button menu, although it is more difficult.

See hidden files

A file with the hidden or system attribute turned on can be seen in the File Manager if you click View, By File Type, Show Hidden/System Files.

The Explorer automatically hides files with certain extensions unless you click View, Options, View and turn off this option.

See free disk space

Both the Explorer and the File Manager show the available disk space in their status bar.

File attributes

The File Manager will display the file attribute for all the files at once in its All File Details view.

The Explorer cannot show file attributes in its window. Using the Explorer, right-click a file and choose Properties to see the file attributes for one file. The common file attributes for multiple selected files will also be shown if you use this method after selecting more than one file.

File size

The File Manager displays a greater degree of precision than the Explorer when giving the file size. The Explorer shows only the number of bytes to the nearest 1KB.

Additional File Manager strengths

The File Manager is very fast. You can ask the File Manager to minimize itself after you start a file by double-clicking it in the File Manager.

Additional Explorer strengths

The Explorer gives you immediate access to the Control Panel, Network Neighborhood, Printer folder, and Fonts folder.

You can use the universal naming convention (UNC) to access a networked drive without having to map it to a drive letter.

Summary

The Explorer is the most powerful tool that Windows 95 provides to manage your computer. Unfortunately, much of its power is hidden.

▶ Use the Explorer to navigate throughout your computer and the network that is connected to your computer.

▶ We show how to make sure that file types aren't hidden from your view.

▶ We reveal the hidden command line parameters that determine how the Explorer behaves.

▶ We show you how to put the Explorer on the desktop, on a launchpad, or just about anywhere that makes sense to you.

▶ If you know how to use the Explorer, you can quickly copy and move files and folders around on your computer.

▶ The Explorer and My Computer come with shortcuts, some of which can be accessed only from the keyboard.

▶ We show you how to size and display the Explorer or multiple Explorers on your desktop.

▶ We compare what the Windows *3.x* File Manager does with how the Explorer handles the same tasks.

Chapter 10

Using Shortcuts to Open up Your Computer

In This Chapter

Shortcuts make your Windows 95 computer a lot easier to use. We discuss:

▶ Putting shortcuts to anything in your computer on your desktop

▶ Viewing any document with a shortcut to the Quick View file viewers built into Windows 95

▶ Starting any program when Windows 95 starts

▶ Single-clicking to start your favorite applications

▶ Copying, moving, opening, compressing, and viewing files easily with Send To

▶ Starting DOS programs and DOS/Windows batch files from icons

▶ Starting different versions of your applications with different icons

▶ Printing files by dragging and dropping them to an icon on the desktop

▶ Making the full power of your computer visible

▶ Making sure your applications can find all their accessory files without having to add folder names to your Path statement in your Autoexec.bat file

What's a Shortcut?

We want to clear up something right away. We use the word *shortcut* to mean two very different things in this book. When we say something like *keyboard shortcut*, we mean a keystroke that does something that otherwise would have taken a bunch of keystrokes or a lot of mousing around. The *shortcuts* we talk about in this chapter refer to icons that represent, and are linked to, applications and documents.

This kind of shortcut is a shortcut in the sense that you don't have to go looking around using the Explorer or My Computer folder windows to find your document or application. You can just put a link or shortcut to it in a convenient place. Double-clicking the shortcut is the same as — sometimes even better than — double-clicking the original file.

Didn't Windows 3.1 have something like shortcuts? Yes, the Program Manager was full of them. You could drag a file from the File Manager and drop it on the Program Manager to create a new Program Item within a Program Group. Double-clicking the Program Item started the application or opened a file with its associated application (if its file type was registered).

Shortcuts have escaped the confines of the Program Manager. They are no longer limited just to files and applications. No longer babies crawling on their hands and knees, they are on their way to high school.

Shortcuts can be recognized by the curved black arrow in the little white box in the lower left side of their icon. This little icon on an icon shows up automatically when you create a shortcut. Take a look at the example in Figure 10-1.

Figure 10-1: A shortcut icon. All shortcut icons have a black arrow in a little white box in the lower left corner of the icon.

An important fact to remember is that if you delete a shortcut icon from the desktop (or anywhere else, for that matter) you have deleted only the shortcut. But if you move an actual file to the desktop and then delete that file's icon, you have deleted the actual file.

If you attempt to delete the icon of a program on your computer, you will receive this warning from Windows 95: "The file *appname.exe* is a program. If you remove it, you will no longer be able to run this program or edit some documents. Are you sure you want to delete it?" If you answer yes, the program file will be sent to the Recycle Bin, (unless you held down the Shift key when you pressed the Delete key or you have configured the Recycle Bin to purge the deleted files). In all these cases, that program will no longer be available. So be careful out there.

Shortcuts Are Great (Here's Why)

Just because one place is a good place to store something doesn't mean that it's a good place to go to get what you stored there. There probably are really good reasons to put some files or applications in a particular folder, but it also makes perfect sense to give yourself a way to get at them quickly.

Disk drives are getting big. The amount of information that can be stored on one can quickly overwhelm the most meticulous person. If you stack a lot of boxes in a room, it's soon going to be hard to get around the room.

Our computers are getting hooked up ever more tightly to other people's computers. We're looking for stuff on their machines and they are doing the same on ours. A gigabyte here, a gigabyte there, and pretty soon it adds up to real chaos.

Shortcuts make all your information much more accessible. Microsoft has made shortcuts flexible and powerful. It isn't obvious at first, but you will soon discover that Windows 95 shortcuts are a huge improvement in the Windows interface. Your personal productivity will greatly benefit from their use.

Put your favorite files and programs on the desktop

Your desktop is an icon container, and the perfect spot for shortcuts. It may remind you of the Windows 3.x Program Manager. You don't really want to put your documents or applications on your desktop. Keep them in the folders that they share with other similar applications and files. For example, keep all your game applications in subfolders of the Games folder, but put shortcuts to your favorite game on the desktop.

Put shortcuts to documents on the desktop — just the ones that you are currently working on. Working on a set of similar documents? Create a shortcut to the folder holding the set of documents.

If you want a bunch of similar applications on the desktop, but not covering the desktop, put a folder (or, even better, a shortcut to a folder) on the desktop and put shortcuts to the applications in the folder. This is sort of like a Windows 3.x Program Manager Program Group.

Want the Explorer on the desktop? Put a shortcut to Explorer.exe on the desktop, but leave the file Explorer.exe itself where it belongs, in the \Windows folder.

Tip

Wouldn't it be easier to drag and drop files to the Quick Viewer, in order to see what is going on inside? Put a shortcut to \Windows\System\Viewers\Quickview.exe on the desktop and rename it Quick Viewer.

If you put a shortcut to your printer on your desktop, you can drag and drop a document to your printer.

Remember — the desktop is itself a folder and a subfolder of the \Windows folder. Its full pathname is C:\Windows\Desktop. You usually don't want to *move* files to the Desktop folder. Instead, you want to *create shortcuts* in the Desktop folder (or on the desktop).

Automatically start programs when Windows starts

You no doubt have some programs that you want to start when you start Windows — a launchpad to start programs with one click, perhaps?

You can put shortcuts to these programs into the Startup folder and leave the program where it is. This is very similar to the Startup Program Group in the Windows 3.x Program Manager.

Undocumented

Want to make sure that the programs start in the order that you want them to? It's easy.

Create a DOS batch file that is nothing but a series of calls to the programs you want to start, in the order that you want, preceded by the "start" command. For example:

```
start Winapp1.exe
start Winapp2.exe
start Winapp3.exe
```

Create a shortcut to this batch file in the Startup folder.

The Start button is full of shortcuts — add more

Like a hierarchical version of the Windows 3.x Program Manager, the Start button menus cascading across the desktop are filled with shortcuts. When you install a Windows 3.x application under Windows 95, it thinks it is creating a Program Group. In fact, it is creating a folder full of shortcuts to the application and its companion files.

Shortcuts in the Start button menus make it easy to get to applications. Click the Start button and follow the menus out to the shortcut to the application you want.

Tip

You can put a shortcut on the desktop (or in any folder) to a folder that holds the shortcuts to a set of documents or applications — shortcuts within a shortcut to a folder. Right-drag a folder from the Start Menu folder (in the Explorer, not from the Start button menu itself) to the desktop and drop it. Here are the steps:

STEPS

Putting a Start Button Menu on the Desktop

Step 1.   Right-click the Start button. Click either Open or Explore.

Step 2.   Double-click the Programs icon if you want a folder further down the hierarchy of Start button menus, for example, the Accessories folder.

Step 3. Right-drag a Start Menu folder to the desktop and click Create Shortcut(s) Here after you drop it.

You now have part of your Start menu on your desktop. You can add or remove menu items with ease just by dropping and dragging.

Single-click to your favorite applications

Want to have single-click access to your applications? Right-drag your most-used applications onto Russell Holcomb's Run launch bar (featured on the shareware CD-ROM that accompanies this book) and drop them there. Right-click a button on the launchpad and change the properties of the shortcut.

Move, copy, compress, print, and view files and folders easily

Put shortcuts to your Briefcase software, default file opener, Quick Viewer, printer, file compression program, or whatever into your Send To folder. Then, whenever you right-click a file or folder, you have the option of sending it to one of these destinations.

Send a file to the shortcut of your default file opener, and it gets opened. Send a file of unregistered type to the shortcut of the viewer, and the viewer does the best it can to display it.

We use the ability to send a file to WinZip (featured on the CD-ROM) all the time. Right-click a file, click Send To, click WinZip, enter the name of the compressed file to be created, and it's done.

The newest version of WinZip for Windows 95 (which you'll find on the included shareware CD-ROM) will add the Add To Zip and Extract To menu items to your right mouse-button menu. When you install WinZip, you are asked whether you want "Explorer Shell Extension." Clicking the check box next to this choice creates these menu items. If you make this choice, you won't need to put a shortcut to WinZip in your Send To folder.

Start DOS programs by double-clicking icons

Put a shortcut to DOS on your desktop. There's already one in your Start button menus, but it's that much closer if it is on the desktop (at least when the desktop isn't covered up).

You can create shortcuts for all your DOS programs. You can use icons from any icon library or from the files that come with Windows 95. DOS programs can be treated like Windows programs. Why not? Most DOS program run fine in a window, just like Windows programs.

Use a shortcut to do more than one thing at a time

Create a shortcut to a DOS batch file that calls a Windows program in addition to calling some DOS functions. This is a neat little way to do programming, as Microsoft does provide a Windows batch language. You can combine DOS and Windows programs in the batch file and they can all do more together. Here's an example that uses a couple of proprietary DOS utilities:

```
echo off
:: The next line switches COM2 from modem to port
c:\util\ams\encom
:: The next line runs the Direct Cable Connection
:: Start /w is used to suspend the batch file processing
start /w c:\Windows\Directcc.exe
:: This utility switches COM2 back to the internal modem
c:\util\ams\modem
```

The Start command is described in Chapter 17.

Modify how a Windows program operates

A shortcut allows you to combine the call to your Windows application with some of its command line parameters. The Windows Explorer shortcut on the Start, Programs menu is a good example of this (see Chapter 9).

If your program has the ability to take command line parameters, you can create different versions and different shortcuts to the same program. Who cares if it is just one program behind the scenes (behind the shortcut)? If it acts differently when you call it with one shortcut than with another shortcut, it might as well be a different program.

Use a different program to open a document

If you have a shortcut to a document, you can change the application that opens or acts on that document. The default shortcut just names the document and its path. Insert the name of the application that you want to act on the document into the definition of this shortcut (in the Target field) to override the file/application association found in the Registry.

The Shortcut Properties sheet for such a shortcut is displayed in Figure 10-2. Notice that the name of the application (and any command file parameter switches) precedes the name of the file.

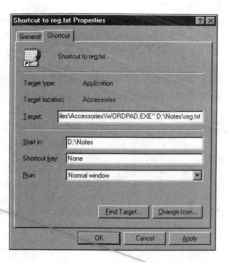

Figure 10-2: The Shortcut Properties sheet for a shortcut to a file ending in the *txt* extension. To override the Windows default file association of files ending in *txt* with Notepad, we have specified that the WordPad application open this file. The file is too big for Notepad.

Put shortcuts to parts of documents on the desktop

You can copy a paragraph from a document and paste a shortcut to it on the desktop. Just highlight the paragraph, click Copy, right-click the desktop, and click Paste Shortcut. The application that opens the document must be OLE-enabled.

The "scrap" on the desktop is how a piece of data or text can be inserted into another document. If you double-click it, the application that created it is invoked, and the scrap is displayed in the application's window.

Send shortcuts through (some of) the mail

You can paste a shortcut to a document into a message. Send the message over Microsoft Mail on your local area network. The recipient can open the document by clicking the shortcut icon if the document is stored in a shared folder or disk drive. All you had to send by mail was the shortcut, not the document. The e-mail post office wasn't bogged down by the document.

You can e-mail shortcuts to to other Microsoft Network users by sending shortcuts to Microsoft Network bulletin boards, chat areas, documents, and so on. Users can double-click the shortcut and go to the targeted area or document.

If both parties are using the Internet Explorer that comes with Micosoft Plus!, you can send an e-mail document over the Internet using the Internet e-mail client for Microsoft Exchange. The e-mail document can contain shortcuts to various Internet sites. The recipient can double-click the shortcuts in the e-mail message, thereby starting the Internet Explorer on their computer and directing the shortcut to the targeted site or document.

Creating Shortcuts

The whole point of shortcuts is to have them in convenient places. These places are the desktop, the Start button menus, the Send To folder, folders on the desktop, and within whatever folder window you regularly have open on the desktop. You can put shortcuts wherever you want, but then, what's the point of some of the possible locations?

Drag and drop to create a shortcut

Undocumented

Shortcuts are created automatically if you drag and drop a binary executable file to a new folder or the desktop. Executable files have *exe*, *com*, or *bat* extensions. However, *bat* files are a major exception to this rule. If you drag a *bat* file to the desktop, it is *moved*— a shortcut is *not* created. (Files that ended with the *pif* extension used to be executable files. They are now shortcuts.)

If you left-drag a binary executable file icon from a folder or Explorer window over another folder window or over the desktop, you will see the little black curved arrow in the lower left corner of the transparent file icon. This tells you that a shortcut will be formed if you release the left mouse button.

Undocumented

You can explicitly force the creation of a shortcut when you drag and drop an icon by holding down the Ctrl and Shift keys. You can also do this by dragging and dropping the icon. In both cases, you will get a right mouse button menu asking if you want to Move Here, Copy Here, Create Shortcut Here, or Cancel the operation. To explicitly create a shortcut with drag and drop, click Create Shortcut(s) Here from the right mouse button menu.

Name that shortcut

Tip

You can change the name of a shortcut. When you create a shortcut, its name is highlighted, giving you the chance to change it immediately. It is a good idea to change the name to something meaningful, rather than a short filename. Don't hold back; make the names work for you.

While the name of the shortcut is highlighted, press F2 to invoke the rename function. If the shortcut isn't highlighted, right-click the shortcut icon and then click Rename on the right mouse button menu.

Write in something useful, but something that doesn't fill up the desktop. Names are wrapped at the edge of the icon grid on the desktop. Single words are shortened with ellipses. Longer names are shortened in a folder windows details view.

Certain symbols can't be used in a shortcut name. They are as follows:

$$/ \setminus : * ? \text{".}< > |$$

Get rid of "Shortcut to"

Tip

Do you get tired of seeing "Shortcut to:" as the first part of your shortcut's name? You can teach Windows 95 to quit putting it on every shortcut that you create. To give Windows 95 the idea of how you want to do things, place one shortcut after another on your desktop. After you place each one, edit the name of the shortcut to remove "Shortcut to."

After seven or eight shortcuts, Windows 95 wises up and quits putting "Shortcut to" in the name of the newly created shortcut. From then on, your shortcuts should have shorter names.

Cut and Paste a shortcut

You can create a shortcut whose first location is the same folder as the application or document itself and then move it to the folder that you want. Right-click an icon in a folder window or Explorer and click Create Shortcut. A shortcut to the file that you right-clicked will appear.

You can then move the shortcut out of this folder to your desired destination by using Cut and Paste. This combined method avoids dragging and dropping. We describe Cut and Paste in Chapter 8.

New and Browse a shortcut

You can create a shortcut first and link it to an application or document second. To do this, take the following steps:

STEPS
Creating a New Shortcut

Step 1.   Right-click the desktop or the client area of a folder or Explorer window. Click New. Click Shortcut. The Create Shortcut dialog box, as shown in Figure 10-3, will be displayed on the desktop.

(continued)

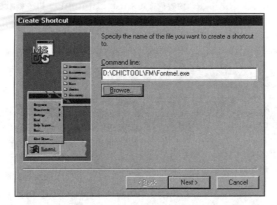

Figure 10-3: The Create Shortcut dialog box. You can type in the path and filename of the application, document, or file that you want to create a shortcut to, or you can click the Browse button to look for the file.

Step 2.   Type in the complete path and filename of the program, document, or file that you want to create the shortcut to. Click the Browse button if you would rather find the file instead of typing in the name.

Step 3.   Click the Next button. You can type in a new name for the shortcut or leave it the same name as the file that you linked to.

Step 4.   Click the Finish button.

Shortcuts on the Desktop

The desktop is like any other folder, except that it is always open on the desktop, so to speak. Drag an application icon from a folder or Explorer window and drop it on the desktop and you automatically create a shortcut.

Right-click the desktop, click New, and then Shortcut, and you are creating a shortcut on the desktop.

Tip

You can create folders on the desktop and put shortcuts in them. This a handy way to put a lot of stuff on the desktop without cluttering it up. To do this, right-click the desktop, click New and then Folder. You can change the folder name at any time.

The new folder is now a subfolder of the C:\Windows\Desktop folder. You can find the Desktop folder using the Explorer and looking in the Windows folder. Click the plus sign next to the Windows folder icon in the folder tree of the Explorer and you will see it (if you have configured the Explorer to show all files with View, Options).

Tip

You can drag and drop shortcuts to the new folder on your desktop. Double-click the new folder to open its folder window. Right-drag icons from another folder window focused on another folder and drop them on the new folder's window. Click Create Shortcut(s) Here.

Creating a Folder and a Shortcut to a Folder

Tip

You don't have to put a folder on the desktop. You can put a shortcut to a folder on the desktop and then put shortcuts in this folder. To do this, use the Explorer to find an appropriate location for a folder that will contain shortcuts. You might create an AllGames subfolder under your Games folder using the Explorer.

STEPS

Creating a Folder and a Shortcut to It

Step 1. Right-click the My Computer icon on the desktop. Click Explore.

Step 2. Expand the folder tree in the left pane of the Explorer window until you see the folder icon where you will place your new folder. Click this folder's name. Make sure that the folder name is highlighted and that its name is in the Explorer window's caption area.

Step 3. Right-click the client area of the Explorer window in the right pane. Click New and then Folder.

Step 4. A new folder icon appears in the right pane. Its name is highlighted. Type in an appropriate name for the folder and press Enter.

Step 5. Right-drag the folder icon to the desktop. Release the right mouse button and select Create Shortcut(s) Here from the menu.

You now have a shortcut to a folder on your desktop. You can double-click its icon on the desktop and the folder's window will be displayed. You can drag and drop icons to it to create shortcuts that will be stored within the folder.

Shortcuts to Folders, Disks, Computers, Printers, and On and On

You can have shortcuts to items other than files, documents, or applications. The following sections describe some suggested shortcut opportunities.

Folders

Let's say that you are working on documents you have placed in the C:\JonesAccount\BillsIssues folder. You can right-drag this folder from a folder window or the Explorer window onto the desktop. Double-clicking the shortcut to this folder provides you with a folder-window view of all the documents in this folder.

Disk drives

Tip

Right-drag a disk icon from the Explorer and drop it on the desktop. The right mouse button menu will let you choose only between Create Shortcut(s) Here or Cancel. This disk icon can be a mapped drive, so a shared resource (folder or drive) from another peer computer (or server computer) can be easily accessed.

Do you want to know the properties of a hard disk whose icon you have on your desktop? Right-click the icon, click Properties, click the Shortcut tab, click Find Target, right-click the target icon in the folder window, and click Properties.

Computers

You can put a shortcut to whole computers on the desktop (or anywhere you like). Right-click the My Computer icon on the desktop and click Create Shortcut. You've got yourself a shortcut on the desktop to something already on the desktop.

Undocumented

You can also do this with networked computers, even computers that you remotely dial into. Just right-drag them out of Network Neighborhood and onto the desktop (or another folder window). If you are dialing into the computer through remote access, you can put a shortcut to the computer on your desktop and initiate the call by double-clicking the computer's shortcut icon.

Printers

Right-drag a printer icon out of your Printers folder and drop it on the desktop. Click Create Shortcut(s) Here. Now you are ready to drag and drop files to the printer.

Control Panel icons

Open the Control Panel (Start, Settings, Control Panel). Right-drag one of the icons from the Control Panel to the desktop or a folder on the desktop, or to a shortcut to a folder on the desktop. Click Create Shortcut(s) Here. Now you have immediate access to whatever that icon does. Want to keep changing your mouse properties? You got it.

Undocumented

We would like to thank Mathias Koenig for his great investigative work in finding the following undocumented features.

Want to put a shortcut to the Device Manager on your desktop? Take the following steps:

STEPS

Creating a Shortcut to the Device Manager

Step 1. Right-click the desktop, click New, and then Shortcut.

Step 2. In the Command line field type

 C:\Windows\Control.exe Sysdm.cpl, System,1

 Click Next.

Step 3. Type **Device Manager** in the Name field. Click Finish.

Undocumented

How about a shortcut to one of the display properties sheets?

STEPS

Creating a Shortcut to the Display Control Panel

Step 1. Right-click the desktop, click New, and then Shortcut.

Step 2. In the Command line field type

 C:\Windows\Control.exe Sysdm.cpl, Display,3

 Click Next.

Step 3. Type **Display Settings** in the Name field. Click Finish.

The format of the above examples is

```
Control.exe {cpl filename}, {applet name}, {tab#}
```

You can find the cpl name of any of the Control Panel icons by searching (using Find as detailed in Chapter 11) for files with the *cpl* extension in the \Windows\System folder. The applet name you can find by looking in the Control Panel. Run any of the Control Panel icons to figure out the tab number, starting with 0 for the first one on the left.

HyperTerminal connections

Right-drag a connection icon out of the HyperTerminal folder (open it from Start, Programs, Accessories). Drop it on the desktop and click Create Shortcut(s) Here. Now when you want to call, double-click the connection's icon on the desktop.

Shortcuts to files far, far away

You can create a shortcut to a document that resides on a computer that you have to dial into with Dial-Up Networking. If you double-click the shortcut for the file, your modem dials the phone and makes the connection to the other computer. Once it gets into the other computer, the linked document is displayed on your desktop.

Mail out shortcuts

You can mail a shortcut by dragging and dropping it into an e-mail message. When the message is received, the recipient can access the file or folder that is linked to the shortcut by double-clicking the shortcut in the mail message. At this writing, this works with Microsoft Mail and with the Microsoft Network.

Paste shortcuts into documents

Microsoft has attempted to blur the line between the shell (the desktop or user interface) and the Windows applications that you use while in Windows 95. The fact that Cut and Paste are now part of the user interface is one example of this.

Another is the fact that shortcuts—which, for the most part—get placed in folders, can also be placed in documents and e-mail messages. You can right-click a shortcut in a folder, click Copy, right-click the client window area in WordPad or Word for Windows, and then click Paste, and the shortcut will be pasted in your document.

This may not do you much good since shortcuts in documents often aren't very useful. But they can be, especially if they are shortcuts to other documents.

You can give someone a document that contains shortcuts to other documents that are found on the Microsoft Network or on the Internet. With the document full of shortcuts, the recipient now has a dynamic document with access to the latest versions of all the included documents referenced by the shortcuts.

Double-click a shortcut in a document, and the appropriate actions will be taken to retrieve that document from wherever it is. Of course, you need to have the Internet Explorer from Microsoft Plus!, Microsoft Exchange, and/or Microsoft Network installed for this technique to work.

And on and on

Do the same for Direct Cable Connections, Dial-Up Networking, Phone Dialer—whatever you want or need on the desktop, in a folder, on the Start button menus, or wherever you want. The idea is to not hold back. Make your computer convenient for you. Put the shortcuts where they do the most good for you.

Don't hide your computer under a bush or an Explorer. Obviously the Explorer is well named, if you have to go exploring for the functionality that you want.

Right-Click to a Powerhouse

Secret

Placing shortcuts in the Send To folder can turn your right mouse button menu into a powerhouse. Send To is found on almost all right mouse button menus. And it doesn't really mean *send to*. It means *drop this file on this application or folder.*

However the recipient application or folder deals with drag and drop is how the application reacts when something is sent to it. You can modify the application's behavior using command line parameters. (See the section below entitled *The target.*)

Applications in the Send To menu are like commands on the right mouse button menu. You can do such things as send files to be compressed in the background, print files, view, or open files with a particular editor.

Tip

Use the Explorer to expand your folder tree and give you a view of the Send To folder under your Windows folder. To see how Send To works, drag and drop a printer icon from your Printers folder to the Send To folder to create a shortcut to the printer. When you right-click a file in a folder or Explorer window (or on the desktop) you can choose to send it to the printer using the Send To menu item.

You can place other items in the Send To folder: a shortcut to a folder on a server computer perhaps; a shortcut to an application that will be used to open files of unregistered types (see Chapter 13); a shortcut to the Quick Viewer (Quickview.exe in the \Windows\System\Viewer folder).

Undocumented

When you use Send To, it acts as though you used your left mouse button and dragged the file or folder that you right-clicked to the application, folder or object in the Send To list. For example, say you are sending (using Send To) a file to a folder. If the file is on the same disk drive (or volume) as the folder, then it gets moved. If it is on another disk drive, it gets copied.

Send To Send To

You can put a shortcut to the Send To folder in the Send To folder! Yes, that's right, although you'll go crazy trying to do this if you don't know the secret.

Why would you do this? If you want to browse for executables or folders that you would want in the Send To folder as targets, you can send them there easily by right-clicking them, clicking Sent To, and then Send To again. A message box appears telling you that you can copy of the executable, and it asks if you want to create a shortcut, which you do.

Undocumented

First of all, attempting to drag the Send To folder from the left Explorer pane into the Send To folder in the right pane doesn't work. All you get is Open and Cancel items on the context menu that appears — not Create Shortcut(s) Here, which is what you want.

The right way to do this is to right-drag the Send To folder to the Desktop and create a shortcut there first. Click the shortcut icon once, and then press F2 and change the icon's name to Send To Folder. You actually *do* want a shortcut to the Send To folder on your Desktop, in case you're ever browsing around your system and find a program you'd like to right-drag into the Send To folder.

You're not done yet, however. Right-click the Send To Folder icon you just created on your Desktop, and then click Copy on the context menu that appears. Navigate to the Send To folder in the Explorer so it is highlighted in the left pane and its contents are displayed in the right pane. Now right-click your mouse anywhere in the right pane where there is *no* other object. On the context menu that appears, click Paste. You've just copied-and-pasted a shortcut from the Desktop to the Send To folder.

Now browse through your whole system, looking for executable files that would be great targets for sending documents to. When you find one, right-drag it to the Send To icon on the Desktop, or right-click it and select Send To Send To Folder.

Create Shortcuts to DOS Programs

You can drag and drop a DOS application file to the desktop or to a folder window just as easily as you can a Windows executable file. A shortcut is created just by dropping it.

You'll probably want to make some changes to a DOS program's shortcut. You might want a different icon than the default MS-DOS icon that you get. You may need to change some other properties. All shortcuts have properties, which we'll get to shortly.

You can create a folder to store the shortcuts to your DOS programs or you can mix these DOS program shortcuts with your Windows shortcuts. It's up to you.

If you have DOS files, such as files that you edit with the DOS Edit program, you can create shortcuts to these and store them on the desktop or in a folder. The DOS programs and DOS files fit right in with the Windows programs and files, as long as they can be run in a Windows DOS session.

Tip You can run a mixture of DOS and Windows programs from a DOS batch file. Windows programs will run from the DOS prompt of a DOS virtual machine, so they can be combined with DOS functions.

You can call a DOS batch file with a shortcut and the batch file can contain lines that start Windows programs. If you include the following command in a batch file, you can have a DOS batch file run a Windows program and wait for you to quit the Windows program to continue processing the commands in the batch file:

```
Start /w {Windows program}
```

We discuss many of the aspects of running DOS programs in Chapter 17.

What's Behind the Shortcut?

Right-click a shortcut and click Properties. A Properties sheet similar to the one shown in Figure 10-4 will be displayed on your desktop.

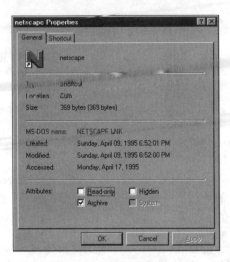

Figure 10-4: A shortcut's General Properties sheet. You can change the file attributes if you like.

A shortcut has two properties sheets: General and Shortcut. The filename of the shortcut (after all, it is a file) has a *lnk* extension. A shortcut is a link (or *lnk*) to another file. The only things you can change on the General Properties sheet are the file attributes of the shortcut file.

Click the Shortcut tab to display the Shortcut Properties sheet, as shown in Figure 10-5.

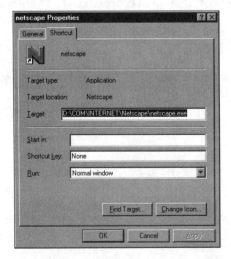

Figure 10-5: A shortcut's Shortcut Properties sheet. The Target field contains the name of the file linked to. It can be changed in numerous ways. The Change Icon button lets you change the shortcut's icon.

The target

The Target field in the Shortcut Properties sheet lists the file that is linked to the shortcut. This field can be modified in numerous ways. If the target file is an application that accepts command line parameters, you can include them after the application name.

Tip

The file in the Target field may be a document or data file that you want to view with an application other than the one assigned to this file's file type in the Registry. You can type the path and filename of the desired application in front of the file's path and filename. You can add command line parameters after the application's name to alter its behavior. For example:

```
C:\Windows\Wordpad.exe /p D:\Myfolder\Thisfile.txt.
```

With this entry in the Target field, the shortcut will print the file Thisfile.txt using WordPad.

Secret

The command line parameters won't work if you drag a file to a shortcut like the above on the desktop. This is also true if you place a shortcut like this in the Send To folder and then right-click a file and send it to the shortcut. Windows 95 acts asif the command line is as follows:

```
C:\Windows\WordPad.exe %1
```

In this command line, %1 is the name of the dragged or sent file. The /p parameter is ignored.

The Start in field

What is now labeled "Start in" used to be called the Working Directory in Windows 3.*x*. This field is blank unless you put something in it. You may need to do so if the application in the Target field needs to find some files in another folder and can't do so without help from you.

If you want, you can make the "Start in" folder the folder that contains the application or the folder that contains the document.

Hotkeys

A *shortcut* key, which we also refer to as a *hotkey,* is a keyboard key combination that runs a shortcut. For example, press Ctrl+Alt+F and up pops FreeCell. Well, not actually, but it could if you defined the hotkey for FreeCell. (If you're in WinWord, it opens the footnote window.)

Hotkeys or shortcut keys are also known as *accelerator keys*. They give you a keyboard method of quickly getting to those applications and files that you use most of the time. Their purpose is to cut down the amount of mousing required to do what you do most often.

The problem with hotkeys is that you have to remember which keyboard combination does what. (You also have to make sure you are not in a program that uses that hotkey for another function.) While a visual user interface gives you the feedback that you are headed in the right direction, a hotkey relies exclusively on your finger memory. But then, to each his or her own.

To define a hotkey, type the letter in the Shortcut field. Crtl+Alt will automatically be added to and precede the letter. The hotkey will then be defined as Ctrl+Alt+{*letter*}. If you want Ctrl+Shift+{*letter*}, then hold down the Ctrl key and the Shift key before you press the letter.

Hotkeys can also be defined for shortcuts to DOS programs. The hotkey field in a *pif* (the shortcut file to a DOS program) operates somewhat differently from a shortcut to a Windows file. See Chapter 17 for more details.

Hotkeys will work only for shortcuts that are on the Start button or in one of the Start menus. You can't have hotkeys to the shortcuts on the desktop, for example.

Want to create a hotkey to call the Task Manager? Why not create one that resembles the Windows 3.1 keystrokes that called it? How about Ctrl+Alt+~? (Ctrl+Alt+*tile*.)

Just define a shortcut to the Task Manager, which you'll find in the Windows folder, and put the shortcut in one of the Start menus. Define the hotkey for this shortcut and you're in business.

Run in which size window?

Most of the time you will want the shortcut to display the application or document in its normal or restored window, i.e. a window that is bigger than the icon on the Taskbar, but smaller than the whole desktop (minus the Taskbar). This field gives you the choice between these three alternatives.

If the shortcut just prints a document, for example, you might as well leave it minimized. If you want the application or document to take over the whole desktop, then make that choice.

Change the shortcut's icon

When you create a shortcut, the icon chosen by Windows 95 will be the first icon referenced in the application's executable file. Often this is adequate. If you have different shortcuts to the same application, though, you will want to distinguish them with different icons. You might pick from among the different icons that may be present in the application's executable file.

You can browse for icons after you click the Change Icon button. Icons can be found in many executable files. You can look in \Windows\Explorer.exe, \Windows\Moricons.dll, or \Windows\System\Shell32.dll for additional icons.

If your shortcut is to a document, then the first icon in the associated application's executable file is chosen. If the document doesn't have an associated application, then the blank document icon is chosen. Just how documents get associated with applications is discussed in Chapter 13.

Tip

Lots of icons are available to use with your shortcuts. You can pick icons from icon libraries available in shareware distribution, or icons from other executable files. The shareware on the CD-ROM that accompanies this book features Iconshow, which searches through all your files and automatically creates icon libraries. This cuts down on the search effort involved in picking a new icon.

Find that target

Tip

If you have a shortcut, you can get back to the file linked to the shortcut by clicking the Find Target button. This is helpful if you want to run the application without any of the command line switches you may have put in the Target field.

A window into the folder that contains the target is opened when you click the Find Target button. The folder is the folder that contains the application if an application is in the Target field, even if there is also a document in the Target field. If there is only a document filename in the Target field, the folder window opens the folder containing the document.

The Find Target button is another shortcut, i.e., a quick way to get to something stored in your computer.

DOS shortcut sheets

If the shortcut targets a DOS file (a file whose file type is associated with a DOS application) or a DOS application, you'll get a whole different set of shortcut Properties sheets than what we have described above. These sheets are so extensive and so interwoven with the workings of DOS programs under Windows 95 that we devote an entire chapter to them. Turn to Chapter 17 for further details.

Undocumented

The DOS Properties sheets are stored in files that used to be called Program Information Files, or *pif*s. The shortcuts that link to Windows files use the *lnk* extension. The shortcuts that link to DOS files use the *pif* extension. You can see these extensions if you use the File Manager or a DOS window. They aren't visible in the Explorer or in a folder window.

There is a folder named \Windows\Pif. This folder can contain the *pif*s that are associated with DOS programs. Anytime you double-click a DOS program name in the Explorer, a default *pif* is created for it in the same folder as the DOS program.

All *pif*s are shortcuts. You can open an Explorer window and focus on a folder that contains a *pif* to see that it has the little black arrow in the white box in the lower left corner of the MS-DOS icon.

If you create a shortcut to a DOS file or application on your desktop, the *pif* is stored in \Windows\Desktop.

Secret

Let's say that you create a shortcut to a Windows file or application. Later you decide to change this shortcut and have it link to a DOS batch file that calls your Windows application after running some other functions. What happens to your shortcut?

It's changed from a *lnk* file to a *pif*. Easy as can be.

This doesn't work the other way. You can't edit the Target field in a *pif* and have it now refer to a Windows file and have the *pif* change to a *lnk* file.

Shortcuts on the Start Button

We discuss how to put shortcuts on the Start button and in the Start button menus in Chapter 11.

A Shortcut to a Shortcut

Earlier in this chapter we showed how to make a shortcut to a folder that contained shortcuts. How about a shortcut to a shortcut?

Right-drag one of the shortcut icons that you have created from its source folder and drop it on the desktop. Click Create Shortcut(s) Here. Now, right-click the shortcut on the desktop and click Properties. If this is a DOS link, or *pif,* you'll need to click the Program tab and look at the Cmd field to see the equivalent of the Target field used for shortcuts to Windows files. If it is a Windows file shortcut, click the Shortcut tab, and look at the Target field.

Notice that the name in the Cmd or Target field is not the name of the shortcut in the source folder, but rather the name of the file that the original shortcut was linked to. A shortcut to a shortcut links to the original target file. A shortcut to a shortcut isn't, but is rather a shortcut to the original file.

Try this out. Place a shortcut to a folder in the folder.

STEPS

Creating a Shortcut to a Folder in that Folder

Step 1. Open a folder window (double-click My Computer) and make its focus some temporary folder or whatever you like, nothing special.

Step 2. Right-click the client area. Click New and then Folder and give the folder a new name.

Step 3. Double-click the new folder icon.

Step 4.   Right-click the client area in the new folder window, click New, and then Shortcut.

Step 5.   Click the Browse button, then browse to the path of the new folder and click Next.

Step 6.   Give the shortcut a new name and click Finish.

You now have a shortcut to the folder stored in the folder itself. Double-click it and see what happens. Try it with the Explorer.

What Happens if I Move or Delete the Linked File?

Shortcuts are linked to a specific item — a file, a folder, and so on. What happens if you move or delete that item when you double-click the shortcut?

If you moved the item, Windows 95 goes to work to find it the next time you open its shortcut. It searches for the file. While it does this, a search box, as shown in Figure 10-6, appears on your desktop.

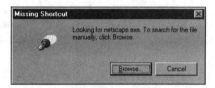

Figure 10-6: The Missing Shortcut search box. If you know where you moved it to, you can help out by clicking the Browse button.

When a shortcut is created it stores the creation time and date of the linked file or folder down to a fraction of a second. It is extremely unlikely that any two files or folders would be created at the same date and time to this level of precision.

Using a built-in function, Windows 95 begins searching for the lost file, folder, or object starting at its original location. You may have edited the file or changed its name — Windows 95 doesn't care, because it is searching on the file or folder's creation time/date that is stored in the shortcut file.

The search method is not foolproof. If you move the target object (say a linked file) from one volume (say the D drive) to another volume (say the C drive), it won't find it. If your shortcut is to a file on a mapped networked drive and not to a file using the universal naming convention, and that mapping of that drive changes (say from D to F), the link to the target is lost.

If the file or folder is deleted, then, of course, when Windows 95 searches for it, it won't find it. As it's looking, it does keep track of the file or folder that is nearest in time/date to the actual linked item. If it can't find what it is looking for, it gives you the option of choosing the item closest in time, which can provide some weird "matches." You may decline.

Shortcuts in the Help Files

The Windows 95 help files are filled with shortcuts that take you to the item that you had a question about. Of course, you may already be there.

The shortcut icon in the help file is a little like the black arrow used to indicate that an icon on the desktop or in a folder window is a shortcut icon. It is a purple arrow pointing to the upper left corner instead of a black arrow pointing to the upper right corner.

Click the shortcut arrows in the help files to take the action that is explained in the sentence surrounding the arrow icon.

Creating Application-Specific Paths

If you start an application from a shortcut, you may find that it won't work because you haven't correctly identified the location to necessary accessory files in the Start In or Working directory (see Chapter 17). You might also want to be able to start an application by clicking the Start button, then Run, and typing in the application's name. You'll have to type in the path to the application's executable file also, unless you specify that complete path to the application in the Registry.

Secret

By editing the Registry, you can associate a set of folders that house the accessory files that are necessary to allow an application to work correctly. In addition, you can specify the complete path name to the application. Michael Giroux, a Windows 95 beta tester, gave us the basis for these steps:

STEPS:

Specifying Paths to Applications in the Registry

Step 1. Double-click Regedit.exe in your \Windows folder.

Step 2. Click the plus signs in the left pane of the Registry to drill down to the following branch:

```
Hkey_Local_Machine\SOFTWARE\Microsoft\Windows
    \CurrentVersion\AppPaths
```

Step 3. Right-click the AppPaths icon in the left pane, click New, then Key. A new key folder will appear in the left pane of the Registry editor. Type in the name of the executable file, including the *exe* extension.

Step 4. Double-click "Default" in the right-pane while the new folder is highlighted in the left pane. Type in the full path name to the executable file in the Edit String dialog box. Click OK.

Step 5. You will now be able to type in the name of the executable file in the Run dialog box and have the application actually run.

Step 6. Define the path to the executable file's associated files by right-clicking the right pane of the Registry editor while the focus is on the new folder.

Step 7. Click New, then New String. Enter the name **Path** in the highlighted name field in the right pane.

Step 8. Double-click "Path" in the right pane. Enter the complete path to the folders that contain the associated files in the Edit String dialog box. If there is more than one folder, separate the path names with semicolons. Click OK.

Step 9. If you have any trouble with these steps, look at the other examples under the AppPaths folder.

The paths that you entered in Step 8 will be added temporarily to your Path statement when you invoke the executable file whether by double-clicking a shortcut to it, or in the Run dialog box, or in the Explorer.

Summary

Windows lets you put links to your applications and files on your desktop, and anywhere you find useful. Shortcuts are an incredibly powerful means of opening up your computer to ease of use.

▶ We show you how to use the power of shortcuts to display your most important applications and documents in areas that they are easy to get to.

▶ We guide you through the many ways of creating shortcuts.

▶ We show you how you can drag and drop files to a desktop file viewer, a desktop printer, or a default file opener.

▶ We show you how to start your most-used applications with one mouse click.

▶ DOS and Windows applications can get along much better under Windows 95 and you can make them even appear to like each other.

▶ If you add application-specific paths to your Registry, you can run applications from the Run dialog box without specifying their paths.

Chapter 11

The Start Button and Finding

In This Chapter

The Start button can be molded to meet your need for a convenient way to get at your applications. We discuss:

▶ Shutting down Windows 95

▶ Optimizing your Start and Programs menus

▶ Deleting unwanted shortcuts to recent documents from your Documents menu

▶ Adding and removing items from your Start button menus

▶ Putting the desktop on the Start button

▶ Running the Start button menus from the keyboard

▶ Creating and saving complex file searches

▶ Using Find to build Start button menus and get rid of unwanted files

Starting

In Chapter 7, we looked at the desktop and the Taskbar. The Start button is attached to the Taskbar. There is a lot going on with the Start button, which is why it gets its own chapter. First, it is the primary entry point into Windows 95. As you change your desktop to match your needs, the Start button continues to provide many useful services.

The Start button is the Windows 95 replacement for the Windows 3.x Program Manager. Like the Program Manager, the Start button gives you a way to quit Windows.

You can also think of the desktop as the Program Manager. You can fill it up with shortcuts. You can put shortcuts to folders on the desktop and fill the folders with shortcuts. These folders then look like Program Groups. But it is the Start button that inherits all the Program Groups and Program Items when you convert your existing Windows 3.x to Windows 95.

Stopping

We start our discussion of the Start button by talking about the Stop button. The most important function you can find on a computer is how to stop it, how to get it ultimately under your control so that if you have any problems you can just stop the whole thing.

Click the Start button. Click Shut Down and select the first menu item, Shut down the computer. We're outta here. We know it seems funny that the Start button is also the Stop button, but there it is.

Clicking Shut Down presents you with the dialog box shown in Figure 11-1. This dialog box gives you four choices. The default is Shut down the computer. You can also choose to Restart the computer, Restart the computer in MS-DOS mode, or Close all programs and log on as a different user.

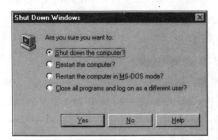

Figure 11-1: The Shut Down Windows dialog box. Make one of four choices.

Shut down the computer

Shut down the computer actually means to shut down Windows 95. You have to turn off the computer yourself.

After the Shut Down dialog box is displayed, you click the OK button. It is best to wait for the screen that displays the message "It is OK to turn off the computer" before you power down with a switch on the computer. If you turn off the power before this, the Registry files may not have been updated with the latest configuration information.

Undocumented

The Windows 95 shut-down screens are Windows bitmap (*bmp*) files. Microsoft gave them *sys* extensions just to keep your prying eyes out of them. If you want to change them, you can by using MS Paint to edit them. Their names: Logos.sys and Logow.sys. You'll find them in the \Windows folder.

Undocumented

After you quit Windows 95, you are back under the control of Io.sys. If you had pressed the F8 key when the Starting Windows 95... message appeared on your screen and started Windows 95 by typing **Win** and pressing the Enter key at the DOS command prompt, you would now be able to get back to real-mode DOS (that is get to the DOS command prompt) by typing **mode co80** and pressing the Enter key while the screen saying "it's OK to turn off your computer" is showing. See additional discussion of this in Chapter 6.

There is a better way to get to real-mode MS-DOS, but this method illustrates that DOS is still there after you quit Windows 95. We don't suggest that you start Windows 95 in this manner, as it is less effective in managing conventional memory. For example, the real-mode compression driver Dblspace.bin is not unloaded to be replaced by the protected-mode double-space driver if you start Windows 95 this way.

Restart the computer

If you have had a problem with Windows 95 and just want to start over again, you can choose Restart the computer. This works the same way as Shut down the computer but doesn't require that you press Ctrl+Alt+Del to restart Windows 95. It also doesn't tell you when you can safely turn off your computer.

Windows 95 saves all its desktop configuration (open folders, for example) and then quits. As soon as it quits, it restarts with a warm reboot.

Restart the computer in MS-DOS mode

Choosing to Restart the computer in MS-DOS mode means closing down Windows 95 and going to the DOS command prompt. Your computer isn't rebooted (not even a warm boot), so when DOS starts, it doesn't read a special Config.sys or Autoexec.bat file. The file DOSstart.bat, found in your \Windows folder, is read at startup. You can get out of MS-DOS mode and back to Windows95 by typing **Exit** or **Win** at the DOS prompt.

To get the full details on how to use this option to run recalcitrant DOS programs turn to the *DOS in MS-DOS mode without a reboot* section of Chapter 17.

Log on as a different user

The option to Close all programs and log on as a different user doesn't even appear if you don't have a network, never installed or used Direct Cable Connection, haven't installed Dial-Up Networking, or haven't enabled user profiles. If you have done any of these things, you will see it.

"Close all programs and log on as a different user" is the same as "Restart the computer" but lets you log on as a different user. Windows 95 keeps track of different users so you can have different desktop and network setups for each. This allows you to get out of the current user's setup and into a new user's configuration. Turn to Chapter 12 for more details.

Click Here to Begin, boing...

Secret

When you first start Windows 95, you get a bouncing message in the Taskbar: "Click here to begin." We haven't seen this message in a while on our computers. The message goes away if you have applications in your Startup folder (or referenced in the Run or Load line in your Win.ini), you left folders open when you last shut down, or there are applications (like the System Agent) in the Notification area on your Taskbar.

If you would like to see this little pest come back, you need to be sure that none of the above conditions are true. In addition, Windows 95 beta tester John Bode tells us to take the following steps:

STEPS

Bring back "Click here to begin"

Step 1.   With no active tasks minimized or running (that is, you want an empty Taskbar), press Ctrl+Alt+Del. Highlight Explorer and click End Task.

Step 2.   Answer No when asked if you want to shut down Windows 95.

Step 3.   In about 15-20 seconds, a dialog box will appear that says the Explorer is not responding. Click End task.

Step 4.   The Taskbar will now run the "Click here to begin" animation. No need to restart Windows 95.

The Start Button Menu

Click the Start button and up pops the Start button menu, as shown in Figure 11-2. This is the first of the cascading menus. The nice thing about the Start button is that it is a starting point. There never was much of a starting focus with the Windows 3.x Program Manager.

Figure 11-2: The Start button menu. Your window into the world of Windows 95.

What is not so great about the Start button is that it takes a lot of mousing to get to where you want to be. Following the cascading menus to get to the application or document that you want can get pretty tedious. Turn to the *Change Menu Display Speed* section later in this chapter for details on how to make menus appear more quickly.

One way to cut down on the extra mousing is to drag an application icon from a folder, the desktop, or an Explorer window and drop it on the Start button. A shortcut is created when you drop an icon for an application, folder, or document on the Start button. This shortcut is immediately available right after you click the Start button. We discuss Start button menu shortcuts in more detail later in this chapter.

The Start button menu has six items. The Programs menu at the top gets you to most of your applications. Next, Documents is a list of the last 15 files that you double-clicked in an Explorer or a folder window. Settings gets you right to the Control Panel, Printers folder, or Taskbar, areas where you can update many Windows 95 properties. Find lets you search your computer, your LAN, or the Microsoft Network (MSN) for files or services that meet criteria you define. Help is a combined help for all of Windows 95. Run lets you type in the name of an application that you want to run or document that you want to work on (its associated application will load along with it).

Programs

Notice the Programs icon. It is expressing the Programs menu's role. The Programs menu acts like a folder window. It is a folder that contains applications. Windows 95 comes with a default setup of applications and accessory programs that get installed in the Programs folder/menu. If you installed Windows 95 in your existing Windows 3.*x* directory, all your previous Program Manager groups are converted to folders and placed in the Programs folder.

You don't have to put just applications in the Programs folder/menu. You can organize it any way you want. You can put documents in the Programs menu just as you could with the Programs Groups in the Windows 3.*x* Program Manager.

Unlike the Program Manager, which had only one level, you can have as many subfolders of the Programs folder/menu as is practical, and they can each have subfolders. Of course, the cascading menus can get pretty complicated after a while.

Everything in the Programs folder can be moved around and organized in whatever manner you desire. It can be flat or hierarchical. The names associated with the icons can be anything you want. Using tools built into the Start button, it is quite easy to change any of this around.

If you set up Windows 95 in a new folder, the Programs menu has three submenus and between two and five applications on its menu. Additional submenus are present if you set up Windows 95 over your existing Windows 3.x directory.

To get to an application, click the Start button, move the cursor over the Programs icon, and follow the cascading menu until you get to the application that you want to run. Click the application once to run it.

Can't find your application? We'll show you how in the *What you can do with Find* section later in this chapter.

Accessories menu

The Accessories menu under the Programs menu contains many of the applications that come with Windows 95. You can use this menu to quickly familiarize yourself with the applications that come with Windows 95.

The Startup menu

If you have applications that you want to start when Windows 95 starts, you will need to put shortcuts to them in this menu/folder. You can later close a program that started when Windows started. If you decide that you want to start it again, go to this menu item and click it.

We show you how to put shortcuts in the Startup folder/menu later in this chapter.

Documents

The last 15 documents that you started by double-clicking in an Explorer or folder window will be displayed in this menu. You can restart a document and its associated application by clicking it once in this menu.

To get on this list, the documents have to be started from an Explorer or My Computer folder window. That way, Windows 95 can grab document name. If you open a document from inside your application, Windows 95 doesn't necessarily know how to put it on this list. Applications written specifically for Windows 95 will have the capability of placing their newly opened document on this list.

The list is a list of shortcuts to the documents. You can delete all the shortcuts at once. Right-click the Taskbar. Click Properties. Click Start Menu Programs. Click Clear. All the shortcuts in the Documents menu are gone and it is empty.

Undocumented

You can also remove shortcuts individually.

STEPS

Cleaning Up the Documents Menu

Step 1. Open an Explorer window.

Step 2. Click the plus sign next to the \Windows folder. Highlight the Recent subfolder under the \Windows folder.

Step 3. The shortcuts to the documents will be in the right pane. You can delete them in any manner you choose.

As you can see, the shortcuts to the recently opened documents are kept in the \Windows\Recent folder. You can edit these shortcuts or delete them as you like. You need to be sure that Show all files is checked under the View Options menu found in any folder or Explorer window. Otherwise, the Recent folder won't be found.

Put a shortcut to your recent documents folder on the desktop

Tip

If you want to be able to quickly edit the contents of your recent documents folder, put a shortcut to it on the desktop. Open the Explorer and focus on the \Windows\Recent folder. Right-drag the Recent folder to the desktop and drop it there. Click Create Shortcut(s) Here. Edit the name of the shortcut folder icon to **Recent Docs** or whatever.

Now you can quickly get to the folder of recent documents and remove the documents that you don't care to have there.

Settings

Settings gets you down deep into Windows 95 if you follow it very far. It contains the Control Panel, Printers folder, and the Taskbar Properties sheets.

The Control Panel

Click the Control Panel menu item to bring up the Control Panel. You'll find lots of applications for configuring your computer and Windows 95.

Tip

The Control panel is a special folder. It is hidden and you won't find it by using the Explorer to see which hard disk folder it is a subfolder of. You will see it in the Explorer in the left pane on the same level as the local hard disks and the Printers folder, Fonts folder, and Dial-Up Networking folder. We discuss the Control Panel in Chapter 16.

The Printers folder

You find all your currently installed printers in the Printers folder. You also will find an icon in this folder that lets you add new printers. The Printers folder is also found in the Control Panel. The Printers folder is a special folder. In the Explorer, you'll find it only in the left pane.

We cover the Printers folder in Chapter 23.

The Taskbar Properties sheets

Clicking the Taskbar item in the Settings menu brings up the Taskbar Properties sheets. This is the same as right-clicking the Taskbar and choosing Properties. The first Properties sheet is the Taskbar Options sheet.

We detail the Taskbar check boxes found in the Taskbar Option Properties sheet in Chapter 7. The Show small icons in Start menu check box lets you change how the Start button menu looks. Check and uncheck this box to see which look you favor.

The Start Menu Programs Properties sheet is where you will find much of the power to add, remove, and move menu items (which are just shortcuts) in the various Start menus. This Properties sheet is shown in Figure 11-3.

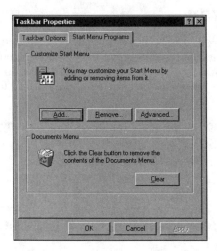

Figure 11-3: The Start Menu Programs Properties sheet.

Add Start menu items

Click the Add button from the Start Menu Properties sheet and you are presented with a Wizard, as shown in Figure 11-4, that will help you add a shortcut to a file in a menu. You can also create new menus (after you have chosen an item to add to a menu). You can place the shortcut in any menu, or create a new menu within which to place the item.

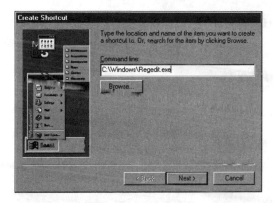

Figure 11-4: The Create Shortcut Wizard. You can browse to find the application file that you want to place as a menu item. You get to choose, in the next Wizard dialog box, where to put the items, or whether to create a new menu and then perhaps place the item there. You choose a name for the shortcut /menu item in the third Wizard dialog box.

You can add items to the Start button menu, to the Programs menu, or to submenus of the Programs menu. If you add a shortcut to a folder in the Start button menu (perhaps a shortcut to the desktop), you can place shortcuts in this folder. You can add shortcuts in the Startup menu to programs that you want to start when Windows 95 starts.

Menu items, which are after all shortcuts, don't display the little black arrow in the lower left corner of their icons. We normally associate this black arrow with a shortcut. Since all menu items are shortcuts, the Microsoft designers felt that there was no need to add the arrow to icons when they are displayed in menus. The menus themselves are not shortcuts, but rather folders.

Remove Start menu items

The Remove button from the Start menu Properties sheet lets you remove menu items or entire menus. Be careful — these removals aren't stored in the Recycle Bin for you to put back in place. The Remove dialog box, as shown in Figure 11-5, lets you navigate among the menus/folder to find the items (or folders) that you wish to remove.

Figure 11-5: The Remove Shortcuts/Folders dialog box. You can highlight the menu item or menu/folder that you want to remove. If you remove a menu/folder you also remove (delete) all the shortcuts in that menu.

Edit, move, add, delete Start menu items — the Advanced button

The full power to edit the menus is unveiled when you click the Advanced button from the Start Menu Properties sheet. You get a version of the Explorer that includes only the Start menu. This clipped Explorer works like any other Explorer window. (The Start Menu folder is set as the root — see Chapter 9 for how this is accomplished.)

You get all the capability you need to move menus from node to node. You can right-drag menu items from another Explorer window and drop them in any menu/folder that you like. You can create new folder/menus in the Start menu or in any submenu/folder.

The Start Menu Explorer, as shown in Figure 11-6, demonstrates very clearly that the Start button menu is a series of folders— special folders, but folders nonetheless. You can manipulate them as you would any other folders.

The menu folders are meant to hold shortcuts. It is best to right-drag an application icon from another Explorer window to the Start Menu Explorer, drop it in the menu/folder that you want, and choose Create Shortcut(s) Here. You will want to edit out the "Shortcut to". . . part.

You can copy or move application icons (and document or folder icons) to the menu folders if you wish, but that really isn't the idea with these menus/folders. Better to just put shortcuts to applications in them.

You'll have to edit the "Shortcut to. . ." out of the application name if you use the Advanced button. You don't have to do this when you use the Add button.

The Start Menu Explorer is especially useful for moving menus about. This is not possible using the Add and Remove buttons.

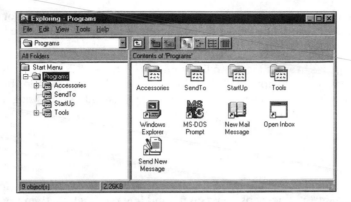

Figure 11-6: The Start Menu Explorer. If you highlight a folder icon name in the left pane, the contents of that folder/menu appear in the right pane.

Find

For a detailed discussion of the Find capabilities, see the section later in this chapter entitled *Find*.

Help

The Start menu Help command gets you to the unified help for all of Windows 95. Click Help and you get the Windows Help window, as shown in Figure 11-7.

Figure 11-7: The Windows 95 Help Contents window. Open any of the book icons by double-clicking it (or highlighting it and clicking the Open button).

Since Windows 95 help is a unified help, you don't have to search a lot of separate help files to find out quite a bit about Windows 95. Click the Find tab to build a complete word index to the help file.

Other help files are connected to the unified Windows 95 help. You access them from their associated applications. Windows help files are found in the \Windows\Help folder, as well as the \Windows, \Windows\System, and \Windows\Command folders.

Run

This is a command line interface. If you want to run a program by typing in its path and name and perhaps some command line parameters, then this is the place for you. This is like calling a program from the DOS command line, especially now that you can run Windows programs from the DOS command line.

The Run box keeps a little history. You can bring up previous commands, edit them, and run them again. The Run Application dialog box is shown in Figure 11-8.

Figure 11-8: The Run Application dialog box. Type in the path and filename of your DOS or Windows application or document. Put in some command line parameters, if you like.

You can type in the name of a document that has an associated application that will open it (as defined in the Registry) and run it. For example, you can type in the name and path of an *ini* file. When you click the OK button, NotePad is invoked and it displays the *ini* file in its client window area.

Right-Click the Start Button

You can right-click the Start button and choose Open, Explore, or Find. Choose Open to display a Start Menu folder window on the desktop. This is a regular folder window focused on the Start Menu folder, a subfolder of the Windows folder.

The Programs folder is a subfolder of the Start Menu folder. Double-click the Programs folder and you open the Programs folder window. The Programs folder's icon is the same icon that you saw next to it in the Start button menu. Folders within the Programs folder use this same icon.

The Programs folder contains the Accessories folder, the Startup folder, and other folders and applications. You can continue opening folder windows by double-clicking these icons.

What you are doing is duplicating, in a folder window fashion, what the Start button menu gives you in cascading menus. Each of the cascading menus is a folder, and within the menus are more menus and therefore more folders.

The Start Menu folder gives you a way of traversing the menus using folders, a different style for those who may wish to use it.

Of course, as the Start menu is also a folder, it is possible to move or drag shortcuts into it and its subfolders.

You can open other folder windows from the Start Menu folder window and navigate back up the parent folders.

Click Explore to bring up a full Explorer window focused on the Start Menu folder. Unlike the Advanced button in the Taskbar Start menu programs Properties sheet, this is a full Explorer. The folder tree in the left pane will take you anywhere you want to go.

The Find command will open up the Find: All Files dialog box. We describe this in the *Find* section later in this chapter.

The Programs Menu/Folder

Secret

Try dragging the Programs folder out of the Start Menu folder and onto the desktop. This will give you another way of knowing that the Start Menu folder is a special folder. You can move the Programs folder onto the desktop using the Explorer window you found when you right-clicked the Start button.

The Programs folder will contain all of the subfolder/menus that it had when it was attached to the Start Menu folder. The Programs folder icon will change to a folder icon, not a folder icon with a window. All the menu items/shortcuts will still be in their proper folders.

The menus will still be attached to the Programs menu item on the Start button menu. All the menus and menu items are still there and functional. The Programs folder and the Programs menu are separate but connected items, as long as the Programs folder is stored within the Start Menu folder.

If you now try to add a menu item using the Add button in the Start Menu Programs Properties sheet, the shortcut will be added to the Programs folder on the desktop, but not to the Programs menu.

We suggest that you leave the Programs folder and its subfolders in the Start Menu folder.

A much better idea is to just place a *shortcut* to the Programs folder on the desktop.

The Start Menu Folder

Secret

You can move the Start Menu folder, \Windows\Start Menu, if you like, and it will maintain its relationship with the Start button menu. This is unlike the Programs folder. Add a menu item using the Add button, and you will find it in the correct subfolder of the Start Menu folder and in the correct menu in the Start button menus.

You can try to delete the Start Menu folder, but you will be asked to designate another folder as the Start Menu folder. If you don't, you won't be allowed to delete it. This is one way of creating a new Start Menu folder and putting in the shortcuts and menus that you want.

You can rename the Start Menu folder, but it keeps the same function.

Secret

The name of the Start Menu folder is stored in the Registry. If you wish to designate another folder as the Start Menu folder, you can change the name of the Start Menu in the following branch of the registry using the Registry editor:

```
Hkey_Current_User\Software\Microsoft\Windows\CurrentVersion\Explorer\Shell  Folders
```

You'll want to turn to Chapter 15 to see how to use the Registry editor. You'll need to restart Windows 95 to have this change take effect.

Drop It on the Start Button

There is an easy way to add menu items to the Start menu. Drag and drop icons from the desktop or from a folder or Explorer window to the Start button. This works only if you have specified Auto Hide Off in the Taskbar Properties sheet.

Shortcuts to the dragged icons are automatically added to the Start button menu. They appear when you click the Start button and are right above the Programs menu item. They have their own little section, as shown in Figure 11-9.

Figure 11-9: The Start button with additional shortcuts. Notice that, as per other menu items, these shortcuts don't have the little black arrow in the lower left hand corner.

These menu items are shortcuts just like the other menu items. The nice thing about them is that the icons are full size so you can see what is going on. These shortcuts appear in the Start Menu folder along with the Programs folder.

The shortcuts dropped on the Start button will order themselves alphabetically.

Tip

The Desktop on the Start Button Menu

A neat trick is to put the desktop itself on your Start button. Since the desktop is also a folder, you can drag it from the Explorer onto the Start button. You will find the Desktop folder under the \Windows folder.

Undocumented

The Desktop folder will, of course, open up to a folder window once you click its icon in the Start menu. You have a Desktop folder window on the desktop. This can come in very handy if the icons on your desktop are covered with other windows. You just put a window to your desktop over them.

This also comes in handy when you use the keyboard to get to the Start button. Press Ctrl+Esc to get to the Start button from anywhere — even full-screen DOS sessions. The Start button comes up, and you can use your arrow keys to get to the Desktop icon. This gives you a quick way to switch to an inactive application if it has a shortcut on the desktop.

In Chapter 8, we show you how to put the desktop on the Taskbar. That way you can get to it with Alt+Tab. This is another way to get to the desktop with another set of keystrokes. The Desktop folder on the Start button will not contain My Computer, Network Neighborhood, or Recycle Bin — but the desktop on the Taskbar does.

Folders in the Start Menu Folder

If you create a folder in the Start Menu folder using the Add button described above, its folder icon comes with folder window icon. The Start Menu folder is a special folder that adds a folder window-like icon to the folder icon of the folder stored within the Start Menu folder. Enough folders there for you?

If the Programs folder is moved from the Start Menu folder, it and all its subfolders revert to their folder icons. Adding further shortcuts to them won't place those shortcuts in the menus.

Control Panel on a Start button menu

You normally get to the Control Panel by clicking the Start button, then Settings, and finally Control Panel. The Control Panel is displayed in a folder window. It is possible to make the Control Panel a menu item in any of the Start menus, and to display it as a menu and not necessarily a folder window. To do so, take the following steps:

Secret

STEPS

The Control Panel as a Menu

Step 1.   Right-click the Start button; click Open. If you want to place the Control Panel on the topmost Start menu, stop here. Otherwise, continue to open up folder windows of menu items until you get to the menu item/folder that you want to contain the Control Panel.

Step 2.   Right-click an open area in the client area of the Start menu's folder window. Click New in the right mouse button menu, then Folder.

Step 3.   The temporary name of the New Folder is highlighted, and you can now type in a new name. Type in the following text exactly as we have printed it here:

```
Control Panel.{21EC2020-3AEA-1069-A2DD-08002B30309D}
```

Step 4.   Press Enter and the New Folder icon is replaced with the Control Panel Icon.

Step 5.   Click the Start button; the Control Panel icon and all the Control Panel icons will appear in a menu.

The long identifier given in Step 3 is unique to the Control Panel. You can find it by using your Registry editor and searching for Control Panel.

You can do the same trick for the Printers and/or the Dial-Up Networking folder. The unique identifiers for these folders are as follows:

Dial Up Network   Dial Up Net.{992CFFA0-F557-101A-88EC-00DD010CCC48}

Printers   Printers.{2227A280-3AEA-1069-A2DE-08002B30309D}

Use these identifiers in Step 3 above to put these folders on the Start menu.

Keyboard Control of the Start Menus

You can run the Start button menus with your keyboard. The most important keyboard combination is Ctrl+Esc, which gets you to the Start button.

If you have defined hotkeys for the shortcuts on the Start button menus, you can start the application immediately without going through the Start button, just by pressing its hotkey combination. We describe how to create hotkeys in Chapters 10 and 17.

Once you press Ctrl+Esc to get to the Start button, you can use your arrow keys, letter keys, and Tab key to navigate. The down arrow key will take you down the Start menu. You can move down until you find the menu item that you want. If it is an application, pressing Enter activates it.

Menu items on the Start menu can be reached by pressing a letter key that corresponds to the underlined letter in their name. If you have added items to the Start button with the same letter, the letter key will take you to them first. The letter keys operate in round-robin fashion, going to the first item that starts with that letter, then the next until it starts over at the top again.

The letter keys work in all the submenus also. There is no designated letter in the shortcut names under the Programs menu, so the first letter is always used.

The arrow keys can also move you through the menus. The up and down arrow keys move you within a given menu. When you get to the bottom, you go back to the top. The right and left arrow keys move you forward and back between the cascading menus. When you reach a menu item that you want to run, press Enter.

Undocumented

If you press Ctrl+Esc and then Esc, the Start button menu will disappear, but your focus will still be on the Start button. You can confirm this for yourself   by pressing Enter after Ctrl+Esc and then Esc. The Start button menu will reappear.

You can change the focus between the Start button, the Taskbar, and the desktop by using the Tab key. Pressing Tab once changes the focus to the Taskbar. Pressing it again focuses on the desktop, and pressing it once again focuses back on the Start button.

If your focus is on the Taskbar you can use the arrow keys to move the focus from button to button. Move the focus to a button of an application that you want to restore or move to the top of the windows on the desktop, and press Enter.

If your focus is on the desktop, particularly on an icon on the desktop, then you can use your arrow keys to move among the desktop icons to focus on the one application or folder you want to open. Press Enter when you are so focused.

It's hard to see visually whether the focus is on the Start button, Taskbar, or desktop. Using the Windows 95 default color scheme makes this identification even more difficult. If the Start button has the focus, you'll see the typical dotted rectangle around the word Start. If the Taskbar or the Start button has the focus, and your color scheme has an Active Window Border color that is different from the 3D Object color (something that is not true for the default Windows color scheme), you will see a border line around the Taskbar. If the desktop has the focus, the Taskbar border will display the Inactive Window Border color, and an icon on the desktop will be highlighted. See Chapter 22 for details on how to change these colors.

Change Menu Display Speed

If you position your mouse pointer over one of the menu items on the Start button menu, you'll notice that after a short delay the menu appears. If instead you click the menu item, the associated menu appears immediately.

You can set the length of the time interval before the menu appears. You can make it appear instantaneously or make it so long that the menus don't pop up until you click the menu item. The current default value for the time delay is 1/4 of a second or 250 milliseconds. To change this value, take the following steps:

STEPS

Change the Menu Display Speed

Step 1.   Double-click Regedit.exe in an Explorer window focused on your \Windows folder.

Step 2.   Click the plus sign next to Hkey_Current_User, and then Control Panel. Highlight Desktop under Control Panel.

Step 3.   Right-click in a clear area in the right pane of the Registry editor window; click New and then String Value.

Step 4.   Type in **MenuShowDelay**.

Step 5.   Double-click MenuShowDelay. Type in the length of the time delay that you want to wait until the menus pop up in milliseconds (thousandths of a second). Type in **0** for no delay, and **100000** for almost never.

Step 6.   Click OK.

Step 7.   Restart Windows 95 to have these values take effect.

Find

Windows 95 includes a search capability. The Windows 3.*x* File Manager has a very rudimentary one but it has been much improved for Windows 95.

You can get to this Find function in a number of ways. Right-click the Start button and click Find. Click the Start button, and choose Find from the Start button menu. You can choose between finding a computer and finding files or folders.

You will also find the Find function in the Explorer. Click Tools, Find on the Explorer menu bar. You can choose between finding a computer and finding files or folders.

Right-click the My Computer icon and click Find to find files and folders. Right-click the Network Neighborhood icon and click Find Computer. Right-click any folder icon and click Find to find files and folder.

The easiest way to find a file or folder? Press the F3 key when the focus is on the desktop, folder window, Explorer, or Taskbar.

Tip

Tip

Just because it says *find* doesn't necessarily limit the usefulness of this function to finding things. For example, you can use it as a filter to list all the executables in a given folder or set of folders in one window.

Finding files or folders

You can find files and/or folders that match the criteria you set in a Find dialog box. You are given a significant number of options to define your search strategy.

File or folder name

Undocumented

If you are looking for a specific file or folder and you know its name, type its name in the Named field, as shown in Figure 11-10. You can search for multiple folders, files or file types. Just separate their names by a comma as in:

```
*.bat, *.sys, *.txt, bill?.*
```

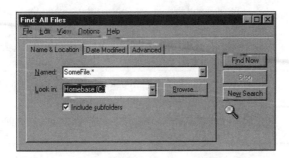

Figure 11-10: The Name & Location dialog box. Enter a file or folder name or partial name. If you know the general area where the file or folder can be found — for example, the disk drive — enter that area.

You can type in a partial name with wild cards. The wild cards are ? and *. The question mark stands for one letter and the asterisk for one or more letters. Table 11-1 shows these and other options.

Secret

Table 11-1	Find Options
Entered In Named Field	*Search Location*
*	All files and folders.
.	All files and folders.
*.	All files.
.	No files or folders.
.exe	No files or folders (because a filename cannot start with a period).

(continued)

Table 11-1 *(continued)*

Entered In Named Field	Search Location
abc	All files and folders with *abc* in name.
exe	All files and folders with exe in name or extension. Most likely executable files.
*.exe	All files with exe in extension only.
abc	All files and folders with *abc* in name
*abc	All files with *abc* as last letters in name (not including extension).
*abc?	All files with *abc* as second to last letters in name (not including extension).
?abc	All files and folders with *abc* at least second letters in name if not later.
?abc*	All files and folders with *abc* as the second through fourth letters in name.
??abc	All files and folders with *abc* at least the third letters in name if not later.
?abc?	All files and folders with at least one letter in front of *abc* and at least one behind in name.
?a?.*	Three-letter file name with middle letter of name given and extension unknown.

Notice that, unlike searching in DOS for file names, you can have the asterisk or question marks in front and still get meaningful results. In fact, the search algorithm is much more flexible and powerful then what was available with DOS or Windows 3.*x*.

In the Look in field, enter the general location for the file or folder. If you know a file or folder is on a certain disk drive, choose that drive letter. If you can narrow it down further, use the Browse button to choose a folder, or type in a path name.

Including subfolders in the search is the default. As you want the search to be a top-down search, leave it checked unless you know the folder the file is in.

Secret

Find will search for your files in hidden subfolders, if you have checked the Show all Files check box in the View options dialog box (click View, Options, Show all Files in an Explorer window menu bar). Find will not find your fonts in the Fonts folder (which has the system attribute set, but is not hidden) if the Look in field in your Find dialog box is set to Windows and not Windows\Fonts. The hidden subfolders under the Windows folder: NetHood, Recent, PIF, SYSBCKUP, ShellNew, SPOOL, INF.

Date Modified

You can limit your search to find a file or folder modified during a certain time period. Click the Date Modified tab to display the Date Modified dialog box, as shown in Figure 11-11.

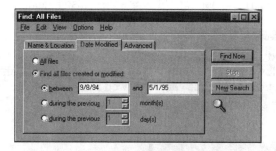

Figure 11-11: The Date Modified dialog box. You can limit the search for files and folders based on the last time/date they were modified. If it is a recently changed file, search for files that have been modified in the last few days.

If you have some idea of the date that the file was modified or the folder created (modified date is the same), you can limit the search criteria to find only files and folders within that time frame.

File type, specific text, file size

You can search for files that contain certain pieces of text, or are of a certain file type, or are at least as big as or greater than a certain size. Click the Advanced tab to display the Advanced dialog box, as shown in Figure 11-12.

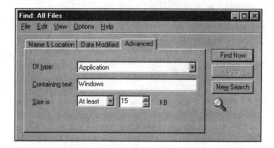

Figure 11-12: The Advanced dialog box. If you know only some text that the file contains, you can use that to find the file.

You can search for all the files that contain a similar piece of text. Maybe all the files that contain *Sincerely Yours.* This is a method of tracking down a file whose name you have forgotten, but whose content you would like to recover.

You can limit the search to a file of a certain type. For example, all text files, all Word for Windows files, or all Quattro Pro files. If you have some idea of the size of the files that you are looking for, this variable is also available.

Starting the search

After you have entered all the criteria, click Find Now. The results of the search are shown in the window below the search criteria dialog boxes, as shown in Figure 11-13. The file and folder icons can be viewed in any of the four standard views (large icon, small icon, list, details) by clicking View on the Find menu bar.

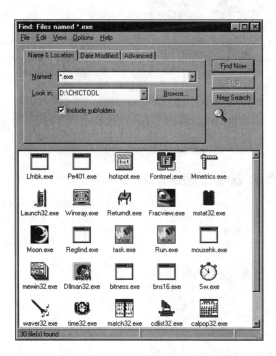

Figure 11-13: The Find results window. In the details view you can order the results by name, name of folder, date, size, and file type, either ascending or descending.

The results window is like a folder window with the addition of the In Folder column in the details view. You can sort the found files and folders by name, name of folder, date, size, and file type, in either ascending or descending order.

If you want to go to the folder that contains a given file or folder, highlight the file or folder in the results window and click File, Open Container Folder in the menu bar.

Saving the search

The search criteria remain after the search is concluded. If you don't like the results of your search you can modify the criteria and do another search. In Windows 3.x the search criteria disappeared after each search. Extreme frustration was one result; other results included the creation of many third-party products for finding files.

You can also save the search criteria to be used again or used later for the basis of a slightly modified search. Specific sets of search criteria are saved to the desktop as icons. Click File, Save Search in the menu bar of the Find window.

What you can do with Find

Tip

You can use Find to locate all the executable files in your games folder and then drag shortcuts to all these games to a newly created games submenu on your Start menu. It is great to be able to see all the executables within the subfolders of a folder that defines a general class of applications. This is especially true if you turn on the large icon view for the found window.

This is a general method of creating menus under the Start button. You can search for all executables on your hard disk and then drag them in groups to new menu/folders. You can also create folders or shortcuts to folders on the desktop and drag documents or executables over to these folders.

It really opens up your computer and lets you see what is hiding under the covers. You'll be surprised at what you have ignored.

Tip

Use Find for file management. You can have it find all the files on your entire hard disk so you can order them by size or age or file type. You can get rid of all the TMP (temporary) files, or all the really old text files.

Finding a computer on your network

You can use a completely different Find function to find a server or computer on your local network. Each computer has a unique name, so you can search for the name.

You can't use wild cards. You have to know the name of the computer that you are looking for — not much of a find utility if you have to know exactly what it is you are looking for.

You need to preface the name of the computer that you are looking for with "\\". This is the universal naming convention for a server — and therefore computer — name.

Searching the Microsoft Network

You also have the option of searching the MSN for services related to a topic. Click Tools, Find, On the Microsoft Network in a folder or Explorer window menu bar.

The search engine will look for a word in a bulletin board or chat room name or description. This search engine will be improved and expanded as MSN matures, allowing for text searches of documents stored on MSN.

Summary

Both the Start button and the Find function can be used to improve ease of use and efficiency.

► We show you how to create and modify the Start button menus to match the way that you work.

► We provide a means to trim the unnecessary files from the recently used files list.

► If you're using the keyboard a lot to control or find that desktop icons are covered up often, you'll appreciate being able to put the desktop on the Start button.

► Windows 95 has a very powerful search engine. You can define intricate searches that are quite useful in file management and for building Start menus and desktop folders.

Chapter 12

Desktop Strategies — Making Windows 95 Your Own

In This Chapter

Windows 95 is a set of tools waiting for an artist. This is a chance to let your creativity shine. We discuss:

▶ Cleaning up the clutter in your Start button menus

▶ Putting the Start button to work with your heavily used applications

▶ Letting loose and just piling it on the desktop

▶ Putting folders on the desktop to hold your shortcuts

▶ Launching programs with one click

▶ Turning a folder window into your Program Manager and using the Explorer as your File Manager

▶ Using the real Program Manager and File Manager as your user interface without giving up of the power of the *new* interface

▶ Adding to the power of Windows 95 to make it a complete operating system

---

It Comes with a Start Button

"But, I don't know where to start."

Microsoft goes for the uncluttered look in Windows 95. Many of its customers thought the Windows 3.*x* Program Manager ugly. In reaction, Microsoft has reduced the desktop to a Taskbar/Start button and a few icons.

You're going to have to build your own virtual computer — which, after all, is the real computer — for yourself. Windows 95 provides the tools, but leaves the design up to you.

Your documents and applications are well hidden on your hard disk or across the network. To create a usable computer, you'll need to bring them forth. You may have expected that it would all be there for you. If that's the case, it's time to leave home and make your own way in the world.

Windows 95 gives you shortcuts, cascading menus off the Start button, a desktop that can contain icons, folders with properties, a powerful browser in the Explorer, a configurable right mouse button menu, a Send To folder, and a moveable/hideable Taskbar. We provide you with a single-click launchpad and collection of add-on utilities to raise your computer's functionality. More tools are undoubtedly available, but these offerings should take you a long way.

A Desktop Strategy

Every single one of you will set up the Windows desktop in a different manner to match your own preferences. Only if a network administrator or system information manager has set up your computer over the network — and enforced a mandatory style (stored on a secure server) — will you be prevented from making the changes that make your computer your own.

Windows 95 provides a great deal of flexibility — although, of course, there will never be enough to completely please any of us. In this chapter, we present five major strategies for designing a Windows desktop. You can ignore all our hard work here and go off on your own or you can start with one of our approaches that most closely matches your own style and build on it.

The major considerations in developing a desktop strategy are getting the tools and putting them close at hand. Windows 95 doesn't include everything that you need in the user interface, so you are going to have to add a number of utilities to make it work for you. We have some and point out areas where you'll need to get more.

Don't hide the power of Windows 95 under a bush. Bring it out, make it accessible, make it easy. Take advantage of additional utilities and make them accessible, too.

Whose Desktop Is This Anyway?

When you first start Windows 95 you get a logon box like the one shown in Figure 12-1. The point of the logon box is to let the computer know who you are and whether you really are who you say you are. Windows 95, in turn, will let you configure your own desktop, so even if other people use the computer they won't mess with your desktop settings.

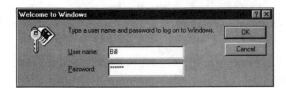

Figure 12-1: The Windows 95 logon box. Type in a user name and a password to protect your desktop.

The logon box will go away and not come back if you correctly configure Windows 95. If you make the logon box go away, you are telling Windows 95 that either you are the only user of this computer or that everyone gets the same desktop with this computer. You are also saying that you are not presently logging onto a network.

You must satisfy the following three conditions to make the logon box go away.

1. You must have a blank password.

2. You must disable user profiles.

3. You can't log on to a network at Windows 95 startup.

If you want your computer to be able to change depending on who is using it, you need to enable user profiles.

To be able to make these choices, take the following steps:

STEPS

Configuring User Profiles

Step 1. Start your computer after installing Windows 95.

Step 2. When the logon box appears, type in a user name, say your first name, and then click the OK button. This enters your password as blank.

Step 3. Click the Start button, then Settings, and then Control Panel.

Step 4. Double-click the Passwords icon in the Control Panel. Click the User Profiles tab. The User Profiles Passwords Properties sheet, as shown in Figure 12-2, will be displayed.

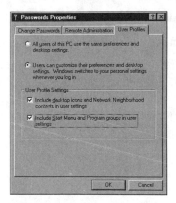

Figure 12-2: The User Profiles Password Properties sheet. Either one desktop for all, or each user gets his or her own.

(continued)

STEPS *(continued)*

Configuring User Profiles

Step 5.   Choose between "All users of this PC use the same preferences and desktop settings" and "Users can customize their preferences and desktop settings." Windows switches to your personal settings whenever you log in.

Step 6.   Click the OK button. You'll be given the option of restarting your computer. To have your changes take effect now, do so, or wait until after you take the next steps.

If you make the choice of the same desktop for all users, any changes that you make to the current user in the Registry, and any changes on the desktop or in the Start menus, will apply to all users. If you let different users customize their own desktops and Start menus, their changes will apply only to their configuration.

You can use the Passwords icon to change your password. You can even change it to blank if you had previously put in another password.

Different users can log onto different servers on the network. To log onto the network when you first start Windows 95, you will have to enter your user name in the logon box. If you want to just get into Windows 95 locally, you won't need to log on to a network, and you can forego the logon box at startup time. To allow for this choice, take the following steps:

STEPS

Configuring Logon Options

Step 1.   Click the Start button, then Settings, and then Control Panel.

Step 2.   Double-click the Network icon in the Control Panel. Click the down arrow in the Primary Network Logon drop-down list, as shown in Figure 12-3.

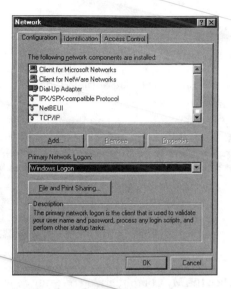

Figure 12-3: The Network dialog box. If you click the Primary Network Logon field, the description field tells you what it does. Right-click it for more detailed information.

Step 3. Choose between Windows Logon, Client for Microsoft Networks, Client for NetWare Networks, or other possible choices.

Step 4. Click the OK button. Restart Windows to have your changes take effect.

If you choose Windows Logon, you are saying you don't want to log onto the network, whatever network that might be. If you are not logging onto a network and you've met the other two conditions, the logon window won't appear the next time you start Windows 95.

If you want to have separate desktops for separate users, be sure to enable User Profiles.

Dealing with the Start Button

If you installed Windows 95 over your existing Windows 3.*x* directory, you will likely find a large number of submenus attached to the Programs menu on your Start button. All your Program Manager Groups have been transformed into menus and folders. Your Program Items have become shortcuts.

Windows 95 has its own collection of menus and shortcuts on the Programs menu as well, and those will only add to the appearance of clutter off the Start button. You'll probably want to reorganize things soon after you set up Windows 95. You may wonder if you can get rid of some of the menus. You also may not remember the functions of the applications that now have shortcuts in your various new menus.

Tip

One way to deal with all this clutter, and still have a manageable set of Start menus, is to drag the menus/folders out of the Programs folder into a temporary holding folder. You can create this new folder, perhaps in the root directory, or maybe on another drive. Take the following steps to clean up your Start menus:

STEPS

Uncluttering Your Start Menu

Step 1.   Right-click the My Computer icon on your desktop. Click Explore.

Step 2.   Be sure that Show all files is turned on, by clicking View, Options in the Explorer menu bar, and then clicking Show all files if it isn't checked. Click OK.

Step 3.   Navigate with the Explorer and highlight a drive or folder that will contain the temporary location for some Start menu items.

Step 4.   Right-click in the right pane client area of the Explorer window, click New, click Folder, and then type in a name like **TempStart**.

Step 5.   Navigate with the Explorer to your Windows 95 folder and focus on the Start Menu folder within the \Windows folder.

Step 6.   Drag (move, not copy) menus (folders) that you want to temporarily move out of the Start menus from the Programs folder over to the TempStart folder.

You can also do this with shortcuts found in the menus, perhaps dragging them to a subfolder of the TempStart folder.

You can use the Explorer to move the menus under the Programs menu around so that they make more sense to you. Unlike the Windows 3.*x* Program Manager, the Start button menus are hierarchical. There are submenus of menus. You might want to arrange these menus in some "natural" order.

The Start button itself

You can place shortcuts right on the Start button by dragging folder, application, or document icons over to it and dropping them on it. You'll want to put only your most heavily used applications on the Start button. Starting such an application requires only that you click the Start button (or press Ctrl+Esc) and click the application icon (or use the down arrow and press Enter). This level of convenience demands that you list just the applications (or folders) that deserve it.

There is a cost to this strategy. The Start button menu gets bigger, takes longer to draw, and these application icons get in the way of getting to the other items on the Start button menus. The icons on the Start button are full size (unless you right-clicked the Taskbar, clicked Properties, and then checked Show small icons in Start menu), so even more room is taken up. So it doesn't bog down, you should restrict the number of icons that you place on the Start button.

The menus on the Programs menu

The Programs menu is the replacement for the Program Manager. You can create a Programs menu that duplicates your Program Groups. You could configure the Programs menu to have only submenus. The submenus of the Programs menu would be analogous to Program Groups in the Program Manager.

The Programs menu can contain submenus (folders) as well as icons for applications (or documents). It's your choice how to mix these different elements.

Tip

If you have just one level of the hierarchy, then you will have submenus of the Programs menu, and these submenus will contain shortcuts to your applications. You can group similar submenus together (for example, all editing and word processing submenus) and put them under a more general submenu (say, editors). This submenu would then be a submenu of the Programs menu.

The Programs menus can be used as often or as little as you like. They require more mousing around to get out to your applications, navigating through the cascading menus. You can keep applications there that you use only once in a while. You can place the applications that you use the least, furthest out in the chain of menus. You can place more useful programs right on the Programs menu itself.

Pile It on the Desktop

Your computer desktop can take it, so why not pile it on? You can throw just about anything that you want on the desktop, but the best idea is to put shortcuts to applications, folders, and documents there. There is little need to hold back; if you have something that you are dealing with right now, put a shortcut to it on the desktop.

The desktop is often easy to get to (especially if you have a large high-resolution monitor) so you may want to put shortcuts to your most heavily used applications on the desktop. But just because shortcuts to your most important applications (in terms of use) end up on the desktop, that doesn't mean that you shouldn't just put anything there. You should.

The desktop is a very convenient temporary storage area. You can right-drag files out of a folder window or the Explorer and drop them there (creating shortcuts when the right mouse button menu appears) without having to open another folder window. You can go back later and drag these shortcuts to wherever you want. You can drop the actual files on the desktop if you like and move them later.

You can even drag text selections out of WordPad (and other Windows 95-aware word processors) documents onto the desktop, which acts like a permanent clipboard.

It's easy to get things off your desktop. Just click, then press the Delete key — or drag the icon to the Recycle Bin. If the icon is just a shortcut, then no harm is done. You've just removed a link to your application or document. If the icon represents a file, however, you've deleted the whole file. That's why it's a good idea to put only shortcuts on the desktop. You reduce the risk of deleting something that you wanted.

Tip

You can create folders on the desktop and put shortcuts in them. You could just as well create folders off the desktop (in the Explorer, for example) and put shortcuts to the folders on the desktop. Then you put shortcuts in the folders.

The desktop becomes the Program Manager. The shortcuts to the folders on the desktop are like Program Groups. It's as though your Program Manager had wallpaper.

Tip

Putting shortcuts to folders on the desktop is particularly convenient when you're working on projects with many different files in many different folders. You can create a folder that will store shortcuts to the files in the project. Put a shortcut to this folder on the desktop (or on the Start button). Now you have a quick way to access all the files in the project.

If the project is divided into recognizable subsets, put the shortcuts to files in each subset into a folder identifying that subset. Put shortcuts of the subset folders into an overall project folder. Put a shortcut to the project folder on the desktop.

If you have a document that you are working on, drag a shortcut to it onto the desktop. Double-click the shortcut and the document opens along with the application that created it.

Sometimes the desktop isn't so convenient, especially if you don't have much real estate. Say you're running at 640x480 on a 14-inch monitor or you're running your applications full screen. You can still use your desktop and you can always get to it. In Chapters 8 and 11, we show you ways to put the desktop on the Start button or on the Taskbar so that you can always get to the desktop, even if it is covered up.

Undocumented

The folder that is the desktop on the Taskbar or on the Start button can also be seen as a variant of the Program Manager. Open the Desktop folder window on the desktop and, in the large icon view, it looks a lot like the Program Manager. Windows 95 gives you many Program Managers: Start button menus, the desktop, folder windows with large icons, and a variation on the Windows 3.*x* Program Manager itself.

Use a Program Launcher

The Windows 95 desktop is not as convenient as we would like it to be. It still requires too much mousing and clicking to get the job done. You can reduce the clicking by putting a launch bar on your desktop.

Tip

A *launch bar*, also called a *launchpad*, is an application that allows you to click an icon once to start it. You'll want to use one to hold icons for those applications that you use all the time. It's like the Taskbar for applications that haven't been started yet. After all, it takes only one click to restore an application from the Taskbar.

The shareware CD-ROM that accompanies this book includes a launcher. It is Russell Holcomb's Run program, as shown in Figure 12-4. It's free so you don't have to increase the cost of Windows 95 just to get what really should have been there anyway.

Figure 12-4: The Run application launcher. Actually, you could launch documents or folders from here, too. Just keep this or an equivalent launcher on your desktop and you can launch a program with a click.

You can drag icons out of an Explorer or folder window — or off the desktop, for that matter — and drop them on the Run launcher. Run treats them pretty much like shortcuts.

You'll want to put Run in one spot on your desktop and leave it there. That way you'll build up "mouscle" memory as to where to find it. Put the most-used applications at the top of the Run bar. If you have two or three applications that you use together, group them on the Run bar, and click them one after the other.

Run is always open, so you don't need to do something to get at it. It is on the desktop, so it can be covered up. But it is also on the Taskbar, so you can uncover it.

Massage the Right Mouse Button Menu

Both the Explorer and My Computer provide navigational windows that give you a view of your computer. Because the Explorer has a folder tree view in the left pane, it has greater navigational abilities, but both display all your folders, files, applications, and documents.

If you right-click any of the objects displayed in these views, you get a right mouse button menu. The right mouse button menu can be changed to provide a significant increase in ease of use. In Chapters 10 and 13, we discuss how to modify the right mouse button menu and add destinations to the Send To menu item.

Tip

You'll want to add a default file opener to the Send To menu, a shortcut to Quick Viewer, a shortcut to a file compression program, and a shortcut to your printer. You may want to add a default file opener for all files of unregistered type to the right mouse button menu itself.

Some of these changes are very easy to make while others require that you edit the Registry a bit.

Turn a Folder Window into the Program Manager...

... and turn the Explorer into the File Manager.

Windows 95 integrates the File Manager and Program Manager functions into the Explorer and folder view windows. The Explorer is just a different type of folder window with two panes. Shortcuts, which are like Program items, are now stored in folders. Shortcuts can be viewed in both the Explorer and folder window views. Large icons can be displayed in the Explorer.

The Program Manager folder window

Undocumented

You can set up your desktop so it resembles the Windows 3.*x* interface but uses the new Windows 95 folders and windows. My Computer resembles the Program Manager, and the Explorer, in details view, looks like the File Manager.

STEPS

Creating a Program Manager-Like Folder

Step 1. Right-click My Computer on your desktop. Click Explore. Navigate until you find a convenient place to store a hierarchy of folders that will be your Program Manager folders.

By convenient, we mean in a folder or attached to the root of the disk drive, where you can easily go back and find these folders that we are about to create. You'll be able to move them later, so it doesn't matter if you don't choose the best spot at first.

Step 2. Create a folder called PMShortcuts. Do this by right-clicking in the right pane of the Explorer when it is focused on the folder or disk drive root that you have chosen to place the Program Manager folders. Click New and then Folder. Type in the name **PMShortcuts**.

Step 3. Highlight the new PMShortcuts folder in the left pane of the Explorer. Right-click the right pane, Click New and Folder. Type in the name **Program Manager**.

Step 4. Continue to right-click the client area of the PMShortcuts folder, adding new folders that are the equivalent of Program Groups. You will place shortcuts to them in the Program Manager folder.

Give these Program Group-like folders a class name that represents all the shortcuts to applications that will be stored within them.

Step 5. After you have created all the Program Group-like folders, right-drag the Program Manager folder icon to the desktop. Click Create Shortcut after you drop it there and change the name to **Program Manager**.

Step 6. Double-click the Program Manager icon and it opens up a Program Manager folder window. Right-drag the other folders from the Explorer and drop them on the Program Manager folder window. Change their names to get rid of Shortcut to...

Step 7. Now you can right-drag shortcuts or application icons from the Explorer, or maybe a Find window, to any of the shortcuts to folders within the Program Manager folder window. To make it easier to drop the shortcuts to the applications on them, you can open these folders first.

You now have a Program Manager folder window that resembles the Program Manager found in Windows 3.x. There is a shortcut to it on the desktop and any time that you want to open it, you can double-click this icon. You can place this icon on the Run launcher, or put it on the Start button. Placing the Desktop folder on the Start button is very similar to placing this Program Manager icon on the Start button.

The Program Manager folder has a shortcut on the desktop so you won't accidentally delete the folder itself. The same is true of all the folders displayed within the Program Manager folder window. All the application icons within these folders are also just shortcuts.

You can leave this Program Manager folder window open on your desktop, just as you could with the Windows 3.x Program Manager.

The Explorer as File Manager

If you choose the details view, the Explorer looks a lot like the Windows 3.x File Manager. It can accomplish many, but not all, of the functions that the File Manager can and quite a few that the File Manager can't. You can certainly use it as a replacement File Manager. For a comparison of the two, see Chapter 9.

Secret

You can't place a shortcut to Explorer.exe in the Startup folder. Explorer.exe contains the complete user interface (desktop, Taskbar, and so on), so it causes a problem to have the Explorer (the user interface) call itself when it starts up. You can put a shortcut to Explorer.exe /n,/e, { *pathname* and *filename*} in the Startup folder. (Yes, the commas are necessary in that command line.) The command line parameters that follow Explorer.exe modify this command to start the Explorer and not the complete user interface.

You don't have to put a call to the Explorer in the Startup folder to still have the Explorer close at hand. When you quit Windows 95, just be sure that the Explorer icon is on a Taskbar button; that is, that the Explorer is active. Next time you start Windows 95, the Explorer is one click away.

You can also place an Explorer icon on the desktop so you can double-click it to start the Explorer. Right-drag Explorer.exe from the \Windows folder using the Explorer to navigate and find itself. Drop Explorer.exe on the desktop and click Create Shortcut. Shorten the name to Explorer.

If you want, you can also place the Explorer on the Run launcher. One of the authors has it in the first slot on the launcher. The Explorer can also be placed on the Start button, and, by default, is in the Programs menu as Windows Explorer.

The Explorer isn't the File Manager. It doesn't have a multi-document interface, so you can't display two folder trees next to each other within the Explorer window. Microsoft wants to get away from the multi-document interface and let the operating system manage multiple documents and applications. You can run more than one copy of the Explorer by double-clicking its shortcut on the desktop twice.

Tip

Want to put up two Explorer windows side by side? Here's how.

Minimize all active windows. If you have created a shortcut to the Explorer on your desktop, double-click it twice. Now, right-click the Taskbar and click Tile Vertically. You now have two Explorer windows side-by-side. The desktop is a multi-document interface.

Use the Real Program and File Managers

Program Manager and File Manager are still there (\Windows\Progman.exe and \Windows\Winfile.exe) and you can use them. No shame in that. You can place shortcuts to the Program Manager and File Manager in the Startup folder, so that they come up every time you start Windows 95. You can choose (in the Properties sheets of their shortcuts) whether they will be restored, maximized, or minimized on the Taskbar when you start.

Program Manager and File Manager act the same as they did in Windows for Workgroups 3.11. That is their charm. You don't have to learn something new and you get all the power of these applications.

The File Manager is quicker than the Explorer. For one thing, it doesn't have to display all the file icons. For another, it doesn't have to go looking for long file names. Of course, you can't use it to display long file names, as it knows nothing about them.

The File Manager can be used to rename groups of files (as long as the file names are less than nine characters), which is something that the Explorer or My Computer folder windows just can't do. The Program Manager will minimize itself after you choose an application if you set it to do so. Folder windows won't do that.

Even if you don't use File Manager or Program Manager as your primary interface, you can place shortcuts to them in your other interface areas and call them when you want to use their power.

If you leave the Program and File Manager active (on the Taskbar) when you quit Windows 95, you won't have to worry about putting them in the Startup folder. They will return to their positions the next time you start up Windows. You will want to put shortcuts to them on the desktop, or the Start button, or in the Start menus, though, so that you can start them quickly if you need to.

You can think about ways to combine the use of the desktop, Start menus, and the Program Manager and File Manager. Some applications, perhaps less-used ones, could go on the Start menus. Just put those applications that you use most often in the Program Manager.

Some of you may have used the File Manager as your primary shell or user interface. The Start menu mimics the File Manager with its hierarchical structure. You might mix and match these two means of getting to your files.

You can change the shell setting in System.ini. For example, you can set shell=Winfile.exe to make the File Manager your shell in Windows 95. You can then quit Windows 95 by quitting the File Manager.

Right-clicking doesn't work in the Program Manager or the File Manager. You won't be able to drag things out of the File Manager and put them on the desktop although you still will be able to drag applications from the File Manager and drop them into a Program Group.

Ctrl+Esc gets you to the Start button, not to the Task Manager. You won't find the Program Group icons in the Program Manager, but rather the fairly ugly minimized application icons common to multi-document interfaces under Windows 95.

Making Windows 95 a Complete Operating System

No matter how good Windows 95 is, it is never going to be good enough. There will always be something that could improve it dramatically. With time, it will age and your needs will change as you see other possibilities.

Microsoft can't provide everything (neither can we), and Windows 95 needs some improvements right now. That's why we have included a CD-ROM containing shareware with this book. Programs on the CD-ROM can add to the basic Windows 95 software set to make a system that you can use every day.

We won't go into all the additional software that we provide right now, but we do want to highlight a few areas worthy of your immediate attention. We want to encourage you to examine the CD-ROM and add the utilities that will make your life with Windows 95 that much better.

We've already mentioned Russell Holcomb's Run launchpad a few times, so we'll concentrate on other software.

A file compressor/decompresser

If you send files over networks or phone lines, or if you want to cut down on the space that your graphics files are taking up on your hard disk, you will want to install WinZip. You are also going to want to make it real handy by placing a shortcut to it in the Send To folder. That way you can highlight a file, or group of files, and send them to be compressed while you go onto something else.

A find/text searcher

Get a grep. You might be in a position where you need all your text files indexed on every word other than *the*. Otherwise, the enhanced Windows 95 Find facility may be enough for you. It isn't enough for us. We need to search through folders for text that we put somewhere but we just can't remember where. We have featured Wingrep on the CD-ROM to do just that. A *grep* is a *generalized regular expression parser*, which is a fancy UNIX way of saying *text searcher*.

A font viewer

Double-click a font in the Fonts folder and you get a nice screen display and the ability to print out a sample of the font. This may be enough for you. If not, check out FontMe! You can compare multiple fonts on the screen at the sizes that you choose, print multiple fonts on the same page, and view all installed fonts.

Communications programs

Windows 95 comes stocked with communications programs, but this is the area where the computer can really shine. You may find yourself wanting a lot more than Windows 95 provides. We have featured a number of Internet communication programs, which are discussed in Chapter 33.

Hardware palette setter

If you set your color scheme to anything other then the default Windows 16-color scheme, then you are going to need this program to be able to choose the color of your insert point bar and I-beam in your word processor. That is why we have featured the Better Colors and Flying Colors program on our included Shareware CD-ROM.

A magnifying glass

Those are pixels there on your desktop. Often you'll need to take a closer look at them. We have featured not one but two shareware programs that help you do that — Extreme CloseUp! and Lens 2.0.

A real word processor

We have provided a shareware word processor that, while not as full featured as Word for Windows 6.0, comes awfully darn close. WordPad, NotePad, Edit, and (if you saved it from Windows 3.*x*) Windows Write may be all you need. But if you have to go to the next level and you don't want to shell out the big bucks for WordPerfect, Word Pro, or Word for Windows, Word Express is the program for you.

A personal address/phone number manager/dialer

Address Manager should do the trick. This full-featured address manager lets you easily divide your mailing list into appropriate groups and keep lots of different phone numbers for each person. One person can belong to many different groups.

An image editor

Lots of graphical information is available out there. Windows 95 comes with a fine paint package and a number of graphics file viewers. Paint Shop Pro 3.0 gives you the extra power you may need to manipulate those images — if just to make yourself some interesting wallpaper.

A calendar/to do list

We include Almanac for Windows NT to give you a handle on your time.

A macro editor

You'll find Morris Wilson's Winbatch, a complete Windows batch file creator.

Summary

Windows 95 is still in the box and waiting for you to assemble it, maybe even add the batteries.

▶ We show you how to dredge up the good stuff and put it where the sun does shine.

▶ We give you a way to clean up the clutter Windows 95 created on your Start menus when you set it up over your Windows 3.x directory.

▶ We encourage you to use the desktop as you would any horizontal surface in your office — pile it on. We also show you how you can keep it neat with folders and shortcuts to folders.

▶ Programs should be easy to get going, so we give you a way to get them up and at 'em with one click.

▶ Want the Windows 3.x retro look? Turn a folder window into the Program Manager.

▶ We show you that you can still use the real Program Manager and File Manager as your user interface.

▶ *Windows 95 Secrets* comes with a CD-ROM packed with add-ons to the "bare bones" Windows 95 operating system. Take advantage of them.

Chapter 13
Documents First

Document-Centric?

Microsoft has touted the "document-centric" nature of Windows 95. What are they getting at? To get perspective, you have to shift your focus to a non-computer-mediated way of dealing with a document.

If you were going to write a personal letter, perhaps to your mother, you might decide to take out a nice piece of stationery, retrieve a serviceable pen from your desk drawer, and begin the letter. Your attention was on the letter first, the paper second, and the writing implement third.

If you were to write the letter on a computer, you would have to start a letter-writing application before you started writing the letter. The letter-writing software package is the container for the letter. It's as though the pen contains the paper and the letter.

Windows 95 lets the letter-writing application take its more "natural" place as the means (perhaps one of many) of getting the words (and numbers, pictures, and sounds) into the document. The document has gained a measure of independence from the application.

This document-centric approach is reflected in a number of Windows 95 features: elimination of the Program Manager and File Manager as two separate and distinct ways of viewing the contents of your computer, integration of their functions into the folder window and Explorer window views, the ability to place new blank documents on the desktop or in any folder window, the Documents menu on the Start button menu, the ability to double-click a file name or icon and have its associated application open it, and the ability to define actions to be taken on a file that are displayed in the right mouse button menu.

Associating Actions with File Extensions

Like Windows 3.1, Windows 95 uses file extensions to define file type. A file with the extension *txt* can be, and is by default, defined as having the file type of text. Certain *actions* can be taken on files that are of a certain file type. For example, music files can be played on sound cards.

Usually the source of the action is an application. For example, files with the extension *ht* contain information necessary to successfully call a bulletin board. The HyperTerminal application is used by the *ht* file to make the call. Other applications that can read *ht* files could also be used.

You can choose (and modify) the actions that will be taken on a file or document from among all the possible actions that are open to you. The available actions depend on what Windows 95 provides and which other applications you have installed on your computer.

File types and their associated actions are defined (registered) in the Registry files. Windows 95 defines more than 50 file types (and their associated actions) before you get a chance to define your own.

Where Are These Actions?

If you right-click a file of a registered (defined) file type, a right mouse button menu will be displayed on the desktop. At the top of the menu are the actions defined for this file type. Whatever actions you define are now available to you. The action at the top of the menu is the default action. If you had double-clicked the file name or icon, this action would have occurred.

It is quite possible for an application to be able to take literally thousands of different actions on a file. Just think of the many different ways that a word processor (with your help) acts on a document. Not all the actions that an application can undertake need or should be defined in the Registry.

It makes sense to define only certain kinds of actions in the Registry. Actions that can be taken without significant additional user input come to mind, such as opening, printing, translating the file from one format to another, playing (musically speaking), and updating.

Creating and Editing File Types and Actions

The file type/action association is fundamental to the document-centric character of Windows 95. Without it, you could not double-click a file name or file icon on the desktop or in a folder window and have it and its application displayed in a window. You would be required to always start an application first and then search for the document with the application's File, Open dialog box.

One of the main points of the Windows 95 desktop metaphor is to make applications subservient to the data or document. This metaphor falls down when you can't get to your data without going through an application. If you can right-click a file and have associated actions appear on the right mouse button menu, it feels like the file or document is in charge.

You can change which file extensions are associated with which actions. You can add (or register) new extensions. When you install Windows 95 over your existing Windows 3.x directory, the setup program reads your existing Windows 3.x Win.ini and Registry files and places all your existing file types and their associated actions in the Windows 95 Registry files.

When you install a new application under Windows 95, all its defined file types and their associated actions are stored within the Registry. This may be just the simple action of opening.

You can edit or add new file type/action associations in either a folder window or an Explorer window. To do so, take the following steps:

STEPS

Creating and Editing File Types

Step 1.   Open a folder or Explorer window. One way to do this is by right-clicking My Computer and choosing either Open or Explore.

Step 2.   Click View, Options in the menu bar of the window. Click the File Types tab. The Files Types dialog box, as shown in Figure 13-1, is displayed.

(continued)

STEPS *(continued)*

Creating and Editing File Types

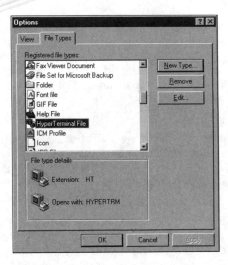

Figure 13-1: The File Types dialog box. All registered file types can be seen by scrolling the Registered file types window.

Step 3.   You have the choice of creating a new registration for an extension (New Type), removing an existing registered extension, or editing the description and associated actions for an existing file type.

Undocumented

If you click a file type in the Registered file types window, the file type extension and the application that is associated with the default action taken on the file type will be displayed in the File Type details box. This box contains a field labeled Opens with. Open is not necessarily the default action. You have the option of choosing any of the actions that you define as the default action. This field should be labeled Default action by.

Creating a new file type

To create a new file type, take the steps above. Then follow these steps:

STEPS

Creating a New File Type

Step 1. Click the New Type button. The Add New File Type dialog box will be displayed, as shown in Figure 13-2.

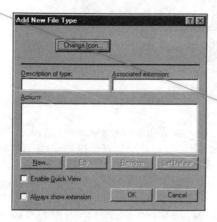

Figure 13-2: The Add New File Type dialog box.

Step 2. Press Tab once. Enter a description of the file type in the Description of type field. The file types are listed in alphabetical order in the File Types dialog box by the first letter of this description. Any name that is relevant to you is OK.

Tip

This field is used to order files in folder and Explorer windows when these windows are in details view and you order by type. When ordered by type, files are not ordered by their extension, as was true under Windows 3.x, but by the alphabetical ordering of the Description of type field.

Step 3. Enter the file extension in the Associated extension field. The extension should be no longer, than three letters if the application can't handle long file names, that is, a Win16 application or one written for Windows 3.x. You don't have to type the period.

You won't be allowed to enter an extension that is already registered. Windows 95, therefore, won't have to choose between applications when you double-click a file.

(continued)

STEPS *(continued)*

Creating a New File Type

Step 4. Click the New button. The New Action dialog box is displayed, as shown in Figure 13-3. Enter an action that you want an application to perform on files of this file type. You might want to first define the default action that an application performs on the file when you double-click it.

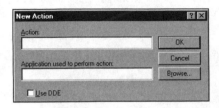

Figure 13-3: The New Action dialog box.

You can use any action name you like. You will associate your action name with an action that you define. You will be able to define a number of different actions and name each.

For example, Open and Print are among the many possible action names. Later, the action names you choose will be used to describe what actions are taken, so you're better off to make them understandable.

Put an ampersand (&) in front of the letter in the action that you want to use to select the action. For example, &Open underlines the letter "O" on right-mouse menus, so you can press the "O" key and then Enter to excute this action from the Keyboard. Capitalize the first letter of the action.

Step 5. Enter the name of an application that will perform the named action and that is associated with the file type. Type in the complete path name prefacing the application filename. Add to the application name the command line parameters that will instruct the application to perform the requested action. You don't have to type in %1 as a command line parameter for the file. It is assumed.

For example, if you want a text file to be printed you might define the action named Print as **C:\Windows\Notepad.exe /p.**

The possible actions that an application can take on files of this type and the macro language of the application program determine which action names make sense. The default action for most applications is Open. If you put the file name of the application in the Application used to perform action field without any command line parameters, the action it most likely will carry out is to open the file that you clicked.

Undocumented

Step 6. You can also use Dynamic Data Exchange (DDE) to modify the behavior of the application by passing it a message. If the application has a macro language, you can use that macro language to make the application behave in all sorts of different ways when you choose some action of the right mouse button menu. Click the Use DDE box to see additional ways to define an action.

Figure 13-4 shows a way to modify how files with extensions other than *doc* can be opened by Word for Windows 6.0 without opening a new copy of Word, if it is already active. If you didn't use DDE to send a message to Word, another copy of Word would be opened when you double-clicked a file with an extension other than *doc*.

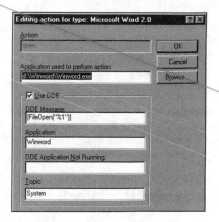

Figure 13-4: Using DDE to modify how a file is opened by Word for Windows 6.0.

Step 7. Click OK when you have finished defining the application's action. You can continue defining new and different actions to take on a given file type by clicking the New button and repeating Steps 1 through 5. Highlight one of the actions when you are done, and click Set Default in the Add New File Type dialog box. This will define the highlighted action as the action that occurs when you double-click the file.

Step 8. Click OK and then OK again. You can change the icon if you want with the Change Icon button before you click these two OK buttons.

You now have a new file type — a new file extension that is associated with a given set of actions that most likely originate in one or more applications. Each action will appear on the right mouse button menu. Right-click a file of this type and you have a menu of actions to take.

Enabling Quick View

There is an Enable Quick View check box in the lower left corner of the Add New File Type or Edit File Type dialog box. Quick Viewers let you see a file on the desktop without having to open (or even own) an application that is normally used to open it. Microsoft ships more than 20 viewers for some common file types. Application developers can ship their own Quick Viewers with their applications. In addition, Systems Compatibility Corp., the makers of Outside In and the Quick View technology, plans to ship Quick View Plus with many more viewers shortly after Windows 95 becomes available.

You can implement this feature for a file type that has an associated Quick Viewer by clicking this box. If you installed the application, it should have checked this box during setup.

Which file viewer will be enabled? The one associated with the application that opens the document.

Always show extension

It is possible to have the extensions of file types that are registered not show up in folder windows or the Explorer. If you want the file extension for this file type to show even though the option to Hide MS-DOS file extensions for file types that are registered is checked in the View, Options, View dialog box of the Explorer, then check the Always show extension box.

Editing an existing file type

Instead of clicking the New Type button in the Options File Types dialog box, click the Edit button after you highlight a file type whose actions, or icons, or associated application(s) you wish to change. You will be presented with a dialog box similar to the Add New File Type dialog box —the Edit File Type dialog box.

You will be able to add new actions, edit existing ones, remove existing ones, or declare a different action as the default. You will also be able to change the icon associated with the file type if you like. You can do all this using steps very similar to the ones detailed in the previous section.

One application associated with two file extensions

Secret

If you scroll carefully through the list of registered file types you will notice that some show two file extensions for one file type. Using the File Types dialog box, it is not possible to create a file type with two extensions and only one entry in the list of file types. But it is possible to do this using the Registry editor. (See the section entitled *Multiple extensions—one application* later in this chapter.)

File associations via the Registry

Undocumented

The File Types dialog boxes are a front end to the Registry — but then so are most of the Properties sheets and dialog boxes that you deal with in Windows 95. You can edit the Registry entries for your file types directly, if you like, using the Registry editor.

STEPS

Editing File Types in the Registry

Step 1. Go to Chapter 15 if you need to learn more about the Registry. If you have put a shortcut to it on your desktop, double-click it. Otherwise, find Regedit.exe in the Windows folder using the Explorer or My Computer and double-click it.

Step 2. Click the plus sign next to HKEY_CLASSES_ROOTS. This branch of the Registry will expand. The first keys shown are the file extensions. They all start with a period. There should be at least 50 keys, all marked with folder icons.

Step 3. Click any of the keys that are file extensions. A file type name will be associated with each one. Look at a few of these names to get an idea of how they are associated with the extension.

Step 4. Scroll down the HKEY_CLASS_ROOTS branch until you pass the extension keys and get to the file type names. Click the plus sign next to a file type name that corresponds to a file type or extension that you previously viewed in Step 3.

Step 5. Click the plus sign next to "shell" under the file type name. Notice that the action names associated with that file type are displayed. Click the plus signs by those action names and then highlight the command key.

Step 6. Notice that the action defined in the New Action or Editing Action dialog boxes is defined here. If DDE is used, you will find references to it under whichever action is was defined for.

Step 7. Use the Registry editor's New, Delete, and Rename menu commands to create new file types or edit existing ones, using the models shown by following Step 1 through 6. You may need to turn to Chapter 15 for more information on how to edit these values.

You may find old file types and file type names that no longer apply. You can prune them out of the Registry if you like.

Change the edit application for batch files

Tip

If you right-click an MS-DOS batch file (files with the *bat* file extension) while it is displayed in a folder window, you will notice that WordPad is used to edit the file. We find Notepad more convenient. To use Notepad instead of WordPad as the editor for *bat* files, take the following steps:

STEPS

Editing the Action Associated with *Bat* Files

Step 1. Open a folder or Explorer window. One way to do this is by right-clicking My Computer and choosing either Open or Explore.

Step 2. Click View, Options in the menu bar of the window. Click the File Types tab.

Step 3. Highlight MS-DOS Batch file in the Registered file types window. Click the Edit button.

Step 4. Wait a minute; the Edit button is grayed out. You can't change the application associated with editing a batch file this way. This is why you need access to the Registry.

Step 5. If you have put a shortcut to the Registry editor on your desktop, double-click it. Otherwise, find Regedit.exe in the Windows folder using the Explorer or My Computer and double-click it.

Step 6. Click the plus sign next to HKEY_CLASS_ROOTS. Scroll down to batfile. Click the plus sign next to batfile. Click the plus signs next to shell and edit.

Step 7. Highlight command. Double-click Default in the right pane of the Registry editor.

Step 8. Type in **Notepad.exe %1**

Multiple extensions — one application

Secret

Using the Registry editor you can create multiple extensions and associate them with one application. If you have Microsoft Word installed, you will notice that the extension *.dot* and *.doc* in the Registry (under HKEY_CLASSES_ROOT) both refer to Word Document. This is how multiple extensions are associated with one application.

Using the Registry editor, you can edit an entry for an extension to change the application that the extension is associated with. Highlight an extension entry in the Registry editor, double-click Default in the right pane of the Registry editor, and type in a new file type name or the name of an existing file type.

If you created a new file type name, you will then need to create a new Key value in HKEY_CLASSES_ROOT by that name. In addition, you will need to define some actions that are associated with that file type. Use the existing keys in this section of the Registry as examples.

Unlike most other areas where we give you a step-by-step procedure, this is a sketchy discussion. Before you take on this task continue reading this chapter and try all the examples. You'll need to go over this section of the Registry extensively before you try to do this yourself.

Editing (not merging) exported Registry files

Tip

Exporting your Registry or a branch of your Registry creates a file with a *reg* extension. The default action for this file type is Merge, as in Merge this file back into the Registry. We find this a bit dangerous. It is easy to change the default action for this file type.

STEPS

Changing the Default Action for an Exported Registry File

Step 1. Open a folder or Explorer Window. Click View, Option on the menu bar. Click the File Types tab.

Step 2. Scroll the Registered file types list down to Registration entries. Highlight Registration entries.

Step 3. Click the Edit button.

Step 4. Highlight Edit in the list of actions. Click the Set Default button.

Step 5. Click the first OK button and the second OK button.

Re-associating RTF files with WordPad

Tip

If you install Word for Windows after you install Windows 95, the Open action for Rich Text Format (RTF) files is associated with Word and not WordPad. If you want to open this type of file with WordPad, edit the Open action associated with RTF files so it points to \Program Files\Accessories\Wordpad.exe instead.

Secret

If you find that your new associations are reverting to their previous association (for example, if after changing the *rtf* association to WordPad, it goes back to Word), you are the victim of Microsoft's not-too-smart Registry association update routines. These go in after a new program is installed and update the Registry based on what is in the [Extensions] section of the Win.ini file.

If you have an old association of *rtf* with Word in the Win.ini file, it may be used to "update" your Registry and wipe out your new change. A way to get around this is to erase this association in the [Extensions] section of Win.ini. Unless you are using ccMail, you can erase this whole section. You might want to keep a copy first, just in case.

Associating more than one program with a given file type

You can define many actions for a given file type. Each of these actions can be associated with a different application. Each action has to have a unique name.

Tip

Files of the file type screen saver have a *scr* extension. Script files used by many different programs also use the *scr* extension. You can create an action, which we call Edit Scripts, that is associated with script files. To do so, take the following steps:

STEPS

Adding an Edit Scripts Option to the File Type Screen Saver

Step 1. Open a folder or Explorer Window. Click View, Option on the menu bar. Click the File Types tab.

Step 2. Scroll the Registered file types list down to Screen Saver. Highlight Screen Saver.

Step 3. Click the Edit button and then the New button.

Step 4. Type **Edit Scripts** in the Action field. Browse to \Windows\Notepad.exe in the "Application used to perform action" field.

Step 5. Click all three OK buttons, one at a time.

Opening Unregistered File Types

If you double-click a file that has an extension not registered, the file will not be opened. Instead, the Open With dialog box, as shown in Figure 13-5, will be displayed. It lists all the programs associated through actions to registered file types.

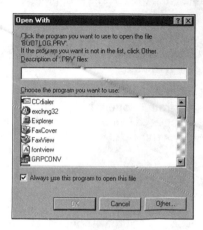

Figure 13-5: The Open With dialog box.

The "Always use this program to open this file" check box is checked by default. If, in general, you want files with this extension to be opened by the application that you are about to choose, then leave this box checked. You can also type in a description of the file type in the Description of '.xxx' files field. Choose a program to open this file by double-clicking the program name in the list box or by clicking the Other button to find the program that you want.

If you just want to open this file now and not worry about establishing an association between its file type and an application, click "Always use this program to open this file" to uncheck this box and double-click an appropriate program to open the file.

This method of opening files of an unregistered type gives you a great deal of flexibility at a cost of having to scroll to find an appropriate application. It also lets you bypass the File Types dialog box to create new file types and associate them with applications.

Opening a registered file type with another application

Sometimes you want to be able to open a file whose file type is already registered and whose open action is associated with an application that you would rather not use this time. If you double-click the file in the Explorer, this application will open it.

Tip

Hold down the Shift key and right-click the file in an Explorer or folder window. An Open With menu item appears on the right mouse button menu. You can choose which application to use to open the file.

The Open With dialog box shown in Figure 13-5 is displayed when you choose Open With but the Always use this program to open this file check box is not checked. If you want to change the associated Open action for this file type to the new application, you'll need to check this box.

Create a default file opener

Secret

You can define a default program that will always open a file of an unregistered type when you right-click it and choose OpenNote without having to go through the rigmarole of the Open With dialog box. A variation on this method lets you open the file with a double-click.

The section below entitled *Easiest Way to View/Open an Unregistered File* includes another way of defining an alternative with a quasi-default file opener. We got a much earlier version of this little gem from Elton Saulsberry, a Windows 95 beta tester. Elton was not the first to figure this one out, but we've lost its origins.

STEPS

Defining a Default File Opener

Step 1.   If you have put a shortcut to the Registry editor on your desktop, double-click it. Otherwise, find Regedit.exe in the Windows folder using the Explorer or My Computer and double-click it.

Step 2.   Click the plus sign next to HKEY_CLASS_ROOTS. Scroll down the left pane until you find Unknown. Click the Unknown folder icon. Click shell.

Step 3.   Click Edit, New, Key. Type **OpenNote**. Highlight OpenNote.

You don't have to name the command OpenNote. You can type what you want here — whatever menu item makes sense to you and corresponds with the action or command that you are about to define.

Step 4.   Click Edit, New, Key. Type **command**. Highlight the Command folder icon.

Step 5.   Double-click the icon labeled Default in the right pane of the Registry editor. Enter the file name and path to the application that you want to use as the default file opener. For example, type **C:\Windows\Notepad.exe %1**.

Step 6.   Click OK.

A variation on the above steps lets you double-click to open a file of an unregistered file type with the default file open application. You need to first examine the **openas** key under the Unknown key because you are going to delete it (and the command key under it) and then put it back in.

The steps to do this are the same as the ones above—but before you take Step 3, examine **openas**, write down the command data, and then delete the openas key. After Step 5, use Edit, New, Key to put the **openas** key and its command key back in as before, but now under OpenNote.

Now when you double-click a file of an unregistered type in Explorer, it will open the file in the specified program. Both OpenNote and Open With will now be on the right mouse button menu when you right-click an unregistered file. You can still use Open With and get the option of opening the unregistered file types with your choice of program.

General actions on any file type

Secret

You can define a set of actions that will apply to any file type or to any unregistered file type. These actions will then appear on the right mouse button menu when you right-click any file or when you right-click any file of unregistered file type. Again, Mathais Koenig showed us this little gem.

In the earlier section entitled *Create a default file opener*, we showed you how to use the Registry editor to create OpenNote, an action that would open unknown file types with Notepad.exe. You were required to use the Registry editor to create this action because the file types **unknown** and **all** are not displayed in the File Types dialog box.

It is possible to display these two "file types" in the File Types dialog box. Once they are displayed there, you can define any actions that you care to for these file types.

Defining Actions for Any File Type

Step 1.   Right-click the desktop, click New, and then click Text Document.

Step 2.   Rename the text document **All.reg**. Click OK when asked about the extension change. (Be sure that you are showing your MS-DOS extensions. To do this in the Explorer, click View, Option, View, and then uncheck "Hide MS-DOS file extensions for file types that are registered." Click OK.)

Step 3.   Right-click the new document icon that you have just created, and choose Edit. Type the following text into the document, save, and close it when you are done:

```
REGEDIT4

[HKEY_CLASSES_ROOT\Unknown]

"EditFlags"=hex:02,00,00,00

[HKEY_CLASSES_ROOT\*]

"EditFlags"=hex:02,00,00,00
```

Step 4.   Right-click the new document icon, and then click Merge.

Step 5.   Open an Explorer or folder window. Click View, Options, and then the File Types tab.

Step 6.   The first entry should now be an asterisk (*), which stands for all file types. Scroll down the file types list to find the Unknown file type.

Step 7.   You can use the methods described in this chapter to add new actions to these "file types."

Change BMP icons to show thumbnail

Secret

Each file type has its associated icon shown in the Explorer, on the desktop, or in folder windows. Instead of a single uniform icon for all your *bmp* files, you can display a crude thumbnail sketch of each of the *bmp* files. Thanks for this secret go to Firas El-Hassan, who sent a message to the Windows 95 beta forum on CompuServe about how to create a unique icon for each graphic. This way you know what you're going to see when you double-click the *bmp* file's icon.

Thumbnails for BMP files

Step 1.   Double-click Regedit.exe in your \Windows folder.

Step 2. Click the plus sign next to HKey_Classes_Root. Scroll down the left pane of the Registry editor to Paint.Picture.

Step 3. Click the plus sign next to Paint.Picture, and highlight DefaultIcon in the left pane of the Registry editor.

Step 4. Double-click (Default) in the right pane.

Step 5. Delete existing value in Value field of Edit String dialog box and type in **%1** instead. Click OK.

Go to an Explorer or folder window and focus on a folder that contains *bmp* files. Click View, Large icons and check out the new thumbnails. They should each display a tiny thumbnail of each bitmap, not the generic paint icon.

Viewing a File Without Starting an Application

If you right-click a file when viewed in the Explorer, in a folder window, or on the desktop, you may be given the option of Quick Viewing it. You are given this option if the file that you right-click is of a registered file type and Windows 95 has a file viewer for that type.

Windows 95 ships with more than 20 file viewers. These viewers know about the file format of the documents of a given file type. They can load quickly, read the document, and display it on your desktop.

Application developers are encouraged to ship file viewers with their applications, so you may have additional viewers stored in the \Windows\System\Viewers folder. Windows 95 ships with Quick Viewers for the file types shown in Table 13-1.

Table 13-1	Files Windows 95 Recognizes
File Extension	*File Type*
asc	ASCII
bmp	Windows bitmapped graphics
cdr	Corel Draw Version 4 and 5
dib	Windows bitmapped graphics (DIB)
dll	Dynamic link libraries (application extensions)
doc	Microsoft Word 2.0, 6.0, WordPad, others *(continued)*

Table 13-1 *(continued)*

File Extension	File Type
drw	Micrographic draw
eps	Encapsulated Post Script
exe	Executable format
gif	CompuServe and Internet graphics
inf	Windows setup files (text)
ini	Windows configuration files (text)
mod	Multiplan Versions 3, 4, 4.1
ppt	PowerPoint Version 4
pre	Freelance Graphics for Windows
rle	Bitmapped graphics (Run Length Encoded)
rtf	Rich Text Format
sam	Ami, Ami Pro
tif	Tagged Image Format
wb1	Quattro Pro for Windows
wdb	MS Works Database
wk1	Lotus 1-2-3 Versions 1 and 2
wk3	Lotus 1-2-3 Version 3
wk4	Lotus 1-2-3 Version 4
wks	Lotus 1-2-3 or MS Works Version 3
wmf	Windows Meta File
wp5	WordPerfect 5
wp6	WordPerfect 6
wpd	WordPerfect demo
wps	MS Works word processing
wq1	Quattro Pro for MS-DOS
wq2	Quattro Pro for MS-DOS Version 5
wri	Windows Write
xlc	MS Excel chart
xls	MS Excel Versions 4 and 5

All you have to do is right-click a file of the above file type or with the above file extension and click Quick View from the right mouse button menu. The file will be displayed on your desktop in a view window. If you want to edit the file and you have the associated application, click the Edit button in the view window and that application will be loaded.

Undocumented

You can create a shortcut on the desktop for the Quick Viewer and drag and drop files to the Quick Viewer from the Explorer or a folder window. Files that aren't associated with any viewer can then be viewed by the default viewer. You will be asked if you wish to do this after you drag a file to the Quick Viewer.

STEPS

Putting a Quick Viewer on Your Desktop

Step 1. Use My Computer or the Explorer to view the \Windows\System\Viewers folder.

Step 2. Right-drag Qvstub.exe to the desktop and drop it there.

Step 3. Change the Qvstub's icon title to **Quick Viewer**.

For an even easier and quicker way to view files without a specific viewer, see the next section.

Easiest Way to View/Open an Unregistered File

If you right-click a file in the Explorer or in a folder window, you will notice the Send To menu. It has an arrow on the right indicating a submenu, which is shown in Figure 13-6. When you first set up Windows 95 this submenu should contain such items as Floppy Disk Drive and/or Fax Recipient.

Figure 13-6: The Send To menu.

The Send To list contains your common destinations. If you often copy files and folders to your floppy disk drive then you want to be sure to put a shortcut to it in the Send To folder.

Undocumented

You can add shortcuts to the Quick Viewer and to your default file opener(s). To view or open a file of an unregistered type, right-click it, click Send To, and then click either the Quick Viewer or the application icon. Here's how to set up Notepad as a file-opening application:

STEPS

Making Notepad Your Default File Opener

Step 1. Open an Explorer window. Be sure that you can see all file extensions. If not, click View, Options to set this.

Step 2. Navigate using the Explorer to the Windows folder and click the plus sign to the left of the Windows folder icon in the left pane of the Explorer window. Highlight the Windows folder icon.

Step 3. Scroll down the right pane until Notepad.exe is visible. Right-drag Notepad.exe to the Send To folder icon in the left pane and drop it there. Click Create Shortcut.

Step 4. Highlight the Send To folder icon in the left pane of the Explorer. Highlight the Shortcut to Notepad.exe icon in the right pane and click it again. Rename this icon **Notepad**.

Step 5. Notepad will now be a choice in your Send To menu. You can place a shortcut to Qvstub.exe in the Send To folder in a similar manner (see the previous section).

Of course, you don't have to choose Notepad as your default file opener. You can also put numerous different shortcuts in the Send To folder.

Documents on the Start Button Menu

If you open a file by double-clicking it (or right-clicking and then choosing Open) in a folder window or Explorer window, a reference to it will show up on a list under the Documents menu item on the Start button menu. The last 15 documents so opened show up on this list.

If you open a document within a Windows 3.x application — using the File, Open menu item, for example — it does not show up on the Documents list.

Undocumented

To clear the Documents list, right-click the Taskbar, click Properties, click the Start Menu Programs tab, and then click Clear. To clear just the documents that you want cleared, open the \Windows\Recent folder in the Explorer or a folder window and delete the undesired documents.

You can put a shortcut to \Windows\Recent on your desktop. This is another way to get to these recently opened documents and also lets you easily edit the list.

New Blank Documents

Creating new blank documents on the desktop, in a folder window, or in an Explorer window is discussed in Chapter 8. Blank documents can be created on the desktop by right-clicking the desktop, clicking New, and then clicking the desired document type.

Tip

If your desired file type isn't on the list, don't worry. Click any file type. When the new blank document shows up on the desktop, its title is highlighted. Type in a new name with an extension of the registered file type that you want. You will get a dialog box asking you if you are sure that you want to change the extension. You do.

The file will still contain the data of the kind that you originally chose, such as text. If you chose to create a new text file but changed the extension to *doc,* the file will still contain plain text until you save it in a Word for Windows format or another word-processing document format.

Adding Items to the New Document Menu

Secret

If you regularly create a document type that isn't on the New menu, you can add a menu item by making a few changes to the Registry. There is a simple way to create a text document with the proper extension and call the correct application when the document is double-clicked. There is a more complex method, which creates the correct document type.

We wish to thank Mathias Koenig for providing much of this information.

The first step is to make sure you have registered the document type in the Registry. Do this by following the steps in the section entitled *Creating a new file type* earlier in this chapter.

The next step is to edit the new file types entry in the Registry. The following steps show you how to do that:

STEPS

Creating an Item on the New Menu

Step 1.   Go to Chapter 15 if you need to learn more about the Registry. If you have put a shortcut to it on your desktop, double-click it. Otherwise, find Regedit.exe in the Windows folder using the Explorer or My Computer and double-click it.

Step 2.   Click the plus sign next to HKEY_CLASSES_ROOTS. This branch of the Registry will expand. The first keys shown are the file extensions. They all start with a period. There should be at least 50 keys, all marked with folder icons.

Step 3.   Click the file extension key that matches the file type that you just created.

Step 4.   Right-click the right panel of the Registry editor. Click New, Key. Change the name of the key to **ShellNew**.

Step 5.   Click the new ShellNew key in the left panel of the Registry. Right-click the left panel. Click New, String Value. Type in the Name **NullFile**.

Step 6.   Exit the Registry editor if you are done.

The file type description for a file with this extension will now be added to the New menu. The file type that is created will be a text file, but it will have the extension that you just picked in the Registry.

Immediately invoke an application with a new file

If you want to have an application called immediately when the new file is created you can add a command string value to the ShellNew key. To do so, take the following steps:

STEPS

Invoking an Application When You Create a New File

Step 1.   Follow the first five steps in the previous section.

Step 2.   If it is not highlighted, click the ShellNew key in the left panel of the Registry. Right-click the left panel. Click New, String Value. Type in the Name **command**.

Step 3.   Double-click **command**. Type in the path and file name of the application that will be invoked. Include a **%1** after the file name to allow
the new file to be opened by the application.

Step 4.   Exit the Registry editor.

Make the new file of the correct file type

If you want to have the new file be the correct file type, you have to stuff some
data into the file so it can be recognized by the associated application. For
example, if you want to create a Windows Write file, you need some header
information at the beginning of the file that identifies it as a Windows Write type
of file.

To do this, you need to store the Windows Write header information in the
Registry. You store it under the ShellNew key associated with the *wri* extension.
The data, which has to be stored in a hexadecimal format, consists of whatever
is included in an empty Windows Write file.

First, you will need to create an empty Windows Write file. Next, you will need
to read this file with a hexadecimal editor, like the one found on the CD-ROM
accompanying this book. Third, you must either type that data into the Registry
after taking the steps detailed below or feed it in using a macro editor.

STEPS

Creating a New File of the Correct File Type

Step 1.   Go to Chapter 15 if you need to learn more about the Registry. If you
have put a shortcut to it on your desktop, double-click it. Otherwise,
find Regedit.exe in the Windows folder using the Explorer or My
Computer and double-click it.

Step 2.   Click the plus sign next to HKEY_CLASSES_ROOTS. This branch of
the Registry will expand. The first keys shown are the file extensions. They all start with a period. There should be at least 50 keys,
all marked with folder icons.

Step 3.   Click a file extension key that matches the file type that you just
created. Click the ShellNew key that you created using the steps in
the first part of this section.

Step 4.   If you created a NullFile entry, delete it by highlighting it in the right
panel of the Registry editor and pressing the Delete key.

Step 5.   Right-click the left panel. Click New, Binary Value. Type in the
Name **Data**.

(continued)

STEPS *(continued)*

Creating a New File of the Correct File Type

Step 6.   Double-click Data. Type in the hexadecimal values that you are reading from the hexadecimal editor that is displaying the contents of your empty file.

Step 7.   Exit the Registry editor when you are finished.

Summary

We describe how to make it easy to get to your documents without having to go through your applications first.

▶ The desktop and folder windows can give you a view of your documents. It is such a bother to have to open an application first to see these documents and work on them. We show you how to get right to the document and let the application take care of itself.

▶ We show you how to create new file types and define actions that can be taken on files of those types — actions that can automate your work.

▶ We show you how to use DDE and the macro languages built into your applications to automate your work even further.

▶ We use the Registry editor to change the assigned edit application for MS-DOS batch files from WordPad to Notepad.

▶ We show you how to create new menu choices for the right mouse button so that you can right-click (or double-click) on your files and have something useful happen.

▶ We give you a couple of ways to create shortcuts to opening and viewing files of unknown file type.

▶ Finally, we describe how to clear the Documents list on the Start button menu and open new blank documents on your desktop.

Chapter 14

The Recycle Bin — Going Through the Trash

In This Chapter

We reveal the secrets and subtleties of deleting files, folders, and shortcuts, including:

▶ Using the Recycle Bin to store your deleted files and shortcuts until you are sure that you want to get rid of them

▶ Seeing how files are stored in these hidden folders

▶ Deleting (and copying, moving, and renaming) files in the common file dialog boxes

▶ Restoring deleted files and folders or moving the files to new locations out of the Recycle Bin

▶ Deleting files over a network

What's Recyclable about the Recycle Bin?

The Recycle Bin doesn't recycle anything but your disk space. If you want to stretch the analogy a bit, you could say that if you delete unused files, you won't have to go out and buy new hard disks, but that is stretching it.

Our take on the use of this symbol for the trash can is Microsoft's realization that people would rather have a Recycle basket on their desktop then a trash can. It is cooler. Right?

So why the Bin part of Recycle Bin? During the early stages of the Windows 95 (then code-named Chicago) beta testing, its name was Recycle.bin. This is a pun. In a Unix file system, "bin" is a standard subdirectory where the "binary" files (executable programs) are stored. Combine the trash-receptacle meaning of the word *bin* with its Unix-world meaning and the nerds at MS got *.bin* on the Chicago desktop. An art designer or somebody in marketing made them get rid of the "." and capitalize the "b."

Secret

Want to change the name of the Recycle Bin to Trash Can? All you need to do is search your Registry for all occurrences of the name "Recycle Bin" and change each one to "Trash Can." Searching and editing the Registry is discussed in Chapter 15.

The Recycled Folders

The Recycle Bin is an alias (a stand-in) for the folders labeled Recycled. These folders are found in the Explorer on every hard disk and every logical drive on the hard disk. (If you have divided the hard disk into multiple drives, such as C, D, and so on, you will see a Recycled folder on each logical drive). The Recycle Bin icon is placed on the same level as the My Computer and Network Neighborhood icons in the Explorer. The Recycle Bin is on the desktop. The Recycled icons are attached like folders to the hard disk icons in the Explorer. They are designated as file type Recycle Bin.

If you double-click the Recycle Bin icon or any of the Recycled icons, you will find the same contents displayed in its folder window. Opening the Recycled icon attached to one hard disk will show the files deleted from the other local hard disks as well.

Microsoft made it a point to have the Recycle Bin on the desktop and not easily removable. The Recycle Bin stores all the files that have been deleted from your hard disks. You have to go to only one place to find all your deleted files.

Secret

It is possible to change the name of the Recycled folders; it just doesn't do any good. If you change **Recycled** to **Wasted**, the next time you start Windows 95, a new Recycled folder is created. You end up with two recycle receptacle icons, both of which show you the same list of deleted files when you double-click them.

Not only do you now have a Recycled folder and a Wasted folder, but how do you erase or get rid of the Wasted folder? It's not so easy.

STEPS

Getting Rid of the Wasted Folder

Step 1.   Click the Start button, Programs, MS-DOS Prompt to open a DOS window.

Step 2.   Change directories to the Wasted directory.

Step 3.   Type **dir /a** to see if any files are stored in the Wasted directory. You are going to purge these files so be sure to restore any that you might want before you do this.

Step 4.   Type **Attrib -r -s -h desktop.ini**.

Step 5.   At the DOS prompt type **del *.*** while you are in the Wasted directory to purge the files in the Wasted directory.

Step 6. Change directories to the root directory of the hard disk partition that contains the Wasted directory (**cd **).

Step 7. Remove the Wasted directory by typing **rd Wasted** at the DOS prompt.

Secret

The Recycled folders are system resources. Windows 95 regenerates them if you change the name of the Recycled folder. It doesn't want you to mess with these resources because it needs them to manage deleted files.

The Recycled folders are indeed folders, but different. The deleted files are displayed with an additional column (Original Location) in the details view of a Recycled folder window. The folder icon is not used. The Recycled folders are hidden so that you can't see them by going to DOS and typing **dir** (although you can type **dir /a** and see them).

The deleted files are stored in these folders but under new names (although you don't see this). An additional file, named Info, is stored in the Recycled folders. Again, you don't see this file (unless you type **dir/a** at a DOS prompt). The deleted files and the Info file are combined to create an entry that looks like the original deleted file entries with the addition of a column listing their original location.

What is really unusual about these Recycled folders is that their folder windows display the names and icons of all the deleted files, not just the ones stored in that particular folder or deleted from that particular logical disk drive. The files deleted from the D drive, however, are actually stored in the Recycled folder on the D drive which you can see for yourself by again typing **dir /a** at a DOS prompt after changing directories to the Recycled folder on the D drive.

The Recycle Receptacle Icons

Both the Recycle Bin and the Recycled folders use a recycling bin as an icon. If there are no files in the Recycling Bin, the icon shows an empty bin. If there are any deleted files in the Recycle Bin, the icon displays white paper stuffed into the bin. This bin is for paper recycling only — no cans or bottles.

If you delete a file and the Recycle Bin was previously empty, the Recycle Bin icon on the desktop changes to its "stuffed with white paper" state. If you drag a file to a Recycle Bin folder window, the recycling bin icon in the folder window's caption area changes from the empty symbol to the "stuffed with white paper" state.

If the Recycle Bin properties have been set to "Remove files immediately on delete," a message box with a shredding paper icon as shown in Figure 14-1 will appear when you mark a file to be deleted. You will be asked for confirmation before the file is purged from the file system.

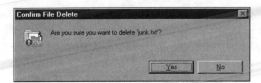

Figure 14-1: The Confirm File Delete dialog box. If you click Yes, the file is "deleted" in the sense that it is lost to the file management system and its space on the hard disk is free to be written over.

What Does the Recycle Bin Do?

Unless you have configured the Recycle Bin to remove files immediately on delete, the Recycle Bin will store the files (and shortcuts, which are stored as files) that you have deleted from your local hard disks using the Explorer or a folder window.

The deleted files will remain in the Recycle Bin until you choose the Empty Recycle Bin option. You may decide to restore a file and it will be returned to its original folder, even if that folder was previously deleted. The folder will be restored simultaneously.

Undocumented

You can't recover deleted folders that don't contain deleted files. Only files are listed in the Recycle Bin folder window, but if you Restore them, if the folders that they were stored in are also restored if they were deleted.

If you delete a folder (and, automatically, all the files contained within it) and that folder had subfolders that were empty, these subfolders cannot be restored. Some transaction software uses empty folders as temporary storage and requires that these folders be always available, so be careful what you delete.

Files or folders are sent to the Recycle Bin when you highlight them in a folder window or the Explorer and press Delete. You can right-click a file or folder and click Delete on the right mouse button menu. You can also drag and drop files or folders to the Recycle Bin icon on the desktop or in the Explorer, or to the Recycled icons in the Explorer or a folder window.

Delete files from file dialog boxes

You can also delete files from the new common file dialog boxes that are used by Windows 95-aware applications. This is done by using the File, Open command, right-clicking on the file to be deleted and selecting Delete from the right mouse menu. Both WordPad and MS Paint use these dialog boxes. If you delete a file from these dialog boxes, it is stored in the Recycle Bin.

It isn't possible to delete files in the older common file dialog boxes such as those used by Windows 3.*x* Write. These are now referred to by Microsoft as Win16 common dialog boxes. The new version of Notepad uses the new common file dialog boxes. An example of the new common file dialog box is shown in Figure 14-2.

Figure 14-2: The Windows 95 common file dialog box. You can highlight a file listed in this box and delete it by pressing the Delete key. You can also drag and drop files to and from this dialog box.

The new file dialog boxes work a lot like folder windows. You can drag and drop files to and from them. You can rename files listed in them. You can create new folders or files. You can't, however, select multiple files or folders in them.

Deleted, what does that mean?

To delete a file means it is moved to the Recycle Bin.

The fact that deleted files are stored in the Recycle Bin means that they weren't "really" deleted. They are still taking up space on your hard disk. If you never get around to emptying the Recycle Bin until your disk is full, you will experience performance slowdowns or problems with other applications as your free disk space shrinks.

What is great about the Recycle Bin is that it allows you to organize and clean up your file system without having to make a decision that you may regret a few minutes later. You are given the opportunity to restore with ease the results of any rash desire to delete something that turns out to be more important than you imagined.

The Recycle Bin provides a trade off between the safety and convenience of not deleting the file until later and the valuable disk space taken up by these deleted items. It is up to you to decide when to choose Empty the Recycle Bin.

Files that are deleted in a DOS session are not sent to the Recycle Bin. If you have an application that deletes files without using an Explorer window, folder window, or the new common file dialogs, these files likewise are not sent to the Recycle Bin. These files are deleted as far as the Windows or DOS file management system is concerned.

When you empty the Recycle Bin or delete a file in a DOS session, its name is altered in the directory listing so it doesn't show up in the file listings in an Explorer window or DOS directory list. The disk space taken up by the file is now available to be written over by new files. If they haven't been written over, files so deleted can be recovered using low-level tools. For additional information, see the section entitled *Undelete and Unerase* later in this chapter.

There are three levels of delete. If you delete a file in a folder window, it is stored in the Recycle Bin. If you delete it from the Recycle Bin, it is deleted from the file management system. If you use low-level tools to wipe the space on the hard disk that it occupied, it can't be recovered. Still, a slightly earlier version of the file may be intact on the hard disk in some other location — and therefore recoverable.

Deleting shortcuts

If you delete a shortcut, only the shortcut goes to the Recycle Bin, not the target file or folder. The original file or application stays right where it was and continues to work fine. You are deleting a file with an extension *lnk*, which designates a shortcut. Only the shortcut to the original file goes to the Recycle Bin.

Right- or left-drag to the Recycle Bin

There are many ways to delete a file. You can drag the file to the Recycle Bin or a Recycled icon or to an opened Recycle Bin or Recycled folder window. If you left-drag the file icon, it is moved to the Recycle Bin. If you right-drag it, you are given the choice to move the file or cancel the move.

You can drag files back out of the Recycle Bin and place them in any folder, not just their original location. If you right-drag a file out of the Recycle Bin to a folder window, you will be given the chance to move the file or cancel the move.

If you right-click a file icon and click Delete from the right mouse button menu, or if you highlight a file icon and press the Delete key you will be asked to confirm your deletion. It doesn't matter if the Recycle Bin has been set to Remove files immediately on delete or not; you will still be asked for confirmation of the deletion.

If you drag a file (either left or right) to the Recycle Bin, you will not be asked for confirmation unless Remove files immediately on delete has been set. The Windows 95 designers assumed that if you were willing to go to all the trouble of dragging the file to the Recycle Bin, you meant it.

You can turn off the delete confirmation message by following these steps:

STEPS

Turning Off Delete Confirmation

Step 1.   Right-click the Recycle Bin icon on your desktop.

Step 2.   Click Properties in the right mouse button menu.

Step 3.   Click the Global tab (if necessary).

Step 4.   Click the Display delete confirmation dialog checkbox so as to uncheck it.

Shift+Del

You can delete files without sending them to the Recycle Bin — in other words, purge them — by highlighting their filenames, holding down the Shift key, and pressing the Delete key. (You can also hold down Shift while clicking Delete on a right mouse-button menu.) The files won't be sent to the Recycle Bin because by deliberately holding down the Shift key, you are telling Windows 95 that you want these files purged. Don't confuse this use of Shift+Delete with the feature in some word processors, which use Shift+Delete to send selected text to the Clipboard. Most newer word processors now also support Ctrl+x to cut to the Clipboard, so if you use this key combination, you won't mix up the meaning of Shift+Delete.

Don't Delete Your Hard Disk

If you right-click a hard disk icon in the Explorer or in a folder window, you won't find Delete on the right mouse button menu. It's not a good idea to delete a hard disk. You can't. But you can delete — or move to the Recycle Bin — all the files on the hard disk by dragging the disk icon to the Recycle Bin.

This is not a good idea, especially if the space taken up by the current files on the hard disk is greater than the space set aside for deleted files in the Recycle Bin. If you delete a hard disk, you are moving all the files on the hard disk to the Recycle Bin. This is not possible if there isn't room for them there.

All this can get quite confusing. The Recycled folders are attached to a hard disk, but they show all the files that have been deleted or moved to the Recycle Bin no matter which hard disk (or disk partition) they were deleted from. If you drag a hard disk icon to the Recycle Bin, are you also deleting the files stored in the Recycled folder?

You Can't Delete My Computer or Other Key Components

You can drag My Computer, Network Neighborhood, and the Recycle Bin and drop them on the Recycle Bin folder window. But when you do, you will just get a beep. Windows 95 won't let you delete these things, thankfully.

The same is true of the Printers folder, Control Panel, Fonts folder, and Dial-Up Networking. You just get a beep. You can try this with the right mouse button drag, which feels safer because it normally has a confirmation menu.

You *Can* Delete a Floppy Disk

Files on a floppy disk are not moved to the Recycle Bin when you delete them. You can drag the floppy drive icon to the Recycle Bin (icon or folder window) and all the files will be purged after you are first advised of that fact and allowed to change your mind. The dialog box that appears displays an icon of a file being shredded as a way to indicate to you that your file will become very difficult to recover if you continue.

If you highlight a file that is stored on a floppy disk and press the Delete key, you will get the same notification. Windows 95 just doesn't provide as much safety for files on floppy disks as it does for files on your hard disks although it does ask every time for confirmation of the deletion (purge).

Going Through the Trash — Retrieving Deleted Files

It is easy to get files back from the Recycle Bin. Just double-click the Recycle Bin icon on the desktop to open the Recycle Bin folder window, as shown in Figure 14-3. Right-click the item that you want to restore to its original location and then click Restore. The file is restored to its original location. If the folder that it was stored in has been deleted, it is restored also.

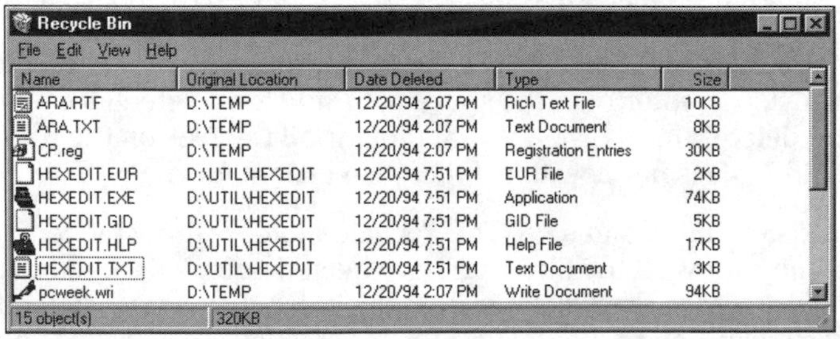

Name	Original Location	Date Deleted	Type	Size
ARA.RTF	D:\TEMP	12/20/94 2:07 PM	Rich Text File	10KB
ARA.TXT	D:\TEMP	12/20/94 2:07 PM	Text Document	8KB
CP.reg	D:\TEMP	12/20/94 2:07 PM	Registration Entries	30KB
HEXEDIT.EUR	D:\UTIL\HEXEDIT	12/20/94 7:51 PM	EUR File	2KB
HEXEDIT.EXE	D:\UTIL\HEXEDIT	12/20/94 7:51 PM	Application	74KB
HEXEDIT.GID	D:\UTIL\HEXEDIT	12/20/94 7:51 PM	GID File	5KB
HEXEDIT.HLP	D:\UTIL\HEXEDIT	12/20/94 7:51 PM	Help File	17KB
HEXEDIT.TXT	D:\UTIL\HEXEDIT	12/20/94 7:51 PM	Text Document	3KB
pcweek.wri	D:\TEMP	12/20/94 2:07 PM	Write Document	94KB

15 object(s)   320KB

Figure 14-3: The Recycle Bin folder window. The second column lists the original location (folder) of the deleted file. Right-click the file you want back and then click Restore from the menu.

You can also just drag the files out of the Recycle Bin and move them to wherever you want. Dragging only moves files in and out of the Recycle Bin, no matter whether you right-drag or left-drag. There are no options for Copy, Create Shortcut, or whatever else you would expect to see with a normal right drag and drop.

Tip

You can use any of the selection techniques discussed in Chapter 8 to choose which files will be moved or restored to their original location. Even Undo Delete is available from the Edit menu on the menu bar of the Recycle Bin folder window. If you right-click the client area of the Recycle Bin folder window, Undo Delete is on the right mouse button menu. That is, it is available if deleting a file was the last file management action that you carried out.

Undocumented

Do you want to check out a graphic or text file that you deleted? Maybe you want to edit it after you deleted it. As long as you haven't emptied your Recycle Bin, you can drag and drop the file from the Recycle Bin onto your application icon. After you're done viewing the file you don't have to worry about deleting it, because it wasn't undeleted in the first place.

If you edited it and want to save its new version, save it to another folder. The Save As name of the file will default to its Recycle Bin name, which is not its original name (even though the original name is shown in the Recycle Bin folder window). This name is used internally by the Recycle Bin to track the deleted files. You may want to change it if you save this edited file to a new folder.

Tip

Unlike moving, copying, or deleting a file, emptying the Recycle Bin is not a recoverable action. You won't find UnEmpty the Recycle Bin on the right mouse button menu. (If the emptied files haven't yet been overwritten by other files, however, you may still be able to get them back with an Undelete utility, as we discuss later in this chapter.)

Emptying the Recycle Bin

As you have seen, dropping a file into the Recycle Bin or pressing the Delete key while highlighting an icon does nothing more than move the files to the Recycle Bin. It certainly doesn't delete them — unless you chose the Remove files immediately on delete option in the Recycle Bin properties sheet. If you want to delete the items in the Recycle Bin, you need to choose the action Empty Recycle Bin.

STEPS

Emptying the Recycle Bin

Step 1.   Double-click the Recycle Bin icon on the desktop.

Step 2.   Click File in the menu bar followed by Empty Recycle Bin.

(continued)

STEPS *(continued)*

Emptying the Recycle Bin

Step 3.   All the files in the Recycle Bin are purged.

If you want to delete only some of the items in the Recycle Bin, select those items first and then click Delete in the Recycle Bin's File menu. Or, you can right-click the items that you want purged and click Delete from the right mouse button menu.

Remove Files Immediately on Delete

You can set a Recycle Bin property to remove files immediately on delete. When you delete a file, it is no longer moved to the Recycle Bin but is immediately purged from the file system.

If you drag files to the Recycle Bin or highlight them and press the Delete key, you are asked for confirmation of the file deletion because now they are purged. This is also true if you right-click a file and choose Delete.

To set the properties of the Recycle Bin, right-click the Recycle Bin icon or client area of the Recycle Bin folder window and choose Properties. The Recycle Bin Properties sheets, as shown in Figure 14-4, will appear on the desktop.

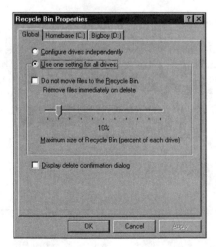

Figure 14-4: The Recycle Bin Properties sheets. You can choose whether to remove files immediately on delete or not. You can choose the maximum size of the Recycled folders on each hard disk and whether to configure the hard disks separately.

In the Recycle Bin Properties sheet, check whether you want the files to be removed immediately on delete or not. You can set the maximum size of the Recycled folder on all or any of the hard disks.

The Recycle Bin and Networks

If the Recycle Bin shows you all the deleted files, then what if you are connected to a local or wide area network? Are you going to see all the deleted files on all the servers in your Recycle Bin? Nope.

Undocumented

You see only the files that you deleted from your local hard disks. It doesn't matter if the server resources (a hard disk or folder) are mapped to a local drive letter or not. You can double-click a Recycled folder on the host or server computer and you still will see only the files that you deleted from your local hard disks.

If you attempt to delete a file on the host, it is the same as if you deleted a file from a floppy disk — it is purged. The deleted file is not saved to the Recycle Bin.

Undelete and Unerase

If a file is purged, it is no longer recognized by the Windows 95 file management system. Files are purged when you choose Empty the Recycle Bin, when you hold down the Shift key and press the Delete key, or when you delete a file and the Recycle Bin Properties sheet has been set to Remove files immediately on delete.

When a file is purged, all that happens is that the first letter of its filename is changed so that it is no longer recognized as a legitimate filename by the file management system. The space taken up by that file is now available for use when other files are written to the hard disk.

DOS 6.x came with an Undelete utility. This utility is not available with Windows 95. But you can use the old DOS 6.x Undelete utility to unpurge files. You just need to be sure to keep this utility around after you upgrade to Windows 95. You'll find Undelete.exe in your old DOS directory.

Undelete works to recover files that haven't been overwritten by new files. It doesn't do much good if more than a short time has elapsed between the time that you purged the file and the time you want to Undelete it. The probability that it has been overwritten increases as time passes.

Undocumented

To use Undelete, you need to run it in MS-DOS mode with the file system locked. One way to do this is to choose Start, Shut Down, and choose "Restart the computer in MS-DOS mode" from the menu. At the DOS prompt, type **Lock**, then **Undelete**. When you are done, type **Unlock** and then **Exit** to relaunch Windows 95. Be sure to copy Undelete.exe to your \Windows\Command directory before you do this, so it will be found when you type Undelete at the DOS prompt.

Symantec has released Norton Utilities for Windows 95. The utilities are integrated with the Windows 95 desktop and user interface. They are right there in the Recycle Bin, as you can see if you right-click the Recycle Bin icon and look at the right mouse button menu. You can also click Properties on the right mouse button menu and see more evidence of the Norton Utilities.

Norton Utilities let you unerase files that have been purged without having to go to MS-DOS mode and using the Undelete utility. They have the same problem to deal with as does Undelete — a file whose name has been altered and a hard disk space that may still contain the purged file's contents but has been marked available to be used by other files. Use the Norton Utilities Unerase as soon as you can after you inadvertently purge a file in order to have a chance to recover it.

Summary

There are three layers of delete. We show you how the Recycle Bin helps you delete files without undue worry.

▶ You can access and manage the Recycle Bin with minimal effort. It is right there on the desktop.

▶ We show you how deleted files are stored in a special hidden system folder that displays their properties in the Recycle Bin manner.

▶ The common file dialog boxes are like mini folder windows. We show you how to use them to delete, copy, move, and rename files.

▶ You can move files into and out of the Recycle Bin with ease to any location that you please. Dragging with either the right or left mouse button works the same.

▶ If you delete files on a floppy or over a network, they really do go away without going to the Recycle Bin first.

Chapter 15

The Registry — The Real User Interface

Ini Files, RIP

It is Microsoft's intention that configuration files, otherwise known as *ini* files, cease to be used by both Microsoft and by other developers. Windows directories throughout the world are filling up with these files. Win.ini and System.ini, Microsoft's main contribution to this blight, have grown as some developers took the easy route and put their applications' vital parameters in these files.

This has led to a number of difficulties as users and system administrators try to access the computer's and user's configurations. There are so many different files that no one can keep track of what is where. In addition, there is no clear-cut systematic distinction between values that are user-specific and those that are machine/software-specific.

Windows 3.1 introduced the Registry (Reg.dat), which stored file association and OLE information. The Registry was greatly expanded in Windows NT and has returned to Windows 95 ready to be the central repository of user and system configuration data.

The fact that Microsoft programmers still use *ini* files, such as Telephon.ini, in Windows 95 means that Microsoft hasn't yet gotten it together to completely make the transition. Telephony (TAPI) was developed before the Windows 95 Registry was ready.

Win.ini and System.ini (and other *ini* files) are provided with Windows 95. These files are still necessary for Windows to operate properly. That is, not all the information they contain has been transferred to the Registry. For example, a list of font substitutes is still kept in Win.ini.

The Win.ini and System.ini files are also retained to maintain compatibility with Windows 3.*x* applications and other, previous methods of storing system and user configuration information.

The Registry Keywords and Structure

The Registry is a storehouse for configuration values and settings that are used to determine how Windows 95 operates. It is supposed to, over time, assume all the functions of the configuration files found in the Windows folder.

The Registry also keeps track of a list of hardware and hardware configurations that the Windows 95 setup and hardware detection routines discovered. If you change your hardware configuration, the Registry is updated.

The keys in the Registry are similar to the bracketed headings found in the Win.ini or System.ini files. Registry keys, unlike *ini* file headings, can and do contain subkeys. While only text strings were allowed in *ini* files, values in the Registry can consist of executable code.

User.dat can store values for multiple users using one computer. Each user has his or her own area of the User.dat file.

The Registry is a database divided into six main branches, as can be seen in Figure 15-1. Each branch is a *handle* to a different set of Key values, hence the names HKEY_CLASSES_ROOT, and so on, shown in Figure 15-1. The branches are described in the following sections.

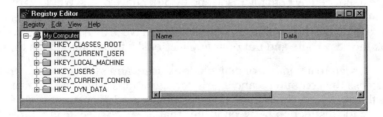

Figure 15-1: The Registry editor. Click a [+] to open a branch of the Registry.

[HKEY_CLASSES_ROOT]

The branch that contains the file extensions and file/application associations as well as OLE data. This branch is an *alias* (simultaneously updated copy) of HKEY_LOCAL_MACHINE\Software\Classes. Changes in this area of the Registry are discussed in Chapter 13.

[HKEY_USERS]

This is User.dat. The desktop configurations, network connections, and information specific to users is kept here.

[HKEY_CURRENT_USER]

The portion of HKEY_USERS that is applicable to the current user. If there is only one user, the default user, then both branches are the same.

Many of the examples of editing the Registry that are used in this book have made the implicit assumption that you are editing the values only for the current user or for the default user. Therefore, many of those changes take place along this branch of the Registry.

If you want to make the indicated changes for other users with different login names, you need to track down the appropriate locations in the HKEY_USERS branch.

There are similar values in this branch and in the next one. The values in this branch take precedence over the values in the next one.

[HKEY_LOCAL_MACHINE]

The computer hardware and its installed software. Multiple configurations for the hardware are stored if the computer can have different configurations, such as hooked up to the network or not, and docked or not.

[HKEY_CURRENT_CONFIGURATION]

The Display settings and the available printers are here.

[HKEY_DYN_DATA]

The Registry keeps data on Windows performance parameters. Their values are stored here. This information is kept in RAM after Windows 95 loads, and is available and is being updated on an ongoing basis. Performance statistics are being recorded and can be viewed using the System Monitor.

Each of these branches is divided into further branches. Each node is a key. You can follow any of the branches out untill you run out of keys and have only data.

Secret

To expand all branches below a node, highlight the node and press Alt+*. That is, Alt plus the numeric keyboard asterisk. To collapse all the branches below a node, click its minus sign, highlight the node, and press F5.

Much of the Registry is not of much use to a user or system administrator. It is maintained by the operating system, configured when you install new software, or better edited through user interface elements in the Control Panel and elsewhere.

We have, however, found wide applicability for editing the HKEY_CLASSES_ROOT branch and the HKEY_CURRENT_USER branch. You may find that the other branches also provide useful areas for individual customization.

The Registry Files

System.dat and User.dat are the two hidden, system, read-only files that make up the Registry. Unlike the *ini* files, they are binary files that can't be read easily with an ASCII file editor. You need the Registry editor to examine the variables and values stored in the Registry.

Actually, it is possible to use WordPad to read the Registry, but you need to export it to a text file first. This is an option found in the Registry editor. The resulting file (if you export the whole thing instead of just a branch) is too big to be read by Notepad. You can make changes to the exported Registry file and import the altered file back into the Registry database, updating the previous Registry entries. We discuss this more in the later section entitled *The Registry Editor*.

There is only one Registry on your computer, but it is made up of the two files — System.dat and User.dat. If there is a policy file (a file with the *pol* extension), it is also part of the Registry. We discuss policy files and their implications for the Registry in Chapter 12. The Registry editor displays the two files as one Registry when you invoke it.

The Registry files and their backups (System.da0 and User.da0) have the DOS file attributes of hidden, read-only, and system. This doesn't prevent them from being displayed in an Explorer or a folder window as long as the View, Option, View dialog box setting (found on the menu bar of an Explorer or folder window) is set to show all files.

System.dat and User.dat are by default stored in the \Windows folder, or the main Windows folder created during installation. (Remember that while we call our folder \Windows, you may have named yours something else, such as Win95 or Win.) If your \Windows folder is on a compressed drive, these files (and their backups) are stored on the boot drive. Other variations are possible with networked computers.

It should be obvious from the names that the System.dat file stores information specific to a computer and to the software to be found on that computer. System.dat tracks the detected hardware and its configuration, as well as Windows and other installed programs (that put their information in the Registry).

Likewise, User.dat stores user-specific information, including mouse speed, color scheme, cursor scheme, wallpaper, accessibility settings, icon spacing, fonts, keyboard layout, keyboard delay and speed, regional settings, Explorer settings, attributes of standard Windows software, and network passwords.

A user's desktop icons and network connections are stored in User.dat. If the appropriate choice is made in the User Profiles Properties sheet (found in the Passwords Control Panel), each individual user can have his or her own Start menu or Program Groups in the Program Manager.

Registry recovery

Every time that you successfully start (or restart) your computer, Windows 95 backs up System.dat and User.dat to System.da0 and User.da0, respectively. If Windows 95 fails to start, you can use the backup files from the last successful start to recover.

There is an additional System.dat backup file, System 1st, It is found in the root directory of your boot drive (or its host). This file was created when you first installed Windows 95 and contains your hardware and software configuration as the Windows 95 setup program understood it.

If your Registry becomes so corrupted that you can't recover it, you can always copy this file over System.dat in your Windows 95 folder.

If Windows 95 fails to start successfully, it will revert to Safe mode. When you find yourself in Safe mode, you know that you have had an unsuccessful start and that the Registry files were not written to their backups. The backup files are the ones that worked the last time there was a successful start.

You will now find yourself in Windows with the words "Safe" on the four corners of your screen. You can recover the last good Registry files from their backup files by double-clicking on the Registry backup recover icon that you will have set up following our instructions, shutting down Windows, and restarting.

STEPS

Installing a Registry Files Backup Recovery Program

Step 1. Using the Explorer, copy RegRecov.bat from the Registry folder on the enclosed shareware CD-ROM to your Windows folder.

Step 2. Double-click this file in the Explorer once you have it stored in your Windows folder and then restart Windows 95. If you want to create a shortcut for it on your desktop (or some other convenient location), follow the next steps.

Step 3. Right-click the desktop. Click New and then Shortcut.

Step 4. Click the Browse button. Find RegRecov.bat in your Windows 95 folder. Double-click it and then click Next.

Step 5. Type in the Name **Registry Recovery**. Click Next. Click Finish.

Step 6. Right-click the Registry Recovery icon on your desktop. Click Properties.

Step 7. Click the Program Tab. Click the Change Icon button, and then the Browse Button. Find Pifmgr.dll in your \Windows\System folder. Double-click it.

Step 8. Click the Cloud and Lightning icon, and then the OK button in the Browse dialog box. Click the Apply button in the Properties sheet.

Step 9. Change the Run field in the Program Properties sheet to Minimized. Click the Close on Exit box. Click the OK button for the RegRecov.bat Properties sheets.

You now have an icon on your desktop that will copy the last successful version of your Registry files over the files that didn't work. To use it, double-click this icon. When it has completed its work, shut down Windows and restart with the recovered files.

The cloud with lightning icon is quite appropriate for this function. It combines the saving-for-a-rainy-day aspect with the lightning-is-now-striking aspect.

Registry backup

Even though the Registry files are backed up after every successful start, it doesn't hurt to make a backup of these files periodically. You also might want to do it just before you edit the Registry. This can be achieved through the use of a DOS batch file. (Isn't it amazing how useful DOS can be?) Such a file is included with the shareware accompanying this book.

STEPS

Installing the Registry Backup Batch File

Step 1.   Using the Explorer, find Regback.bat in the Registry folder on the enclosed shareware CD-ROM. Copy it to your Windows folder (or any folder that you find convenient)

Step 2.   Right-click the desktop. Click New and then Shortcut.

Step 3.   Click the Browse button. Find Regback.bat in your Windows 95 folder. Double-click it and then click the Next button.

Step 4.   Type in the Name **Registry Backup**. Click Next. Click Finish.

Step 5.   Right-click the Registry Backup icon on your desktop. Click Properties.

Step 6.   Click the Program Tab. Click the Change Icon button, and then the Browse button. Find Pifmgr.dll in your \Windows\System folder. Double-click it.

Step 7.   Click the Umbrella icon, and then the OK button in the Browse dialog box. Click the Apply button in the Properties sheet.

Step 8.   Change the Run field in the Program Properties sheet to Minimized. Click the Close on Exit box. Click the OK button for the Regback Properties sheets.

Be sure you have room on your hard disk for the Registry files (approximately 500-600K). You can copy these files from your Windows folder to a floppy disk if you like or edit the batch file to save these files directly to a diskette.

Tip

In the previous section we wrote about a Registry file recovery batch file that used the Registry backup files automatically created each time Windows 95 starts successfully. You may wish to use the backup files that you have created manually instead of these files as the Registry files. If so, you will need to copy the files created by the manual backup process over System.dat and User.dat.

The manual backup process creates two files — System.dak and User.dak. You can use the batch file RegMan.bat, which you will find in the Registry folder on the enclosed shareware CD-ROM. Copy this batch file to your Windows folder (or any folder that you find convenient). You can place a shortcut to it on the desktop or to any location that you like. Follow a variation of the previously given steps, choosing a different icon.

The Registry Editor

In a number of chapters in this book, we reveal how to use the Registry editor to change a value or add a key. Microsoft has created numerous user interface elements — the Control Panel, dialog boxes, and Properties sheets — designed to let you change the values stored in the Registry without having to resort to directly editing it. It is Microsoft's hope that these elements are enough. They aren't.

If you can make the changes you need without using the Registry editor, by all means do so. Changes made through Properties sheets and dialog boxes are reflected immediately in changes in the behavior of that portion of the operating system affected by the values stored in the Registry.

Changes made using the Registry editor may not be used until the next time you start Windows (and the Registry values are read and stored in memory). We have indicated throughout the text when the changes you make take effect immediately versus when you need to restart Windows.

Making changes to Registry values using Windows 95 user interface elements is the safest means of changing these values. It is quite possible, using the Registry editor, to delete or alter vital elements of the Registry. Some changes may prevent Windows 95 from operating correctly.

One precaution that you can take to recover from such an unfortunate editing session is to make a backup of the Registry files before you edit them. If you have copied our Registry backup batch file to your hard disk and made a shortcut to it, you can run it every time before you edit the Registry. You can even edit the shortcut that you use to start the Registry editor to call Regback.bat first.

If you engage in a course of action that damages the Registry, you still have your automatic backups. If you restart Windows after an editing session that has gotten out of hand, and Windows can't start successfully, you always can go to the backups.

On the other hand, you may have done some damage during your editing session—perhaps made some inadvertent changes that you really don't remember and didn't want to make anyway—but not enough damage to prevent Windows 95 from starting. In this case, an intentional backup before editing would be very handy because Windows 95 will start successfully after your rash of editing. Now the backup and your master are identical — and both contain settings that you don't want.

If you backup intentionally before you make editing changes, you can always recover to your intentional backups. Otherwise, you will have to manually undo your egregious labors.

Starting the Registry editor

You'll find the Registry editor in the \Windows folder. The Windows 95 setup/installation does not place it on any of the Start menus. Microsoft is not that eager for the uninitiated to use this tool. The application file name is Regedit.exe. Your system administrator may have removed it from your computer.

If you are going to use the editor, it is a good idea to create a shortcut to access it. Place the shortcut on the desktop or in the Start Menu folders. If you don't know how to create shortcuts, you shouldn't be messing around with the Registry editor (unless you are following our explicit step-by-step instructions).

Editing with the Registry editor

Chapters throughout this book contain discussions that point to areas of the Registry to be edited. Let's take a minute to see what the editing commands are and how to use them.

To edit the Registry it helps to get to a location that has some useful keys, constants, and values. We'll use the current desktop in the following steps as an example of a very fruitful location.

STEPS

Editing the Registry

Step 1. Click the plus sign to the left of HKEY_CURRENT_USER. Click the plus sign to the left of Control Panel, and then the one next to Desktop. (The name HKEY refers to the fact that it is a handle to a key. The Registry is filled with keys that eventually have data attached to them.)

Step 2. Highlight the WindowMetrics name next to its folder icon. Notice that the right pane is now filled with constant names (Names) and values (Data).

Step 3. In Chapter 7, we showed you how to create a new constant (MinAnimate) to turn off the sliding windows effect. If you haven't created this constant, you can do so now (you can easily get rid of it or change its value so that your current configuration remains the same).

Step 4. Right-click in the right pane of the Registry editor (but not a constant name or value). A New button, as shown in Figure 15-2, appears. Highlight the New button, and a new menu appears. You can choose to create a Key, a String Value, a Binary Value, or a DWORD Value. The key and/or any of the constants will be attached to the WindowMetrics key.

(continued)

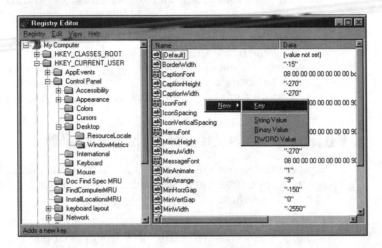

Figure 15-2: Inserting new keys or values in the Registry. Right-click the right pane of the Registry editor to insert new keys or constants.

Step 5. Right-click next to the Desktop key in the left pane of the Registry editor. As shown in Figure 15-3, the right mouse button menu will give you the choice of collapsing this expanded branch of the Registry; creating a New Key, String Value, or Binary Value; Finding a text or numerical string in the local branch; or Deleting or Renaming the Key.

It is not a good idea to delete or rename a key unless you know exactly what you are doing. Adding a new key or value (actually a constant that has a value, which the Registry editor refers to as Data) may change the way the Windows 95 operates, but it won't do any damage.

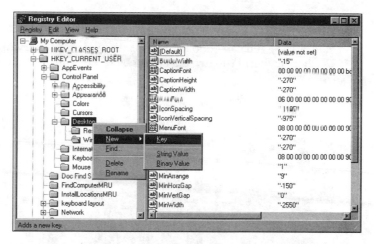

Figure 15-3: Right-click next to a key in the left pane of the Registry editor to quickly access a right mouse button menu.

Step 6. Right-click a constant in the Name column in the right pane of the Registry editor. A right mouse button menu appears, allowing you to modify the constant's value, delete the constant and its value, or rename the constant.

Step 7. The Edit menu on the Registry's menu bar provides similar choices to those found on the right mouse button menu when you right-click next to a key or a constant. The Edit menu changes depending on whether you have highlighted a key or a constant. You can't highlight a value (or Data).

Editing the Registry consists of adding or deleting keys, adding new constants and their values to be associated with the keys, and modifying those constants and their values — pretty straightforward. It's knowing what keys, constants, and values to add, rename, or delete that's the trick.

Exporting and importing the Registry

It is possible to export the Registry to an ASCII file with the *reg* extension. The keys, constants, and values stored in System.dat and User.dat are written out to an ASCII text file that can be read by WordPad. The size of the file for the whole Registry is about 500K (before additional applications are registered).

You can export the whole Registry or just a branch of the Registry. To export either, choose Registry, Export Registry File in the Registry's menu bar. To export a branch, highlight the branch in the left pane of the Registry before you choose to export it.

Choosing Registry, Export Registry File displays the common file dialog box with an added modifier extension attached at the bottom, as shown in Figure 15-4. You can choose to export the whole Registry or just a branch by clicking one of the two check boxes at the bottom of the dialog box.

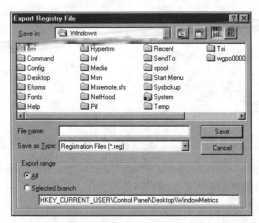

Figure 15-4: The Export Registry File dialog box. You can determine how much of the Registry is exported (the highlighted branch or all of the Registry) by clicking one of the two check boxes at the bottom of this dialog box.

You should export the Registry or a branch of the Registry into a file with a *reg* extension, as is the default in the Export Registry dialog box. The *reg* extension will be added automatically if you type in a file name. The exported Registry is a text file. Using the *reg* extension makes it easy to merge or import the Registry or its branch later if you edit the exported file.

The exported Registry file can be read easily by WordPad. Right-click the exported file and choose Edit on the right mouse button menu. Don't double-click the file, as the default action for a file of this file type is to merge it back into the Registry. Figure 15-5 shows how part of an exported Registry file looks in WordPad.

Tip

The exported text file encloses the key name, including all preceding key names, in square brackets. The constant names are enclosed in double quote marks. String values associated with the constant names are also enclosed in double quotes. DWORD values (double word in either decimal or hexadecimal format) begin with *dword:*. Binary values begin with *hex:*.

Searching an exported Registry file

One reason to export a Registry file is to be able to search it quickly. The Registry editor has a find facility, but it is slow. You can bring the exported Registry text file into WordPad and use its binoculars icon to find a text or numeric string much quicker then you can find the same string searching the Registry.

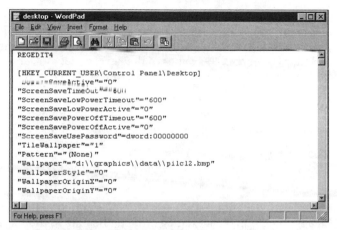

Figure 15-5: The Control Panel\Desktop key area in the Registry exported to a text file. The key values are surrounded by square brackets. The constants and their string values are surrounded by double quotes.

This can be quite useful when investigating the structure of the Registry or trying to find that constant name whose value you want to change. You can have both the Registry editor open and on your desktop, and the exported Registry file open in WordPad. Search for the constant name in WordPad. Then, in the Registry editor, click the plus signs next to the Registry keys to expand the branch of the Registry that contains the constant that you are looking for.

Editing an exported Registry file

Of course, you can edit the Registry directly, so why would you export it, or a branch of it, to edit? If you wanted to make a lot of changes, the editing capabilities of WordPad are much more powerful then those provided by the Registry editor. You can make large-scale changes, as you can see in the example in the section later in this chapter entitled *Adding a Windows Write file type definition to the New menu*.

The Registry editor allows only certain kinds of values to be typed into the fields for keys, constant names, or values. This prevents many of the errors that you might otherwise encounter by just editing the export Registry file.

You edit an exported Registry file so that you can import or merge it back into the Registry. If you are not comfortable doing this, then make all your Registry changes either though the Windows 95 Properties sheets or dialog boxes, or directly in the Registry editor.

Importing or merging a text file into the Registry

Once you have exported a branch or all of the Registry and edited it, you can put it back in. Now might be a good time to back up the Registry using the procedure outlined previously in the *Registry backup* section of this chapter.

Merging and importing are the same thing. Double-click an exported Registry file (a file with a *reg* extension) and it is imported or merged into the Registry. Right-click an exported file and you will see that the first choice on the right mouse button menu is Merge. The values of the keys, constants, and data in the exported text file overwrite or are added to the values stored in the Registry.

Of course, you can create a text file with the correctly formatted key, constant name, and data values from scratch and import it into the Registry. You will need to review exported files until you understand the format.

You can also import a Registry file (actually a text file that has been correctly formatted) by clicking Registry, Import Registry File in the Registry editor's menu bar.

If you are just importing a branch, then the branch is added to the Registry. If the branch is a new version of an existing branch, the data in that branch in the Registry is added .

Double-click to edit a Registry file

We would rather edit an exported Registry file by double-clicking it and merge it by right-clicking it and choosing Merge from the right mouse menu. This is safer and more in line with the rest of the Windows 95 interface. To make this change, take the following steps:

STEPS
Making Editing the Default Behavior for Registry files

Step 1. Open an Explorer Window. Click View, Options. Click the File Types tab.

Step 2. Scroll down the Registered file types window to Registration Entries. Highlight Registration Entries. Click Edit.

Step 3. Highlight Edit in the Actions window. Click the Set Default button.

Step 4. Click OK in the Edit File Type dialog box and OK in the File Types dialog box.

Backing up the Registry with export and import

A nifty way to back up and protect your Registry is to export it to a text file. If there is a problem with your Registry, you can import the earlier saved version of the exported Registry.

Export the Registry, using the Registry editor, to a name like Backup.reg. You can always edit this file if you like. When there is a problem with your Registry you can import this file back in to the Registry by right-clicking it and choosing Merge.

Adding a Windows Write file type definition to the New menu

Secret

Windows Write is a small editor—sort of a word processor—that comes with Windows 3.x. Microsoft did not include Windows Write with Windows 95. It has not been revamped to take advantage of the new common file dialog boxes, the print preview facility, and other Windows 95 features. That doesn't mean it is not useful—it is awfully fast—and if you have saved your copy from Windows 3.x, you can still use it.

You have to be sure that you save Write.exe to another name before you set up Windows 95 over your existing Windows 3.x folder. You can then copy it back over the phony Write.exe that Windows 95 constructs in your \Windows folder. This phony Write.exe just calls WordPad.

You can create a file type definition for Windows Write by editing the Windows 95 *wri* extension file/program association with WordPad using View, Options, File Type in an Explorer Window. Review the section entitled *Creating a new file type* in Chapter 13 to understand how to do this or follow the steps below.

Secret

After you have changed the association of *wri* files from WordPad to Window Write, use the instructions in the *Adding items to the New document menu* section of Chapter 13 to create a new menu item for Windows Write files. The problem with these instructions is that unless you know the file header for a Windows Write file, you won't be able to have the New menu item actually create a Windows Write file for you. It will instead create a text file with a *wri* extension.

Even if you know what the Windows Write file header is, it will take a long time to type it in using the Registry editor. This is where the ability to export a branch of the Registry, edit it, and merge it back in comes in handy.

STEPS

Adding Windows Write to the New Menu

Step 1. Back up your Registry using the shortcut to the Regback.bat icon created earlier in the *Registry backup* section of this chapter.

Step 2. Copy the Windows 3.1x version of Write.exe and Write.hlp to your Windows 95 folder.

Step 3. Open an Explorer window. On the menu bar click View, Options.

(continued)

STEPS (continued)

Adding Windows Write to the New Menu

Step 4. Click the File Types tab and scroll down the list box of file types until you get to the Write Document entry. Highlight it.

Step 5. Click the Edit button. Highlight the open action and click the Edit button. Type in **C:\Windows\Write.exe,** assuming that your Windows 95 folder is named Windows and is stored on drive C. Click OK.

Step 6. Highlight the print action and click the Edit button. Type in **C:\Windows\Write.exe /p.** Click OK.

Step 7. Highlight the print to action. Click the Remove button. Click OK. Click the Close button. Click the next Close button.

Step 8. Right-click the Write.reg file in the Registry folder of the shareware CD-ROM and choose Merge to merge it into the Registry. Double-click on your Registry shortcut on the desktop.

Step 9. Traverse the Registry to the following key: [HKEY_CLASSES_ROOT]\.wri\ShellNew.

Step 10. If there is a NullFile under the ShellNew key constant, delete it and its empty value. Double-click the constant name "Data" to display the Edit Binary Value dialog box, as shown in Figure 15-6.

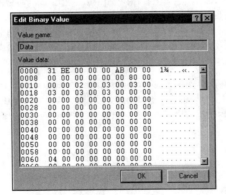

Figure 15-6: The Edit Binary Value dialog box. You edit the binary value in this dialog box by highlighting the values you want to replace and typing in new ones. It is a tricky process.

Step 11. You can compare the values in the Edit Binary Value dialog box with the values in the Write.reg file. Right-click the Write.reg file and click Edit. WordPad will display the file.

Step 12. Now, if you right-click the desktop, choose New, and then Choose Write Document, an empty file with the header of a Windows Write file will be created. When you double-click its icon on the desktop, Windows Write will start and there will be no dialog box asking you whether you want to convert this text file.

The method used to create this item on the New menu is generally applicable to other applications. We have created a Registry file with the correct file header information that can be merged into the Registry. Here's how you can do this for your application:

Secret

STEPS

Creating an Empty Header File to Merge into the Registry

Step 1.   The Write.reg file was created from an empty Windows Write file. We started Windows Write, clicked File, New in its menu bar and then File, Save. We named the file Empty.wri. You can do something similar with your application.

Step 2.   Install the hex editor that comes with the enclosed shareware CD-ROM. Open the new empty file with this editor.

Step 3.   Print the output of the hex editor to a file using the generic/text printer attached to a file. Edit the text in this file in a word processor such as Microsoft Word that has macro capabilities. Massage it into a format that looks like what you find in the Write.reg file.

Step 4.   Once you have a file that looks like Write.reg, but changed to apply to your application, follow the steps in the previous section (making variations that are applicable to your program) to create a modified Registry entry for your application. You will now be able to create files using the New menu that have the correct format for your application.

Editing other people's Registries

The Registry editor gives you the option of editing Registries on other computers that you are networked to over a dial-up line, Direct Cable Connection, or LAN. This feature requires a Windows NT server on your network to provide user-level (as opposed to share-level) network security.

In addition, if you are going to let your Registry be edited by someone else on your network, you must configure your networking options on your computers to add the Remote Registry service. Only other users who have user-level access to your computer will be able to edit (or use their Registry editor to view) your Registry.

Setting user-level security

If you have a Windows NT server on your network, set your computer to use user-level security by taking the following steps:

STEPS

Setting User Level Security

Step 1.   Click the Start button, then Settings, then Control Panel.

Step 2.   Double-click the Network icon.

Step 3.   Click the Access Control Tab. Click the User-level access control check box. Type in the name of the Windows NT server that keeps the list of users of groups.

A system administrator will be responsible for maintaining the user groups on the Windows NT server. It may be that only the system administrator has access to your Registry.

Setting up a computer to allow its Registry to be edited

You can set up your computer to be a Registry server. That is, you allow people at other computers to edit or view your Registry. To so this, take the following steps:

STEPS

Configuring Your Computer as a Registry Server

Step 1.   Click the Start button, then Settings, then Control Panel.

Step 2.   Double-click the Network icon.

Step 3.   Click the Add button. Double-click the Service icon in the Select Network Component Type dialog box.

Step 4.   Click Microsoft in the Manufacturers window of the Select Network Service dialog box, and Microsoft Remote Registry in the Network Services window.

Step 5.   Click OK and then OK again. You will have to restart your computer for this change to take effect. You may need to obtain the source floppy disks or the Windows 95 CD-ROM to get the files for this service.

Using the Registry editor to edit someone else's Registry

If another computer user on your network has set up their computer as a Registry server and you have user-level access to their computer through a list kept on a Windows NT server, you can edit their Registry. Double-click your Registry editor icon. Click Registry, Connect Network Registry in the Registry editor's menu bar. Type in the name of the computer containing the Registry you are going to edit.

When you are done, Click Registry, Disconnect Network Registry.

First, you'll need to add the software that enables you to do this. It doesn't come on the Windows 95 diskettes, but it's there on the Windows 95 CD-ROM. You'll find it in the \Admin\Nettools\Remotreg folder. Use the Add/Remove Programs icon in the Control Panel to add this software using Windows Setup. Be sure to click Have Disk and then browse to the correct folder.

The DOS Version of the Registry Editor

It is possible to edit the Registry from the DOS command prompt. This is useful if you are having difficulties starting Windows 95. To go to the DOS prompt without starting Windows, press F8 at the Starting Windows 95 notification.

If you type **Regedit /?** at the DOS command prompt, you will get a little help on how to import and export the Registry. You will need to use the program Edit to edit the exported Registry. Use Regedit to import the edited exported Registry file back into the Registry.

The DOS Regedit syntax is as follows:

```
REGEDIT {/L:system} {/R:user} filename1
REGEDIT {/L:system} {/R:user} /C filename2
REGEDIT {/L:system} {/R:user} /E filename3 {regpath}
/L:system       Specifies the location of the System.dat file
/R:user         Specifies the location of the User.dat file
filename1       Specifies the file(s) to import into the Registry
/C filename2    Specifies the file to create the Registry from
/E filename3    Specifies the file to export the Registry to
regpath         Specifies the starting Registry key to export from
                (Defaults to exporting the entire Registry)
```

You can export and edit the whole Registry or just a branch of it. Don't import a branch back into the Registry with the /C (create) option. This will create a Registry with only one branch.

Summary

If you can edit the Registry, you have complete control of Windows 95.

▶ We show you how to get that extra margin of safety by manually backing up your Registry using our batch files and desktop shortcuts.

▶ We also provide you with a means of recovering from fatal conditions in the Registry.

▶ We describe a number of keystroke shortcuts for easier and faster editing and display of the Registry.

▶ As an example of how to use Registry export to edit the Registry, we bring Windows Write back to life and show you how to create Windows Write files of the proper type from the New menu.

▶ We introduce you to editing Registries across a LAN.

▶ If there is a real problem starting Windows 95, we tell you how to edit the Registry in DOS.

Chapter 16

The Control Panel and Properties Sheets

In This Chapter

We cover the Control Panel and general features of Properties sheets.

▶ Quick ways to get to the Control Panel settings

▶ Installing and removing Windows applications

▶ Creating a bootable startup disk

▶ Controlling your multimedia hardware and drivers

▶ Configuring Windows 95 for your local currency, time, and dates

▶ Associating sounds with Windows 95 events

▶ Locating those missing parameters in Properties sheets

What Will You Find Where?

Windows 95 has to keep track of itself and the computer it is running on. You need a way to see (and change) your Windows 95 configurations. Thousands of little pieces of information running around in your computer need to be right for everything to work.

In the Control Panel, you'll get a handle on most of your computer's hardware and the software drivers that work with it. You'll also find the Fonts folder there (it's also in your Explorer) and the settings for currency, dates, time, and other location-specific information.

Properties sheets, an innovation with Windows 95, provide another means to get at the parameters that define your files, and in some cases, your hardware.

Many of the specific Control Panel settings are described in the chapters in *Part IV: Plug and Play*. In this chapter, we discuss the Control Panel settings that aren't described there.

Getting to the Control Panel

It's easy to get to the Control Panel. Just click the Start button, Settings, and then Control Panel. You'll see the Control Panel, as shown in Figure 16-1. But that's not the only way to get to the Control Panel, nor is it necessarily the most convenient.

Figure 16-1: The Control Panel. Double-click any icon to change the settings associated with that icon.

Following are some suggested ways to get to the Control Panel:

- If you want to use the Display Control Panel (the Display icon in the Control Panel), right-click the desktop and click Properties.

- You can get to the Date/Time Control Panel by double-clicking the clock on the Taskbar.

- The Fonts and Printers folders are accessible through the Explorer (C:\Windows\Fonts and the Printers folder below the Control Panel in the Tree window, respectively).

- You can get to the System Control Panel by right-clicking My Computer and clicking Properties.

- Access the Modem Control Panel by clicking the HyperTerminal application in your Start menu (if you installed it). Click Files and then Properties in the HyperTerminal menu and then the Configure button in the New Connection Properties sheet.

- You can also get to the modem through the System Control Panel, by choosing the Device Manager tab in the Properties sheet, selecting Modem, and then choosing the desired modem.

- To get the Network Control Panel, right-click the Network Neighborhood icon on the desktop and choose Properties.

Desktop Shortcuts to the Control Panel

If you want a shortcut to an icon in the Control Panel, open the Control Panel, right-click on an icon, and click Create Shortcut. You'll see a dialog box saying you can't create a shortcut in the Control Panel and asking whether you want to place the shortcut on the desktop instead. You can certainly make that choice.

Shortcuts to Control Panel icons make it easy to get at the specific settings that you want changed. While the Control Panel is a reasonable organizing folder for these items, you may have one or two that you change a lot. Bring them out to the desktop.

We provide more details on how to make shortcuts to the Control Panel icons in the *Control Panel Icons* section of Chapter 10.

Control Panel Settings

Most of the Control Panel settings are discussed in other chapters. Here, we discuss those that aren't covered elsewhere. Table 16-1 lists the settings discussed in other chapters.

Table 16-1	Settings Covered In Other Chapters
Control Panel Icon	*Chapter*
Add New Hardware	19
Date and Time	7
Display	22
Fonts	20
Keyboard	21
Mail and Fax	32
Microsoft Mail Postoffice	32
Modems	25
Mouse	24
Network	34
Passwords	32 and 34
PC Cards	19
Printers	23
System	19

Add/remove programs

The Add/Remove Programs Control Panel gives you three functions:

- Installing and removing programs that utilize the Windows 95 version of Install Shield

- Installing or removing programs that are covered by the Windows 95 setup routines or that have *inf* files consistent with the Microsoft standard for install files

- Creating a bootable startup diskette, as described in Chapter 3

Install/Uninstall

Microsoft has attempted to provide a standard Windows application installation and setup procedure so you don't have to fathom a new procedure every time you install a new piece of software. By licensing portions of the Install Shield installation software and integrating it into Windows 95, Microsoft provides application developers with a tool that will help you install and uninstall their programs.

To install a piece of compatible software, click the Install button, as shown in Figure 16-2.

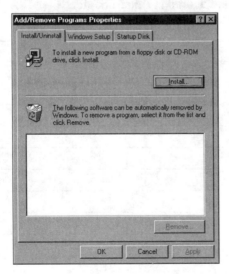

Figure 16-2: The Install/Uninstall dialog box. Use this method to install software that utilizes the built-in Install Shield procedures. Developers of small shareware applications may opt not to use these.

Installations that you make using these tools are tracked. The Registry is updated correctly and enough information about the setup is retained so you can uninstall the software.

Windows Setup

Applications that have accompanying *inf* files (control files that install the application without user input) can be installed and removed through the Windows Setup dialog box, as shown in Figure 16-3. Click the Have Disk button to install an application that has an accompanying *inf* file. This is an easy way for a developer to provide for a quick and dirty installation procedure.

Figure 16-3: The Windows Setup dialog box. Click Have Disk if your diskette contains an *inf* file.

The optional applications that were installed when you first installed Windows 95 can be uninstalled. If you didn't install something when you installed Windows 95 the first time, you can install it here.

Other applications or add-ons that use this *inf* method are added to the list of applications shown in the Components list box. They are treated like any other Windows 95 components.

Startup Disk

You are given the opportunity to create a startup disk when you set up Windows 95. If you didn't do it then, need another disk, or your computer came with Windows 95 already installed and set up and you didn't get a startup disk, you can create one here by clicking the Create Disk button in the Startup Disk dialog box.

Multimedia

Audio, video, MIDI, CD music, and Advanced Settings — the Multimedia Control Panel gives you some control over very basic multimedia parameters, such as volume, size of video playback, MIDI scheme, volume of CD headphone playback, and installed multimedia drivers.

Most of the action with multimedia is in the Multimedia menu on the Start button or comes from third-party applications that you probably received with your multimedia hardware. Microsoft provides only a basic mechanism for integrating multimedia into Windows 95. It depends on other developers to produce the really cool stuff.

Lots of multimedia software or content titles have multimedia applets that control how to play their video clips and listen to their sounds. Most of your interaction with multimedia will take place through the interfaces defined by these applications.

Regional settings

Where are you and where is your computer?

The best thing about regional settings (and date/time) is the world map, as shown in Figure 16-4.

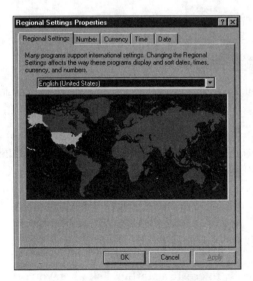

Figure 16-4: The Regional Settings world map. It looks like some of the world is not taken into account. Other versions of Windows 95 can handle the languages in these countries.

Regional settings have to do with how date, time, money, and numbers are sorted and displayed. Windows 95 keeps track of which country has which customs regarding these most core symbols of civilization. If the application you are using is smart enough to ask in advance, it can display these values correctly.

You can set the particular configuration yourself (from among many options) if you need to make adjustments.

Sounds

The Sounds Control Panel lets you associate a given sound with a given Windows event. Sounds are files with the *wav* extension. Windows 95 understands wave files and can "play" them through your sound card.

Windows 95 comes with lots of new sounds that you can associate with Windows events (if you installed them). You can also purchase CD-ROMs full of wave files, or download sound files from online services or bulletin boards, or get them over the Internet.

The new sounds that come with Windows 95 are arranged as sound schemes so you can apply them all at once to all the designated Windows events. This makes it a lot easier. Before you apply them all, check to make sure that your sound equipment and sound drivers can play the wave files.

You can test the sounds by highlighting a sound and clicking the play button to the right of the Preview window, as shown in Figure 16-5.

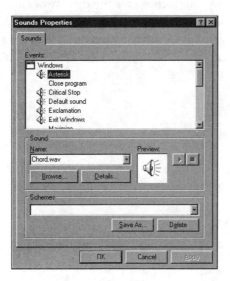

Figure 16-5: The Sound Control Panel. Highlight a Windows 95 event, Browse for a sound, and then click the triangular play button next to the Preview window.

Properties Sheets

Right-click an object and click Properties. This is how to display an object's
Properties sheet(s).

Pretty much anything you see on your desktop has a Properties sheet, except,
interestingly enough, Control Panel settings. Often the Control Panel settings
are Properties sheets — for example, the Display Control Panel contains the
desktop's Properties sheets.

Every file has a similar Properties sheet. Every shortcut to a Windows program
has a similar Properties sheet, as does every shortcut to a DOS program.

Like settings in the Control Panel, most Properties sheets are discussed in
the relevant chapter, such as Chapter 10. We mention Properties sheets here
because we want to point out that they are a general phenomenon. While they
aren't universal because you will run lots of Windows 3.x applications that
don't use them, they will become more common as developers integrate
them into applications.

Summary

The Control Panel settings let you configure hardware and software drivers.

▶ We show you how to quickly get to the different Control Panel settings.

▶ You can install and remove Windows applications through a consistent interface.

▶ You'll want to be able to choose your settings for the display of currency, time,
and date.

▶ The Control Panel has a setting for associating sounds with Windows 95 events.

Part III
DOS Secrets

Chapter 17

Meet the New DOS... Same as the Old DOS....

In This Chapter

Who says DOS is dead? Sure, it doesn't have that much to do anymore, but lots of DOS programs could use a friendly C> prompt. We discuss:

▶ The relationship between Windows 95 and DOS

▶ The real concerns of Windows 95 users regarding DOS

▶ Designing the DOS *screen* in a DOS *window*

▶ Editing shortcuts to DOS programs to make them work better with Windows

▶ Private DOS in MS-DOS mode — letting DOS programs work even when they're cranky

▶ Writing Windows/DOS batch files

▶ Finding the Windows folder

The Who?

We hope, like the Who, we don't get fooled again. By our appropriation of this song lyric, we mean to point out the issue of what this "DOS" is that we are dealing with in Windows 95. Is Windows 95 really a *revolution* or is it an *evolution* from the previous mix of DOS and Windows as a combined operating system?

This chapter deals with three subjects. First, we look at DOS as that thing that starts up before Windows 95 takes command. Second, we examine the part of DOS you get with Windows 95. Third, we cover how to best run DOS programs. DOS, the former operating system — now reduced to being a part of Windows 95 — will not be our main emphasis. After all, the point of *Windows 95 Secrets* is to make your life easier as a user, not to debate the fine points of operating system philosophy.

If you would like to understand the finer points of how DOS and Windows 95 commingle, you'll want to get Andrew Schulman's excellent book *Unauthorized Windows 95* (Programmers Press, IDG Books, 1995). Yes, it is published by the same company that publishes this book, but we still think it is a great book despite the fact that our publisher would love us to praise it.

We'll give you a little bit of the flavor of Schulman's book here, as it applies to how DOS and Windows 95 actually work on your computer. You will also want to turn to Chapter 18 for further discussion on conventional and expanded memory.

DOS and Windows, Together at Last, at Least

Microsoft says that Windows 95 is an integrated operating system. Does that mean that DOS 7.0 and Windows 95 come in the same box? Or does it mean something more radical, that Windows 95 is a whole new operating system that leaves DOS with but a small role to play?

Andrew Schulman argues in his book that Windows has been a real operating system since 1988 with the advent of Windows/386 2.x. What he means is that Windows code has been handling the requests that programs make of the computer, and, if needed, Windows hands those requests to DOS to do some of the work. With the advent of Windows for Workgroups 3.11, and especially the 32-bit file access that came with it, DOS has had even less of the grunt work to do.

32-bit file access, which was introduced with Windows for Workgroups 3.11, is (according to Schulman) "pre-beta" code for the disk/file access subsystem of Windows 95. In Windows for Workgroups, 32-bit file access really did not work well, failing under some conditions. For example, certain legitimate DOS-read functions cause Windows for Workgroups with 32-bit file access to halt with a "system integrity" error. In Windows 95, it is hard to turn off 32-bit file access, and we have not seen any reports of difficulties with it.

It is the fact that Windows is first in line to deal with disk access requests that makes it an operating system. Windows makes the decision about how these requests will be handled and uses some of the DOS code routines if they are useful. Windows 95 treats DOS as a real-mode driver.

Schulman states early in his book:

> If I had to explain how Windows 95 relates to DOS in 25 words or less, I'd say this: *Windows 95 relates to DOS in the same way that WfW 3.11 does.* Windows provides 32BFA [32-bit file access]. For non-file calls, it calls (in V86 mode) the real-mode DOS code in WINBOOT.SYS *[now called Io.sys in the released version of Windows 95].* Windows 95 is a genuine operating system; so were WfW 3.11, Windows 3.1 Enhanced mode, and Windows 3.0 Enhanced mode.

It Sure Looks Like DOS

Of course, as a user, it sure looks like DOS when you start your computer. Right there is a text screen with familiar messages. The first text messages are probably output from your BIOS.

The Basic Input/Output System (BIOS) chip(s) used to play a much more important role. In the days before 386 systems, the BIOS chips contained the only code that told DOS enough about the hardware to allow DOS to talk to said hardware. Soon, DOS programs were bypassing the BIOS in order to get directly at the hardware and speed their screen display. Later, DOS bypassed the BIOS to use its own descriptions of the hard disk to provide quicker access. Now, Windows — and especially Windows 95 — keeps its own account of the hardware and provides all the hardware drivers it needs.

This doesn't mean the BIOS is ignored by Windows 95. Instead, once the hardware description is read from the BIOS, Windows uses its own routines to interact with the hardware.

Soon after the BIOS display (if any), your screen will give you the reassuring message "Starting Windows 95." But where did this message come from? Well, from DOS, of course. The file Io.sys sits in the boot tracks of your hard disk and starts after the BIOS completes its work. Io.sys *is* DOS.

Many of you may think of Command.com as DOS. But Command.com is only the user interface (the *shell*) for DOS. It can easily be replaced by another user interface, such as 4DOS.

Io.sys does the work of reading Config.sys and, by leading Command.Com, excuting Autoexec.bat. Even if these files don't exist, Io.sys does much of the work that they would have done, such as loading Ifshlp.exe and Setver.exe. The last thing Io.sys does is start Windows by sending out the instruction Win.com as though it were a line in Autoexec.bat.

This Windows startup process is discussed in much more detail in Chapter 6.

The data structures and routines created by Io.sys are still there after Windows 95 starts up and are called upon by Windows 95 (in virtual 86 mode) as it needs them. As more Windows components are rewritten using 32-bit equivalents, Windows needs less and less of Io.sys.

A Thing on a Thing

The facts that you first boot into real-mode DOS, that you have DOS-looking text on your computer screen, and that DOS is necessary for Windows to run, create the perception that Windows is "a thing on a thing." IBM, in its marketing of OS/2, does as much as it can to foster this perception.

Microsoft wants us to see Windows 95 as a "real" operating system, which it is. In order to enhance that perception, Microsoft constructed Io.sys so that Windows 95 is automatically called without your having to put a line in your Autoexec.bat file to call Win.com. It also made it somewhat difficult to get to DOS outside of a Windows DOS box.

It couldn't go all the way, because so many people still rely on DOS programs and continually whined about it to Microsoft. They were unable to get all their DOS programs to run in Windows DOS sessions, so Microsoft had to provide "MS-DOS mode." Early in the beta test cycle, Microsoft tried to get this mode to work with all DOS programs with a stub of Windows 95 still loaded in memory, but couldn't. Some DOS programs required that the processor be reset with a warm boot before they would work.

Therefore, Windows 95 provides two "MS-DOS modes." One is a warm boot and one has a Windows 95 stub. DOS is running your computer in both cases.

Command.com is called in the Autoexec.bat file that starts MS-DOS mode. This allows you to "exit" this second instance of the command line interface (exit MS-DOS mode) and carry out the next line of Autoexec.bat, which is a call to reload Windows 95 (and return to Windows 95).

Windows has difficulty running DOS programs that use memory managers not in compliance with the Windows memory manager specification. This affects DOS games especially. DOS games really eat up computer resources and often don't want to cooperate with Windows at all. It is this issue of DOS games — the last, as yet, unconquered territory for Windows — that forced Microsoft to include MS-DOS mode.

By making DOS harder to get to and by automatically starting Windows 95, Microsoft is trying to change our perception about whether Windows is a "real" operating system. Of course, the fact that your screen still looks like a DOS screen before Windows starts dilutes that message. Too bad they just didn't switch your VGA display card into graphics mode using Io.sys and then display the messages that Io.sys, Autoexec.bat, and Config.sys throw up on your screen in a message box.

We assume they didn't because this would cause some incompatibility. Microsoft must have thought about it. Of course, they display in VGA mode the Windows 95 logo screen (Logo.sys), but it doesn't start early enough to dispel the dreaded image of DOS on your screen.

Windows 95 is not "a thing on a thing." Ignore the man behind the curtain. Windows 95 is the *real* thing.

The Real DOS Concerns of Windows 95 Users

There is an issue beyond perceptions. Aren't there some problems with DOS that make Windows 95 unstable, that "crash the system?"

Windows 95 is an operating system that makes compromises, like any operating system. It compromises "crashability" in exchange for performance, given minimum resources. Minimum resources in this case means 4MB of memory and a 386 DX or 486/25 processor.

These compromises are not really related to DOS as a real-mode driver for Windows. They would be there anyway, however Windows 95 was designed, as long as Windows 95 had to fit within these computer resources.

Some Windows programs use conventional memory resources and this can be seen as a DOS problem. Windows 95 does a good job in reducing the consequences of this bad behavior, but it still allows these programs to put parts of themselves into conventional memory. Turn to Chapter 18 for more discussion of this issue.

Windows 95 makes most DOS 16-bit drivers unnecessary. This is a great benefit. Not only is Windows 95 more stable than earlier versions of Windows because the new 32-bit drivers are more stable, but this also lessens the demands on conventional memory and the upper memory blocks (UMBs). DOS and some Windows programs benefit from this reduced demand. This increased stability is particularly noticeable in video card drivers.

Writing video drivers for Windows 3.x was much more difficult than writing them for Windows 95. Microsoft has provided with Windows 95 a mini-driver module that video card manufactures use to write their own drivers. Microsoft has also written many video drivers itself.

The new video drivers allow greater integration with Windows. The Display Properties sheet illustrates some of that increased integration. Windows display resolution can be changed on the fly — something that was possible with only a few manufacturers' video drivers previously.

What's Left of DOS?

What does it mean that DOS comes in the same package as Windows 95? DOS itself means a lot of different things. It is Io.sys, which sits in the boot tracks and boots up DOS 7.0 when the BIOS is finished. Io.sys definitely comes with Windows 95.

The DOS routines perform some of the low-level tasks of controlling the hardware and providing pointers to active applications. This is the part of DOS that is called by the VxDs that make up Windows 95. This DOS is running in V86 mode in the system virtual machine. It definitely comes with Windows 95.

On top of DOS is Command.com: the DOS user interface and the DOS prompt. A new and bigger version of Command.com comes with Windows 95.

DOS includes also DOS commands (both internal to Command.com and external) and the files that were previously stored in the DOS directory. Windows 95 doesn't create a DOS directory but puts most of its "DOS" files in the C:\Windows\Command folder.

The internal DOS commands (Dir, Copy, CD, and so on) are those resident in Command.com. The external DOS commands (Xcopy, Find, Mem) are those DOS files that are separate executable programs.

All the internal DOS commands found in DOS 6.x are still there in the DOS that comes with Windows 95. But only some of the DOS external commands (executable files) that came with DOS 6.x come with Windows 95.

Secret

Windows 95 doesn't come with a virus checker, an undelete program, or DOS based backup. These were big new functions that came with DOS 6.2x. Microsoft decided to drop virus checking in Windows 95 and let others provide that functionality.

Windows 95 comes with a Recycle Bin, but files deleted from the DOS prompt (or over the network or on diskettes) don't go to the Recycle Bin. If you want to undelete files deleted at the DOS prompt, you have to use the DOS 6.2x Undelete command or a package from another developer such as Norton Utilities for Windows 95.

Windows 95 does come with a Windows-based backup program that works with floppy-based tape backup hardware. More extensive backup software (for example, for SCSI tape drives) is provided by other developers.

To find out how to undelete files at the lower DOS levels by using the DOS 6.2x Undelete command, turn to Chapter 14.

The remaining DOS commands

Microsoft claims that DOS commands are now native Windows 95 commands. They certainly are in the sense that they have been changed to work with long filenames and the VFAT (Virtual Fat Allocation Table, the DOS file system). All the previous internal DOS commands are available and have been updated.

Table 17-1 lists the DOS external commands that come with Windows 95.

Table 17-1	DOS External Commands in Windows 95
Filename	*Definition*
Attrib.exe	Show or change file attributes
Chkdsk.exe	Check disk and provide status report (use ScanDisk instead)
Choice.com	Accept user input in a batch file
Debug.exe	Debug hexadecimal editor and viewer
Deltree.exe	Delete tree (directory and subdirectories)
Diskcopy.com	Full copy of diskettes
Doskey.com	Edit command lines, recall them, create macros

Filename	Definition
Edit.com	File editing application
Extract.exe	Extract files from a cabinet file
Fc.exe	Compare two files
Fdisk.exe	Low-level disk partitioning and configuration
Find.exe	Find text in a file
Format.com	Format a disk
Label.exe	Label a disk
Mem.exe	Display memory use
Mode.com	Mode of port or display, or code page (character set)
More.com	Pause for output one screen at a time
Move.exe	Move files (copy and delete original)
Scandisk.exe	Fix disks
Share.exe	File locking
Sort.exe	Sort the contents of a file
Start.exe	Run a Windows program
Subst.exe	Substitute a drive letter for a directory
Sys.com	Create a system disk
Xcopy.exe	Extended file and directories copy
Xcopy32.exe	Improved version of Xcopy.exe, called by Xcopy.exe

You can't copy long file or folder names with Xcopy.exe (or Xcopy32.exe) in MS-DOS mode (even when you use double quotes around the file names), but you can in a Windows DOS session.

Secret

Xcopy /k copies the file attributes correctly but not the directory attributes. This is an acknowledged bug in Windows 95.

The use of all these commands, and the internal ones also, can be discerned from the online DOS help. Type the command and add /? before pressing Enter.

DOS 6.2x came with a DOS help program. You could find out extensive information about DOS commands by just typing "help" at the DOS prompt. This Help program wasn't updated for the Windows 95 version of DOS commands, nor was it shipped with Windows 95 in spite of our pleas on the Windows 95 beta forum. It wasn't even put in the \Other\Oldmsdos folder.

If you have DOS 6.2x around, you might want to make sure the Help program is available to you. You could copy it into the \Windows\Command folder, as this folder is on the path, and you will then be able to get to the Help program just by typing **help *command*** at any DOS prompt. The help information will be somewhat out of date, but still useful.

DOS Edit

Windows 95 ships with a new version of DOS Edit. Written by a contractor to Microsoft, Emory Horvath, it is a nifty little editor and quite useful for dealing with text and batch files. You can easily create a shortcut to it and put it on your Start menu or your desktop (see Chapter 10). You'll find Edit.com in your \Windows\Command folder.

Undocumented

Edit can load up to nine files and can have two windows open at any one time. It can use up to 5.5 MB of virtual memory to load and manage files, handling files up to 64,000 lines. The maximum line length is 1024 characters. It doesn't require Windows 95 to run, and should run on any processor equal to or greater than a 286. It requires only 160 KB of conventional memory.

It's great for looking for text in binary files and has a switch on its File Open box just for that option. The Edit command's File Open dialog box defaults to opening files with any extension — a big improvement over the early version if you use it to edit batch files.

Secret

The Edit command doesn't recognize a mouse double-click setting in the Registry. If you have set your middle mouse button on a Logitech mouse to double-click (as described in Chapter 24), it won't work with Edit. You'll have to remember to double-click with the left mouse button.

Config.sys commands

A number of commands are used only in your Config.sys file. They include:

break	files	rem
buffers	include	set
country	install	shell
device	lastdrive	stacks
devicehigh	menucolor	submenu
dos	menuitem	switches
drivparm	numlock	verify
fcbs		

DOS commands that are no longer around

The following DOS commands did not come with Windows 95:

append	interlnk	recover
assign	intersvr	replace
backup	join	restore
comp	memcard	ramdrive.sys
dosshell	memmaker	romdrive.sys
edlin	mirror	share
ega.sys	msav	smartmon
fasthelp	msbackup	tree
fastopen	power	undelete
graftabl	print	unformat
graphics	print.sys	vsafe
help	qbasic	

Some of these external DOS command files can be found in the \Other\Oldmsdos folder on the Windows 95 source CD-ROM. They are the MS-DOS 6.22 versions and haven't been updated.

Cautions about some DOS commands

Chkdsk has been superseded in functionality by Mem.exe and Scandisk.exe. Scandisk is now both a Windows program and a DOS program that checks for problems with your disk (hard or floppy). Mem gives you a great deal more information than Chkdsk about your available conventional memory. Chkdsk /f is rejected both in a Windows DOS session and in MS-DOS mode. You can type it, but you just get a message that you "Cannot obtain exclusive access to drive X."

Share.exe is not needed in Windows DOS sessions. A virtual device driver takes care of file locking. You can still use it in MS-DOS mode.

Subst.exe hasn't fully worked for quite a while. It doesn't work with networked drives and fails with Fdisk, Format, and Sys. It will work just fine in a Windows DOS session or in MS-DOS mode to substitute a drive letter for a path or folder name. This makes it easier to use really old DOS programs that weren't designed to use path names.

Do not use the earlier DOS Append utility. It prevents Windows 95 and Windows-based applications from creating valid path names for the files they are using.

Wonderful DOS commands

If you want to change or view the attributes of a large set of files, the File Manager or the Attrib command are really your only choices. You can change the attributes of only one file at a time in the Explorer by right-clicking each filename and changing the properties displayed on the General Properties sheet — a slow and tedious task.

If you want to rename a set of files, once again it is either the File Manager or the DOS Ren command. To compare files you'll need to use either Fc.exe or the file-matching shareware that we feature on the shareware CD-ROM accompanying this book.

Modifying DOS commands

You can modify some DOS commands so they do by default just what you want them to. You do this by setting the value of certain environmental variables. For example, if you wish to change the default behavior of the Dir command, you may add the following line to your Autoexec.bat file (or a batch may file that runs when you start a Windows DOS session):

```
set dircmd=/p /l /o:-d
```

This line modifies the Dir command to pause after each screen full of listed files, display the filenames in lower case, and order the filenames in descending date order.

You can modify the copy command by setting the value of *copycmd*.

How do you know which modifiers to use when changing these commands? They are the same ones you could type in manually when you enter the command. Type **copy /?** or **dir /?** at the Command prompt and press Enter to see the available modifiers.

Doskey lets you define macros, so you can redefine any of the DOS internal or external commands, as long as you run them after you load Doskey and the macro definitions (most likely in your Autoexec.bat file or in a batch file that is run when you start a Windows DOS session). For example, if you want to redefine the Mem command to pause after each page of information, add the following to your batch file:

```
c:\Windows\Command\Doskey
Doskey mem=mem.exe $* /p
```

The Mem command is now changed to mean "Mem with the page pause modifier." The symbol $* means "include whatever is typed after Mem on the comand line." For more information on DOSKEY, type **doskey/?** at the command prompt.

Shortcuts to DOS commands

Further modifications can be carried out by using Shortcuts to MS-DOS programs (also known as *pif*s) to call the DOS commands. Some of these are carried out automatically. To see what we mean, take the following steps:

STEPS

Creating a Shortcut to Mem.exe

Step 1. Using your Explorer, navigate to the C:\Windows\Command folder. Right-click Mem.exe. Click Properties.

Step 2. Click the Program tab. Notice that the Command line field has the following entry:

```
C:\WINDOWS\COMMAND\MEM.EXE /c /p
```

This entry modifies the Mem command to display greater details about memory allocation, and to pause after displaying one page of information. These commands were automatically added to the command line.

Step 3. Click OK.

Step 4. Press the F5 key to refresh the Explorer window. Scroll through the Command folder until you find the MS-DOS icon next to the Mem command. It will be right below the Mem.exe file and its type (in details view) will be listed as Shortcut to MS-DOS Program.

Step 5. Double-click the Shortcut to Mem icon.

You will notice that this opens a Windows DOS session, displays the memory details, and then pauses, waiting for you to press another key. You will want to change this Shortcut a little, so it doesn't close on exit.

You can create a Windows shortcut for any of the DOS commands. You can put these shortcuts anywhere that makes sense to you — on your desktop, in the Start menus, in a DOS folder with a shortcut to your desktop. In this way, the DOS commands become Windows programs.

If you have parameters or filenames that often change relative to a DOS command, add a question mark after the DOS command name in the command line, such as **EDIT?**.

DOS commands you shouldn't run

We want to be sure to cover a few DOS commands and applications that must *never* be run while in a Windows DOS session or in MS-DOS mode.

Don't ever run any disk utilities that haven't been updated to work with long filenames, unless you have saved your long filenames. This includes Norton Utilities Version 8 and previous versions as well as any earlier versions of Central Point disk utilities. You can run earlier versions of Norton Disk Editor, but do so by pressing F8 at the Windows 95 startup message and getting to a command prompt.

Don't ever run backup programs that are unaware of long filenames unless you have saved your long filenames with lfnbk.exe (Long filename backup). This program saves the long filenames and restores them after you run the older DOS-based Backup program.

You won't be able to run Chkdsk /f. Don't run Fdisk, Format C: (but Format A: and Format B: are fine), or Sys C: while in a Windows DOS session.

Don't ever run any disk optimization packages other than Defrag (which comes with Windows 95) if they haven't been updated for long filenames. Don't run programs that change your hard disk interleave from a Windows DOS session.

Windows has a built-in disk cache. Don't run third-party disk cache programs that aren't specifically designed for Windows 95.

Don't ever run utilities that undelete files unless they have been specifically designed for Windows 95. You can use the DOS 6.*x* version of Undelete using the steps provided in Chapter 14.

The Path and Windows 95 applications

The default path that is set if you don't have an Autoexec.bat file is

```
C:\Windows;C:\Windows\Command
```

This assumes, of course, that your Windows 95 folder is called Windows and that it is on the C: drive.

You can add additional folders to the path if you have an Autoexec.bat file. You can also change the path in a batch file that you run when you open a DOS window.

Undocumented

Windows 95 applications can set a pointer to the folder that contains their executable files. The reference is stored in the Registry at H_KEY LOCAL_MACHINE\Software\Microsoft\Windows\CurrentVersion\AppPaths.

When a Windows 95 application starts, the shell looks at the entry at this location and appends the folder(s) referenced to the path.

You can set up references at this location in the Registry so you don't have to type in the full path name in front of an executable file's name when you use the Run menu item to run a program. This also works with the Start command in DOS batch files.

Use the Registry editor to add folder references patterned after the ones already in the Registry at the above location for your own Windows applications that don't know about this new Windows 95 feature. You can then reference the applications in Start commands without using their full path name.

Running DOS Programs

Our major concern in this chapter is providing you with the tools to make it easier to run DOS programs, both in Windows DOS sessions and in MS-DOS mode. You'll find significant improvements relative to Windows 3.*x* in Windows 95's ability to run DOS programs, and we want you to be able to take advantage of these improvements.

You can run DOS programs:

- Before Windows 95 starts by booting to a command prompt
- After Windows 95 starts in a Windows DOS session
- By quitting Windows to get to MS-DOS mode without a reboot
- By warm booting to MS-DOS mode with a call to send you back to Windows with an exit command

DOS before Windows

To get to the DOS prompt before Windows 95 starts, press F8 when you see the message that Windows 95 is starting. Choose the sixth menu item, Command prompt only. You can edit your Msdos.sys file to have your computer automatically start at the DOS prompt or have a menu of choices appear before Windows 95 starts (For more information, see Chapter 6).

Undocumented

Windows 95 hasn't loaded yet, but the commands in your Config.sys and Autoexec.bat files (if you have such files) are executed. You won't have access to any hardware devices like your mouse, CD-ROM, or sound card unless you have loaded their 16-bit drivers. Windows 95 loads the 32-bit drivers for these devices only when Windows 95 is loaded.

Unless you have configured your Autoexec.bat and Config.sys files to work with DOS programs that you would normally start before you start Windows 95, it is unlikely you will have these 16-bit drivers loaded. Windows 95 doesn't need them and can, by itself, provide these services to DOS programs that run in Windows DOS sessions.

To increase conventional memory, you may want to load your 16-bit drivers and DOS TSRs in the upper memory blocks. If your DOS program requires expanded memory you will want to have an expanded memory manager loaded by a line in your Config.sys file. Turn to Chapter 18 for more details.

Secret

At this point, since Windows 95 hasn't loaded, you are in DOS 7.0. You have real-mode direct disk access, not 32-bit file/disk access. If you want disk caching, you are going to need to run SmartDrive (Smartdrv.exe). Chkdsk /f works just fine (whereas it will not work in MS-DOS mode).

While it is certainly possible to run your DOS programs by booting up DOS instead of Windows 95, it may not be the best method. You will probably want to optimize Autoexec.bat and Config.sys to run Windows 95, not DOS programs. DOS programs can be run in MS-DOS mode with their own individually optimized Autoexec.bat and Config.sys files, so this is a better place for them. DOS programs can also be run in Windows DOS sessions, which provide 32-bit drivers thereby reducing demands for conventional memory.

DOS in Windows

If your DOS programs run in Windows DOS sessions, by all means run them there. Windows 95 creates a "virtual machine" for each Windows DOS session. As far as your DOS program is concerned, it is running in its own computer.

Each Windows DOS session is its own virtual machine. Each virtual machine can be different. You can run a number of them at once. Each is preemptively multitasked. This means no one session can hog all your computer's resources.

You have the option of setting a number of virtual machine operational parameters. You determine what the computer looks like to the DOS program by editing Windows DOS session Properties sheets. These were previously known as Program Information Files, or *pif*s.

The easiest way to run a DOS program in Windows 95 is to double-click its icon in a folder window or the Explorer. In many cases, the DOS program will just run and that's all there is to it. You can create shortcuts to DOS programs and documents and treat them just like you would shortcuts to Windows programs and documents. Shortcuts to DOS programs and *pif*s are one and the same.

You can also run a DOS program from the Run menu command in the Start button menu. Click the Start button, then click Run. Type in the full name of the program including its path. Type in any command line parameters after the program's name.

Undocumented

If you want to run the DOS internal commands like Copy from the Run command, you will need to use something like the following syntax:

```
command /c copy filename lpt1
```

The /C switch allows you to run internal commands.

If you have an application that writes a Postscript file to disk and later you want to send that Postscript file to the printer to be printed, there is no "Windows" way to do this. You have to copy the file to the printer port as per the example above — one good reason to keep DOS around. (Note that the previous example will not eject the last page of text files from laser printers; you must do this manually.)

Windows 95 provides Windows DOS sessions with 32-bit file access to the hard drive as well as disk caching. This significantly speeds hard disk access by DOS programs. DOS programs have full mouse functionality (if they are designed to use a mouse) without having to load a 16-bit mouse driver. There is no need for 16-bit sound card drivers, CD-ROM drivers, or network drivers, as these services are provided by Windows 95 32-bit drivers.

DOS programs can be run in a window or full screen. You can switch a DOS session between windowed and full-screen modes by pressing Alt+Enter. Data that is displayed in a DOS window can be cut and pasted into a Windows 95 window. You can switch between DOS sessions with Alt+Tab.

There is an MS-DOS Prompt item in your Start menu. Click the Start button, then Programs, and MS-DOS Prompt. This is a generic Windows DOS Session. You can run a DOS program in the Windows DOS session from the DOS prompt. You can open multiple Windows DOS sessions by choosing this Start menu item.

Given all these features you get when you run your DOS programs in a Windows DOS session, you might conclude that Windows 95 provides a better DOS than DOS. If all DOS programs were able to take advantage of the DOS box, this would surely be the case.

DOS in MS-DOS mode without a reboot

If your DOS program won't run in a Windows DOS session, no matter how you set the properties of its virtual machine, you'll need to run it in MS-DOS mode. You don't have to quit Windows to use this version of MS-DOS mode, but you are given that option when you do quit Windows.

To quit Windows to MS-DOS mode without rebooting, take the following steps:

STEPS

Quitting Windows to MS-DOS Mode

Step 1.   Click the Start button.

Step 2.   Click Shut Down.

Step 3.   Click Restart the Computer in MS-DOS mode.

Step 4.   Click Yes.

Undocumented

All but a 4K stub of Windows is unloaded from memory, and the file Dosstart.bat is run. This file is found in your Windows 95 folder. It was created when you first installed Windows 95 and consists of the calls to DOS TSRs that were remarked out of your previous DOS/Windows 3.x Autoexec.bat file.

You can edit the Dosstart.bat file so it calls the TSRs that are appropriate (like Smartdrv.exe and/or a 16-bit mouse driver) for when you start MS-DOS mode. Because you are not doing a warm boot when you start non-rebooted MS-DOS mode, you will be unable to start any 16-bit drivers you would have normally called from a Config.sys file that you configured for DOS. If you need to load these drivers to run DOS programs in MS-DOS mode, either load them in the Windows 95 Config.sys file or use the warm boot version of MS-DOS mode.

Secret

If you wish to access your CD-ROM while in MS-DOS mode, you'll need to load your real-mode CD-ROM driver in your Config.sys file or load it in a private Config.sys if you use the reboot version of MS-DOS mode. In addition, Mscdex.exe, which is normally loaded by your Autoexec.bat, is needed. When Windows 95 is installed, Mscdex.exe is remarked out (because Windows 95 has its own 32-bit protected-mode version of Mscdex.exe) and the unremarked call from your previous Autoexec.bat file is moved to Dosstart.bat. The real-mode CD-ROM driver in your Config.sys file is not remarked out.

When you go to MS-DOS mode, Mscdex.exe is called by Dosstart.bat, and because the real-mode CD-ROM driver has been previously loaded, you will now be able to access your CD-ROM drive in MS-DOS mode. If you remove the real-mode CD-ROM driver from your Config.sys (perhaps to reclaim the conventional memory it uses), you won't be able to access your CD-ROM in MS-DOS mode without a reboot. In addition, you will get a series of error messages about Mscdex.exe unless you also remove it from Dosstart.bat.

If you have plenty of conventional memory even when you load the real-mode CD-ROM driver, you will be able to play your CD-ROM-based DOS games without having to go to rebooted MS-DOS mode. If this is not the case, you will want to load your real-mode CD-ROM drivers in private Config.sys files, and Mscdex.exe in private Autoexec.bat files.

Undocumented

A shortcut to a DOS program is automatically created when you exit to MS-DOS mode in this manner. You'll find it in the Windows 95 folder. It is called **Exit to dos.pif.**

Undocumented

You can also get to this version of MS-DOS mode by creating a shortcut to MS-DOS (a *pif*) that doesn't create its own Autoexec.bat and Config.sys files. This is an option in the Advanced Program Settings Properties sheet, which we discuss later in this chapter in the section entitled *Advanced button*.

When you exit this MS-DOS mode, your computer reboots back to Windows 95 (if you have configured your Msdos.sys file so you normally boot to Windows 95). Unlike rebooted MS-DOS mode, your computer is rebooted only once in switching from Windows 95 to DOS and back to Windows.

DOS in MS-DOS mode with a reboot

Windows 95 restarts (warm boots) your computer when it goes into rebooted MS-DOS mode. You exit this mode back into Windows 95 by typing **exit** at the command prompt and pressing Enter. Your computer is again restarted (warm booted) and Windows 95 reloads.

Undocumented

A restart is a warm boot. Io.sys runs again and reads Msdos.sys, Config.sys, and Autoexec.bat. Be careful: If you have edited your Msdos.sys file so that BootMulti=1 and the default boot is to DOS 6.2 (BootWin=0), you will restart to your previous version of DOS instead of MS-DOS mode. A way around this is to press F4 at reboot time to boot to Windows 95. You'll also need to do this when you exit MS-DOS mode.

To get to rebooted MS-DOS mode, you first need to create an icon with the proper properties. We show you how to do this in the *MS-DOS mode* section of this chapter. Each DOS program that uses MS-DOS mode can have its own icon with these properties.

DOS in a Box

A DOS program running in a Windows DOS session can be displayed either in a window on top of the Windows desktop or full screen. A DOS window can have a Toolbar just like any respectable Windows program (see Figure 17-1). If your DOS window doesn't have a Toolbar, click the system menu on the left side of the DOS window caption area, then select Toolbar.

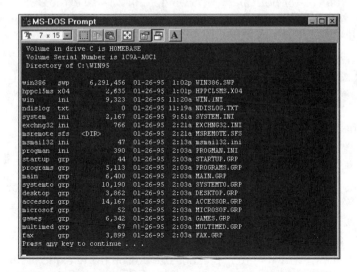

Figure 17-1: A Windows DOS session. Notice the Toolbar. The caption area is at the top of the window. The system menu is on the left end of the caption area.

You can use the DOS window Toolbar to:

- Change the DOS font size and thereby the DOS window size
- Mark, and copy and paste text to and from the DOS window and the Clipboard
- Expand the DOS window to full screen
- Change the properties of the shortcut to the DOS application
- Choose to not suspend the DOS program when it is in background (doesn't have the focus)

DOS window vs. DOS screen

There is a difference between a DOS screen and a DOS window. In full-screen mode, there is no DOS window and the DOS screen is the same as your computer's screen. A DOS screen on the desktop is contained within a DOS window. In Figure 17-1, it is the area underneath the Toolbar and inside the edges of the DOS window.

Often you will want to see the whole DOS screen inside the DOS window, because this is how DOS programs are designed to operate — designed under the assumption that you can see all the DOS screen. If you can't see the complete DOS screen in the DOS window, it may be more difficult to run the DOS program effectively.

The DOS window is smaller than the DOS screen if you can see horizontal or vertical scroll bars or both in the DOS window. In this case, the DOS window is a window on the DOS screen and you can see only a part of the DOS screen at any one time.

Sizing and locating the DOS Window

There are three ways to change the size of a DOS window and/or a DOS screen:

- Set the DOS font size to Auto and drag the edge or corner of the DOS window.
- Change the DOS font size.
- Set the DOS font size to a fixed size and drag the edge or corner for the DOS window.

Drag a DOS Window with font set to Auto

First, set the font size to Auto in the font size box on the left side of the DOS Toolbar. You should be able to see the whole DOS screen. If not, click one of the corners of the DOS window and the DOS window and screen will shrink to fit.

Now, stretch or shrink the DOS window by dragging one of its corners. The whole DOS screen will stretch and shrink along with the DOS window. The DOS font will change size to match the changing whole DOS screen size (after you release the mouse button).

Dragging the DOS window will not smoothly resize it. The DOS window resizes in increments that correspond to multiples of the available font sizes.

Tip

It is possible to drag a side of the DOS window but it is quite a bit easier to drag from a corner. Because the DOS window widths and height jump in increments that are multiples of the fixed ratios of font pixel width to height, the window may get a lot shorter all of a sudden or not expand at all in another direction. Dragging by the corner opens up possible moves along both axes, making dragging somewhat smoother.

If you have clicked the maximize button in the DOS window caption area, you won't be able to resize the DOS window. In fact, the resize arrows won't appear if the DOS window has been maximized. The DOS window is already maximized anyway if the whole DOS screen is visible and the font size is fixed. That is the meaning of maximum DOS window size (with fixed font size) — the whole DOS screen is visible.

If the font is set on Auto, maximizing the DOS window will enlarge the font size and consequently the DOS screen. The DOS window will be the largest it can be and still be within the boundaries of the desktop.

As you adjust the DOS window size, you are adjusting the size of a full DOS screen. Everything on the DOS screen is displayed in the window. Nothing is scrolled. There is no window on a DOS screen that allows you to see only part of the DOS screen at a time.

Size the DOS window by changing the font size

The DOS window and the DOS screen will automatically resize themselves if you change the font size. Just pick a new font (other than Auto) in the font size box on the left end of the DOS window Toolbar.

The DOS screen must be completely visible — no scroll bars. If there are scroll bars and you resize the screen to be smaller than it was, the DOS screen and window will shrink to the new size and the scroll bar may disappear, if you shrink it enough.

If you call for a larger font, and the DOS window is smaller than the DOS screen, the DOS screen and the font will increase in size, but the DOS window will not. The scroll bars will stay right where they are.

Drag the DOS window edges or corner

Set the DOS fonts to a fixed size. You can shrink the DOS window so that only part of the DOS screen shows. The resize arrows move the DOS window edges smoothly. When you release the mouse button, the scroll bars appear. You now have a window on your DOS screen.

If the DOS window is maximized, the resize arrows, correctly, do not appear.

Relocate the DOS window

To relocate the DOS window, drag its caption bar. The DOS window remembers its new size and location. This information is stored in its *pif*. The next time you start this DOS application the window will be located in the same place with the same font at the same size.

Choosing the DOS display fonts

Windows 95 provides 25 different fonts for displaying text in a DOS window. Sixteen of the fonts are fixed-pitch TrueType fonts (Courier New) and 9 are the bitmapped Terminal fonts. More details about fonts are available in Chapter 20.

If you have installed Microsoft Plus!, Courier New has been replaced as the DOS font by Lucida Console. You can see the differences between these two fonts by moving Lucida Console out of the Fonts folder and comparing DOS windows with the Courier font, which will automatically be used if Lucida is not found.

Secret

You won't be able to move Lucida Console unless you restart Windows 95, press F8, and boot to the command prompt. You can then use the DOS Move command to move Lucida Console to another folder.

These fonts aren't used when DOS is displayed at full-screen size. The font built into your computer's ROM is used instead.

There are two methods for choosing between different fonts for displaying DOS commands and programs in a window. The first is as follows:

STEPS

Choosing a DOS Font, First Method

Step 1. If your DOS application is displayed at full-screen size, press Alt+Enter to get DOS into a window.

Step 2. If the DOS window does not have a Toolbar, click the system menu in the upper left corner of the DOS window and select Toolbar.

Step 3. Click the arrow on the font size combo box at the left end of the Toolbar.

Step 4. Use the scroll bar on the font list box to review the choices.

Step 5. Choose a font size and type.

The second method is as follows:

STEPS

Choosing a DOS Font, Second Method

Step 1.   Click the "A" icon at the right end of the DOS window Toolbar.

Step 2.   Choose a font from the Font size list, as shown in Figure 17-2. A preview of the DOS window size appears along with a preview of the font itself.

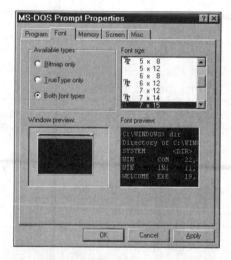

Figure 17-2: The Fonts Properties sheet. When you choose a font from the list in the upper right corner, the result is displayed in the bottom two windows.

Step 3.   Click OK.

Secret

If "Both font types" is checked in the Available types area, only 23 fonts are shown, in addition to Auto. This is in spite of the fact that 25 fonts are available (16 TrueType and 9 bitmapped). There is an overlap of the 4x6 and 7x12 TrueType and bitmapped fonts. Only the bitmapped fonts for these sizes are shown when this box is checked.

To choose the TrueType font for these two font sizes, click the TrueType only check box. These fonts of the same size look quite a bit different.

Auto font

If you want the font to change based on the size of the DOS window, choose the font size -Auto. As you drag the window, Auto will choose the one that best fits your DOS window size from among 23, 18, 16, or 9 fonts (depending on your choice of available fonts).

Mark, copy and paste text to and from the DOS window and the Clipboard

The Toolbar in a DOS window makes it easy to mark and copy data and text to and from the Clipboard. You can copy data and text into DOS documents from Windows documents and vice versa.

STEPS

Copying DOS Data to the Clipboard

Step 1.   To start marking data (or text), click the dotted square icon next to the font size list box on the left side of the Toolbar.

Step 2.   Move your mouse pointer to anywhere just outside the area that contains the data or text that you want to copy to the Clipboard.

Step 3.   Press and hold the left mouse button.

Step 4.   Drag the mouse pointer until the rectangle that you are dragging with your mouse pointer completely covers the desired data or text.

Step 5.   Release the mouse button.

Step 6.   Click the copy icon, which is the dual-page icon to the right of the mark icon in the Toolbar, or press Enter.

To paste text or data from the Clipboard to your DOS application, position your cursor in the DOS document, and click the paste icon, which is the icon with the Clipboard in the DOS window Toolbar to the right of the copy icon.

Changing Directories in a DOS window

Undocumented

Here's a cool trick from Kaleb Axon, a Windows 95 beta tester. It an interesting way to change directories in a DOS window.

STEPS

Changing Directories in DOS

Step 1.   Open a DOS window by clicking the Start button, Programs, MS-DOS prompt.

Step 2.   Open an Explorer window by, for example, right-clicking My Computer, then Explore. Navigate in the Explorer to any folder or sub folder.

Step 3.   Type **cd** at the DOS prompt in the DOS window. Press the space bar.

Step 4.   Drag and drop a folder icon from the Explorer window to the DOS window.

Step 5.   Notice that the folder name is placed on the DOS command line.

This is an example of a general class of behaviors. Drag and drop works with DOS, sort of. While you can't drag and drop text from a Windows 95 application into a DOS application, it is possible to drag and drop file names to the command line of a DOS application. You can, of course, copy text from a Windows application to the Clipboard and paste it into a DOS text editing application.

Connecting a DOS window to the Explorer

Want to be able to quickly open a DOS window into the current directory while you are navigating about your hard disk in the Explorer? This makes it easy to use DIR to look more closely at the files in that folder.

STEPS

DOS Windows and Folder Together

Undocumented

Step 1.   Open an Explorer window.

Step 2.   Click View, Options, File Types from the menu bar.

Step 3.   Click the Folder icon and the Edit button.

Step 4.   Click New.

Step 5.   In the Action field type **MS-DOS Prompt.**

Step 6.   In the "Application used to perform action" field, type **C:\Windows\Command.com /k cd.**

(continued)

STEPS *(continued)*

DOS Windows and Folder Together

Step 7 Click OK, then OK again, then Close.

Step 8. Right-click any folder icon in the Explorer window. Click MS-DOS prompt in the right mouse button menu

Step 0. A DOS window is opened by Step 8. If the folder icon was on a different drive letter (volume) than the C: drive, you will need to type in the letter followed by a colon and a carriage return to go to the folder that you right-clicked.

You now have a new right mouse button menu command associated with any folder. This gives you a quick way to open a DOS window on any current folder in the Explorer.

Expand the DOS window to full screen

You can run DOS in a DOS window or you can run it at the full-screen size. It's easy to switch back and forth. Press Alt+Enter to switch between the two modes. If you have the Toolbar turned on, you can switch to full screen by clicking the icon with four arrow heads in the middle of the Toolbar.

Change the properties of the shortcut to the DOS application

Click the Properties icon in the DOS window Toolbar. It is the fourth icon from the right and looks like a hand holding a sheet of paper at the top of the paper. We discuss the effect of changing these properties in the *Editing Shortcut Properties Sheets* section later in this chapter.

Background

Click the background button on the Toolbar to *not* suspend the DOS application while it is in the background; that is, when the DOS application doesn't have the focus. See the *Background* section later in this chapter.

Closing a DOS application

Under normal circumstances you exit your DOS application by whatever means the developer of your DOS program provided. If you clicked the Close on Exit box in your DOS application's *pif*, the DOS window would also close when you exited your application.

If you are unable to exit normally, you can exit by clicking the "x" caption button on the right end of the DOS window caption area. You will get a warning message if the "Warn if still active" box is checked in the DOS application's *pif.*

Using Windows 3.x, you exited from the DOS command prompt in a Windows DOS session by typing **exit** and pressing Enter. You can now just click the "x" caption button. Placing an X.bat file on your path, containing the single line **EXIT**, also gives you a simple way to end a DOS session. Simply press the X key, and then press Enter to exit.

Creating a Virtual Machine for DOS Programs

Windows creates a "virtual machine" for every DOS program that you start from Windows (every Windows DOS session). You have the option of designing this "virtual machine." Instead of interacting with your computer hardware (the real machine), the DOS program interacts with something that it "sees" as a real machine: the virtual machine.

If you start your DOS programs from the MS-DOS prompt in the Start menu, they will run in the virtual computer associated with that MS-DOS prompt. This virtual machine is defined by Properties sheets stored in the shortcut to the DOS prompt program stored in the \Windows\Start Menu folder. You can edit these Properties sheets to redefine the virtual machine associated with the Start menu's MS-DOS prompt.

When in a folder window, the Explorer, or File Manager, you double-click an icon that represents a DOS program, you will automatically create a shortcut. This is also true if you choose Run from the Start button. This shortcut to a DOS program will be stored in the same folder the DOS program is stored in. If a shortcut is already there, a new one isn't created.

If you delete or move the shortcut, double-clicking the DOS application's icon in the Explorer will create a new shortcut in the folder that contains the DOS application, unless you moved the shortcut to the \Windows\Pif folder. If the DOS program doesn't execute, the shortcut won't be created.

These shortcuts to DOS programs are like shortcuts to Windows programs. The properties of a shortcut to a DOS program, a *pif,* are different from those of a shortcut to a Windows program, because the Properties sheets of a shortcut to a DOS program define a virtual machine.

Double-click a shortcut to a DOS program and the program starts. You can move these shortcuts and copy them. You can place them on your desktop or on your Start menus. You can have multiple shortcuts for one DOS program, just as you can have multiple, and different, shortcuts for Windows programs or documents.

Shortcuts to DOS can be associated with document files instead of programs, just like Windows shortcuts. The DOS applications that open these documents can be associated with the document's extension. See Chapter 13 for details on how to associate application with document extensions.

Undocumented

While the task of identifying the needs of each and every possible DOS program is too daunting for Microsoft to attempt, Windows 95 comes with Apps.inf, which can be found in the \Windows\Inf folder. Apps.inf provides the basic virtual machine configuration for over 300 DOS applications. You don't have to do anything to access this file; it is used automatically to help create shortcuts for the DOS programs referenced in it.

Often the default shortcut that is created when you double-click a DOS application icon works just fine.

Undocumented

Many DOS software developers include *pif*s with their DOS applications. *Pif*s created for Windows 3.*x* are compatible with shortcuts to DOS programs for Windows 95. You can place them wherever they are appropriate for your work.

Secret

When a shortcut is created automatically, it has the same name as the DOS program, but a different extension: *pif*. You won't see this extension even if you have chosen View, Options, View in the Explorer and unchecked "Hide all MS-DOS file extensions for file types that are registered." Likewise, you won't see the *lnk* extension used for shortcuts to Windows programs. You will see the file type "Shortcut to a MS-DOS Program."

There is a difference between starting a DOS program at the MS-DOS prompt within a Windows DOS session and double-clicking the DOS program icon in a folder window.

Secret

- If you are starting the DOS program from the MS-DOS prompt in a Windows DOS session, no shortcut is created.

- If you double-click the DOS executable program icon, or run a DOS program by choosing Run from the Start button, a shortcut is created.

You can also create a shortcut by right-clicking a DOS program icon and clicking Create Shortcut.

Creating multiple shortcuts

It is possible to create multiple shortcuts that are all associated with the same DOS program. By setting different properties in each shortcut, it is possible to start the DOS program in different configurations by double-clicking the different shortcuts. Here's how:

STEPS

Creating Multiple Shortcuts

Step 1. Double-click a DOS program's executable icon in the Explorer (or in a folder window).

Step 2.   Exit the DOS program.

Step 3.   Use the Explorer to display the folder that contains the DOS program.

Step 4.   Click the shortcut associated with your DOS program. Press F2.

Step 5.   Type in a new filename for the shortcut.

Step 6.   Right-click the shortcut, choose Copy. Right-click the right pane of the client area of the Explorer and choose Paste.

Step 7.   Click the new shortcut and press F2. Type in a new name for this shortcut.

Step 8.   Repeat Steps 6 and 7 to create new shortcuts associated with the same DOS program.

Step 9.   Edit each of these shortcuts for different properties, as detailed in the following sections. You can move these shortcuts to different folders or onto the desktop or Start menus.

Opening program information files (pifs)

If you are familiar with editing *pif*s using Windows 3.*x*, you'll notice the Pif Editor is gone. Good riddance.

In its place, you can easily change the properties that are stored in a DOS program's shortcut. The shortcut stores these changes in Properties sheets. You simply right-click a DOS application's icon and change its properties. We show two ways to open the Properties sheets. Our example DOS application is Command.com. Here's the first method:

STEPS

Opening a DOS Application Properties Sheet

Step 1.   Use the Explorer to view the \Windows folder.

Step 2.   Right-click the icon labeled Command.com and then select Properties. The shortcut hasn't been created yet, if it wasn't already. Only after you make a change to any one of the Properties sheets and then click the OK button will a shortcut be created.

If a shortcut has already been created for a DOS application, you can use the Explorer, perhaps in conjunction with the Find tool, to find the shortcut. Once you have found it, right-click it and choose Properties. You can open the shortcut associated with any DOS program in this same manner.

The following steps describe another method:

STEPS

Getting to a DOS Shortcut

Step 1. Using the Explorer, find Command.com in the \Windows folder. Double-click Command.com.

Step 2. Click the system menu on the right side of the DOS window's caption area, or right-click the caption area. (If yours is a full screen Windows DOS session, press Alt+Enter to make it a windowed DOS session.)

Step 3. Choose Properties from the right mouse button menu.

Step 4. You can now change the properties of the virtual machine. They will be stored in the shortcut.

This method can be used whenever you are running a DOS program in a window. If you have the Toolbar turned on, you can also click the Properties icon.

Editing Shortcut Properties Sheets

There are seven Properties sheets (six shown as tabs) associated with a DOS program. Click the tabs at the top of the Properties sheets dialog box to switch between them. The first one, the General Properties sheet, is for any DOS or Windows file or folder. You won't see this General Properties sheet if you have the DOS application window open and click on the Properties icon, the system menu, or the caption area.

Program Properties sheet

The Program Properties sheet is the meat of the matter. Take a look at Figure 17-3 to see what we mean. A Properties sheet contains the command line for the DOS program, its working directory, an optional startup batch file that runs before the DOS application, a shortcut key/hotkey definition, a window configuration, and buttons to change the associated shortcut's icon and define MS-DOS mode. You'll find a big chunk of DOS program functionality here.

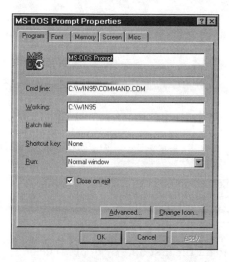

Figure 17-3: The Program Properties sheet. Define the title of the application, its command line, working directory, startup batch file, hotkey combination, state of the DOS window, and icon. Also say whether the application needs to run in MS-DOS mode or not.

The Program Properties sheet for a shortcut to a DOS program is a lot like the shortcut Properties sheet associated with Windows programs. Figure 17-4 shows the similarities. Where there are differences, we point them out below.

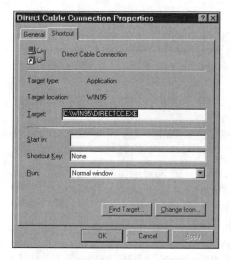

Figure 17-4: The Shortcut Properties sheet for a Windows shortcut. The shortcut's title is given. Target is like Cmd line. Start in Working is similar to Program Properties. Both Properties sheets have Run and Hotkey fields. Both have Change Icon buttons.

Notice that the Programs and the Shortcut Properties sheets have titles, command lines (Target and Cmd line), working directories (Start in and Working), Hotkeys and Run fields, and Change Icon buttons. For more on shortcuts, see Chapter 10.

Title

A name appears in a DOS application's title bar. The title bar appears when the application is running in a window and not in full-screen mode. The name is on the left-most side of the title bar. This is the name in the first field of the Programs Properties sheet, the title field.

If you leave the Title box blank, the name of the shortcut is put in this field. This title is also the icon title on the Taskbar.

Command line

When you start a DOS program for the first time by double-clicking its icon in a folder window, you automatically create a shortcut that contains the complete path name of the DOS application in the command line field. The command line can contain the driver letter, folder name, filename, extension, and any command line parameters.

It is possible to set the values for what are referred to as *environmental variables* in your Autoexec. bat file and other DOS batch files. You do this with a Set command. These variables can be used in the command line in a Properties sheet to insert their associated values into the command line. You use the following form:

```
%variablename%
```

For example, if you used in Autoexec.bat the command **Set location = ABC**, the command line **c:\%ABC%\Myprog.exe** in a Properties sheet would run the program Myprog in the ABC directory.

Secret

If you move the DOS program or want the shortcut to refer to another program, you can edit this command line. Unlike shortcuts to Windows applications or documents, a shortcut to a DOS program or document will not go looking for the associated DOS program or document if you move it. You have to edit the command line to give it a new location.

The Shortcut Properties sheet has a Find Target button. There is no such button in a shortcut to a DOS program. You have to navigate to the DOS application's folder by yourself, using the Explorer or a folder window.

If your DOS program can accept different command line parameters, and you want to avail yourself of the opportunity to type them in whenever you start the DOS program, you need to add a space and question mark at the end of the command line string. Only one question mark is needed, no matter how many parameters your DOS program can accept. Figure 17-5 shows what the command line dialog box looks like.

Figure 17-5: The command line dialog box. Enter a question mark after the program name in the command line of a DOS shortcut and you get to specify the command line parameters every time you start this DOS application.

If you use the same command line parameters every time, just type them in the command line field after the program's path name. It is possible to have multiple shortcuts associated with one DOS program, each with different command line parameters, and perhaps one with a question mark.

Any parameters you type after the shortcut name when you run a shortcut from the Run command on the Start button menu *override* the parameters that you specified in the command line field in the program's property sheet. For example, doing a command like Run Myapp.lnk /abc forces your app to use the parameter /abc instead of whatever command line you defined in the shortcut. This is one way to use one set of switches to start the application most of the time, and use a different set occasionally.

The command line can contain a DOS application name and a filename, something like C:\Windows\Command\Edit.com C:\Windows\Temp\New.txt, for example. The shortcut will be a shortcut to the document, just like a Windows shortcut to a document.

If the DOS application is associated with a file extension, a *lnk* shortcut to a DOS document can easily be created. Right-click a document with that extension and click Create Shortcut. This creates a Windows shortcut, a file with the *lnk* extension, not a *pif*. You have to create the association between the file extension and the DOS program first. Turn to Chapter 13 for details.

A *lnk* file can be changed to a *pif* just by adding the DOS application name in front of the document filename in the command line field of the shortcut Properties sheet. For example, assume you have a shortcut to a text file that is normally associated with Notepad. You can edit the command line in the shortcut Properties sheet for this document to use Edit.com instead. When you do, the *lnk* file turns into a *pif*.

You can't create a *lnk* shortcut from a *pif*. If you right-click a *pif* and choose Create Shortcut, you'll create another *pif*.

Working directory

The working directory is the folder that is meant to contain files that work in conjunction with your DOS application or the data or text files you edit with the DOS application. What's in this field will direct the DOS program to search this directory for any files it needs. Whether an entry is needed here or not depends on the DOS program.

Tip

For example, one of the authors runs the DOS program Doom (don't so many misguided souls?). The Doom shortcut is stored in \Windows\Desktop. The command line for Doom is d:\games\doom\doom.exe. The working directory for Doom is d:\games\doom. If the working directory field is blank, Doom 1.2 won't run when the Doom shortcut icon is double-clicked. Heretic, another product from id Software, the developers of Doom, doesn't require an entry in the working directory field.

Batch file

You can run a DOS batch file before your application starts up.

This is one way to set certain environmental variables for a DOS application before you run it. For example, put the following line in this batch file:

```
Set Mydir=C:\thisone
```

Alternatively, you can load TSR programs in the batch file before your primary DOS application starts. You then can access the TSR from within that DOS application — without using memory in every DOS session by loading that TSR prior to starting Windows.

Hotkey(s)

Undocumented

You can make an entry into the hotkey field (it's labeled Shortcut key) to define a set of keys that you press at the same time to start a DOS application. Hotkeys work only for shortcuts that are in the Start menus. If your shortcut is on the desktop, defining a hotkey won't do you any good.

Hotkeys are used to allow you to start an application from the keyboard without mousing around. People who use DOS applications in full-screen mode and want to quickly start and switch between applications are particularly fond of them.

While the field name is singular, as in Shortcut key, it is best to assign a *set* of keys to be pressed together as one hotkey. That way, you can define three keys that probably won't be used for something else in one of your applications that may be open at the time you press these three keys. For example, you could define Ctrl+Alt+D to start the MS-DOS prompt window.

If you use the Ctrl, Alt, and/or Shift key, it is easy to press and hold down one or two of these keys first while you then press the last key, most likely a letter key. These keys are modifier keys and usually your applications won't react to them until another key is pressed. This makes it easier to press three keys at once.

Even if another application has the focus and you are in full-screen DOS mode, the hotkeys will work. The hotkey takes precedence. If you define a hotkey combination that is used in an application, that application loses the ability to use that combination. The keyboard combination opens another application instead.

Tip

For example, if you define a hotkey as Shift+d without Ctrl or Alt, you would be unable to type a *D* (capital *d*) in your word processor. Or if you define a hotkey as Ctrl+Shift+D and that combination is used in your spreadsheet for some function, the spreadsheet will not be able to see that combination, because Windows will grab it before the spreadsheet can get ahold of it — even if the spreadsheet has the focus.

Undocumented

Your hotkey should (by convention) include either an Alt or Ctrl key, plus a function key or printable key. The Windows 95 help files say it has to, but it doesn't. You can include the Shift key in the combination, but not the keys Backspace, Enter, Esc, PrintScreen, Spacebar, or Tab. Crtl+Shift or Ctrl+Alt plus a letter key is often a good combination. Windows applications often leave combinations with these keys undefined so you can define macros with them.

Something else to try is Ctrl or Alt in combination with the punctuation keys (period, comma, etc.). Windows applications rarely use these combinations.

If you just want to switch to running applications, an easier way to do this is to press Alt+Tab. This allows you to switch to any running application, DOS *or* Windows. You can also use Ctrl+Esc to get to the Start button menu.

Tip

If you happened to set a hotkey for a shortcut, and you later want to get rid of it, you can't just delete the key combination from this box, then save the shortcut. The previous key assignment isn't actually deleted unless you succeed in entering None in the box. And you can't just type the word *None* — you must place your cursor in the box and press Backspace to specify None.

Undocumented

There is a hotkey definition field in the shortcut Properties sheet of a *lnk* file also. While hotkeys work the sameway in some types of shortcuts (*pif* and *lnk*), entering keystrokes into the hotkey field is different. You can press the *d* key and have it entered into the hotkey field when editing the properties of a shortcut.

If you do the same for a *lnk* file, Ctrl+Alt+ will be automatically added before the *d*.

It is also not a good idea to redefine such keystrokes as F1 (help) as a hotkey. This reduces the functionality of Windows 95. Many applications also use the combinations Ctrl+F1, Ctrl+Shift+F1, and so on.

Run — Normal, Minimized, Maximized

What size window do you want to start your DOS application in?

If your font is set to Auto sizing, you can have a maximized DOS window that fills up the desktop as much as possible. DOS windows are sized based on the height-to-width ratio of the DOS font used and are limited by the size of the desktop. If you choose Maximized with Auto font sizing, you'll get a large DOS window.

If you have a fixed DOS font size, the Maximized setting will display a DOS *window* that encompasses a whole DOS *screen* at the set DOS font.

If you choose Normal, you will get a DOS window that is the restored size. If the maximized and restored size are the same because you are using a fixed DOS font size, and the DOS window is big enough to display the whole DOS screen, the only difference between Normal and Maximized may be the location of the window.

If you choose Minimized, the DOS application opens as an icon/button on the Taskbar. This is great for running DOS programs that don't require any interaction with the user (as is true of many batch files).

Close on exit

The Close on exit box is a very nice feature. If you want to run a quick DOS batch file, you can have it show up only as an icon/button on your Taskbar and make it go away as soon as it carries out its work.

In many cases you will want the DOS window to close after you have completed working with the DOS application or document. This is the way all Windows programs work; nothing is left open after you quit them. The only reason you would want to leave the DOS window open is if you wanted to run another DOS program after you finished working on the one that you are currently running.

You can open a DOS window with just the DOS prompt, as you do when you click the MS-DOS prompt icon in the Start menu. Even with Close on exit checked, the DOS prompt is there ready for you to run the next DOS program. You don't exit the command prompt DOS window until you type **exit** at the prompt or click the "x" caption button in the upper-right corner of the DOS window.

Tip

If your DOS program does some work, writes some output to the DOS screen, and then quits, you are not going to be able to see what the output was if you check Close on exit. Lots of DOS programs do this, so uncheck this box if you want to see their output.

If you quit a DOS application and the DOS window is still on the desktop, the title bar of the DOS window states that the application is inactive. To get rid of the DOS window, click the "x" caption button.

Change Icon button

The Change Icon button is pretty straightforward. You are given a choice of icons contained in C:\Windows\System\Shortcutmgr.dll, as shown in Figure 17-6. If your current icon is contained in another file, the icons in that file are displayed. You can choose a new icon from among those displayed, or Browse through other files for other icons.

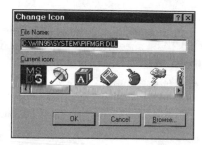

Figure 17-6: Choose an icon. Use the scroll bar to move to the right or left and then double-click on the icon you want. If you want to get an icon from another file, click Browse.

The CD-ROM with this book features a shareware program, Icoshow, that will collect all the icons on your hard disk into a file (or set of files). This makes it much easier to find just the right icon.

The Browse button brings up the common File Open dialog box. You use this dialog box to find the file that contains the icons you want to use.

Advanced button

Clicking Advanced displays the Advanced Program Settings Properties sheet shown in Figure 17-7. Click the MS-DOS mode check box to allow your computer to be switched to MS-DOS mode when you double-click the MS-DOS icon associated with this Properties sheet.

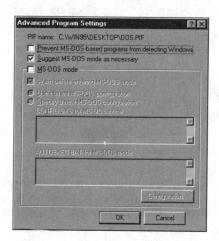

Figure 17-7: The Advanced Programs Settings Properties sheet. Clicking the first check box tells the DOS box to try to fool any program that checks to see if it is running under Windows by telling it that it isn't. Clicking the second check box asks Windows to see if the DOS program you run could better use MS-DOS mode. The third check box turns on the MS-DOS mode. Double-click a DOS program icon that has this check box checked and your computer is switched to MS-DOS mode.

Many DOS programs that didn't run well under Windows 3.x will run fine in the Windows DOS session under Windows 95. Some of these Windows-unfriendly DOS programs would check to be sure they weren't running under Windows in order to warn you to quit Windows before running them.

Tip

If you have such a program that can, in fact, run in the Windows 95 DOS session, you can send a message to it when it asks if it is running under Windows that it is not (when, of course, it is). This allows it to run in a Windows 95 DOS session (hopefully) successfully.

Windows programs will by default run from the DOS prompt of a Windows DOS session (using the Start command). If you click the first check box in the Advanced Programs Properties sheet, Windows 95 will no longer be able to recognize that you typed the name of the Windows program at the DOS prompt and Windows programs will not run from a Windows DOS session.

Windows will check to see if there are incompatibilities in a DOS program that will most likely prevent it from running successfully in a Windows DOS session. The default is to "Suggest MS-DOS mode as necessary" if such incompatibilities are found. If you uncheck the second check box, you run the risk of running a badly behaved DOS program in your Windows DOS session.

Clicking the MS-DOS mode check box and Specify a new MS-DOS configuration enables the lower portion of the Properties sheets and lets you edit the Config.sys for MS-DOS mode and Autoexec.bat for MS-DOS mode fields. You switch your computer into MS-DOS mode by double-clicking a DOS program icon that has the MS-DOS mode check box checked.

If you choose the MS-DOS mode, the rest of the Properties sheets don't apply and are blank. We discuss MS-DOS mode in its own section below, so we'll quit talking about it here.

Fonts

For details on the Fonts Properties sheet, see the section earlier in this chapter entitled *Choosing the DOS display fonts*.

The Memory Properties sheet

The amount of memory available to a DOS program running in a Windows DOS session depends on the configuration of the Autoexec.bat and Config.sys files, if any, and whether DOS TSRs and 16-bit drivers are loaded in conventional memory or in the upper memory blocks (UMBs). Further details can be found in Chapter 18.

Windows 95 will provide DOS programs with expanded, extended, and/or DOS protected mode memory. The DOS programs must comply with Windows extended, expanded, and/or DPMI memory specifications in order to be able to use this memory.

Because Windows 95 makes extensive use of 32-bit protected-mode drivers that do not use conventional memory or UMBs, it can provide up to 612K of conventional memory for DOS programs that run in Windows DOS sessions.

The Memory Properties sheet, as shown in Figure 17-8, is divided into four sections that mirror the types of memory available to DOS programs. You can set the amount of memory of each type available to your DOS program in each of these sections.

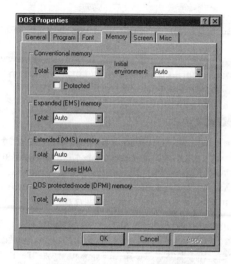

Figure 17-8: The Memory Properties sheet. You can set the amount of available conventional, expanded, extended, and/or DPMI memory. The default is Auto, which means "let the DOS programs determine how much they need or want." Some DOS programs don't do a good job of restraining themselves and need to be limited in their memory acquisition.

Conventional memory

The maximum available is about 612K under the best of circumstances. DOS games and other large programs will likely take all they can get. The only reason to limit the amount of conventional memory available to a DOS program is to let it load slightly quicker. This may help on slower computers, but won't be noticeable on faster ones.

Tip

You could create a separate shortcut, for example, for "small" DOS sessions in which you plan to run only DOS commands such as Dir, Del, and so on. Setting conventional memory at 160K would be adequate for these tasks. This would conserve physical memory for other applications while a "small" DOS session is running.

Protected

Does your DOS program contain a bug? Does it write to memory in areas that it shouldn't? If so, click the Protected check box to help protect Windows from crashing because of bugs caused by your DOS application.

When the protected box is checked, the MS-DOS system memory area is write-protected so your DOS application can't write into this area and corrupt it.

Environment

If you are running a batch file to set environment variables before your DOS application runs, you might want to expand the size of the environment that stores these variables. You may have a smaller environment size in your common Config.sys file. Use this variable to set aside a larger environment for environment variables that are particular to your DOS application.

Expanded (EMS) memory

DOS programs that make use of expanded memory that meets the LIM 4.0 specification can be provided with expanded memory by Windows itself. Windows includes its own expanded memory manager separate from Emm386.exe. DOS games like Xwing use expanded memory for handling sound effects and music. Some DOS spreadsheets use expanded memory.

You can set the value for expanded memory to Auto if you want the DOS program to determine how much it needs, or you can limit its appetite. Some DOS programs don't know when they have enough, so you'll want to say when enough is enough.

If you have a Config.sys file with a line calling the MS-DOS expanded memory manager (Emm386.exe), and if the parameter "noems" is on that line, expanded memory will not be available to DOS programs running in Windows DOS sessions. The Memory Properties sheet will be altered to show this state of affairs, as shown in Figure 17-9.

For most DOS programs, you can set expanded memory equal to zero. If you have any DOS programs that use expanded or extended memory, these programs should have their own shortcuts.

Extended (XMS) memory

In case your DOS application makes use of extended memory in a way that is compatible with running under Windows, the XMS memory settings allow you to specify the amount of available extended memory.

Applications that use DPMI (DOS Protected Mode Interface) — which Microsoft prescribes as the correct way to access extended memory under a multitasking environment — can use this extended memory. (DPMI applications obtain extended memory through Himem.sys or other "XMS managers".)

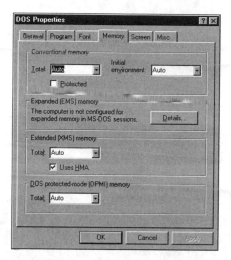

Figure 17-9: The Memory Properties sheet with no expanded memory available. If you have a line like Device=Emm386.exe noems in your Config.sys file, there will be no enhanced memory available to your DOS programs.

HMA

If DOS or other 16-bit drivers are loaded high in your Config.sys file, checking Uses HMA doesn't do anything. Otherwise, you can use this memory like extended memory.

The High Memory Area (HMA) is the first 64K of extended memory. It is the only part of extended memory that an application running under DOS can access while still in real mode. Very few DOS applications currently use this memory area. This is unfortunate, because if they did, they would be able to add almost 64K to the amount of conventional memory available to them (unless the line DOS=High is in your Config.sys file). The Windows memory manager, Himem.sys, and all other compatible memory managers make this 64K area available to Windows or any program that requests it.

The rule for the Uses HMA check box is: if you start two shortcuts under Windows — both using the HMA — Windows will switch this memory between them in turn, so they can both benefit from using it.

If you turn *off* this HMA check box, an application started from that shortcut cannot access any HMA from within Windows, even if it would otherwise be capable of doing so.

If DOS or a DOS application, however, claims the HMA *before* you start Windows, then no Windows application or shortcut to a DOS program can ever use it.

DOS applications that can use the HMA generally make this fact very well known in their publicity and documentation. You can leave this check box *on*, unless you know that two particular applications using it at once would conflict. In that case, turn it off for the application that requires less memory.

DOS protected-mode memory

Some DOS programs use this specification for turning extended memory into something that DOS programs can use.

The Screen Properties sheet

The default setting for a new shortcut is to run your DOS application windowed on the Windows 95 desktop. This makes the DOS programs look and feel more like Windows programs, which is a nice touch.

Tip

MS-DOS programs that run in VGA graphics mode can run in a window on the desktop. This wasn't the case in Windows 3.x. DOS games that rely on hand-eye coordination will probably run too slowly in a window. You'll want to run them at full-screen size.

You can always switch between full-screen and windowed with Alt+Enter.

Starting a Windows DOS session in a small window takes slightly more memory than starting it full-screen. So if your application won't start in a window, check Full-screen. You get to choose how your DOS program first comes up, by choosing Full-screen or Window, as shown in Figure 17-10.

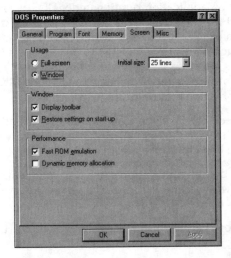

Figure 17-10: The Screen Properties sheet. Select how your DOS program will be windowed.

Initial size — number of lines displayed

If your video display driver can provide support for more than 25 lines of DOS text in a DOS window or full-screen display (and most VGA or higher-resolution systems can) this section will be active. You can change the number of lines displayed in the first box.

This works great for a windowed DOS session, even one that merely displays the good old DOS C> prompt. When you configure Windows for a number of screen lines greater than 25 — let's say 50 — DOS commands *know* that the screen now contains that many lines. For example, the command dir /p, which halts a directory listing at the end of each screen page, now halts scrolling the display after showing 50 lines instead of 25.

DOS applications themselves vary in their support for higher-than-25-line screens. Some applications automatically adjust to the number of lines in effect when they start up. Other applications, presuming that no one would ever have a display with more than 25 lines, are hard-coded to force themselves into that mode every time.

No matter how high the number of DOS screen lines you configure Windows for, Windows won't open a windowed DOS session any taller than your screen will allow. If you specify a number of lines that would make a windowed DOS session extend beyond the top and bottom of your screen (with the DOS screen font you're using), Windows creates a window only the height of your physical screen — with scroll bars so you can see the rest.

Most VGA adapters support 25-, 43-, and 50-line modes, although if yours doesn't, this setting won't change anything. A 43-line display takes up less room on your display than a 50-line display, while still giving you a lot more information than the bad old 25-line display.

Restore settings on start-up

You can change your font, window size, and position while running your DOS application. If your want your original values to be used the next time you start the application, click this box.

If you exit your DOS application and close the DOS window while you are in full-screen mode, the next time you start this application it will come up in full-screen mode.

Fast ROM emulation

Applications that display text run faster if the Fast ROM Emulation box is checked. This allows Windows to use faster routines in RAM if the application normally uses standard ROM BIOS calls to write text to the screen. You must turn the setting off if garbage appears on the application's screen or you lose control of its mouse when you run it under Windows.

Dynamic memory allocation

If your DOS application switches between text and graphics modes, you can be sure to always have enough memory for the graphics mode or release this memory for other programs when in text mode. This switch appears to be written in the most part for Microsoft Word for MS-DOS.

Check this box if you want to let other programs use the small amount of extra available memory when the DOS application goes into text mode.

The Misc Properties sheet

Microsoft had no place else to put these various properties of the DOS virtual machine, so it created a miscellaneous Properties sheet. Not too original, but what the heck. The Misc Properties sheet is displayed in Figure 17-11.

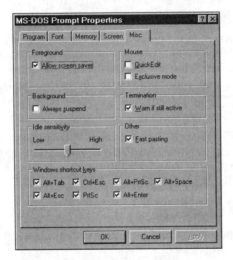

Figure 17-11: The Misc Properties sheet. This is the grab bag of the DOS Properties sheets. Whatever didn't fit elsewhere is here.

Allow screen saver

Screen savers can be pretty unruly. If you want to allow your screen saver to start up even though you are in full-screen DOS mode, check Allow screen saver underneath Foreground.

Screen savers can interfere with DOS communications or terminal emulation programs, which is the biggest reason to turn off this box.

Background

If you are running a DOS communications program in the background, you won't want to check Always suspend.

Background means when the application doesn't have the focus. If the DOS application is running in full-screen mode and you can see it, it has the focus. If it is running in a window and the window caption area is highlighted, it has the focus.

DOS communications applications often run in the background as you download files while going on to some other task in the foreground. Other DOS applications don't do anything while they don't have the focus, so you might as well suspend them to give all the computer's resources to the foreground task.

Idle sensitivity

This setting, when turned to high, enables Windows to stop giving DOS applications any time slices if Windows determines that the application is doing nothing but waiting for you to press a key. This cutoff can make foreground Windows applications run faster when a DOS session that needs no time slices is running in the background.

Whether Windows *correctly* determines that a DOS application is idle, however, varies from application to application.

Newer DOS apps can detect when they are running under Windows and send it a message whenever they are merely waiting for a keystroke. This makes your whole system run faster, since Windows doesn't have to give time slices to that application until you start using it again.

Tip

The Idle sensitivity option is intended for older kinds of DOS apps. The rules for its use with the newer kind of program are not intuitive. You should set this option according to one of the following three rules:

1. If the application is an older one, and does not do *anything* in the background that is important, turn Idle sensitivity to high.

2. If the application does something once a second, or intermittently when a certain event occurs (such as midnight), turn Idle sensitivity to low.

3. If the application is a newer, Windows-aware type, turn Idle sensitivity to low. Your applications will all run a little faster if Windows gets the "idle" message directly from these applications and does not have to test for it.

Unfortunately, it is difficult to determine whether a particular DOS application does or does not send this "idle" message to Windows. If the documentation doesn't mention this feature, you have to assume that it hasn't been added to the program.

Mouse

You don't want to check the QuickEdit box if your DOS application uses a mouse. Checking this box makes it easier to use your mouse to mark, cut, and paste selections to the Clipboard, but it does this at the cost of disabling the mouse for other actions.

Normally, making a selection to cut or copy to the Clipboard requires clicking the mark icon in the Toolbar of a DOS window. Checking this box allows you to bypass setting the selection mode, which would otherwise require clicking the mark icon.

This setting is useful if you are cutting and pasting a great deal of data back and forth between DOS and Windows or other DOS applications.

If you check Exclusive mode, you lose your Windows mouse pointer while this DOS application is in the foreground. The only reason to do this is if the DOS programs won't use the mouse correctly unless it exclusively controls it.

Tip

To get your Windows mouse back while this DOS application is in the foreground, press Alt+Space and then P. This will bring up the mouse and the Properties sheet. You can then click Misc and uncheck this box.

Termination

You can exit your DOS application in a number of ways. If your DOS application is Command.com (the DOS prompt), you can type **exit** and press Enter. If you are in some other DOS application, you exit that application in the fashion determined by the application. If you have chosen close on exit, the DOS window closes.

You can also close a DOS window just by clicking the "x" caption button. If you are at the DOS prompt, the DOS window closes without further ado. If you are in a DOS program, you may want to close this DOS program first before you close the DOS window. This way, you can be sure you have saved any unsaved data to your disk.

To be sure you are given a warning to close your DOS application before you close its DOS window, click Warn if still active.

Other

Some old DOS programs can take input only so fast. They expect you to be typing, not piping stuff over from some Windows file. If you paste data into your DOS application and it has trouble with it, uncheck Fast pasting.

Windows shortcut keys

Windows has a defined set of what we call hotkeys that it labels shortcut keys. It grabs them first whenever you press them. If your DOS program wants these keys for its own uses, you have to configure a shortcut for that application that tells Windows to back off and let the keystrokes go to the DOS application.

Table 17-2 lists these hotkeys and their definitions.

Table 17-2	Windows Hotkeys
Hotkey	**Definition**
Alt+Tab	Tab from one active application to another. Switches to graphics mode if DOS is in full-screen text mode. This is the "cool switch." Windows 3.x has a text-mode version of the cool switch that doesn't switch to graphics mode when you switch between full-screen DOS applications.
Alt+Tab+Click	If your DOS application is in full-screen mode, and you press and hold the Alt+Tab key combination, clicking any mouse button brings up the desktop.
Ctrl+Esc	Switch to graphics mode, if necessary, from full-screen DOS, display the desktop and the Taskbar, and click the Start button.
Alt+PrtSc	Copy the active window to the Clipboard. If the DOS application is in a DOS window, copy it as a graphic; if the DOS application is in full-screen text mode, copy it as text.
Alt+Space	Click the system menu.
Alt+Esc	Switch to the next active application.
PrtSc	Copy the complete desktop, including all windows, to the Clipboard. If in full-screen DOS text mode, copy all the text to the Clipboard.
Alt+Enter	Switch between full-screen and DOS window.

Undocumented

Using the Alt+Enter command changes the Window setting in the shortcut's Screen Properties sheet. You may want your DOS application to come up the same way you set it the first time and not the way you left it the last time. To preserve the settings in a shortcut's Properties sheets, you can set the shortcut's file attribute to read-only. Right-click the shortcut icon, click Properties, and then click Read-only.

If PrtSc is unchecked, the Print Screen key will send the current DOS screen to the printer in the same way it would under the DOS operating system, if the Windows DOS session is in full-screen mode.

To let the DOS application use any of these keystrokes while it has the focus or is in full-screen mode, uncheck the box associated with the appropriate keystrokes.

MS-DOS Mode

If your DOS program doesn't work in a Windows DOS session, you have the option of running it in MS-DOS mode (real-mode DOS). Rebooted MS-DOS mode works by shutting down Windows 95, performing a warm reboot, and booting into MS-DOS after calling a second copy of Command.com. You exit MS-DOS mode and Windows 95 is restarted.

Non-rebooted MS-DOS mode doesn't require a reboot before DOS starts. It runs the Dosstart.bat file right after it switches to DOS mode. You can exit back to Windows 95 by typing **exit** at the DOS prompt.

To get to a command prompt (the DOS prompt) in rebooted MS-DOS mode, you need to create a shortcut for Command.com with the proper properties. You can put the icon associated with this shortcut on your desktop, in one of your Start menus, or wherever is convenient. You can create properly configured shortcuts for every DOS application that requires MS-DOS mode.

Creating an MS-DOS mode shortcut

To create an MS-DOS mode icon and shortcut for your desktop, carry out the following steps:

STEPS

Creating a Shortcut for MS-DOS Mode

Step 1. Open the Explorer and navigate to your Windows 95 folder. Find Command.com.

Step 2. Right-click Command.com and click Properties.

Step 3. Click the Program tab and then the Advanced button.

Step 4. Click the MS-DOS mode box. Click the Warn before Entering MS-DOS mode to uncheck it if you don't want a warning before you switch to MS-DOS mode.

Step 5. The default is to use the current MS-DOS configuration. This means that you won't need to reboot to get to MS-DOS mode. If you are going to want private Autoexec.bat and Config.sys files for this DOS application, you will want to check the Specify a new MS-DOS configuration box. See the next section.

Step 6. Click both OK buttons, the first on the Advanced Program Settings dialog box, and the second one on the Properties for Command dialog box.

Step 7.   Using the Explorer window, right-drag the MS-DOS icon labeled Command from the Windows 95 folder to the desktop. Click Move here.

Step 8.   The icon name Command will be highlighted. Press F2 and type **MS-DOS mode.**

You now have an icon on the desktop that will get you to the non-rebooted MS-DOS mode (real-mode DOS) and give you a DOS prompt. The MS-DOS mode created in this fashion will use versions of the same Autoexec.bat and Config.sys files, if any, that are read when Windows 95 starts, as well as the Dosstart.bat file.

Private Autoexec.bat and Config.sys files

Each MS-DOS mode shortcut can have its own private Autoexec.bat and Config.sys files. The information used to create these files will be stored in the shortcut. The files will be created when you switch from Windows 95 to rebooted MS-DOS mode; that is, when you double-click the icon associated with the shortcut.

Having private Autoexec.bat and Config.sys files is a great idea. Each DOS program that runs in rebooted MS-DOS mode can have its own special configuration or drivers and DOS TSRs that work just right for it. You can also create a MS-DOS mode shortcut just for the command prompt, but with Autoexec.bat and Config.sys files that are completely independent of those used to start Windows 95.

Previously, the only way to have different startup configurations was to create a multiconfiguration Config.sys file by creating different sections of your Config.sys file as documented in your MS-DOS manual.

At startup, you then chose from a menu which set of drivers and DOS TSRs you wanted to be loaded. It was often necessary to have a multiconfiguration Config.sys file in order to have enough conventional memory for some DOS programs, or to allow for enhanced memory for other DOS programs.

Allowing completely different Autoexec.bat and Config.sys files is a much cleaner and easier-to-understand solution to the problem of multiple configurations. (Of course, the best solution is to have one configuration that works for all programs.) You create and save in the shortcut the information necessary to create the Autoexec.bat and Config.sys files that work with your DOS application.

Creating private Autoexec.bat and Config.sys data

To see how to create private Autoexec.bat and Config.sys files, you will use the shortcut that you just created for Command.com. It is already configured to start in MS-DOS mode.

STEPS

Creating Private Autoexec.bat and Config.sys Files

Step 1. Right-click the MS-DOS mode icon on the desktop (assuming you created it using the steps in the previous section entitled *Creating an MS-DOS mode shortcut*).

Step 2. Click Properties, click the Program tab, and then the Advanced button. The Advanced Program Settings dialog box will be displayed on your desktop, as shown in Figure 17-12.

Figure 17-12: The Advanced Program Settings dialog box. You can create your own private Autoexec.bat and Config.sys files by typing what you want in these files in the bottom two fields of this dialog box, or by clicking the Configuration button.

Step 3. Click the MS-DOS mode box.

Step 4. Click the Specify a new MS-DOS configuration box. The bottom half of this Properties sheet becomes active.

Step 5. Type in what you want in your CONFIG.SYS for MS-DOS mode and AUTOEXEC.BAT for MS-DOS mode fields. You can get a head start by clicking the Configuration button. This will display the Select MS-DOS Mode Configuration Options dialog box shown in Figure 17-13.

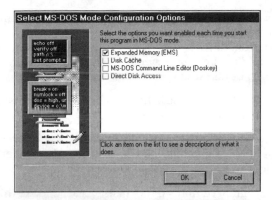

Figure 17-13: The MS-DOS Mode Configuration Options dialog box. As you highlight each option, its description is provided in the status area. You can check and uncheck options until you click OK.

Step 6.   Choose the options that you want from the Select MS-DOS Mode Configuration Options dialog box. If you highlight an option, its description is displayed in a status bar. You can highlight it before you click its check box.

Step 7.   Click the OK button in the Select MS-DOS Mode Configuration Options dialog box. All your options will be used to fill the CONFIG.SYS for MS-DOS mode and AUTOEXEC.BAT for MS-DOS mode fields. You can further edit these fields now.

Step 8.   Click both OK buttons, the first on the Advanced Program Settings dialog box, and the second on the Properties for MS-DOS mode dialog box.

Editing private Autoexec.bat and Config.sys data

Secret

You should carefully edit the CONFIG.SYS for MS-DOS mode and AUTOEXEC.BAT for MS-DOS mode fields. They may include lines from your Autoexec.bat and Config.sys files that are read before Windows 95 starts. You may not want some of these lines in the private Autoexec.bat and Config.sys files for MS-DOS mode.

These fields may also include some instructions that are (by default) carried out by Io.sys. For example:

    SET TMP=C:\Windows\Temp
    SET TEMP=C:\Windows\Temp

You may want to delete these lines or edit them.

Tip

If you choose to install the expanded memory manager (Emm386.exe), 16-bit drivers and DOS TSRs can be loaded in UMBs, and will be by default, if you choose them from the Select MS-DOS Mode Configuration Options dialog box. You need to add the **noems** or **ram** parameter to the line with the Emm386.exe driver (after Emm386.exe).

Disk caching in MS-DOS mode is handled by the 16-bit driver Smartdrv.exe. It will be loaded high if Emm386.exe is used.

If you want to have an easily accessible history of your previous DOS commands while in MS-DOS mode, load Doskey. It is also loaded high if Emm386.exe is loaded with the **noems** or **ram** parameter.

If your DOS program requires direct disk access, choose this option from the Select MS-DOS Mode Configuration Options dialog box. The command **Lock** is added as the last line in your private Autoexec.bat file.

Tip

You'll need to add a 16-bit mouse driver to your private Autoexec.bat or Config.sys file if you want to have a mouse in rebooted MS-DOS mode.

Where are the private files?

Secret

The lines that you added to the CONFIG.SYS for MS-DOS mode and AUTOEXEC.BAT for MS-DOS mode fields are stored in the MS-DOS mode shortcut you created for your DOS application or for Command.com. You can use Edit.com to see this for yourself. To do so, take the following steps:

STEPS

Seeing the Internals of the MS-DOS Mode Shortcut

Step 1.   Click the Start button, then Programs, then the MS-DOS prompt.

Step 2.   Type **Edit** and press Enter.

Step 3.   Click File, Open on the menu bar. In the Directories field scroll to C:\Windows\Desktop.

Step 4.   In the Files field, scroll to **MS-DOS mode.pif** and double-click it.

You'll see the lines from your CONFIG.SYS for MS-DOS mode and AUTOEXEC.BAT for MS-DOS mode fields at the bottom of the file. Be sure *not* to save this file when you are finished looking at it.

The private files exposed

Secret

When you switch to rebooted MS-DOS mode, new private Autoexec.bat and Config.sys files are created just for that session. The lines in the shortcut used to start this MS-DOS session are used to create these files. The existing Autoexec.bat and Config.sys files used to start Windows 95 are stored in temporary files with the extension *wos* (Windows Operating System?).

When you exit MS-DOS mode (by typing **exit** at the DOS prompt, or by quitting your DOS application if the Close on exit check box is checked), the private Autoexec.bat and Config.sys files are deleted, and the temporary Autoexec.wos and Config.wos files are renamed to their original names.

This is an example of what a temporary private Autoexec.bat looks like:

```
@ECHO OFF
SET TMP=C:\Windows\Temp
SET TEMP=C:\Windows\Temp
SET WINPMT=$p$g
SET Path=C:\Windows;C:\Windows\Command
LoadHigh C:\WINDOWS\SmartDrv
LoadHigh C:\WINDOWS\Command\DOSKey
Lock
REM
REM The following lines have been created by Windows. Do not modify them.
REM
CALL C:\WINDOWS\COMMAND.COM
C:\WINDOWS\WIN.COM /WX
```

Notice that Command.com is called to create the DOS prompt in the MS-DOS mode session. Command.com was already loaded before this Autoexec.bat was read, so this is a second copy of Command.com. You exit from MS-DOS mode by typing **exit** at the DOS prompt and pressing Enter.

Exiting from this Call allows the next line of the Autoexec.bat file to be carried out. The next line is the call to restart Windows with the /WX switch. This switch starts Windows 95 with the message that Windows is restarting, which is displayed on your screen in text mode.

When MS-DOS mode starts, it displays the following message, a text-mode message, that Windows 95 is starting the MS-DOS based program.

This is an example of what a temporary private Config.sys file looks like:

```
DOS=SINGLE
Device=C:\Windows\Himem.sys
DeviceHigh=C:\Windows\Emm386.exe noems
DOS=HIGH,UMB
```

You don't need to load the memory manager, Himem.sys, unless you want to load Emm386.exe and thereby provide access to the UMBs and expanded memory.

Tip

You must add the noems parameter manually. This parameter allows upper memory to be used as UMBs. There is no reason for DeviceHigh= in line three. This line is automatically written when you choose to load the expanded memory manager option from the Select MS-DOS Mode Configuration Options dialog box. Emm386.exe is loaded in conventional memory, so it might as well read Device=.

Creating a Distinct Prompt for DOS

You can create a prompt used in Windows DOS sessions that is different than the DOS prompt you see in MS-DOS mode (or before Windows 95 starts up). You can also create a different prompt for every different MS-DOS mode shortcut.

Windows 95 prevents you from starting another instance of itself if you type **Win** at a DOS prompt while in a Windows DOS session or in MS-DOS mode. (If you try, it just displays a warning message.) But you still might find it desirable to remind yourself — in full-screen DOS sessions — whether you are running a Windows DOS session or an MS-DOS mode session.

There is a good reason to have a reminder that you are in a DOS session under Windows 95. While it is safe to turn off your PC while in DOS before Windows starts (or MS-DOS mode), it is not such a good idea when at a DOS prompt in a full-screen Windows DOS session. Even in rebooted MS-DOS mode, you will want to return to Windows so your Autoexec.bat and Config.sys files get renamed correctly.

DOS prompt for Windows DOS sessions

Tip

You can alert yourself to the fact that you are in a Windows DOS session by adding a line to your Autoexec.bat file. This line might look like the following:

```
SET WINPMT=Press ALT+ENTER or type EXIT to return to Windows 95.$_$_$P$G
```

The $_ symbols insert blank lines between your message and the normal Path and Greater-than signs used in the default prompt. (pg means path and greater than symbol). Be sure to make this all one line in Autoexec.bat.

After shutting down and restarting Windows 95 so this Autoexec.bat file is executed, you should be able to see your new prompt inside a Windows DOS session.

If you type **SET** by itself in a Windows DOS session, you can see what's happening. The SET command displays the contents of the DOS environment. In Windows DOS sessions, Windows reverses the meaning of SET PROMPT and SET WINPMT. SET WINPMT is either equal to PG (which is the default) or whatever your normal prompt setting is in your Autoexec.bat file. SET PROMPT is equal to your longer message.

DOS prompt for MS-DOS mode sessions

Just as you can create a distinctive DOS prompt for your Windows DOS sessions, you can also create unique DOS prompts for every different MS-DOS session type. Each shortcut that is used to start a DOS program in MS-DOS mode can have its own Autoexec.bat file. Edit the Winpmt settings used when creating these Autoexec.bat files, and you can have unique prompts.

You can create and edit the CONFIG.SYS for MS-DOS mode and AUTOEXEC.BAT for MS-DOS mode fields for a given MS-DOS mode shortcut using the Select MS-DOS Mode Configuration Options dialog box. If you do, the Winpmt setting from your Windows 95 Autoexec.bat is placed by default in your AUTOEXEC.BAT for MS-DOS mode field. You can edit it or replace it with a more appropriate choice.

You can create a distinct DOS prompt for your shortcut that just opens with Command.com. You might want to set a prompt by adding the following line to your AUTOEXEC.BAT for MS-DOS mode field:

```
SET WINPMT=Type EXIT and press Enter to return to Windows 95.$_$_$P$G
```

A Way Cool DOS Banner Instead

A distinctive DOS prompt is nice, but a DOS banner is way cool. It sits at the top of your DOS window (as well as in full screen) and quietly informs you that you are indeed in DOS.

The wording, "Press Alt+Enter or type Exit to return to Windows 95," certainly reminds you that you are in a Windows DOS session, but this black-and-white prompt is tiresome, especially as you watch it repeated over and over again, every time you type a command.

Therefore, you can replace boring DOS prompts with a colorful prompt. To utilize a prompt like this, you need to have the DOS screen and keyboard driver Ansi.sys loaded in your Config.sys file. Add this line anywhere in Config.sys:

```
Device=C:\Windows\Command\Ansi.sys
```

If you want to load this driver in the UMBs, make it Devicehigh= (but be sure to include the calls to the real-mode expanded memory manager, Emm386.exe, first, as well as DOS=High,UMB).

If you have a third party replacement for ANSI.SYS with a slightly different name (such as FANSI.SYS), change the DEVICE= line to reflect the name and location of your version of this driver. If you've just added this line to CONFIG.SYS, you must shut down Windows and restart to make the change take effect (but don't do that just yet).

Next, you must add a new line to your Autoexec.bat batch file. Put this line (and only this line) in the file Winpmt.txt. You'll find this file on the shareware CD-ROM included with this book. You can copy and paste this line from this file into your Autoexec.bat or you can type it out as shown below.

The Windows prompt is one long line, in ANSI.SYS's terse jargon which we explain later in this book:

```
SET WINPMT=$e[s$e[f$e[0;30;46m$e[K DOS Session In Windows 95
$e[16CAlt+Tab to switch; type Exit to close$_$e[0;40;37;1m$e[K$e[u$P$G
```

(Notice again, this is one long line in your Autoexec.bat file, and part of is not put on a second line like it must be when printed in a book.)

Now that you have edited both your Autoexec.bat and Config.sys files, you can shut down Windows and restart so these changes take effect.

Open a Windows DOS session (click the Start button, click Programs, and click the MS-DOS prompt icon). You should see something like Figure 17-14.

Figure 17-14: A Windows DOS session with our new banner prompt. Notice that the banner hangs out at the top of the window and doesn't bother the C> prompt.

This prompt is an improvement over the plain C> prompt in many ways. First of all, it's all on the top line, so it isn't repeated on every line down the side of the screen as you type commands. And instead of listing EXIT as the only command to return to Windows, it gives you the alternative of Alt+Tab, which lets you Tab to another active application. You can, in fact, *hold down* the Alt key and press Tab repeatedly to see a listing, one after another, of all other running applications that you can switch to. Release the Alt key, and that application becomes the foreground. (In case you have a BIOS that doesn't support Alt+Tab, use Alt+Esc instead.)

Of course, this banner prompt is most useful in full-screen mode. Press Alt+Enter to switch to full-screen mode, as shown in Figure 17-15:

```
DOS Session In Windows 95       Alt+Tab to switch; type Exit to close




Microsoft(R) Windows 95
  (C)Copyright Microsoft Corp 1981-1994.



C:\>
```

Figure 17-15: A Windows DOS session in full screen mode.

The banner line is re-drawn every time the C> prompt appears. But if you're in the midst of a long DOS command, such as a DIR /P command that lists a directory longer then one screen page, the banner conveniently disappears until another C> prompt is available.

If your system has a fast video ROM BIOS, or this ROM is copied into fast "shadow RAM" by your PC, this re-drawing of the banner shouldn't noticeably affect the performance of your DOS session.

A banner for MS-DOS mode

You can create a similar banner for your shortcut that switches Windows to MS-DOS mode. You want a different message because you can't switch to another application with Alt+Tab while you are in MS-DOS mode.

You will need to make the same types of editing changes to your CONFIG.SYS for MS-DOS mode and AUTOEXEC.BAT for MS-DOS mode fields that you made to Autoexec.bat and Config.sys in the previous section. We have included a prompt you can use for your MS-DOS mode shortcut in the file Msmdpmt.txt. You will find it on the shareware CD-ROM with this book.

Be sure to edit the MS-DOS mode shortcut's CONFIG.SYS for MS-DOS mode field to include the reference to Ansi.sys. You have to load this 16-bit driver when you enter MS-DOS mode.

You can create unique banners for each of your different MS-DOS mode shortcuts. But if the DOS application associated with a given shortcut uses the full screen (as almost all of them do) it doesn't make any sense, because you'll never see it.

Making your own prompt using Ansi.sys

If you want to design your *own* banner prompt (or a prompt that shows up in any location you like), you'll need to know how to change the Set Winpmt= statement that creates this type of banner. First, we'll explain what each element of the Ansi.sys statement that creates the banner does. In the following three tables, , the characters "$e" are interpreted by Ansi.sys as an escape character ASCII number 27 and these Prompt strings are known as "escape commands."

In this table, which takes apart the Prompt= statement item by item, each element is shown on the left and what it does is explained on the right.

Table 17-3	Ansi.sys Commands
Command	*Action*
Set Winpmt=	Sets the DOS prompt in a Windows DOS session or in a MS-DOS mode session equal to the following
Command	*Action*
$e[s	Saves the present cursor location
$e[f	Moves the cursor to row 1, column 1; the setting $e[2;3f would move it to row 2, column 3
$e[0;30;46m	Resets colors to 0, then sets them to cyan and black; the number for each color is explained below
$e[K	Erase line from the current cursor position to end
DOS Session ...	Writes this text string to the screen
$e[16C	Moves cursor 1 space to the right
Alt+Tab to switch; ...	Writes this text string to the screen
$_	The prompt command to start a new line
$e[0;37;40;1m	Sets colors to black and white, intensified
$e[K	Erases the line immediately beneath the banner
$e[u	Restores the cursor to its original location
PG	The prompt command to display Path and ">" sign

The preceding explains almost all the Ansi.sys commands available. However, if you are designing your own prompt, you might also need the commands in Table 17-4:

Table 17-4	Commands for Designing Your Own Prompt
Command:	*Action:*
$e[B	Moves cursor 1 line down (for a new C:\> prompt)
$e[*n*A	Moves the cursor up *n* rows
$e[*n*B	Moves the cursor down *n* rows
$e[*n*C	Moves the cursor right *n* columns
$e[*n*D	Moves the cursor left *n* columns
$e[2J	Clears the screen with current colors and moves the cursor to the Home position: row 1, column 1

And if you want to design your own colors, you need the following chart of numbers that stand for each available color:

Table 17-5	Commands for Choosing Colors
Command	*Action*
0	Resets all attributes to light gray on black
1	Intensifies the foreground (text) color
4	Underlines text (on monochrome systems)
5	Makes the foreground text blink
7	Reverse video on
8	Canceled (invisible) text; black on black
30	Black foreground
31	Red foreground
32	Green foreground
33	Yellow foreground
34	Blue foreground (underlined on mono)
35	Magenta foreground
36	Cyan foreground
37	White foreground

(continued)

Table 17-5 *(continued)*	
Command	*Action*
40	Black background
41	Red background
42	Green background
43	Yellow background
44	Blue background
45	Magenta background
46	Cyan background
47	White background

The colors in the table are set using the command

```
$e[color1;color2;...;colorNm
```

where *color1* is one of the numbers in the list of Color Attributes. You may have as many of these attributes in the same command as you need. They must be separated by semicolons (;) and the command must end with a lowercase *m*.

You usually begin a color command with a zero (0) to reset everything — turn blinking off, for example — then continue with the numbers for foreground color (the text color) and background color. If you use the number *1* as one of the attributes, the text color is made brighter (intensified). Intensified colors are not always what you would expect. Intensified yellow is yellow, but "un-intensified" yellow is actually brown.

You could set all your DOS sessions to black text on a light gray background (similar to Windows' own black-on-white color scheme) by using the following in your Winpmt= statement:

```
$e[0;30;47m
```

If you set your Winpmt to this color, don't forget to then clear the entire screen to this color scheme. This requires the DOS command CLS in batch files you start from Windows. Using white on black in DOS sessions is easier.

Windows/DOS Batch Files

In Chapter 15, we describe three DOS batch files for backing up and restoring your Registry files. These batch files all have accompanying shortcuts and icons that make them look like Windows programs. They run in minimized windows so their buttons only last for a few seconds on the Taskbar. You can sort of see their commands in action as they flash by on their buttons, if your Taskbar button are large enough.

While these particular DOS batch files use only DOS commands, they do something very important to Windows (back up and restore the Windows 95 Registry), and at the same time they look a lot like Windows programs.

DOS batch files are no longer just DOS batch files. They now contain the Start command, which allows them to start Windows programs. Windows programs can be run and their internal macro languages used to carry out further commands. Batch files can pause until the Windows program has completed its work.

The Start command has the following format:

```
START {options} program
START {options} document.ext
```

The options are as follows:

/m	Run the new program minimized (in the background)
/max	Run the new program maximized (in the foreground)
/r	Run the new program restored (in the foreground). The default.
/w	Wait. Does not return until the other program exits.

A batch file can run Windows programs; it can run in a minimized window so it doesn't open a window that looks like DOS; it can start from a shortcut icon; and it can run Windows application macros. DOS batch files are now Windows batch files.

You can use any DOS or Windows command in a batch file. You can also use the following commands that are specific to batch files:

Call, If, Choice, Pause, Echo, Rem, For, Shift, Goto

These commands are documented in the DOS 6.2x help file. If you have DOS 6.2x still on your computer, you can change directories to the DOS 6.2 directory in a DOS window and type **Help batch**.

Commands you can use in batch files

A number of DOS commands work only in batch files. These mostly control the flow of the execution of the commands in the batch file. They are as follows:

call
choice
echo
for
goto
if
pause
rem
shift

Launching batch files from macro languages

In other cases, you might want to start a DOS batch file from within a Windows application. For example, you could command a Windows application to start a batch file in order to send a listing of the current directory to your printer — a common task that almost no Windows application can perform.

To do this, you would create a macro within your Windows application, assuming it has something like Winword's WordBasic or Excel's macro language. In Excel, a macro to start a batch filename MyBatch.bat (from a shortcut) would look like the following:

```
RunMyBatch
=EXEC("mybatch.bat")
=RETURN()
```

In WordBasic, this same action would appear something like this:

```
SUB MAIN
SHELL "mybatch.bat", 3
END SUB
```

These examples illustrate a good reason why you should define shortcut files to run all your batch files (or define a single, master shortcut file that you rename over and over for each of your batch files). Be sure that the shortcut for a batch file you run from a Windows macro language has Always suspend (under Background) unchecked, or Windows may switch away from the batch file before it is finished carrying out its tasks. This would return control to the Windows application that launched the batch file *prior to the batch file's completion.* This could lead to errors that might be hard to diagnose.

Finding the Windows folder

A full-blown Windows program can always find the folder that contains Win.com (C:\Windows) by asking Windows through a published Application Programming Interface (API) call. But what about a batch file?

The developers of Windows created an environmental variable specifically to meet this need in batch files. If you open a Windows DOS session and type **SET** by itself (no parameters), you'll see the current DOS environment strings. One of them should be something like windir=C:\WINDOWS. This variable's value is the directory that contains WIN.COM — the directory C:\WINDOWS, in this case. Of course, if the Windows folder was always C:\Windows there would be little point in having this environmental variable.

Unfortunately, this variable is of little use in its original form. This is because batch files always treats the names of environmental variables as ALL CAPS. You might try to use the "windir" variable in a batch file, as in this line:

```
COPY A:\MY.DLL %WINDIR%\MY.DLL
```

DOS looks for a variable named WINDIR, which should have the value C:\WINDOWS. But Windows names its windir variable in all *lowercase*. Therefore, there is no match. A DOS batch file can't *see* the variable at all.

There are two fixes.

First, the brute-force method: You can use the shareware hexadecimal editor we feature on the shareware CD-ROM to change the string windir to WINDIR in Win.com. If this string is in all caps, DOS batch files can test for it.

But if you'd rather not perform this surgery, you *can* write a batch file that uses the value of windir correctly.

The following batch file (Wintest.bat) tests for the existence of the string windir= in the environment, and jumps to the label NOWIN if it isn't found:

```
@Echo off
SET|FIND "windir=">C:\TEMP_1.BAT
COPY C:\TEMP_1.BAT C:\TEMP_2.BAT
IF NOT EXIST C:\TEMP_2.BAT GOTO :NOWIN
C:\TEMP_2.BAT
:NOWIN
DEL C:\TEMP_1.BAT
ECHO Windows 95, where are you?
```

The first line pipes the output of the SET command into FIND, which is case-sensitive. FIND writes the line it finds into a temporary file. If no line contains "windir=", this will be a 0-byte file. This will be the case if you booted Windows 95 to the Command prompt. It will also be true if you are in MS-DOS mode. It will not be true if you are in a Windows DOS session.

The second line copies the temporary file to a new name. Due to a feature of COPY (which thousands of batch files now rely upon), if the first file is a 0-byte file, the second file will not be created.

The third line, therefore, tests for the existence of the second file. If there is none, no "windir=" was in the environment.

If the batch file was run in a Windows DOS session, however, TEMP_2.BAT will contain a single line:

```
    windir=C:\WINDOWS
```

Running TEMP_2.BAT executes this line, which runs a file (which you must create) called WINDIR.BAT and feeds it a single parameter: the directory name. (DOS considers a single equals sign to be a blank, so this line looks like WINDIR C:\WINDOWS to DOS.)

WINDIR.BAT does your *real* work starting with the line as follows:

```
    @echo off
    SET WIN-DIR=%1
    DEL C:\TEMP_2.BAT
```

The replaceable parameter "%1" has the value C:\WINDOWS. This is just what you want. This batch file leaves an environmental variable, %WIN-DIR%, available for future use (until this DOS session is terminated or the PC is rebooted).

You can then create and use any batch file that uses the environmental variable %WIN DIR%. Both of these batch files can be found on the shareware CD ROM included in the back of this book. You might want to copy both these files to your C:\Windows\Command folder (or wherever you have stored your Windows 95 DOS files).

Using the Clipboard in DOS Sessions

The Windows Clipboard is an extremely useful area of memory for Windows applications. Microsoft almost didn't ship an updated version of the Clipboard with Windows 95 but was persuaded to do so by its beta testers. You'll find it in the \Other folder on the Windows 95 CD-ROM.

DOS applications recognize the Clipboard/Clipbook

In Windows applications, highlighting some text and then pressing Ctrl+Insert copies the text into the Clipboard. Pressing Shift+Delete has the effect of *deleting* the text from the application while moving it to the Clipboard. In either case, moving the cursor to another location or another application, then pressing Shift+Insert, pastes the text into the new location. These same actions can be accomplished with a mouse by clicking Edit Copy, Edit Cut, and Edit Paste — choices that appear on the main menu of almost all Windows applications. After performing any of these actions, you can view the contents of the Clipboard memory area by running the CLIPBRD.EXE program that is included with Windows. This program is actually a *viewer* of the Clipboard, not the Clipboard itself. The Clipboard memory area can contain many types of data other than text — bitmapped graphics, Windows metafile graphics, and so on.

DOS applications, however, vary widely in their support for the Windows Clipboard. Many DOS apps (such as Edit.com) can't use it directly. But other programs, such as Microsoft Word for DOS, have choices right on their menus for copying to and pasting from the Clipboard. (This assumes that Windows is running and, therefore, a Clipboard exists.)

You can copy text *from* a DOS application *into* the Clipboard; simply use the mark and copy icons in the DOS Toolbar. If you are in full-screen text mode in a Windows DOS session, simply press the Print Screen key. If you are in a window, Alt+PrtSc prints your DOS window in graphics mode to the Clipboard.

To paste text *from* the Clipboard *into* a DOS application, run the DOS application in a window and click the paste icon on the Toolbar. The text is placed in the DOS application at the location of the cursor in the DOS application.

If the text that appeared in your DOS application is missing a few characters, the program may not be able to receive keystrokes as fast as the Clipboard is capable of sending them. In this case, you need to change the DOS application's shortcut to turn the Fast Pasting option *off.*

End runs around the Clipboard

If you have major problems making a DOS application accept material from the Windows Clipboard (and you've tried the method explained above), there may be a formatting conflict. All three applications involved in a cut-and-paste — the source of the material, the Clipboard, and the recipient of the material — must have *some* format in common in order for the transfer to work.

To get around this, you may have to first save the material into a file on your hard disk. You can then merge this file into your DOS application to transfer the material. It's commonly known that you can save text into a plain-text file on disk using the Windows Notepad. But to save textual material that has *formatting* you don't want to lose, such as bold and italic type or different type sizes, try saving it with Windows Write as a Microsoft Word format file. Many DOS programs can import Microsoft Word files, complete with formatting.

A possibility for graphics is to save the graphic in a *pcx* format on disk using MS Paint or another format using Paint Shop Pro. Then try to open this file in your DOS application.

Can't start a DOS app?
Delete stuff in the Clipboard

If you can't start a DOS session because of low memory, the Clipboard may, surprisingly, be the cause. The Clipboard can handle almost anything, though any large objects that you copy stay in memory until you copy something else.

You might think that the solution to this problem would be to start the Clipboard application, then click Edit, Delete. This displays a dialog box asking you to confirm (by clicking OK) the clearing of whatever is taking up memory in the Clipboard. But there's a better way.

Secret

If you are in a low-memory situation, simply copy *a single character* into the Clipboard from any application. This erases whatever was previously in the Clipboard and releases the corresponding amount of memory, except what's needed for the one character. You needn't leave your current application or answer any dialog boxes.

Now try to run whatever program would not start earlier due to lack of memory.

Using the Print Screen Key in DOS Sessions

We want to emphasize that you can Print Screen to the printer when running a DOS application (or Command.com). If you uncheck the PrtSc check box in the shortcut associated with the DOS application, your text (or graphics) goes to the printer instead of the Clipboard.

Getting a Directory Listing

It's hard to print out a directory (folder) listing from Windows. You can focus on a folder using your Explorer or a folder window. You can send this view of your folder to the Clipboard by pressing Alt+PrtSc. You can then print this view by pasting it into a new empty MS Paint file and printing from MS Paint.

This will work only if your whole folder view can be seen in one screen (unless you wish to do this multiple times).

DOS gives you a better way.

STEPS

Printing a Directory Listing from DOS

Step 1.   Click the Start button, then Programs, then the MS-DOS prompt.

Step 2.   Use the cd, or *change directory,* command to move to the folder or directory whose file listing you are interested in printing.

Step 3.   Type in the command **dir > dir.txt** and press Enter. If you have redefined your dir command to pause for each page, type this instead: **dir /-p > dir.txt**. This transfers the directory listing to a file that can then be printed.

While it is possible to print the directory listing directly to the printer with dir > lpt1:, this method will fail to eject the last page from a laser printer.

Step 4.   Navigate using your Explorer to the directory whose listing you have just printed. Right-click dir.txt to select this file in the Explorer. If you can't find dir.txt, press F5 to refresh your file listing in your Explorer.

Step 5.   Click Print on the right mouse button menu.

Increasing Files in Config.sys vs. System.ini

All applications open files when they run. DOS provides a method to set aside enough memory to keep track of the various files that applications may need to read and leave open. This memory area is set aside by a statement in the Config.sys file such as FILES=30. This allows DOS to reserve memory for the names that applications use to manipulate files; these names are called *file handles.*

When you start a DOS application in a Windows DOS session that uses a lot of open files, you may see the following error message:

```
Insufficient File Handles, Increase Files in Config.sys
```

This message is in error, and changing the FILES= statement in your CONFIG.SYS will not cause it to go away. Instead, the message should advise as follows:

```
Add "PerVMFiles=15" to the [386Enh] section of SYSTEM.INI.
If 15 is not enough file handles, increase the number to 20.
```

The number of file handles specified in the Config.sys file relates to the number of file handles that are available to applications. The PERVMFILES= statement in System.ini refers to the number of file handles that can be open per virtual machine under Windows. Without any PERVMFILES= statement in System.ini, Windows defaults to only 10 file handles allowed within a DOS session. This may not be enough for some DOS applications.

Windows recommends 30 file handles in Config.sys. You should change the file handles per virtual machine in System.ini only if you receive an error message. Each file handle requires a very small amount of memory — only a few bytes under DOS.

The number of handles specified by the FILES= line in Config.sys and PERVMFILES= in System.ini combined cannot be greater than 255 (although it is unlikely anyone would need to approach this limit).

Summary

Windows 95 provides a better virtual machine for DOS programs. Lots of DOS programs can run in Windows DOS sessions.

▶ Windows 95 takes over even more of the functions formerly provided by DOS. We discuss which is the real operating system.

▶ Windows programs can use conventional memory, which is always in short supply. We discuss the impact of this design flaw.

▶ Windows 95 provides a DOS window for the DOS screen. The DOS screen has access to 20 different fonts and can be extensively manipulated by the DOS window.

▶ DOS programs can have shortcuts to them just like Windows programs. These shortcuts also define the virtual machine that surrounds the DOS program.

▶ If you can't run the DOS program in a Windows DOS session, you should be able to run it in MS-DOS mode (real-mode DOS). Each program can have its own Autoexec.bat and Config.sys files.

▶ Batch files now work with both DOS and Windows programs so that you can use DOS batch files for Windows programming.

Chapter 18

Configuring Windows 95 Memory

In This Chapter

The issue of memory is the issue of our common DOS heritage. If you use DOS programs that demand large amounts of conventional memory or expanded memory (DOS games perhaps?) you will do well to study this chapter. We discuss:

▶ Determining whether you need to be concerned about memory

▶ The six most important memory issues

▶ Getting more conventional memory for your DOS programs

▶ Using MS-DOS mode to provide just the memory that you need tailored for each DOS application

▶ Cleaning up your Autoexec.bat and Config.sys files — or eliminating them altogether

▶ Using Mem to see your memory use

Why Worry about Memory?

Why should end users have to be concerned about the issue of how memory is configured or used on their computer? After all, you should be able to just buy enough memory to run your programs and leave it at that. The fact that it hasn't been that way has made Windows just that much more difficult to use.

Windows 95 does a significantly better job in dealing with memory issues than Windows 3.x. Most of the fixes are under the surface, and you won't have to worry about them. It may be that you can install Windows 95, eliminate (or greatly pare down) your Autoexec.bat and Config.sys files, and go on your merry way. This should be your starting point.

If you have done this and things are working well for you, you don't need to be concerned about memory optimization. Go on to another chapter.

If you are still losing memory and performance because of obsolete items in Config.sys and Autoexec.bat, read on.

Windows 95 Memory-Handling Improvements

The major memory improvement made in Windows 95 is the introduction of a broad list of 32-bit protected-mode drivers. These drivers replace 16-bit DOS drivers that were required to be loaded in conventional memory (the first 640K of RAM in your system) or upper memory blocks (UMBs, the memory between 640K and 1MB in your system). This reduced the amount of memory available for DOS programs running either stand-alone or in Windows DOS virtual machines. (DOS programs depend in large part on the first 640K of RAM on your PC. To the extent that you have video, SCSI, sound, and network drivers in that memory area, less memory is left to run DOS programs. This partially explains why owners of PCs with multimedia upgrade kits and multiple add-on boards often have trouble running DOS programs under Windows 3.1. To find out more about DOS virtual machines, turn to Chapter 17.)

These new 32-bit drivers are loaded when Windows 95 is loaded. For example, a properly configured Windows 95 computer with a DoubleSpace/DriveSpace hard disk will first load a 16-bit driver in conventional memory. When Windows 95 is loaded, the 16-bit driver is removed from memory and the 32-bit driver takes over.

Tip

You no longer have to load mouse drivers in Config.sys or Autoexec.bat. The Windows 95 mouse drivers are 32-bit and support the mouse both for Windows programs and for DOS programs running in Windows DOS sessions. But 16-bit mouse drivers are not automatically removed from memory, so you'll need to be sure to remove instructions to load them from your Autoexec.bat or Config.sys files.

CD-ROM and sound card drivers that were previously loaded in conventional memory or in UMBs have for the most part been replaced by protected-mode drivers. Your sound card and CD-ROM will work with Windows programs and for DOS programs running in Windows DOS sessions (also known as DOS Windows sessions or windowed DOS sessions).

Network drivers that could eat up lots of conventional memory as well as UMBs have been replaced with protected-mode drivers. This is true for the Windows Network, NetWare, and TCP/IP networks. Other network providers have been encouraged by Microsoft to provide protected-mode drivers for their networks.

In addition, you no longer have to use Smartdrv.exe to provide a RAM cache for your hard disk reads and writes. Smartdrv.exe is a 16-bit driver that takes up conventional memory or UMBs. Disk caching is built into Windows 95 and works for all Windows programs and DOS programs running in Windows DOS sessions.

Starting with Windows for Workgroups 3.11 (WFWG), you no longer had to load Share.exe for those programs that needed it (like Word for Windows). WFWG 3.11 came with a VxD, a protected-mode version of share called Vshare.386. Vshare is now part of Vmm32.exe and is automatically loaded when Windows 95 starts. Sharing works for all Windows programs and DOS programs running in Windows DOS sessions.

Windows 95 does not provide the benefits of 32-bit protected-mode drivers to DOS programs that need to run in MS-DOS mode or before Windows 95 starts (or if you press F8 and start at the command line). If you run DOS programs that need a mouse or access to a CD-ROM in MS-DOS mode, you will need to load those 16-bit drivers in Autoexec.bat or Config.sys (or in Autoexec.bat and Config.sys files that are created on-the-fly when you run specific DOS programs).

In addition to use of these 32-bit drivers, Windows 95 also provides greater Windows resources and greater cleanup of abandoned Windows resources. We discuss this further later in this chapter.

When to Worry about Memory

There are six major memory issues with Windows:

- Configuring your memory so you can run DOS programs that require large amounts of conventional memory and/or expanded memory

- Having enough hard disk space so the Windows swap area for virtual memory is large enough to handle all your active applications as well as the Windows 95 components

- Running out of Windows resources when you have a number of Windows applications open

- Windows applications written for Windows 3.x that can (and often do) spring memory leaks, eating up resources until they are all gone

- Windows programs that use significant amounts of conventional memory, which is always limited

- Unrecognized memory address conflicts between video and network cards in upper memory

In this chapter we concentrate most on the first issue, configuring memory for running DOS programs. So let's look at the other issues first.

Hard disk space for virtual memory

You'll want to turn to Chapter 27 to get the full story on virtual memory. Windows 95, like its predecessor, Windows 3.x, uses your hard disk to "swap" programs and data out of RAM when it needs this memory to accomplish your more pressing tasks. Unlike Windows 3.x, Windows 95 doesn't ask you to create a permanent swap file for maximum performance. It handles swapping automatically.

It is a very good idea to let Windows 95 have plenty of room on your fastest hard disk for swap space. Depending on the amount of RAM that you have (more RAM calls for more hard disk swap space — see Chapter 27), it is best to be sure there is at least 20MB of unused hard disk space available.

If you don't have enough hard disk space, so that the swap file takes up every bit of it, you will get an error message about not being able to write User.dat, a file that is part of the Registry. Windows 95 produces information about the state of the machine dynamically and every so often writes it out to User.dat in the background. If you don't have enough hard disk space, it can't be written

Again, turn to Chapter 27 for more information on swap space.

Windows 95 resources

Windows 3.x often runs out of resources and displays error messages that blame limited memory as the problem. This is very frustrating to users who just purchased 16MB of memory and are quite willing to yell back at their machines that they have plenty of "memory."

If you receive such a message when using Windows 3.x, what is really happening is that one of your applications asked for more system resources and Windows 3.x ran out of them. You may have plenty of unused memory (RAM) and plenty of swap space left, but you just can't use them because of a limitation in the ability of Windows 3.x to assign system resources.

Resources are essentially lists (referred to as *heaps*) of memory. The lengths of the lists under Windows 3.x are quite small. The lists can be much longer with Windows 95. The lists point to areas of memory where user interface elements (and other items) are stored — things like dialog boxes, windows, and so on.

System resources under Windows 3.x employ four 16-bit heaps. Three of the heaps are part of the User resource, which manages the user interface portion of Windows. One is the Graphic Device Interface (GDI) resource, which manages drawing objects to the screen. As these lists are 16-bit heaps they can address only 64K of memory each, a total of 256K of memory to store the objects used in the user interface and displayed on your screen.

If one of your applications asks Windows 3.x for more objects and one of the heaps has already allocated all the memory on its list, the out-of-memory message is generated.

Windows 95 has greatly expanded the lists for the GDI and User resource areas in Windows 95. George Moore from Microsoft has reported that, "In addition to all of the things in User and GDI which were moved to the 32-bit heap Device Contexts and Logical Font structures in GDI are moved to the 32-bit heap. This means that the old system-wide limit on the number of Device Contexts has been raised from around 150–200 to over 10,000. In addition, you can now also easily load many, many more TrueType fonts than you ever could under Windows 3.1."

In Windows 95, the three heaps in User have been replaced by one 32-bit heap with the ability to address 2 gigabytes of memory — probably enough for the next couple of years. The 16-bit heap for the GDI is maintained for compatibility reasons (essentially some programs managed this heap directly without going through the Windows application program interfaces (APIs), and changing it to a 32-bit heap would break these programs). Some of the elements that were in the GDI heap have been moved to the 32-bit User heap, as George Moore points out.

Table 18-1 shows how system-wide resources have been increased in Windows 95.

Table 18-1	System-Wide Resources Then and Now	
Resource	*Windows 3.1*	*Windows 95*
Window/menu handles	about 299	32K (each)
Timers	32	Unlimited
Listbox items (per listbox)	8K	32K
Listbox data (per listbox)	64K	Unlimited
Edit control data (per control)	64K	Unlimited
Regions	All in 64K	Unlimited
Physical pens, brushes, etc.	All in 64K	Unlimited
Logical fonts	All in 64K	750-800
Installed fonts	250-300	1,000
Device contexts	200 (best case)	16K

Windows 3.x programs spring memory leaks

Many applications written for Windows 3.x have the unfortunate habit of asking for system resources and then not giving them back after they quit. The longer you run Windows 3.x, the fewer resources you have until you finally run out of resources and are forced to start Windows again.

These same programs will have the same problems running under Windows 95, but Windows 95 has two new defenses. First, with greater system resources, the problems will show up less often. Second, Windows 95 cleans up after Win 16 applications (those written for Windows 3.x), making sure that the resources they were allocated get back in the common pool.

It can do this only after all Win 16 apps (excluding those that have been specifically tagged as Windows 95-aware) have quit. Windows 95 must wait because Win 16 apps can share the same resources. Therefore, you have to be sure that you quit all your old Win-16 applications every now and then to get the resources back.

Windows 95 cleans up the resources used by 32-bit applications if they don't do it properly themselves.

Piggy Windows programs

Some Windows programs, 16-bit drivers, and even 32-bit protected-mode video drivers use up lots of conventional memory. If you tried to run a couple of these oinkers, you would soon see the error message saying you were out of memory when, again, you had plenty of memory. In this case you ran out of conventional memory.

The problem here is poor programming. The writers most likely included fixed memory segments in their programs, which under Windows 3.x, have to be allocated out of the limited pool of 640K of conventional memory. Microsoft has fixed most of this problem in Windows 95 by loading these structures in extended memory instead of conventional memory.

One program that tracks the amount of available DOS memory is the Norton System Watch applet that comes with the Norton Utilities Version 8. Another is the System Information portion of Norton Desktop for Windows. You can use either of these programs to see whether your free DOS memory gets low as you start and use your regular Windows applications.

Windows 95 automatically provides a good deal more DOS memory than Windows 3.x because it substitutes 32-bit protected-mode drivers for the 16-bit drivers that work with Windows 3.x. These 32-bit drivers reside in extended memory. In many cases, you have to check and make sure to remark out the 16-bit drivers from your Config.sys and Autoexec.bat files.

Under Windows 95, these piggy programs will have more conventional memory available to them. Given that portions of the programs that were previously loaded in conventional memory are now loaded in extended memory, they should be less of a problem than under Windows 3.x. It is hoped that newer 32-bit versions of these applications won't use fixed memory segments to nearly the same extent. You may have to upgrade your applications if this continues to be a problem for you. Just because the program is a newer version doesn't mean its authors have fixed the problem.

In this chapter, we concentrate on increasing conventional memory for DOS programs that require much more than even these piggy Windows programs. Any increases in conventional memory will also help these programs work better.

Memory Conflicts

Windows 95 should be able to identify most, if not all, potential memory conflicts. These occur when a video, network, or some other card uses a memory address between A000 and FFFF without revealing that address to

Windows. This used to cause serious configuration difficulties for Windows 3.*x*. Windows 95 is much better at spotting these cards and not using the forbidden memory addresses.

The Device Manager will highlight any detected memory use conflicts. You can also use the Device Manager to reserve memory address ranges for use by hardware devices.

Memory conflicts are discussed in detail in the *Troubleshooting Memory Conflicts* section near the end of this chapter. The Device Manager is revealed in all its glory in Chapter 19.

The Short of It — More Conventional Memory

Before we go into all the gory details, we want to give you some quick tips on how to get the most conventional memory possible if you need it to run your DOS programs or if your Windows programs are running out conventional memory.

DOS programs in Windows DOS sessions

Tip

If you want to have the largest amount of conventional memory for Windows programs and DOS programs that can run in Windows DOS sessions, you'll need to have a Config.sys file that starts off looking like this:

```
Device=Himem.sys
Device=Emm386.exe noems
DOS=High,UMB
```

Pull from your Config.sys and Autoexec.bat files any references to 16-bit drivers that have 32-bit replacements with Windows 95. Load high any DOS TSRs that you want easily available to all DOS virtual machines in your Autoexec.bat as:

```
LoadHigh C:\Windows\Command\Doskey.exe
```

If you need enhanced memory for your DOS programs running in Windows DOS sessions, change the **noems** parameter after Emm386.exe to **ram.**

If you still need more free UMBs in order to get drivers or whatever out of conventional memory, and there isn't a memory conflict with your video or network card, change the second line in your Config.sys to:

```
Device=Emm386.exe i=b000-b7FF noems
```

or

```
Device=Emm386.exe i=b000-b7FF ram
```

You can see if this area of memory is available by using the Device Manager as detailed in the *Troubleshooting Memory Conflicts* section later in this chapter.

Pull all unneeded references to FILES, STACKS, and so on in Config.sys and go with the default values (which we detail later in this chapter in the section entitled *Cleaning Up Config.sys and Autoexec.bat*). Don't load the DoubleSpace or DriveSpace compression drivers in UMBs.

DOS programs in MS-DOS mode

Tip

If you need to run DOS programs in MS-DOS mode (that is, you have really tried to run them in a Windows DOS session and they won't work), modify your MS-DOS mode *pif*s which create private Config.sys and Autoexec.bat files. These private files can be associated with each program that runs in MS-DOS mode or with MS-DOS mode in general. They are stored in a *pif* file for that program or in the *pif* for the icon associated with MS-DOS mode in general. See Chapter 17 for more details.

You don't have to change the values in the Config.sys or Autoexec.bat files associated with Windows (or even have such files) because MS-DOS mode restarts (warm boots) your computer and uses its own set of files. If you start your computer and press F8 to go to the DOS prompt before you go into Windows 95, you won't have the same Config.sys and Autoexec.bat files that started in MS-DOS mode.

Modify the private files using the tips given in the preceding section. Include your 16-bit drivers and DOS TSRs in your private Config.sys and Autoexec.bat files. Otherwise the DOS programs can't use your mouse, CD-ROM, and so on. Include your DoubleSpace or DriveSpace driver in Config.sys as:

```
Devicehigh=C:\Windows\Command\Drvspace.sys /move
```

Load all the 16-bit drivers high as discussed earlier. You may need to fiddle with the order of these drivers to get them all to load in UMBs. You may not have room to put them all there and will have to put some of them in conventional memory. Later in this chapter, we discuss fiddling in more detail.

The PC Memory Map

Before we continue with the issue of configuring memory to run DOS programs, here's an overview of how memory is structured on personal computers. If you already understand this structure, then go right to the next section.

Figure 18-1 shows a memory map that applies to most 386, 486, and Pentium computers with 16MB of memory. 16MB equals 16384K of RAM. The first 640K of the first megabyte of RAM is addressed from 0-640K (0000h-9FFFh), and the next 384K is addressed starting at 1024K (10000h). The rest of RAM starts at 1408K (16000h) and continues through 16768K (106000h).

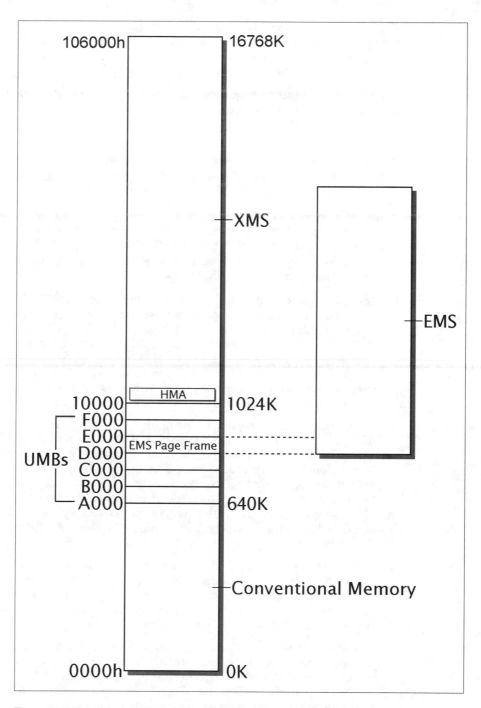

Figure 18-1: This diagram shows a PC with 16MB of RAM (640K of conventional memory plus 15744K of extended memory = 16384K plus 384K of UMBs, for a total of 16768K). EMS memory is taken from the extended memory by using EMM386.exe or other third-party memory managers, or is given to DOS programs running in Windows DOS sessions by Windows 95 itself.

The Windows 95 Device Manager uses a slightly different memory address notation than is standard for DOS and Windows 3.x. For example, the address A000 (notation used in DOS) is shorthand for 000A0000 (the notation used by the Device Manager).

The first notation recognizes the fact that we were concentrating our attention on a small range of memory below 1MB, so it ignores anything smaller than a paragraph (16 bytes). Therefore, it drops the three higher digits and ignores the first digit.

The second notation points out the fact that Windows can address FFFFFFFF (4,294,967,295) bytes of memory using its flat-memory, protected-mode model. All eight places are used as in 000A0000. We use the notations interchangeably.

You should be concerned with six types of memory: *conventional memory, UMBs,* and *extended memory* are the first three. Portions of DOS can be loaded into the *high memory area* (HMA), the fourth. DOS applications also use a fifth type of memory, *expanded memory. Virtual memory,* the sixth, is a combination of RAM and swap space on your hard disk.

- *Conventional memory* is the first 640K of memory in your PC. DOS applications run in this memory. Real-mode drivers that start before Windows 95 starts use this memory unless they are loaded into UMBs. DOS TSRs that are loaded before Windows 95 starts use this memory. Windows also uses this memory when it switches to Virtual 86 mode in order to access some DOS device drivers and PC hardware. Some Windows programs use significant amounts of conventional memory. Windows can put some (or all) of its translation buffers in conventional memory.

- *UMBs* are memory addresses where hardware devices and software drivers may be accessed by DOS and Windows. Exactly 384K of memory addresses are reserved for UMBs, and it is always located just above the first 640K of conventional memory. Much of this memory can't be used to relocate 16-bit drivers and DOS TSRs from conventional memory, since it is used by the ROM on your video card and/or network card and the system ROM. The 64K EMS page frame, if any, is located here. UMBs can be used by 16-bit drivers and DOS TSRs if the parameter **ram** or **noems** is after EMM386.exe in your Config.sys file.

- *Extended memory* (also called XMS, for eXtended Memory Specification) is the memory above conventional memory and the UMBs. It begins at the 1MB line, which is the same as 1024K (640K + 384K). If you have 16MB of RAM in your system, the first 640K is conventional memory, and the rest begins at the 1024K line and is counted upward from there.

- The first 64K of extended memory (minus 16 bytes) is called the *high memory area* (HMA), and is used by DOS, Windows, and a few other programs. No more than one program can be loaded into HMA, which is typically a part of DOS. Loading DOS in HMA saves about 46K in conventional memory. The DOS buffers also get loaded here.

- *Expanded memory* (also called EMS, for Expanded Memory Specification) is a special type of memory that requires at least 64K of address space in the UMBs. On a 386 and higher, expanded memory is usually provided by an expanded memory manager, a program that converts extended to expanded memory as required. Expanded memory requires a 64K page frame somewhere below the 1MB line in order to function. The Emm386.exe file provided by Windows 95 is an expanded memory manager. Additionally, QEMM, 386Max, NetRoom, and other products available from other software vendors provide somewhat more functionality than the Microsoft utility.

- *Virtual memory* is the combination of RAM that can be addressed by Windows 95 and the dynamic swap file space on your hard disk. Windows 95 manages this combined memory to allow you to load a significant number of applications at once without running out of physical (RAM) memory. The programs that are actually doing something are in RAM, while those sitting idly by have been swapped to the hard disk.

We discuss the UMBs a lot in this chapter. This is because you can increase the amount of conventional memory available under Windows 95 by moving device drivers and DOS itself from conventional memory into UMBs and into HMA.

UMBs from A to F

The 384K of UMBs can be thought of as six separate areas, each of which is 64K in size. These six blocks are known as A, B, C, D, E, and F. This is due to the fact that the address of the first byte of memory in the A block is A000 (pronounced "A thousand") in hexadecimal numbering.

The A block is used for the addresses of the RAM on your VGA or higher video board. When the board is in graphics mode (as opposed to text mode), the 64K of address space at A000 is used by Windows to write information into the RAM on the board. No matter how much RAM the board has physically installed — 256K, 512K, or more — the same 64K block is used to write to all video memory.

The B block is used for two purposes. The first 32K, which begins at B000, is used when a VGA or higher resolution video board is in monochrome graphics mode. These memory addresses would be used, for example, if you were using a monochrome monitor and the Windows VGA monochrome driver. The second 32K, from B800 to C000, is used for VGA or higher text mode. A portion of this address space is used when you are at a DOS prompt and type a command. The DOS output is written to B800, where it appears on your screen as text characters.

The C block is used for the read-only memory (ROM) chip that is present on all VGA and higher video adapters. This chip always begins using address spaces at C000. From that point, the chip may claim 16K, 24K, or more, depending on the complexity of the adapter and how many video modes it supports.

The D block has no reserved function, but often is claimed by memory managers for the 64K page frame required for the use of expanded memory.

The E block is often unused on AT- and EISA-bus machines, but is usually claimed by machines with a Micro Channel Architecture (MCA) bus. MCA machines include a unique set of ROM chips that reside at addresses starting at E000 and continue toward F000. These chips contain instructions in ROM that are used when OS/2 is running. For those people who are not using OS/2, many memory managers can claim these addresses for other purposes.

Finally, the F000 block is reserved on all PCs for the ROM chips that hold the basic input-output system (BIOS) — instructions that run low-level functions, such as writing to disk drives.

Knowing the purpose of each UMB can help you claim more conventional memory for both Windows and DOS applications running under Windows 95.

Windows Memory Management

Windows 95, in concert with two real-mode memory managers, manages all the memory on your computer, both real and virtual. One of the memory managers, Himem.sys, must be loaded before Windows 95 can start. It is loaded automatically by Io.sys if you don't have a Config.sys file or don't refer to it in Config.sys.

The other memory manager, Emm386.exe, is not needed unless you want to load 16-bit drivers or DOS TSRs in UMBs or provide expanded memory for DOS programs not running in windowed DOS sessions under Windows 95. You have to reference Emm386.exe explicitly in a Config.sys file to use it.

Windows has its own expanded memory manager that provides expanded memory for DOS programs running in Windows DOS sessions. It can also place Windows translation buffers and a 64K page frame in upper memory.

Himem.sys

Io.sys is the first thing loaded when you start Windows 95. Himem.sys is automatically loaded by Io.sys with the /testmem:on switch unless your computer has a Config.sys file with a line in it like:

```
Device=Himem.sys /testmem:off
```

Without this line in a Config.sys file, Io.sys issues an instruction to load Himem.sys. Himem.sys is a real-mode driver that takes about 1K of conventional memory.

Himem.sys must be loaded for Windows 95 to load. If you erase this file from your computer, you will not be able to start Windows.

As Himem.sys is loaded by default by Io.sys, there is no need to put the above sample line in your Config.sys file unless you are going to add parameters to this line (not too likely) or load Emm386.exe. Himem.sys has to be loaded before Emm386.exe is loaded, and Io.sys will read Config.sys before it loads

Himem.sys. So if it finds Emm386.exe in Config.sys and tries to load it, it hasn't already loaded Himem.sys unless Himem.sys is in Config.sys.

Io.sys loads Himem.sys with the test for extended memory on (/testmem:on) but with verbose off. It doesn't appear as though the test for memory is really turned on in spite of this reference in the Io.sys as it doesn't make any difference in the load time for Windows 95. You can turn on the testmem switch in the Config.sys file or, if you would like to see the reports of any errors that Himem.sys encounters, the command line parameter /v turns verbose on.

You don't have to do anything for memory management to be invoked when you start your Windows 95 computer. You had to add a line to your DOS 3 through DOS 6.2 Config.sys to load Himem.sys if you wanted to run Windows 3.*x*. Windows 95 will run because Himem.sys is loaded automatically. You don't even have to have a Config.sys file.

Himem.sys is a memory manager that allows Windows programs to use extended memory. Windows can provide expanded or extended memory to DOS programs that run in DOS sessions under Windows 95.

Emm386.exe

Himem.sys does not provide expanded memory to DOS programs that run in MS-DOS mode (or before Windows 95 starts up). It also doesn't manage UMBs. If you want to take real-mode drivers (and portions of DOS) out of conventional memory and place them into upper memory, you must load Emm386.exe (and Himem.sys) in Config.sys.

If you are not running DOS programs that require expanded memory in MS-DOS mode, and if your DOS programs do not need additional conventional memory, and you are not having problems with some Windows programs that are caused by low available conventional memory, don't do any of this. Relax. Go to another chapter.

Emm386.exe can be found in the Windows folder. It is a real-mode driver that takes up about 3K of conventional memory. It also takes up about 150K of extended memory to provide mappable memory. If you don't need it, don't use it.

To make the UMBs available for loading 16-bit drivers and portions of DOS, you'll want to create a Config.sys file that starts off as follows:

```
Device=Himem.sys
Device=Emm386.exe noems
DOS=High,UMB
```

The second line loads Emm386, the real-mode manger for expanded and upper memory, with a parameter (**noems**) that tells it to not set aside a 64K page frame for handling expanded memory and thereby not provide any expanded memory. All upper memory that Emm386.exe marks as available can be used for loading 16-bit drivers, TSRs, and portions of DOS.

The **noems** parameter means that no expanded memory will be available for DOS programs whether they are running in Windows DOS sessions under Windows 95 or in MS-DOS mode. It doesn't matter where you set the EMS value in the DOS *pif*, if **noems** has been specified in Config.sys, no EMS will be available to DOS programs.

If you want to set aside a page frame in upper memory so that you can provide expanded memory for DOS programs, then instead of the parameter **noems**, use the parameter **ram**. This allows both EMS memory and the use of UMBs for 16-bit drivers and TSRs.

Using the parameter **ram** decreases by 64K the amount of UMBs that can be used to store 16-bit drivers and DOS TSRs. If they can't fit in UMBs, they will be loaded in conventional memory.

If you don't include the second line in your Config.sys (or don't have a Config.sys file), Windows is free to allow EMS memory in DOS sessions under Windows as you see fit. You can set the limit of the EMS memory for each DOS session in its *pif*. See Chapter 17 for further details.

The third line loads a portion of DOS into HMA — a 64K area just above the 1024K boundary — instead of in conventional memory. It also directs DOS to manage the UMBs so that 16-bit drivers and TSRs can be loaded there and still retain their connection to conventional memory and DOS. If UMB is not included in this line (or in a separate line of the form DOS=UMB), no drivers are loaded into UMBs.

A number of specific and esoteric parameters can be used with Himem.sys and Emm386.exe. You can find out more about them if you still have DOS 6.2*x* on your computer. You can open up a Windows DOS session, changing directories to your old DOS directory and typing **Help Emm386.exe** or **Help Himem.sys.** Windows 95 doesn't come with a DOS Help command.

Loading drivers in UMBs

If you are going to load your 16-bit drivers into the UMBs, you need to use Devicehigh= in Config.sys and/or Loadhigh in Autoexec.bat. Here's an example Config.sys that loads the real-mode DriveSpace driver in upper memory :

```
Device=c:\Windows\Himem.sys /testmem:off /v
Device=c:\Windows\Emm386.exe noems /v
DOS=High,UMB
Devicehigh=C:\Windows\Command\Drvspace.sys /move
```

You would not want to load this particular driver in upper memory unless you were running DOS programs in MS-DOS mode with no private Autoexec.bat and Config.sys files. This is because Windows 95 automatically unloads this real-mode driver if it is loaded in conventional memory.

An Autoexec.bat that loads Doskey.exe (a DOS TSR) in a UMB would look like this:

```
LoadHigh C:\Windows\Command\Doskey.exe
```

How Windows Uses Upper Memory

Windows looks for space in UMBs for two different purposes:

- It places an expanded memory page frame, 64K in size, in an unused area above 640K. If an expanded memory manager was loaded in Config.sys, Windows "inherits" the settings for that EMS page frame.

- Windows claims another area, approximately 16K in size, for DOS translation buffers. These buffers are used by Windows to transfer data to and from real-mode devices such as disk drives. If there is not enough space left in UMBs, Windows takes the equivalent amount of space out of conventional memory.

Windows doesn't need EMM386.exe to accomplish these tasks. It has its own built-in expanded and UMB memory manager.

Memory for DOS Programs

You can run DOS programs in a Windows DOS session, in MS-DOS mode, or before Windows 95 starts (if you press F8). Each mode provides a different amount of conventional memory for DOS programs. MS-DOS mode makes available about 3K less conventional memory than starting a DOS program at the DOS command prompt before Windows 95 starts (if they both use the same Autoexec.bat and Config.sys files). See Chapter 17 for more details.

Windows provides each DOS program in a Windows DOS session with a "virtual machine." The memory available to the virtual machine is determined by what was loaded by Io.sys, Autoexec.bat, Config.sys, and Windows. Windows 95 provides protected-mode drivers that are used by DOS programs running in Windows DOS sessions. These protected-mode drivers aren't available to DOS programs running in the MS-DOS mode or that were started before Windows 95 is loaded.

Io.sys automatically loads Drvspace.sys in conventional memory if it detects a DoubleSpace or DriveSpace compressed drive and there isn't a line in a Config.sys file loading the driver in UMBs. This real-mode driver is removed from conventional memory and replaced by a protected-mode driver loaded in extended memory when Windows loads. It is not removed from the UMBs if it was loaded there.

You may need to run DOS programs that can't run in the Windows DOS sessions (for whatever reasons) and need resources that require 16-bit drivers. You will either have to load these drivers before Windows 95 starts or load them in each MS-DOS mode session. Each DOS program that has to run in MS-DOS mode can have its own private Autoexec.bat and Config.sys files. Again, Chapter 17 provides more details.

If these 16-bit drivers are loaded by Autoexec.bat and Config.sys, they can be loaded into UMBs. This increases the amount of conventional memory available to DOS programs that do run in Windows DOS sessions and provides more conventional memory for the DOS programs run in MS-DOS mode.

The DoubleSpace/DriveSpace driver can be loaded into conventional memory and it won't take up any conventional memory in a virtual machine because it is replaced by the 32-bit driver. DOS programs that run outside the Windows DOS sessions will have less available conventional memory because the real-mode DoubleSpace/DriveSpace is taking up conventional memory.

If you run DOS programs that require expanded or extended memory in a Windows DOS session, the *pif* associated with that DOS program can be configured to tell Windows to provide the required expanded or extended memory. Windows won't be able to allocate expanded memory to DOS programs if the line:

```
Device=Emm386.exe noems
```

or:

```
Device=Emm386.exe frame=none
```

is in Config.sys. You don't need a line in your Config.sys file (or even a Config.sys file, for that matter) for Windows 95 to be able to provide expanded memory to DOS programs running in Windows DOS sessions.

Examples of available memory for DOS programs

You can configure Config.sys and Autoexec.bat different ways to load different drivers and make them available to DOS programs. Here are the consequences of these configurations.

No Config.sys or Autoexec.bat

If you don't have Config.sys or Autoexec.bat and no real-mode drivers or DOS TSRs, and you used the default values for variables such as FILES and STACKS (more about this later in this chapter), you will find that on a representative computer, a Windows DOS session has about 604K of conventional memory available. In MS-DOS mode, 606K is available (if the MS-DOS mode is configured without its own Config.sys and Autoexec.bat).

If the computer had a hard drive compressed with DoubleSpace or DriveSpace, the respective values would be 604K and 556K of conventional memory. Because Windows 95 replaces the real-mode compressed disk driver that was automatically loaded in conventional memory with a protected-mode driver, the Windows DOS session's conventional memory is not reduced at all.

Minimum real-mode drivers in Config.sys

Assume you were to use a Config.sys to allow access into the UMBs to load the real-mode compressed disk driver, as shown previously in the Config.sys file. The respective values for conventional memory would be 612K for a Windows DOS session, and 623K in MS-DOS mode.

Some real-mode drivers that were loaded in conventional memory by Io.sys are now automatically loaded into UMBs. These include Ifshlp.sys, Setver.exe, and Command.com, as well as Drvspace.sys. This accounts for the increased conventional memory across the board.

While the DOS programs have more memory outside of Windows 95, they are without the services of the protected-mode drivers for a mouse, CD-ROM, sound card, network, and so on. If your DOS programs need these services, you can have their 16-bit drivers loaded into the UMBs or conventional memory.

All the real-mode equivalents of the protected-mode drivers mentioned in the previous paragraph (minus the network drivers) should be able to be loaded into the UMBs as long as there is no need to provide expanded memory for any of the DOS programs.

Too many 16-bit drivers and enhanced memory

Things begin to get tight in conventional memory as you continue to pile on the real-mode drivers or set aside 64K of UMBs for a page frame for enhanced memory. There just isn't enough room after a while, so some of the drivers are placed in conventional memory.

Using the following Config.sys and Autoexec.bat files, which include 16-bit drivers for a sound card, mouse, and CD-ROM, as well as set aside 64K of UMB for enhanced memory, you end up with 562K of conventional memory in MS-DOS mode and 545K in a Windows DOS session. (LH is shorthand for LoadHigh):

```
Devicehigh=C:\Windows\Command\Drvspace.sys /move

Path=C:\Windows;C:\Windows\Command
LH C:\Logitech\mouse
LH C:\Windows\Mscdex.ese /s /d:mscd001 m:10
Device=C:\Windows\Himem.sys /testmem:off
Device=C:\Windows\Emm386.exe ram
DOS=High,UMB
Devicehigh=C:\Sound\Mtmcde.sys /d:mscd001 /p:310 /a:0 /m:64 /t:s /i:5
```

If your DOS programs run in this reduced conventional memory, it is no problem. Unfortunately, many DOS programs want at least 600K of conventional memory plus expanded memory to boot. If they can run in the Windows DOS session, you can quit loading these 16-bit drivers and have plenty of conventional memory.

This example doesn't show the results of loading a 16-bit network driver, which would have reduced the conventional memory that much more,

More Memory for DOS Programs

There are numerous ways that you can claim additional UMBs in order to provide more conventional memory for DOS programs.

Claiming the space used by the page frame

If you have large DOS programs that need lots of conventional memory but don't require expanded memory, you can get more memory for these programs by disabling the creation of a 64K page frame in upper memory when you load EMM386.exe in your Config.sys file.

If you are using Emm386.exe, do this by adding **frame=none** to the command line in Config.sys, as in:

```
device=c:\windows\emm386.exe frame=none
```

This parameter also works with Qemm386, but varies with other memory managers. The parameter **frame=none** does not work in some configurations. It usually frees a little more memory than putting **noems** on the Emm386 command line. But if **frame=none** does not work in your system (Windows 95 won't start, for example), go back to using the **noems** parameter.

If you eliminate the page frame in your memory manager in Config.sys, you should also keep Windows 95 from creating one. To do this, place a line in the [386Enh] section of your System.ini file with NotePad or Sysedit, as follows:

```
[386Enh]
NoEMMDriver=TRUE
```

By preventing the creation of the 64K page frame in Emm386 and in Windows, you open up this much space to load additional device drivers and memory-resident programs into UMBs. Drivers that wouldn't load high before you reconfigured your memory managers may now fit just fine.

Claiming the space used by translation buffers

Windows 95 tries to load approximately 16K of translation buffers in the UMBs. Only if it is prevented from doing so will it take up 16K of conventional memory.

You can see Windows move its translation buffers to conventional memory by taking the following steps.

STEPS

Showing the Memory Used by Translation Buffers

Step 1. Rename Config.sys and Autoexec.bat to filenames that won't be used by Windows 95.

Step 2. Reboot Windows 95 and open a Windows DOS session.

Step 3. Type **mem /c/p** at the DOS command prompt, press Enter, and write down how much conventional memory is available.

Step 4. Exit the Windows DOS session and then restart Windows 95. As the Starting Windows 95 message appears on your screen, press F8 and then boot to the command prompt.

Step 5. Type **Win /d:x** to start Windows 95 in the debug mode and exclude it from using the UMBs.

Step 6. Open a Windows DOS session. Type **mem /c/p** and press Enter. Write down the amount of conventional memory available.

Step 7. Rename the files that you created in Step 1 back to Autoexec.bat and Config.sys.

The difference in the two measurements of conventional memory is the size of your translation buffers. If Windows finds room for these buffers in the UMBs, it will place them there. If there is not enough room, they go into conventional memory.

If you fill up your UMBs with 16-bit drivers, you might be able to get more conventional memory for DOS applications under Windows by loading one of the smaller drivers into conventional memory instead of UMB. Even a 1K device driver might be taking up a 16K address space that could be used for Windows translation buffers.

One other thing might be preventing Windows from finding a free 16K space in UMB. If an expanded memory manager claims all UMBs, Windows may find there are none for it to use. Emm386.exe doesn't do this.

Tip

If Windows is forcing its translation buffers into conventional memory, try setting aside a 16K area of UMBs from your expanded memory manager. Emm386.exe allows you to do this by adding the switch /win to the command line in Config.sys, followed by an equals sign and the exact addresses to exclude. For example, if you want to exclude the last 16K of the D000 block, you would put the following line in Config.sys:

```
device=c:\Windows\Emm386.exe /win=dc00-dfff
```

Getting the best of conventional and upper memory

If you have fit the translation buffers and page frame into upper memory as well as you can and your DOS programs are still not getting enough conventional memory to run, you can add another trick to your arsenal: claiming the monochrome UMB area.

If you run Windows with a VGA or super VGA color driver, it is likely that no program is using the memory area that starts at B000. Additionally, DOS text-mode programs rarely use all of the text-mode memory that starts at B800 and continues to C000. (IBM XGA adapters, however, do use the B000 area to store information, so don't use the following technique with them.)

Even if you have a monochrome monitor or a laptop with a monochrome display, you may be able to use this technique. Instead of using the VGA with Monochrome Display driver that comes with Windows, try switching to the color VGA driver. Many monochrome displays simply use shades of gray when color information is output and will work fine with color VGA drivers.

To find out if your display driver uses this area of upper memory, take the following steps:

STEPS

Determining Memory Usage

Step 1. Click the Start button, then Settings, and then Control Panel.

Step 2. Double-click the System icon in the Control Panel. Click the Device Manager Tab in the Properties sheet.

Step 3. At the top of the tree, Computer should be highlighted. If not, highlight it.

Step 4. Click the Properties button. Click the Memory button on the View Resources page of the Computer Properties dialog box, as shown in Figure 18-2.

The memory addresses used by your video card and video driver as well as the system ROM are shown on this dialog box. As you can see in Figure 18-2, the memory between 000B0000 and 000B7FFFF is marked "Unavailable for use by devices." This memory is marked to be used by the monochrome portion of your video driver.

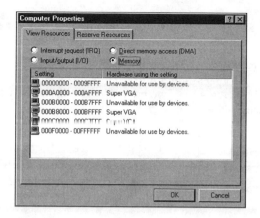

Figure 18-2: The View Resources dialog box in the Computer Properties sheet. The memory addresses used by the display adapter and system BIOS are shown.

You can use this memory range if it is marked "Unavailable for use by devices." To give your expanded memory manager access to the monochrome B000 area, use an include parameter in Config.sys similar to the following:

```
device=c:\Windows\Emm386.exe i=b000-b7ff ram
```

This statement instructs your memory manager to use the entire block between B000 and B800 (the address B7FF is one byte lower than B800 in hexadecimal numbering). This block is often avoided by memory managers since VGA adapters can be switched into monochrome mode by programs at any time. But if you don't use such programs, this area can be managed safely by your 386 memory manager.

If you give access to this area to your memory manager in Config.sys, you should also specify this to the Windows 386 memory manager. This is not absolutely necessary, since Windows inherits Emm386.exe settings, but it makes this memory available if you ever disable Emm386.exe for any reason. To do so, add an include line to the [386Enh] section of System.ini with Notepad or Sysedit, as follows:

```
[386Enh]
EMMInclude=B000-B7FF
```

When you restart Windows and run Mem in a DOS session, you may find that a substantially larger amount of conventional memory is now available (if 16-bit drivers couldn't previously be loaded in the UMBs). There is now more room to locate Windows translation buffers, a page frame (if you use one), 16-bit drivers, and DOS TSRs.

Cleaning Up Config.sys and Autoexec.bat

As you can see from the previous sections, after you install Windows 95 on a computer that already has DOS 5.0 or DOS 6.x and Windows 3.x installed, you will benefit from examining Config.sys and Autoexec.bat files. These files may contain references to 16-bit drivers that you no longer need. You may be able to get rid of these files entirely.

The major functions of Config.sys were to set a series of system values and to load 16-bit drivers. Io.sys now sets most of these values, and the 16-bit drivers may be replaced by 32-bit drivers that Windows or Io.sys will load automatically.

Io.sys sets the following values that were normally set in Config.sys in Windows 3.x:

```
FILES=60
FCBS=4
BUFFERS=30
LASTDRIVE=Z
STACKS=9,256
```

It also sets the Path equal to C:\Windows;C:\Windows\Command; the prompt equal to pg; TMP=C:\Windows\Temp; and TEMP=C:\Windows\Temp.

If these values work for you, there is no need to have them repeated in Config.sys or Autoexec.bat. The Windows 95 Setup program may have already modified these files, changing your path statement and remarking out redundant lines. You can take out the 16-bit drivers that you don't need anymore if you can run your DOS programs without them.

The DOS buffers get loaded into the HMA so you may be able to increase their number if needed without affecting conventional memory.

Troubleshooting Memory Conflicts

Windows 95 relocates some extended memory from addresses above 1MB to UMB addresses between 640K and 1MB. Problems occur when Windows relocates memory into a block that is also used by a device like a video board or a network adapter. Boards like this require some address space between 640K and 1MB to operate. Windows attempts to identify all UMBs in use, but this attempt may not always be successful.

Conflicts can also occur if the real-mode expanded memory manager loads 16-bit drivers or DOS TSRs into upper memory areas used by other devices. Before you continue troubleshooting, remark out the line in Config.sys that loads Emm386.exe and therefore force all the drivers and DOS TSRs to be loaded in conventional memory.

You can check for memory conflicts between different devices by using the Device Manager. Known conflicts are highlighted in the Device Manager.

STEPS

Checking for Memory Conflicts

Step 1.   Click the Start button, then Settings, then Control Panel.

Step 2.   Double-click the System icon in the Control Panel. Click the Device Manager tab in the System Properties sheet.

Step 3.   At the top of the tree, **computer** should be highlighted. If not, highlight it.

Step 4.   Click the Properties button. The View Resources memory dialog box will be displayed.

Any memory conflicts that Windows 95 detects will be displayed in this dialog box.

The addresses between 640K and 1MB that Windows relocates memory into are referred to in the Device Manager in hexadecimal numbering as 000A0000 to 000FFFFF.

Tip

One way to test whether some form of memory conflict is causing a problem is to force the expanded memory manager built into Windows to stop using these memory addresses. You do this by forcing Windows not to use these blocks. To do so, take the following steps:

STEPS

Excluding Windows from Using UMBs

Step 1.   Shut down and Restart Windows.

Step 2.   At the Starting Windows 95 message on your screen, press F8 and then choose to boot to the command prompt.

Step 3.   Type **Win /d:x** to start Windows 95 in the debug mode and exclude it from using the UMBs.

If you have remarked out the line in your Config.sys that refers to Emm386.exe (if such a line exists), and are running Windows 95 in this debug mode, nothing should be loaded into the upper memory area. If the problem goes away, you know that there was a memory conflict.

Start finding out where the conflict was by unremarking the line in Config.sys containing Emm386.exe. If it contains a memory-include parameter, such as i=b000-b7ff, erase it. Restart Windows in debug mode and see if the problem is still absent. If it is, you know that Windows is causing the problem by loading some of itself into an area in upper memory that is used by a conflicting card.

Now you will want to find out just what memory addresses are in conflict. To do so, take the following steps:

STEPS

Excluding Memory

Step 1. You use the System.ini file to exclude memory from use by Windows 95. This may seem old-fashioned now that we have the Registry and a way to reserve memory using the Device Manager, but trust us, it is easier this way.

Step 2. Double-click the Sysedit icon. You'll find it in \Windows\System if you haven't already put a shortcut to it on your desktop in the System Tools menu on your Start button.

Step 3. Add the following lines to the [386Enh] section of System.ini:

```
EMMExclude=A000-AFF
EMMExclude=B000-B7FF
EMMExclude=B800-BFFF
EMMExclude=C000-C3FF
EMMExclude=C400-C7FF
EMMExclude=C800-CBFF
EMMExclude=CC00-CFFF
EMMExclude=D000-D3FF
```

Step 4. Save System.ini, shut down, and restart Windows.

If the problem goes away when you restart Windows with these excluded memory addresses, a memory conflict was definitely present in the first half of the upper memory. Only one or two of the reserved address ranges is actually needed to resolve the problem, however — not all of them.

Step 5. If the problem didn't go away, comment out the above lines (by placing a semicolon in front of EMMExclude) and add these lines.

```
EMMExclude=D400-D7FF
EMMExclude=D800-DBFF
EMMExclude=DC00-DFFF
EMMExclude=E000-E3FF
EMMExclude=E400-E7FF
EMMExclude=E800-EBFF
EMMExclude=EC00-EFFF
```

Shut down and restart Windows.

Step 6. To determine which ranges are necessary, comment out the bottom half of the lines (by placing a semicolon in front of EMMExclude) and restart Windows. If the problem recurs, comment out only the bottom *two* lines, and so on. By this method, you should be able to isolate the culprit within only about four trials (if just one line is at fault). This is faster than trying the lines one at a time.

Using Mem to Determine Available Memory

We have mentioned the Mem command a few times in this chapter. If you were to type **Mem /c/p** within a Windows DOS session, you would see something like Table 18-2:

Table 18-2		Results Produced by Mem			
Modules using memory below 1 MB:					
Name	**Total**		**Conventional**		**Upper Memory**
SYSTEM	34,109	(33K)	9,101	(9K)	25,008	(24K)
	1,920	(2K)	1,600	(2K)	320	(0K)
HIMEM	1,120	(1K)	1,120	(1K)	0	(0K)
EMM386	3,200	(3K)	3,200	(3K)	0	(0K)
WIN	2,048	(2K)	2,048	(2K)	0	(0K)
vmm32	79,392	(78K)	3,536	(3K)	75,856	(74K)
COMMAND	7,504	(7K)	7,504	(7K)	0	(0K)
COMMAND	10,016	(10K)	0	(0K)	10,016	(10K)
DRVSPACE	39,472	(39K)	0	(0K)	39,472	(39K)
IFSHLP	2,816	(3K)	0	(0K)	2,816	(3K)
SETVER	688	(1K)	0	(0K)	688	(1K)
DOSKEY	4,448	(4K)	0	(0K)	4,448	(4K)
Free	627,008	(612K)	627,008	(612K)	0	(0K)

Memory Summary:			
Type of Memory	**Total**	**Used**	**Free**
Conventional	655,360	28,352	627,008
Upper	158,624	158,624	0
Reserved	393,216	393,216	0
Extended (XMS)	15,570,016	?	16,744,448
Total memory	16,777,216	?	17,371,456
Total under 1 MB	813,984	186,976	627,008
Largest executable program size		626,976	(612K)
Largest free upper memory block			0 (0K)
MS-DOS is resident in the high memory area.			

Mem tells you which DOS programs, 16-bit drivers, or TSRs are loaded in memory, how big they are, and where in memory they are loaded (conventional or UMBs). You can see how much conventional memory is available, the size set aside for UMBs, and how much is used. Reserved memory is the memory between 640K and 1024K (384 * 1024 bytes).

There are some errors in this report because Mem has been run inside a Windows DOS session and not before Windows 95 starts. The question mark in the column/row "Used extended memory" clues you in to the fact that Free Extended and Total Free memory are incorrectly calculated.

You can also run Mem before Windows 95 starts or in MS-DOS mode. Mem has a number of command line switches that alter its behavior as follows:

```
MEM [/CLASSIFY | /DEBUG | /FREE | /MODULE modulename] [/PAGE]

   /CLASSIFY or /C    Classifies programs by memory usage. Lists the size
                      of programs, provides a summary of memory in use,
                      and lists largest memory block available.
   /DEBUG or /D       Displays status of all modules in memory, internal
                      drivers, and other information.
   /FREE or /F        Displays information about the amount of free
                      memory left in both conventional and upper memory.
   /MODULE or /M      Displays a detailed listing of a module's memory
                      use. This option must be followed by the name of a
                      module, optionally separated from /M by a colon.
   /PAGE or /P        Pauses after each screenful of information.
```

Mem is invaluable in determining how well you are doing in placing 16-bit drivers and DOS TSRs into UMBs.

Using MSD to Examine Memory Configuration

Another way to see what programs are loaded into UMBs is to start your PC and press F8 at the "Starting Windows 95" message and then choose option 5 on the menu, Start only the Command Prompt. At the DOS prompt, type **MSD**. This starts the Microsoft Diagnostic program.

The MSD utility provides screens that show the use of upper memory and any devices that are loaded there. Microsoft uses this utility when people call for technical support. Strangely, MSD can provide unreliable information when used in a DOS session under Windows, so run it from a plain DOS prompt instead.

Undocumented

MSD isn't automatically installed by Windows 95 Setup. You'll find it on the Windows 95 source CD-ROM in the Other folder.

Optimizing UMB Usage with MemMaker

You can use MemMaker to place as many 16-bit drivers and DOS TSRs as possible into the UMBs. MemMaker sort of automatically reconfigures Config.sys and Autoexec.bat to place device drivers in upper memory. You can do this yourself by changing Device= to Devicehigh= in your Config.sys, and putting Loadhigh (or LH) in front of any DOS TSRs in Autoexec.bat.

MemMaker won't move the lines around in your files that make the calls to your DOS TSRs and 16-bit device drivers. You can put the largest ones first, and that should help get more of these things into upper memory.

To run MemMaker, edit Msdos.sys and add or change a line so the [options] section reads:

```
BootGUI=0
```

This allows you to keep booting to the DOS prompt automatically during the multiple booting MemMaker process instead of going into Windows 95. You can change this back after you're done.

You'll find MemMaker on the Windows 95 source CD-ROM in the Other\Oldmsdos folder.

Third-Party Expanded/UMB Memory Managers

You can use a third-party expanded/UMB memory manager to get additional space in the upper memory area. Memory managers like QEMM, 386 to the Max, and NetRoom are more aggressive than Emm386.exe in going after this address space.

Windows 95 cuts down on the need to be so aggressive by introducing 32-bit protected-mode drivers that aren't loaded into UMB and don't take up conventional memory. You will need to be extra aggressive only if you have to load 16-bit drivers and large DOS programs.

Managing Memory with Multiple Config.sys Configurations

You can also use a Config.sys that is set up for multiple configurations to allow for different memory setups. Much of the reason for doing this is wiped out by MS-DOS mode and the ability to tailor each private Config.sys and Autoexec.bat file in this mode for each DOS application. See Chapter 17 for details.

Multiple configurations in Config.sys allow you to set different startup parameters for any number of menu options. You can choose whether to have expanded memory available to DOS programs, whether to load anything high or not, whether to be on a network or not.

Turn to Chapter 6 for details on how to create a multiconfiguration Config.sys file.

Windows 95 and DOS Games

So let's finally get to the real point of this chapter. How can your get your games to work under Windows 95?

Most games written for PCs are written for DOS. This is because doing so gives the game's author access to the hardware and therefore the best chance at getting the best performance. Since the games market is highly competitive and very technically sophisticated (compared to the business market), game authors really have to know how to deal with the hardware.

Until Microsoft introduced WinG and a games software development kit, games that relied on Windows suffered. Game makers didn't care if their programs even worked with Windows in Windows DOS sessions. They figured that their clients would just exit Windows (or not even start it) to run the game. DOS games often have memory managers that conflict with the Windows memory management specification.

Microsoft is of course very interested in having games work in Windows and with Windows. They are embarrassed that this "technical" part of the market considers Microsoft and Windows a stumbling block to performance.

Consequently, Microsoft programmers have worked hard to make sure that Windows 95 can run DOS games in Windows DOS sessions. That doesn't mean they always succeeded. Of course, the fact that it is quite a bit more difficult to get to DOS in Windows 95 than with Windows 3.x makes it in Microsoft's interest that DOS games succeed in working in Windows DOS sessions.

Try your DOS games first in a Windows DOS session. You may need to provide expanded memory (like for Xwing) or make other changes to the Windows DOS session properties. If they don't work, try the DOS games in MS-DOS mode with their own Config.sys and Autoexec.bat files.

If that doesn't work, you can always start the DOS game before Windows starts. See Chapter 17 for more details.

Summary

Previous versions of Windows when combined with existing DOS programs taught us all to be very careful about how we configure memory. In a lot of cases it was way too difficult.

▶ Windows 95 makes memory management a lot easier by reducing the drain on conventional memory.

▶ We show you how to see if you are suffering from afflictions that could be caused by memory problems.

▶ We give you a lot of ways (and show you the quick and dirty ways) to give your DOS programs more conventional memory.

▶ We also show you how to get more upper memory so you can get more conventional memory.

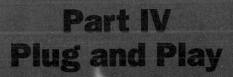

Part IV
Plug and Play

Chapter 19

Plug and Play — Device Management

In This Chapter

Windows 95 "captures" your PC hardware. Microsoft provides a raft of 32-bit drivers for almost everything under the sun. We discuss:

▶ What's so great about plug and play?

▶ How Windows 95 works with existing hardware and new plug and play devices

▶ Automatic hardware detection during and after setup

▶ Adding new hardware drivers

▶ Untangling resource conflicts

▶ Setting up multiple hardware configurations (profiles)

▶ Why you can define only one monitor

▶ Why CD-ROMs and sound cards mess with your parallel ports

So What's All the Hoopla?

Microsoft has made a very big deal about Plug and Play. A consortium of hardware manufacturers and software developers have agreed to a standard that allows easier installation and tracking of PC hardware independent of the operating system. Windows 95 is the first commercial manifestation of an operating system that completely embraces this standard.

Unlike the Apple Macintosh, nobody (not even Microsoft) owns the PC hardware and software standards. Therefore, a great deal of cooperation is required among companies that would like nothing better than to grind each other into the ground to arrive at standards that offer great benefits to the customer.

Everyone knows it is relatively difficult to set up PC hardware (and accompanying hardware drivers), especially when your computer is filled with cards from different manufacturers. The major difficulties are:

- Assigning hardware interrupts, of which there are only 16 — some of which are used by the basic computer hardware

- Assigning non-conflicting I/O addresses so each add-on card can have its own unique address

- Assigning Direct Memory Access (DMA) channels (in non-PCI bus cards) so there is no conflict

- Installing PC Cards (formerly known as PCMCIA cards) that adhere to different standards

- Setting monitor parameters to automatically work with your video card

- Making sure there are no memory blocks used (especially by video and network cards) that conflict with memory assignments, particularly in upper memory

- Recognizing and highlighting conflicts so they can be resolved

- Gracefully handling multiple hardware configurations for one computer; for example, docking stations with portables

- Recognizing when the hardware configuration changes so the operating system and Windows 95-aware application software can take the appropriate action

Microsoft realized that many of its support calls had to do with hardware conflicts of the first three types. Hardware manufacturers realized that it was more difficult to sell add-on devices (in particular multimedia kits) when they were so difficult to install.

The first order of business for plug and play was to make it easier to install hardware and resolve any conflicts with the hardware interrupts, the I/O address, memory ranges used, and the DMA channel used, if any. Windows 95 solves most of these problems automatically and gives you the tools to solve the rest of them.

32-bit Drivers

Haven't we talked about this elsewhere? Windows 95 is a 32-bit operating system (for the most part) and one big part of that is its 32-bit drivers. All the new device drivers get loaded into extended memory and they don't take up conventional or upper memory.

Not only are they 32-bit, but they have lots of new features, features that come about because they have more room to wiggle in extended memory. The Device Manager and the Add New Hardware Wizard install these new drivers for the hardware that they detect. When you run Windows 95 Setup, 16-bit drivers are cast aside for the new 32-bit drivers.

16-bit Drivers

If you need to run 16-bit drivers, you're going to have to use the older installation routines that come from the manufacturers. Only in relatively rare circumstances, however, will you need to run 16-bit drivers.

Undocumented

There is a list, Ios.ini, in your Windows 95 folder that contains the names of the hardware driver files that can be (and are) *safely* replaced by 32-bit drivers in Windows 95. *Safe* just means that the 32-bit driver implements at least all the functionality of the 16-bit driver. If you find that your real-mode driver is on the list but provides functionality missing from the replacement 32-bit driver, you can delete it from the list and reinstall the driver (unremark the call to it in Config.sys).

If you have 16-bit drivers that aren't replaced, you'll find them listed in the Device Manager with a yellow exclamation mark. You can remark out the drivers in Config.sys and Autoexec.bat, install more generic drivers using the Add New Hardware Wizard (details later in this chapter) and reboot your computer.

Plug and Play BIOS and Devices

You may have a computer that doesn't have a plug and play BIOS and has no plug and play cards. That's fine. Windows 95 will do its best to search for and identify the hardware you have installed and then install the appropriate drivers.

You may have a computer without a plug and play BIOS, but with some plug and play devices. That's fine also. The plug and play devices will give Windows 95 a little more flexibility in configuring the hardware resource usage so there are no conflicts among the devices.

You may have a computer with a plug and play BIOS *and* plug and play cards. Great! Windows 95 can work with the plug and play BIOS to configure your computer automatically so there are no conflicts among hardware devices.

Hardware Detection

Windows 95 Setup detects installed hardware and drivers for a broad range of pre-plug and play hardware as well as the new stuff.

Undocumented

The installation files contain a database of existing hardware and drivers that is found in specific *inf* files and coordinated by the Msdet.inf file. You will find these files in the \Windows\Inf folder. The detection routines are non-invasive and do their best to determine just what you've installed over the years from one of a zillion different manufacturers.

Undocumented

Hardware detection won't be able to determine what monitor you have, unless it is plug and play compatible, so you'll need to pick a monitor from the list of monitors.

It may register your modem as generic, so if you know what modem you have, you will want to go back later and specify that modem. Knowing the right modem assures you that the correct initialization string is used when running Windows 95-aware communications software.

Undocumented

Hardware detection most likely will assign your hard drive, diskette drives, and disk controller cards to the generic category, unless you have specific SCSI controllers. You may have manufacturer-specific hard disk driver software, but you won't want to use it unless it has been updated for Windows 95 and is 32-bit. Windows 95 Setup will remark Config.sys lines that call these older drivers.

IDE drives that are 1 gigabyte and larger often come with software that allows them to be partitioned even in a computer with a BIOS that doesn't understand drives larger than 524MB. Windows 95 can work with Ontrack's Disk Manager 6.03 and other partition software of this nature.

Detecting your display adapter is probably the most difficult problem for hardware detection because there are so many. Microsoft has written a series of display drivers, and Windows 95 Setup does its best to install the correct driver. You may need to install a display driver that doesn't have all the functionality of your previous Windows 3.*x* driver and wait for the manufacturer to update the driver for your video card. You can also install the Windows 3.*x* driver (and lose some Windows 95 display driver functionality), if you like.

Undocumented

Hardware detection will find only one keyboard, even if you have a portable with an external keyboard plugged into it. Both keyboards will be live. If your external keyboard is an extended keyboard, and the one on the portable is not, you will want to make sure the extended keyboard driver is installed (or install it if it isn't).

Undocumented

Your BIOS is checked to determine if you have Automated Power Management features compatible with the APM 1.0 and APM 1.1 standards. If you do, there will be an APM icon in your Control Panel. You can use this icon to control the power control settings of your portable.

Lots of portables have a BIOS that is not really compatible with APM 1.0 or 1.1 (as far as Microsoft is concerned). So even if you have control of your power saving configuration through your BIOS settings, you may not have an APM icon in your Control Panel. You just won't have the convenience of power management through Windows. Look in the Device Manager under System Devices for other APM features, which may or may not work on your portable.

Windows 3.*x* didn't do a thorough job of checking for APM features in your BIOS. When it didn't find exactly what it was looking for during setup, it didn't install Windows-based APM at all. Windows 95 does a better job, but still will find BIOSes that are incompatible and not add an APM icon to the Control Panel.

Windows 95 can support multiple mice simultaneously. If you have a trackball built into your portable as well as a serial mouse attached to a serial port, Windows 95 Setup will recognize and install two mouse drivers. Both mice should work. If only one driver is installed, you can install the other after initial setup. The mice will most likley be on different interrupts, so you won't have to do any interrupt conflict resolution. If not, see the *Device Manager* section later in this chapter.

If you install Direct Cable Connection (DCC), your serial and parallel ports will also be classified in the Device Manager as modems. They aren't really modems, of course, but storing this definition in the modems device type is a convenient place to keep track of the fact that DCC will work over these ports. DCC finds all available ports when it uses hardware detection to see what is available. You can remove ports from the modems list using the Device Manager, if in fact these ports are being used exclusively for mice or other devices.

Windows 95 Setup installs a Dial-Up Adapter if you direct it to install DCC and Dial-Up Networking (DUN). No piece of hardware is itself a Dial-Up Adapter, other than your ports or your modem. Again, this is a convenient label to put on a capability. All the necessarily network protocols and services are bound to this pseudo device. The Dial-Up Adapter is referenced as a network adapter device in the Device Manager.

Hardware detection finds your serial and parallel ports. Serial ports are defined as plug and play compatible devices if they have the 16550A UART or better. If an extended capability parallel (ECP) port is found, you will have to configure it after setup. For details, see Chapter 23.

CD-ROMs and sound cards are detected first through their signature drivers that are called from Config.sys and Autocxec.bat. These calls to drivers are remarked out and 32-bit drivers are installed instead.

Detection after Setup

Hardware detection takes place during Windows 95 Setup, but you can also force it to happen later, or you can install a driver for a specific device which may or may not be physically installed yet. You use the Add New Hardware icon in your Control Panel, as we discuss later in this chapter in the section entitled *Adding New Hardware Drivers*. You use this icon to install new drivers for your devices.

If you physically install new hardware without using the Add New Hardware icon, and the device is plug and play compatible, it will notify Windows 95 that it has been installed and a driver will be installed automatically. You will be prompted for the diskette that contains the driver, unless Windows 95 can find the source files on your hard disk or CD-ROM drive.

The Registry of hardware

Information about installed hardware and its drivers is kept in the Registry. The original entries are made during Windows 95 Setup. You can use the Registry editor to view the hardware drivers installed on your computer. To see how to invoke the Registry editor, turn to Chapter 15.

Undocumented

You'll find references to your hardware under the HKEY_LOCAL_MACHINE keyword, specifically under the Enum (enumeration) subkey. It's easy to use the Registry editor to view the values stored there.

When you start Windows 95, a dynamic hardware tree is created based on information in the Registry. This tree is stored in RAM and can be viewed using the Registry editor under the HKEY_DYN_DATA key word and the Config Manager\Enum subkeys. Looking at this data is not particularly enlightening.

The hardware tree in RAM is updated every time the hardware configuration changes. Microsoft's favorite example is when you plug your portable into a docking station. We assume they have a lot of these over at Microsoft's Redmond campus.

It is a much better idea to use the Device Manager to manage your hardware configuration. The Device Manager's user interface is a lot more informative and understandable. You should use the Registry editor only if the Device Manager is not working for you and you understand the effect of the changes that you are making.

Adding New Hardware Drivers

In a perfect world, you would physically install your new device, such as a printer, in your computer (or perhaps plug it into a port). The drivers for that device would be automatically installed and the device activated. If you install a plug and play compliant device, this *almost* happens.

You may need to turn off the computer first so you don't inadvertently cause any electrical damage when you install a card in a slot. You may be asked for a diskette from the device's manufacturer that contains the drivers needed to use the device. The drivers for that device may have been shipped with Windows 95 either on diskettes or CD-ROM and you will be asked to insert a diskette or the CD-ROM.

Double-clicking the Add New Hardware icon invokes the Add New Hardware Wizard, as shown in Figure 19-1.

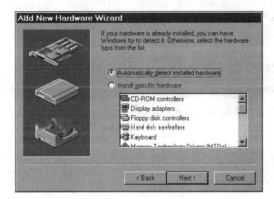

Figure 19-1: The Add New Hardware Wizard. The hardware detection routines can be invoked to find your pre-plug and play device. If you know what driver you want installed, you can pick the manufacturer and model by clicking Install specific hardware.

If the device is not a plug and play device, you may need to double-click the Add Hardware icon in the Control Panel to inform Windows 95 that it needs to check for the new hardware and add a new driver. You can have the Wizard automatically detect your installed hardware (and thereby find the device that you just installed). Alternately, you can direct the Wizard to install a specific driver by providing it with a manufacturer and model designation or pointing it toward an installation diskette from the manufacturer.

Getting the Settings Right

Windows 95 can resolve potential conflicts between plug and play devices, setting their IRQ, I/O, memory address, and DMA channel requirements so all these devices can cooperate. It needs your help to do this for pre-plug and play (which Microsoft insists on calling *legacy*) devices.

We know this is not how plug and play is supposed to work in a plug and play operating system, but Windows 95 has to encompass the past. Pre-plug and play cards and devices can't automatically be configured. You may need to move some jumpers or run a hardware-specific DOS-based configuration program that changes the settings on a given card. You can do this before running the Add Hardware Wizard or after you determine the conflicts.

Secret

After the Add Hardware Wizard finds your hardware, or after you direct it to install a driver for a specific device, a window detailing the settings specified for that device is displayed, an example of which is shown in Figure 19-2. The driver settings have been configured by the Wizard to not conflict with any existing settings for another installed hardware. *But these settings may have nothing whatever to do with the actual settings or available settings for your device.*

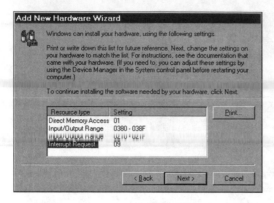

Figure 19-2: The Add New Hardware Wizard's resource settings window. The Wizard has determined the settings that it would like to see you set your device to. You may not be able to do this, given the limitations of your device. These settings will not conflict with any other existing hardware that you have installed. Don't try to change them just yet.

You cannot change these driver settings at this time, even if you know they don't match the actual device settings. The Wizard did not interrogate your device to see what settings you actually had or what settings were possible (unless it's a plug and play device). Understand that the Wizard is not so smart at the moment. You are going to have to provide the smarts to get this process completed.

Secret

Continue with the Add Hardware Wizard, clicking the Finish button in the last window. The drivers for the new device are now installed. You will find them in the Device Manager, as described later in this chapter, if you care to look for them. *Don't use the Device Manager to change the settings at this time, as it will do no good.* We'll get to that in a minute.

You now have the option of reconfiguring your device to match the driver settings just assigned to it, changing your device to other settings that don't conflict with the driver settings for other hardware, or leaving your device settings as they are and changing the driver settings for your device in the Device Manager. The actual settings for your device may be determined by jumpers or by device settings stored in ROM on the device. If you need to make changes on your device, you may need to turn off the computer to set jumpers or run a DOS application that allows you to change the device ROM settings.

Using the Device Manager, as described in the next section, you can make sure that the actual settings for your device do not conflict with existing hardware drivers. If they do, you are going to have to change them. Remember, we are talking about the *actual* device setting, not the driver settings *taken from those available* which the Add New Hardware Wizard just assigned to your device.

If you need to change ROM settings on the device, open a DOS window and run your device-specific configuration routines found on the manufacturer's diskette now. Change the settings on your device so there is no conflict with existing hardware drivers. When you are done, you are ready to shut down Windows 95.

If you need to change jumpers on a device, shut down Windows 95 and turn off your computer. If you change jumpers, be sure the new device settings don't conflict with existing hardware drivers. For details, see *The Device Manager* section that follows. Restart your computer after you have made the changes.

Your device may have a limited range of choices allowed for the various resource settings. Limiting the number of IRQs available to a device reduces its price, but at the cost of high user dissatisfaction when conflicts become irresolvable. Do your best to move around device resource usage to avoid conflicts, but you may not be successful. You may have to purchase an improved device, hopefully plug and play enabled.

To get the actual device settings and the driver settings as recorded in the Registry in sync, you need to use the Device Manager. Using the Device Manager now — and not before — you will be able to make changes in the resource settings for your new device driver that match the device's actual settings. After you make these changes, you may need to restart your computer once again to get the new values to take hold.

The Device Manager

The Windows 95 Control Panel is filled with icons that let you manage your computer's hardware and drivers. We outline what some of these icons do in Chapter 16, and the rest in the many hardware-specific chapters in this book. If you have a question about a specific piece of hardware, turn to the chapter that focuses on that hardware.

The Device Manager is part of the System icon in the Control Panel. It provides a general view of all hardware installed on your computer. Sometimes the Device Manager and the hardware-specific icons overlap in functionality, sometimes something can be done only in one or the other.

The Device Manager provides a very powerful view of your computer. Nothing like this has been available before, even from third-party software developers that created Windows-specific diagnostic tools. The Device Manager supersedes MSD (the Microsoft Diagnostic tool) that came with Windows 3.*x* but was never documented by Microsoft. The Device Manager is much easier to use and much more powerful than MSD.

To get to the Device Manager, take the following steps:

STEPS

Starting the Device Manager

Step 1. Click the Start button, click Settings, and then Control Panel.

Step 2. Double-click the System icon in the Control Panel and click the Device Manager tab. The Device Manager window is shown in Figure 19-3.

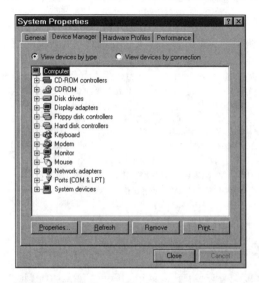

Figure 19-3: The Device Manager. To print your system configuration, highlight Computer and click Print. To view more information about each type of hardware device, double-click an item in the window, or click the plus signs next to the device types. Double-click a specific device to display its properties.

Devices are listed in the Device Manager. Click the plus sign to the left of a device type to see the installed devices. Double-click a device name to display its Properties sheets. You can also highlight a device and click Properties.

IRQs, I/O, memory addresses, DMA channels

If you highlight Computer in the Device Manager window and click Properties, you will get a wonderfully powerful window that shows all the hardware interrupt request settings for your computer, as shown in Figure 19-4. You now know just what hardware is using just what interrupt. You'll see what interrupts (between 0 and 15) are available.

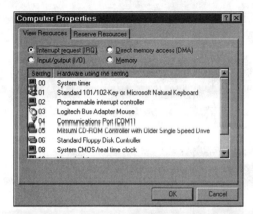

Figure 19-4: The View Resources Interrupt request window. You can't change anything here, but you do get a consolidated view of interrupt usage.

You can view other resources in other windows by clicking the buttons at the top of the View Resources window. The consolidated I/O, memory addresses, and DMA channel usage are displayed in each window — very helpful.

When Computer is highlighted, you can also print a system summary or a summary of all devices. This list will be useful if you later install pre-plug and play devices.

Specific device drivers

The device drivers installed in your computer are by default displayed by type in the Device Manager. Clicking the plus sign next to a device type displays the device drivers installed. Double-clicking a device driver's name displays its Properties sheets, as shown in Figure 19-5.

Changing device driver settings

If you have plug and play devices, you should let the hardware detection routines in Windows 95 determine what the resources settings should be. If you set them manually, the settings become fixed and Windows 95 can't adjust them to avoid conflicts.

To change the resources assigned by Windows 95 to a device to match the actual settings for that device and to avoid any conflicts with other devices, take the following steps. If your device driver settings don't match the device's settings, the device driver entry in the Device Manager will have a yellow exclamation sign on it.

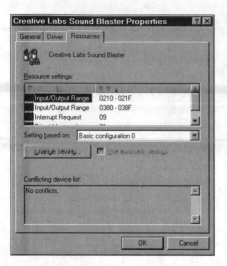

Undocumented

Figure 19-5: The Resource Properties sheet for the Creative Labs Sound Blaster. (These values are actually incorrect so don't use them.) You can change them in the Device Manager.

STEPS

Changing a Device's Resource Settings

Step 1. Double-click the specific device in the Device Manager window.

Step 2. Click the Resources tab in the Properties sheets for the device.

Step 3. Double-click a resource type in the Resource settings field. If this resource can be changed, a dialog box such as that shown in Figure 19-6 will be displayed. Use the scrolling arrows in the field to change the values of the resource requested.

Your device driver may allow different basic configurations that in turn allow for different resource values and the ability to change some resources in one configuration but not in another. Click the down arrow in the Basic configuration drop-down list to see if there are other configurations. If there are, you can try them to see what difference this makes in allowable resource values.

If the Use automatic settings box is checked, you'll need to click it to uncheck it.

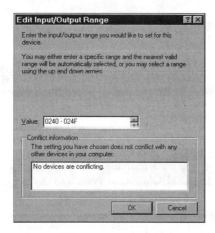

Figure 19-6: The Edit Input/Output Range dialog box. This dialog box is specific to changing an I/O resource. Other resources display different dialog boxes.

Step 4.   Click the OK button in the resource dialog box to accept the changes that you have made. Click the OK button in the Resources Properties sheet to accept all the changes and get out of this particular Properties sheet.

Step 5.   You may be asked to restart your computer to allow the new resource settings to take effect.

Throughout this process, be sure you haven't introduced any new resource use conflicts. If you printed a copy of the system summary, you will have a ready reference on resource use. Also, the Device Manager will track conflicts for you and warn you when you have created them.

Changing device drivers

It is possible to install new device drivers for some devices through the Device Manager. You may want to do this when you get a new driver from your hardware manufacturer, perhaps downloading it from a bulletin board.

You could, of course, install the new device driver by using the Add New Hardware Wizard. When you invoke the Add New Hardware Wizard you are asking it to install the driver (or a new driver) for a device. (Of course, the Wizard will also search for your installed hardware and tell you what it found and install drivers to match.)

You can also change the device driver in the Device Manager.

STEPS

Installing a New Device Driver

Step 1.   Double-click the specific device in the Device Manager window.

Step 2.   Click the Driver tab in the Properties sheets for the device if it has one.

Step 3.   Click Change Driver. This will cause the Select driver dialog box to be displayed. You can select from among the drivers that came with Windows 95. Or click the Have Disk button if you have a new driver on a diskette, CD-ROM, or on your hard drive.

Step 4.   Click OK in the Select Device dialog box to accept the new device driver. Click OK in the Driver Properties sheet to accept the changes.

Step 5.   Restart your computer to allow the new driver to take effect.

Resolving resource conflicts the easy way

There is another way to resolve resource conflicts. Windows 95 help contains a Hardware Conflict Troubleshooter. It gives you a little background on resource conflicts and then leads you to the same places that we just covered. It's kind of cute, though.

STEPS

Starting the Hardware Conflict Troubleshooter

Step 1.   Click the Start button, and then Help.

Step 2.   Click the Contents tab, and then double-click Troubleshooting.

Step 3.   Click "If you have a hardware conflict."

Step 4.   Follow the suggestions and shortcuts to the Device Manager.

Hardware Profiles

We have *hardware profiles* for different hardware configurations on one computer, *user profiles* for different users on the same computer, and *Exchange profiles* for different mail services. Windows 95 presents us with quite a prolific world.

You don't need hardware profiles If you have a plug and play computer with plug and play devices. Windows 95 can automatically load the hardware drivers that it needs based on the hardware it detects and stores in the hardware tree in RAM. Change the configuration (by pulling the portable from the docking station, for example), and Windows 95 reconfigures itself dynamically.

The static hardware profiles are a bit of a kludge. A menu comes up in DOS full-screen text mode before the Windows 95 desktop is displayed and asks you to choose your current configuration.

Tip

You have to set up the hardware profiles manually. You install all the drivers for all the hardware configurations for all the profiles and then assign the proper set of drivers to each profile. The hardware doesn't have to be installed at the time that you install the drivers. You can just install the drivers and make any changes that you need to later if there is a difference between the device settings and the resources settings that you choose.

To create multiple hardware configurations, take the following steps:

STEPS

Creating Multiple Hardware Configurations

Step 1. Use the Add Hardware Wizard to install all drivers applicable for all your configurations. Tell the Wizard what to install if you don't have all the hardware installed at the moment. You can run the Add Hardware Wizard in each hardware configuration and have it search for the installed hardware if you like. This will also build up a base of installed hardware.

Step 2. Double-click the System icon, and then the Hardware Profiles tab. Original Configuration will be highlighted in the Hardware Profiles Properties sheet.

Step 3. Click the Copy button and then type a name for the new profile. You will probably want to rename the original profile to a new descriptive name also.

Step 4. Click the Device Manager tab. Now go through each device and check or uncheck it depending on which Hardware Profile it goes with, as shown for a keyboard in Figure 19-7.

(continued)

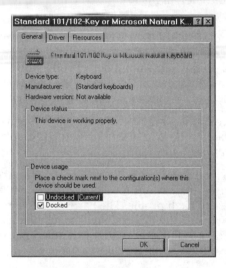

Figure 19-7: The Keyboard Properties sheet. The keyboard is connected physically to the computer in one profile, but not the other.

Step 5.   After completely defining the hardware available under each Hardware Profile, exit the Device Manager and restart Windows 95. You can then choose which Hardware Profile is currently valid.

Monitors — you get only one

Secret

Perhaps you have a portable that in one configuration uses its built-in LCD screen, and in another uses an external monitor. Too bad you can't define multiple monitors in Windows 95. In fact, you can't do much of anything with monitors in the Device Manager (other than remove them). You need to use the Display icon in the Control Panel, or right-click the desktop and choose Properties, then click the Settings tab, and finally click Change Display Type to do anything at all with them.

Since you can't have two monitors defined, you can't assign one to one Hardware Profile and another to another profile. This is not a real good state of affairs.

If you have a portable computer, you will need to use your BIOS routines, your built-in keyboard shortcuts, or hardware-specific utilities to switch between an LCD display and an external monitor.

Hot swapping and hot docking

A plug-and-play compatible computer can notify Windows 95 when the connection with a docking station is made or broken. This will trigger a reconfiguration of the hardware tree, making Windows 95 aware of the new hardware.

Windows 95-aware applications can take advantage of this by responding to messages that are sent regarding the hardware change. Windows 3.x programs will have no idea what is going on. You will have to make sure you have saved any files you are editing on a remote hard disk, while using, for example, Word for Windows, before you pull your portable out of the docking station.

Sound Cards, CD-ROMs, and LPT Ports

Secret

Windows 95 doesn't flag interrupt conflict between sounds cards, CD-ROMs, etc., and the LPT1 and LPT2 ports. LPT1 and LPT2 use interrupts 7 and 5 respectively. Many sound cards and CD-ROMs are also set by default to use these very same interrupts. In spite of this conflict, the Device Manager doesn't inform us that it exists.

Device Manager is silent on this conflict because printers connected to these parallel ports really don't use these interrupts. In some ways they are up for grabs.

The problem is that the Direct Cable Connection *does* use these interrupts when it is configured to use a parallel cable. DCC is at its fastest when it uses the parallel ports and will be slowed by a factor of three if it finds a sound card or CD-ROM drive using these interrupts. The only way you notice this is by testing the speed of communication across these ports.

Detlog.txt, Setuplog.txt, and Ios.log

Undocumented

If you are using any 16-bit drivers, there are three files, the first two found in your root directory and the third in your Windows 95 folder, that can give you another look at your hardware. Detlog.txt is a record of the hardware detection process. Setuplog.txt details what files were installed. Ios.log tracks your real-mode drivers.

You can simply read these files with Notepad to get a little added insight to your configuration.

Setuplog.txt is used if you inadvertently erase a file that is crucial to the proper running of Windows 95. You can use Windows 95 Setup to verify files instead of installing them. The Setuplog.txt file is reviewed during the setup process to see what you installed.

In Summary

Microsoft has made a concerted effort to bring a new level of standardization to the PC world. By providing an extensive list of 32-bit device drivers and giving manufacturers a new model for creating new ones, it has improved the utability of Windows 95.

▶ Windows 95 deals both with existing and plug-and-play hardware, providing a way to track it all.

▶ Hardware detection routines built into Windows 95 do a robust job of matching your hardware to Windows 95 needs.

▶ We show you how to add new hardware drivers to match your devices.

▶ The major benefit of plug and play is the automatic resolution of hardware conflicts. It isn't automatic with non-plug-and-play hardware, but it is easier.

▶ If you have multiple hardware configurations, Windows 95 can be directed to the current configuration.

▶ Watch out for the fact that you can only install one video monitor.

▶ You will likely find a conflict between your sound cards and CD-ROM drivers and your parallel ports.

Chapter 20

Fonts

In This Chapter

We examine how text is displayed on the screen and printed on the printer. We detail the differences between screen fonts, printer fonts, True Type, and PostScript fonts. We show:

▶ How text is displayed on the screen and printed on the printer

▶ The differences between screen fonts, printer fonts, TrueType fonts, and PostScript fonts

▶ Viewing, installing, and uninstalling fonts using the new Windows 95 font installer

▶ The essentials of a bitmapped font

▶ The advantages of scalable fonts such as TrueType

▶ How to set the magnification factor for Windows 95 and what it does to your fonts

▶ What screen fonts are used for and why

▶ Why TrueType fonts are so popular

▶ Why PostScript fonts continue to be used by design professionals

▶ Making your own TrueType fonts

▶ Reproducing documents that contain fonts you don't have

What Are Fonts?

Text is displayed on your screen or printer through the medium of typefaces or fonts. The characters will look different depending on which font or typeface is used to display the text.

A *font* is a set of character shapes of a given size, weight, style, and design. For example, Courier 12-point regular or Times New Roman 12-point bold are different fonts. A *type family* or *typeface* is a family of fonts of a similar design with different sizes and weights, including italic, bold, condensed, and expanded versions of the same design. In Windows terminology, *font* is often used to mean a font file or a typeface. Following the Windows convention, we use *font* in this book to mean font or typeface, interchangeably.

Most of the fonts available for Windows 95 use the Windows 3.*x* ANSI character set. Symbol and Wingdings, two TrueType fonts that come with Windows 95, are exceptions. If you want to use unusual characters, you may need to purchase additional fonts that include those characters. If you installed multilingual support, Arial, Courier New, and Times Roman fonts provide a new 652-character set. More details on character sets can be found in Chapter 21.

Using Fonts in an Application

Windows 95 applications have access to a common Font box. You can see what the font looks like in the Sample window of the Font dialog box, as shown in Figure 20-1.

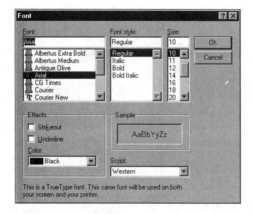

Figure 20-1: The Font dialog box. This box is used by WordPad and can be used by other applications to make it easy to choose a font.

WordPad, a word processing applet that comes with Windows 95, uses the Font dialog box to allow the user to change font style. Click Format, Font on WordPad's menu bar to bring it up.

The Script field shown in Figure 20-1 refers to the character set used by the font. Western refers to the Windows ANSI character set, DOS/OEM to the IBM PC-8 character set, and Symbol to one of many non-standard character sets. Turkish, Cyrillic, Central European, Greek, Baltic, and so on, refer to other character sets. These designations will appear only if you have installed fonts that support these additional characters, which you can do by installing multilingual support while setting up Windows. See Chapter 21.

Where Are the Fonts Installed?

To see what fonts you currently have installed, click the Start button on the Taskbar, then Settings, Control Panel. Double-click the Fonts folder icon in the Control Panel. A Fonts folder window displaying the extended font names and font file icons of the fonts that come with Windows 95 is shown in Figure 20-2.

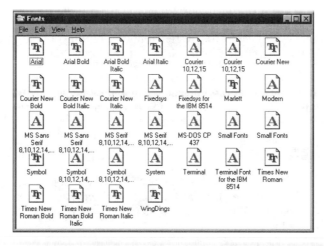

Figure 20-2: The Fonts folder window showing the standard screen (raster) and TrueType fonts that come with Windows 95.

All the fonts that come with Windows 95 are stored in the \Windows\Fonts folder. To see the Fonts folder, take the following steps:

STEPS

Finding the Fonts Folder

Step 1.   Right-click the My Computer icon on the desktop. Click Explore.

Step 2.   Click View, Options in the Explorer menu bar. Be sure that the Show all files radio button is checked. Click OK.

Step 3.   Click the plus sign to the left of the icon that represents your hard drive that stores your Windows folder, most likely the C: drive.

Step 4.   Click the plus sign next to the Windows folder icon in the Explorer. Click the Fonts folder icon.

The fonts stored in the \Windows\Fonts folder are shown with their filenames and font icons in the right pane of the Explorer. The font files stored in the \Windows\Fonts folder are displayed differently than fonts stored in other folders. The large icon view in Figure 20-2 displays their long font name. In the details view, the first column shows the long filename, the second the filename, the third the size and the fourth the date.

Secret

Not all the font files stored in the \Windows\Fonts folder will be displayed in the Fonts folder window or the Explorer view of the fonts. You need to open a DOS window to see that either 8514sys.fon or Vgasys.fon is not displayed. Only one of these fonts is defined as the System font (depending on your screen resolution) and the \Windows\Fonts folder displays only that font.

Fonts don't have to be physically stored in the \Windows\Fonts folder in order to be displayed in that folder (and therefore "installed"). Placing shortcuts in \Windows\Fonts to fonts stored in other folders installs those fonts.

Installing Fonts

Previous versions of Windows stored the font files in the \Windows\System directory. This was a terrible place, as it mixed them with all the rest of the Windows files. By default, Windows 95 stores fonts in their own folder, the \Windows\Fonts folder.

When a TrueType font is installed, it is by default copied to the \Windows\Fonts folder. Even though there is only one special \Windows\Fonts folder, you can have many different folders on your hard disk and store font files in them.

You can use the Windows 95 font installer to install new fonts (that is, make them visible to Windows applications). The font installer will also copy font files into the \Windows\Fonts folder or leave them where they are, as you desire.

You can have multiple folders that store fonts, and install references (shortcuts) to them in the \Windows\Fonts folder with the Windows 95 font installer.

To install new fonts, take the following steps:

STEPS

Installing TrueType Fonts

Step 1. Click the Start button, then Settings, Control Panel. Double-click the Fonts folder icon in the Control Panel.

Step 2. Click File on the Fonts folder window menu bar and then Install New Font. The Add Fonts dialog box, as shown in Figure 20-3, will appear on the desktop.

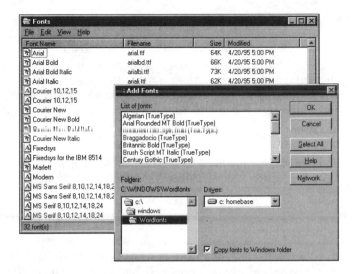

Figure 20-3: The Add Fonts dialog box.

Step 3. The default action is to place a copy of the font file in the
\Windows\Fonts folder. The "Copy fonts to Windows" folder is
automatically rechecked every time you take Step 2. If you copy that
font to the \Windows\Fonts folder and it was previously stored in
another folder on your hard disk, you might want to delete it from
its original location. You probably wouldn't want to do this if it
came from a network hard disk or from your original diskettes.
Uncheck the "Copy fonts to Windows" folder if you are going to
leave the font file where it is (on your hard disk or on a network
server's hard disk) and just place a *shortcut* to it in your
\Windows\Fonts folder.

Step 4. Use the Add Fonts dialog box to browse to find the location of the
fonts that you wish to install. Select the fonts that you will be installing from the list box and click OK.

If the "Copy fonts to Windows" folder is not checked, you will notice
that only shortcuts are added to the \Windows\Fonts folder.

TrueType fonts and font packs that worked with Windows 3.*x* will also work
with Windows 95. The font installers that worked with Windows 3.*x* installed
their TrueType fonts to the \Windows\System directory. You can use the
above steps to move fonts from the \Windows\System directory to the
\Windows\Fonts folder.

Tip You can install fonts from TrueType font packs using the Windows 95 font
installer and ignore the Windows 3.*x* font installers that come with these fonts.

Uninstalling and/or deleting a font

If you delete a font file that is stored in the \Windows\Fonts folder, it is both uninstalled (the font is no longer available to Windows 95 applications) and deleted (the font file is removed to the Recycle Bin). If you delete a shortcut in the \Windows\Fonts file to a font file that is stored in another folder, the font is uninstalled but the font file is not deleted. Only the shortcut is deleted.

To uninstall a font and delete its font file stored in the \Windows\Fonts folder, open the Fonts folder window by clicking the Start button, then Settings, Control Panel. Double-click the Fonts folder icon in the Control Panel. Right click the font icon or filename, and select Delete from the right mouse button menu.

If you have another copy of the font file stored in another folder, you can later reinstall it.

You can uninstall a font by deleting its shortcut in the \Windows\Fonts folder. The original font file is not deleted, but the font is no longer available to be used by Windows 95 applications and won't be displayed in the \Windows\Fonts folder.

Highlight a font's shortcut in the \Windows\Fonts folder and press Delete. Answer Yes to the message asking if you want to delete the font.

Viewing fonts

You can see a sample "printout" of a font by double-clicking its icon in any folder window or in the \Windows\Fonts folder. Figure 20-4 shows what Arial Bold looks like.

Undocumented

A font's icon is shown in the Fonts folder if it is installed. If a font is not installed you can still view it by opening the folder window where the font is stored and double-clicking its icon. You can produce the same "printout" by double-clicking a font file wherever it is stored.

Most text editing and word processing applications will list only TrueType or printer fonts in their font lists. To keep these font lists manageable you will want to install only the fonts that you use. You can use Windows 95's built-in font viewing capability to decide whether you want to install a particular font.

Tip

Numerous more sophisticated font viewers and font managers are available from other vendors. The CD-ROM included with this book features font utilities that provide additional capabilities for the display and printing of all your fonts.

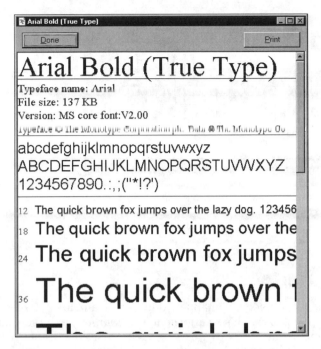

Figure 20-4: Sample "printout" of the Arial Bold TrueType font. Double-click a font icon in a folder window to see how the font looks at various point sizes.

The Kinds and Types of Fonts

You can slice and dice the fonts available for Windows into a number of different categories. One cut gives you the bitmapped fonts versus the scalable fonts. Another gives you screen fonts, printer fonts, and scalable fonts that work with both the screen and the printer. There are fixed-pitch and proportional fonts. And then there are the DOS fonts. As you shall see, these categories overlap.

Bitmapped fonts

Bitmapped (or *raster*) fonts are fixed-size fonts. The typeface is stored in a font file on your hard disk. Each character is a pattern of a fixed number of dots. An example of a bitmapped screen font is MS Sans Serif.

Secret

The MS Sans Serif 10-point font stored in the file Sserife.fon is constructed on a grid that is 16 dots high. The grid varies in width up to 14 dots (with an average of 7), depending on the width of each proportionally spaced character. In Figure 20-5, the lower case letters *a, b, c,* and *d* are shown on their dot grids.

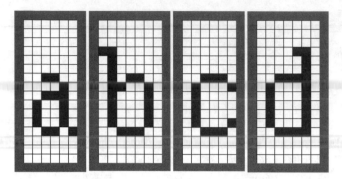

Figure 20-5: The lowercase letters a, b, c, and d in MS Sans Serif 10 point. Screen fonts are created on a grid of dots.

Scalable fonts

Secret

First a word on terminology. Bitmapped fonts can be and are enlarged to display larger point sizes. This enlargement is accomplished by replacing each dot in a bitmapped font with two, three, or more dots. This results in rather ugly blocky fonts. You might think of this as a crude form of scaling, but this is *not* what is meant by that term in the context of Windows 95 scalable fonts.

Scalable fonts such as TrueType fonts are stored in files on your hard disk (or in your printer's ROM) as descriptions of each character. This description includes an outline of the font as well as *rules* (known as *hints*) used when displaying the font. When scalable fonts are displayed on the screen (or printed on paper) they are rendered by a font-rendering algorithm that takes this description and turns it into dots. In other words, they are *rasterized*. An example of a scalable font is Times New Roman, which is a TrueType font created by Monotype, licensed by Microsoft, and included with Windows 95.

Scalable fonts have a number of advantages over bitmapped fonts.

■ First, they can be displayed over a wider range of point sizes and magnifications and still look good. Having a large number of fixed-sized bitmapped fonts (in different sizes) to cover such a wide range would require significantly more hard disk space. As noted above, enlarging bitmapped fonts on the fly to display larger font sizes produces jagged fonts. Windows can't shrink bitmapped fonts to display sizes smaller than the smallest size font stored in a font file.

■ Second, scalable fonts can be used for both your screen and printer. You don't need one set of bitmapped screen fonts (in a limited number of sizes) and another set of bitmapped printer fonts in the same sizes. The rasterizer takes advantage of the highest resolution available on your printer.

- Third, a scalable font description method provides a standard that font foundries can use for every printer and font size. This considerably reduces the work required to create a font. At the same time, it vastly expands the market because one font can be used on all printers with Windows printer drivers. Fonts become much less expensive. Printer manufacturers can concentrate on producing printers (and printer drivers for Windows) and not on creating fonts (which they aren't very good at anyway).

- Fourth, the likelihood that your printer and your screen correspond greatly increases with scalable fonts. Both the printer rasterizer and the screen font rasterizer are reading from the same book (using the same font description).

Bitmapped fonts have their advantage. Each font is created by hand to look its best on a video monitor (or particular printer) at a certain resolution (dots per inch, or dpi). A team of human beings has taken the time necessary to make each sized font the best it can be. Compare the examples of TrueType and screen fonts shown later in this chapter.

Tip

If you want to check out the difference in rendering speed between bitmapped and scalable fonts, launch the Character Map applet (under the Accessories menu on the Start button). Go through each character set, one at a time, and look at bitmapped fonts and TrueType fonts. The first time a character set using a TrueType font is viewed will take a second to render the characters. Character sets using bitmapped screen fonts such as MS Sans Serif are rendered instantaneously. After the first viewing, you won't be able to tell the difference in rendering time between the characters using a TrueType font or a screen font.

A crude form of scalable fonts included with earlier versions of Windows were known as *vector* fonts. The font descriptions are stored as sets of coordinates that make up the letters as stick figures. There are three vector font files — Modern.fon, Script.fon, and Roman.fon. These files have the same extension in their filename as the bitmapped fonts making it a little more difficult to differentiate them.

Modern.fon is installed by default, but the other fonts will be installed only if you install a plotter.

Screen fonts

 Screen fonts are bitmapped fonts used (for the most part) to display icon titles, dialog box text, help files, the file and folder names in the Explorer, and so on. It is expected that you won't use these fonts to create text documents. In fact, you can't see them in the font drop-down boxes in Microsoft Word for Windows.

Unless a printer manufacturer has created matching printer fonts, screen fonts will not be printed, even if you were to create a document using these fonts.

The printer driver instead substitutes printer fonts of the same or similar size and prints your text using those fonts.

When you first install Windows 95, titles in the title bars of folder windows, titles under the icons on the desktop, menu items, application or document names on the Taskbar buttons, file and folder names in the Explorer, and text in dialog boxes use either the screen font MS Sans Serif 8 point or MS Sans Serif 10 point, depending on your screen resolution. It is possible to change fonts and use TrueType fonts or other screen fonts. See Chapter 22 to determine which fonts can be used for these screen text entities.

Printer fonts

 Printer fonts can be either bitmapped or scalable fonts. They can be stored in your printer's ROM, in cartridges plugged into your printer, or downloaded from your computer's hard disk to your printer's RAM.

Microsoft does not supply printer fonts with Windows 95 or with Windows 3.1, although it did with Windows 3.0. Printer manufacturers provide these fonts. Many laser printer manufacturers provide built-in (ROM) PostScript or PostScript-compatible fonts. Hewlett-Packard provides built-in scalable TrueType-compatible fonts in its LaserJet 4 series. The HP 4L fonts are shown in Figure 20-6.

Albertus Medium	AaBbCcRrXxYyZy
Albertus Extrabold	**AaBbCcRrXxYyZz**
Antique Olive	AaBbCcRrXxYyZz
CG Times	AaBbCcRrXxYyZz
Coronet	*AaBbCcRrXxYyZz*
Letter Gothic	AaBbCcRrXxYyZz
Univers	AaBbCcRrXxYyZz
Univers Condensed	AaBbCcRrXxYyZz

Figure 20-6: These printer fonts are stored in ROM in the HP LaserJet 4L printer. You can print with these fonts and purchase compatible TrueType fonts for display on the screen.

Printer manufacturers may also provide screen fonts that work with their printer fonts. If the printer fonts are bitmapped fonts, most likely the screen fonts are as well.

Undocumented

The printer fonts stored in your printer's ROM will not show up on your hard disk but they will show up in the font dialog boxes in your word processor or text editor. The printer driver passes along the information about the printer fonts to your word processor so you can create a document using these fonts. Unless you have installed the corresponding screen fonts, the text created using the printer fonts is displayed on your screen using a screen font that matches in size the desired printer font.

Scalable fonts that work with both the printer and the screen

Adobe introduced the first successful scalable font technology used on personal computers when it brought out PostScript. Later, Microsoft integrated its own TrueType technology into Windows 3.1 (making it a major reason to upgrade from Windows 3.0).

Microsoft (and Apple) went into competition with Adobe by providing TrueType technology as a no-charge addition to the operating system. It's hard to compete when your competitor gives away its product (or bundles it with something you are going to have to purchase anyway). Adobe continues to be successful partly because most imagesetting service bureaus are more familiar with PostScript Type 1 fonts than with TrueType fonts.

When PostScript became available, type designers could create computer-based type to one specification and sell it to anyone who used a PostScript device. With the advent of TrueType, a second specification allowed type designers to create fonts in a different popular format.

Proportional and fixed-pitch fonts

Almost all the fonts used with Windows are proportional fonts; that is, each character has a width that varies with each character's shape. This means that the letter *l* would take up less space than the letter *m* since the width of an *m* is more than the width of an *l*.

Every character in a fixed-pitch font has the same width. Courier, Fixedsys, and Terminal are fixed-pitch screen fonts. Courier New is a TrueType fixed-pitch font. Fixed-pitch fonts are used, for example, to display text coming from computer bulletin boards when using HyperTerminal. DOS applications often use fixed-pitch fonts. You may also want to use fixed-pitch fonts in some of your correspondence. (Make the person you're corresponding with think that you are using a typewriter!) Check later in this chapter for graphical examples of fixed and proportional fonts.

DOS fonts

DOS fonts are fixed-pitch fonts used in windowed DOS sessions — DOS Windows. The DOS fonts in Windows 95 are stored in three files, Vgaoem.fon (or 8514oem.fon), Dosapp.fon, and Courier.ttf.

Microsoft Plus! includes Lucida Console, a TrueType font that replaces the Courier New font as the DOS TrueType font.

As DOS fonts are also screen fonts, we cover them in more detail later in this chapter.

Font Sizes

Secret

The term *font size* is used in Windows Properties sheets and dialog boxes to refer to four quite different ideas. The first use refers to the height of characters when printed on paper. The second is the magnification factor used to display characters (and other items) on the screen. It is measured in pixels per "logical" inch. The third refers to the "small" and "large" sets of screen fonts. The fourth is the size in pixels of the fonts used in windowed DOS sessions (also called *DOS Windows*).

Font sizes, using the first definition given above, are denoted in *points*. There are 72 points per inch. As an example, the screen font file Coure.fon contains three fonts: one each of 10, 12, and 15 points. Font height in points is measured from the top of the lower case *f* (the *ascender*) to the bottom of the lower case *g* (the *descender*) plus any invisible space (called a *shoulder*) that the font designer has added to the top or bottom of the letters.

When text is printed on paper, its size is fixed. For example, 24-point text will be one-third of an inch high (24 divided by 72 equals $^1/_3$). On paper, an inch is an inch, and, in the United States at least, letter-sized paper is $8^1/_2$ by 11 inches.

Unlike paper, computer monitors and their associated graphics adapters come in four major different nominal sizes and five major different screen resolutions. You, the operator, can change the size of the display area (the desktop) just by turning some knobs on the monitor.

Computer screens are usually farther away from our eyes then the distance that we comfortably hold a book or a sheet of paper. To be perceived as being the same size, text on a computer needs to be bigger than its corresponding print on the paper. The "apparent" height of an image decreases as you move back from it.

So, most likely 24-point text will be magnified to display larger than one-third of an inch high on your Windows desktop.

The logical inch

Undocumented

Enter the *logical inch*. Twenty-four point text displayed on your Windows desktop will be one-third of a logical inch high, although it will be printed at exactly one-third of an inch high on your printer. Text most likely will be displayed larger than it will be printed. This means that, on your monitor, the logical inch will most likely be larger than the printed inch.

The logical inch is a magnifier. The size of the logical inch divided by one inch gives the value of the magnification. The actual size of the logical inch is dependent on the size of your monitor, the resolution of your graphics card, how large you have adjusted your image size, and which value of the magnification factor internal to Windows 95 (as you may recall, this is the second meaning of the term font size) you have chosen. The magnification values available to you are Small Fonts, Large Fonts, and Custom. Custom allows a wide range of values. Font size — magnification factor — is set in the Display Settings Properties sheet. More details are available in Chapter 22.

So how big is a logical inch? One of the authors has a Compaq 14-inch SVGA monitor connected to one of his computers. While 14 inches is its nominal dimension, the actual diagonal size of the image of the Windows 95 desktop on the screen is approximately 13 inches.

Most monitors used with PCs that run Windows are constructed to have greater width than height. They use the ratio of 4 (width) to 3 (height). The height of the desktop image on our 14-inch monitor is 7 $^7/_8$ inches and its width is 10 $^3/_8$ inches.

The screen resolution on this computer is set to Super VGA, or 800 x 600 pixels, (notice the 4-to-3 ratio of width to height). Therefore, our dots per inch (dpi) resolution is approximately 76 pixels per inch.

So, do we know how big a logical inch is yet?

We can set the magnification factor to Small Fonts (96 pixels per logical inch), Large Fonts (120 pixels per logical inch), or Custom (a wide range of values). Given these values and our calculation of our screen resolution of 76 pixels per inch, we can calculate the size of the logical inch.

Secret

For the small font magnification, the size of the logical inch is 96 pixels divided by 76 pixels, or about 1 $^1/_4$ inches. For large font magnification it is about 1 $^5/_8$ inches.

We have calculated the size of the logical inch, but to test our calculation we need to closely examine the characters on our screen to see that they displayed at the correct size.

Windows screen fonts are designed on grids of dots. The screen fonts come in two sets. The large screen font set was designed to be used with a high resolution display (1024 × 768). The fonts are built on a grid of dots assuming 120 dots per logical inch. The small screen font set was designed for VGA resolution (640 × 480). The fonts assume a grid of 96 dots per logical inch. The small screen font set is not to be confused with the font typeface Small Fonts that is provided in both sets.

Small screen fonts are used by Windows 95 when the magnification factor is set to Small Fonts (96 pixels per logical inch). Not surprisingly, large screen fonts are used when the magnification factor is set to Large Fonts (120 pixels per logical inch). You can, of course, display TrueType fonts (which don't come in sets). TrueType fonts will be magnified by the same amount as screen fonts.

Figure 20-7 shows the letters *T*, *f*, and *g* as designed for the MS Sans Serif 24-point screen font from the small font set. Figure 20-8 shows the same letters from the large screen font set.

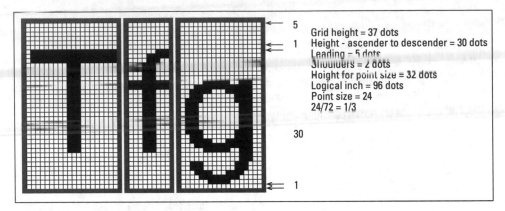

Figure 20-7: Small fonts: MS Sans Serif font at 24 points. You can count the number of dots used to create this font.

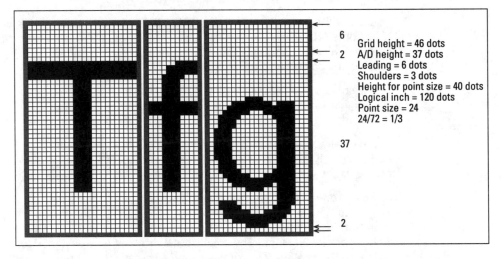

Figure 20-8: Large fonts: MS Sans Serif font at 24 points. More dots were used to create this larger font.

The height of the 24-point type using a font from the large screen fonts set is 40 dots (for MS Sans Serif — 46 dots minus the 6 dots of internal leading). We are assured by Figure 20-8 that the font designers have correctly named and designed this font because 24 points is one-third of a logical inch and 40 dots is one-third of 120 dots.

Tip

If each dot on the font design grid corresponds to one pixel on the screen, text displayed in a 24-point font will be 40 pixels high. The one-dot-to-one-pixel relationship can be confirmed by using a magnifier utility (we have featured Extreme CloseUp and Lens 2.0 on the shareware CD-ROM included with this book) that lets you see and count the pixels of displayed text and compare them with the design grid. Our calculation of the size of the logical inch is confirmed.

Undocumented

Text shown on the display when the magnification factor is set to Large Fonts is about 60 percent bigger on the screen than when printed. It is about 25 percent bigger when using the Small Fonts magnification factor. Again, because you are normally farther away from a screen than you are from a piece of paper, characters may appear to your eyes to be the same size on both.

The logical inch is not restricted to fonts, but is used throughout the internals of Windows. For example, if you were to set the Image Attributes size under the Options menu in MS Paint to one inch, you would notice that the displayed square is 96 pixels by 96 pixels if you choose Small Fonts mode. It's 120 pixels by 120 pixels if you choose Large Fonts mode, and 144 pixels by 144 pixels if you choose Custom at 150 percent magnification. There is more discussion of this issue in Chapter 22.

The magnifier

Previous versions of Windows had only two magnification levels — small fonts and large fonts. You could change the size of the characters displayed on your screen by using the setup icon to switch between these two font sizes or between different screen resolutions.

In Windows 95, you have the choice, using the Display Settings Properties sheet, of changing the font size to Small Fonts, Large Fonts, or Custom. Custom allows you to specify a magnification factor (in pixels per logical inch). Font size, as the words are used in this Properties sheet, is the magnifier used to increase (or decrease) the size that the characters are displayed on the screen while not changing the size at which characters are actually printed.

The magnification factor chosen using Custom is arbitrarily (but neatly) set to 100 percent for Small Fonts or 96 pixels per logical inch. Small Fonts and Custom Font Size set to 100 percent are the same thing. Our example monitor at SVGA resolution displayed 76 pixels per inch. On this monitor, 100 percent magnification displays characters that are 25 percent bigger on the screen then on paper.

Magnification of 125 percent corresponds to 120 pixels per logical inch (Large Fonts), 150 percent equals 144 pixels per logical inch, and 200 percent equals 192 pixels per logical inch. Selecting a Custom size (or choosing Small or Large Fonts) just tells Windows how much to magnify the size of the text displayed on the desktop.

Can you comfortably read the text?

"Man is the measure of all things" — *Protagoras*

You should care about how big the text is displayed on the screen so you can read it in comfort. The size of text you can comfortably read is also often a function of the size of your monitor. The larger the screen size, the more text size modes can be used comfortably.

Lots of different kinds of text are displayed on desktops. These include the icon titles, the file and folder names in the Explorer, the text in menus, the text in dialog boxes, the text in WordPad documents, and so on. You have the option of changing the size, weight, style, and family of fonts used to display this text. See Chapter 22 for details on how you can change all of these text entities.

If you are comfortable reading text on a piece of paper that is 18 inches away from your eyes (a pretty normal distance) then you will be comfortable reading text of the same point size on the computer screen at 2 feet if it has been increased in size by 33 percent. If you are using Small Fonts (which magnifies the text by 25 percent) then you will want to be a little closer than 2 feet from your computer monitor (22 to 23 inches).

Can you see enough text?

Tip

The SVGA monitor referred to previously displays about 6 vertical inches of text in WordPad if the WordPad Toolbar, format bar, ruler, and status bar are turned on and WordPad is at its maximum window size. If font size is set to Small Fonts, 25 lines of text (in Courier New 12 point) are visible on the screen. This is a little less than half a page's worth of text. If font size is set to Large Fonts, then only 19 lines of text, or a third of a page of printed text, displays.

The size of the font that is used to display text on the desktop increases when we change from Small Fonts to Large Fonts or go to larger sizes with the Custom option using the Display Settings Properties sheet. Therefore, we see less text displayed. After all, our Windows 95 desktop stays the same size. Microsoft Word for Windows has a zoom feature that is equivalent to changing the font size or using custom font sizes, although it changes only the displayed size of the fonts in the Word for Windows client area and not the size of the fonts used in dialog boxes, and so on. This feature is often used in Word for Windows so the user can shrink the font size enough that one full line of text is on screen while editing.

Larger monitors with higher-resolution display adapters can display greater amounts of text — they have more logical inches on the display. Go to Chapter 22 for further detailed comparisons.

Screen Fonts in Detail

 Microsoft supplies the screen fonts used in Windows, although other manufacturers can, if they wish, supply screen fonts — perhaps ones that match their printer fonts.

Secret

Screen fonts are bitmapped fonts. The screen fonts are stored in screen font files that end in the extension *fon*. These files may contain fonts of one or more font sizes. Windows creates, on the fly, the bold, italic and bold italic versions of screen fonts from the regular bitmapped version, which is the only version that is stored in the bitmapped screen font file.

Table 20-1 lists the screen font files that Microsoft ships with Windows 95.

Table 20-1	Windows 95 Screen Fonts by Font Set
Font Filename	*Somewhat Esoteric Embedded Typeface Name*
Large screen fonts	
8514fix.fon	Fixedsys for the IBM 8514
8514oem.fon	Terminal Font for the IBM 8514
8514sys.fon	System (Set #6)
Courf.fon	Courier 10, 12, 15 (8514/a resolution)
Seriff.fon	MS Serif 8, 10, 12, 14, 18, 24 (8514 resolution)
Smallf.fon	Small Fonts (8514/a resolution)
Sseriff.fon	MS Sans Serif 8, 10, 12, 14, 18, 24 (8514 resolution)
Symbolf.fon	Symbol (8514 resolution)
Small screen fonts	
Vgafix.fon	Fixedsys (Set #6)
Vgaoem.fon	Terminal (US) (Set #6)
Vgasys.fon	System (Set #6)
Coure.fon	Courier 10, 12, 15 (VGA resolution)
Serife.fon	MS Serif 8, 10, 12, 14, 18, 24 (VGA resolution)
Smalle.fon	Small Fonts (VGA resolution)
Sserife.fon	MS Sans Serif 8, 10, 12, 14, 18, 24 (VGA resolution)
Symbole.fon	Symbol (VGA resolution)
DOS fonts	
Dosapp.fon	MS-DOS CP 437

Table 20-2 shows fonts by typeface.

Table 20-2	Screen Fonts by Typeface	
Typeface	*Font Filename*	*Character Set*
Fixed space fonts		
Fixedsys	8514fix.fon	Windows 3.0 ANSI
	Vgafix.fon	Windows 3.0 ANSI
Terminal	8514oem.fon	DOS/OEM
	Vgaoem.fon	DOS/OEM
	Dosapp.fon	DOS/OEM
Courier	Coure.fon	Windows 3.0 ANSI
	Courf.fon	Windows 3.0 ANSI
Proportional fonts		
System	8514sys.fon	All Windows 3.0 ANSI
	Vgasys.fon	
Sans Serif	Sserife.fon	
	Sseriff.fon	
Serif	Serife.fon	
	Seriff.fon	
Small Fonts	Smalle.fon	
	Smallf.fon	
Symbol	Symbole.fon	Symbol
	Symbolf.fon	Symbol

Undocumented

Windows 95 stores the references to the screen fonts (other than the DOS fonts) in the Registry files System.dat and User.dat. This is what that information looks like:

```
[HKEY_LOCAL_MACHINE\SOFTWARE\Microsoft\Windows\CurrentVersion\fontsize]
[HKEY_LOCAL_MACHINE\SOFTWARE\Microsoft\Windows\CurrentVersion\fontsize\96]
"Description"="Small Fonts"
[HKEY_LOCAL_MACHINE\SOFTWARE\Microsoft\Windows\CurrentVersion\fontsize\96\System]
"vgasys.fon"="fonts.fon"
"vgafix.fon"="fixedfon.fon"
"vgaoem.fon"="oemfonts.fon"
[HKEY_LOCAL_MACHINE\SOFTWARE\Microsoft\Windows\CurrentVersion\fontsize\96\User]
"serife.fon"="MS Serif 8,10,12,14,18,24 (VGA res)"
"sserife.fon"="MS Sans Serif 8,10,12,14,18,24 (VGA res)"
"coure.fon"="Courier 10,12,15 (VGA res)"
"symbole.fon"="Symbol 8,10,12,14,18,24 (VGA res)"
```

```
"smalle.fon"="Small Fonts (VGA res)"
[HKEY_LOCAL_MACHINE\SOFTWARE\Microsoft\Windows\CurrentVersion\fontsize\120]
"Description"="Large Fonts"
[HKEY_LOCAL_MACHINE\SOFTWARE\Microsoft\Windows\CurrentVersion\fontsize\120\System]
"8514sys.fon"="fonts.fon"
"8514fix.fon"="fixedfon.fon"
"8514oem.fon"="oemfonts.fon"
[HKEY_LOCAL_MACHINE\SOFTWARE\Microsoft\Windows\CurrentVersion\fontsize\120\User]
"seriff.fon"="MS Serif 8,10,12,14,18,24 (8514/a res)"
"sseriff.fon"="MS Sans Serif 8,10,12,14,18,24 (8514/a res)"
"courf.fon"="Courier 10,12,15 (8514/a res)"
"symbolf.fon"="Symbol 8,10,12,14,18,24 (8514/a res)"
"smallf.fon"="Small Fonts (8514/a res)"
```

All the screen fonts whose font filenames begin with 8514 or whose names before the *fon* extension end in an *f*, such as Sserff.fon, are large fonts (designed on a dot grid of 120 dots per logical inch). Those font files that begin with VGA or whose names end in an *e*, as in Sserfe.fon are the small fonts (96 dots per logical inch).

Font point sizes

It is convenient to have a consistent method of referring to font size across all kinds of fonts. For example, a 9-point font is $9/72$ of a (logical) inch high. The (small font set) font file Vgafix.fon contains one font of size 9 points. It was created on a grid that is 15 dots high and 8 dots wide. The top 3 dots are line spacing (or internal leading) and are not used to draw the character. The characters are therefore 12 dots high (from the top of the ascender to the bottom of the descender with no shoulder).

A small screen font 12 dots high would be a 9-point font because 12 dots times the ratio of 72 points per logical inch divided by 96 dots per logical inch equals 9 points: (12*72)/96 = 9. The arithmetic doesn't always produce integers. For example, the MS Serif font file Serife.fon has a 10-point font that is 13 dots high and is therefore actually a 9.75-point font.

Fixed-pitch screen fonts

There are four fixed-pitch screen fonts. Each is designed for a different application or purpose. Three are used in communicating with the world of fixed-pitch font computers and operating systems and one is used to mimic a typewriter. These fonts reach back into the past.

Tip

The lower-case *r* is shown in Figures 20-10, 20-12 and 20-14 for each of the fixed-pitch fonts. You can use these figures (in conjunction with Extreme CloseUp) to identify which font is being used in Windows 95 to display a given text entity. Start Extreme CloseUp and use it to look at an *r* in your icon titles on your desktop. For an example, see Figure 20-9. Compare what Extreme CloseUp shows you with what you see in the figures for each screen and TrueType font to determine which font is in use on your display for that text entity.

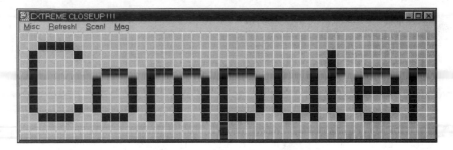

Figure 20-9: Extreme CloseUp view of part of the My Computer icon title in 16x magnification with the grid on. Each grid point represents a pixel or a dot on the grid used to create the screen font, or a pixel that is the result of the rasterization of the TrueType font.

Fixed-pitch system fonts

The Fixedsys fonts are fixed-pitch fonts used by Notepad to display ASCII (and Windows ANSI) characters. You can also use them in HyperTerminal to display text coming from the host computer. This font is basically a holdover from the days when Windows 2.x and previous versions of Windows used it as the system font to display the text in menus and dialog boxes.

The font file Vgafix.fon contains a 9-point font, and 8514fix.fon contains an 11-point font. The 11-point large Fixedsys font was designed on a grid 10 dots wide and 20 dots high. The height from the ascender to the descender is 16 dots and the shoulder is 2 dots above the ascender. The point size calculation is as follows: (16+2) times 72 divided by 120 dots per logical inch, which results in 10.8, or 11 points. See Figure 20-10 for a comparison of weights. Throughout this chapter, we use the *r* character to show differences between various fonts.

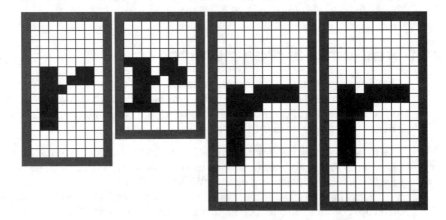

Figure 20-10: Lower case *r* from VGAfix.fon, VGAoem.fon, 8514fix.fon, and 8514oem.fon font files, from left to right respectively.

Terminal fonts

The Terminal fonts use the OEM, or the original IBM PC-8 (bit), character set. This is the standard character set used by DOS programs. For more information about character sets, see Chapter 21.

Like Vgafix.fon, the screen font file Vgaoem.fon contains a 9-point font and 8514oem.fon contains an 11-point font.

These fonts are used by the Clipboard to display DOS text. You can copy text from a Windows application into the Clipboard, switch the Clipboard to display the text in the OEM font (click View; see Figure 20-11), and paste the text into a DOS application. Most of the time there is no point in switching to the OEM font because the actual characters you are copying back and forth are the same in the Windows application as in the DOS application. Character with an ASCII number greater than 127, however, differ between Windows and DOS applications. See the character set discussion in Chapter 21 for a comparison of the Windows ANSI and the DOS/OEM character sets.

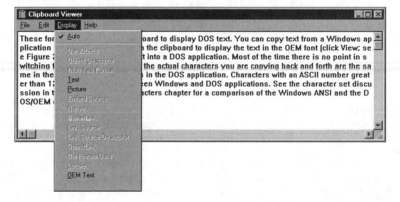

Figure 20-11: You can change from Windows ANSI to OEM character set in the Clipboard by using this menu to switch between these character sets.

Secret

The Vgaoem.fon file provides one of the DOS fonts, 8 x 12 (which is also found in the Dosapp.fon file) and the 8514oem.fon file provides another DOS font, 10 x 20.

Windows will not boot unless these files are stored in the \Windows\Fonts folder on your computer. Nor can you delete them from the Fonts folder.

DOS fonts

The DOS fonts share the typeface name Terminal with the OEM fonts. These fonts are used only in DOS Windows sessions. Your DOS window uses eight bitmapped screen fonts from the Dosapp.fon file. The DOS window can also use the TrueType fixed font, as shown by the letter *r* in Figure 20-12.

Figure 20-12: DOS fonts 4 x 6, 5 x 12, 6 x 8, 7 x 12, 8 x 8, 8 x 12, 10 x 18, and 12 x 16.

One line in the System.ini file determines which DOS screen fonts are used by windowed DOS applications. Find the line woafont=dosapp.fon in the [386enh] section.

Secret

The Dosapp.fon file contains eight fonts. They were designed using a grid of 96 dots per logical inch. There are not separate sets of large and small DOS fonts. The DOS fonts are the same (pixel) size irrespective of what magnification factor or font size you set. The windowed DOS session will be the same physical height on your desktop irrespective of which font size you choose in the Display Settings Properties sheet.

The DOS font size drop-down box on the Toolbar of a windowed DOS session (or on the DOS Fonts Properties sheet, as shown in Figure 20-13) gives the size of the pixel grid that was used to create each of the DOS screen fonts — first their width and then their height. Dosapp.fon contains the screen fonts created on grids of sizes 4 x 6, 5 x 12, 6 x 8, 8 x 8, 8 x 12, 7 x 12, 10 x 18, and 12 x 16 dots. The additional DOS screen font, 10 x 20, is found in the 8514oem.font file.

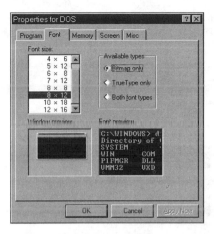

Figure 20-13: The DOS Fonts Properties sheet.

A DOS window can also use a set of fixed-pitch fonts created from the TrueType font Courier New. These fonts are included in the DOS window font drop-down box when you check Both font types in the DOS Fonts Properties sheet.

A DOS window using the 8 x 12 font will be 300 pixels high (12 pixels × 25 lines), not including the DOS window caption bar and Toolbar height. On a 14-inch monitor at SVGA resolution, this DOS window is about 4 inches high, or over half of the screen height (600 pixels). This same DOS window on a monitor with 1280 ×1024 resolution is less than 30 percent of the height of the screen.

On a 15-inch inch monitor with a resolution of 1024 × 768, DOS text using the 7 × 12 DOS screen font will be smaller (78 percent of the height) than the same DOS text on the same monitor at SVGA (600 × 800) resolution (0.131 inches vs. 0.168 inches). A wide range of DOS text font sizes are required to be sure that everyone's eyes are comfortable using DOS programs in a window, given the wide variety of display resolutions and monitor sizes.

Courier fonts

The Courier screen font comes in 10, 12, and 15 points, in both the small and large screen size. These Courier fonts' sizes are a subtle joke. As Courier is a fixed-pitch font, you might be tempted to think that the above point sizes refer to *pitch* as in characters per inch. Fifteen characters per inch, a standard size in old-fashioned line printers, requires a small font, while 15-point Courier is bigger than 12-point Courier.

The Windows font developers are having a little fun at our expense. They remember that these three sizes, 10, 12, and 15 pitch, were standards. They encourage us to think in this wrong headed-fashion (by providing Courier in these three sizes, and not, say, 10, 12, and 14 points).

The small fonts stored in Coure.fon were created on grids of 8×13, 9×16, and 12×20 dots for the 10-, 12-, and 15-point fonts respectively. For a comparison, see Figure 20-14. The large fonts in Courf.fon were created on grids of 9×16, 12×20, and 15×25 dots. Courier uses the Windows ANSI character set.

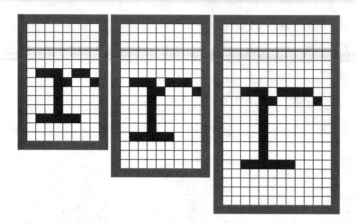

Figure 20-14: Courier screen font in 10, 12, and 15 points. That's 15-point Courier, not Courier at 15 characters per inch.

Courier can be used to display fixed-pitch text in HyperTerminal (although you may want to use a font that uses the DOS/OEM character set) or in your personal letters. Almost all printers have a corresponding Courier print font — at least 10 and 12 point.

Just because screen fonts are created and stored on a fixed-size grid doesn't mean that you can't display them in a larger size. Windows contains code that will enlarge a screen font and display it at a larger size. The results aren't very pretty as the code doesn't take the time to do any filling and smoothing, but it gets the job done quickly.

There is a TrueType font — Courier New — that pretty much replaces Courier. The advantages include better looking fonts at larger than 24 points and perhaps better correspondence between the font size you see on the screen and the font size printed in your letter to Aunt Sally.

Proportional screen fonts

Proportional fonts are used throughout the Windows 95 user interface. You can, if you wish, use a fixed-pitch font like Courier for your menu items, or window titles, and so on, but proportional fonts take up less room. The boxes that the text inhabits (which adjust to the font size and length of the text within them) are therefore smaller and more manageable.

System fonts

The system font comes only in 10-point bold and bold italic. It can be used for text entities like window titles or menu items. Because it comes only in bold, it can't be used for the finer things in life. While it was once an important font for displaying all sorts of Windows text entities, it has fallen into disuse in Windows 95.

Secret

If all your font files are erased from your hard disk you cannot boot your computer in Windows and will get a Gdi.exe error message.

But if the font files Vgasys.fon and Vgaoem.sys (assuming that you last chose Small Fonts in Display Settings Properties sheet) are still in the Windows\Fonts folder, you would be able to start and use Windows. These two files (or their equivalent large fonts files (8514sys.fon and 8514oem.fon) are the minimum font files needed to make Windows work. Figure 20-15 shows the lower case r for the two sizes of system fonts.

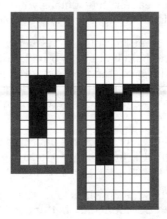

Figure 20-15: Lowercase r from Vgasys.fon and 8514sys.fon screen font files. These are the system font files from the small font and large font cases.

The Terminal font in the OEM font files (Vgaoem.fon or 8514oem.fon) is needed to give the DOS window a font. The system font is used for all the text entities in Windows if there is no other font.

MS Sans Serif fonts

MS Sans Serif is the default font for all Windows 95 screen text entities. Depending on your resolution, either 8 or 10 points is used. The MS Sans Serif font files, Sserife.fon, and Sseriff.fon, each contain six fonts in 8, 10, 12, 14, 18, and 24 points, as shown in Figure 20-16. Larger MS Sans Serif fonts will be constructed automatically by the Windows 95 screen font rasterizer if you choose to display bigger screen fonts. They will look a bit crude, though.

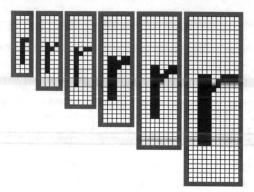

Figure 20-16: MS Sans Serif in six sizes — 8, 10, 12, 14, 18, and 24 points — from the Sserife.fon file.

This font is Microsoft's replacement for its earlier Helv font, as you can see from the font substitution table in the Win.ini file in your Windows folder.

Unlike the System font, which it also pretty much replaces, MS Sans Serif comes in regular and italic in addition to bold and bold italic. This broader range of weights accounts for its appeal as a Windows 95 standard font for menu items, icon titles, and so on. For example, a MS Sans Serif 10-point bold does well as the window title text. MS Sans Serif 10-point regular does better for menu items (purely a personal opinion).

MS Sans Serif is, of course, a sans serif font. Sans serif fonts have less elaboration in their design then serif fonts. A capital T, for example, doesn't have little vertical lines at the end of the horizontal line in a sans serif font.

The System font is a sans serif font and so is the Fixedsys font. These fonts do well expressing text entities on the screen. Serif fonts are better used for the body of text documents.

MS Serif fonts

Like MS Sans Serif, this replacement for the earlier Tms Rmn font comes in six font sizes: 8, 10, 12, 14, 18, and 24 points. If you like serifs, then this is the font for you. Check out the MS Sans Serif font in Figure 20-17.

Figure 20-17: MS Serif in 8, 10, 12, 14, 18, 24 points. Like the previous figure, these are taken from the small fonts set.

Small fonts

These are indeed small fonts — in 2, 3, 4, 5, 6, 7 points. The small font set and large font set each have a file that contains Small Fonts — smalle.fon and smallf.fon.

It is not easy to construct a good-looking and meaningful font when the grid size you have to work with is 2 dots wide and 3 dots high, which it is for some of the wider characters in the 2-point font in the large small font file, smallf.fon. The larger point sizes of the Small Fonts can actually display some useful information. The 7-point size is the smallest that can be clearly read on most popular monitor/adapter combinations. This makes it a reasonable choice for icon titles and the like when space is at a premium.

Small fonts are used to display TrueType text if it gets too small to be seen legibly and to display greeked text in the print preview dialog box. Small fonts are shown in Figure 20-18.

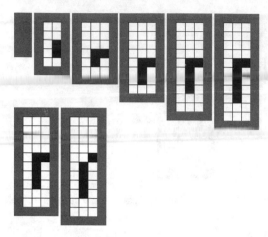

Figure 20-18: Small fonts in 2, 3, 4, 5, 6, and 7 points, including two sans serif fonts in sizes 6 and 7 point. These are taken from the Smalle.fon file.

Secret

The small font file Smalle.fon also contains two San Serif fonts, one 6 points and one 7 points.

Symbol font

The character set used for the Symbol font has nothing in common with the Windows ANSI or OEM character sets. The Symbol font files contain characters at the same point sizes as the MS Sans Serif and MS Serif. Use the Character Map application to display the Symbol character set.

TrueType Fonts

What very much helped make Windows 3.1 a successful product was the addition of TrueType — typeface outlines that Windows smoothly scales to any size on any Windows-supported monitor and printer.

This capability meant that Windows could use the same typefaces to display a document that it used to print the document. It no longer mattered whether a Windows user's printer contained the same typeface as the font used to display the text of a document on the desktop. Windows prints its TrueType faces to any printer with the ability to print graphics or download fonts.

TrueType is integrated into Windows 95. When you send a document to another person or company and you use one of five TrueType typeface families included with Windows 95 — Times New Roman, Arial, Courier New, Symbol, and Wingdings — the recipients of your document can view it on their monitors and print it on their printers exactly the way you saw it on your monitor and printer.

Microsoft Plus! comes with additional TrueType fonts files, including Book Antigua, Comic Sans, Lucida Console, Lucida Sans Unicode, News Gothic MT, and OCR-A.

If you install Windows 95 multiple language support (either during initial setup or later using the Add/Remove Programs Control Panel), the 652 character versions of Arial, Courier New, and Times Roman are installed.

Freedom from screen fonts and printer fonts

Before TrueType, Windows required that a set of specific fonts be built for every point size that you might require on your printer. These printer fonts required several megabytes of disk space for a complete set, especially when larger sizes were desired. Furthermore, to display these printer fonts on screen required building of a separate set of screen fonts in a different format.

TrueType almost completely eliminated this confusion. If you don't like the typefaces included with Windows 95, you can buy TrueType fonts from a variety of vendors. Once you install these fonts, all sizes of that typeface are immediately supported by all applications, displays, and printers.

The TrueType fonts that come with Windows 95

As shown in Table 20-3, Windows 95 ships with six TrueType font families: Arial, a Helvetica sans serif font; Times New Roman, a Times Roman serif font; Courier New, a fixed-pitch font to replace the Courier screen font; Symbols, a replacement of the Symbols screen font; Wingdings, which use dingbats as characters, and Marlett, a TrueType font used to create desktop "furniture."

Table 20-3	Windows 95 TrueType Families
Typeface	*Font Filename*
Fixed space fonts	
Courier New	Cour.ttf
	Courbd.ttf
	Couri.ttf
	Courbi.ttf
Proportionally spaced fonts	
Arial	Arial.ttf
	Arialbd.ttf
	Ariali.ttf
	Arialbi.ttf *(continued)*

Table 20-3 *(continued)*

Proportionally spaced fonts	
Times New Roman	Times.ttf
	Timesbd.ttf
	Timesi.ttf
	Timesbi.ttf
Non text fonts	
Marlett	Marlet.ttf
Symbol	Symbol.ttf
Wingdings	Wingding.ttf

When TrueType fonts are installed (or when Windows 95 is first installed) references to them are placed in the Registry. The Registry entries for the installed TrueType fonts looks like this:

```
[HKEY_LOCAL_MACHINE\SOFTWARE\Microsoft\Windows\CurrentVersion\Fonts]
"Arial (TrueType)"="ARIAL.TTF"
"Arial Bold (TrueType)"="ARIALBD.TTF"
"Arial Bold Italic (TrueType)"="ARIALBI.TTF"
"Arial Italic (TrueType)"="ARIALI.TTF"
"Courier New (TrueType)"="COUR.TTF"
"Courier New Bold (TrueType)"="COURBD.TTF"
"Courier New Bold Italic (TrueType)"="COURBI.TTF"
"Courier New Italic (TrueType)"="COURI.TTF"
"Times New Roman (TrueType)"="TIMES.TTF"
"Times New Roman Bold (TrueType)"="TIMESBD.TTF"
"Times New Roman Bold Italic (TrueType)"="TIMESBI.TTF"
"Times New Roman Italic (TrueType)"="TIMESI.TTF"
"Wingdings (TrueType)"="WINGDING.TTF"
"Symbol (TrueType)"="SYMBOL.TTF"
"Modern (Plotter)"="MODERN.FON"
"MS-DOS CP 437"="DOSAPP.FON"
"Fixedsys for the IBM 8514"="8514FIX.FON"
"Terminal Font for the IBM 8514"="8514OEM.FON"
"System (Set #6)"="8514SYS.FON"
"Courier 10,12,15 (8514/a res)"="COURF.FON"
"MS Serif 8,10,12,14,18,24 (8514 res)"="SERIFF.FON"
"Small Fonts (8514/a res)"="SMALLF.FON"
"MS Sans Serif 8,10,12,14,18,24 (8514 res)"="SSERIFF.FON"
"Symbol 8,10,12,14,18,24 (8514/a RES)"="SYMBOLF.FON"
"Fixedsys (Set #6)"="VGAFIX.FON"
"Terminal (US) (Set #6)"="VGAOEM.FON"
"Marlett (TrueType)"="MARLETT.TTF"
```

Secret

A helpful reader (Hellmut Golde, Professor Emeritus, Department of Computer Science and Engineering at the University of Washington) points out that you can edit the Registry (at the preceding location) and place your fonts where you want. For example

```
"Arial (TrueType)"="F:\Fonts\ARIAL.TTF"
```

This creates a shortcut in the \Windows\Fonts folder to the Arial font in the Fonts folder on drive F, which you can easily see when you open the \Windows\Fonts folder. Of course, it is easier just to move all the fonts to a convenient folder and then install them in the \Windows\Fonts folder without moving them. The steps are detailed in the previous Installing Fonts section of this chapter.

Tip

TrueType fonts are stored as font descriptions in files with the file extension *ttf*. Previous versions of Windows required an accompanying file with the same filename as the TrueType font file, but with a different extension — *fot*. The *fot* files merely provided Windows with the location of the *ttf* file. These files are no longer needed and can be erased from your hard disk.

Unlike screen font files, the font descriptions are not patterns of dots on a grid, but consist of a font outline and rules (hints) for rendering the font. The description is used by one of the TrueType font rasterizers in Windows to render the fonts as a pattern on dots (pixels on the screen, ink dots on the paper). Compare the results of the TrueType font rasterization with the previous figures that display the dot patterns for screen fonts.

We have constructed pseudo-grid patterns for the TrueType fonts based on the closest screen font. For Arial we used the grid from MS Sans Serif, for Times New Roman, the grid from MS Serif, and for Courier New, the Courier screen font grid. We had to widen only the middle grid for Times New Roman by one pixel — this is for the 14-point font.

Using these grids taken from bitmapped screen fonts allows you to more closely compare the quality of hand-tuned screen fonts and those generated by the TrueType rasterizers. You might review the following three TrueType font renderings in Figures 20-19, 20-20 and 20-21 and compare them with their corresponding screen fonts in Figures 20-16, 20-17, and 20-14.

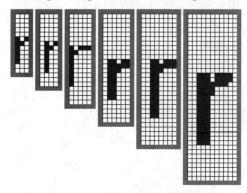

Figure 20-19: The lower case *r* in Arial at 8, 10, 12, 14, 18, and 24 points. Compare these r's with those MS Sans Serif r's in Figure 20-16.

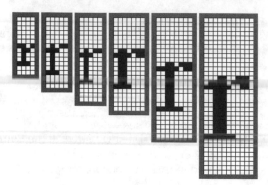

Figure 20-20: The lowercase *r* in Times New Roman at 8, 10, 12, 14, 18, and 24 points. Compare these r's with those MS Serif r's in Figure 20-17.

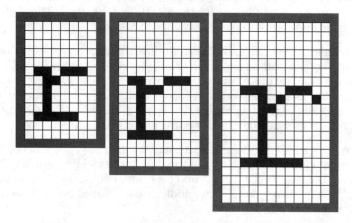

Figure 20-21: The lowercase *r* in Courier New Roman at 10, 12, and 15 points. Compare these r's with those Courier r's in Figure 20-14.

Microsoft sells other TrueType fonts — in particular, Font Packs 1 and 2. More information on some of the unusual characters sets available in those font packs is given Chapter 21.

Marlett

The Marlett font provides some of the "furniture" for the Windows 95 desktop. You don't want to delete this font. The minimize, maximize, and close button on the right end of any Windows caption area are constructed using this font.

The emergence of the Metafile format

For many years, one of the nice features of the Macintosh environment compared to Windows has been support for Encapsulated PostScript (EPS) graphics files. These files can contain line drawings, photographs, and text — almost any graphical material. When printed to a PostScript printer, an EPS file (which is a vector graphics format that can also contain bitmapped information) can be scaled to any size without becoming jagged, as opposed to the more limited *bmp* graphics files (which is a raster or pixel-based graphics file format).

Windows, in fact, has long supported its own scalable graphics format — Windows Metafile, or WMF.

By specifying type in a Metafile as, say, Times New Roman, anyone with Windows can print a file that includes text at any size to any device supported by Windows. A recipient of these documents could revise the text and save it as files that would print to any printer. Unlike EPS files, Windows Metafiles do not require a PostScript device.

Send your favorite typeface

TrueType gives you the ability to send TrueType faces to anyone, including typesetting service bureaus, without violating the copyright of the owner of the typeface. This is made possible by a TrueType feature called *font embedding* — you simply include the typefaces required by the document in an encoded form within the document itself.

Font embedding is a response to a serious problem within the PostScript service industry. A PostScript typesetter, such as a Linotronic 300, will not print a PostScript job unless the typesetter contains *exactly* the same typefaces that were used in the preparation of a document. If a document calls for a typeface with a name unknown to the device, it will often substitute a Courier font or not print at all. In either case, expensive service bureau time is wasted.

Many PostScript users, therefore, copy their special PostScript typefaces — Helvetica Black for headlines, say — onto a disk and send them along with their print job to the service bureau. This is a copyright violation (which is widely ignored), wastes service bureau time in downloading the fonts, and doesn't always work.

TrueType solves this problem by allowing typefaces to be embedded into a document in an encrypted form. This encryption, which is easily supported by any application, prevents the recipient of a document from removing the typeface file and using it without paying for it. But the document can be viewed on any monitor and printed to any device supported by Windows — complete with the exact fonts used by the document's originator.

Microsoft has built three levels of usability into TrueType font embedding.

- In the first, most restrictive level, a vendor of TrueType faces may choose *not* to allow them to be embedded into documents for transmission. In this case, applications that support font embedding simply refrain from embedding those typefaces. The recipient of the document must purchase the required typefaces or substitute a generic typeface like Times or Helvetica.

- At the second level, a TrueType vendor may choose to allow *read-only embedding*. A document embedded with read-only typefaces may be viewed and printed, but not edited. (If the document could be edited, the original contents could be deleted and the file used over and over again to produce other documents, with no payment to the owner of the typeface.) This kind of document could be edited if the embedded typefaces were deleted first. Read-only embedding will probably become the standard for commercial vendors of TrueType faces.

- The third and most useful level of font embedding is *read-write embedding*. When read-write TrueType faces are embedded in a document, that document can be freely edited and saved by the recipient, as well as viewed and printed. Furthermore, applications are expected to give the user of such a document the option of permanently installing the embedded typefaces into Windows so other applications and documents can also use the faces. This type of embedding is most appropriate for free and public-domain TrueType faces likely to become widely available.

All of the TrueType faces included in Windows 95 are read-write enabled. This allows you to embed these faces into documents you send to people who, for whatever reason, have Windows but deleted the TrueType faces from their system.

More significantly, Microsoft has made an arrangement with Bigelow & Holmes, a scalable type vendor in Menlo Park, California, to circulate 22 additional TrueType faces — all of which are read-write enabled. When you embed any of these faces into a document and send out a copy of the file, the recipient of that document can not only read, print, and edit your document, but can also permanently install the typefaces on his or her own Windows system. These faces then can be used by the recipient to create other documents. Since these Bigelow & Holmes faces are licensed to allow this kind of read-write capability, you are not violating the copyright on these typefaces by sending them to your friends and associates in this way — as you would be if you sent copies of, say, Adobe Type 1 typefaces.

The 22 typefaces in this set are called the Lucida family (pronounced LOOSE-id-dah). This name derives from the fact that these typefaces are designed to be easy to read, and therefore lucid, on low-resolution devices like computer monitors and low-end printers. A few of the Lucida faces, for example, are sturdy serif and sans serif designs that reproduce well when sent to fax machines. Other faces provide a variety of symbols, such as mathematics and engineering characters. The Lucida typeface set is available for well under $100 from most major computer software dealers.

PostScript vendors have developed kinds of universal, interchangeable typefaces that solve the problem of recipients of PostScript documents who do not own the typefaces needed to print those documents. In particular, Adobe Systems, the inventor of the PostScript language, has created Multiple Master typefaces, which can stretch to emulate many serif and sans serif typefaces. But these typefaces do not serve the same purpose as typefaces that can be directly embedded into documents, like TrueType.

PostScript

The best-known type scaling program for Windows is probably Adobe Type Manager (ATM). After you install ATM, you have 13 scalable outlines on your hard disk: Times, Helvetica, and Courier (in four weights: roman, italic, bold, and bold italic), and Symbol (in a single weight). Purchasing the Adobe Plus Pack gives you the additional 22 typefaces normally found in PostScript printers: Avant Garde, Bookman, Century, Helvetica Compressed (useful for spreadsheets), Palatino, Zapf Chancery, and Zapf Dingbats.

One of the advantages of ATM is that you can configure it to scale type on the screen at a certain point size and above. This is useful because of the horrible truth about VGA — a VGA screen simply doesn't have enough pixels to accurately represent the shape of letters below 15 points in size.

Below that size, the hand-tuned screen fonts look better than fonts scaled on the fly by a type scaler. The TrueType scaler quits drawing fonts on the screen below 6 points (smaller sizes are represented by the Small Fonts screen font).

For a comparison of the look of fully-formed characters, and the on-screen representation of these characters created by Windows screen fonts, TrueType, and ATM, see Figure 20-22.

One of the disadvantages of ATM is that it scales only typeface outlines that are in Adobe's own Type 1 format. While this is a popular standard, it is by no means the only format in which scalable typefaces are sold.

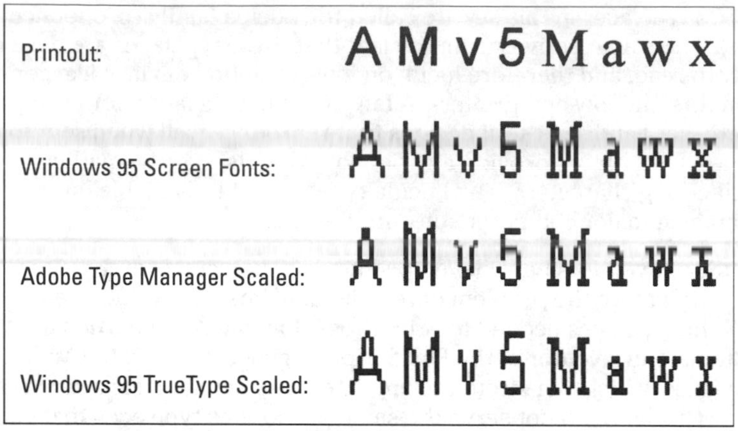

Printout:	A M v 5 M a w x
Windows 95 Screen Fonts:	A M v 5 M a w x
Adobe Type Manager Scaled:	A M v 5 M a w x
Windows 95 TrueType Scaled:	A M v 5 M a w x

Figure 20-22: The differences between the look of typefaces when printed and the look of the same typefaces on a Windows screen. The first line is printed on an HP LaserJet. The second line shows the 10-point screen font (MS Serif and MS Sans Serif) The third and fourth lines show the same 10-point type scaled for a VGA screen by Adobe Type Manager and the TrueType rasterizer built into Windows 95, respectively. (Each font has been enlarged to show detail.) At this size, none of the screen fonts has enough pixels to show anything like the true shape of the characters. But the hand-tuned screen fonts are easier to read and closer to the desired shape of these characters than those scaled by ATM and TrueType.

Differences between PostScript and TrueType Faces

The pros and cons of TrueType versus PostScript Type 1 outlines have been debated since the Apple/Microsoft announcement of TrueType at the Seybold Desktop Publishing Conference in 1990. It is impossible to declare a simple winner and loser, as long as such die-hard advocates for each technology as Microsoft and Adobe Systems still support their divergent paths. But a few generalizations can be made.

TrueType is included in Windows; PostScript isn't

The most obvious statement, but perhaps the most influential over time, is that TrueType faces are built into Windows and PostScript faces are not.

Furthermore, Microsoft cites industry studies that show that only 2-3 percent of Windows users in the U.S. have a PostScript printer, while the overwhelming majority have some kind of LaserJet-compatible printer.

Windows users can easily add ATM or another third-party type scaler that works with Type 1 outline faces. Adobe encourages this even more by bundling ATM essentially for free with such Windows applications as Lotus Ami Pro and 1-2-3 for Windows, Adobe PageMaker and Persuasion, Ventura Publisher, Micrografx Designer, and many others.

But many more Windows users employ the TrueType faces that are built into Windows than add separate scaler programs.

PostScript is built into typesetters; TrueType isn't

Almost all high-end typesetting is conducted with computerized imagesetters programmed with built-in PostScript interpreters. Most serious graphic arts professionals (especially publication designers) use Macintoshes instead of Windows and almost all of them prefer PostScript over TrueType because of its dominance in high-end typesetters.

Tip

On the other hand, it is easily possible to send output containing TrueType fonts (either directly or in the form of a PostScript print file) to a PostScript device. Windows automatically converts TrueType fonts into the exact same fonts in Type 1 format either when creating a print file or before the fonts are sent directly to the printing device. But there appears to be no compelling reason for professional designers to switch from PostScript to TrueType (or from a Macintosh to Windows) since their existing technology is working well.

TrueType fonts are less costly; some are cheap

The battle continues over which fonts have the highest quality, but TrueType fonts have won the war regarding price. Many TrueType fonts are available at a dollar a font and less. You can try out shareware TrueType fonts before you buy. TrueType font packs are sold by Microsoft, Monotype, and many others.

FontChameleon from Ares Software offers the ability to build an almost unlimited number of TrueType fonts in a package that lists at $295. You'll find details about FontChameleon later in this chapter.

TrueType hints are in the font; PostScript's (mostly) aren't

Hints are instructions in a computer program that make scalable type look better on displays and laser printers.

These hints are necessary because computer monitors and printers don't have enough dots to truly follow the shape of most typefaces at smaller sizes. The hinting instructions reshape the letterforms so they don't have odd pixels sticking out where curves would normally appear, or have pixels missing where fine strokes in a character would normally be less than one pixel thick.

TrueType and PostScript faces provide hinting instructions in very different ways. But in both cases, hints are most useful with 18-point type and smaller on a computer display such as a VGA monitor, and 12-point type and smaller on a 300-dpi laser printer. Hints aren't necessary, no matter what size the type is, on 600-dpi printers (which includes high-end laser printers), nor are they necessary on imagesetters, which typically feature resolutions of 1270 or 2540 dpi.

The essential difference between TrueType and PostScript typefaces is where the hinting instructions are placed. TrueType hints are actually part of the typeface file itself. The program that scales TrueType for the screen and printer has little hinting information of its own, but reads what is contained in each typeface file.

PostScript faces, by contrast, contain little hinting information. The rasterizer program for PostScript faces, such as ATM, is smart enough to use that limited information to figure out exactly how each character should be reshaped to retain a legible design in small screen or printer sizes.

The upshot of this difference is that PostScript typefaces, once perfected, seldom need to change. If better hinting methods are discovered or changes need to be made in order to accommodate new kinds of output devices, these changes can be made to the PostScript rasterizer program in an update. The typeface files themselves should be unaffected.

The inclusion of hinting instructions in the typeface file itself is a boon to typeface vendors, who can compete with each other for sales on the basis of arguments that they have the best-hinted faces available. This also means that type buyers must become aware of the subtle differences between typefaces from competing vendors (all type is definitely not the same).

TrueType and Type 1 differ on device independence

Device independence means that a printed document looks the same whether it is printed on a 300-dpi laser printer, a 2540-dpi typesetter, or any other resolution device. *Looking the same* means that each printout of the document should have the same number of lines and the same number of pages, regardless of the resolution of the printer. The most important factor that allows a document to print out exactly the same way on printers of different resolutions is that the spacing of each individual character is the same at all resolutions.

Device independence has always been a selling point for PostScript typefaces and printers. But PostScript is by no means perfect in this regard. Any experienced typesetting service bureau can tell you horror stories about print jobs that came out perfectly when printed to a PostScript laser printer but were several lines longer or shorter when printed on an imagesetter (ruining the carefully formatted job).

Microsoft states that this happens because PostScript Type 1 characters suffer from rounding errors. Each character in a PostScript typeface counts as a certain width on a line. A character at a small size, such as 10 points, might be 7.5 pixels wide on a computer monitor. But because it is impossible for an application to give a character half a pixel, this character spacing is rounded up, giving the character a whole 8 pixels.

Over the length of a line, these rounding errors add up. When the document is printed on a PostScript printer of a different resolution, this character spacing rounds differently, which can result in different line breaks and a different layout for the whole job.

Some applications, such as Adobe PageMaker, compensate for these rounding errors by allowing the user to specify that the spacing of characters should be performed using the resolution of the ultimate printing device, no matter what the current printer is. But most applications do not include these fine adjustments and this can result in a different appearance for documents printed on two different PostScript devices.

TrueType attempts to handle these rounding errors by giving applications more information about each character. An application that supports TrueType can add up all the fractional pixel widths of each character on a line. The application then must round off only the pixel count at the end of each line, not the pixel count for each character. This theoretically results in TrueType documents with a rounding error of only one pixel per line, instead of many.

Even this is enough to throw off the word wrap of a line — a difference of a single pixel can mean that a word like *a* or *I* will fit at the end of one line instead of wrapping to the beginning of the next line. But the improved spacing information in TrueType faces may lead to an improved portability of documents across all types of printers.

Printing with TrueType and PostScript fonts

Tip

Turn to Chapter 23 to see a further discussion of the interaction between these scalable fonts and your printer. In particular, we discuss in detail LaserJet- and PostScript-compatible printers.

How Hinting Affects the Look of Your Work

Hinting is such an important component of computer typefaces that it's worth knowing how hinting technology can change what you get when you display or print text.

Hinting affects the process of converting a typeface into a type font. All scalable, outline typefaces start out as a perfect, ideal shape for a set of characters. Since monitors and printers can handle only squarish pixels, not ideal shapes, these outlines must be converted into bitmaps of the correct size and shape. The ideal outline of a set of characters is called a typeface. When a typeface has been scaled to a particular size, the resulting pattern is called a font. The program that converts the typeface shapes into recognizable bitmaps is called a rasterizer because most printers are raster (bitmap) devices rather than vector-drawing devices, such as plotters.

If the pixels in a monitor or a printer were infinitely small, typeface hints would not be necessary. All type fonts would appear perfect.

In fact, this is exactly what happens on high-end typesetters; 1270-dpi imagesetters and 600-dpi laser printers have enough resolution to print any font and do not need hints.

But this is not the case with most laser printers and monitors. Below 13 points on a 300-dpi laser printer, and 19 points on a 96-dpi VGA screen, a typeface outline can fall in place on the grid of pixels in such a way so that not every letter will look the way you would expect it to look.

Take as an example the capital letter *H* in a sans serif typeface, as shown in Figure 20-23. The letter *H* has only three lines: two vertical lines, called stems, and a horizontal line, called the crossbar. To display these lines on a monitor, the shape of the *H* must turn on a certain pattern of pixels.

In Figure 20-23, the capital *H* is shown superimposed over a grid of pixels on the face of a monitor. A typeface rasterizer program will normally turn on a pixel (make it black) if the center of the pixel falls inside the outline of a letter. But in the case of Figure 20-23, the letter *H* does not fall neatly on the grid. If you turn pixels on using a mechanical system that considers only the center point of each pixel, you get the result shown in Figure 20-24. The right stem of the letter is twice as thick as the left because the outline falls over two center points on the right-hand side. Meanwhile, the crossbar disappears from the image because it does not enclose the center of any pixels. Almost no one would find this bitmap recognizable as the letter *H*.

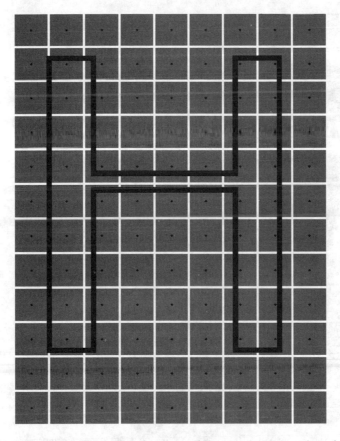

Figure 20-23: The outline of a sans serif *H* covers the center points of several pixels on the face of a computer monitor.

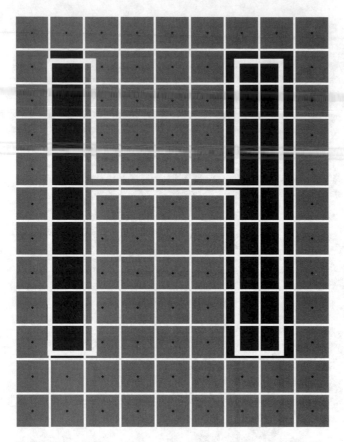

Figure 20-24: Without hinting, only pixels inside the original outline would be turned on, creating a stem on the right that is two pixels wide instead of one pixel, and a crossbar that doesn't show up at all.

Hints in the typeface help to correct this problem. The rasterizer, reading the hinting instructions, detects that both stems are supposed to be equal in width, and therefore one stem cannot be two pixels wide while the other is only a single pixel wide. The rasterizer also detects that the crossbar is an essential element of the outline, which cannot be allowed to earn less than one pixel.

Therefore, the rasterizer effectively moves the outline of the character so it is better aligned with the bitmap grid. The result is shown in Figure 20-25. Both stems now turn on only one pixel, and the crossbar turns on one pixel also. This is much more recognizable as the letter *H*. The shape of the letter has been slightly distorted to get this result — the crossbar is no longer at the height it was originally, for example — but at the low resolution of this particular monitor, there was no choice if the character was to be readable at all.

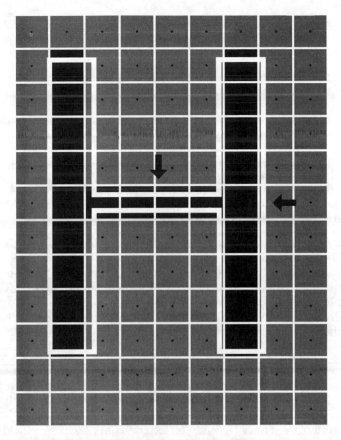

Figure 20-25: With hinting, the font rasterizer knows how to "move" the outline so the strokes are better aligned with the pixel grid; this turns on exactly one pixel for each of the three strokes in the letter.

Secrets of Arial and Times New Roman

Other differences between the TrueType faces that come with Windows and their PostScript counterparts are worth knowing. It is commonly believed that the Times New Roman and Arial typefaces included in Windows are exactly equivalent to the Times and Helvetica included in PostScript printers, but this is not the case.

The Times and Helvetica typefaces resident in the original PostScript printers were licensed by Adobe Systems from their creator, the Linotype Corp. Times and Helvetica are registered trademarks of Linotype and cannot be used to describe type products from other vendors without paying royalties to Linotype. This is why many other type vendors use substitute names.

Bitstream, for example, uses Dutch and Swiss as the names for its outline designs, while Microsoft used the abbreviations Tms Rmn and Helv in Windows 3.0 and earlier.

When the TrueType faces were being prepared for Windows 3.1, Microsoft licensed typeface outlines and the corresponding trademarked names from the Monotype Corp., a competitor of Linotype. Times New Roman is derived from the original typeface developed for the Times of London is the early 1900s. Arial is a sans serif typeface designed to be similar to Helvetica. These names are different enough from Linotype's trademarks to avoid legal problems. Since PostScript printers cannot print typefaces with the same names as the ones built into the printers, these different names also help avoid printer problems.

But how identical to Times and Helvetica are these TrueType faces? As you can see in Figure 20-26 they are not actually identical at all.

The first line in Figure 20-26 is the PostScript Helvetica provided by Adobe Systems. The second line is the TrueType Arial included in Windows 95. Many characters differ only slightly between the two typefaces, but they do differ. The uppercase *G* has a downward spur in Helvetica, but not in Arial. The uppercase *R* has a vertical leg in Helvetica, while the leg in Arial is diagonal. The finishing strokes of the lowercase *a* and numeral *1* differ between faces, and the % sign is made up of perfect circles in one but ovals in the other.

Differences between Adobe Times, on the third line of Figure 20-26, and TrueType Times New Roman, on the fourth line, are more subtle but still present. The loops of the uppercase *B* droop slightly more and are wider in Times New Roman than in Times. Times New Roman's *M* and *N* are slightly broader, and the tips meet when normally spaced, as in the word *HYMN*. The upper-left serif of the Times New Roman letter *N* is not the same thickness as the upper-right serif of the M, as they are in Adobe Times. The lower stroke of the letter *e* flares outward much more in Times than in Times New Roman and the % signs in both typefaces are completely different.

No one is going to reject one of your memos or proposals because it is format-ted in Arial rather than Helvetica, of course. Based on the differences in design, many people would find the TrueType versions of these typefaces more graceful than the Adobe versions.

Tip

It's simply important to recognize that TrueType faces are *not* the same as PostScript faces. They may act differently, they may space differently, and they may appear differently. There are certainly many reasons to use TrueType faces. But you shouldn't assume that typefaces based on different technologies can be interchanged at will. You can mix them and match them, but be aware that a difference as small as a single pixel can sometimes mean that a block of type will fit on a single line or that it will *not*.

Figure 20-26: Adobe Helvetica (top line) and TrueType Arial (second line) exhibit differences in the shape of their letters. The "tail" of the *G, R, a,* and numeral *1* differ, as do the circular parts of the percent sign. Adobe Times Roman (third line) and TrueType Times New Roman (fourth line) show subtle differences, too, as in the droop of the TrueType *B,* the serifs of the TrueType *MN* characters, and the upstroke of the *e* character.

Font Monger — Making Your Own Faces

Windows' TrueType rasterizer works only on TrueType faces, not Adobe Type 1 faces or other font files you may have purchased from other sources. TrueType, of course, will work alongside ATM, SuperPrint, and other third-party type scalers. You simply install one of these third-party packages and let it scale the typeface outlines it knows how to scale.

ATM, for example, can scale a typeface outline called Helvetica, because that typeface comes with ATM and is in a Type 1 file format that ATM can handle. If you request the typeface Arial, however, the built-in TrueType rasterizer takes over and builds the font for you. This works even when you mix different typeface formats in the same document.

But you might find it most convenient for all of your typeface files to share a single format. By converting them all to TrueType — or to Type 1 or whatever — you could turn off all your type scalers and use only one, consuming a little less memory.

Fortunately, someone has come up with a solution just for this problem. Ares Software is the creator of Font Monger, a conversion utility for outline typeface files.

Font Monger exists in versions for the Apple Macintosh as well as PCs with Windows. The Apple version converts typefaces from Adobe's hinted Type 1 format to hinted TrueType format, or the reverse.

Font Monger for Windows converts additional typeface formats, since the PC world has more alternative formats than are found in the Mac environment. In addition to converting Type 1, Type 3, and TrueType formats, Font Monger for Windows also converts HP's Intellifont and URW's Nimbus formats. All conversions can be performed in any direction, from any format to any other.

This utility not only allows you to convert your existing typeface library to work with Windows, it also lets you use one of the formats to produce type that runs under drawing applications like CorelDraw! and font-manipulation utilities like ZSoft's SoftType. Additionally, typeface outlines produced by Font Monger can be used in graphical environments other than Windows, such as GeoWorks Ensemble, NeXT, and the PenPoint tablet-oriented operating system.

Finally, you can add your own company logo, fractions, or other symbols into any typeface, making these characters available from your keyboard. Font Monger can convert selected characters or whole typefaces into EPS files, Windows Metafiles, or Adobe Illustrator files. These files can then be edited or redrawn, and inserted back into a typeface.

For more information, contact Ares Software at 561 Pilgrim Dr., Suite D, Foster City, CA 94404, 415-578-9090.

FontChameleon — One File, Many Fonts

Ares' latest product, FontChameleon, isn't a font utility, but an actual synthetic master font. The difference between FontChameleon and ordinary font files, however, is spectacular. Ares Software has found a way to pack almost every text typeface you can think of into a single file. This means that you can install typefaces like Avant Garde Gothic and Bookman *on demand*.

Even better, you can modify typefaces, or combine two different faces into an original creation of your own design. Much like the morphing effect you see in special-effects movies, you'll be able to tell FontChameleon to give you a typeface that's "80 percent Avant Garde and 20 percent Bookman." You can watch the effect change as you tweak the settings.

When Adobe Systems had a monopoly on the PostScript language, it priced individual PostScript font families higher than some major applications.

Then Microsoft created a price war by offering the 44 faces in its TrueType Font Pack below $50 (with the Windows 3.1 upgrade). In response, other TrueType vendors began selling their faces as libraries, rather than individually. Now, Ares may shift type sales toward single, low-cost files from which you can create as many typefaces as you like.

Ares has figured out the essential characteristics of all text typefaces. All type designs start with the outline of a basic alphabet, then dress it up with serifs and so on. But far from merely copying the outlines of other type vendors, Ares has generated its own master outline, and manipulates it endlessly, a kind of parametric technology.

It shoots a big hole in Adobe's Multiple Master type technology. Multiple Masters allow a magazine designer to distort one or two typefaces into enough shapes to fill a whole publication. But only 14 Multiple Master families are currently available and they're expensive. When a designer has 4 *billion* faces to choose from, that's a selection.

As a product, FontChameleon can generate more than 200 fonts and resides on two diskettes. The program takes only 2MB of disk space but allows you to generate an almost unlimited assortment of TrueType and PostScript Type 1 fonts.

FontChameleon takes advantage of the fact that almost all typefaces in Western languages share the same basic skeleton. Ares has spent years creating small "descriptor" files (about 3K in size) that capture the details that make, say, Times Roman different from Arial.

The FontChameleon package lists for $295 and is available at discounted prices through software stores and most direct-mail vendors.

Among the 200 fonts generated by FontChameleon are Ares faces similar to Avant Garde, Bodoni, Bembo, Century, Cheltenham, Franklin Gothic, Frutiger, Futura, Galliard, Garamond, Gill Sans, Kabel, Melior, Palatino, Serif Gothic, Serifa, Trump Mediaeval, and Univers.

But beyond these classic typefaces, FontChameleon offers a powerful capability to anyone who's ever wanted a face that was exactly the right width, height, and weight. You can adjust any of these font characteristics with sliders in FontChameleon's main window. And you can actually morph two typefaces to create a totally new font to your liking.

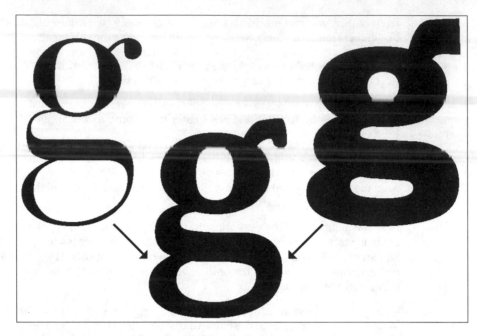

Figure 20-27: Bodoni can be "morphed" with Franklin Gothic Heavy to create a new font with its own interesting characteristics.

For an example of morphing, see Figure 20-27. In the hands of a skilled desktop publisher, many specialized faces can be created.

Parametric technology will undoubtedly trickle down into desktop applications. You'll be able to tell your word processor to generate a font that's, say, two percent smaller, so your newsletter will fit into 16 pages instead of 16 1/2. And electronic publishers will distribute magazines-on-a-disk, with Chameleon providing the fonts. And imagine a laser printer with over four billion possible faces built in.

How's the output quality? Surprisingly good. FontChameleon is tuned for best output on high-resolution printers but also looks good on laser printers.

The latest version of FontChameleon includes descriptors that define some true serif italics in the main package. The shape of italic letters is quite different than normal letters. Additional packages of about 80 descriptors are expected to list for about $89.

In some faces, FontChameleon's output may not give you the same smooth quality at small sizes on a laser printer that you would get from hand-tuned font packs. If you just want one or two type families to replace dull old Times Roman, get the Bitstream TrueType Font Pack or the Agfa Discovery TrueType Pack.

But if you want the ultimate in a customizable type library, you have only two choices — FontChameleon and Font Works.

Font Works — Create Fonts Found in Documents

The font wars have moved to a new intensity. Another product promises to end font headaches for Windows users by supplying — on the fly — virtually any font required by any document. This product, from ElseWare Corporation of Seattle, Washington, is called Font Works.

Although FontChameleon and Font Works appear to be similar technologies at first glance, they are based on very different philosophies. FontChameleon, for example, allows you to easily modify the look of its fonts. You simply move a slider bar with your mouse to make a font condensed or expanded, lighter or darker, and so on. You can also create interesting new fonts by morphing a serif typeface with a sans serif typeface, as discussed in the preceding section.

Font Works is based on a "synthetic" font technology that can also, in theory, modify and blend font outlines. But these features are not present in the shrink-wrapped version (list $130).

You might think this would be a weakness, but ElseWare considers it a strength. The company's interviews with MIS directors revealed a major problem in corporations: documents created on one machine would not display or print properly on other machines. The cause was that the intended fonts were not present on the target PC or printer. The MIS people did not want the ability to create more fonts — they wanted to make sure that every document would look as it was supposed to, no matter what fonts were used originally.

This is what Font Works specializes in. When you install Font Works, its 150 included typefaces take up about 2MB of hard disk space. The program also changes the Fonts.fon line in System.ini so it loads Fontwork.fon, a 19K file that remains in memory. Font Works then transparently builds any font required by any document if your system does not have that font installed.

We tested this with the typeface families Garth Graphic, from the Agfa Discovery TrueType Pack, and Lucida Sans, from the Microsoft TrueType Font Pack 1. After creating documents using variations of these faces, we deleted the fonts from the system. Normally, Windows would substitute Times New Roman or worse the next time we opened these documents. But with Font Works running, Windows had no trouble displaying and printing ElseWare's own Wilmington and Teras Sans faces. These fonts are width-matched to the originals, so a document prints with the same line and page breaks. ElseWare says Font Works supports 2,000 third-party fonts by name.

Beyond its database of font names, Font Works is built on a sophisticated font-matching scheme called Panose. Panose is the name of the company that created the font-matching scheme. The Panose numbering system — adopted by Microsoft, Agfa, Bitstream, and other type vendors — is what TrueType fonts use to identify their weight and other characteristics. Applications that support Panose (the list includes Adobe PageMaker 6 and Lotus WordPro) can substitute fonts with much greater accuracy than just using Times Roman.

The font quality is pretty good for office laser printer work.

FontChameleon will appeal to users who want the ultimate in type selection. Font Works is more likely to find a niche in future printer/display systems designed to handle anything you throw at them.

For information on Font Works, contact ElseWare Corp., 101 Stewart St., Suite 700, Seattle, WA 98101; 206-448-9600.

Summary

- ▶ We show you how to use the font installer that is built into Windows 95 to view both installed and uninstalled fonts, as well as to install and uninstall them.
- ▶ We examine the construction of both bitmapped and TrueType fonts and look closely at each of the fonts that comes with Windows 95.
- ▶ We detail the differences between screen fonts, printer fonts, TrueType fonts, and PostScript fonts.
- ▶ We show how to adjust the magnification that is used to size all the text displayed on your screen.
- ▶ We show you how your TrueType fonts can be sent in a PostScript file to your image setting service bureau.
- ▶ We give you a number of ways to create your own fonts and to be assured that the fonts referred to in whatever documents you receive are correctly recreated even if you don't have those fonts on your computer.

Chapter 21

Keyboards and Characters

In This Chapter

We show you how to type in the characters available to you in Windows 95, how to pick a keyboard layout for easier access, and how to use shortcuts to run Windows 95 from the keyboard. We reveal:

▶ The relationship between fonts and characters

▶ What characters and what eight character sets come with Windows 95

▶ The five ways to type (or insert) little-used characters into your documents

▶ Modifying your keyboard layout to more easily enter these little-used characters

▶ Creating multilingual documents

▶ Windows shortcut keys that can speed up your work

▶ Speeding up your keyboard

▶ Changing your keyboard driver if you get a new and different keyboard

Fonts and Characters

There is a relationship (although it is complex one) between the characters you see on your keyboard's keys and the characters that appear on your screen when you press those keys. For one thing, what that character looks like depends on which font you are using. For another, you can type characters that may not appear on your keyboard, for example ©, ™, ®, $^{1}/_{4}$, $^{1}/_{2}$, $^{3}/_{4}$, é, õ, ä, ¢, £, or ¥.

The characters that are displayed on your screen are stored on your computer's hard disk in font files. Each font file has at least 224 character definitions (known as a character set) stored in it. A font is a visual expression of a character set. When you purchase a packet of fonts, the characters come with it at no additional charge (this is a typographer's little joke).

As explained in Chapter 20, TrueType and bitmapped screen fonts ship with Windows 95. The TrueType fonts consist of font descriptions for each character and the ability to scale the font across a wide variety of sizes. TrueType fonts work with both the screen and the printer. The bitmapped fonts are for display on the screen, and consist of dots on a grid.

For a complete understanding of fonts, this chapter should be read in conjunction with Chapters 20 and 22.

Windows Character Sets

The fonts that ship with Windows 95 are based on eight different character sets. Three of the TrueType fonts (Arial, Courier New, and Times New Roman) use the Windows ANSI character set defined when Windows 3.1 and TrueType fonts were developed. This character set is also known more esoterically as the *ISO 8859-1* or *Latin-1* character set.

The bitmapped screen fonts (Courier, Fixedsys, MS Sans Serif, MS Serif, and System) use an earlier version of the Windows ANSI character set, which defined fewer characters between positions 0130 and 0159.

The bitmapped screen font Terminal and the bitmapped DOS fonts used in windowed DOS sessions all use the DOS/OEM character set. This is also referred to as the IBM PC-8 (which stands for 8 bit) or Code Page 437 character set. This character set was developed by IBM when it created the first IBM PC. This same character set is stored in ROM in U.S.-made PCs and used by full-screen DOS programs.

Three additional TrueType fonts ship with Windows 95 — Symbol, Marlett, and Wingdings. They have their own particular characters and don't relate to the previous "standards." Figure 21-1 shows the characters from the TrueType fonts Times New Roman, Symbol, and Wingdings with their corresponding character number. The Times New Roman characters display the Windows ANSI character set.

Undocumented

The Marlett font contains the Windows 95 "furniture." The caption button symbols for minimize, maximize, and quit are found in this font. Because the symbols in the buttons are fonts, it is easy to resize these buttons. Be sure not to delete this font from your \Windows\Fonts folder.

The Windows 95 source CD-ROM comes with a second set of True Type font files for Arial, Courier New, and Times New Roman. These files contain 652 characters instead of 224. The additional characters are from central European languages, which use the Greek, Turkish, and Cyrillic alphabets. The original 224 characters are the same in the extended multilingual font sets and the original font sets. The extra characters are accessible only when you use the appropriate keyboard driver or software.

Microsoft Plus! includes Lucida Sans Unicode for an even greater number of characters. Microsoft Plus! also includes Lucida Console, which replaces the True Type DOS fonts that come with Windows 95.

The Windows 95 TrueType Character Sets

Windows 95 includes three kinds of TrueType faces: Text typefaces (Times New Roman, Arial, and Courier New), Symbol, and Wingdings. To access characters that cannot be typed directly from the keyboard use the Character Map applet, use the special keystroke combination defined by your word processor, or:

　　1) Make sure the Num Lock light is *on*.
　　2) Hold down the Alt key while typing the appropriate number on the numeric keypad.
　　3) Release the Alt key.

Windows ANSI character set (Times New Roman font)
　Symbol character set
　　↓　　↓　Wingdings character set
Character Number →　　98　b　β　ℒ

Num	ANSI	Symbol	Wing	Num	ANSI	Symbol	Wing	Num	ANSI	Symbol	Wing	Num	ANSI	Symbol	Wing	Num	ANSI	Symbol	Wing	Num	ANSI	Symbol	Wing	Num	ANSI	Symbol	Wing
32				64	@	≅		96	`	‾		128	€			160				192	À	ℵ		224	à	◊	→
33	!	!	✏	65	A	Α		97	a	α		129				161	¡	Υ		193	Á	ℑ		225	á	〈	↑
34	"	∀	✂	66	B	Β		98	b	β	ℒ	130	‚			162	¢	′		194	Â	ℜ		226	â	®	↓
35	#	#		67	C	Χ		99	c	χ	ℳ	131	ƒ			163	£	≤		195	Ã	℘		227	ã	©	↖
36	$	∃		68	D	Δ		100	d	δ	≜	132	„			164	¤	⁄		196	Ä	⊗		228	ä	™	↗
37	%	%		69	E	Ε		101	e	ε	ℳ	133	…			165	¥	∞		197	Å	⊕		229	å	Σ	↙
38	&	&		70	F	Φ		102	f	φ	♐	134	†			166	¦	ƒ		198	Æ	∅		230	æ	⎛	↘
39	'	∋		71	G	Γ		103	g	γ	♑	135	‡			167	§	♣		199	Ç	∩		231	ç	⎜	←
40	(	(	☎	72	H	Η		104	h	η	≈	136	ˆ			168	¨	♦		200	È	∪		232	è	⎝	→
41	)	)		73	I	Ι		105	i	ι	♓	137	‰			169	©	♥		201	É	⊃		233	é	⎡	↑
42	*	∗	✉	74	J	ϑ		106	j	φ		138	Š			170	ª	♠		202	Ê	⊇		234	ê	⎢	↓
43	+	+		75	K	Κ		107	k	κ		139	‹			171	«	↔	★	203	Ë	⊄	✂	235	ë	⎣	↖
44	,	,		76	L	Λ		108	l	λ	●	140	Œ			172	¬	←	✳	204	Ì	⊂		236	ì	⎧	↗
45	-	-		77	M	Μ		109	m	μ	○	141				173		↑	✴	205	Í	⊆		237	í	⎨	↙
46	.	.		78	N	Ν		110	n	ν	■	142				174	®	→	✳	206	Î	∈		238	î	⎩	↘
47	/	/		79	O	Ο		111	o	o	□	143				175	¯	↓	✴	207	Ï	∉		239	ï	⎪	⇒
48	0	0		80	P	Π		112	p	π	□	144				176	°	°	⊕	208	Ð	∠		240	ð		⇦
49	1	1		81	Q	Θ		113	q	θ	□	145	'			177	±	±	⊕	209	Ñ	∇		241	ñ	〉	⇧
50	2	2		82	R	Ρ		114	r	ρ	□	146	'			178	²	″	◇	210	Ò	®		242	ò	∫	⇩
51	3	3		83	S	Σ		115	s	σ	•	147	"			179	³	≥	◻	211	Ó	©		243	ó	⌠	⇔
52	4	4		84	T	Τ		116	t	τ	◆	148	"			180	´	×	◇	212	Ô	™		244	ô	⎮	⇕
53	5	5		85	U	Υ		117	u	υ	◆	149	•			181	µ	∝	◎	213	Õ	∏		245	õ	⌡	⇗
54	6	6		86	V	ς		118	v	ϖ	✤	150	—			182	¶	∂	☆	214	Ö	√		246	ö	⎞	⇘
55	7	7		87	W	Ω		119	w	ω	✦	151	–			183	·	•	◷	215	×	·	◁	247	÷	⎟	⇖
56	8	8		88	X	Ξ		120	x	ξ	◻	152	˜			184	¸	÷	◶	216	Ø	¬	▷	248	ø	⎠	⇙
57	9	9		89	Y	Ψ		121	y	ψ	⊠	153	™			185	¹	≠	◵	217	Ù	∧		249	ù	⎤	□
58	:	:		90	Z	Ζ		122	z	ζ	⌘	154	š			186	º	≡	◴	218	Ú	∨		250	ú	⎥	□
59	;	;		91	[	[		123	{	{	⊕	155	›			187	»	≈	◐	219	Û	⇔	⊂	251	û	⎦	✗
60	<	<		92	\	∴		124					✦	156	œ			188	¼	…	◓	220	Ü	⇐	⊃	252	ü	⎫	✓
61	=	=		93	]	]		125	}	}	"	157				189	½			221	Ý	⇑	∩	253	ý	⎬	⊠
62	>	>		94	^	⊥	♈	126	~	~	"	158			·	190	¾	—	◌	222	Þ	⇒	∪	254	þ	⎭	☑
63	?	?		95	_	_		127					159	Ÿ		•	191	¿	↵	←	223	ß	⇓	←	255	ÿ		

Figure 21-1: The Windows 95 TrueType character sets.

The Windows ANSI character set

The Windows ANSI characters numbered 0 through 127 are identical to their counterparts in the IBM PC-8 character set. (These characters are also called the ASCII or lower ASCII character set, after the American Standards Committee for Information Interchange, which codified them decades ago.) The next 32 characters, 128 through 159, are mostly punctuation marks, although some character numbers are left unused. Of special interest are the curly single and double quotes. Characters 128 through 159 are followed by 32 characters of legal and currency symbols, then 32 characters of uppercase accented letters, and finally 32 characters of lowercase accented letters.

One way to access the characters numbered above 127 is to hold down the Alt key, type a *zero* (0) on the numeric keypad, then type the three digits of the character's number. This extra zero is already included in the character numbers shown in Figure 21-1. This is the most basic method of accessing these additional characters. Better methods are detailed later in this chapter.

You must add a leading zero — as in 0189 — when using this method to insert characters numbered 128 through 255. This is because Windows is downward compatible with the IBM PC-8 character set, which is used by DOS applications. The IBM PC-8 character set already uses the Alt+*number* method, and Windows allows you to enter characters in this way, too. For example, Alt+171 inserts a one-half symbol in both DOS and Windows. (Characters in the IBM PC-8 character set that do not exist in Windows, such as line-draw characters, are ignored or converted into other keyboard characters.)

The difference between the Windows 3.0 ANSI and the Windows 3.1 version is that fewer characters between character numbers 0128 and 0160 are defined in the older version. As this character set is not used for TrueType fonts you have little need to be concerned about it when creating documents. In Figure 21-2, the Windows 3.0 ANSI character set is shown in MS SansSerif.

Font designers are supposed to base their TrueType fonts on the Windows ANSI (post Windows 3.1) character set or on the new Windows ANSI 652-character set that includes the previous 224 Windows 3.1 ANSI characters. That is, their fonts are supposed to be an expression of the same characters as defined by the Windows ANSI character set. Font designers generally stick to this standard unless they are designing a special-purpose font like Wingdings.

	!	"	#	$	%	&	'	(	)	*	+	,	-	.	/	0	1	2	3	4	5	6	7	8	9	:	;	<	=	>	?
@	A	B	C	D	E	F	G	H	I	J	K	L	M	N	O	P	Q	R	S	T	U	V	W	X	Y	Z	[	\	]	^	_
`	a	b	c	d	e	f	g	h	i	j	k	l	m	n	o	p	q	r	s	t	u	v	w	x	y	z	{	|	}	~	.
.	.	.	.	.	.	.	.	.	.	.	.	.	.	.	.	.	.	.	'	'	.	.	.	.	.	.	.	.	.	.	.
	¡	¢	£	¤	¥	¦	§	¨	©	ª	«	¬	-	®	¯	°	±	²	³	´	µ	¶	·	¸	¹	º	»	¼	½	¾	¿
À	Á	Â	Ã	Ä	Å	Æ	Ç	È	É	Ê	Ë	Ì	Í	Î	Ï	Ð	Ñ	Ò	Ó	Ô	Õ	Ö	×	Ø	Ù	Ú	Û	Ü	Ý	Þ	ß
à	á	â	ã	ä	å	æ	ç	è	é	ê	ë	ì	í	î	ï	ð	ñ	ò	ó	ô	õ	ö	÷	ø	ù	ú	û	ü	ý	þ	ÿ

Figure 21-2: The pre-Windows 3.1 Windows ANSI character set as used by the current bitmapped screen fonts. It is shown in MS SansSerif.

It is important that font designers use the Windows ANSI character set. As computer users, we are interested in easily accessing the ANSI characters no matter what text font we are using. If the copyright symbol is displayed when we use Times New Roman, we would like that to also be the case if we are using Coronet. This will be true only if the copyright symbol is present in the Coronet font and it has the same character number as it has in Times New Roman.

The DOS/OEM character set

The number of total characters possible under the Windows 3.1 ANSI standard is the same as under DOS — 224, due to the number of possible combinations in an 8-bit byte, minus the 32 nonprinting "control" characters. But, more international characters and symbols are available in Windows because the ANSI set eliminates the line-drawing and math characters that are part of the IBM PC-8 set. By moving IBM's math characters into a new Symbol font, and deleting the line-draw characters entirely, Windows adds support for several accented letters needed in various languages, as well as copyright and trademark symbols and the like. (Most Windows word processing applications can draw lines without having to use text characters.)

The IBM PC-8 character set is shown in Figure 21-3. In the U.S. keyboard layout, the main keyboard provides keys for each of the alphabetic characters and punctuation marks, numbered 32 through 127. Under DOS, you access the other characters by holding down the Alt key, typing the appropriate character number on the numeric keypad (with the NumLock light on), and then releasing the Alt key. Alt+157, for example, produces "¥," the Japanese Yen symbol. Notice that using this method with the DOS/OEM character set does not require the additional zero for the characters above character number 127, as is true of the Windows ANSI characters.

Although the IBM PC-8 character set seems a chaotic jumble of letters and signs, there is a natural order of sorts (no pun intended). For instance, the first 32 characters are control codes (including tab and carriage return characters), the next 32 are punctuation and numerals, the next 32 include capital letters, and exactly 32 places above that are their lowercase equivalents.

CTRL & PUNC:		ALPHABETIC:		ACCENTS & LINE DRAW:			MATH:	
0 ■	32	64 @	96 `	128 Ç	160 á	192 └	224 α	
1 ■	33 !	65 A	97 a	129 ü	161 í	193 ┴	225 β	
2 ■	34 "	66 B	98 b	130 é	162 ó	194 ┬	226 Γ	
3 ■	35 #	67 C	99 c	131 â	163 ú	195 ├	227 π	
4 ■	36 $	68 D	100 d	132 ä	164 ñ	196 ─	228 Σ	
5 ■	37 %	69 E	101 e	133 à	165 Ñ	197 ┼	229 σ	
6 ■	38 &	70 F	102 f	134 å	166 ª	198 ╞	230 µ	
7 ■	39 '	71 G	103 g	135 ç	167 º	199 ╟	231 τ	
8 ■	40 (	72 H	104 h	136 ê	168 ¿	200 ╚	232 Φ	
9 ■	41)	73 I	105 i	137 ë	169 ⌐	201 ╔	233 Θ	
10 ■	42 *	74 J	106 j	138 è	170 ¬	202 ╩	234 Ω	
11 ■	43 +	75 K	107 k	139 ï	171 ½	203 ╦	235 δ	
12 ■	44 ,	76 L	108 l	140 î	172 ¼	204 ╠	236 ∞	
13 ■	45 -	77 M	109 m	141 ì	173 ¡	205 ═	237 ø	
14 ■	46 .	78 N	110 n	142 Ä	174 «	206 ╬	238 ∈	
15 ■	47 /	79 O	111 o	143 Å	175 »	207 ╧	239 ∩	
16 ■	48 0	80 P	112 p	144 É	176 ░	208 ╨	240 ≡	
17 ■	49 1	81 Q	113 q	145 æ	177 ▒	209 ╤	241 ±	
18 ■	50 2	82 R	114 r	146 Æ	178 ▓	210 ╥	242 ≥	
19 ■	51 3	83 S	115 s	147 ô	179 │	211 ╙	243 ≤	
20 ■	52 4	84 T	116 t	148 ö	180 ┤	212 ╘	244 ⌠	
21 ■	53 5	85 U	117 u	149 ò	181 ╡	213 ╒	245 ⌡	
22 ■	54 6	86 V	118 v	150 û	182 ╢	214 ╓	246 ÷	
23 ■	55 7	87 W	119 w	151 ù	183 ╖	215 ╫	247 ≈	
24 ■	56 8	88 X	120 x	152 ÿ	184 ╕	216 ╪	248 °	
25 ■	57 9	89 Y	121 y	153 Ö	185 ╣	217 ┘	249 ·	
26 ■	58 :	90 Z	122 z	154 Ü	186 ║	218 ┌	250 ·	
27 ■	59 ;	91 [	123 {	155 ¢	187 ╗	219 █	251 √	
28 ■	60 <	92 \	124 |	156 £	188 ╝	220 ▄	252 ⁿ	
29 ■	61 =	93]	125 }	157 ¥	189 ╜	221 ▌	253 ²	
30 ■	62 >	94 ^	126 ~	158 ₧	190 ╛	222 ▐	254 ■	
31 ■	63 ?	95 _	127	159 ƒ	191 ┐	223 ▀	255	

Figure 21-3: The IBM PC-8 Character Set. In addition to nonprintable control codes, punctuation, and alphabetic characters, the PC-8 character set includes accented and line-draw characters, and math symbols. The latter are accessed using the Alt key and the numeric keypad.

Easily Typing the Less-Used Characters

As is clear from Figure 21-1, Windows 95 provides a broad array of characters that do not appear on your keyboard. These characters include fractions, footnote superscripts, copyright and trademark symbols, and many others. Even if you are using a French, German or other European-style keyboard, you only get a few different characters defined on your keyboard, mostly for the accented letters.

If you are using a full-featured word processor such as Word for Windows, WordPro, or WordPerfect, you have easy access to many of these additional characters without using one of the methods we are about to describe. Not all the extra characters are easy to get at in your word processor, and some may require that you insert them from a Character Map-like dialog box. Also, you have access to this method only from within your word processor.

Using the first method we describe below, Windows lets you easily type in these additional characters. You need only press a simple two-key combination to insert symbols such as © into text in any Windows application. Other methods to access these characters are awkward.

For example, you can, as we've explained above, turn NumLock on, hold down Alt, type a number on the numeric keypad, then release the Alt key. Alt+0169, for instance, inserts the © symbol.

Or you can start the Character Map applet, select a symbol, and insert it into your word processing document. This does require that you switch between applications. The advantage of this method is that you get to see all the characters (even if they look pretty small on high resolution monitors). The Character Map applet can be found by clicking the Start button and traversing through the Programs and Accessories menus.

One method we describe allows you to type characters like these directly into your documents using only one or two keystrokes, pretty much like you would in the full-featured word processors. You can switch this ability on and off at any time (by switching between keyboard layouts), and use it in conjunction with the Character Map applet or the Alt+*number* method whenever you wish.

Later in this chapter, we describe another method using the Compose applet that is almost as simple. It allows you to type even a broader range of less-used characters without resorting to the keypad.

The U.S.-International keyboard layout

This first method requires the U.S.-International keyboard layout. Most Windows users, in the U.S. at least, use the plain United States keyboard layout with the English (American) language. This layout corresponds with the keys on typical U.S. keyboards. Each key inserts a lowercase letter and an uppercase letter, and that is it. There are no keys for extra symbols or accented letters, such as the *é* in *café*.

There are three keyboard layouts associated with the U.S.— plain, Dvorak, and International. When you switch to the U.S.-International keyboard layout, most of the keys on a regular U.S. keyboard gain a third or a fourth meaning. The *C* key, for example, gives you access to the copyright symbol (©) and cent sign (¢), as well as the normal uppercase *C* and lowercase *c*.

You don't need to have a U.S. keyboard to use the U.S.-International keyboard layout. Any of the keyboard layouts provided by Windows works with any of the U.S. or European keyboards. It's just that the character that you see on the keyboard may not be the character that you see displayed when you press a key.

Undocumented

Some problems with the U.S.-International keyboard: the Shift+Tab doesn't do a back tab, and you will have to resolve some conflicts with your word processor regarding Alt+Ctrl key redefinitions.

Installing the U.S.-International keyboard

To switch to the U.S.-International keyboard layout, take the following steps:

STEPS

Installing the U.S.-International Keyboard Layout

Step 1. Open the Control Panel by clicking the Start button, choosing Settings, and then Control Panel.

Step 2. Double-click the Keyboard icon.

Step 3. Click the Language tab.

Step 4. Double-click the first (and most likely only) entry in the Language and Layout window. Click the Properties button.

Step 5. Open the drop-down box in the Keyboard Layout field in the Language Properties sheet by clicking the down arrow on its right side and choosing United States-International, as shown in Figure 21-4.

Figure 21-4: The Keyboard Properties sheet somewhat covered over by the Language Properties sheet.

Step 6. Click OK next to this layout.

Step 7. Click OK on the Keyboard Properties sheet. You will be asked to insert your Windows 95 source CD-ROM or diskettes.

The change is available immediately in all applications.

While the U.S.-International keyboard layout is in effect, the *right* Alt key on your keyboard is turned into an "Alternate Character" key. When you hold down this key (alone or with the Shift key), most of the keys on your normal U.S. keyboard gain new meanings.

We refer to this Alternate Character key as AltChar. The location of this key on extended 101-key keyboards and the meaning of each of the keys in the U.S.-International keyboard layout are shown in Figure 21-5. When using the U.S.-International keyboard, the AltChar is the same as Ctrl+Alt. This can lead to conflicts if the Ctrl+Alt key combinations are redefined in your word processor.

Figure 21-5: The United States-International keyboard layout.

The normal character is shown on the left of each key, while the character inserted when you hold down AltChar or Shift+AltChar is shown on the right.

Unusual characters on the keyboard

You gain access to many categories of characters by switching to the U.S.-International keyboard. For clarity's sake, we break them into the following categories:

- Legal characters, such as the copyright symbol (©), registered trademark (®), and the section mark (§) and paragraph mark (¶) used by lawyers.

- Currency symbols, such as the British pound (£), Japanese yen (¥), the cent sign (¢), and the international generic currency symbol (¤).

- The fractions one-fourth ($^1/_4$), one-half ($^1/_2$), and three-fourths ($^3/_4$), and the degree symbol (°), useful when typing addresses like 120$^1/_2$ Main St. or recipes (300°).

- Superscripts from one to three (^{123}), useful for inserting footnotes into a page of text, or for expressions like x^2. Windows 95 doesn't offer superscript numbers higher than three, but Windows NT provides a full set of superscript and subscript numbers, from 0 to 9.

- True multiplication and division symbols ($\times \div$), so you don't have to use a lowercase x and a forward slash (/) in your documents.

- Open and closed quote marks (' '), also called "smart quotes," which look like the quote marks used in professionally typeset magazines and newspapers.

- Accented characters, so you can correctly spell words like *résumé* and *mañana.*

The U.S.-International keyboard actually provides two different ways to insert accented letters into your documents. This ability is becoming more important as more Americans have names that include accented letters, such as Frederico Peña, the U.S. Secretary of Transportation at this writing.

The first way to insert accented letters is to hold down the AltChar key and press one of the letters on your keyboard that has an accented alternate character. For example, AltChar+E produces the accented *é,* while AltChar+N produces the accented *ñ.*

The second way is to use what are called *dead keys.* These are keys that do nothing until another key on the keyboard is pressed.

On the U.S.-International keyboard, five keys are converted into dead keys. These are:

- The *circumflex* or "hat" over the "6" key (^), which is used in words like *crêpes Suzette*

- The *back quote* ('), which produces a *grave accent* (*grave* rhymes with "Slav" or "slave") in words like *à la carte*

- The *tilde* (~), used in words like *jalapeño*

- The *apostrophe* ('), which produces an *acute accent* in words like *exposé;* and

- The *double-quote* ("), which produces an *umlaut* or *dieresis* in words like *naïve*

When you press one of these dead keys, Windows shows nothing on your screen until you press another key. Then, if that key is a letter that has an accented form, such as most vowels, the appropriate accented letter is inserted into your document. If not, such as the letter *t,* both the accent and the *t* are inserted, one after the other. If you want to insert just an accent itself, you press the corresponding dead key, followed by the spacebar, and Windows inserts just the accent.

This behavior produces a small irritation when using the apostrophe and double-quote key on your keyboard. When you press the apostrophe, which is common in contractions like *don't* and possessives like *Brian's,* you don't see the apostrophe until the second letter is typed. But you don't get an apostrophe at all if you type an unusual contraction, such as Hallowe'en. With the U.S.-International keyboard, pressing the apostrophe and then *e* produces the letter *é,* unless you remember to press the spacebar after the apostrophe.

This is a very minor problem, because most English contractions end in *s* or *t,* not in vowels. But it is a more serious problem with the double-quote key, which is used to begin sentences that are quotations, such as "Are you there?" Sentences often begin with *A, E,* and other vowels, and you must remember to press the spacebar after the double-quote key when typing any such sentence.

If you ever use symbols or accented characters, the advantages of using the U.S.-International keyboard far outweigh the slight disadvantage of remembering how to use the quotation marks. But because it *is* irritating, we wish Microsoft hadn't used the apostrophe and double-quote key as dead keys. Instead, they should have used the colon (:) and the semicolon (;). The colon looks like an umlaut, and the bottom of the semicolon resembles an acute accent mark. Since colons and semicolons are always followed by spaces or carriage returns in normal English usage, you wouldn't need to remember to press the spacebar before pressing a vowel after these keys. If a letter immediately followed a colon or semicolon, you could be sure that it was meant to be an accented letter.

In any case, using the U.S.-International keyboard is usually better for users of U.S. keyboards than switching to an entirely different keyboard layout to type in another language, such as French. You can use the Control Panel's Keyboard Properties sheet, of course, to add keyboard layouts in addition to (or instead of) U.S. layout. There are 26 available keyboard layouts. But this almost always moves some alphabetical keys to new positions that are customary in those locales. For example, the top row of alphabetical keys on keyboards sold in France starts out with the letters AZERTY, not QWERTY, as on U.S. keyboards. Unless you're a touch typist who learned to type on keyboards in a different country, it's better to stick with the U.S.-International keyboard.

What if you don't have an extended keyboard?

For users with older 84-key keyboards (the ones on the original IBM AT, with 10 function keys on the left side), the U.S.-International keyboard provides another way to access alternate characters. This is necessary, of course, because 84-key keyboards do not have two Alt keys and therefore cannot convert one into an AltChar key.

Holding down Ctrl+Alt while pressing a letter is the same as holding down the right Alt key (the AltChar key) while the U.S.-International keyboard is in effect. Shift+Ctrl+Alt does the same thing as Shift+AltChar.

Unfortunately, these parallel methods are in force even if you are using a 101-key extended keyboard. This means that you must take care when using a macro language in your word processor to redefine Ctrl+Alt keys or Shift+Ctrl+Alt keys to run macros. These macro definitions overrule the meaning of letters that have an alternate form when used with the AltChar key. In other words, a macro that has been defined to run when you press Ctrl+Alt+A will take precedence over AltChar+A. Instead of AltChar+A inserting *á* into your document, the macro will execute.

Switching between keyboard layouts in one language

It is possible to set up two (or more) keyboard layouts and easily switch between them. You can switch back and forth between the U.S. and the U.S.-International keyboard if you like. This can help solve the irritation of the poor definition of the dead keys referred to above.

Undocumented

You'll need to use the steps described in the section later in this chapter entitled *Setting up and using multilingual identifiers*. Choose the language "English (American)" and associate the U.S.-International keyboard layout with it and "English (Australian)" and associate the U.S. keyboard layout with it. You now have two language identifiers on your Taskbar that are in fact the same language (almost) but refer to two different keyboard layouts. You switch between layouts by choosing one or the other language identifier.

The only problem this will cause occurs if you have two spelling dictionaries in your word processor, one for the U.S. and one for Australia. The text that you typed while you were typing Australian (using the plain U.S. keyboard layout) will be proofed by the Australian spelling dictionary.

Accessing unusual characters in Word for Windows 6.0

For an example of how a full-featured word processor handles non-standard characters see Table 21-1. The elements in this chart were taken directly from the Word for Windows 6.0 help files (and edited to improve clarity).

Table 21-1	Shortcut Keys for Inserting Accented Letters in Word for Windows 6.0
Character:	**Keystrokes**
à, è, ì, ò, ù, À, È, Ì, Ò, Ù	Ctrl+ ` (accent-grave), the letter
á, é, í, ó, ú, ý, Á, É, Í, Ó, Ú, Ý	Ctrl+' (apostrophe), the letter
â, ê, î, ô, û, Â, Ê, Î, Ô, Û	Ctrl+ ^ (caret), the letter
ã, ñ, õ, Ã, Ñ, Õ	Ctrl+ ~ (tilde), the letter
ä, ë, ï, ö, ü, ÿ, Ä, Ë, Ï, Ö, Ü, Ÿ	Ctrl+: (colon), the letter
å, Å	Ctrl+@, a or A
æ, Æ	Ctrl+&, a or A
œ, Œ	Ctrl+&, o or O
ß	Ctrl+&, s
ç, Ç	Ctrl+, (comma), c or C
, D	Ctrl+' (apostrophe), d or D
ø, Ø	Ctrl+/, o or O
¿	Ctrl+Alt+?
¡	Ctrl+Alt+!
©	Ctrl+Alt+C
®	Ctrl+Alt+R
™	Ctrl+Alt+T
… (ellipsis)	Ctrl+Alt+period
' (single opening quotation mark)	Ctrl+ ` (accent-grave), `
' (single closing quotation mark)	Ctrl+'(apostrophe),'
" (double opening quotation mark)	Ctrl+ ` (accent-grave)," (double quote)
" (double closing quotation mark)	Ctrl+'(apostrophe)," (double quote)

AutoCorrect (a feature of Word for Windows 6.0) is by default automatically set to replace straight quote marks with the typesetter's quote marks. You won't have to use the last four keystroke combinations in the table if you leave this setting at its default.

Undocumented

There are some conflicts between the U.S. International keyboard layout and Word for Windows 6.0. The Word team within Microsoft has chosen to redefine a number of the Ctrl+Alt shortcut keys, so many of the AltChar+*letter* shortcuts don't work as indicated. Fortunately, you have a number of options if you want to use the convenient U.S.-International keyboard layout with Word for Windows.

First, many of the keys on the U.S.-International keyboard that conflict with a Winword shortcut key have a different shortcut key than that listed in the table. You can just use these shortcut keys instead of AltChar+*letter*. For example, in Winword, to get the letter ä, type **Ctrl+:** (Ctrl + colon). On the International keyboard layout you type AltChar+A, but Winword defines Ctrl+Alt+A as "Insert Annotation."

Second, you can remove 13 of the 16 Winword shortcut keys that conflict with this keyboard layout. Fortunately these shortcut definitions are held in the Normal.dot template. You can easily change or eliminate these shortcut key combinations in Normal.dot or whatever template you use with Winword.

STEPS

Easing Use of the U.S.-International Keyboard with Winword

Step 1.   Double-click your Winword icon. Choose File, New from the menu.

Step 2.   You can make the changes to the Normal.dot template or to a new template. You can always go back later in the Explorer and rename Normal.dot to Normal.old and your New template to Normal.dot if you want it to be the default template.

Step 3.   If you want to make changes to Normal.dot, click the OK button in the New dialog box. If you want to make a new template based on Normal.dot, click Template and then OK.

Step 4.   Choose Tools, Customize from the Winword menu and click the Keyboard tab. Click the template that you want changed in the lower right corner window of the Customize dialog box.

Step 5.   Choose Categories, as shown in Table 21-2, and scroll the Commands window through the alphabetically organized commands until you find the ones listed in Table 21-2.

Table 21-2	Word for Windows Shortcut Keys that Can Be Removed		
Category	*Command*	*Predefined Shortcut*	*Alternate*
File	FilePrintPreview	Ctrl+Alt+I	Ctrl+F2
Edit	GoBack	Ctrl+Alt+Z	Shift+F5
Edit	RepeatFind	Ctrl+Alt+Y	Shift+F4
View	ViewNormal	Ctrl+Alt+N	
View	ViewOutline	Ctrl+Alt+O	
View	ViewPage	Ctrl+Alt+P	
Insert	InsertAnnotation	Ctrl+Alt+A	

Category	Command	Predefined Shortcut	Alternate
Insert	InsertEndnoteNow	Ctrl+Alt+E	
Format	ApplyHeading1	Ctrl+Alt+1	
Format	ApplyHeading2	Ctrl+Alt+2	
Format	ApplyHeading3	Ctrl+Alt+3	
Table	TableUpdate AutoFormat	Ctrl I Alt I U	
Windows and Help	DocSplit	Ctrl+Alt+S	

Step 6. In the Current Keys field of the Customize dialog box, highlight the Shortcut key from the table that you want to remove. Click Remove.

Step 7. Repeat Steps 5 and 6 until you have removed all the shortcut key definitions that you want. The changes are made immediately to your template file or Normal.dot.

Step 8. If you are creating a new template file, click the File, Save menu item when you are done.

The third conflict involves the fact that two Winword shortcut keys that conflict with the U.S.-International keyboard layout cannot be so easily redefined. They are:

Add a command to a menu   Ctrl+Alt+ = (Equals sign)

Remove a command from a menu   Ctrl+Alt+ - (Minus sign)

Another shortcut key has been defined to insert the trademark symbol with Alt+Ctrl+T. It can be easily removed using the Winword character map if you so desire.

You can, of course, choose to ignore these three conflicts and pick the × and ¥ characters from Winword's built-in character map choosing the Insert, Symbol menu item.

Or you can define a new AltChar+*letter* shortcut for the three orphan symbols by using Winword's built-in character map, highlighting them one at a time, and clicking the Shortcut button.

The Five ANSI Accents

One reason that many English-speaking computer users aren't more familiar with the accented letters in the ANSI set is that these letters seem to be a jumble of random, unrelated symbols. Actually, all the accented letters in the ANSI character set fall into one of five types:

1. Characters with an Acute Accent:

Á É Í Ó Ú Ý á é í ó ú ý

2. Characters with a Grave Accent (*grave* rhymes with "Slav" or "slave"):

À È Ì Ò Ù à è ì ò ù

3. Characters with an Umlaut (also called a *dieresis*):

Ä Ë Ï Ö Ü ä ë ï ö ü ÿ

4. Characters with a Circumflex (also informally called a "hat"):

Â Ê Î Ô Û â ê î ô û

5. Characters with a Tilde, or an Iberian or Nordic Form:

Ã Æ Ç Ð Ñ Õ Ø ¡ ¿ ã æ ª ç ñ õ ø º ß

These accented characters largely occupy the positions numbered 0192 through 0224 — the uppercase letters start at 0192, while the lowercase versions are exactly 32 positions higher. On non-U.S. keyboards, those accented characters that are common in the national language are assigned to keys, so that pressing, say, the "ñ" key on a Spanish keyboard automatically inserts ANSI character 0241 into the document.

You should note that, when accented characters are used in your documents, they still sort correctly in alphabetical order. Windows applications use the "sort value" of each letter, not the numerical ANSI value, so characters are sorted *a, á, b, c*, not *a, b, c, á*, as their numerical value might suggest. The actual sort order is determined by the sort rules associated with the locale that you set in the Regional Settings Properties sheet.

Using accented letters

Since it isn't very useful to have access to accented characters if you don't know *when* to use them, Table 21-3 includes words in common English usage that contain accents. Many of these words started out as phrases in languages other than English, but became an accepted part of the English vocabulary long ago.

Table 21-3	Accented Words in Common Usage	

Words and Phrases

à la carte	décor	naïveté
à la mode	découpage	negligée
adiós	déjà vu	passé
appliqué	déshabillé	paté
après ski	discothèque	pièce de resistance
attaché	émigré	pied à terre
Au révoir	exposé	piña colada
bête noire	fête	protégé
café	fête champêtre	raison d'être
cause célèbre	fiancé	répondez s'il vous plaît (RSVP)
coup d'état	fiancée	résumé
coup de grâce	fin de siècle	risqué
crème de menthe	habitué	roman à clef
crème fraîche	jalapeño	sautéed
crêpe	lamé	soufflé
crêpes Suzette	maître d'hôtel	tête-à-tête
débridement	mañana	très chic
déclassé	moiré	voilà!
décolletage	naïf	
décolleté	naïve	

Proper Names

Condé Nast	Estée Lauder	Les Misérables
Crédit Suisse	Hermès	Moët & Chandon
Crédit Lyonnais	Lancôme	Nestlé
Dom Pérignon	Lazard Frères & Co.	Plaza Athénée

(continued)

Table 21-3 (continued)

Place Names

Ascunción, Paraguay	Genève, Switzerland	San José, Costa Rica
Belém, Brazil	Medellín, Colombia	São Paulo, Brazil
Bogotá, Colombia	México	Tiranë, Albania
Brasília, Brazil	Montréal, Canada	Valparaíso, Chile
Córdoba, Argentina	Perú	Zürich, Switzerland
Curaçao, Lesser Antilles	Québec, Canada	
Düsseldorf, Germany		

One argument for using these accents in your documents is, as a job counselor once wrote, "It's naïve to spell résumé wrong." Would anyone discriminate against a job applicant because the word *résumé* wasn't spelled accurately in their application? We would rather not find out. Many people, especially those who have learned two or more languages, consider a person's use of accents a clue to their overall level of education. (For the record, some English dictionaries allow either *résumé, resumé,* or *resume* to mean the same thing — but not the *American Heritage Dictionary* or the *New York Public Library Desk Reference,* which use only the first spelling.)

Besides your self-interest in how the words on your job applications are spelled, we live in a world that is growing smaller and closer by the day, and people appreciate it when their names and those of their home towns are spelled correctly — regardless of their country of origin. Since Windows makes it possible to include accented characters just like any character on the keyboard, it's in our best interest to know and use the "extra" characters that don't appear on a visible key.

Windows provides many ways to access different symbols and characters when you write — it's up to you to find ways to use these characters more expressively in your documents.

Redefine keys into any character string using Compose

Unusual characters that you usually use, as well as oft-repeated names and phrases, can be a pain to type. We often have to look up the oddly spelled names of companies and friends that we work with, which takes even more time.

Compose, a tiny Windows application available on CompuServe, allows you to insert virtually any character or character string into your documents by pressing just two or three keys on your keyboard. In its default configuration, Compose uses the Right Ctrl key as its "compose" key. You **press and release** your Right Ctrl key, then press any combination of keys that are defined. We emphasize **press and release** because so often you **press and hold down** the Ctrl key while you press and release another key. This is not the case with Compose.

Compose comes with more than 100 such "hotkey" sequences defined for you. For example, pressing and releasing Right Ctrl, the letter Y, and an equals sign inserts a Japanese Yen symbol (¥) into your document. You can type the Y and = in any order, in uppercase or lowercase. Or you can change these options to insert a different character when you change the order or the case.

As you might expect, Compose is easily capable of handling all Windows upper ANSI characters. It is much easier to remember the predefined Compose sequences for these characters — Right Ctrl, the letter e, and an apostrophe produces the accented *é* in *café,* for instance — than the equivalents (Alt+0233, in this case).

You can make the Compose "hotkey" sequence include up to five characters, so acronyms can be expanded easily to any reasonable length. Because Compose was created by Jerry Cummings of Digital Equipment Corp., the sequence Right Ctrl, D, E, C, is predefined for you to insert Digital Equipment Corporation. This can be changed or deleted, of course.

Other defaults are more useful. Pressing Right Ctrl, D, and a space inserts into your documents the current date. T and a space inserts the current time, and DT inserts both. For some reason, these assignments can't be changed, but you *can* determine the format used for the date and time. Compose picks up these formats from the preferences you set in the Control Panel's Regional Settings Properties sheet. Click the Options, Options menu in Compose to choose between long or short date formats.

The only other combination you can't change is Right Ctrl followed by two spaces. This brings up a really nifty scrolling character insert box. You can insert any character from any typeface you have installed into your document. It's easier to make out each character in this box than it is in the Character Map applet — because you can enlarge the character font size when searching for, say, that special Wingdings character.

You can always see what "hotkey" sequences are defined by clicking the Compose icon in the Taskbar and then clicking the Compose, Define Sequences menu item. To add a new sequence, just type in the sequence in the blank box on the lower-left corner of the Define Sequences dialog box and the resulting string of characters that you want in the box on the lower-left corner.

You can download the Compose utility from CompuServe. Type **GO DECPCI** and then download the file Compos.zip from the DEC Unsupported Library.

On the CD-ROM that accompanies this book, we've featured several other utilities that redefine the keyboard. To access these utilities, run Setup.exe. Click Tools and then select "Utilities for redefining the keyboard" to read about and install these programs.

Accessing more hidden characters

A little-known benefit of Windows 95 is that it includes a bundled typeface containing several clip-art-like characters. This face is called Wingdings, and it can definitely add interest to your documents — once you know what characters are there to be used.

Microsoft also offers the Microsoft TrueType Font Pack, which gives you an additional *44* TrueType faces. This set consists mainly of typefaces similar to the 35 that are found in PostScript printers. But buried beneath these familiar typefaces are four unusual fonts, each with more than 200 symbols — one of which might be just perfect to make a point in your next newsletter, fax, or spreadsheet.

The situation is that *every* Windows 95 user has access to hundreds of characters that are not visible on any keyboard. And those users who have the Microsoft TrueType Font Pack have access to more than 1,000 symbols, bullets, arrows, and other designs that printers call *dingbats*. All this is available with almost no way for the average person to know which characters are there.

To be fair, it must be said that Microsoft does provide the Character Map applet with Windows 95 to try to help people access these symbols. When you start this map, it displays all 224 characters that appear in a Windows font (but not the 652 characters in a multilingual font). Unfortunately, the Character Map window is small (and can't be resized), so it's difficult to use it to browse through your type collection. You can use the Compose utility's preview feature to see bigger versions of the characters.

To give you a place to see many of these characters and symbols, we've collected all the characters (other than the extended multilingual fonts) available to Windows 95 users into two charts. Figure 21-1, which is at the beginning of this chapter, is for all Windows 95 users, while Figure 21-6 is for those who have the TrueType Font Pack. These charts are suitable for photo-copying and tacking onto the nearest bulletin board for the next time you need just the right symbol.

In these figures, about half the characters can be inserted into a document by pressing a key on your keyboard. Pressing the *w* key, for example, inserts character number 119 into your document. If you're using a text typeface, such as Windows 3.1's Arial, the inserted character is, in fact, a *w*. But if you're using Wingdings, the same keystroke inserts a diamond-shaped bullet (♦).

We use many of the higher-numbered special characters all the time. Windows makes it easy for us to use a long dash for emphasis — like this — by typing Alt+0150. Bullets to set off paragraphs are found at Alt+0149.

The Microsoft TrueType Font Pack Character Set

The TrueType Font Pack includes four TrueType faces with numerous special characters: Lucida Bright Math Extension, Math Italic, and Math Symbol; and Monotype Sorts. To access characters that cannot be typed directly from the keyboard:

1) Make sure the Num Lock light is *on*.
2) Hold down the Alt key while typing the appropriate number on the numeric keypad.
3) Release the Alt key.

Lucida Bright Math Extension character set
Lucida Bright Math Italic character set
Lucida Bright Math Symbol character set
↓ ↓ ↓ Monotype Sorts character set
Character Number → 64 \ ϕ ≫ ✠

32				
33	(	Γ	+	✁
34	)	Δ	=	✂
35	[	Θ	−	✃
36	]	Λ	·	✄
37	⌊	Ξ	×	☎
38	⌋	Π	∗	✆
39	⌈	Σ	÷	✇
40	⌉	Υ	⋄	✈
41	{	Φ	±	✉
42	}	Ψ	∓	☛
43	⟨	Ω	⊕	☞
44	⟩	α	⊖	✌
45	∣	β	⊗	✍
46	‖	γ	⊘	✎
47	/	δ	⊙	✏
48	\	ϵ	◯	✐
49	(	ζ	∘	✑
50	)	η	•	✒
51	(	θ	≍	✓
52	)	ι	≡	✔
53	∣	κ	⊆	✕
54	∣	λ	⊇	✖
55	∣	μ	≤	✗
56	∣	ν	≥	✘
57	∣	ξ	⪯	✙
58	∣	o	⪰	✚
59	∣	π	∼	✛
60	∣	ρ	≈	✜
61	⟨	σ	⊂	✝
62	⟩	τ	⊃	✞
63	/	υ	≪	✟

64	\	ϕ	≫	✠
65	{	χ	≺	✡
66	}	ψ	≻	✢
67	{	ω	←	✣
68	}	ε	→	✤
69	⌊	ϑ	↑	✥
70	∣	ϖ	↓	✦
71	⌈	ϱ	↔	✧
72	∣	ς	↗	★
73	{	φ	↘	✩
74	}	↼	≃	✪
75	⟨	↽	⇐	✫
76	⟩	⇀	⇒	✬
77	/	⇁	⇑	✭
78	\	·	⇓	✮
79	/	·	⇔	✯
80	⟩	▹	↖	✰
81	⟨	◃	↙	✱
82	⟩	0	∝	✲
83	⌈	1	′	✳
84	⌉	2	∞	✴
85	⌊	3	∈	✵
86	⌋	4	∋	✶
87	∣	5	△	✷
88	∣	6	▽	✸
89	∣	7	/	✹
90	∣	8	·	✺
91	∣	9	∀	✻
92	∣	.	∃	✼
93	⎨	,	¬	✽
94	⎬	<	∅	✾
95	∣	/	ℜ	✿

96	∣	>	ℑ	❀
97	\	⋆	⊤	❁
98	/	∂	⊥	❂
99	∣	A	ℵ	❃
100	∣	B	𝒜	❄
101	⟨	C	ℬ	❅
102	⟩	D	𝒞	❆
103	⊔	E	𝒟	❇
104	⊔	F	ℰ	❈
105	∮	G	ℱ	❉
106	∮	H	𝒢	❊
107	⊙	I	ℋ	❋
108	⨀	J	ℐ	●
109	●	K	𝒥	❍
110	●	L	𝒦	■
111	⊗	M	ℒ	❏
112	⨂	N	ℳ	❐
113	∑	O	𝒩	❑
114	∏	P	𝒪	❒
115	∫	Q	𝒫	▲
116	∪	R	𝒬	▼
117	∩	S	ℛ	◆
118	⊎	T	𝒮	❖
119	∧	U	𝒯	◗
120	∨	V	𝒰	❘
121	∑	W	𝒱	❙
122	∏	X	𝒲	❚
123	∫	Y	𝒳	❛
124	⋃	Z	𝒴	❜
125	⋂	♭	𝒵	❝
126	⨄	♮	∪	❞
127				

0128			∩	❨
0129			⊎	❩
0130	⊔		∧	❪
0131	⊔		∨	❫
0132	ˆ		⊢	❬
0133	⌢		⊣	❭
0134	⌢		⌊	❮
0135	˜		⌋	❯
0136	∼		⌈	❰
0137	∼		⌉	❱
0138	[		{	❲
0139	]		}	❳
0140	⌊		⟨	❴
0141			⟩	❵
0142			∣	
0143			‖	
0144			↕	
0145	}		⇕	
0146	√		\	
0147	√		≀	
0148	√		√	
0149	√		⨿	□
0150	∣		∫	□
0151	√		∇	□
0152	⌈		⊔	
0153	‖		⊓	
0154	↑		⊑	
0155	↓		⊒	
0156	⌜		§	
0157			†	
0158			‡	
0159	⌟		¶	

0160				
0161	ı	‾	◆	❡
0162	⌈	ˆ	♥	❢
0163	⌉	(	♠	❣
0164	[	)	‾	❤
0165	]	[	ℂ	❥
0166	⌊	]	△	❦
0167	⌋	Ⅎ	∈	❧
0168	⌊	Ɔ	∋	♣
0169	⌋	ℇ	Π	♦
0170	[illegible]	℧	Σ	♥
0171	[illegible]	ℊ	+	♠
0172	[illegible]	ℏ	∟	①
0173	[illegible]	ℨ	∠	②
0174	[illegible]	ℏ	∡	③
0175	[illegible]	ƛ	∢	④
0176	[illegible]	ℓ	∬	⑤
0177	[illegible]	ℶ	∭	⑥
0178	[illegible]	λ	∴	⑦
0179	[illegible]	ℸ	∵	⑧
0180	[illegible]	𝔸	∶	⑨
0181	[illegible]	𝔹	‥	⑩
0182	[illegible]	ℂ	∸	❶
0183	[illegible]	𝔻	∹	❷
0184	[illegible]	𝔼	∺	❸
0185	[illegible]	𝔽	∻	❹
0186	[illegible]	𝔾	∽	❺
0187	[illegible]	ℍ	∾	❻
0188	[illegible]	𝕀	∿	❼
0189	[illegible]	𝕁	≂	❽
0190	[illegible]	𝕂	≃	❾
0191	[illegible]	𝕃	≅	❿

0192	[illegible]	𝕄	≈	➀
0193	[illegible]	ℕ	≊	➁
0194	[illegible]	𝕆	≋	➂
0195	[illegible]	ℙ	≌	➃
0196	[illegible]	ℚ	≎	➄
0197	[illegible]	ℝ	≏	➅
0198	[illegible]	𝕊	≐	➆
0199	[illegible]	𝕋	≑	➇
0200	[illegible]	𝕌	≒	➈
0201	[illegible]	𝕍	≓	➉
0202	[illegible]	𝕎	≔	➊
0203	[illegible]	𝕏	≕	➋
0204	[illegible]	𝕐	≖	➌
0205	[illegible]	ℤ	≗	➍
0206	[illegible]	⪅	≘	➎
0207	[illegible]	⪆	≙	➏
0208	[illegible]	⋖	≚	➐
0209	[illegible]	⋗	≛	➑
0210	[illegible]	⋘	≜	➒
0211	[illegible]	⋙	≝	➓
0212	[illegible]	⩽	≞	➔
0213	[illegible]	⩾	≟	→
0214	[illegible]	⋞	≣	↔
0215	[illegible]	⋟	≦	↕
0216	[illegible]	⊀	≧	➘
0217	[illegible]	⊁	≲	➙
0218	[illegible]	⪷	≳	➚
0219	[illegible]	⪸	⋚	➛
0220	[illegible]	⪙	⋛	➜
0221	[illegible]	⪚	⪞	➝
0222	[illegible]	⪛	≿	➞
0223	[illegible]	⪜	⋓	➟

0224	[illegible]	⪺	⋓	➠
0225	[illegible]	⪻	⊏	➡
0226	[illegible]	⫅	⊐	➢
0227	[illegible]	⫆	⊚	➣
0228	[illegible]	◀	⊙	➤
0229	[illegible]	▶	⊜	➥
0230	[illegible]	≬	⦶	➦
0231	[illegible]	⋔	⊞	➧
0232	[illegible]	∣	⊟	➨
0233	[illegible]	∥	⊠	➩
0234	[illegible]	⋈	⊡	➪
0235	[illegible]	⌢	⊨	➫
0236	[illegible]	≌	⫤	➬
0237	~	∮	⊩	➭
0238		∯	⋞	➮
0239		∰	⋟	➯
0240			⊴	
0241		∮	⊵	➱
0242		∮	⊸	➲
0243		⋉	⧟	➳
0244		⋊	⟜	➴
0245		⋋	⊹	➵
0246		⋌	⊼	➶
0247		⊻	⊽	➷
0248		⊛	⊾	➸
0249		⊪	⊿	➹
0250		⊦	⋐	➺
0251		⫞	⋑	➻
0252		⊧	⋒	➼
0253		⫣	⋓	➽
0254		⟍	⋏	➾
0255			⋎	

Figure 21-6: The Microsoft True Type Font Pack Character Set.

The Wingdings character set takes these special symbols much, much farther. Many Wingdings characters are pictorial. This includes keyboard and mouse symbols (Alt+55 and Alt+56), and electronic mail symbols (Alt+42 through Alt+47).

Finally, Microsoft's Font Pak contains a whole grab-bag of symbols: Monotype Sorts; more than 200 arrows, pointing hands, and bullets from a grand old type foundry; and three math symbol fonts from the upstart Lucida typographers (who also created Wingdings).

All of these characters are laid out for you in Figures 21-1 and 21-6. Look through them with an eye for a particular character that you might use in your work. Chances are you'll find it.

Microsoft isn't the only source for fonts, of course. More symbols (and even better TrueType faces) are available from a variety of vendors. Agfa Compugraphic has converted many trademark and corporate images into TrueType format (call 800-424-8973 or 508-658-0200). Casady & Greene offers Keycap faces for computer documentation, as well as a range of Russian and other language sets (call 800-359-4920 or fax 408-484-9218). For more details, see the discussion that follows regarding additional special purpose fonts.

Using Multiple Languages

Many North American companies routinely use different languages in their documents. Companies in the southern U.S. often produce documents containing both English and Spanish text, while Canadian documents often include both English and French.

In WordPad, Word for Windows 2.0, and 6.0 and other word processors, text may be marked as belonging to a particular language. By default, text in Winword documents is marked as the language you have selected in the Control Panel. But one section could be marked English (American), while another section is marked French (Canadian), for example. Text as small as a single word or character can be marked as a particular language.

The ability to mark sections of text as different languages can be very important when spell-checking, hyphenating, and using a thesaurus. If utilities in that language are installed, Word for Windows automatically uses the appropriate utility when operating on any section of text.

This ability to keep track of what text is in what language has been moved into the operating system in Windows 95, so many applications can take advantage of this capability now.

In addition, Windows 95 makes it easy to switch between different languages and, if you like, between different keyboard layouts. You can set up a number of different language identifiers and choose between them as you write a multilingual document. Each language that you use has an identifier, and you just pick which language the next section is going to be in by picking the identifier.

Setting up and using multilingual identifiers

You use the Keyboard Properties sheet in the Control Panel to set up multilingual identifiers. These identifiers will be displayed on your Taskbar, as shown in Figure 21-7.

Figure 21-7: Language identifiers on the Taskbar. The Taskbar in this figure is set to the right edge of the desktop, so the submenu "pops out" to the left.

To create these identifiers, you need to go to the Keyboard Properties sheet in the Control Panel. Follow these steps:

STEPS

Adding Multilingual Identifiers

Step 1.   Open the Control Panel by clicking the Start button, choosing Settings, and then Control Panel.

Step 2.   Double click the Keyboard icon.

Step 3.   Click the Languages tab.

Step 4.   Click Add.

Step 5.   Open the drop-down box in the Language field by clicking the down arrow on its right side.

Step 6.   Pick the language that you want and click OK on the Add Language dialog box. The default keyboard layout for that language or location will be displayed next to the language.

Step 7.   If you want a different keyboard layout, click Properties and choose a new layout.

Step 8.   Repeat Steps 4 through 7 until you have all the language identifiers that you will be using regularly.

Once you have set up a list of language identifiers, you can choose among them by picking one from the Taskbar, or by pressing Alt+Shift. Move your mouse pointer to the Taskbar and over the language identifier. Click the identifier. The list of identifiers pops up. Click the identifier of the language that you wish to use from the list.

Using the Left Alt+Shift key combination rotates through the list. You have to release the Alt key before you press the next Shift key.

The Left Alt+Shift shortcut key can be changed to Ctrl+Shift if you like, or no shortcut key at all in the Keyboard Language Properties sheet.

One language/keyboard layout combination is set as the default. Highlight the combination that you want as your default in the Keyboard Language Properties sheet and click Set as Default.

Multilingual documents

If you have installed Multilanguage Support either during the Windows 95 setup process or later using the Add/Remove Programs icon in your Control Panel, you can write documents using Greek, Turkish, Cyrillic, or Central European character sets. Installing Multilanguage Support installs Arial, Times New Roman and Courier New fonts with the extended Windows ANSI character set containing 652 characters.

Once you have set up multilingual identifiers, as described in the previous section, you are ready to start typing in a foreign language. Of course, your keyboard keys often won't have the correct characters engraved upon them (check out Greek, for example), so you'll need to make up a chart that tells you which characters show up in your document when you type specific keys.

All you need to do to switch between languages and keyboard layouts is press Alt+Shift. To test this, start WordPad. Type in text and then press Alt+Shift to switch your language/keyboard layout to Greek (assuming you set up a Greek identifier). The font list box in the WordPad format bar will switch from a font identified as Western to one identified as Greek. Greek letters will now appear in your document as you type.

Multilingual proofing tools

If you find yourself using different languages frequently, you should probably obtain one or more of Alki Software Corp.'s Proofing Tools packages. The packages' manual alone is valuable for its extensive charts showing the location of Windows characters and the layout of every different keyboard language supported by Windows. More importantly, each Proofing Tools package provides a spelling checker, thesaurus, and hyphenation utility for a different language supported by Microsoft Word for Windows.

Alki offers Proofing Tools packages for the following languages: Danish, Dutch, English-British, Finnish, French, French-Canadian, German, Italian, Norwegian, Portuguese, Portuguese-Brazilian, Spanish, and Swedish. (The Finnish and Portuguese packages contain spelling and hyphenation utilities but not a thesaurus.)

Each package has a list price of $99.95, but is $89.95 if obtained directly from Alki. The company also sells a Comprehensive Thesaurus for Word for Windows (list $79.95, $39.95 from Alki), which contains three times the synonyms of the thesaurus that comes with Winword, and a Comprehensive Spelling package (list $79.95, $69.95 from Alki), which adds 74,000 medical, legal, and business terms to Winword's spell-checker.

Alki Software Corp. can be reached at 300 Queen Anne Ave. N., Suite 410, Seattle, WA 98109, 800-669-9673 or 206-286-2600.

Using Upper ANSI Characters in E-mail

The Internet and many other e-mail systems will handle only the lower ASCII character set. CompuServe's WinCIM and its internal e-mail system handle the full Windows ANSI character set. You can also use Microsoft Exchange to send e-mail with these additional characters. Now all your buds in Germany and France will finally appreciate receiving letters from you.

Some Characters Say What You Mean

When documenting Windows applications for the average user, you might find yourself wondering how to represent certain keystrokes that the user is supposed to press.

Windows is full of important key combinations that are, frankly, hard to remember. In this book we indicate key combinations like this by capitalizing the first letter of special keys on the keyboard. For example, to bring up the Windows Start button we write, "press Ctrl+Esc." To switch among running applications, press Alt+Esc.

But Elizabeth Swoope finds that this isn't enough, and has actually done something about it. She teaches a microcomputer literacy course to beginners, and says, "Some of my students just didn't 'get it' when I used ENTER or [Enter] or <Enter>, no matter how carefully I explained it." So she created her own TrueType and PostScript shareware fonts, which show every key on the keyboard as a tiny keycap.

There are many retail versions of fonts that show the PC keyboard, of course. But Swoope didn't find them useful, because they were too "arty." By rendering each keycap as a three-dimensional object, or with an artistic shadow border, these keycap characters actually became too small to read clearly when inserted into 10-point or 12-point type — the same size as the body copy of Swoope's documentation.

Swoope's fonts, shown in Figure 21-8, are simple, two-dimensional shapes that reproduce well at small sizes.

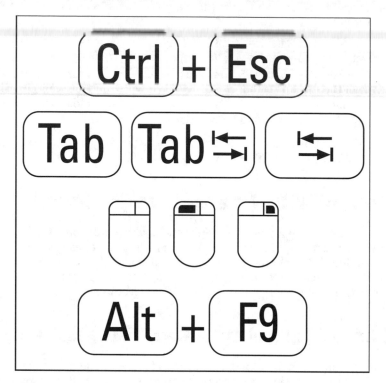

Figure 21-8: Examples of characters in the RRKeyCaps TrueType face.

One font, RRKeyCaps, includes all the "gray keys" on a typical PC keyboard. Different variations are provided for certain keys, such as Tab. Sometimes the word *Tab* is printed on the key, sometimes a double-headed arrow, sometimes both. The variations allow you to choose the Tab key that looks like the one on the keyboards in your company.

Another font, RRKeyLetters, includes key caps for punctuation marks, such as periods and commas. When you register, you receive a complete set of both fonts, with all the letters of the alphabet.

We have featured the RRKeyCap font and a sampler font with characters from both the Keyletter and Winsym fonts on the enclosed shareware CD-ROM. To download the latest versions of these fonts from CompuServe, type **GO DTPFORUM**. Select the PC Fonts library, then download RR-PT#.ZIP (TrueType) or RR-PP#.ZIP (PostScript), where "#" is greater than 2, representing whatever is the latest version number.

To register, or to obtain printed documentation by mail, send $49 (Louisiana residents add tax) to: Elizabeth Swoope, RoadRunner Computing, P.O. Box 21635, Baton Rouge, LA 70894; CompuServe: 76436,2426; 504-928-0870.

Using Keyboard Shortcuts

In this section, we examine the many shortcuts assigned to key combinations like Ctrl+Insert and Ctrl+A by Windows and Windows applications. Additionally, you may want to redefine key combinations that aren't used by *any* Windows applications in order to support your own macros.

You can specify that you have to press and release shift keys like Ctrl and Alt *before* pressing the letter key of the combination if you check the proper settings in the Accessibility Properties sheet. You'll find it under the Accessibilities icon in the Control Panel.

The most important (and poorly documented) shortcuts

Despite the ease-of-use publicity about Windows, a novice Windows user is confronted with a bewildering array of new objects to click and shortcut keys to learn. These shortcut keys are difficult to memorize, and some shortcuts are not documented at all. Once learned, furthermore, these shortcuts are difficult to remember because many of the key combinations are confusingly similar and do not follow any logical pattern.

Pressing Alt+Esc, for example, switches you from your current application to other applications running under Windows, while Alt+F4 exits the application that is running. Quick — do you remember which is which? Why is the act of exiting assigned to an F4 key combination instead of one based on the "escape" key?

Windows and Windows applications are full of other inconsistencies in the way they use shortcut keys — even in applications that were all written at Microsoft itself. Despite what you've heard that "all Windows applications work the same way," even as common an action as File Save is assigned to Ctrl+S in Windows MS Paint but Shift+F12 in Microsoft Excel and Word for Windows. And Windows Notepad has no shortcut key for File Save at all!

Worse, all Windows applications that support multiple, smaller windows (*child windows*) inside their main application window allow you to jump quickly from child window to child window by pressing Ctrl+Tab. But not Word for Windows — Ctrl+Tab actually inserts a tab character inside document tables. To cycle through child windows in Winword requires Ctrl+F6.

Despite these inconsistencies, there *are* many shortcut keys that work the same way in all or most Windows applications. We have gathered many of these in Table 21-4. You'll find other shortcut keys in Chapters 6, 10, and 17.

Table 21-4	Windows 95 Shortcut Keys
Key or Combination	*Effect*
Alt or F10	Pressed and released without any other keys, activates an application's menu bar. Then you can pull down any menu with the keyboard by moving to the menu name with a cursor arrow and pressing Enter or down arrow.
Alt+{*letter*}	Activates the choice on an application's menu that has an underlined letter corresponding to the letter you pressed. Works the same way if you press and release Alt, then press the letter on the main menu.
Alt+Down Arrow	Displays the contents of a drop-down list (such as color schemes available in the desktop Properties sheet). This is a toggle.
End	Moves to the end of a line (in a word processor).
Ctrl+End	Moves to the end of a document (in a word processor).
Enter	Selects a choice that is highlighted on a menu or in a dialog box.
Alt+Enter	Switches a DOS application that is running full-screen to running in a small window (and back). This doesn't work to toggle Windows applications from full-screen to a small window and back. If you have highlighted an icon, Alt+Enter is the same as right-click and then clicking Properties.
Esc	Closes a dialog box or drop-down menu without taking any action.

Key or Combination	Effect
Alt+Esc	Switches to another application running under Windows in a round-robin fashion each time you press this combination.
Ctrl+Esc	Brings up the Start Button menu and the Taskbar. The icons that represent applications are covered up by the Start Button menu if the Taskbar is on the right or left of your desktop.
Alt+F4	Closes the current application. If the current application is the Taskbar, this also exits Windows after you give confirmation.
Ctrl+F4	Closes a child window, in Windows applications that support the Multiple Document Interface (File Manager, Word for Windows, and so on).
Home	Moves to the beginning of a line (in a word processor).
Ctrl+Home	Moves to the beginning of a document (in a word processor).
Alt+Hyphen	Pulls down an application's multi-document control menu — the small icon at the extreme left of the application's main menu — which controls the size and other aspects of the document's child window. Do not confuse this with the System icon or the Control menu (see Alt+Spacebar), which controls the application itself. This is just above the multi-document control menu icon.
PrintScreen	Copies the entire Windows display to the Clipboard. It then can be pasted into MS Paint or another graphics application and printed.
Alt+PrintScreen	Copies only the currently active window to the Clipboard. This could be the current foreground application or a dialog box that has the keyboard focus within that application. May not work on 84-key keyboards and computers with old BIOS chips. In that case, try Shift+PrintScreen instead.
Spacebar	Toggles a choice that the selection cursor is on in a dialog box (see Tab).
Alt+Spacebar	Pulls down the Control menu, the icon in the extreme upper left corner of an application's window, which controls that application's size and other aspects.
Tab	Moves the selection cursor (a dotted rectangular box) to the next choice in a dialog box.
Shift+Tab	Moves the selection cursor in reverse order.

(continued)

Table 21-4 *(continued)*

Key or Combination	Effect
Alt+Tab	Switches to the application that was the current application before the application you are presently in. Switches back when pressed again. May not work on 84-key keyboards and computers with old keyboard BIOS chips.
Alt+Shift+Tab	Switches between applications in the opposite direction as Alt + Tab
Alt+Tab+Tab	Hold down Alt and press Tab. Continue holding Alt and pressing Tab. Release the Alt key when the icon of the application you want to switch to is highlighted. Switches in turn to every application running under Windows (same as Alt+Esc) but displays only the icon and application name. May not work on 84-key keyboards and computers with old keyboard BIOS chips.
Ctrl+Tab or Ctrl+F6	Jumps to the next child window in an application that supports the Multiple Document Interface, such as File Manager. (Ctrl+F6 in Word for Windows.)

The following keys are used before the Windows 95 graphic appears on your screen, while the message "Starting Windows 95" appears. These keys are used to modify how Windows 95 starts up.

Startup Keys

Key	Effect
F4	Start the previous operating system. Boot MS-DOS. If Windows 95 has been installed in its own directory on the computer that has the MS-DOS 6.*x* or previous DOS operating system, then this key will start DOS instead of Windows. This also works for OS/2 and Windows NT.
F5	Safe mode startup of Windows 95. This allows Windows 95 to start with its most basic configuration, bypassing your Autoexec.bat and Config.sys files and using the VGA driver for video and not loading any networking software. This is used if there are any problems starting Windows 95.
Shift+F5	Command line start. Boots into real-mode version of DOS 7.0. MS-DOS, Command.com and Dblspace are loaded low, taking up valuable conventional memory. Bypasses Config.sys and Autoexec.bat.
Ctrl+F5	Command line start without compressed drives. The Dblspace.bin and Drvspace.bin files are ignored, and double-spaced and drive-spaced drives are not mounted.
F6	Safe mode startup (like F5) but with the addition of the network.

Key	Effect
F8	Go to the following menu before startup:

```
1.      Normal
2.      Logged (\BOOTLOG.IXI)
3.      Safe mode
4.      Safe mode with network support
5.      Step-by-Step confirmation
6.      Command prompt only
7.      Safe mode command prompt only
8.      Previous version of MS-DOS
```

Key	Effect
Shift+F8	Interactive start that goes through Config.sys and Autoexec.bat one line at a time and lets you decide if you want each line read and acted upon. Also goes through each command that Io.sys initiates before it carries out the commands in Config.sys.

Alt+Tab+Tab — the task switcher

Other shortcut key combinations allow you to switch among running applications. These include Alt+Esc, which opens a different application every time you press it, and Alt+Tab, which switches from your current foreground application to the application you previously used, and back.

But the best way to switch among your running applications isn't documented at all. Just *hold down* the Alt key while you press the Tab key several times, pausing slightly between each press. Unlike Alt+Esc, which switches applications and re-draws the window for every application in turn, Alt+Tab+Tab switches applications but shows only the application's icon and name. Alt+Tab+Tab is a much faster method than Alt+Esc to cycle through all your running applications until you find the one you want. Simply release the Alt key when the desired application's icon is highlighted, and that application's window will be fully drawn and becomes the foreground.

Alt+Esc and Alt+Tab+Tab work with both Windows apps and DOS apps running under Windows, whether these apps are running full-screen, in a smaller window, or minimized as an icon on the Taskbar.

84-key keyboards and computers with older keyboard BIOS chips may not recognize the key combination Alt and Tab. IBM's BIOS for its enhanced-AT 101-key keyboard was one of the first to accept the Alt key as a way to modify the meaning of the Tab key. Test your keyboard to see which combinations of keys you can take advantage of. If you have a 101-key keyboard, you shouldn't have a problem with Alt+Tab+Tab or any of the other possible combinations.

Using the humble Shift key

Behold the lowly Shift key. You hold it down while you type, and all you get is a capital letter, right? Not quite. Beneath the Shift key's humble reputation lies a world of undocumented functionality.

Many Windows users know the most basic ways the Shift key has been redefined. One of the first lessons for a new Windows user, for example, is the fact that holding down the Shift key in a word processor while pressing an arrow key actually highlights text, instead of just moving the cursor. Holding down Shift while clicking your mouse in text also highlights everything between the current insertion point and the place you clicked (in most word processors).

Other functions of the Shift key are much less well known. When you use the straight-line tool in MS Paint, for example, holding down Shift forces the line you draw to be perfectly horizontal or vertical. Similarly, when you use the box or oval tools, Shift forces these shapes into perfect squares or circles, respectively.

Undocumented

When you double-click a document icon or filename in a folder window or in the Explorer and hold down Shift, you will most likely put the document into the print queue. The Shift + double-click combination brings up the second defined action for that document type (document type, as in, for example, text file or WordPad file) and usually the second action is print. You can find out just what actions are defined for your document type by clicking View, Options in the Explorer. For more on this topic, see Chapter 13.

If you have redefined any application menu items — by writing a Word for Windows macro to modify the File Print routine, say — you can often force the app to revert to the original, built-in procedure by holding down Shift while clicking that menu choice. (To defeat Winword's AutoExec macro, however, you must start the application with the command Winword /m.)

There is a convenient Startup folder. Shortcuts placed in this folder are automatically loaded by Windows every time you start it. But if you hold down Shift when you see the Windows 95 logo — and keep it down until the Taskbar is displayed on your desktop — the Startup group is completely ignored! This is *very* handy if something in the startup group is hanging Windows. Or you might try this just to get Windows up and running quickly for some short task.

If you hold down Shift as soon as you see the text message "Starting Windows 95...", your Config.sys and Autoexec.bat files are ignored.

If you are using the File Manager, you can use the Shift key to display the existence of subdirectories in the File Manager only when you *care* to see them.

Clicking, say, the drive C icon with your mouse displays the top-level directories of that drive. You can also press Ctrl+C to display drive C.

It's undocumented that holding down the Shift key while clicking the drive icon forces File Manager to display all levels of directories on that drive. This does not work in the Windows 95 Explorer.

The Shift key works as a keyboard shortcut, too. When you press Ctrl+Shift+C, File Manager changes to drive C and displays all subdirectories, and so forth.

Fixing the Shift key

One of the *worst* features of the Shift key in Windows is that Microsoft repeated a mistake that IBM made with its first DOS PCs.

On an old IBM Selectric typewriter (and virtually every typewriter in the world), pressing the Shift key releases your Caps Lock key, if it was already on. This is because after typing a heading in all caps, you probably want to start a new paragraph with a capital letter, then continue typing lowercase letters, as usual. Millions of touch-typists do this without thinking.

The IBM PC, however, does this wrong. If you have the Caps Lock key on, and press the Shift key, you get a *lowercase letter!* This is because the BIOS uses the Shift key to reverse the state of any key that is pressed, and no one at IBM checked to see what would happen if Caps Lock was on at the same time.

While this is an obvious and simple mistake to correct, no other PC manufacturer has ever done so, because of Livingston's Law of Compatibility: the dumber the mistake that IBM built into the original PC, the more slavishly it will be copied by compatible makers.

After years of putting up with this foolishness, we've found a utility that can return the Shift key to its time-honored and intuitive function in every Windows application.

It's called WinKey and it's just $15. Lest you think reprogramming the Shift key isn't much functionality for a utility, WinKey has plenty of other features.

Besides returning Shift to its original Selectric behavior, WinKey allows you to configure the Shift key so it *doesn't* turn off Caps Lock if you press a non-alphabetical key, such as a numeral or an underscore. This is great when you're typing API functions such as **WM_COMMAND** in C programs, or spreadsheet functions such as @sum.

You can also use WinKey to switch the Ctrl and Caps Lock keys, if you're subjected to a keyboard that doesn't give you freedom of choice on those keys. (Since there's always room for two keys to the left of the *A* key, we don't know why more companies don't put Caps Lock and Ctrl, in that order, to the left of *A*, as Digital Equipment Corp. does on some keyboards.)

Finally, you can use WinKey to force NumLock and ScrollLock on or off. ScrollLock enables cursor keys to be used to scroll the screen in Excel, and invokes DEC-style VT-100 function keys in Windows Terminal.

You can obtain a registered version of Winkey for $15.00. Contact DataGem Corp., 1420 NW Gilman #2859, Issaquah, WA 98027; 206-391-4415; CompuServe 75540,762.

A hotkey and desktop shortcut for screen savers

By right-clicking the desktop, clicking Properties, and then the Screen Saver tab, you can choose which screen saver you want displayed.

Screen savers were originally designed to prevent ghostly images from permanently "burning in" on monochrome monitors that displayed the same application day after day. The "rotated-L" of Lotus 1-2-3 spreadsheets, for example, might still be visible even after you'd exited the program.

Modern color monitors don't have the severe burn-in problems of monochrome monitors. But screen savers still have their uses. You can blank your screen when you leave the room, or when someone walks in, if the document you're working on is at all confidential or personal. You can even blank the screen just to be able to clear your mind for a few moments without your work staring you in the face.

Since all these uses for a screen saver require an immediate response time (rather than waiting 30 minutes or whatever for the saver to kick in), you may find it irritating that Windows provides no easy way to launch its screen saver instantly from a hotkey combination.

Undocumented

You can, of course, start your screen saver by right-clicking the desktop, clicking the Screen Saver tab, and clicking Test — the saver will then begin. But there is a much faster method, which isn't in the Windows manual. If you've obtained any compatible savers from companies other than Microsoft, the following steps should work with them, too.

STEPS

Creating a Hotkey to Your Screen Saver

Step 1. Use the Explorer to view your Windows folder. Click the Details View button on the Toolbar and then the Type button to arrange the filenames by type. Scroll down to the screen saver files. You should see Flying Windows.scr and Flying Through Space.scr, and any other screen savers you may have.

Step 2. Scroll the left pane of the Explorer and, clicking on the plus signs, display the \Windows\Start Menu\Programs\Startup folder. Maybe you don't want this particular behavior, but it does give you the ability to hotkey to your screen saver later.

Step 3. Right-drag the screen saver that you want from the left Explorer window pane to the \Windows\Start Menu\Programs\Startup folder. Click Create Shortcut on the popup menu. This will launch your screen saver every time you restart Windows. If you don't want this, however, right-drag the saver into a Start menu folder other than startup.

Step 4. Click the \Windows\Start Menu\Programs\Startup folder in the left pane of the Explorer. Right-click the shortcut to your screen saver icon in the right pane of the Explorer and click Properties. Click the Shortcut tab and the Shortcut key field to move your cursor to that field.

Step 5. Press a key that will be preceded by a Crlt+Alt key combination to be your hotkey combination. For example, press the letter *s,* and the hotkey combination Ctrl+Alt+S (this is the split window shortcut key combination in Word for Windows 6.0) will appear in the Shortcut key field.

Step 6. You can, at the same time, create a shortcut to the screen saver icon on the desktop. Right-drag the screen saver icon from the Explorer onto the desktop and drop it there. Choose Create Shortcut from the popup menu. Don't define a hotkey for this shortcut.

CapsLock Notification

If you find yourself accidentally hitting CapsLock, you can provide yourself with a little notification so you won't end up typing something LIKE THIS. You'll need to install the Accessibility option when you install Windows 95 or later using the Add/Remove Programs icon in the Control Panel.

STEPS

Turning on CapsLock Notification

Step 1. Click the Start button, then Settings, and then Control Panel.

Step 2. Double-click the Accessibilities icon.

Step 3. Click the Toggle key check box. Click OK.

You will now hear a tone every time you press the CapsLock, NumLock, or ScrollLock keys. The tone for enabling the key function is different from the tone for disabling it.

DOS National Language Support

When you install Windows 95, the setup routines read your existing Autoexec.bat and Config.sys files to determine if you are using something other than a U.S. keyboard layout, and require a character set other than the standard Code Page 437 to display characters on your computer screen. If it finds the National Language Support calls in these files, it keeps them in the new Autoexec.bat and Config.sys files and chooses the appropriate keyboard layout for Windows 95.

If you wish to change your keyboard layout or use another language, it is quite easy to do in Windows 95, but not so with DOS applications. You will need to reconfigure your Autoexec.bat and Config.sys files to reflect this change if you want your DOS programs to display the correct characters.

You'll need your DOS documentation for all the numerous details regarding National Language Support for DOS.

Making the Keys Repeat Faster

If you use your arrow keys a lot (and who doesn't), you'll want your cursor to rip around your documents at the fastest speed possible. The key repeat rate and the delay time before the key repeats itself are set in the Keyboard Speed Properties sheet.

To change the keyboard speed:

STEPS

Changing Key Repeat Rate and Delay Time

Step 1. Open the Control Panel by clicking the Start button, choosing Settings, and then Control Panel.

Step 2. Double-click the Keyboard icon.

Step 3. Move the sliders as shown in Figure 21-9.

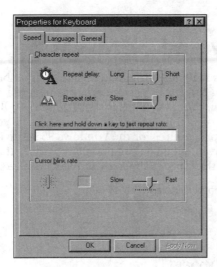

Figure 21-9: The Keyboard Speed Properties sheet.

Step 4. Test it out by placing your cursor in the test field.

Step 5. Click OK.

The Keyboard Speed Properties sheet is, like all Properties sheets, the user interface to the Registry, where all this information is stored. The information about the keyboard is stored in the User.dat file in the Windows folder. It is part of the information that is particular to a given user. This is what the exported ASCII file version of it looks like:

```
[HKEY_USERS\.Default\Control Panel\Keyboard]
"KeyboardSpeed"="31"
"KeyboardDelay"="0"
```

This Registry entry states that there is the least delay that Windows 95 gives before the key press is repeated, and that the key repeat rate is as fast as possible. We have put in a number of values greater than 31, and it has made no difference. If you set the sliders in the Keyboard Speed Properties sheet all the way to the left, the values stored in the Registry are 0 and 3 respectively.

Secret

If you have a portable computer and an external keyboard, the speed and repeat rate settings may not be applied to them when you first start Windows 95. You'll have to run the Keyboard Control Panel every time you start Windows 95 and reset these settings. You can put a shortcut to the Keyboard Control on your desktop to help with this process. For details, turn to Chapter 10.

If You Get a New and Different Keyboard

Almost all keyboards sold now are based on and compatible with the PC/AT Enhanced Keyboard (101/102-Key) standard. If you have a different keyboard attached to your computer, when you install Windows 95 it should be detected and the correct keyboard drivers installed. If you change your keyboard or the hardware detection procedures for the Windows 95 setup didn't install the correct keyboard driver, then you can manually identify the keyboard to Windows 95 and get the correct keyboard drivers installed.

To change the keyboard driver:

STEPS

Changing the Keyboard Driver

Step 1. Open the Control Panel by clicking the Start button, choosing Settings, and then Control Panel.

Step 2. Double-click the Keyboard icon.

Step 3. Click the General tab.

Step 4. Click the change button.

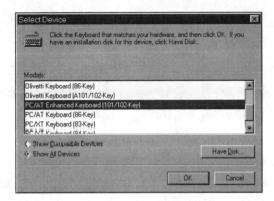

Figure 21-10: The Keyboard General Properties sheet.

Step 5. Choose a new keyboard driver from the list, as shown in Figure 21-10.

Behind the Keyboard Properties Sheets

Information about your keyboard type, layout, and language is stored in the Registry in the System.dat and User.dat files in the Windows folder. You can use the Registry editor and search on *keyboard* to see how it is stored.

Further hardware and driver properties of the keyboard can be found by double-clicking the System icon in the Control Panel, clicking the Device Manager tab, clicking the plus sign next to the Keyboard icon, highlighting your keyboard description, and then clicking the Properties button. There is not much you can change (unless you want to change the keyboard driver, which is more easily done following the instructions in the earlier section).

Keyboard layout definition files are stored in the \Windows\System folder and have an extension *.kbd. Only those files necessary for your keyboard layouts will be stored there. If you have previously installed other keyboard layouts and have now uninstalled them in the Keyboard Language Property sheets, you can remove their associated files. The files, which are listed in Table 21-6, are quite small so there is no need to remove them unless you are tight on hard disk space.

Table 21-6:	Keyboard Layout Files It's Safe to Remove
Description	**Filename**
Belgian	kbdbe.kbd
Brazilian	kbdbr.kbd
British	kbduk.kbd
Canadian Multilingual	kbdfc.kbd
Danish	kbdda.kbd
Dutch	kbdne.kbd
Finnish	kbdfi.kbd
French	kbdfr.kbd
French Canadian	kbdca.kbd
German	kbdgr.kbd
German (IBM)	kbdgr1.kbd
Icelandic	kbdic.kbd
Italian	kbdit.kbd
Italian 146	kbdit1.kbd
Irish	kbdir.kbd
Latin American	kbdla.kbd
Norwegian	kbdno.kbd
Portuguese	kbdpo.kbd
Spanish	kbdsp.kbd
Swedish	kbdsw.kbd
Swiss German	kbdsg.kbd
Swiss French	kbdsf.kbd
United States	kbdus.kbd
United States Dvorak	kbddv.kbd
United States International	kbdusx.kbd

Summary

We detail the characters that are available to you in Windows 95 and how to make it easy to type those that are not shown on your keyboard. We also discuss keyboard shortcuts and hot keys. Finally, we tell you how to modify properties of your keyboard driver to, for example, increase the key repeat rate. We provide:

- ▶ Lists of the character sets that come with Windows 95 and which fonts they are associated with.

- ▶ Tables of characters so you can find just the ones you want to spice up your documents.

- ▶ Five methods for typing in characters that don't show up on your keyboard.

- ▶ Steps for creating multiple keyboard layouts, as well as multiple language documents.

- ▶ Details on how to use a utility that will not only access these characters but lets you enter user-defined character strings with a few keystrokes.

- ▶ A table of all Windows 95 hot keys.

- ▶ Instructions on how to fix the Shift key so it works the way a touch typist would expect.

- ▶ Details on creating a hot key (and desktop icon) to bring up your screen saver at a moment's notice.

- ▶ Steps for modifying your keyboard speed.

Chapter 22

Displays

In This Chapter

We discuss monitors, video cards, and the Windows 95 software that drives them.

▶ What to look for in monitors

▶ What to look for in graphics cards

▶ Choosing a monitor/graphics card combination

▶ Installing video cards

▶ Changing the screen magnification

▶ Making the desktop and all the elements on it look the way you want them to by changing their color, size, font, and font color

▶ Creating a fancy desktop background and picking a screen saver

▶ Setting up Energy Star monitors and cards

First a Little Terminal-ology

Your fingers are typing on the keyboard and your eyes are looking at the computer screen — no, at the monitor; no, at the display; no, at the image on the computer's screen; no, at the desktop; no, at the wallpaper; well, how about that big colorful thing that sits on top of your desk. Hey, we've all got to get together on this so we, the authors, can write something meaningful but not be straight-jacketed by the words.

■ The *monitor* is what sits on your desk or on top of your computer. It contains the display or the screen upon which Windows 95 is displayed. There is most likely a colorful image on the screen, surrounded by a thin black border. The thickness of the border depends on how you adjust your monitor. This image forms the background for everything placed "on top" of it — "on top" in the sense that it obscures the image.

■ The *image* is what appears when you start Windows 95. It can be a single color, even just black, though it's hard to tell the difference between it and the black borders when it is black. The image can have a pattern like tiled bricks or it can be a photograph. The image can be just about anything you want it to be — this is an area of great personal freedom. This image is the image of your *desktop*. Things that obscure it are things on your desktop.

■ When we refer to the *screen*, to the *display*, or to the *desktop*, what we really mean is this *image* on your display. After all, if we direct your attention to your monitor, it is doubtful that we are asking you to concentrate on its *bezel* (the plastic edge around the display). We tend to use these words interchangeably unless there is a reason to make a particular distinction. This is the case when we refer to adjusting the controls on your monitor.

The image on your screen is sent to the monitor by your *graphics adapter* — also called a *display card, display adapter, video card, video adapter,* or *graphics board.* Computers that can run Windows 95 have video cards (or graphics chip sets on their motherboards) that are capable of displaying graphical images. We may use any of the preceding terms to refer to the graphics adapter that sends to the display (and often does much of the creation of) the Windows 95 images.

Monitors — Size, Flicker, Clarity

Dozens of technical specifications define the performance of monitors. It used to be that in order to make an intelligent decision you had to understand most of these parameters. The marketplace has winnowed down the meaningful differences to just a few.

Size

If you've got a Windows computer, odds are that you have a 14-, 15-, or 17-inch monitor to go with it — especially if you are using it at work. With 17-inch monitors near or less than $800 at street prices (actually, it's quite difficult to buy them on the street itself), more middle and upper-middle income people are choosing them for their home multimedia play/work/net surfing stations as well as using them at work.

Monitors come with displays in the following nominal sizes: 14, 15, 17, 21, or 23 inches and beyond. The point of a bigger monitor is this: Either you can display more information on it or what you put on it can be bigger. It's an either/or proposition that depends on you which way to go. We give you a system for making that trade-off later in this chapter.

If you have a portable, your screen is a nominal 9 or 10 inches. Liquid crystal display (LCD) screens are just too expensive to make any bigger. You already know that trade-off if you've used a portable. Don't buy one without the option of plugging in an external monitor. Be sure the portable's video chip set can support a higher resolution on external monitors.

Flicker

You don't want any flicker on your monitor. Go to a computer store and check monitors out side by side. Set the resolution of the video card driver in the computer store at the level you want. If the store is running Windows 95, you'll see how to do that later in this chapter. There should be plenty of fluorescent light in the store to create a good test bed. Turn up the contrast and brightness.

If you're looking at the monitor's specs, get one with a refresh rate, or vertical frequency, of 72 Hz or better. Don't have anything to do with interlaced video cards or monitors that require interlacing to display high resolutions. Within hours or minutes, your eyes will hate the flicker caused by interlacing and you'll have wasted your money.

Clarity

Your Windows desktop is made up of phosphorus, unless you are using the LCD screen on a portable. The image can be quite muddy if the "dot pitch" on your monitor isn't fine enough. Don't buy a cheap monitor with .31 mm dot pitch. Don't you value your eyes? Get one with a dot pitch no greater than .26 mm or .28 mm.

Graphics Adapters — Resolution, Speed, Colors

Graphics cards are one of the most heavily advertised computer hardware items out there. You, no doubt, have seen plenty of technical jargon in their ads. We'll just stick to what's important.

Resolution

You'll want a card that matches the criteria you determine from the next section. You really won't be happy if you push your monitor beyond a certain resolution for its size. Table 22-1 lists some reasonable upper limits.

Table 22-1	Monitor Size and Maximum Resolution Limits
Nominal Monitor Size	*Suggested Maximum Graphics Card Resolution*
14-inch	800 x 600
15-inch	1024 x 768
17-inch	1280 x 1024
21-inch	1600 x 1280

Of course, this is non-interlaced resolution. You weren't even thinking about using the interlaced option, right?

Speed

If you are going to use a higher resolution card, you'll want to get a faster card because you don't want to fall behind yourself. The more pixels you push, the slower it goes. If you're now at 800 x 600 pixels, you need a boost to get your performance back to where you were at 640 x 480 pixels.

All video cards today (except the very cheapest) are accelerated. You can follow their ratings in computer magazines if you want to get some idea of their relative acceleration. Many of the video cards sit in a VESA or PCI local bus slot, giving them a fast connection to the processor. The processor is handing the video card the primitive video instructions as fast as it can. It is nice not to have to wait on a slow bus to get these instruction to the video card.

You won't need the fastest cards (and won't have to pay the premium for them) if you are not doing desktop publishing, imaging, multimedia (video images running as though they were on video tape), or CAD. Of course, multimedia continues to be a hot button, and it eats computer processing (and high-definition TV bandwidth) alive.

If you are going to have your children spend their formative years looking at Microsoft's Encarta (a CD-ROM based encyclopedia), then a fast card (and a fast quad-speed or better CD-ROM drive) may be just what you are looking for. A card that provides video acceleration (as distinct from graphics acceleration) does not, in fact, speed up the display of videos. What it can do is scale up the video size, say from 160 x 120 pixels to 320 x 240 pixels, without losing speed as measured in video frames per second.

Colors

More colors equals more memory required on the video card. More colors at higher resolutions equals even more required memory. Most Windows video cards come with 1MB or 2MB of dynamic RAM (DRAM) or video RAM (VRAM). VRAM is faster and more expensive. One type of DRAM, called EDO, or *extended data-out memory,* is almost as fast as (and is cheaper than) VRAM. Again check the card specifications and see what *color depth* (how many colors) is supported at what resolutions.

Some cards come with 4MB of VRAM. They can handle 24-bit, or 16,777,216 colors, at high resolution. Unless you are doing fancy artwork or color publishing, you don't need more than 256 colors. This is the fat middle of the market. Most CD-ROM videos come in 256 colors. Be sure to get at least 256 colors at the resolution you desire.

Choosing a Monitor/Card Combination

The bigger the monitor, the higher the resolution of the video card, the more they cost. You can easily find out the costs in the mail-order marketplace, but what about the benefits?

If you match a bigger monitor with the graphics adapter running at a moderate resolution, then you get the benefit of larger text on the screen. Larger text is *easier on the eyes as long as you can place the larger monitor as close to you as you can place a smaller monitor.*

The closer the monitor is to you, the bigger the text appears to your eyes, and the easier it is to read. If you have the monitor as close as you want and you still want the text bigger (without reducing how much material you see), then you need to get a bigger monitor.

There is a cost to increasing the size of the text on the screen by increasing the magnification factor. For a given size monitor, you see less text if the text is bigger.

If you match a bigger monitor with a higher resolution video card (running at a high resolution setting) you get the benefit of having more room to put stuff on your desktop. This is referred to as more *real estate.*

Just what stuff are we talking about here? That depends. If you were just running one application, say at maximum size, it would give you a bigger view of that application with more items in the application showing. For example, you would see more lines and more sentences in a word processor, more cells in a spreadsheet, more of the image in a paint package, more of the page in a page layout package, and more lines in a computer-aided design (CAD) system.

If you are running multiple applications on your desktop, you have more room to place the other applications where you can bring them to the top of the desktop easily. You can tile applications side by side. If you bring up dialog boxes in an application — a Find dialog box in a word processor, for instance — you can place it to the side and not in the way of the words.

Now might be a good time to review the section in Chapter 20 in which we discuss font sizes, in particular the discussion of the "logical" inch (also see the section below on the "displayed" inch). The short of it is this. The objects on the screen are magnified. On a 14-inch display with a video card set at 800 x 600 resolution and font size or magnification set to 96 pixels per logical inch (Small Fonts), text is 25 percent larger than its printed size. On a 17-inch display with the same video resolution, you see the same amount of text, but now the text is 44 percent larger than its printed size.

Picking a monitor from the list

When you install Windows 95, you will be given the chance to tell Windows 95 which monitor you are using (if it isn't plug and play). Be sure to do so, because this sets the limit on the available video resolutions found in the Display Settings Properties sheet.

You can always go back and use the Add New Hardware icon in the Control Panel to change the monitor.

Setting Windows magnification

Windows 95 allows you to set the magnification of the font size used by the desktop. This is a lot like the zoom capabilities built into full-featured word processors. They allow you to increase the displayed size of the text in their client window without actually going to a larger point size font. This capability makes it easier to see what you are writing.

Changing the magnification factor for the desktop changes more than just the displayed size of text in a client window. It changes the size of most things on the desktop. Icons, icon titles, and the spacing between icons are affected. So is the text in window titles and in menus, including the Start menu. Dialog boxes get bigger when you increase the font size.

Microsoft built in this ability to change the displayed size of objects on the screen to allow for greater flexibility in configuration of the Windows desktop. You get to choose what size is comfortable for you.

The magnification factor is set arbitrarily to equal 100 percent at 96 dots per inch — this is also referred to as the Small Font size. In Chapter 20, we demonstrate that the actual magnification of the text display on one of our screens, compared to the same text printed on paper, is 125 percent for the display and video resolution. The actual magnification you will experience depends on the size of your display, the resolution you have set for your video card, and the font size you have chosen.

To set the font size (or magnification), carry out the following steps:

STEPS

Changing the Windows Magnification Factor

Step 1. Right-click the desktop. Click Properties. Click the Settings tab to get the Display Settings Properties sheet.

Step 2. Under Font Size choose either Small Font, Large Font, or click the Custom button. Small Font gives you 100 percent magnification and Large Font gives you 125 percent, or 120 dots per inch.

Step 3. If you chose Custom, use the Custom Font Size dialog box to choose a magnification factor. You can type in an amount, use the drop-down box to choose an amount (150% is the next step up after Large Fonts), or click and drag the ruler.

Step 4. Click OK in the Custom Font Size dialog box when you have chosen a magnification factor and OK on the Display Settings Properties sheet. You will be asked to restart Windows so the changes can take effect.

You have to restart Windows every time you change font size or color depth. You can change the resolution without restarting.

The "displayed" inch

If you choose Custom to set the Windows magnification factor, you get to see the Custom Font Size dialog box with its on-screen ruler, as shown in Figure 22-1. This ruler measures the "logical" inch or, more descriptively, the "displayed" inch.

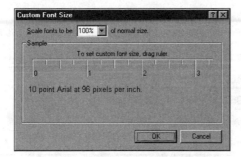

Figure 22-1: The Custom Font Size dialog box with its "logical" or "displayed" inch ruler.

If you have Windows 95 set at the small fonts magnification factor, your Custom Font Size dialog box will look like the one in Figure 22-1. The text on the screen will be displayed assuming 96 pixels per logical or displayed inch. If, at your screen resolution and monitor size, your monitor displays fewer than 96 pixels per actual inch, then the displayed inch will be bigger than an inch long.

The displayed inch is equal to the magnification factor or font size that you choose times the resolution or dots per inch that your screen displays divided by 96 dots per inch.

Place a physical ruler over the ruler displayed on the screen and see how much bigger (or smaller) the displayed inch is compared to an actual inch. The ratio of the size of the displayed inch to the actual inch is the magnification of the text on your screen. An inch of text is displayed at the size of the displayed inch.

Getting comfortable first

Sit down in front of your system and/or a friend's computer. Adjust the monitor and keyboard to a comfortable position. Is it easy to read the text displayed on the screen? Adjust the text size by using the zooming function in a word processor or, if you are using Windows 95, by changing the font size in the Display Settings Properties sheet. Do you notice an improvement?

Table 22-2 is a comparison of monitors of different sizes paired with video cards of different maximum resolutions and a range of font sizes or magnifications. It gives you the actual increase in the size of the text displayed on the screen over its size on the printed page for each of the combinations. While given in percentages, it is the ratio of the "displayed" inch to the actual inch.

Table 22-2	Magnification by Monitor Size and Video Card Resolution				
	Video Resolution				
	VGA	**SVGA**	**1024 x 768**	**1280 x 1024**	**1600 x 1280**
14-inch monitors (actual size 13 inches — 7.8 inches high x 10.4 inches wide)					
96 (Small Font)	156%	125%	98%		
129 (Large Font)	195%	156%	122%		
144 (150%)	NA	187%	146%		
15-inch monitors (actual size 14 inches — 8.4 inches high x 11.2 inches wide)					
96 (Small Font)	168%	134%	105%		
129 (Large Font)	210%	168%	131%		
144 (150%)	NA	202%	158%		
17-inch monitors (actual size 15 inches — 9 inches high x 12 inches wide)					
96 (Small Font)	NA	144%	113%	84%	
129 (Large Font)	NA	180%	141%	105%	
144 (150%)	NA	216%	169%	127%	
150 (200%)	NA	288%	225%	169%	

(continued)

	Video Resolution				
	VGA	SVGA	1024 x 768	1280 x 1024	1600 x 1280
21-inch monitors (actual size 19 inches — 11.4 inches high x 15.2 inches wide)					
96 (Small Font)	NA	NA	143%	107%	86%
129 (Large Font)	NA	NA	178%	134%	107%
144 (150%)	NA	NA	214%	160%	128%
150 (200%)	NA	NA	285%	214%	171%

The monitor sizes are the nominal or advertised size or diagonal dimension of the display. The second monitor size is the average actual diagonal dimension of monitors in the class.

The height and width of the desktop image is given in inches, assuming a 3-to-4 ratio of length to height.

Video card resolution names are by common name or resolution value in pixels.

Font size is given in the values used in the Custom Font Size dialog box, and in the Display Settings Properties sheet. The first value is dots per logical inch, the value in parentheses is the magnification factor.

NA = Not applicable

Use your experience working with your computer or your friend's computer and the information in Table 22-2 to see what size monitor, card resolution, and font size are most comfortable for your eyes. Say you find that a 14-inch monitor at SVGA resolution and Large Font size is about right. This corresponds to 156 percent magnification. If you later use a 15-inch monitor at 1024×768 resolution, set the font size at 150 percent to get the same magnification.

Use Table 22-2 to put a number on your comfort zone. Given how far away you normally are from the monitor, this number represents how much bigger you want the text on your display. Use this number to gauge the value of using a larger monitor at a higher resolution.

You can also use the table to see how to adjust your monitor, video card resolution, and font size. It doesn't make any sense to set up your monitor in a manner that will give you a value for your magnification that is far away from your comfort zone. You can use the chart to see which setting would be right for you.

Real estate

The trade-off with text size on the screen is real estate. The bigger the displayed text, the smaller the size of your "lot" — unless you get a bigger monitor. This is where Table 22-3 comes into play.

Table 22-3	Number of 12 pt. Lines in WordPad by Monitor Size and Video Card Resolution				
	Video Resolution				
	VGA	SVGA	1024 x 768	1200 x 1024	1600 x 1280
14-inch monitors (actual size 13 inches — 7.8 inches high x 10.4 inches wide)					
96 (Small Font)	24	31	40		
129 (Large Font)	20	25	33		
144 (150%)	NA	21	27		
15-inch monitors (actual size 14 inches — 8.4 inches high x 11.2 inches wide)					
96 (Small Font)	24	31	40		
129 (Large Font)	20	25	33		
144 (150%)	NA	21	27		
17-inch monitors (actual size 15 inches — 9 inches high x 12 inches wide)					
96 (Small Font)	NA	31	40	55	
129 (Large Font)	NA	25	33	45	
144 (150%)	NA	21	27	36	
150 (200%)	NA	16	20	27	
21-inch monitors (actual size 19 inches — 11.4 inches high x 15.2 inches wide)					
96 (Small Font)	NA	NA	40	55	69
129 (Large Font)	NA	NA	33	45	56
144 (150%)	NA	NA	27	36	46
150 (200%)	NA	NA	20	27	34

The monitor sizes are the nominal or advertised size or diagonal dimension of the display.

The second monitor size is the average actual diagonal dimension of monitors in the class.

The height and width of the desktop image is given in inches, assuming a 3-to-4 ratio of length to height.

Video card resolution names are by common name or resolution value in pixels.

Font size is given in the values used in the Custom font size dialog box, and in the Display Settings Properties sheet. The first value is dots per logical inch, the value in parentheses is the magnification factor.

NA = Not applicable

Like Table 22-2, Table 22-3 is a comparison of monitor size, video resolution, and font size. Only now the basis of comparison is the number of lines of 12-point text that can be displayed on the screen in WordPad, assuming that WordPad is maximized.

For example, a 15-inch monitor at 1024×768 resolution can display 33 lines of text, a little over half a page, when the font is set to Large Fonts. A 21-inch monitor at 1600×1280 resolution can display 46 lines of text. The size of the text is about the same on both monitors — 131 percent magnification on the 15-inch monitor and 128 percent on the 21-inch monitor. (These magnification numbers are taken from Table 22-2.)

One measure of the value of going from a 15-inch monitor/video card combination to a 21-inch monitor with a higher resolution card is the increase in the number of lines of text that can be displayed without scrolling. The increase is from 33 to 46 lines of text. This is what you are buying when you purchase the bigger monitor and higher resolution card.

Caveats

These tables are still not the whole story about the value of monitors and video resolution. Additional real estate can be valuable just to have more of everything on the screen. For example, you might want to have your Taskbar always on top, a column of icons on the left side of the desktop always visible, and pieces of utility applications peeking around the corner of your main application. The value of quick access to other applications may be great enough to justify the cost.

You can adjust the spacing between icons, and the size of different text entities on your desktop, independently of the overall magnification. With these adjustments you can do more with less. We consider them in more detail later in this chapter.

Installing Video Card Drivers

Microsoft provides video drivers for a wide range of video cards. Previously, the company supplied only the most basic video drivers and expected the video card manufacturers to produce their own drivers that showcased the special features of their cards. This was a way for video card manufacturers to distinguish themselves in the marketplace.

The new video drivers from Microsoft are 32-bit protected-mode drivers and offer faster performance with Windows 95 than older 16-bit video drivers. Microsoft's 32-bit video drivers also have been extensively tested with Windows 95 so they are less likely to cause problems than drivers provided by the video card makers. You can use the older 16-bit drivers from the video manufacturers with Windows 95 if your video card does not have a 32-bit video driver from Microsoft or supports features that Microsoft's drivers don't.

Setup

When Windows 95 is installed, Setup attempts to determine what type of video display adapter is installed in your computer. It examines the chip set on your video adapter. If you already have Windows 3.0 or 3.1 installed, Setup attempts to match your previous video resolution and color depth.

If the video driver that Microsoft supplies with Windows 95 can't run at the settings of your previous version of Windows, then the new video settings will default to VGA values (640 × 480 pixels by 16 colors) or, if it can, 640 × 480 pixels at 256 colors. You will have the opportunity to make changes to this resolution after Windows 95 is installed.

Wait a minute. Where are the instructions for installing the Windows 95 video drivers? Well, that's it. When you set up Windows 95, the video card driver for your card is installed automatically.

You have the option of picking a different driver during the installation process when you are asked to confirm the hardware list as detected. Click the video driver and then Change to choose from a list of all the available Microsoft-developed video drivers. See further instructions in the next section.

Installing a new video driver

If you change your video card, or Setup hasn't correctly detected your video card, you can install another video driver. If you are changing video cards, you can install first the new video driver, exit Windows 95, install the new video card after powering down the computer, and reboot Windows. Also, you could change the video driver to the Standard Display Adapter (VGA) driver, shut down Windows 95, power down your computer, install the new video card, reboot Windows 95, install the new video driver, and reboot Windows 95.

If you install the new video card without having first installed the new driver, Windows may boot up in Fail-Safe mode, which is VGA, and then you can change the video driver.

STEPS

Changing the Video Driver

Step 1.　Right click the desktop. Click Properties. Click the Settings tab to display the Display Settings Properties sheet. Click the Change Display Type button.

Step 2.　Click the Change button in the Adapter Type portion of the Change Display Type dialog box. The Select Device dialog box will appear and the Show Compatible Devices check box will be checked.

Step 3.   Only your current chosen video driver and the Standard Display Adapter (VGA) driver will be shown. Click the Show All Devices check box, as shown in Figure 22-2, to get the complete list of video drivers for Windows 95.

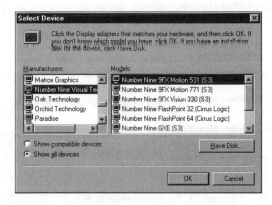

Figure 22-2: The Select Device dialog box showing a number of video drivers that come with Windows 95.

Step 4.   Click the video driver for the card that you have or will install in your computer.

Step 5.   If you have a diskette from the video card manufacturer that contains its Windows driver for this card, insert that diskette into your floppy disk drive and click Have Disk. After you have indicated the correct diskette drive letter, click OK on the Install from Disk dialog box.

Step 6.   Click the OK button in the Select Device dialog box. Your video card driver will be installed. The Adapter Type listed in the Change Display Type dialog box will change to the new video card driver name. The Manufacturer, Version, and Current files fields may also change to reflect this new driver.

Step 7.   Click the Cancel button in the Change Display Type dialog box. The new video driver has already been installed and you are not canceling that installation.

Step 8.   Make whatever changes you want to the colors, resolution, and font size fields. Click OK or Apply Now.

Step 9.   A message box appears, asking you to reboot Windows 95. If you want the new video driver to take effect now, you should do so.

Microsoft-supplied video drivers

Time has moved on. If you want to run Windows 95 at all, you are going to have to have a VGA video card or better. Microsoft no longer ships video drivers for EGA, Hercules monochrome, or IBM CGA with Windows. You might be able to use the video drivers from previous versions of Windows, but Microsoft doesn't stand behind them anymore.

Microsoft has dropped a number of other previously supported video drivers. The Paradise driver has been supplanted by the Western Digital driver, which encompasses the complete line of cards built with Western Digital chips. These chips are used on most Paradise cards.

The Texas Instruments Graphics Adapter (TIGA) driver is no longer supported by Microsoft, although the previous Windows 3.1 version should work with Windows 95. The VGA with Monochrome Display driver has been incorporated into the new Standard Display Adapter (VGA) with the monochrome setting.

In addition to standard VGA and Super VGA drivers, Microsoft ships video drivers for more than 150 video cards manufactured by 28 different manufactures. You can see the list of cards supported by clicking Show All Devices in Step 3 above.

Installing Windows 3.1 drivers

If there are problems with the new drivers, it is possible to install video drivers that worked with Windows 3.1.

STEPS

Installing Windows 3.1 Video Drivers

Step 1.   Right-click the desktop. Click Properties. Click the Settings tab to display the Display Settings Properties sheet. Click Change Display Type.

Step 2.   Click the Change button in the Adapter Type portion of the Change Display Type dialog box. The Select Device dialog box will appear and the Show Compatible Devices check box will be checked.

Step 3.   Click Have Disk. Insert the manufacturer's Windows 3.1 driver diskette in your diskette drive. Alternatively, browse to the directory that contains the Oemsetup.inf file for that video driver.

Step 4.   Choose the configuration from the alternatives presented.

Step 5.　Click the OK button in the Select Device Dialog. Your video card driver will be installed. The Adapter Type listed in the Change Display Type dialog box will change to the new video card driver name. The Manufacturer, Version, and Current files fields may also change to reflect this new driver.

Step 6.　Click the Cancel button in the Change Display Type dialog box. The new video driver has already been installed and you are not canceling that installation.

Step 7.　Make whatever changes that you prefer to the fields to adjust colors, resolution, and font size. Click OK or Apply Now.

Step 8.　A message box appears, asking you to reboot Windows 95. If you want the new video driver to take effect now, do so.

Reinstalling if there are problems

Windows 95 may start in Safe mode or display an error message that it can't use the video driver choices you have implemented. If this happens, you can easily go back to the Display Setting Properties sheet and install a new video driver. Windows 95 will start in VGA mode if it can't start in any other video mode.

Changing Resolution, Color Depth, and Magnification

A real nifty feature of Windows 95 is that you can change the display resolution of your monitor without having to restart Windows, or pick out a new display driver, or set up Windows from DOS. Windows 95 still has to restart if you change the number of colors displayed or the font size, but it does that automatically.

To view the Display Settings Properties sheet, right-click the desktop, click Properties, and then the Settings tab. You can choose between Desktop Area (screen resolution in pixels), Color Palette, and Font Size, as shown in Figure 22-3.

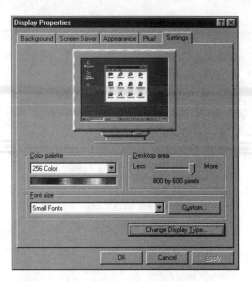

Figure 22-3: The Display Settings Properties sheet.

Not all combinations of Desktop Area and Color Palette will be available to you. What is available will depend on how much video memory is installed on your display adapter card, the maximum video resolution of your card and driver, and the capabilities of your monitor.

Choose a new Desktop Area by moving the slider to the left or right. As you do so, the monitor graphic in the dialog box changes to give you an idea of the relative changes you can expect at the different resolutions. When you click OK you are asked whether you want to keep the new values. Click Continue and the desktop will be rebuilt within a few seconds.

Choosing a different color depth (the number of colors that can be displayed on the screen at any one time) requires that you restart Windows after you make your choice, if you want it to take effect. You will also have to restart Windows 95 if you choose a different font size.

Quickly Change Video Resolution

The shareware CD-ROM accompanying this book features a video resolution utility, Vidres.exe, which you can use to quickly change video resolution without having to go to the Display Properties sheet. You can use it to change color depth also, but this requires restarting.

Microsoft also supplies a simple utility that is essentially a shortcut to the Settings Properties sheet of the Display icon in the Control Panel. Quickres.exe creates a small icon on the Taskbar next to your clock (the notification area). Double-click this icon to display the Display Setting Properties sheet. The utility is in the Windows 95 Resource Kit.

To see how to create your own shortcut to the Display Settings Properties sheet, turn to the *Control Panel Icons* section of Chapter 10.

Changing the Size, Color, and Font of Objects on the Desktop

You have the power to make a number of changes in the way your desktop and the objects on it look. We strongly recommend that you make any number of changes to get the most pleasing and easy to read desktop possible. The default Windows scheme for colors and fonts is OK, but it is the least common denominator. It assumes the worst hardware. You can do much better.

There are limitations and strengths to your video card, video driver, and monitor combination. These are reflected in the range of choices you have in setting values in the Display Settings Properties sheet. You have made certain choices regarding the number of colors you can display and the magnification of text (and other object's) size. Within the limits set by those choices you have the ability to make further refinements.

These refinements are made in the Display Appearance Properties sheet, which is shown in Figure 22-4. To view the Display Appearance Properties sheet, right-click the desktop, click Properties and then the Appearance tab.

Figure 22-4: The Display Appearance Properties sheet.

The top half of this Properties sheet is a mock display of typical desktop objects. As you click an object, the value in the Item field changes to the name of that object. The name that appears may not necessarily be what you interpret as what you were pointing at, so it can be a bit frustrating. For example, you may click the word Disabled in the menu bar in order to change the color of disabled menu items, but what you get in the field labeled Item field is Menu.

Well, there is no accounting for taste.

The bottom half of the Display Appearance Properties sheet has eight attribute fields. These allow you to make changes in the color, size, font style, font size, and font color associated with the desktop objects listed in the Items field. The complete collection of all the attributes of all the desktop objects is referred to as a *scheme*.

The schemes

All properties of the desktop objects that you can change can be stored in a scheme. If you change the attributes of a number of desktop objects, it's a good idea to store these changes, plus the values that you didn't change, in a named scheme.

Windows 95 comes with 28 predefined schemes. You can add your own. You can modify these schemes, but it's a better idea to save your modifications under a new name.

To see how schemes work, pull down the drop-down list in the Schemes field and highlight, with your mouse, various schemes. Once one scheme is chosen, you can move to other schemes that start with the same letter by pressing that letter's key on the keyboard.

The schemes are more powerful then those that came with Windows 3.1. They don't include only color schemes (thus the origin of the use of the word schemes) but also sizes, font styles, font sizes, and font colors as well.

Be sure to check out the Windows Standard Large and Extra Large schemes. Notice that many of the schemes are set up for 256-color displays — another reason to get a video card that supports this color depth.

The changes you make to the attributes of the desktop objects are saved in the unnamed "current" scheme. These changes will be lost if you switch to a named scheme and then try to go back.

The schematic values are stored in the Registry. You don't save any real space by deleting any of the existing schemes. You might want to delete some of your test schemes.

Once you design a scheme, you'll probably stick with that one for a while. Different users can have different schemes on the same computer as they are stored in the user portion (User.dat) of the Registry if the User Profiles option has been enabled (see Chapter 12).

When you want to save a scheme, click the Save As button and type in the new name.

The items

There are 18 desktop objects in the drop-down box in the Items field. Twelve are displayed in the mock desktop window at the top of the Display Appearance Properties sheet. Some, like Horizontal and Vertical Icon Spacing, would be difficult to show on the mock desktop.

If you click an object on the mock desktop, its name appears in the Item field and its attribute values are shown in the other fields. You can also pick a desktop object from the drop-down list.

Lots of objects on your desktop aren't listed in the Items drop-down list. There are names on the list that mean more than it appears from their name. Which desktop objects actually have their attributes changed is often not straightforward. Some changes require direct editing of the Registry.

Table 22-4 lists the attributes associated with every desktop object in the Item drop-down box. This table not only gives you a list of all the desktop objects but also an idea in advance of what you can change.

Table 22-4	Attributes of Desktop Objects				
Item	**Color**	**Font**	**Size**	**Font Color**	**Font Size**
3D Objects	x			x	
Active Title Bar	x	x	x	x	x
Active Window Border	x	x			
Application Background		x			
Caption Buttons	x				
Desktop		x			
Icon	x		x	x	
Icon Spacing (Horizontal)	x				
Icon Spacing (Vertical)	x				
Inactive Title Bar	x	x	x	x	x
Inactive Window Border	x	x			
Menu	x	x	x	x	x
Message Box			x	x	x
Palette Title	x		x	x	
Scroll Bar	x				
Selected Items	x	x	x	x	x
Tool Tips		x	x	x	x
Window		x			x

Table 22-5 is a list of the desktop objects listed in the Item drop-down box and what they mean.

Table 22-5	What Names of Desktop Objects Mean
Name of Item	**What Is It?**
3D Objects	Setting the color for 3D Objects also sets the colors for Message Boxes, Title Bars, Scrollbars, Caption Buttons, Taskbar, Window Borders, and Dialog boxes. The colors associated with some of these items can be reset directly by invoking those items.
Active Title Bar	The horizontal strip at the top of an active window. Setting the font style and size here also sets the font style and size used by the Taskbar.
Active Window Border	Thin (sizable) line around window with focus. It is two pixels in from the actual border. Dialog boxes that are active don't get one. As you make it thicker you also increase the thickness of the Inactive Window Border.
Application Background	Background color of the window client area. Can be seen in applications that have multiple documents within their client window.
Caption Buttons	The buttons in the upper-right corner of the window caption area. You can't change their color independently of 3D Objects.
Desktop	The color of the desktop itself; the background color of the icon titles. If your desktop is completely wallpapered, you won't see this color except behind the icon titles.
Icon	The size of icons and the font style and size used by the icon titles. Can only be black or white, depending on the desktop color. Font style and size is also used by the Explorer and folder windows.
Icon Spacing (Horizontal)	In pixels. Space between large icons on the desktop and in folder windows. This value changes with magnification or font size in Display Settings Properties sheet.
Icon Spacing (Vertical)	Same as horizontal icon spacing, except vertical.
Inactive Title Bar	The horizontal strip at the top of an inactive window. Contains the caption buttons.
Inactive Window Border	Thin (sizable) line around windows without the focus. See Active Window Border.

Undocumented

Undocumented

Name of Item	What Is It?
Menu	The menu area below the window caption area. You can change all five attributes. The text changes are also reflected in the Start menu and in all other menus.
Message Box	Not dialog boxes or Properties sheets. Just little messages, often error messages, that pop up on your desktop.
Palette Title	Unknown, no visible effect.
Scrollbar	You can't set the color of scrollbars through this Properties sheet.
Selected Item	Block of color around the menu item that your mouse pointer has clicked, often a bright color and contrasting text color to indicate quickly where you are.
Tool Tips	Little boxes with text that appear when you leave your mouse pointer over items like a button on the Taskbar. The Tool Tip font size also sets the size of the text in status bars.
Window	A major item. The color of the client window area. For example, in your word processor, the color of the background.

Undocumented (first magnifying glass icon, next to Palette Title / Scrollbar rows)

Undocumented (second magnifying glass icon, next to Tool Tips row)

Changing the color of disabled text and Explorer items

Secret

One item that you might want to change is the color of disabled menu items. You can see it in the mock desktop window, but you can't get to it in the Items field. You can change it in the Registry, though. This color not only changes the color of the disabled menu items, it also changes the color of the squares around the plus signs in the Explorer and the color of the dotted lines connecting Explorer items in its left window pane. Here's how to change how disabled menu items are displayed:

STEPS

Changing the Color of Disabled Menu Items

Step 1. Double-click Regedit.exe in your Windows folder.

Step 2. Click the plus signs next to HKEY_USERS, .Default, and Control Panel in the Registry editor window.

If you are have enabled User Profiles, you can choose your name or any user name instead of .Default.

(continued)

STEPS *(continued)*

Changing the Color of Disabled Menu Items

Step 3.   Click Colors. Click Gray Text in the right window pane.

Colors will not exist as an item in the Registry unless you have previously changed one of your desktop colors and saved them.

Step 4.   Click Edit, Modify on the menu bar.

Step 5.   Type in an RGB value for the color you want for the disabled menu items.

Step 6.   Click Registry, Exit on the menu bar.

Step 7.   The next time you start Windows, the new colors will be used.

Color

Most of the following discussion about colors assumes you have configured your video card driver to display 256 colors. Differences due to the use of 16-color drivers are mentioned throughout the text.

You can change the color and/or font color of many desktop objects. For example, you can change the color and font color of the menu bar. You'll want to make the font color contrast with the desktop object color so that you can read the text.

Changing the color of 3D Objects changes the color of everything but Tool Tips, Desktop, Application Background, and Window. The 3D Objects color is also the color used for the Taskbar, status bars, toolbars, dialog boxes, and so on.

If you have wallpaper covering your desk, the color of the desktop won't show up except as background to the icon title text.

The major color that you see on your desktop when you open an application or a document is the one labeled Window color. It is the background color for your text. The default color is bright white. This can be quite hard on the eyes, especially if the contrast and brightness on your monitor are turned up, you are in a highly lit room with fluorescent lights, and your monitor's refresh rate is less than 70 Hz. You should try out other Window colors to see how your eyes feel.

The Window color is also dithered with the 3D Objects color to create the color for Scrollbars. The Application Background color is different from the Window color. For example, in Microsoft Word you'll see the Application Background color behind a document when you minimize a word document. The Window color is the background color of the document.

The Color pick box

When you click the Color button when the value in the Items field is Menu, a Color pick box, as shown in Figure 22-5, appears. The pick box contains 20 solid colors. The top 16 are always the same colors. The bottom 4 can change. If you are using 16-color mode, the bottom colors just repeat 4 of the previous colors.

Figure 22-5: The Color pick box.

Pick the color that you want for the desktop object highlighted in the Item field by clicking a color. Figure 22-5 isn't in color, so of course you can't see which colors are displayed in the Color pick box by looking at this figure.

Windows reserves 20 colors for use with the desktop objects. If your video card and video driver support 256 colors, 236 additional colors are available to be used by the application. For example, the producers of a Video for Windows file can use whatever additional 236 colors they desire in the palette for the video. It is these 20 colors that are displayed in the color pick box.

The Color dialog box

The Color pick box has an Other button that opens the Color dialog box and in some cases allows you to choose from a larger number of colors. It is shown in Figure 22-6.

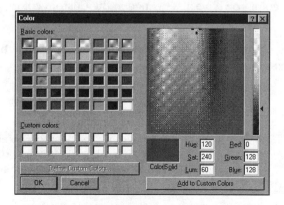

Figure 22-6: The Color dialog box.

If you have set your color depth at 256 colors, the increased colors are colors created by *dithering*, or combining, the first 16 colors displayed in the Color pick box. Forty-eight colors are shown in the Basic colors grid of the Color dialog box. Thirty-two of them are dithered colors, and the other 16 are the same 16 solid colors shown in the Color pick box. The last 4 colors in the Color pick box are not shown in the Basic Colors grid.

Undocumented

Dithered colors are displayed in the Color dialog box when the selected desktop object can use a dithered color. Names of those objects include 3D Objects (some items whose colors are set by 3D Objects can use dithered colors), Active Window Border, Desktop, Application Background, and Inactive Window Border.

If a desktop object can't use a dithered color, then only the 16 colors from the Color pick box are displayed on the Basic colors grid. The colors are just repeated to fill the 48 slots.

Defining and using custom dithered colors

You can define custom dithered colors to be used with desktop objects that can use dithered colors. The only solid colors that are available are the 20 from the original Color pick box.

STEPS

Defining Custom Dithered Colors

Step 1.   To define a custom dithered color, either move the cross-hair cursor over the color matrix, type in RGB values, or type in Hue, Saturation, and Luminosity values.

Step 2.   Click the Add to Custom Colors button.

Step 3.   Click the color you have just defined in the Custom colors grid.

Step 4.   Click OK.

Step 5.   Your custom defined dithered color will now be used by the desktop object highlighted in the item field.

Undocumented

You will not be able to define dithered custom colors for desktop objects that can't use dithered colors. The Color | Solid box (which is right below the color matrix and switches its name from Color | Solid to Color) shows only solid colors as you move the cross hairs around the color matrix.

The solid colors will be one of the 20 colors from the Color pick box. It is most likely that you will find only the first 16 colors if you move the cross hair about the color matrix. The bottom 4 colors are shown only in the Color | Solid box when the cross hair is within a very small area of the matrix around their color position.

The color of the cursor and text select mouse pointer

Secret

If there is one big problem with choosing colors for the desktop objects it is the cursor color.

The *cursor* is that vertical line in your word processor that corresponds to the text insertion point. The mouse pointer becomes an I-beam (referred to as the *text select pointer*) when it is inside the client window of your word processor. Windows 95 includes a variety of custom *.ani and *.cur files that let you change the appearance and color of the text select mouse pointer, but not the color or appearance of the cursor. The color of the cursor and the text select pointer is determined by which palette slot is used by the Window color (see Table 22-5).

The color of the cursor is the color in the slot that is the "inverse" of the slot where the Window color is stored. The 20 Windows colors that you see in the Color pick box are stored in the slots 0 through 9 (the dark colors) and 246 through 255 (the bright colors). If the Window color is the color in slot 8, then the cursor color is the color in the "inverse" slot, 247 (255 minus 8).

This "inverse" color may not be your choice for a cursor color that contrasts sharply with the Window color (and therefore makes your cursor and the text select mouse pointer more visible). Microsoft does not give you any way to change this color or the slot chosen as the inverse of the Window color slot.

This is a major failing, in our humble opinion, of the Windows 95 (and 3.x) color scheme. We have done our best (repeatedly) to point this out to Microsoft. Because you cannot choose the color of your cursor, you are quite restricted in the colors you can easily choose for your Window (or text background) color.

Check all the schemes that Microsoft provides. You will notice that the Window color is either white, black, or light gray. This is no coincidence. The color found in each of the inverse slots for each of these Window colors contrasts with them (by design).To change the color stored in the palette slot used for the cursor, you need to use software that can change the hardware palette of your video card.

We have fortunately found a shareware application that will allow you to change your palette so that you can change the cursor colors. You'll find the shareware program "Better Colors" on the *Windows 95 Secrets* CD-ROM.

If you merge the file Colors.reg (also found on the CD-ROM) into your Registry (using the steps in the section *Registry Values* found later in this chapter), you'll notice that in any of your text-editing or word-processing packages, the text cursor is a medium gray over a light green background. You can use the Better Colors program to change the cursor color to something like dark blue, which shows up very nicely over light green.

To see which palette slot stores the Window color and which stores the cursor color, you can use Palette.exe, a Microsoft Windows utility that you can find on the Microsoft Download Service (see Chapter 1 for more about that) or on the Microsoft Network.

The button colors

Buttons are actually made up of six colors, two of which you have control over from the Display Appearances Properties sheet. You can change the color of the text on the button and the color of the button face (by setting the color of 3D Objects). The other four colors are the colors that surround an actual button and make it look like a button. There are two lines of colored pixels on the right and bottom of the button and two lines using other colors on the top and left sides.

The four colors are referred to in the Registry as ButtonShadow, ButtonDkShadow, ButtonLight, and ButtonHiLight. The outside line of pixels on the bottom and right side are ButtonDkShadow. The pixels above and to the left use ButtonShadow. The outside lines on the top and left are ButtonHiLight. Inside these lines the pixels are ButtonLight.

Two of the four colors, ButtonShadow and ButtonHiLight, are also used to display text in disabled buttons.

If you are familiar with the Color applet in the Control Panel of Windows 3.1, you will remember there were two button colors in addition to the button face color and the button font color listed. You had the ability to change the ButtonShadow color and the ButtonHiLight Color through the Colors applet. Not so in Windows 95.

Secret

Changing the button face color (3D Objects) changes the colors of many desktop objects including status bars, Toolbars, Scrollbar buttons, Caption Buttons, and Properties sheets. It doesn't change the four colors associated with the buttons. You can change these four colors in the Registry.

STEPS

Changing the Four Button Colors

Step 1. Double-click Regedit.exe in the Windows folder.

Step 2. Click the plus signs next to HKEY_USERS, .Default, and Control Panel in the Registry editor window.

If you are have enabled User Profiles, you can choose your name or any user name instead of .Default.

Step 3. Click Colors. Click ButtonDkShadow or any of the four color names in the right window pane.

If you haven't changed the colors of desktop object previously, there won't be a Colors item in the Registry.

Step 4. Click Edit, Modify on the menu bar.

Step 5.   Type in an RGB value for the color you want for that color. Yes, you are going to have to be familiar with how to use RGB values in order to make sense of this step. You can use the Color dialog box with the Custom colors field to learn how to do this. Choose only colors from the 20 Windows colors.

Step 6.   Do this for all four of your button colors.

Step 7.   Click Registry, Exit on the menu bar.

Step 8.   The next time you start Windows 95, the new colors will be used.

Undocumented   Windows 95 can easily wipe out these changes that you have made to the button colors. If you change to another scheme and back to your scheme, your changes will be gone, unless you save your scheme first under a new name.

STEPS

Updating Four Button Colors

Step 1.   Right-click the desktop. Click Properties. Click the Appearance tab to display the Display Appearance Properties sheet. Click the highlighted item in the Item field and then click Button. Choose the button face color that you want.

Step 2.   Click Apply Now to apply this button color to your desktop objects.

Step 3.   Click the Save Now button, type in a name for this scheme, and click OK.

Step 4.   Pull down the Scheme drop-down list and choose another scheme. Click Apply Now.

Step 5.   Pull down the Scheme drop-down list and choose the scheme that you just saved. Click Apply Now.

Step 6.   The four button colors will be automatically updated to the colors you set in the Registry.

This is not a particularly great way to get these colors to update. Microsoft should have written Windows 95 so it updated these four button colors when you chose the button face color. Unfortunately, they didn't.

Fonts

Windows 3.1 gave you the power to change the colors of the desktop objects and the sizes of the borders. Windows 95 also lets you change these objects' size and fonts. You can choose which font to use — both screen fonts and TrueType fonts. You can choose the font point size, whether it is regular, bold, or italic, as well as its color.

These are excellent improvements over Windows 3.1. Given the wider use of larger monitors and higher resolution video cards, it has become more important for end users to be able to adjust the size of their desktop objects. We encourage you to make adjustments until you find the right combination.

The font point size, multiplied by the ratio of the displayed inch to an actual inch, determines the displayed size of the text entities on the desktop. Increasing the font size or magnification in the Display Settings Properties sheet increases the size of the displayed fonts, although their "point size" remains the same.

The default font and font point size is 8-point MS Sans Serif (10 points at higher resolutions). This is a screen font that is specifically designed to look good on VGA resolution screens. It looks fine on Super VGA screens. It looks good at 10, 12, 14, 18, and 24 points. It doesn't look so good at other point sizes.

Arial, a TrueType font, looks almost as good on the screen as MS Sans Serif at these point sizes, and better at other point sizes.

Some combinations of font, font point size, and font size will not work. For example, MS Sans Serif at 8 points and 75 percent magnification does not result in smaller displayed fonts on the desktop. MS Sans Serif is a screen font and isn't displayed below 8 points.

If the font were Arial, then this combination *would* reduce the size of the displayed text.

You cannot change the font in the item labeled 3D Objects, which also means that you don't have control over the dialog box font. (The font used for the text on the Taskbar buttons is controlled through the Active Title Bar font settings.) As dialog boxes are automatically sized based on the font size, you don't have independent control of the dialog box size. Dialog box size is determined by the font size in the Display Setting properties sheet. Windows 95 dialog boxes, by default, use the MS Sans Serif 8-point font (or 10 points for high resolution displays).

Changing the System font size

It is possible to change the font size used by dialog boxes, tabs, and the contents and index pages of the Windows 95 help files. Right-click the desktop, click Properties, click the Settings tab, and then click the Custom button. Setting a large custom font size increases the size of the dialog boxes and allows for a larger font to be used for text that is displayed in dialog boxes, and so on.

The displayed size of all the text shown on your screen is changed no matter what the point size of its font. If you have a small monitor with a video adapter set to a low or moderate resolution, the dialog boxes may no longer fit on your screen.

You can mix this magnification method of setting displayed font sizes (especially for those text entities whose font sizes can't be directly set in the Display Appearances Properties sheet) with font size settings for text entities, whose values can be set in the Display Appearances Properties sheet.

Be sure to read the discussion in Chapter 20 regarding fonts.

Size

Review Table 22-4 earlier in this chapter to see which items can have their size changed. The vertical and horizontal icon spacing values don't change the size of the icons, just their distance apart. You can change the size of the title bars, the menu bar height, the width of vertical scrollbars, the height of horizontal ones, and the thickness of window borders.

Many of the various size properties interact with each other, and often with font sizes. For example, if you increase the size of the caption buttons, this in turn increases the height of the title bar. If you choose a bigger font point size for the menu bar, the menu bar height increases so it can still contain the menu bar text within it.

Icons on the desktop are normally 32 pixels by 32 pixels. You can increase (or decrease) their size in the Display Appearance Properties sheet. Since these icons were originally created by hand on a 32×32 pixel grid, multiplying them by some factor will produce icons that won't look as sharp as the originals.

Icon size is automatically changed (in some cases) when you change video resolution. You can change it back to the original 32×32 size easily enough in the Display Appearance Properties sheet.

It is easy to make the changes in Icon size and Icon spacing, as well as Icon font sizes, so you can play with these a bit to see what you like. If only you could as easily make changes in all the text objects shown on your desktop.

Registry values

The values set in the Display Appearances Properties sheet are stored in the Registry. To see how to view these values, follow the steps in the section earlier in this chapter entitled *Changing the Color of Disabled Text and Explorer Boxes*. The values are stored in the following areas:

```
[HKEY_USERS\.Default\Control Panel\Appearance\Schemes]
[HKEY_USERS\.Default\Control Panel\Colors]
[HKEY_USERS\.Default\Control Panel\Desktop\WindowMetrics]
```

We have included an exported Registry branch that you can import to change the colors of your desktop. Its name is Color.reg and it is found in the Registry folder on the CD-ROM that accompanies this book. To import it into your Registry, take the following steps:

STEPS

Importing Color.reg into Your Registry

Step 1.   Save your current color scheme if you are not using one of the schemes that comes with Windows 95.

Step 2.   Open an Explorer window focused on the Registry folder on the accompanying CD-ROM.

Step 3.   Right-click Color.reg. Click Merge.

Step 4.   Restart Windows 95.

Step 5.   Right-click your desktop. Click Properties. Click the Appearance tab.

Step 6.   Click the Save As button, enter a name for this color scheme, and click OK.

The Desktop Wallpaper

Talk about a mixed metaphor — when was the last time you put wallpaper on a real desktop? Not likely.

The color of your desktop is chosen in the Display Appearances Properties sheet. The desktop is one of the items listed in the Items field. If you don't put up any wallpaper, this is the color you get as the background color on your screen. If you do put up some wallpaper, this is the background color of the titles of the icons on the desktop.

You choose a graphic, pattern, or wallpaper to be the background inert visual representation of your desktop on your computer screen. Your desktop feels more like a clear piece of glass on top of this graphical representation. The Taskbar and folders appear to lie on the glass.

Right-click the desktop and click the Properties menu item on the popup menu. The Display Background Properties sheet will pop up on your desktop. As shown in Figure 22-7, you can choose either Pattern or Wallpaper to create a graphical background.

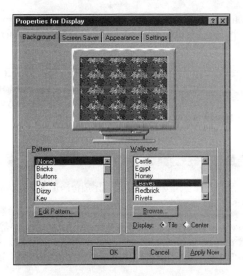

Figure 22-7: The Display Background Properties sheet.

Two-color patterned wallpaper

Wallpaper is something of a misnomer. We normally think of wallpaper as patterned paper. There can be all kinds of wallpaper in Windows 95.

Windows 95 comes with lots of little graphical patterns that are repeated to create a two-color patterned wallpaper. To create this type of wallpaper, click (None) in the Wallpaper window. Choose a pattern from the Pattern window. One color in the pattern is your desktop color and the other is black.

Repeated picture element wallpaper

Another type of wallpaper is created by using the picture elements listed in the Wallpaper window and checking the Tile box below it. The picture elements (small *bmp* files) are repeated to create a pattern. The pattern can contain more than two colors and completely cover the Window or background color.

Big-picture wallpaper

If you want to have one non-repeating graphic element as your wallpaper, then choose from among the *bmp* files available and click the Center box. You can also use the Browse button to find your *bmp* file. If your *bmp* file is the same size as your current display resolution (the same number of horizontal and vertical pixels), then the picture from the *bmp* file will fill out the whole desktop. If it is smaller than the display resolution, there will be a border around the picture made up of your window or background color.

You can tile large pictorial elements, but they will be cut off on one or more sides if the elements are not exactly $1/2$, $1/3$, etc., the size of your screen resolution.

It is great fun to have a very splashy photo up on your desktop. You can download graphics files from CompuServe, America Online, Microsoft Network, the Internet, other services, and many bulletin boards. Using Paintshop Pro 3.0 from the shareware found on the CD-ROM accompanying this book, you can size the bitmapped graphics to the resolution of your screen.

Using RLE files as graphic backgrounds

The wallpaper list box neglects to display Run Length Encoded (RLE) files, although they can be used as graphical backdrops.

This RLE format is just an ordinary bitmap file (like the bitmap wallpaper files included with Windows that are provided as wallpaper, such as Leaves.bmp or WinLogo.bmp) after it has been compressed into RLE format.

Monochrome bitmap files, before compression, contain one bit of data for every pixel displayed on the screen — the first bit is black, the second bit is black, the third bit is white, and so on. Sixteen-color bitmaps require *four* bits of data to represent every pixel, because each pixel could be one of 16 (or 2^4) possible colors.

When a bitmap file, however, is converted to an RLE file, it takes less space on disk. The RLE file contains such information as "2 pixels of black, 12 pixels of white, 20 pixels of blue," and so on. The file stores the number of pixels (the *run length*) of each color instead of storing the meaning of each individual pixel.

You can convert any bitmap file that's in the Windows proprietary *.bmp* format to an RLE file by using a graphics program that can read and write both formats. Paint Shop Pro, a program featured on the CD-ROM that accompanies this book, is perfectly suited to do just that.

In order to use an RLE file as a background graphic, do the following:

STEPS

Using RLE files as Background

Step 1. Right-click the Desktop, then select Properties and then click the Background tab.

Step 2. Click Browse, type ***.rle** in the File Name box of the Browsing for Wallpaper dialog box and press Enter.

Step 3. Double-click various folder names in the right hand list box to navigate to the folder that stores the RLE file you want to use as background.

Step 4. Double-click the RLE file.

Choosing a Screen Saver

Windows 95 comes with a number of different screen savers. You can buy additional ones from third-party software developers.

STEPS

Choosing a Screen Saver

Step 1. Right-click the Desktop, select Properties.

Step 2. Click the Screen Saver tab, and then double-click a Screen Saver in the list box, as shown in Figure 22-8.

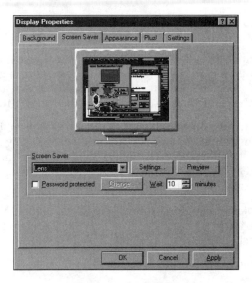

Figure 22-8: The Display Screen Savers Properties sheet.

(continued)

STEPS *(continued)*

Choosing a Screen Saver

Step 3. You can view the screen saver in full-screen mode by clicking the Preview button.

Step 4. Change various settings by clicking Settings.

Energy Star Settings

If you have a monitor and video card that both conform to the VESA specifications for Display Power Management Signaling (DPMS), you can set the timings for initiation of low-power standby and shutoff. This allows you to reduce the power consumption of the monitor if you have not used the keyboard or mouse for a given time period.

The time out settings for low-power standby and shutoff are found in the Display Screen Saver Properties sheet. They show up only if you have the appropriate hardware.

Plug and Play Monitors and Cards

Windows will not know what kind of monitor you have if it isn't plug and play compatible. You should choose your monitor model during the setup process. You can install a new monitor by clicking the New Device applet in the Control Panel, clicking Next, clicking Install a specific device, and then clicking Monitor.

It is important to tell Windows 95 which monitor you have because the proper values for the maximum display resolution will be used by the Display Setting Properties sheet. Some monitors require that their scan rates be set by a program called from Autoexec.bat. If yours requires such a program, choose your display resolution to match your scan rate.

Undocumented

You need a real-mode utility to set the refresh rate for an ATI Stealth 64. Only the ATI Mach 64, Cirrus Logic, and S3 Windows 95 drivers look in the Registry to set the refresh rate.

To set the monitor refresh rate in the Registry take the following steps:

STEPS

Setting the Monitor Refresh Rate

Step 1. Double-click Regedit.exe in your Windows folder. Click the plus sign next to the key values in the left hand pane to get to the following key:

HKEY_LOCAL_MACHINE\System\CurrentControlSet\Services\Class\Display\0000\DEFAULT

Step 2. Right-click the right pane of the Registry editor, and click String Value. Enter the name **RefreshRate.**

Step 3. Double-click RefreshRate and enter the value **-1** for automatic rate setting, or a number for a specific value of the refresh rate.

Step 4. Click OK and then restart Windows.

The video cards are detected by Windows whether they are plug and play compatible or not. Plug and play video cards will also implement the VESA DPMS specification.

LCD Displays and External Monitors

Some Windows 3.1 video drivers that came with portable computers would switch resolutions automatically to the lower 640 x 480 if the external monitor wasn't plugged in. Windows 95 video drivers will sort of do this. Sort of, because they don't do it elegantly. They drop back to a basic VGA with 16 colors.

There isn't a way built into the Windows 95 video drivers to switch between an external monitor and an LCD display — no settings in the Display Settings Properties sheet. You have to either change your BIOS setting, run a small program in Autoexec.bat, or use a keyboard switch (for example, Ctrl+Alt+Comma). The keyboard switch will probably work only when you are in full-screen DOS mode.

If you have configured your Display Settings to, for example, $800 \times 600 \times 256$, and you have unplugged your external monitor on a portable with a 640×480 LCD screen, you will be informed that your display settings are incorrect and given the opportunity to change them and restart Windows. This takes place on the desktop so Windows has already switched video modes to VGA, but it hasn't found it necessary (or helpful) to go into Safe mode. You can ignore the requests to change video modes and continue in VGA mode on your LCD screen or switch to $640 \times 480 \times 256$ if your video chip set/memory can handle this mode. Later, when you plug back in your external monitor and restart Windows 95, it will maintain your desired $800 \times 600 \times 256$ video mode if you haven't changed modes.

This is all rather crude, and we can only hope that either Microsoft or other video display driver developers improve their offerings to allow for transparent switching between LCD screens and external monitors.

Microsoft Plus!

Microsoft Plus! adds themes, font smoothing, full window drag, additional fonts, the Internet Explorer and lots more.

Themes are expanded schemes. Themes include not only desktop colors, sizes and fonts, but mouse pointers, wallpaper art, screen savers, icons, and sounds.

After installing Microsoft Plus!, double-click the Themes icon found in the Control Panel. You can mix and match themes to create your own theme by unchecking various parts of a theme, applying it, and then bringing up another theme and unchecking the parts of it that you have previously chosen. You can use portions of your current settings, if you like, by unchecking parts of themes before you apply them.

To enable font smoothing and full window drag, right-click the desktop, click Properties and then click the Plus! tab. Font smoothing uses anti-aliasing to make fonts appear smooth on white backgrounds. Gray pixels are added around letters to give the appearance of smoother fonts. This works only if your Window color (the text background color in your word processor) is white.

Full window drag means your active restored-size window will repaint itself as you move it about the screen. The default mode is an outline of the window that is dragged around with your mouse pointer. You need a fast video card for this to work in an acceptable manner.

You can also change the icons used for My Computer, Network Neighborhood, and the Recycle Bin in the Display Plus! Properties sheet. You'll find icons from other themes in the Plus! Themes folder. You can choose any icons you want.

You can take any *gif* or *bmp* format picture (found in places like Internet World Wide Web home pages) and transform it into your desktop background by right-clicking it while viewing it with the Internet Explorer and choosing Save As Wallpaper.

Summary

- ▶ We provide you with the information that you need to make your computer screen look the way the you want it to look.
- ▶ We discuss the important properties of monitors and video cards — those properties that still differentiate monitors and cards in the marketplace.
- ▶ We give you a set of tables with which you can define the benefits of a particular monitor and graphics card combination.
- ▶ We lead you step-by-step through the video card driver installation process.
- ▶ We show you how to change the size of all the elements on your desktop.
- ▶ We show you how to change the color, font, and so on of all the desktop elements and the background and screen savers you'll see on your display.
- ▶ We discuss the Microsoft Plus! features of themes, font-smoothing, and full-window drag.

Chapter 23

Printer Drivers

In This Chapter

We discuss the Windows 95 print subsystem, the software that drives physical printers. We go over each area that has been improved since Windows 3.x and discuss:

▶ Using the Printers folder to install, configure, and manage your printers

▶ Putting a shortcut to each of your printers on your desktop

▶ Dragging and dropping documents to any of your printers

▶ Making the drag and drop to a printer icon do anything you want it to

▶ Turning off DOS print spooling or printing Windows files directly to the printer

▶ Configuring enhanced parallel ports (ECP and EPP)

▶ Printing TrueType fonts correctly on PostScript printers

▶ Printing to a printer that isn't physically connected to your computer

▶ Semi-automatically installing networked printer drivers

The Improvements

Windows 95 doesn't introduce any radical changes to the Windows printing subsystem. Printer drivers in Windows 3.x were already based on a universal driver that gave printer manufacturers a big head start toward producing specific printer drivers for their printers. Microsoft later used this approach to write a more complete core video driver and thereby improve the stability of Windows 95.

But lots of incremental improvements increase configuration flexibility and provide for faster and more stable printing.

32-bit printer driver

Like all the other drivers that come with Windows 95, the printer driver has been moved to the 32-bit world. This means it spools the print jobs as threads, which can be preemptively multitasked. The 32-bit driver gives the print subsystem more control over the printing process, including bidirectional communication with the printer.

Each printer has its own print queue. You can have multiple printers connected to different ports, all printing at the same time and all managed by a different queue manager.

The print queue managers do a better job of spooling print jobs to the printers. They are aware of when the printer is ready for more data and don't send it until it is.

New universal print driver

The new universal print driver that communicates with the printer-specific mini drivers and the rest of the operating system comes with enhanced capabilities in Windows 95. It supports 600-dpi laser printers. It can download TrueType outlines to printers that support the PCL language (the HP LaserJet printer control language) so the fonts can be rasterized on the printer without using the resources of the computer.

It supports Hewlett-Packard's HPGL/2, a plotter language. CAD and similar applications can send their HPGL output to a printer instead of a plotter.

Unified printer control interface

Windows 3.x has a Printer icon in the Control Panel (for printer installation and configuration) and a separate Print Manager icon (for print queue management), initially found in the Main program group in the Program Manager. Printer configuration, installation, and the print queue management functions have been combined in Windows 95. They are now associated with the individual printer icons found in the Printers folder. Instead of one Printer icon for all installed printer drivers, each printer has its own icon.

Each printer icon represents a separate print queue manager and a separate set of printer driver Properties sheets. All the configuration information for each printer is set for that printer only. Configuration variables that were global in Windows 3.x can now be set individually. Each print queue can be managed separately and simultaneously.

Spooling EMF, not RAW printer codes

When your document is printed, the document file has to be translated into the printer's codes that instruct the printer on how to print each character. Microsoft refers to these printer codes as the RAW (we capitalize it here because Microsoft does in order to balance it against EMF or *Enhanced Metafile Format*) data. The printer driver/translator/spooler (the Print Manager) that came with Windows 3.x would translate your document into the RAW data and create a temporary file which was then spooled to the printer.

This translation process would begin as soon as you told your application to print your document. During the translation process, you were not able to continue working with your application. You couldn't bring up another document and work on it. The Print Manager would also begin printing the document while translating it. When the translation process was complete, you were allowed to return to your application while the translated temporary file continued to be spooled to the printer in the background.

Translation is a lengthy process. In Windows 95, both translation to RAW data and print spooling have been moved to a background thread. You don't have to wait for the translation to RAW data to finish before you can continue working with your application. Your document is instead translated to Enhanced Metafile Format (EMF), which is a much higher-level, and more-compact format than the RAW data. This reduces the initial translation time and more quickly returns you to your application.

The translation from EMF to RAW takes place in the background, leaving you free to continue your work. The temporary EMF file is spooled and translated as it is sent to the printer. EMF is built into the Graphic Device Interface (GDI) module of Windows 95.

If you run into problems spooling EMF files, you can switch to the old way of spooling RAW data files instead. We show you how later in this chapter in the section entitled *Details*.

PostScript printer drivers spool PostScript files to the PostScript printer. There is no EMF translation available for PostScript printers. PostScript is already a high-level page description language, like the Enhanced Metafile Format, so there is little or no benefit in translating first to EMF and then from EMF to PostScript. The PostScript printer driver translates your document to a temporary PostScript file, spools this file, and starts sending it to the printer as the drivers creates the temporary file.

DOS and Windows printing work together

Under Windows 3.*x*, the printing of DOS files was not managed by the Print Manager. DOS files were not spooled, and there were device contention conflicts if you tried to print DOS and Windows applications simultaneously.

The Windows 95 printing subsystem spools DOS print files, so you can print from any application and let the operating system handle the printer. The printer ports are virtualized, so the DOS application thinks it is printing to a real port, when in fact it is printing to the Windows 95 print subsystem. You can turn off DOS print spooling.

DOS print files are not translated into EMF print files. Rather, the translation occurs as the files (as RAW data files) are spooled. This still releases the DOS application faster than would be the case without a spooler. The spooler is not available in MS-DOS mode.

Off-line printing

If you don't have a printer currently hooked up to your computer, you can still create print files. They will be printed automatically the next time you get connected to a printer and use the queue manager to put the printer back online. To be able to do this, you must first install on your computer a printer driver that references a printer connected to a network server or to another computer over a peer-to-peer network. This network can be as simple as the Direct Cable Connection (DCC) program, which lets your laptop computer connect to your desktop computer.

Undocumented

Off-line or deferred printing is useful whenever your computer is not connected to a networked printer. Unfortunately, you can't use it with a local printer that, for whatever reason, is not currently connected to your computer. It is possible to pause printing while you reconnect your local printer, if for some reason it was off-line when you started printing. Pausing does not save the print jobs for later printing.

Off-line printing works only for printing to non-local (networked) printers.

Bidirectional communications

For years, users couldn't have cared less what a printer had to say to them. Now we all realize that things would be a lot easier if the printer were smarter.

Plug and play printers can provide the Windows 95 printer installation routines all the information they need to set up the printer without you having to answer any questions about manufacturer, model, and so on.

Some printers can send status reports to the printer driver reporting "paper jam" or "out of paper," for instance. This helps if the printer is down the hall. Even more detailed status reports are available from sophisticated plug and play printers.

Support for enhanced parallel port

There has even been progress in the mundane (to some people) world of parallel ports. The EPP and ECP specifications for parallel ports allow for higher speed and improved bidirectional communication. This is most evident using devices that can deal with these new higher speeds. See the section later in this chapter entitled *Configuring ECP and EPP Ports*.

PostScript

The Windows 95 PostScript printer driver was jointly developed by Adobe and Microsoft. The fact that Microsoft is willing to credit Adobe with joint development speaks volumes about Adobe's power and prestige, and Microsoft's desire to have a well-respected printer driver.

The PostScript printer driver is used for all PostScript printers. A separate *spd* (Simplified PostScript printer description) or *ppd* (PostScript printer description) file is used to modify the driver to reflect the features of each PostScript printer. These files can be found in the System folder contained in the Windows 95 folder. The filenames are shortened versions of the printer name.

The Windows 95 PostScript driver includes PostScript Level 2 support as well as numerous incremental upgrades to better handle more complex PostScript documents.

Printer shortcuts

Because each printer has its own associated icon in the Printers folder, you can place shortcuts to each printer driver on your desktop (or into any other folder that you want). If you want to print to the printer, drag and drop your document file onto the shortcut.

If you drag a printer icon from the Printers folder, a shortcut is automatically created when you drop it. No need to hold down Ctrl+Shift keys.

Print without installing printer drivers first

You may have installed a local printer by installing its drivers on your computer. You can print to that printer. If you want to print to another printer on your network, you don't necessarily have to install the printer drivers beforehand. This comes in handy, as there could be all sorts of printers out there on an extensive network and it is a bit of a pain to manually install drivers for all the 800 different printers that Windows 95 supports.

In order to print to a printer, you need to have a printer driver for that printer installed on your computer. The printer driver installation process can be semi-automatic. Microsoft calls this "point and print."

If you are on a network, and there are shared printers available on the network on computers running Windows 95, Windows NT, or Novell NetWare, you can print to that printer, which will semi-automatically install the printer driver for that printer on your computer.

If the networked printer is connected to a Windows 95 computer, all the information about that printer and the location of the files associated with it are stored in the Registry of the computer that the printer is connected to. Point and print uses this information to change your Registry, copy the appropriate files from the other Windows 95 computer, and install the printer driver on your computer.

See the section later in this chapter entitled *Point and Print* for details on how to set up your computer to use and share this capability.

Network printer management

Both Digital Equipment Corporation and Hewlett Packard provide printer server software that eases the job of managing their printers that are connected directly to NetWare, Microsoft, and Digital networks. A Windows 95 computer becomes a network print management station.

NetWare print services

A computer running Windows 95 can serve as a single-printer, NetWare-compatible print services provider when connected to a Novell NetWare print server. A NetWare print server can send print jobs to a printer connected to a Windows 95 computer as long as that computer is also running MS Client for NetWare and MS Print Services for NetWare. The Windows 95 computer providing print services does not need to be running MS File and Printer Sharing for NetWare. All of these programs come with Windows 95.

The Windows 95 computer does not need to be a dedicated print services provider and can be used to carry out other tasks. It can manage only one local printer for the NetWare server. MS Print Services for NetWare runs in the background and has minimal effect on foreground tasks.

No need for logical port redirection

Using Windows 3.x required that you assign a network printer to a specific logical port if you wanted to print to it. This is no longer necessary as long as your network supports the universal naming convention (UNC) for naming its server, folders and printers. When you install a network printer, its UNC name is, retained and used to direct the output to the correct printer, for example, \\Billserver\HP5.

If your network doesn't support UNC (the 16-bit networks that worked with Windows 3.x do not), you can still redirect printer output to logical ports LPT1 through LPT9 through the Capture Printer Port button in the Details Properties sheet. Some DOS programs may require that you print to a logical port and not to a printer through a UNC port name.

The Printers Folder

Unlike Windows 3.x, you'll find that most printing functions are consolidated in the Printers folder. You can get to the Printers folder in one of four ways:

1. Click the Start button, click Settings, then click Printers

2. Double-click My Computer, double-click the Printers folder icon

3. Right-click My Computer, click Explore, click the Printers folder icon in the left-hand pane of the Explorer

4. Use any of the above methods, but click the Control Panel folder instead of the Printers folder, then double-click the Printers folder in the Control Panel

Your Printers folder window will look something like the one shown in Figure 23-1. You won't have all the printer icons shown in this figure until you install some printers (or have them installed for you). Each installed printer driver has its own printer icon in the Printers folder.

Figure 23-1: The Printers folder window. There are the Add Printer icon and the icons for each of the installed printers. Double-click the Add Printer icon to install a new printer. Double-click a printer icon to view its print queue. Right-click a printer icon, then click Properties, to view a printer driver's properties. Right-click the client area of the Printers folder window and click Capture Printer port to redirect printer output out a logical port to a network printer. Right-click a printer icon and click Set As Default to change the default printer.

You'll find most everything to do with printers in the Printers folder. You can:

■ Install new printer drivers

■ Delete printer drivers you are no longer using

■ Change the characteristics of your printer driver

■ View and manage the print queues (pause and purge print jobs)

■ Set the default printer

■ Give LPT*x* names to printers connected to networked servers (redirect logical printer ports to networked printers)

Printer driver installation and configuration and print-queue management were combined in Windows 95 to make it easier to get at the important printer functions. So what is outside the Printers folder that relates to printing?

■ The Fonts folder, where you'll find the fonts that are installed on your computer (See Chapter 30 for details on fonts.)

■ Printer and communication port configurations, including the new enhanced parallel port, which you will find in the Device Manager under the System icon in the Control Panel

■ The Add Printer Wizard (which matches the one in the Printers folder), found by double-clicking the Add New Hardware icon in the Control Panel and choosing to add a printer

- Enabling of the Print Sharing capability, which you will find under the Network icon in the Control Panel

- Dragging a shortcut to a printer to the desktop because you can't drag a printer icon out of the Printers folder

- The Printer Preview capability, a systemwide dynamic link library (DLL) that can be incorporated by developers into their applications, an example of which is found in WordPad

- The common print dialog box, which can be used by developers and is used by Microsoft in WordPad

- Shared printers, which are attached to servers on your network and can be viewed by double-clicking their icons in the Explorer

- Network printer management tools from DEC and HP

The shared printers will also show up in your Printers folder if you print to them, drag and drop them to the Printers folder, or double-click them.

Tip

The Device Manager tracks most of the hardware attached to your computer, but it doesn't track your printers. Only the Properties sheets associated with the particular printer store the parameters of a printer driver. The Device Manager does track the printer port parameters.

Drag and Drop to a Printer Icon

You can drag and drop a file icon displayed in a folder window or the Explorer (or on the desktop) to a printer's shortcut icon on the desktop, to a printer icon in the Printers folder, or to the printer's queue window. With this action you are telling Windows 95 to invoke the application that is associated with the print command for this file type and then execute the application's print command.

If you just want to quickly print a file, or a group of files, this is an easy way to do it. The associated application is invoked and you may see the document in the application's window on the desktop while the document is spooled to the printer. The application is closed as soon as the document is completely spooled.

This is the same action that would take place if you right-clicked a document file and chose Print from the right mouse button menu. The actions listed at the top of this menu are the ones defined for the file type in the Registry and found in the File Types dialog box. We discuss this in detail in Chapter 13.

If you drag and drop to a networked printer icon in a shared folder view and that printer isn't currently installed on your computer, you are also instructing Windows 95 to start the printer installation process.

Defining an action named *print* for a given file type and associating that action with a specific application's print command connects the user action of dragging and dropping a file of that type on the printer icon with the specified application's print command. You define the print action using the method detailed in Chapter 13.

Undocumented

You can define the "print" action to be something other than print, if you like. This will allow you to drag and drop a file to a printer icon and have this other action take place. For example, you can define the print action to invoke a file translator that converts the specified file type into another file type. This will make it easy to convert files of the former type by dragging and dropping them to any printer icon.

Many file types already have the print action defined for them by default or when you installed their associated Windows application after you installed Windows 95.

Installing a Printer Driver

The Printer Driver Installation Wizard pretty much installs the printer driver for you. You just have to respond to its not-too-difficult questions.

Other Windows 95 documentation often refers to installing a printer. That really means installing a printer driver, in other words, installing software. This is confusing, because the natural meaning of installing a printer is to physically place a printer next to a computer and connect a printer cable between them. You'll have to do a little translation in your head when you see the words "Install a printer."

If you install Windows 95 into your existing Windows 3.*x* directory, Windows 95 Setup will automatically install the printer drivers for the printers that you have previously chosen. On the other hand, if you install Windows 95 to a new folder, you will be asked during Setup to install a new printer. The Add Printer Wizard will be called, and you answer the questions.

After Windows 95 is installed, you can invoke the Add Printer Wizard (to add additional printer drivers) by opening the Printers folder and double-clicking the Add Printer icon. If your printer is plug and play compatible, the Add Printer Wizard can communicate with it, find the correct printer driver, and install the correctly configured printer driver itself.

Otherwise, the Add Printer Wizard asks you for the manufacturer's name and printer model before it proceeds to find the correct files from the Windows 95 source diskettes or CD-ROM. To do this it uses the *inf* files, Msprint.inf and Msprint2.inf, found in the Inf folder under your Windows 95 folder.

If you have a printer that isn't covered in these two *inf* files, you can click the Have Disk button, if you have a printer setup diskette from your printer manufacturer. This diskette will need to include an *inf* file for the new printer.

If the printer is connected to a serial port and is not plug and play-compliant, you will have the option of changing the port's baud rate, and so on. You can also choose a meaningful name for the printer, so if you share it on a network, others will know where to go to find their output.

After you set up the printer for the first time, you should choose to print a test page. Not only does this check out the printer, but it leads to a Windows 95 help-based printer troubleshooter, if there is a problem. This troubleshooter asks you questions about the test page and other printer items to help you track down problems with your printer driver configuration.

You can also invoke the printer troubleshooter from the Windows 95 Help Contents menu. Click the Start button, click Help, click the Contents tab, double-click Troubleshooting, and then double-click the first item under Troubleshooting.

You can install a printer driver for a networked printer in the same manner that you install a printer driver for a local printer. The only difference is that you will be asked for the server and printer name. Type in the name using the UNC. Your network must support this convention if you are to install a net-worked printer this way.

You can install a printer driver on your computer for a printer on a network in a couple of other ways, a few of them are a little more automated. See the section entitled *Point and Print* later in this chapter for details.

Printer Driver Properties Sheets

Each printer driver has its own icon in the Printers folder. Attached to each printer icon is a raft of Properties sheets for the numerous properties that can be customized for each type of printer.

Properties that were previously global for all printer drivers have been moved to each printer driver's Properties sheet. For example, you can determine for each printer whether to print directly to the printer or through a print queue.

Getting to a printer's Properties sheets

You get to a printer driver's Properties sheets by right-clicking its icon in the Printers folder and clicking Properties on the right mouse button menu. Also, you can highlight a printer icon in the Printers folder and click File, Properties on the menu. If a printer's print queue window is open, click Printer, Properties on the menu.

If you have a shortcut to a printer on your desktop, you will not be able to get to the printer's Properties sheets by right-clicking the shortcut icon and clicking the Properties menu item. This will just get you the properties of the shortcut. You need to double-click the printer shortcut icon and then click Printer, Properties in the menu of the printer queue.

You can also get to some of the printer Properties sheets through the printer setup options in your application. You would normally click File and then Printer or Printer Setup in the menu of your application. New 32-bit applications can use the common print dialog box DLL to get to the printer Properties sheets. These Properties sheets will not exactly match the ones connected to the printer's icon in the Printers folder.

Basic printer Properties sheets

There are too many printer Properties sheets to go through all of them in this book. Besides, we want to focus on the undocumented aspects of the printer drivers, not those features that are obvious.

You can find out what the various radio buttons and fields on these printer Properties sheets do by right-clicking them and then clicking the What's This button. You can also click the question mark in the upper-right corner of the Properties sheet and then click an area of interest in any of the sheets.

Here, we'll go over a few printer Properties sheets to give you an idea of the range of possible properties that can be set. After that, we give you some guidance on how to deal with some of the less well-explained printer driver properties.

The Graphics Properties sheets for a LaserJet compatible printer and a PostScript compatible printer are shown in Figures 23-2 and 23-3. The specific graphics properties depend on the features available in the printer and the printer driver.

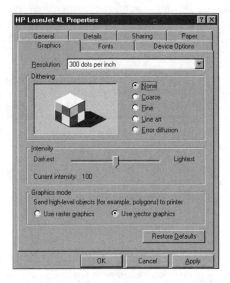

Figure 23-2: The Graphics Properties sheet for a Hewlett Packard 4L printer. You get to determine the quality of the graphics output (traded against time to produce the output and per sheet costs). Resolution doesn't affect text unless printed as graphics (a setting on another sheet).

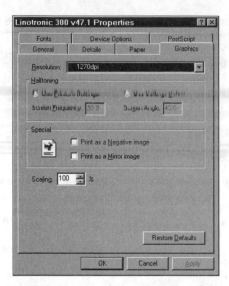

Figure 23-3: The Graphics Properties sheet for a Linotronic 300. The Linotronic would normally be found at a service bureau. You would send PostScript out from your application to a file using this driver and then send the file to the service bureau. The Linotronic can produce film. The Special section flips or reverses the image.

Separator page

The General Properties sheet is the same for each printer. One of the options is to specify a separator page the printer will output between print jobs so that they can be more easily kept separate. Separator pages are useful if many different people print to one printer.

The separator page can be blank, or contain a graphic that more easily identifies it. The graphic needs to be a Windows Metafile Format (WMF). Files of this type have the extension *wmf*.

Undocumented

Microsoft doesn't ship any applications with Windows 95 that can produce Windows Metafile files. You have to purchase an application that creates such files if you want to be able to create a separator page with a graphic on it. We feature Paint Shop Pro 3.0 on the shareware CD-ROM, which allows you to create (or convert) bitmap files to WMF.

Details

All Windows 95 printer drivers have a Details Properties sheet, which is shown in Figure 23-4. This is where you tell the printer driver that the printer has been moved to another port, or decide to print to a file instead. Use the "Print to the following port" drop-down list to do this.

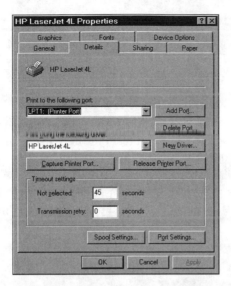

Figure 23-4: The Details Properties sheet. Change the port to which you are printing (after you physically reconnect your local printer). Redirect output to a named LPT port to a network printer with the Capture Printer Port button. Turn off the spooling of DOS print jobs with the Port Settings button. You can even switch to one of the other printer driver Properties sheets by using the "Print using the following driver" drop-down list. You can also update your printer driver from a diskette using the New Driver button.

Undocumented

If you change the "Print to the following port" field to a networked printer path, and that printer is of the same type as the printer whose properties you are currently viewing and editing, you will switch the current printer to the networked printer as soon as you click Apply or OK. This is probably not what you want to do, as you lose your driver to your current printer. It's better to add a networked printer than to switch connections in this field.

If you move the networked or local printer, you can use the Add Port button and this field to move the path to your networked or local printer.

Logical printer port redirection

The Capture Printer Port button allows you to redirect output from a named LPT port to a network printer. You can set up nine redirections (LPT1 through LPT9) and specify if they will be valid the next time you reboot your computer. If you do, Windows 95 will connect to the servers where these printers are located every time you restart your computer while connected to your network.

Add a port

If you want to connect to a different printer, or your networked printer has moved, click the Add Port button. The network path to your already installed network printer will already be shown in the list of ports. You can type in the path to a networked printer for later use.

DOS print spooling

You can turn off DOS print spooling using the Port Settings button. Most of the actual port settings (the I/O address and IRQ setting) are found in the Device Manager.

Print directly to the printer with no spooling

You can also turn off spooling and print directly to the printer (with no intermediate temporary file) by clicking the Spool Settings button. You can also choose between the RAW or EMF spool file data format in the Spool Settings Properties sheet. If there is no spooling, it has to be RAW.

If you are printing to a file, the bottom third of the Details Properties sheets will be grayed out. These properties are not used when printing to a file instead of to a physical printer.

Fonts

All the printer drivers have Fonts Properties sheets. Unlike the case with Details Properties sheet, each type of printer has a different kind of Fonts Properties sheet.

HP font installer

Tip

The HP printer driver allows you to install HP Intellifonts using the Install Printer Fonts button. This brings up HP's font installer, which has the old Windows 3.x look to it. Newer HP printers have a number of built in TrueType fonts that can be matched with TrueType font packs from Microsoft or HP. You would install these fonts using the Fonts folder. See Chapter 20 for more about fonts.

Even if you don't have a newer HP compatible printer with built-in fonts, it's a better idea to install TrueType fonts than the screen versions of the HP Intellifonts. Again, don't use this font installer to install TrueType fonts.

TrueType fonts on PostScript printers

Tip

It's easy to use TrueType fonts and print to a PostScript printer or PostScript file that you will take to a service bureau. In almost all cases, unless you are doing a quick draft document, you will want to check "Always Use TrueType fonts" on the Details Properties sheet and send them to the printer as Outlines.

If you treat TrueType fonts in this manner, your document, as printed, will match the one you saw on the screen. There won't be any shifting of spacing as built-in PostScript fonts are substituted for TrueType fonts, which would be the case if you didn't use this option.

Click the "Always Use TrueType fonts" radio button on the fonts Properties sheet of your PostScript printer, as shown in Figure 23-5. This setting is not the default. Then click the Send Fonts As button and choose Outlines in the Send TrueType Fonts as drop-down list, which is shown in Figure 23-6.

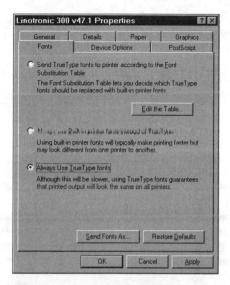

Figure 23-5: The Fonts Properties sheet for the Linotronic 300. Click the Always Use TrueType fonts radio button, then the Send Fonts As button.

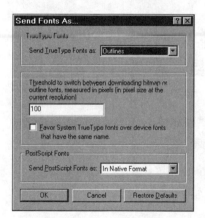

Figure 23-6: The Send Fonts As Properties sheet. Click the down arrow in the Send TrueType Fonts as drop-down list and pick Outlines.

Sharing

Tip

You can have drivers for printers that you don't actually have — no problem with that. For example, if you want to create a PostScript file for a Linotronic 300 that is many miles away in a service bureau, you install a printer driver for it on your computer and write to a file. The file created when you print to the Linotronic can then be shipped out through your modem to the bulletin board at the service bureau for printing later that day or overnight.

One thing that you can't do with printer drivers that are configured to print to a file is share the printer (because there isn't any printer there to share). If you have an actual printer connected locally and you've enabled print sharing (using the Network icon in your Control Panel), you will have a Sharing Properties sheet for your printer. You can choose to share a local printer or not.

You can also get to the Sharing Properties sheet by right-clicking a local printer's icon in the Printers folder and clicking Sharing on the right mouse button menu. For more details, see the section later in this chapter entitled *Sharing a Printer*.

PostScript

The PostScript driver has its own PostScript-specific Properties sheet as shown in Figure 23-7. The Advanced options let you do such wonderful things as getting rid of the Ctrl+D at the beginning or end of your PostScript output so you don't have to manually edit them out if you run over a Unix network to a PostScript printer.

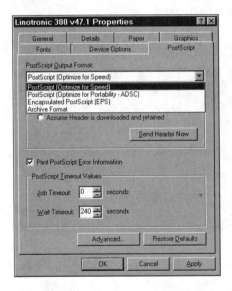

Figure 23-7: The PostScript Properties sheet. Choose an Output Format depending on whether you are printing to a local printer or a file, or to a file to be incorporated into another file. Click the Advanced button for more options.

You have the option of five different PostScript output formats. The default Optimize for Speed is fine for local printers. If you're printing to a file for off-site printing, you might want to try Optimize for Portability - ADSC, which stands for Adobe Document Structuring Conventions.

Defining your own printer

If you have installed the Generic/Text Only printer driver, you can define escape sequences (printer commands) that control your specific printer and set the various font sizes and types. In most cases you don't have to do this, because Microsoft has included printer drivers for 800 different printers with Windows 95. But the capability is there if you run into the 801st.

Use the Device Options and Fonts Properties sheets associated with the Generic/Text only printer driver to define the printer codes for your particular printer.

Tip

Installing the Generic/Text Only printer is a great way to produce text-only output from applications that don't have an option to save unformatted text-only files.

Deferred Printing

You can print documents using a printer driver for a networked printer that isn't currently connected through the network to your computer. The print jobs will be spooled and can be printed later when you reconnect to the printer through the network. The print jobs are tracked in the print queue for that printer, and when you put the printer online, they are automatically printed.

One use of deferred printing is to create documents on a portable, print them to the print queue, and then print them later when you connect your portable to a computer (perhaps your desktop computer) with a printer. The portable has to have a printer driver for the desktop's printer installed as a networked printer. The portable and the desktop computer need to be connected with the Direct Cable Connection (DCC) or through another network connection. See Chapter 30 for more on connecting laptops and desktops.

You can also use Dial-Up Networking (DUN) to phone in from the portable to the desktop computer and print your documents at the office while you are on the road or at home. You will need to have the desktop computer configured as a DUN server.

If you are on a network and printing to a networked printer and you lose the connection to that printer, your print jobs will be spooled until the connection is reestablished and you place the printer online. The printer driver for the networked printer will display itself as off-line as soon as the network connection is broken.

Even if you are presently connected to the networked printer, you can take it off-line (for you) by right-clicking its icon in your Printers folder and clicking Work Off-line.

Undocumented

If you take a networked printer off-line by right-clicking its icon in the Printers folder and checking Work Off-line, the icon in the Printers folder is ghosted. If you have a shortcut to that icon on your desktop, it is not ghosted when the printer is placed off-line. If you double-click the shortcut icon on the desktop, you will see in the window caption area the message that the printer is off-line.

Secret

If you attempt to print to MS Fax, and the phone goes off-hook and is then hung up again by MS Fax before you send the fax, your local printer will go off-line. You can then print to a local printer off-line and have it print later when you put it back on line again.

Printing to a file

Tip

It is always possible to create a print file for a specific printer and later manually send this file to the printer. To do so, change the Print to the following port field in the Details Properties sheet for that printer's driver from a specific port to File. When you print your document, a new file will be created that contains the document formatted with the printer codes for that specific printer.

When you later connect to the printer you can copy the file to the printer port. You actually need to use the DOS Copy command. You can't drag and drop the print file to the printer icon, which makes the most sense (visually), but doesn't work.

Undocumented

You can run the DOS copy command from the Run box on your Start button menu if you like. Assuming that your print filename is File1.hp, you would type the following command in the Run command line:

```
command /c copy /b file1.hp lpt2:
```

This would copy the file of print commands to the second parallel port (which could also be redirected to a networked printer). For some trickier approaches to printing files, turn to the *Printing Postscript Files* section below.

The whole point of deferred printing is to get around this tiresome technique of manually copying print files to the printer port. Unfortunately, deferred printing works only for networked printers and not for local printers that are presently off-line.

Printing to an off-line PostScript printer

You can also use the above technique to print to an off-line (off premises) PostScript printer. You can install a PostScript driver on your computer for your target PostScript printer. You can have the PostScript driver print to a file. Then you transfer this file on a diskette or over the phone lines to the location with the PostScript printer. Using the DOS Copy command, you can then print the PostScript file on the printer.

Print Postscript Files

Windows users will often create print files of PostScript output on computers that don't have PostScript printers connected to them or to the network to which the computer is connected, if any. They can then take this PostScript output file to a computer with a PostScript printer and copy the file (which is just a series of ASCII commands and parameters) to the printer.

Copying a file to the printer is a DOS-based function, but we can configure Windows 95 to carry out this function without obviously opening a DOS window and issuing the DOS copy command or using the Start, Run dialog box.

Undocumented

There are a number of ways to do this. First, you can create an association between the *ps* file extension and a command that copies the file to the printer. Second, you can create a batch file and shortcut that consists of the DOS commands to send the file to the printer. Third, you can additionally place the shortcut to the PostScript printing batch file in the Send To folder.

The batch file is generic, so it will send any file to the printer, not just PostScript files.

PostScript print output files generally have a *ps* extension. To create an association to this file type, take the following steps:

STEPS

Create a Print Command Associated with PostScript Print file

Step 1. Open up your Explorer and click View, Option, File Types on menu bar.

Step 2. Click New Type.

Step 3. Type in **PostScript Print Output file** in the Description of type field, **ps** in the Associated extension field, and **PostScript Commands** in the Content type field.

Step 4. Click New and the type **Copy to Printer** in the Action field and **C:\Windows\Command.com /c Copy /b %1 Lpt1:** in the "Application used to perform action" field. Click OK.

Lpt1: can be replaced by another printer port designator, or by the UNC name of a networked printer.

Step 5. Click the Choose Icon button, and browse through the offered files to find an appropriate printer type icon. Click OK.

Step 6. Click OK and then Close.

You can now double-click any file with a *ps* extension and it will be printed on your PostScript printer. Unfortunately, with this method the DOS window will flash briefly.

To create a batch file and an accompanying shortcut that will print any file (and not flash a DOS window) take the following steps:

STEPS

Create a Print Batch file

Step 1. Double-click Edit.com in your \Windows\Command folder (if you haven't already made a shortcut to this nifty DOS editor).

Step 2. Type in **C:\Windows\Command.com /c Copy /b %1 Lpt1:**

Step 3. Click File, SaveAs and save the file as Ps.bat.

Step 4. Right-drag and drop a shortcut associated with Ps.bat to your desktop. You could also try another method to create a shortcut on your desktop. Right-click Ps.bat, click Create Shortcut. Right-click the shortcut that is created in the same folder as Ps.bat, click Cut. Right-click the desktop and click Paste.

Step 5. With the new shortcut on the desktop highlighted, press F2 and rename the shortcut something like "Print Files."

Step 6. Right-click the shortcut, click Properties, and then click the Program tab.

Step 7. Change the Run field to Minimized and click the Close on exit check box to turn it on. Click the Change Icon button and find an appropriate icon for this shortcut that prints PostScript files. Click OK.

Step 8. Right-click a PostScript print output file in a folder or Explorer window and click Copy in the right mouse button menu.

Step 9. Right-click the new Shortcut on the desktop and click Paste. The PostScript file will be copied to the PostScript printer. A button will appear briefly on the Taskbar as the file is copied.

The file is treated as a DOS file and will be spooled to the printer if you haven't turned DOS print spooling off.

You can place this shortcut in the Send To folder, which is under the Windows folder. If you do that, you can right-click the PostScript (or text) file and click Send To in the right mouse button menu. You can then copy the file to the printer by clicking the shortcut's icon in the Send To menu.

Troubleshooting with Windows 95 Help

If you are having trouble printing, you can use the Troubleshooting section of the help system to track down the problem. Instead of being a semi-meaningless collection of statements of the obvious, Windows 95 help is actually useful in the real world. The printer troubleshooter can pinpoint a problem for you, as long as you answer the questions correctly.

To get to the printer troubleshooter, click the Start button, then Help, then the Contents tab, then double-click the Troubleshooting book icon. The printer troubleshooter is the first item (this placement lets you know what causes the most problems).

Configuring ECP and EPP Ports

Windows 95 Setup will detect whether you have an *extended capabilities port* (ECP) or *enhanced parallel port* (EPP), but it won't set up the port for you. If you want high-speed communication, you will have to enable ECP support yourself. Here's how:

STEPS

Configuring ECP Support

Step 1. Click the Start button, then Settings, then Control Panel.

Step 2. Click the System icon in the Control Panel, then the Device Manager tab.

Step 3. Click the plus sign next to the Ports icon (or double-click the Ports icon).

Step 4. If Windows 95 Setup actually detected an ECP or EPP parallel port in your computer you will find it under the Port icon. Double-click it (or highlight it and click the Properties button), and then the Resources tab.

Step 5. Click the down arrow in the Settings Based on drop-down list. Click Basic Configuration 2.

Step 6. In the Resource Settings window, click the Interrupt Request Resource Type and then click the Change Settings button.

Step 7. Type in the interrupt request (IRQ) value in the Edit Interrupt Request dialog box using the value provided by the manual for this ECP or EPP card (or computer). Click OK.

(continued)

STEPS *(continued)*

Configuring ECP Support

Step 8. Click the Direct Memory Access button in the Resources Properties sheet.

Step 9. Type in the Direct Memory Access (DMA) value using the value provided by the manual for this card in the Direct Memory Access dialog box. Click OK.

Step 10. Restart Windows 95 to allow the changes to take effect.

Notice that all this activity takes place in the Device Manager, outside the realm of the Printers folder.

Network Printer Management Tools

The Digital Equipment Corporation and Hewlett Packard network printer server-management software is designed to help manage their networked printers. You can use these tools to manage these printers from your Windows 95 computer.

The management tools are found on the Windows 95 CD-ROM in the \Admin\Prttools\Decpsmon and \Admin\Nettools\Hpjetadm folders. The software can be installed using the Add/Remove Programs icon in the Control Panel.

STEPS

Installing Digital and HP Network Printer Management Tools

Step 1. Click the Start button, Settings, and then Control Panel.

Step 2. Double-click the Add/Remove Programs icon in the Control Panel, and then click the Windows Setup icon.

Step 3. Click the Have Disk button, then Browse.

Step 4. Browse to either of the folders: \Admin\Prttools\Decpsmon or \Admin\Nettools\Hpjetadm on your Windows 95 CD-ROM.

Step 5. A file with the *inf* extension will be highlighted in the 16-bit common file dialog box. Click OK.

Step 6. Click the OK button on the Install from Disk dialog box.

Step 7. Click the check box next to the component name for the printer server management software that you are about to install and click Install on the Have Disk dialog box.

Step 8. Click OK on the Add/Remove Programs dialog box.

The printer server program that you chose will be added to your hard disk and a shortcut to it is now found in the System Tools menu on your Start menu (under Programs, Accessories).

Sharing a Printer

It is possible to share your printer over your network so others can use it to print their documents. There are two basic ways to do this. The first is to configure your computer as a server (either a file server, a print server, or both). Your computer can become a file and print server on a peer-to-peer network like Microsoft Windows Network, or on a server-based network like Novell NetWare or Windows NT networks.

Unlike Windows NT or Novell servers, the Windows 95 file and print server doesn't have a database that can track users and maintain user-level security. If you want to have the kind of security that allows users to use your resources by group or user name instead of by password, you'll need to use these other servers.

If you are on a NetWare network, the second way to share your printer is to set up MS Print Server for NetWare on your Windows 95 computer and use your computer to service the NetWare print queue on the NetWare server. The Windows 95 Print Server for NetWare cooperates with the NetWare print server to print the jobs that are queued by the NetWare server. We discuss this second method in the next section.

Enabling print sharing

To share your local printer with others on a network you must first enable Print Sharing. To do so, take the following steps:

STEPS

Enabling Print Sharing

Step 1. Click the Start button, Settings, and then Control Panel.

Step 2. Double-click the Network icon. Click the Add button.

(continued)

STEPS *(continued)*

Enabling Print Sharing

Step 3.   Highlight Service in the Select Network Component Type dialog box and click Add.

Step 4.   Highlight Microsoft in the Select Network Service dialog box. Then highlight either File and Print sharing for Microsoft Networks or File and Print sharing for NetWare Networks. If you are installing print sharing for another network and you have a diskette from the manufacturer, click Have Disk instead. Click OK.

Step 5.   Click the File and Print Sharing button.

Step 6.   In the File and Print Sharing dialog box, which is shown in Figure 23-8, check "I want to be able to allow others to print to my printer(s)."

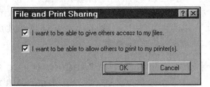

Figure 23-8: The File and Print Sharing dialog box. Click the check box next to the resources that you want to share.

Step 7.   Click both OK buttons.

You will have to restart your computer to have any changes you made take effect.

Actually share it

To share a printer, take the following steps:

STEPS

Sharing a Printer

Step 1. Click the Start button, Settings, and then Printers.

Step 2. Right-click the icon of the printer that you want to share and then click the Sharing menu item on the right mouse button menu.

Step 3. You'll see the Sharing Properties sheet as shown in Figure 23-9. Click Shared As.

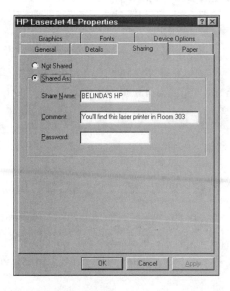

Figure 23-9: The Sharing Properties sheet. Click Shared As to allow your printer to be used by others. You can give a useful comment and name to help others know if they want to use your printer and where to find the output.

Step 4. Fill out the three Shared As fields.

Step 5. Click OK.

Your computer is now a full-fledged print server. If you are using a NetWare network, you can use the Windows 95 computer as a complete print server and off-load the extra resource use from your NetWare server.

If you are using a Windows NT or NetWare server to provide user-level security, you won't see the Password box that appears in Figure 23-9. The users who can access your printer will be determined by the database of users that you have specified have access to your resources. This list of groups and users is kept on the Windows NT or NetWare server.

To specify on which server the list of users is kept, take the following steps:

STEPS

Specifying User-Access Control

Step 1.   Click the Start button, Settings, and then Control Panel.

Step 2.   Double-click the Network icon. Click the Access Control tab.

Step 3.   Click the User-level access control radio button.

Step 4.   Type in the name of the server that has the list.

Microsoft Print Services for NetWare

If you are on a NetWare network, you can set up your Windows 95 computer to be a print services provider for a NetWare server. Instead of being an independent print server, you can use MS Print Server for NetWare to configure your computer to de-spool print jobs from a NetWare print server and print them on its local printer.

To configure your printer as an independent print server, run File and Print Sharing for NetWare. You won't need to do this if you are configuring your computer as a print services provider for a NetWare print server.

Your computer will log on to the NetWare print server and then poll the print queue on the server for print jobs. To install MS Printer Services for NetWare, take the following steps:

STEPS

Installing MS Print Services for NetWare

Step 1.   Click the Start button, Settings, and then Control Panel.

Step 2.   Double-click the Add/Remove Programs icon. Click the Windows Setup tab.

Step 3.   Click Have Disk.

Step 4. In the "Copy manufacturer's files from" field, type in the volume letter designator for your CD-ROM and the path **\Admin\Nettools\Prtagent.**

Step 5. The file Mspsrv.inf will be highlighted in the 16-bit common file dialog box. Click OK.

Step 6. Click OK in the Install from Disk dialog box.

Step 7. Click the check box next to the Microsoft Print Server for NetWare and click the Install button on the Have Disk dialog box.

Step 8. Click OK in the Add/Remove Programs dialog box.

Now that MS Print Services for Network is installed, you need to enable it. First check your NetWare print server and make sure that it is operating correctly. To do so, take these steps:

STEPS

Enabling MS Print Services for NetWare

Step 1. Click the Start button, Settings, and then Printers.

Step 2. Right-click the icon for the local printer that will be used to print jobs coming from the NetWare print queue. Click Properties in the right mouse button menu.

Step 3. Click the Print Server tab. Click the Enable Microsoft Print Server for NetWare button.

Step 4. In the NetWare Server field, click the drop-down list and choose the NetWare server. In the Print server field, choose the NetWare print server names whose queue your Windows 95 computer will service.

Step 5. Adjust the print queue polling time interval.

Step 6. Click OK.

Point and Print

You can install a printer driver on your computer for a networked printer in the normal fashion by using the Add Printer Wizard. Just double-click the Add Printer icon in the Printers folder.

When you do this, the Wizard will find the printer driver files necessary to install that printer driver. Of course, you will need to know exactly what kind of printer you are installing so you can tell this to the Add Printer Wizard, and you will have to have the printer driver source diskettes or CD-ROM handy.

Semi-automated printer driver installation

A better way to install printer drivers for a networked printer is to drag and drop the networked printer's icon to your desktop or your Printers folder. You can also double-click the networked printer's icon in the shared resources folder view of the server. You can also drag and drop a document icon to the networked printer icon in its shared folder window. Finally, you can right-click the networked printer's icon and click Install.

Drag and drop a document to a networked printer icon

When you print a document by dragging and dropping it to the icon of a networked printer that you haven't yet installed, you invoke a version of the Add Printer Wizard.

STEPS

Installing a Networked Printer by Drag and Drop Printing

Step 1.   Open a folder view of a document file or shortcut to a document file.

Step 2.   Be sure you have the shared resources folder window open for the server whose printer you are going to install.

Step 3.   Drag and drop a document icon to the printer icon in the shared resources folder view. The message box shown in Figure 23-10 will appear.

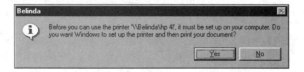

Figure 23-10: A message box telling you that you've got to set up the printer driver on your computer.

Step 4.   Click the Yes button. The Add Printer Wizard (networked printer installation version) appears, as shown in Figure 23-11. If you want to assign a logical printer port to your networked printer, click Yes that you want to print from MS-DOS programs and then click the Next button. MS-DOS programs often require that you print to an LPT port.

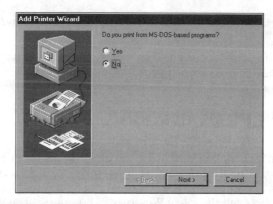

Figure 23-11: The networked printer installation version of the Add Printer Wizard. If you don't want to capture a printer port, click Next. Otherwise, click the MS-DOS radio button and then Next.

Step 5. Finish answering the Wizard's questions. Give the printer a name that gives you a clue when you print to it.

The printer drivers for the networked printer are now installed. When you open your Printers folder window, you'll see an icon for the networked printer there.

Undocumented
Now that you have installed the networked printer, you can drag and drop documents to either of its icons to print documents. The networked printer's icon in the Shared Resources folder or in your local Printers folder are treated exactly the same. Double-click either and you will see the same printer queue. Only the icon in the Printers folder is ghosted if the networked printer is off-line.

Undocumented
You can put a shortcut to a networked printer on your desktop, just as you can a local printer. If your network connection is DCC, you can't invoke the connection if it isn't set up by double-clicking the networked computer's icon. You have to make the connection first before the networked printer can be seen.

Drag and drop a networked printer icon

The networked printer icon should be visible to you in the Explorer or in a Shared Resources window that is focused on the network server computer. You can drag and drop the networked printer's icon from the Explorer or folder window to your desktop or to your Printers folder window or icon.

Double-click the networked printer icon

If you can see the icon that represents the shared printer on the networked computer, just double-click it. That moves its printer drivers over to your computer and puts its icon in your Printers folder.

Enabling point and print

Printers that are shared on networked Windows 95, Windows NT, and NetWare servers can be installed with point and print. If you are printing to a Windows 95 print server, all the information about the printer drivers and the drivers themselves are stored there. You don't have to do anything to allow the drivers to be transferred to the client Windows 95 computer. The Windows 95 printer server must be running File and Print Sharing for NetWare or File and Print Sharing for Microsoft Network.

Point and print to a NetWare server

If you want to be able to have Windows 95 client computers point and print to your printers managed by a NetWare printer server, you're going to need to do a little more work. You'll have to copy the driver files that are used for each of the printers managed by that server to a directory on the server. It turns out that this is a bit less than point and print and a lot like the Add Printer Wizard.

Set up a NetWare print server for point and print

If you have administrative privileges on the NetWare server that you are logged onto, you can configure the server to store the needed printer drivers and auxiliary files. Take the following steps to do so:

STEPS

Configuring a NetWare Server to Store Point and Print Files

Step 1. Right-click a NetWare print queue icon displayed in the NetWare Shared Resources window. Click Point and Print Setup in the right mouse button menu.

Step 2. Click Set Printer Model. In the Select dialog box, highlight the manufacturer and model of the printer associated with the printer queue on the NetWare server. Click OK.

Step 3. Right-click the same NetWare printer queue again, then click Set Driver Path.

Step 4. Type a path and directory name that is valid for the NetWare server and in which you will store the printer driver files for this printer.

Step 5. Open Msprint.inf or Msprint2.inf in your Inf folder with NotePad. See which files are going to be copied when you install this printer. Extract these files from your Windows 95 CD-ROM or diskette source cabinet files and copy them into the directory you just created on your NetWare server.

You now have the printer driver source files on your NetWare server. This makes it somewhat easier to point and print to a NetWare printer from a Windows 95 client computer.

Point and print to a NetWare printer

Now that you have set up your NetWare server to allow for point and print (after a fashion), you can use it to install printer drivers on a Windows 95 client computer. To do this, take the following steps:

STEPS

Installing Printer Drivers from a NetWare Server

Step 1. Log on to a NetWare server from a client Windows 95 computer.

Step 2. In the Network Neighborhood on the client computer, double-click the NetWare server's icon. A folder window displaying the resources of the NetWare server will be displayed.

Step 3. Drag and drop a printer icon from the NetWare window to your local Printers folder window. The Add Printer Wizard will be activated.

Step 4. Type in the name of the new printer.

Your NetWare networked printer drivers are now installed on your local Windows 95 computer.

Summary

Windows 95 arrives with a significant number of improvements in printing capabilities. You'll see what improvements have been made.

▶ We discuss how the new Printers folder unites almost all of the print functions in Windows, making it easier to manage your printers.

▶ Because each printer has its own icon, you can put a shortcut to each printer on your desktop. Now you can drag and drop documents to just the printer that you want without having to change the default printer.

▶ You can define drag and drop to a printer to be any possible action, not just printing.

▶ DOS files are by default spooled to the printer through the Windows 95 print spooler. This alleviates printer device contention.

▶ Windows 95 supported enhanced parallel ports to give you higher speeds and more bidirectional communication between printer and computer.

▶ We show you how to print TrueType fonts correctly on PostScript printers.

▶ You can print to a print queue and have your files printed later when you actually connect to your printer.

▶ You can have the appropriate print drivers semi-automatically installed when you print to networked printers.

Chapter 24

The Mighty Mouse (Other Pointing Devices, Too)

In This Chapter

Mouse support has improved significantly in Windows 95, bringing about a mouse that is friendlier, more powerful, and more useful. We describe:

▶ The improvements in the 32-bit protected-mode mouse driver

▶ Improving mouse responsiveness and making it easier to double-click

▶ Turning your mouse pointer into a nifty animated cursor

▶ Turning your middle button into a double-click button

▶ When to use double-click and how to get around using it

▶ The power of the right mouse button and why you'll want to use it often

Mouse Basics

In this chapter, we don't mean *mouse* exactly, but whatever pointing device you use that acts like a mouse, be it a trackball, BallPoint, InPort, pen and tablet, or one of the other devices that are variants on these themes. All these devices are used to move the mouse pointer about the screen.

The Windows user interface is a point-and-click interface. The mouse is the instrument you use to point and click. Windows 95 has made the mouse more important than it was in Windows 3.x by making it more powerful.

Windows 95 supports, right out of the box, a broad variety of mice from different manufacturers. All Microsoft mouse-compatible mice, of course, are supported as though they were, in fact, manufactured by Microsoft. Explicitly named are mice manufactured by Logitech, Kensington, Compaq, and Texas Instruments (TI). There is generic support for various "standard" mice.

Mouse models that are supported include serial mice, bus mice, PS/2 mice, TI QuickPort BallPoint mouse, Compaq LTE trackball, and Kensington Serial Expert mouse, as well as all models compatible with these models.

Existing Windows 3.x mouse drivers will work as before. When you set up Windows 95, it will remark out calls to the older mouse drivers in your Autoexec.bat and Config.sys files if the new Windows 95 mouse drivers support your mouse. If you have a Windows 3.x mouse driver that provides features not found in the Windows 95 mouse driver, you can continue to use it or upgrade to a new Windows 95 version if available separately from your mouse manufacturer.

Mouse Driver Improvements

The Windows 95 mouse drivers are 32-bit protected-mode drivers. They take up zero conventional memory, leaving more room for your DOS programs. You can remove any references to your old mouse drivers like Mouse.com or Mouse.sys in your Autoexec.bat or Config.sys files if the setup program has not already done so.

The mouse driver supports MS-DOS programs both in full-screen and windowed DOS sessions. This is a big plus since it eliminates the need to remember to load Mouse.com or Mouse.sys before starting a DOS program. It also saves precious real-mode memory, below 640K RAM. Using Windows 3.x, you were required to load a separate MS-DOS mouse driver to support a mouse in DOS sessions. Only if you run MS-DOS programs that use a mouse in MS-DOS mode — a mode that unloads Windows 95 and all its 32-bit protected mode-drivers and reloads real-mode DOS — will you need to load the real-mode mouse drivers. You can configure a shortcut to load them into memory at the time you switch to MS-DOS mode.

A serial mouse can be connected to serial ports COM1 through COM4. Previously a serial mouse could be connected only to COM1 or COM2.

The new Windows 95 mouse driver supports future plug and play mice. These mice will automatically be recognized and installed during setup. Pre-plug and play mice can be detected by the Windows 95 hardware detection routines.

Windows 95 includes an improved Mouse Control Panel with greater functionality. Mouse manufacturers are still able to substitute their own control panels for this one, or add to it.

You can define the middle button of your Logitech three-button mouse to substitute for a double-click.

All along, the mice used with PCs and compatible computers have had at least two buttons, but the right one didn't do anything in Windows itself. Some Windows programs took advantage of the right button. The Borland C++ compiler, for example, used it extensively. Now Microsoft has decided to define the behavior of the right mouse button in Windows 95. In Windows 95, clicking the right mouse button brings up a menu of available options for the current program or item in Windows itself.

By defining what the right mouse button does, Microsoft has greatly increased the ease of use of the Windows interface. That is, it has if you learn how to use the right button without thinking.

Setting Up Your Mouse Driver

The Windows 95 installation and setup procedures include automatic hardware detection. You will want the setup program to correctly identify your mouse. The correct mouse drivers will be installed if your mouse is plugged in.

If your mouse isn't detected properly, you can easily add it using the steps detailed later in this chapter in the section entitled *Adding a mouse driver*.

If your mouse isn't supported by the mouse drivers that come with Windows 95, you can still use your existing mouse drivers. If you have installed Windows 95 in your existing Windows directory without first deleting Windows 3.*x*, your mouse drivers will still be functioning. The calls to these mouse drivers will still be in your Autoexec.bat and/or Config.sys files.

Changing an existing mouse driver

You can change to a different mouse driver or add a new Windows 95 mouse driver if you find that the one you have installed is incorrect. To change an existing mouse driver:

STEPS

Changing an Existing Mouse Driver

Step 1.   Click the Start button, then go to the Settings, Control Panel and double-click the Mouse icon.

Step 2.   Click the General tab and the Change button. The Select Device dialog box, as shown in Figure 24-1, will appear.

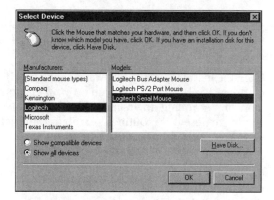

Figure 24-1: The Select Device dialog box. Highlight a manufacturer and then a mouse model. Click OK. You will have to restart Windows after you choose a new mouse driver.

(continued)

STEPS *(continued)*

Changing an Existing Mouse Driver

Step 3. Another way to have the Select Device dialog box appear for a mouse driver is to double click the System icon in the Control Panel. Next, click the Device Manager tab in the System Properties sheet and click on the View Devices by Connection check box. Then click on the Properties button, click the Driver tab in the specific mouse's Properties sheet, and then click the Change Driver button.

Step 4. In the Select Device dialog box, click Show all devices.

Step 5. Choose a mouse manufacturer and model from the dialog box. If the mouse you have isn't listed and you know that it is not compatible with the models listed and you have a mouse driver diskette, click the Have Disk button.

Step 6. Click OK until you have exited all the dialog boxes.

Step 7. Restart Windows 95 to have the mouse driver take effect.

Adding a mouse driver

You can add a mouse driver if you add a mouse after you have installed Windows 95.

STEPS

Adding a Mouse Driver

Step 1. Click the Start button, then Settings, Control Panel. Double-click the Add New Hardware icon. Click Next.

Step 2. Click the Install specific hardware check box if you know what kind of mouse is physically installed on your computer. Click the Mouse icon after scrolling down in the hardware list. You can have the hardware detection routines search for and detect your mouse, but this takes a few minutes. Click Next.

Step 3. Choose a mouse manufacturer and model from the Select Device dialog box. If the mouse you have isn't listed and you know that it is not compatible with the models listed and you have a mouse driver diskette, click the Have Disk button.

Step 4.   If you have a mouse driver diskette, put it in your disk drive and click the OK button if the correct path to your diskette drive is shown. Otherwise, type the correct path before clicking OK.

Step 5.   Click Finish.

Step 6.   Restart Windows 95 to have the mouse driver take effect.

You can install mouse drivers that were written for Windows 3.x if you don't find one that works with your mouse. Be sure to try to install one of the new ones first before you install an older driver. Just because your mouse and the mouse driver don't have the same names doesn't mean one of the new drivers won't work — try a few first.

Undocumented

To install a Windows 3.x mouse driver or a mouse driver that didn't come with Windows 95, click the Have Disk button in Step 3 above. You need to have a diskette with the mouse driver on it. The diskette needs to include a mouse setup file. This file has an *inf* extension and defines how to install the mouse drivers.

Configuring Your Mouse Driver Properties

Use the Mouse Control Panel to set the properties of the mouse driver. Using the Mouse Control Panel, you can change the responsiveness or speed of the mouse pointer relative to your movements of the mouse. You can switch the function of the right and left mouse buttons for left-handed operation.

You can change the double-click time interval. A longer interval counts two separate mouse clicks that have a greater separation in time as a single double-click. You get to pick from a collection of mouse pointer icons, including animated pointers that correspond to a range of mouse functions. Turn the hourglass pointer into a spinning world, for example. Since Windows 95 uses the same *.ani* cursor file format as Windows NT, you will be able to select from a wide variety of shareware and freeware animated icons available on online services such as CompuServe, as well as on the shareware on the CD-ROM that accompanies this book.

For use with an LCD screen, you can add mouse pointer trails by setting the number of ghost images that get left behind (briefly) at the mouse pointer's former location.

STEPS

Configuring the Mouse Driver

Step 1.   Click the Start button, then Settings, and Control Panel. Double-click the mouse icon that looks like a white right-handed soap bar.

Step 2.   The Mouse Buttons Properties sheet allows you to switch the handedness of the mouse buttons and set the speed at which you have to click the mouse twice in order to get the two clicks to count as a single double-click. Figure 24-2 shows the Mouse Buttons Properties sheet.

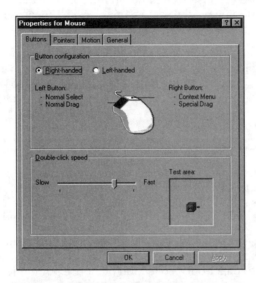

Figure 24-2: The Mouse Buttons Properties sheet. You can swap the left and right mouse buttons and shorten or lengthen the time interval between mouse clicks that will count as a double-click.

Changing the handedness of the mouse buttons

Click the Left-handed check box to switch the left and right mouse buttons. On a three-button mouse these are the two outside buttons.

Changing the double-click speed

To adjust how fast you need to double-click, do the following:

STEPS

Changing Double-Click Speed

Step 1. Move the double-click speed pointer to the left to increase the time interval size allowed between two mouse clicks that are counted as one double-click. Move the pointer to the right to increase the speed with which you must twice click the left mouse button (assuming a right-handed configuration) in order for it to count as a double-click.

Step 2. To test your double-click agility, click twice in the test area. If your two clicks count as one double-click, the jack-in-the-box goes up or down.

Secret

The range of the slider is between 900 milliseconds (nine-tenths of a second) at the left end and 100 milliseconds (one-tenth of a second) on the right end. This makes the middle of the slider equal to half a second.

Changing the double-click height and width

Secret

Windows 3.*x* allowed you to determine the size in pixels of a box around the location of the mouse pointer where the first click of a double-click takes place. The mouse pointer must be located within this box for a second click to count as part of the double-click. The variables DoubleClickWidth and DoubleClickHeight could be inserted into the [Windows] section of the Win.ini file. If these variables were not included in Win.ini, the default size of the box was four pixels on a side.

To change the size of the double-click box (which defaults to four pixels) under Windows 95, you have to edit the Registry. Here's how:

STEPS

Changing the Size of the Double-Click Box

Step 1. Double-click the Registry editor icon on your desktop (or click Regedit.exe found in the \Windows folder in an Explorer window).

Step 2. Click the plus sign next to HKEY_CURRENT_USER and then Control Panel. Highlight Desktop in the left pane of the Registry editor.

(continued)

STEPS *(continued)*

Changing the Size of the Double-Click Box

Step 3.   Right-click in the right pane, away from any of the entries. Click New, then String value.

Step 4.   Type the name **DoubleClickWidth** and press Enter.

Step 5.   Double-click the entry made in Step 4. Type the desired width (in pixels) of the double-click box. Click OK.

Step 6.   Repeat steps 3-6, but this time type **DoubleClickHeight** and specify the desired height in pixels.

Step 7.   If you misspell any of the names, highlight them and press F2.

Step 8.   Shut down and restart Windows 95 to have these new values take effect. You can test them using the jack-in-the-box in the Mouse Properties sheets.

Using different mouse pointers

You can (and we feel should) use some of the newer static and animated cursors available to work with Windows 95. They are a lot of fun and often better designed than the Windows standard ones.

Microsoft Plus! comes with lots of animated cursors. Some will be stored in the \Windows\Cursors folder and some in the \Plus!\Themes folder. Only a few animated cursors come with Windows 95; these cursors are stored in the \Windows\Cursors folder.

You must have your display card driver set to at least 256 colors in order for animated cursors to work. See Chapter 22 for details about display cards.

Secret

Some cards that can display 256 colors have video drivers that don't work with animated cursors. The Diamond Viper is one such video card. You'll need to test your card and driver with one animated cursor to make sure that it works.

Secret

Animated cursors don't work if you use 16-bit real-mode hard disk drivers instead of the 32-bit protected-mode drivers that come with Windows 95. Your Config.sys file will reference these drivers if you are using them. You can also check in the Device Manager (see Chapter 19) to see if you are using 32-bit hard disk drivers.

If you did a custom Windows 95 installation, as is our recommendation, you need to be sure to install the mouse pointers initially (as an accessory) if you want to have them available to you now. If you didn't install them at that time, you can double-click the Add/Remove Programs icon in the Control Panel, click the Windows Setup tab, click Accessories, and check Mouse Pointers to install them.

STEPS

Changing Mouse Pointers

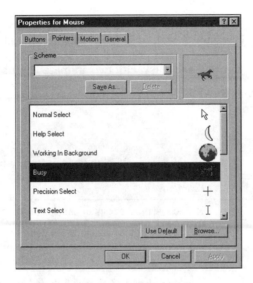

Figure 24-3: The Mouse Pointers Properties sheet. Each mouse function has an associated mouse pointer.

Step 1.   Click the Pointers tab to display the Mouse Pointers Properties sheet, as shown in Figure 24-3. Starting with Normal Select, scroll down the list of pointer functions and their associated pointers. Click on different pointers as you go down the list.

Step 2.   To change a mouse function to use another mouse pointer, click that mouse function. Click the Browse button. You will see a listing of the animated cursors stored in the \Windows\Ani folder (if you have created this folder) or other cursors in the \Windows\Cursors folder. As you highlight them, each of the mouse pointers is shown in the preview window.

Step 3.   Double-click the cursor that you want to be the replacement for the existing pointer.

Tip

The CD-ROM that accompanies this book contains a number of interesting animated and static cursors you can use to replace some of your existing pointers. We suggest you create a folder called Ani as a subfolder of your \Windows folder and move your animated cursors into this folder, even the ones currently stored in the \Windows\Cursors folder. This way it is easy to get at the animated ones with the Browse button, as they will be in the first folder under the Windows folder in the upper left side of the Browse dialog box.

Files that contain animated cursors use the *ani* extension. Files that contain static cursors use the *cur* extension.

Tip

We further suggest you do not replace the mouse pointers associated with Normal Select, Precision Select, or Text Select with animated cursors. They will be too distracting. Go ahead and replace the mouse pointers associated with Working in Background and Busy with two animated icons that express waiting.

Table 24-1 details the different mouse pointers associated with the different mouse functions.

Table 24-1	Windows 95 Mouse Pointers
Pointer	*Function*
Normal Select	The normal mouse pointer for selecting items.
Help Select	Click the ? button in the upper right corner of a dialog box, move this mouse pointer to an area that you want information about, and click again.
Working in Background	Windows 95 or a 32-bit multithreaded application is busy but using a background thread, so you can proceed with something else if you want.
Busy	Windows 95 or an application is busy trying to accomplish some task before it can proceed.
Precision Select	This cursor can be used to guide your eye to its center for careful selection.
Text Select	The I-beam. This cursor is seen in word processors. You position it to select text.
Handwriting	This cursor appears when you have switched to a mode in an application that is expecting handwritten or ink input from you.
Unavailable	If you drag a file icon over an area or application that won't accept the file if you drop it there, this cursor appears to remind you of that fact.
Vertical, Horizontal, Diagonal Resize	The double-headed arrow cursors that appear when you position your mouse pointer along the edges of a sizable window.

Move	Click the Move command in the system menu of a window and this cursor will appear. You can move the window with your arrow keys.
Alternate Select	The only place we have seen this cursor used is in the FreeCell solitaire card game.

There is a very important cursor that is missing from this list. It is the cursor that shows the insertion point within text editors and word processors. It tells you where your current insertion point is, that is, where text will be displayed if you start typing.

If you change the color of your windows using the Display Control Panel, it is very important to be able to set the color of the insertion point cursor so it will show up on top of the background color you choose. You would choose to do this if you prefer a background color other than stark white. For more details, see Chapter 22.

Microsoft Plus! comes with its own sets of cursors that work with various themes. You can edit these cursors and use them independently of the themes. To changes themes and therefore cursors, double-click Master Theme Selector in the Control Panel. The cursors associated with themes are stored in the \Program Files\Plus!\Themes folder.

Changing mouse pointer speed

Undocumented

Speed is a bit of a misnomer. What you are determining is *how much faster* the mouse pointer moves as you move the mouse faster. This is a semi-complicated multiplier of the already-set ratio of mouse pointer movement to mouse movement.

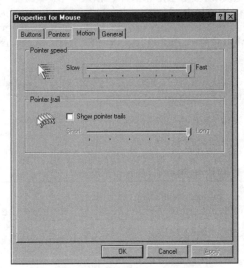

Figure 24-4: The Mouse Motion Properties sheet. Change the responsiveness of the mouse pointer to movements in the mouse. Add trails to the mouse pointer on LCD screens. The units for MouseThreshold1 and 2 are pixels.

The ratio of mouse pointer movement to mouse movement has already been set by your mouse and video driver. The pointer speed values multiply this ratio so that the mouse pointer moves even faster if you move the mouse faster. Each one of the tick marks in the Pointer speed slider, which is shown in Figure 24-4, corresponds to a different set of values for Mouse Speed, MouseThreshold1, and MouseThreshold2. These values are shown in Table 24-2.

Table 24-2	The Pointer Speed Values						
Slider Position	*1*	*2*	*3*	*4*	*5*	*6*	*7*
MouseSpeed	0	1	1	1	2	2	2
MouseThreshold1	0	10	7	4	4	4	4
MouseThreshold2	0	0	0	0	12	9	6

If you move your mouse slowly, the mouse pointer moves slowly. If you move the mouse quickly, the mouse pointer moves even more quickly if the MouseSpeed is greater than zero.

Windows compares the number of pixels the mouse pointer has moved during the time interval between mouse interrupts against the mouse thresholds. The mouse sends out interrupts periodically. If you move the mouse quickly, the mouse pointer movement will exceed the number of pixels of one or both of the mouse thresholds.

If the MouseSpeed is set to 1 and the mouse pointer movement exceeds the number of pixels given by the value of MouseThreshold1, the mouse pointer speed is double the normal rate. If the MouseSpeed is set to 2 and the mouse pointer movement exceeds the MouseThreshold2, the mouse pointer speed is quadrupled. If it exceeds MouseThreshold1 it is doubled, the same as if MouseSpeed is set to 1.

Play with this mouse speed slider a bit to see what you are comfortable with. It depends on whether you have a trackball or a mouse, among other things.

STEPS

Changing the Mouse Pointer Speed

Step 1. From the Mouse Properties sheet, click the Motion tab to display the Motion Properties sheet. Move the speed slider to the left to decrease the travel of the mouse pointer across the screen relative to the speed of travel of the mouse across the mouse pad. Move the slider to the right to increase the responsiveness of the mouse pointer movements to the speed of the mouse.

Undocumented

Step 2. You won't be able to test the speed difference unless you click the Apply button. You might want to try a few different speeds and click the Apply button after each.

Changing mouse speed values in the Registry

Secret

You may wonder how we determined the values set by the Pointer speed slider. They turn out to be the same values set by the mouse driver in Windows 3.*x*. But to determine the actual values, we checked the values set by the slider by looking in the Registry. The way we did it turns out to be generally quite useful and bears detailing.

STEPS

Seeing Your Registry Values Change

Step 1. Display the Mouse Motion Properties sheet on your desktop as per the preceding set of steps.

Step 2. Also display the Registry editor, Regedit.exe. You can do this from the Explorer by double-clicking \Windows\Regedit.exe.

Step 3. Open the Registry editor to HKEY_CURRENT_USER \Control Panel\Mouse. Highlight Mouse, as shown in Figure 24-5. If you don't see this Mouse branch in the Registry, check the undocumented feature at the end of this section.

Step 4. Click on the Mouse Motion Properties sheet. Move the Pointer speed slider. Click Apply.

Step 5. Click on the Registry editor and press the F5 key. You will see the values of MouseSpeed, MouseThreshold1, and MouseThreshold2 change.

Step 6. Repeat Steps 4 and 5 to check all the values assigned by the Pointer speed slider. You can do the same thing with the speed slider for double-clicking.

Step 7. Exit the Registry editor.

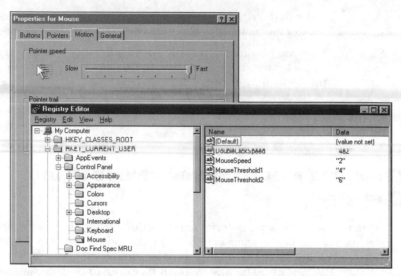

Figure 24-5: The Mouse Motion Properties sheet and the Registry editor working together.

Secret

The values set in a user interface to the Registry are immediately reflected in the Registry. These new values are also the ones used by the applications that rely on them.

Undocumented

You can also edit the values directly in the Registry. These new values aren't used by the mouse. The mouse uses 0, 0, 0 instead, meaning no acceleration. You have to restart Windows to have these values read and used.

If you have User Profiles enabled for this computer, there will be a separate mouse setting for each user. If you edit these values in the Registry, you'll need to follow the branch that applies to the particular user.

You have to make some changes in your mouse speed values (through the Mouse Control Panel) before the Mouse branch will show up in the Registry. You may need to make these changes and quit Windows 95 before you see the changes, as it takes Windows a while to write these changes back out of memory to the disk files that contain the permanent copy of the Registry.

Undocumented

You will find the Mouse branch in HKEY_CURRENT_USER if you made the changes to mouse speed as well as in the HKEY_USERS branch. If you have disabled User Profiles in the Passwords Control Panel, these branches are the same. The HKEY_CURRENT_USER branch is an alias for the current user found in the HKEY_USERS branch.

Numerous values are not stored in the Registry unless they are different than the default values. For example, if you don't make any changes in the mouse double-click speed, you won't find an entry for it in the Registry.

Changing the pointer trails

Pointer trails, which leave "ghosts" of the mouse pointer in the mouse pointer's former position, are really useful only on LCD screens where the mouse pointer can be easily lost. Otherwise they are just a distraction. (The default is no pointer trails at all.) Here's how to modify them:

STEPS

Changing the Number of Pointer Ghosts

Step 1.   On the Mouse Motion Properties sheet, click the Show pointer trails check box and then move the Pointer trail slider to the left and right. You will see the effect immediately.

Step 2.   To apply changes that you have made to the mouse pointer, click OK.

Creating Your Own Mouse Pointers

Windows 95 comes with a number of static and animated mouse pointers that you can assign to different mouse pointer functions. Microsoft Plus! comes with more. This book comes with a shareware CD-ROM that has even more.

You can use these mouse pointers, you can edit them to create your own pointers, or you can create your own static and animated pointers. The Windows 95 source CD-ROM contains two programs that help you create cursors and then string cursors together to create animated pointers.

These programs, Imagedit.exe and Aniedit.exe, are found in the \Admin\Reskit\Apptools\Aniedit folder on the Windows 95 CD-ROM. You can copy them to your \Program Files\Accessories folder (or any folder you like) on your hard disk. They have an accompanying setup *(inf)* file, and you can use the Add/Remove Programs icon in your Control Panel to "install" them if you like. Use the Windows Setup tab, click the Have Disk button, and then browse to the folder on the hard disk that holds these applications. (Installing sets up an association of Aniedit.exe with the file type *cur*.)

Use both of these programs to look at existing animated and static cursors to get an idea of how they are created.

What Is Missing in Mouse Configuration?

There is no way to set the mouse pointer to snap to the active button or item in a dialog box, as is possible with some other mouse drivers, including the ones that come with the Windows 3.*x* Microsoft mouse. This can substantially cut down on the amount of mouse movement — although it can also be annoying as the mouse moves to unexpected places.

The mouse doesn't wrap around the edge of the screen. When it goes off the left edge, you can't have it come in the right edge.

You don't have ability to define the middle mouse button. (We discuss one definition that you can make later in this chapter.)

All these missing features and more will be available from software provided by mouse manufacturers and from Microsoft for Microsoft mice.

Built-In Trackballs and Mice

Undocumented

If you have a built-in trackball in your portable, you can still use a plug-in serial mouse along with it without having to disable the trackball. Both mice are detected by Windows 95 and both are functional at the same time.

If you add a serial mouse later or enable the internal trackball (using your BIOS setup) after Windows 95 is installed, you have to force Windows 95 to detect the "new" hardware (unless these are plug and play devices). Use the Add New Hardware icon in the Control Panel and select the Install specific hardware check box. Follow the steps in the section earlier in this chapter entitled *Adding a mouse driver*.

A generic built-in trackball will most likely be supported by the Microsoft PS/2 Port Mouse or Standard PS/2 Port Mouse drivers in Windows 95.

The Mouse in a DOS Box

If you have a DOS program that is mouse-aware — that is, it can accept and use mouse movements and mouse button presses — Windows 95 will automatically allow you to use your mouse with the DOS program in a DOS Windows session. You don't have to do anything special to let it know that you are using a mouse; Windows 95 passes along mouse movements and button presses to the DOS program.

In previous versions of Windows, if you wanted to have your mouse available for your DOS programs, you had to load DOS real-mode mouse drivers with calls in your Autoexec.bat or Config.sys files. The mouse drivers that ship with Windows 95 are clever enough to handle both Windows and DOS (in DOS Windows sessions), so you don't need to load your old mouse drivers.

On the other hand, if you run DOS programs that use a mouse in the MS-DOS mode, you will need to load real-mode mouse drivers when you enter that mode. This is possible because MS-DOS mode gives you the option of creating specific Autoexec.bat and Config.sys files for that mode. See Chapter 17 for details.

You have two options for modifying how the mouse works with your DOS programs while running in a Windows DOS session. These are specified in the Properties sheet for a given DOS application or for your general DOS Windows sessions.

First, you can select an option that disables the mouse functions of the DOS program (if it has any) and dedicates the mouse to marking, copying, cutting, and pasting between the DOS program and Windows programs or other windowed DOS programs. This is particularly useful if the DOS program is not mouse-aware.

The other option forces the mouse to work only within the DOS client window area and only under control of the DOS program. Both options are found on the DOS Misc Properties sheet. They are the QuickEdit and Exclusive modes. You set them by right-clicking on a DOS program's shortcut icon and clicking Properties. Turn to Chapter 17 for more details on how to set these options.

Double-Clicking with the Middle Mouse Button

Logitech builds and sells more mice than Microsoft (although not more at retail) and most of its mice (and trackballs, for that matter) have three buttons. If the mouse that came with your computer has three buttons, it is very likely a Logitech mouse. Look on the undersurface of the mouse for a label.

Logitech sells a piece of software — the Mouse Control Center — that lets you define the middle button function as well as the right button and a number of other useful mouse parameters. The default setting for the Logitech middle button is double-click, which we very much prefer to use rather than double-clicking the left mouse button.

Secret

You can set the middle button of the Logitech Mouse using the Logitech mouse driver that Microsoft ships with Windows 95 by editing the Registry.

STEPS

Making the Middle Mouse Button Double-Click

Step 1.   Be sure to install the Logitech mouse driver that comes with Windows 95 first. See the steps in the earlier section entitled *Setting Up Your Mouse Driver*.

Step 2.   Use the Explorer to find Regedit.exe in the \Windows folder. Double-click it.

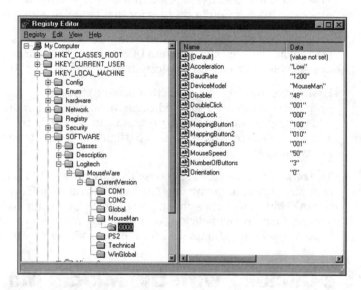

Figure 24-6: The Registry editor. Edit the valued named DoubleClick by double-clicking it. To get the middle key to be a double-click, change this value to 1.

Step 3.   Click the plus signs to the left of HKEY_LOCAL_MACHINE \SOFTWARE\Logitech\MouseWare\Current Version. Figure 24-6 shows the Registry editor at this location for a particular mouse (in this case, the Logitech MouseMan).

Step 4.   Click the plus sign next to your Logitech mouse type. Click the 0000 key.

Step 5.   Double-click the DoubleClick key in the right pane. Change the value from 000 to 001.

Step 6.   Restart Windows 95 to have this change take effect.

This double-click definition doesn't work with Microsoft Edit. We use Edit all the time to edit Autoexec.bat, Config.sys, and other text files.

This double-click definition doesn't work if you have configured the mouse to be a left-handed mouse.

Placing the Mouse Icon on the Desktop

You can have ready access to the way your mouse behaves if you place a shortcut to the Mouse Control Panel on your Desktop.

STEPS

Putting the Mouse Icon on the Desktop

Step 1. Click the Start button, then Settings, Control Panel.

Step 2. Right-drag the mouse icon to the desktop.

Step 3. Drop the mouse icon on the desktop and click Create Shortcut.

Step 4. Press F2 and type in a new name for the shortcut to the Mouse Control Panel.

If you have a Logitech mouse and want to have the purple mouse icon on your desktop (Microsoft provides only the soap-bar-like icon in the Control Panel with its Logitech driver), you can change the shortcut icon. Here's how:

STEPS

Putting the Logitech Purple Mouse Icon on the Desktop

Step 1. Right-click the Mouse shortcut on the desktop. Click Properties. Click the Shortcut tab.

Step 2. Click the Change icon button. Click the Browse button and search for your old Logitech driver directory ("lmouse," perhaps?).

Step 3. When you find a Logitech executable file like Wmousecc.exe, double-click it.

Step 4. Choose the mouse icon you want, and click OK.

Step 5. Click OK.

Your Mouse in the Device Manager

Double-click the System icon in your Control Panel, then click the Device Manager tab and you'll see an entry for Mouse as well as one for Ports. These two entries list the driver files for the mouse and serial ports, as well as display the characteristics of the serial ports.

The Ports section of the Device Manager stores the address and interrupt of the serial port to which your mouse may be attached. If there are conflicts between these assignments and other port hardware in your computer, they will be highlighted. For details on dealing with ports, turn to Chapter 25.

Double-Clicking Versus Single-Clicking

It is not always clear when you are supposed to double-click to initiate an action and when a single click is sufficient. Windows 95 was designed to cut down on the use of the double-click. While double-clicks are not now required, they are often the easiest way to initiate an action.

A *click* means a press and release of the left mouse button. A *double-click* is two clicks within a set time interval. A *right-click* is a click of the right mouse button.

Tip

What is the keyboard equivalent of a double-click? Move the highlight to the icon with the arrow keys. When the item that you wanted opened is highlighted, press Enter.

Double-clicking to open

All icons on the desktop can be opened by double-clicking them. *Open* has multiple meanings. If the icon is a folder, it means open a folder window to display its contents. If the icon represents an application, it means start the application. If the icon represents a document, it means start the application associated with the document and open the document within the application.

Open is often the default action associated with the double-click, but you can choose or define other actions that will take place instead. For example, you could choose the Explore action, a variation on Open that means open in the Explorer mode. If this action is chosen as the default action, then double-clicking an icon on the desktop results in the Explore action. See Chapter 13 for more details.

Double-clicking a filename or icon in a folder window will often open it. Double-clicking a filename or folder name in a common file dialog box (a dialog box associated with File, Open) will open it within the associated application.

If a folder icon is displayed in the left pane of the Explorer, all that is required is a single click to open it and display its contents in the right pane. To display a folder's contents, you have to double-click its right-pane displayed icon.

Double-clicking is used because Windows makes a distinction between highlighting or selecting a file, application, or its icon and taking some action, such as opening or being opened. One may select a group of icons that represent files that you may wish to move to another folder. You don't want the documents to be opened, but you do want to select them. You can select each of them with a single click.

It is this requirement to make a distinction between selecting an icon and having it take some action that requires you to differentiate. Double-clicking is just one means of providing this differentiation.

Where single-clicking works

You don't have to double-click to open a file because Windows 95 provides an alternative — right-click and choose an action for the right mouse button menu. The first action shown on the menu will often be Open.

If a file or application is active and its icon is on a button on the Taskbar, you only have to single-click the icon to restore the application or file or have it displayed on the top of the desktop. With Windows 3.x, minimized icons required double-clicks to restore their associated applications.

Single-click items on the Start menus to open their associated applications. Items in Windows 3.x Program Groups required double-clicks to start them.

The Explorer requires only that you single-click the plus symbol next to the folder icons in the folder tree to open a branch of the folder tree. The File Manager required a double-click of the folder icon. (Single-clicking on the plus symbol in Explorer also is a faster way to navigate your hard disk than clicking on a folder in Explorer.)

The Windows 3.x Task Manager required a double-click on the desktop. Right-click the Windows 95 Taskbar to get similar functions.

In all cases where a double-click was required under Windows 3.x for an action, a single-click, two clicks (one to highlight an icon and one of an associated button), or a right-click and click of a menu item can be used in Windows 95.

The Right Mouse Button Stuff

Windows 95 makes extensive use of the right mouse button. This is a fantastic improvement in the ease of use and functionality of the Windows user interface.

The right-click is not always implemented consistently. Programs written for Windows 3.*x* don't use the right mouse button in the same manner as programs that were written for Windows 95. But you can always just right-click and see what happens. You can't get into any trouble, i.e., you can't start something that you don't want to with just a right-click.

Tip

You can right-click nearly everything that you see on the desktop, including the desktop. You can right-click anything within a folder window or within the Explorer. Our advice is to right-click anything and everything just to see what happens.

Tip

What is the keyboard equivalent of the right mouse button? Shift+F10.

Right-clicking My Computer

Right-click the My Computer icon on the desktop and you have the choice of opening a My Computer folder window or opening the Explorer. You can also map or disconnect network drives, find files or computers, or bring up the System Properties sheets, including the Device Manager.

Right-clicking the Start button

Right-clicking the Start button gives you the following options:

1. Opening the Start Menu folder widow with the Programs folder icon in the client window area

2. Opening the Explorer with the Programs folder in the right pane

3. Finding a file in the Start Menu folder

Tip

This can be quite useful for making changes in the folders and icons associated with the Programs menu. You can use the Explorer focused on the Start Menu folder and the Programs folder to edit and move folders and icons. This will change the menus that drop down off the Programs menu.

Right-clicking the Taskbar

The Taskbar is sort of a replacement for the Windows 3.*x* Task Manager. The Task Manager was invoked by double-clicking the desktop. To switch to another running application (task switching) you double-clicked a name from the Task List. (Notice all the double-clicking.)

The Taskbar includes the icons of the running tasks or applications or folders; they can be brought to the top of the desktop with a single click. Right-click the Taskbar and you have the options of:

1. Cascading the currently open windows on the desktop

2. Tiling these windows horizontally or vertically

3. Minimizing (or undoing the previous minimization) all the open windows

4. Editing the properties of the Taskbar

Turn to Chapter 7 for more details on using the Taskbar.

Right-clicking the date

Same as right-clicking the Taskbar, with the addition of allowing you to adjust the settings for the date and time.

Right-clicking a file or document icon

Right-clicking a file icon presents you with multiple actions in the right mouse button menu, including opening the file with its associated application. If the document has an associated Quick Viewer, then you can quickly view its contents by choosing this option.

You can also engage in file management functions such as delete, copy, cut, and rename.

Shift+right-clicking on a file

If the file is of a registered file type, Shift+right-click gives you another menu option, Open With, that allows you to open the file with another application.

Right-clicking a folder icon

The right mouse button menu for a folder is similar to that of a file. Opening a folder doesn't start an application but rather reveals in a folder window the files and folders stored within the folder. You can move, share, link, rename, or delete a folder from the right button menu, as well as bring up its Properties sheets.

A folder can be opened in the folder window view or in the Explorer view.

Right-clicking a shortcut

Right-clicking a shortcut brings up the same right mouse button menu as would appear if you were to right-click the target of the shortcut. The difference is that the Properties menu item on the right mouse button menu brings up the Properties sheet of the shortcut and not the Properties sheet of the target.

Right-clicking the desktop

Right-click while the mouse pointer is anywhere on the desktop — although not too close to any icon or the Taskbar.

You have the options of:

1. Arranging or lining up the icons on the desktop

2. Placing a new folder, file, or shortcut on the desktop

3. Opening the Display Properties sheet

The last item is the same as double-clicking the Display icon in the Control Panel.

Right-clicking in the client area of a folder window

The client area of a folder window is similar to the desktop. If you right-click in the client area of a folder window you get about the same options as you do when you right-click on the desktop. You don't get the Display Properties sheet and you get the option of changing how the icons are displayed in the folder window: Large icons, Small icons, List, or Details.

Right-clicking the title bar of the active application

Place your mouse pointer in the title bar in the window of the application with the focus (a window has focus if the title bar is blue, assuming you are using standard Windows colors) and click the right mouse button. You will be rewarded with the system menu.

The system menu is programmable so it can change from application to application. The standard functions that are available include moving, sizing, and closing the window or application.

This also works for a folder window or for the icon of an application on the Taskbar.

Right-clicking in a dialog box

Dialog boxes are a little different than most windows that show up on your desktop. There are common resource dialog boxes that are used by 16-bit Windows 3.x and other common dialog boxes used by 32-bit Windows 95 applications. Many Windows applications have their own unique dialog boxes.

Dialog boxes that have question mark caption buttons in the upper right corner are Windows 95-compliant. If you right-click on something within one of these dialog boxes it is the same as clicking on that question mark.

A What's This? button will pop up next to where you right-clicked in the dialog box. If you click the button, an explanation of what the thing does that you clicked will appear.

Right-clicking in a 16-bit File Open dialog box

Common resource dialog boxes for 16-bit Windows 3.x applications include the File Open and Fonts dialog boxes. If your application uses those and you right-click within them, a What's This? button will appear.

Other dialog boxes for Windows 3.x applications will not respond to right-clicks. If you right-click on a filename, you may get the What's This? button.

Right-clicking in a 32-bit File Open dialog box

Right-clicking on a filename in a 32-bit Windows 95 common resource File Open dialog box will highlight the filename and get you a right mouse button menu with options to open the file, and so on. Right-clicking in other places will give you other menus that are appropriate. In some areas you will get the What's This? button.

Figure 24-7 shows the 32-bit File Open dialog box with a right-click on the first filename.

Figure 24-7: The File Open dialog box. Right-click a filename in the box to bring up the right mouse button menu.

Right-clicking in the client area of an active application

You can right-click within the application, say right on the face of a document in your word processor. If the application is Windows 95-aware, a right mouse button menu will appear. In a word processor, for example, you may have the option of copying, cutting, or pasting text. The right mouse button provides menu options that are easier to get at than making choices off the menu bar.

Summary

The nice thing about the mouse in Windows 95 is that it is a lot more useful. You need to know what these new functions are so you can be comfortable with its enhanced power.

▶ A new Mouse Control Panel lets you easily change the responsiveness of the mouse pointer to mouse movements.

▶ Animated cursors can be used to replace some of the duller mouse pointers.

▶ The middle button on your Logitech mouse can be turned into a double-click button.

▶ The need for double-clicking has been reduced.

▶ The right mouse button has been empowered.

Chapter 25

Modems, Serial Ports, and Parallel Ports

In This Chapter

Modems and ports (serial and parallel) are communications devices. Windows 95 automatically detects them and helps you set them up. We discuss:

▶ Configuring your modem driver

▶ Getting behind the configuration routines and changing modem driver parameters

▶ Manually controlling which ports can be used by the Direct Cable Connection (DCC) and adding ports that were inadvertently removed

▶ Configuring your serial and parallel ports

▶ Testing for the presence of an advanced serial port chip

Hello, World

When the personal computer was envisioned and designed, the focus of its communication facilities was the monitor, the keyboard, and the printer — the electronic typewriter model. Serial ports and modem communications were peripheral considerations, so to speak. This legacy has hung on.

Computer-mediated communication is now a central concern. The widespread use of laptop and portable computers in business has accelerated the desirability of reliable, easy to use, fast communications links. Inexpensive high-speed fax/modems, the advent of commercial Internet access providers, and the adoption of graphical user interfaces for online services all speak to a popular interest in electronic communications.

Windows 3.x was not up to the task of effectively handling these communications demands. High-speed communications (over 9600 bits per second, or *bps*) required third-party replacements to the Windows 3.x serial port driver (Comm.drv). Personal computers required a new chip, the 16550A Universal Asynchronous Receiver/Transmitter (UART), to keep up with the data flow through the serial port or modem.

When Microsoft began designing Windows 95, it was already clear that the operating system's communications capabilities had to be much stronger than Windows 3.x. At the minimum, a new communications driver was required. At best, communications would be seamlessly integrated into the basic functionality of the operating system.

Windows 95 Communications

Microsoft had to make changes to the basic operating system to reduce the frequency and duration of time intervals during which the CPU would not be able to deal with data coming into the serial and parallel ports. The use of 32-bit protected-mode drivers has reduced the amount of mode switching required of the processor.

The designers of Windows 95 provided a way for applications to determine which one gets to use the modem or port without having to unload one of the applications. By defining a common modem interface, all communications packages can communicate with the modem at a high level.

The new communications driver is Vcomm.drv. Combined with Unimodem, the universal modem driver, Windows 95 provides high-level services that developers can use to make their communications packages easier to use and more cooperative.

One modem for all communications software

You have to configure a modem only once, and any communications package that is supported by Windows 95 doesn't have to know how to configure the modem itself. Modem configuration was not a feature provided in earlier Windows versions. Every communications package had to know about a large number of different modems in order to properly initialize them and utilize their capabilities.

Communications packages built for Windows 95 don't have to know which command strings to send to get the modem moving. They can send higher level, more general, and more abstract commands that will work on any modem Windows 95 recognizes. Communications software providers can turn their resources to other, more fruitful areas of product design.

Windows 95 ships with seven communications facilities built in: the phone dialer, Direct Cable Connection (DCC), Dial-Up Networking (DUN), the Microsoft Network online service, HyperTerminal, Microsoft Exchange, and Microsoft Fax. Numerous other communications capabilities are built on top of these facilities, including chat, remote network administration (Net Watcher), online registration, CompuServe e-mail, System Monitor, and others. All operate through the interface that defines the capabilities of the modem within your computer.

Microsoft Plus! comes with a Microsoft Mail API extension to Microsoft Exchange for Internet e-mail. In addition, Microsoft provides Internet Explorer, a WorldWide Web browser.

Windows 3.*x* communications support

Your existing Windows 3.*x* communications applications will still work with Windows 95 because the old communications driver (Comm.drv) hasn't changed and is still used by these applications. While Comm.drv thinks that it's talking directly to the hardware, it now talks to the new communications driver, Vcomm.drv.

Only one Windows 3.*x*-style communications application can have access to the modem at a time. Windows 95-style communications applications can share the modem. For example, Microsoft Fax can be active and set to wait for a fax while you use HyperTerminal to connect to a bulletin board. While the phone line is off-hook, Microsoft Fax can't answer an incoming call, but you don't have to unload the fax software while you make the HyperTerminal call.

Some applications replaced Comm.drv with their own communications port drivers. These applications will still work with Windows 95. The replacement communications drivers work with Vcomm.drv instead of directly with the communications hardware.

Configuring Your Modem

After Setup's hardware detection program identifies an internal or external modem, you're automatically prompted to configure it. If you install a modem later, or declined to configure your modem during initial setup, you can engage the Modem Configuration Wizard from the Control Panel.

STEPS

Configuring a Modem

Step 1.   Click the Start button, Settings, and then Control Panel. Double-click the Modems icon. If you have not already installed a modem, the Install New Modem Wizard will start. Otherwise you'll see the Modems General Properties sheet as shown in Figure 25-1. If a modem driver is listed, you can still add another (by clicking Add) or remove the existing one (by clicking Remove).

Step 2.   If no modem has yet been configured, the Modem Configuration Wizard will automatically start. Otherwise, click Add to bring it up, as shown in Figure 25-2. Choose your modem type and click Next.

(continued)

STEPS *(continued)*

Configuring a Modem

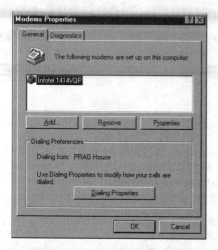

Figure 25-1: The Modems General Properties sheet.

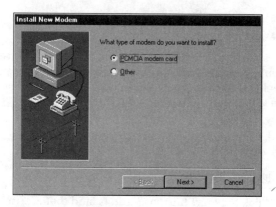

Figure 25-2: The Install New Modem Wizard.

Step 3.   You can choose whether to have the Windows 95 hardware detection routines look for your modem or you can select it from the list of explicitly supported modems. You can change the selection during this configuration process, so it doesn't hurt to let Windows 95 try to detect your modem. Be sure you are not running any communications programs, because they won't allow access to the modem. Check the "Don't detect my modem box," as shown in Figure 25-3, if you want to do it yourself. Click Next.

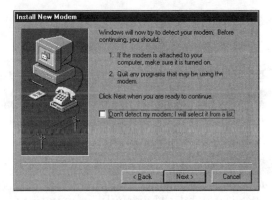

Figure 25-3: The second dialog box of the Install New Modem Wizard.

Step 4. If you choose to have Windows 95 detect the modem, it will take a few seconds to query the modem to determine its type and which communications port it is using. Not all modems can be detected. The fall-back position for the detection routines is Standard modem at a certain speed, such as 9600 bps. Click Change if you don't think the modem that has been detected is correct or you think you can do a better job.

Step 5. If you are choosing your own modem, or you clicked Change, then you have a list of modem manufacturers in the next Install New Modem dialog box, as shown in Figure 25-4. Scroll the left box to find the manufacturer of your modem. Highlight its name. Scroll the right box to choose the model of your modem. Click Next.

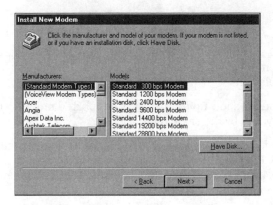

Figure 25-4: The modem selection dialog box in the Install New Modem Wizard.

(continued)

STEPS *(continued)*

Configuring a Modem

If you have a diskette from a modem manufacturer that includes a Windows 95 setup routine for the modem, click Have Disk instead. Modems manufactured after the release of Windows 95 may have these diskettes. Microsoft will publish setup files for new modems on the Microsoft Network.

Step 6.   If your modem is not listed, select Standard Modem Types. Once selected, you can specify its speed, if you know that value. Click Change after Windows 95 has detected your modem as Standard. Highlight Standard Modem Types in the list of manufacturers and then the correct speed in the list of models. Click Next.

Step 7.   If you choose the modem from the list yourself, you will need to tell Windows 95 which port it is connected to. Most modems are serial modems, so you will have a choice of Com ports. Lpt ports are also available for parallel port modems. After highlighting your port, click Next.

Step 8.   The first time you set up a modem, you will be asked for your area code, the number required to get an outside line, whether you are using tone or pulse dialing, and to choose from a list of country codes. This location information defines where you are making the call from and how to make it. See Chapter 26 for more on telephony issues.

Step 9.   Click Finish. The modem name will appear in the Modems General Properties sheet.

If Windows identifies your modem as Standard and you have a better idea of what your modem is, go ahead and set the driver to your best guess. You can always replace it.

If yours doesn't show up on the list of supported models, try selecting a model similar to yours by the same manufacturer.

Tip

If your modem is unnamed — generic as far as you can tell — try setting it as a Hayes, U.S. Robotics, Practical Peripherals, or Microcom modem. If you have a generic 14.4Kbps modem, try the Boca Research Bocamodem 14.4Kbps V.32bis Data-Fax modem.

Under the Hayes manufacturers list, there are two models for Hayes-compatible models at 2400 and 9600 baud. Try one of these.

What you are doing is making a choice about the initialization string for the modem and various other strings that control basic modem functions. These strings, while different for different modems, often have enough in common that strings for one modem will work with another.

Testing your modem configuration

Tip

You can test whether your modem configuration is the right one by calling the Microsoft Network. Click Online Registration in the Windows 95 Welcome message box. If you have told the Welcome box to go away, get it back by double-clicking Welcome.exe in your Windows folder using the Explorer, or Signup.exe in the \Programs Files\The Microsoft Network folder.

If you have already registered for the Microsoft Network, double-click the Microsoft Network icon on your desktop.

Tip

If you have an external modem and the hardware detection routines did not find it, then you may have an incorrect cable connecting your serial (or parallel) port to your modem. Either that or your port may be incorrectly set up.

Changing basic global modem settings

You can adjust some of the properties associated with your modem by clicking the Properties button when the modem driver is highlighted in the Modems General Properties sheet.

STEPS

Changing Modem Driver Settings

Step 1. Click the Start button, Settings, and then Control Panel. Double-click the Modems icon. Highlight your modem in the list.

Step 2. Click Properties. This will bring up the Properties sheets for your modem. The specific modem's General Properties sheet, as shown in Figure 25-5, will appear.

Step 3. An alternate and equivalent way of carrying out Steps 1 and 2 is to click the System icon in the Control Panel. Then click the Device Manager tab, click the plus sign next to the Modem icon, click the icon associated with your modem, click Properties, and then the Modems tab.

Step 4. Change the values you want in your modem's General Properties sheet. The maximum speed at which your modem can receive data depends on what kind of error correction protocol it has and the speed of your CPU. For instance, 14.4Kbps modems that implement the V.32bis standard when combined with a fast 80486 processor may be able to sustain 57.6Kbps with compression. If you find your communications applications are reporting high error rates, reduce this maximum value.

(continued)

Changing Modem Driver Settings

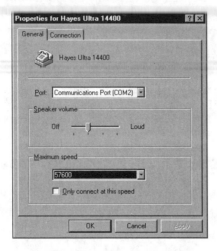

Figure 25-5: The General Properties sheet for modems. You have already chosen which port, so unless you move the modem, you won't want to change that. You can set a global volume for the speaker and the maximum speed your computer/modem combination can handle.

Changing the basic modem connection properties

Each connection — each bulletin board, Internet service provider, friend with a computer and a modem, or server at work that you connect to using your modem — requires unique connection settings. You can determine the default choices that are used until you modify them for a given connection.

STEPS

Setting Modem Connection Properties

Step 1.   Carry out Steps 1-3 in *Changing Modem Driver Settings* from the preceding section. Click the Connection tab. The specific modem's Connection Properties sheet will appear, as in Figure 25-6.

Step 2.   The values of 8, n, and 1 for data bits, parity, and stop bits are probably just fine. Change them only if you are attaching to new services that regularly call for other values.

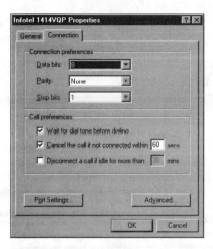

Figure 25-6: The Modem Connection Properties sheet. You can determine the global default values of the data bits, parity, and stop bits.

Step 3. Uncheck the "Wait for dial tone before dialing box" if you are calling outside the U.S.; Windows 95 is a little U.S.-specific here. If you purchased a modem in a country different from the country you are presently calling from, you may need to uncheck this.

Step 4. You can set how long you have to wait for the connection to be made by setting the time interval in the field labeled "Cancel the call if not connected within."

Step 5. To make certain the phone is hung up after a set time of idleness, check the last field in this dialog box.

Step 6. Click OK.

These values can be changed for each connection, so you want to make the changes only if you are creating new connectoids (see below) that regularly use values that are different from the defaults created by your Windows 95 Setup.

Changing more advanced connection settings

These global connection settings can be changed by specific connection settings (referred to as *connectoids*) as determined by your communications software. The command strings that are associated with these settings are sent to the modem when it is first initialized. A given communications package can ask the Windows modem driver to send to the modem other command strings that override these values.

Tip

The Extra settings field allows you to put in a specific command string that is sent to the modem along with the initialization string. It is normally used to put the modem into a debug mode in order to track communications errors. Don't use it unless you are familiar with your modem's commands.

STEPS

Setting Advanced Connection Properties

Step 1.   Carry out the steps in the previous sections to change driver settings or basic connection properties as appropriate.

Step 2.   Click the Connection tab and then Advanced. The Advanced Connection Settings Properties sheet, as shown in Figure 25-7, will appear.

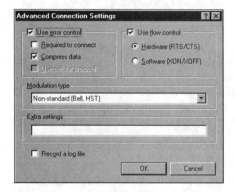

Figure 25-7: The Advanced Connection Properties sheet.

Step 3.   The Advanced Connection Settings dialog box lets you add to the string that Windows 95 normally sends when initializing or preparing your modem for communication. You can type additional strings in the Extra Settings field. Do not type in the attention (AT) command. It is sent automatically by the modem initialization string.

Step 4.   Choose Use error control and Compress data if you are sending data to modems or services that support these functions. Some, such as CompuServe, do not. If you are using software compression (for example, compressed SLIP with your Internet service provider), hardware compression checked here may be a source of conflict which is indicated by very slow communications. You can turn off either compression mode.

Step 5.   Choose Use flow control (*handshaking*) if you are running at 9600 bps or better. If you have an external modem, and the modem cable has the RTS and the CTS lines, use hardware flow control.

Step 6. If you are using a cellular modem, click the Use cellular protocol box to reduce errors over multiple cellular connections.

Step 7. The default setting for Modulation Type is standard. This is the fall-back low-speed communications standard if two modems can't communicate at a higher speed. If you experience trouble communicating with a given site at 300 and 1200 bps, switch from standard to non-standard.

Step 8. You can choose to keep a log file that will help with debugging a connection. The file, Modemlog.txt, will be in your Windows folder.

Step 9. Click OK.

Changing 16550 UART settings

If your serial port uses a 16550A UART, you can set the size of its receive and transmit buffers by clicking Port Settings in the Modem Connection Properties sheet.

The same Port Settings button is associated with each connectoid. To verify it, right-click a connectoid, for example in the HyperTerminal folder. Then click Properties, Configure, click the Connection tab, and there it is. Each connectoid can have its own Advanced and Port Setting values.

Changing any modem settings

The file Modems.inf and the files starting with Mdm in the \Windows\Inf folder contain the modem's manufacturer and model information displayed in the New Modem dialog box. Modem manufacturers can ship a file with their modem on a diskette that provides equivalent information about their new modem. Plug and play modems contain the pertinent information on a ROM chip.

Secret

Each modem model has an associated initialization string or set of initialization strings that are defined in the modem setup files. Additional strings for hanging up the modem, setting it in auto answer mode, turning on or off the speaker and setting its volume, data compression, tone or pulse dial, and so on, are provided in the modem's setup, or *inf,* file.

You can edit the information in these files if you want to change the values used when a modem is configured using the above steps. Change the *inf* file before you add the particular modem driver. From the Explorer, double-click the *inf* file that has a name resembling the manufacturer of your modem. You then can edit it with Notepad. Be sure to make a backup file first.

After a particular modem driver is added to your Windows 95 configuration, you have the option of changing any of the settings associated with the modem by using the Registry editor. Turn to Chapter 15 if you are not familiar with how to edit the Registry.

Go to the following branch of the Registry:

`[HKEY_LOCAL_MACHINE\System\CurrentControlSet\Services\Class\Modem]`

There may be a number of modems specified on this branch, each designated as a branch and starting with the branch key numbered "0000". This area of the Registry is shown in Figure 25-8.

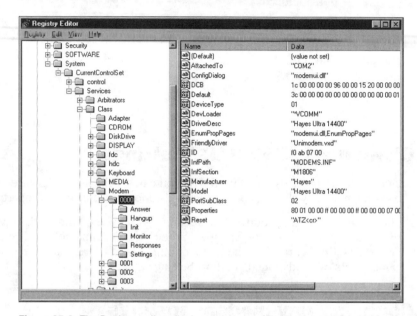

Figure 25-8: The Registry editor displays that area of the Registry that contains the modem configuration information. Click the plus signs at each of the names in the branch shown to get to this area. (The names on the branch now have minus signs in front of them.)

If you have set up DCC, there will be modems in the DriverDesc field labeled Serial cable between 2 PCs. Find the branch that corresponds to your modem driver by checking the DriverDesc field for its familiar name as you highlight each key starting with 0000.

Expand the branch for your modem by clicking the plus sign in front of its designated number to see the additional key values that can be edited. You can edit the Answer, Hangup, Init, Fax, and Settings values. You may want to make a copy of System.dat and User.dat in your Windows folder before you make these changes.

Test and Interrogate Your Modem

You can find out if your modem is working and what values are stored in its registers. To do this, you need the Windows 3.*x* communications package, Terminal, which allows you to talk directly to your modem.

You'll find Terminal.exe still in your Windows folder if you have upgraded over Windows 3.*x*. Otherwise you may need to retrieve it from your Windows 3.*x* diskettes.

Double-click Terminal.exe in a folder window (or in the Explorer). To check if the modem is working, type **atz** or **ath** or **ate1m1v1.** If the modem returns *OK,* then it is there and listening to you.

You need your modem manual to continue interrogation. Send command strings, as shown in the preceding paragraph, taken from your manual. Send the **ati?** command, with the **?** replaced by, one at a time, the numbers **2** through **9.** This should tell you what kind of modem you have.

You can also send AT commands from a terminal window associated with a particular connection. If you have created a connectoid for HyperTerminal, take the following steps:

STEPS

Sending AT Commands in HyperTerminal

Step 1. Right-click a HyperTerminal connectoid. Click Properties.

Step 2. Click Configure and then the Options tab.

Step 3. Click the Bring up terminal window before dialing check box.

Step 4. Click OK. Click OK again.

Step 5. Double-click this connectoid. Click Connect.

Step 6. A terminal window will appear on your desktop. Type in the AT commands and see what response you get.

Step 7. Press F3 to cancel the attempted connection when you are done.

Step 8. Click Cancel.

A modem diagnostic dialog box can be invoked by double-clicking the Modems icon in the Control Panel, clicking the Diagnostics tab, highlighting the port to which your modem is attached, and then clicking the More Info button. Various AT commands are sent to your modem and their response is reported as shown in Figure 25-9. It's not too interesting unless you know from looking in your modem's manual what the correct responses are supposed to be.

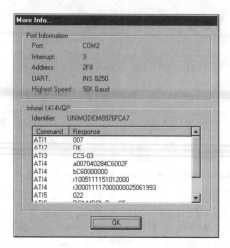

Figure 25-9: The More (Modem) Info dialog box.

Serial and Parallel Ports as Modems

In Chapter 30, we discuss DCC, which lets you hook two computers together using a serial or parallel cable.

DCC keeps track of your serial and parallel ports as though they were modems. When you first click DCC, hardware detection routines determine which serial and parallel ports are available. They create modem designations for each of these ports and allow you to choose between Serial Cable on COM*x* and Parallel cable on LPT*x*. The modem descriptions and properties of each port are stored in the Registry in the area referred to in the *Changing any modem setting* section of this chapter.

These are not real modems, but the Modems area of the Registry is a convenient place to keep track of the fact that these ports are available to be used by DCC. These port connections do not show up on the list of modems when you click the Modems icon in the Control Panel.

There are two ways to see which ports the hardware detection routines have found. You can click the Start button, then Programs, Accessories, and Direct Cable Connection. Clicking Change and then Next produces a list of ports available for DCC.

The other way is to click the Start button, then Settings, and Control Panel. Double-click the System icon and the plus sign to the left of the yellow phone Modem icon. A list of all "modems" will appear, including your serial and parallel cables on ports if you have previously run DCC.

Using this second method, you have the option of removing certain ports that you won't be using with DCC — perhaps ports that are being used only by your mouse, for instance. If you remove a port/cable that you decide later to use with DCC, you must restore it manually.

To add back a removed port, take the following steps:

STEPS

Adding a Removed Port

Step 1. Click the Start button, then Programs, Accessories, and finally Direct Cable Connection.

Step 2. Click the Change button, then Next, and then Next again.

Step 3. Click the Install New Ports button.

Configuring Serial Ports

You have the option of changing serial port settings as well as a port's address and interrupt value. All changes to serial and parallel ports are made through the Device Manager, found under the Systems icon in the Control Panel.

Changing serial port settings

Windows 3.*x* included a Ports icon in the Control Panel. The functions of this Ports icon are now subsumed in the Device Manager. Using the Device Manager, you can change the port speed, data bits, stop bits, parity, and flow control (handshaking). If you are using this serial port for a connection, the settings for that connection override these settings.

STEPS

Changing Serial Port Settings

Step 1. Click the Start button, Settings, and then Control Panel. Double-click the Systems icon. Click the Device Manager tab.

Step 2. Click the plus sign to the left of the Ports icon in the Device Manager Systems Properties sheet. You will see a listing of all the serial and parallel ports connected to your computer.

(continued)

STEPS *(continued)*

Changing Serial Port Settings

Step 3.   Highlight the serial port you want to change and click the Properties button. Click the Port Settings tab

Step 4.   Using the Port Settings Properties sheet as shown in Figure 25-10, you can change the values for speed, data bits, stop bits, parity, and flow control (handshaking).

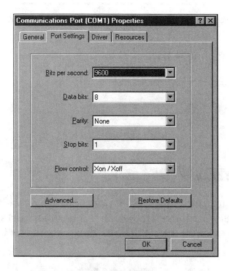

Figure 25-10: The Communications (Serial) Port's Port Settings Properties sheet.

These port settings are similar to the basic global connection settings for a modem. You'll want to set these settings only when you use the port with a device, perhaps a scanner, a printer, or even a mouse. The specific software that uses the port may override these settings. Each communications package's connection can have a different setting.

Each connectoid, whether for HyperTerminal or DUN, can override these port settings.

Serial port address and interrupt values

During setup, Windows 95 will recognize the serial ports that are already installed in your computer. Serial ports in personal computers with ISA buses (not MCA or EISA) have default values for addresses and interrupts. Table 25-1 lists those values.

Table 25-1	Default Address and Interrupt Values	
Port	Address	Interrupt
COM1	03F8h	4
COM2	02F8h	3
COM3	03E8h	4
COM4	02E8h	3

You can remove any special utilities or debug scripts you had in Autoexec.bat to handle problems with Windows recognizing your modems. Previously, some Windows 3.*x* users had problems with internal modems set to COM4, which failed to operate if there was no COM3. Other users had trouble with serial mice on COM2 if COM4 was present but COM3 wasn't. These problems have been fixed in Windows 95.

You'll notice in Table 25-1 that COM1 and COM3 share the same interrupt. The same is true for COM2 and COM4. If you have devices on the higher numbered COM ports, they will be in conflict with devices on the port they share the interrupt with. You can't use both devices at the same time if they share an interrupt and you are using a computer with an ISA bus.

If one device is, say, a scanner and the other is a modem, then it is unlikely that you will use them both at the same time, so sharing an interrupt is OK. If one is a mouse and another is a printer, your mouse will go haywire when you are printing. You can change the interrupts so there is no conflict.

Changing serial port addresses and interrupts

You can configure your serial port addresses and interrupts to avoid conflicts between devices that can't share the same interrupt. You can have a modem on COM3 and a mouse on COM1 and use different interrupts for each device. Your serial port hardware must support the new interrupt number and you must change the configuration switches on the hardware to match the interrupts that you choose in Windows 95.

Secret

The address and interrupt information for each port is stored as a basic configuration. Only one basic configuration is active at any one time for a given port. The default basic configuration of the COM1 serial port is Basic configuration 0. For the COM2 serial port it is Basic configuration 2. Each serial port can be set to use one of nine basic configurations.

Serial port Basic configurations 0, 2, and 4 are non-editable. You can change the interrupt on Basic configurations 1, 3, 5, 6, 7. Either the serial port address or the interrupt can be changed in Basic configuration 8.

Basic configurations 0 and 1 are designed for COM1; 2 and 3 for COM2; 4 and 5 for COM3; and 6 and 7 for COM4.

Use the Communication Port's Resources Properties sheet to choose which basic configuration to use for each port.

STEPS

Changing Serial Port Addresses and Interrupts

Step 1. Click the Start button, Start, Settings, and then Control Panel. Double-click the Systems icon. Click the Device Manager tab.

Step 2. Click the plus sign to the left of the Ports icon in the Device Manager Systems Properties sheet. You will see a listing of all the serial and parallel ports connected to your computer.

Step 3. Highlight the communications port that you want to change and click the Properties button. Click the Resources tab. As shown in Figure 25-11, the Resources Properties sheet for the communications port will appear on the desktop.

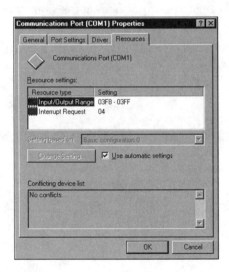

Figure 25-11: The Communications Port Resources Properties sheet. You can edit any of nine basic configurations.

Step 4. You have the option of changing the Input/Output Range or the Interrupt Request settings. Each of these settings is stored with a numbered Basic configuration. Click Use Automatic Settings to uncheck the default settings. Click the drop-down list in the "Setting based on" field to see the possible basic configurations. Highlight a basic configuration.

Step 5.   Highlight either Input/Output Range, i.e. the address of the serial port, or Interrupt Request. Click the Change Setting button. If you get a message that this setting can't be changed, try another configuration. Basic configurations 0, 2, and 4 are not editable. Basic configurations 1, 3, 5, 6, and 7 have editable interrupts. Basic configuration 8 has editable address and interrupt values.

Step 6.   You can give the port a new address if documentation for the port hardware indicates support for the new address. Highlight the Input/Output Range. Click Change Setting. The Edit Input/Output Range dialog box, as shown in Figure 25-12, will appear on the desktop.

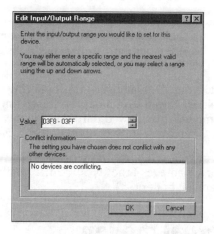

Figure 25-12: The Edit Input/Output Range dialog box. Change the value of the port address by scrolling through the available addresses. The lower field reports whether a hardware device driver is already using this address.

Step 7.   Scroll through the various available addresses to set a new address for this port. You are warned if there is a conflict with another hardware device driver.

Step 8.   To change the interrupt, highlight Interrupt Request and click Change Setting. You can then change the interrupt value and will be warned if there is a conflict.

Step 9.   Click OK. Click OK again.

Step 10.   Restart Windows 95.

Better Serial Ports

Over the lifetime of PC-compatible architecture, the UART chip that is used to control serial ports has evolved. It began in the IBM PC as the 8250. In the AT class machines it was upgraded to a 16540. The current chip of choice in Intel 486 and Pentium-based PCs is the 16550A.

Undocumented

The 16550A has two advantages over its predecessors. First, it incorporates a 16-byte buffer. By buffering incoming and outgoing data, the 16550A UART can accumulate characters without losing them, while waiting for its interrupt request to be serviced by the CPU. Second, the 8250 and the 16540 UARTs send an interrupt to the CPU whenever they receive a character. The 16550A can send one interrupt to service all the characters in the buffer.

By accumulating characters while waiting for the CPU to be available, the 16550A greatly enhances the reliability of high-speed communications, which is a very important feature, given our increased usage of the serial port as a networking device.

Undocumented

Windows 3.x didn't take much advantage of this buffering capability of the 16550A UART. It didn't use it to transmit data and used only a single byte of the buffer in the receive mode. This allowed third-party software developers to find a niche in the market by creating additional COM port drivers to replace Comm.drv.

Windows 95 takes full advantage of the 16650A UART, enabling the full 16 bytes of the receive and transmit buffers.

Testing your internal modem for a 16550A UART

You can test whether your internal modem includes a 16550A UART.

STEPS
Testing an Internal Modem

Step 1.   Set up your modem driver, as per the steps in the *Configuring Your Modem* section earlier in this chapter.

Step 2.   Click the Start button, Settings, and Control Panel. Double-click the Modems icon.

Step 3.   Click the Diagnostic tab. Highlight the port with your modem attached. Click More Info.

The More Info dialog box will tell you which UART you have.

Configuring Parallel Ports

The Windows 95 user interface for configuring parallel ports is almost the same as that used for serial ports. Unlike the eight basic configurations available for a serial port, there are only four basic configurations available for a parallel port. Basic configurations 0 and 2 do not have interrupts.

Tip

Windows 95 by default does not assign an interrupt to a parallel port. The interrupt is rarely needed for printing. The previous standards have been to assign Interrupt 7 to LPT1 and LPT3, and Interrupt 5 to LPT2. Here's how to change addresses and interrupts:

STEPS

Changing Parallel Port Addresses and Interrupts

Step 1. Click Start, Settings, and Control Panel. Double-click the Systems icon. Click the Device Manager tab.

Step 2. Click the plus sign to the left of the Ports icon in the Device Manager Systems Properties sheet to see a listing of all serial and parallel ports connected to your computer.

Step 3. Highlight the parallel port that you want to change and click Properties. Click the Resources tab.

Step 4. You have the option of changing the Input/Output Range or the Interrupt Request settings. Each of these settings is stored with a numbered basic configuration. Click on the drop-down list in the Setting based on field to see the possible basic configurations. Highlight a basic configuration.

Step 5. Highlight either Input/Out Range, i.e. the address of the serial port, or Interrupt Request. Click Use Automatic Settings to uncheck this check box and allow settings other than the default ones. Click Change Setting.

Step 6. You can give the port a new address if you like. Highlight the Input/Output Range. Click the Change Setting button. Change the address setting with the arrow buttons.

Step 7. To change the interrupt, highlight Interrupt Request and click Change Setting. You can then change the interrupt value and will be warned if there is a conflict. There isn't an interrupt displayed with every basic configuration.

Step 8. Click OK. Click OK again.

Step 9. Restart Windows 95.

How Many Serial and Parallel Ports?

Windows 3.x could handle up to four serial ports and nine parallel ports. The four serial ports shared the two interrupts. Using up to nine parallel ports required an add-in board.

Windows 95 can logically address up to 128 serial and 128 parallel ports — the same as previous versions of MS-DOS. Most computers come with far fewer actual serial and parallel ports. Some manufacturers sell add-in cards that give you additional ports. These are useful for handling such tasks as answering multiple modems or collecting data from laboratories.

Port Values Stored in Win.ini

To maintain compatibility with existing Windows 3.x applications, port information is stored in the Win.ini file. If you make changes to the serial port settings, for example, they are reflected in changes to the settings in the Win.ini as well as in the Registry. Therefore, don't edit Win.ini directly. Use the Device Manager (click the System icon in the Control Panel) to make changes in the Port Settings Properties sheet. The changes will show up in both places.

Printer port information, i.e. which printer drivers have been set up and which ports they are connected to, comes from the Printers folder. It is stored both in the Registry and Win.ini.

Tables 25-2 shows a typical set of entries for port information in your Windows 95 Win.ini file.

Table 25-2	Port Information in Win.ini
Entry	**Explanation**
[Ports]	Ports section heading
LPT1:= LPT2:= LPT3:=	Possible parallel ports
COM1:=9600,n,8,1,x COM2:=9600,n,8,1,x COM3:=9600,n,8,1,x COM4:=9600,n,8,1,x	Serial port settings. 9600 bits per second, no parity, 8 data bits, 1 stop bit, xon/xoff
FILE:=	Print to a file
FAX:=	Print to a fax
PUB:=	Fax rendering
\\OurServer\hp=	Network printer

```
[Devices]
Linotronic 300 v47.1=PSCRIPT,FILE:
HP LaserJet 4L=HPPCL5MS,LPT1:
Microsoft Fax=WPSUNI,FAX:
Rendering Subsystem=WPSUNI,PUB:
Server's HP=HPPCL5MS,\\OurServer\hp

[PrinterPorts]
Linotronic 300 v47.1=PSCRIPT,FILE:,15,45
HP LaserJet 4L=HPPCL5MS,LPT1:,15,45
Microsoft Fax=WPSUNI,FAX:,15,45
Rendering Subsystem=WPSUNI,PUB:,15,45
Server's HP=HPPCL5MS,\\OurServer\hp,15,45
```

The [Devices] section, which lists the available printers, is useless and is necessary only for compatibility with Windows 2.x applications.

The [PrinterPorts] section lists again the available printers, the ports they are attached to, and their time-out settings in seconds. The first time-out is how long to wait for the printer to report that it is alive. The second is how long to wait for the printer to respond to an attempt to communicate with it before reporting an error.

See Chapter 23 for further discussion of printer issues.

Previously, the base I/O port address and the IRQ values were stored on the COMxBASE and COMxIRQ lines (where x is a number between 1 and 4) in the [386Enh] section of the System.ini file in the Windows folder. These lines are no longer operative. If you wish to edit your System.ini with Notepad, you can remove these lines.

Null Modem Cables

If you are going to use Direct Cable Connection across serial ports, you will want to use null modem cables to connect two Windows 95 computers. When you ask for a *null modem*, sometimes the sales people at the computer store will know what you're talking about, and sometimes they won't. This is not exactly a brand name. It's easier to pick these items out of a mail order catalog. If you need to be specific, the following tables describe the connections for null modem cables.

Table 25-3	Serial 9 Pin to 9 Pin Null Modem cable	
Signal	*Host serial port pins*	*Guest serial port pins*
Transmit Data	3	2
Receive Data	2	3

(continued)

Table 25-3 *(continued)*

Signal	Host serial port pins	Guest serial port pins
Request to Send	7	8
Clear to Send	8	7
Data Set Ready and Data Carrier Detect	6,1	4
Signal Ground	5	5
Data Terminal Ready	4	6,1

Table 25-4	Serial 25 Pin to 25 Pin Null Modem Cable	
Signal	Host serial port pins	Guest serial port pins
Transmit Data	2	3
Receive Data	3	2
Request to Send	4	5
Clear to Send	5	4
Data Set Ready and Data Carrier Detect	6,8	20
Signal Ground	7	7
Data Terminal Ready	20	6,8

Summary

Windows 95 allows for a great deal of control over your ports and modems.

▶ You can change the address and interrupt value for serial or parallel ports to avoid conflicts with other hardware devices.

▶ You can configure your modem once and this configuration will be used by all Windows 95-aware communications software.

▶ You can determine whether your internal modem has an advanced serial port chip.

Chapter 26

Telephony and the Phone Dialer

In This Chapter

Windows 95 provides a powerful resource for indicating to communications applications the characteristics of the location you are dialing from. We show you how to use the Dialing Properties sheet for:

▶ Putting in the numbers that you have to dial to get an outside line or a long-distance line

▶ Automatically using calling cards to bill calls correctly from out-of-town locations

▶ Defining alternative dialing methods for unusual situations

▶ Formatting phone numbers so you can dial them from anywhere

▶ Designating the first three digits of a phone number in your area code as requiring long-distance dialing

▶ Setting up speed dialing with the Phone Dialer

Where Am I Calling From?

Microsoft provides a resource in Windows 95 for keeping track of where you are. What problem are they trying to solve?

If you consider for a moment your garden variety communications package, you will be aware of the fact that it keeps track of the phone numbers of the computer services that you use. That is, it keeps track of the area codes and local numbers. It also knows that if you placed an area code in the phone number it has to dial a 1 to make a long-distance call.

If you stay in one place (say, your office) and have your calls billed to one number (most likely the number you are calling from), you need to know only the number that you are dialing. Your communications software knows how to complete the call because the billing and other information required are implicit.

If, on the other hand, you and your computer travel around at all, to successfully dial out with your computer you need to know not only where you are calling *to* but the special features of the phone system you are dialing *from*. In addition, you will want to be able to easily choose the long-distance carriers that will handle your calls and how they will bill you.

Different locations have different means of accessing outside lines or long-distance carriers. For example, calling from the office may require prefixing your calls with a 9, while calling from home will not. Calling from a hotel may require using a credit card and dialing into a specific long-distance carrier. A phone number may be local when you're calling from home and long distance when you call from the office. Some phones have only pulse dialing services. Some locations require special calling methods.

All these situations can be handled with the Dialing Properties sheet.

Preliminary Location Information

The first time you set up your modem (see Chapter 25 for details) you encounter the Location Information dialog box as part of the Install New Modem Wizard shown in Figure 26-1. At that point all you need to do is type in your area code.

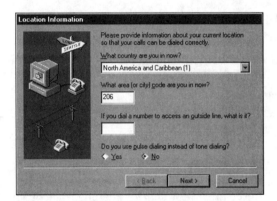

Figure 26-1: The Location Information dialog box.

You have the option of changing the country code, typing in a number required to get an outside line, and choosing whether or not to use pulse dialing. All these values can be changed later using the Dialing Properties sheet.

Dialing Properties Sheet

The Dialing Properties sheet makes it possible for you to define the characteristics of the (perhaps numerous) locations you will be calling from. Your office and/or home location will most likely be ones that you define right away. Define others as you need them.

One of the easiest ways to go to the Dialing Properties sheet is through the Modem Control Panel. Double-click the Modems icon in the Control Panel and then click the Dialing Properties button.

You can also access the Dialing Properties sheet in these Windows 95-aware communications programs: the Phone Dialer, Dial-Up Networking, Hyper-Terminal, and Microsoft Exchange. Here is how to get to the Properties sheet using the Phone Dialer.

STEPS

Accessing the Dialing Properties Sheet

Step 1. Click the Start button, then Programs, and then Accessories. Click the Phone Dialer icon.

Step 2. Click Tools, Dialing Properties in the menu bar of the Phone Dialer. The Dialing Properties sheet, as shown in Figure 26-2, will appear on your desktop.

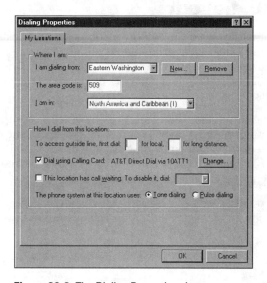

Figure 26-2: The Dialing Properties sheet.

The Dialing Properties sheet is independent of the application that you use to call it up. It works the same for all Windows 95 Telephony Application Programming Interface (TAPI) applications.

Setting up a new location

The particular characteristics of each location are stored by location name. Location names can be anything: Grandma's house, Home Office, HO with ATT, Michigan — direct, Timbuktu — pulse. When you set up a new location, put in names that are unique and meaningful to you.

A location name stands for a location and for the unique dialing sequence used to make the phone call. This includes whether you use a calling card, have to dial a number to get an outside line, and so on. If the number being dialed out is in the international format (see the section later in this chapter entitled *Format for the Numbers That You Dial Out*), the information stored in the location is used to create the sequence of numbers dialed to place the call correctly.

Click the New button to define a new location. Then type in the new location name.

Each location will have an area code. The area code field will accommodate a number up to 29 digits in length, but is most likely no more than 5 digits in length. A location will also have a country code. The drop-down list contains 242 country codes so you should be able to find yours.

Defining how to dial out

Your location may require that you enter a number to get an outside line or another number to be able to make a long-distance call. The long-distance access number may be used to get a line that is used for special billing purposes. You may have multiple such billing numbers at work and may want to set up separate locations for each such number.

Tip

Call waiting can interfere with modem access. If the line you are using at a given location has the call waiting feature, you will want to turn it off for the duration of your call when you are using a modem. Call waiting in the U.S. is normally disabled either by *70, 70#, or 1170. These three choices are displayed in the drop-down list to the right of the call waiting check box.

You have the choice of pulse or tone dialing with your modem. If the local telephone office can handle only pulse dialing, you will need to click that check box.

Credit card calls

The procedures for making credit cards calls (or using a specific long-distance carrier) are uniform enough in most cases to allow for their automation. Specific phone numbers to long-distance carriers (AT&T, British Telecom, MCI, U.S. Sprint, and others) are included with Windows 95 and you can add to the basic list. If you are using a calling card and not just accessing a specific carrier, you'll need to type in your card number, which will be encrypted when it is stored on your hard disk in the Telephon.ini file.

Check the Dial using Calling Card box if you wish to specify a specific long-distance carrier or bill your calls from the location that you are defining to a calling card. Remember, this is a part of the location definition. You can have different location names for the same physical location but with different calling cards.

Checking the Dial using Calling Card check box for the first time for a given location definition will automatically display the Change Calling Card dialog box, as shown in Figure 26-3. If you have previously checked this box, you can click the Change button to display the Change Calling Card dialog box.

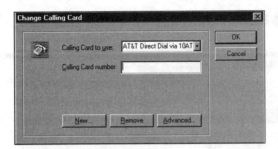

Figure 26-3: The Change Calling Card dialog box. There are originally 22 calling card numbers in the drop-down list from numerous long-distance vendors including AT&T, British Telecom, Carte France Telecom, MCI, Telecom Australia, U.S. Sprint, and others. You can also add calling cards not on this list.

If the drop-down list includes one of the long-distance carriers that you wish to use, click it, type in your calling card number, and click OK.

Adding a long-distance carrier/method to your list

If your long-distance carrier is not on the list, or you want to access your carrier through another method, you need to create a new carrier listing. You can also use the following steps to define another dialing method to match your situation. It is not required that you use this dialog box only for calling cards or accessing other long-distance carriers. You can use it to dial a string of numbers that you need for other purposes.

STEPS

Adding a New Long-Distance Carrier

Step 1. Click the New button in the Change Calling Card dialog box. The Create New Calling Card dialog box will appear. Type in a name to identify a carrier and a method. Click OK.

(continued)

STEPS *(continued)*

Adding a New Long-Distance Carrier

Step 2. The Change Calling Card dialog box will now be on top of your desktop with the new long-distance carrier number in the Calling Card to use field. Click the Advanced button.

Step 3. The Dialing Rules dialog box, as shown in Figure 26-4, is displayed. When this dialog box is first displayed, the fields are empty. Figure 26-4 shows the box after fields are filled.

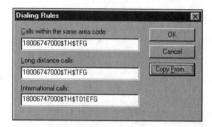

Figure 26-4: The Dialing Rules dialog box.

Step 4. In the three fields in the Dialing Rules dialog box, you will need to enter the access phone number of the long-distance carrier as well as a series of instructions about how to dial the number. The easiest method of doing this is starting with a set of rules for an existing similar long-distance carrier. Click the Copy From button in the Dialing Rules dialog box. This will display the Copy Dialing Rules dialog box, as shown in Figure 26-5.

Figure 26-5: The Copy Dialing Rules dialog box. There are 21 calling card dialing rule sets (plus direct dial, which is empty) in this list.

Step 5.   Click a dialing card name/method from the list and click OK. The dialing rules associated with that calling card and method will be copied into the three fields in the Dialing Rules dialog box.

Step 6.   Edit the fields in the Dialing Rules dialog box by starting with either blank fields or using a template from one of the existing calling cards. Notice that in most cases, at least the long-distance and international calls fields start with a phone number to the long-distance carrier (perhaps just a five-digit prefix) and then include instructions on how to dial the remaining numbers. The dialing rules are given below.

Step 7.   Click OK until you return back to the Phone Dialer. You now have defined the properties of a given location as well as a new long-distance carrier.

The dialing rules

Each of the long-distance carriers/methods has a set of three templates of dialing rules: local, long-distance, and international. You can add a long-distance carrier to your list and edit the dialing rules to match those required by that carrier. The template of dialing rules are not necessarily associated with any long-distance carrier but can be used to define any dialing method.

The templates of dialing rules are a series of numbers, letters, and punctuation marks that are typed into the fields in the Dialing Rules dialog box. When the number is dialed these rules are read and carried out.

Here is an example template of dialing rules:

1- (800) 674-7000 THT01EFG

This is a variation on the template for international dialing shown in Figure 26-4. The rules in this template are as follows:

1. Dial the number 1 - (800) 674-7000.

2. Wait for the "bong" tone ($).

3. Using touch tone, send the calling card number (TH).

4. Wait again for the "bong" tone ($).

5. Using touch tone, send 01 (T01).

6. Send the country code, area code, and local number (EFG).

Spaces, hyphens, periods, and parentheses are ignored.

The dialing rules shown in Table 26-1 allow for the wide variety of circumstances necessary to complete a phone call throughout much of the world.

Table 26-1	Dialing Rules
Code	**Represents**
0-9	Number to be dialed
#	Touch tone pound sign
*	Touch tone star
!	Hook flash
,	Pause for two seconds
@	Wait for a ringing tone followed by five seconds of silence
$	Wait for the calling card tone — the "bong" tone
?	Prompt user for input
E	Country code
F	Area code
G	Local phone number
T	Dial the following number using touch tone
P	Dial numbers using pulse dialing
W	Wait for a second dial tone
H	Your calling card number

Waiting for the 'bong'

Undocumented

Your modem may not support the option of waiting for the "bong" tone. It will ignore the $ and dial your calling card number before the phone company is ready to receive it.

If this is the case, try substituting the @ symbol for the $ in your version of the dialing rules. You modem may respond to this. If not, you can also substitute commas (,,,, instead of $) to force an eight-second wait until the calling card number is sent.

Suppressing the 1 prefix

Your company phone system may dial the prefix 1 for you when you dial long-distance numbers. You can use the Change Calling Card dialog box to create a set of dialing rules that suppresses the prefix 1 for all calls made from work.

STEPS

Creating Dialing Rules to Suppress the 1 Prefix

Step 1. Click the Start button, Settings, and Control Panel. Double-click the Modems icons, and then the Dialing Properties button.

Step 2. Click the New button and type in a name that describes your office location and phone system.

Step 3. Click the Dial using Calling Card check box. Click the New button. Type in a description for the dialing method used at your office, perhaps a name that describes the dialing rules. Click the OK button.

Step 4. Click the Advanced button and then type in the following rules:

Calls within the same area code	G
Long-distance calls	FG
International calls	011EFG

Step 5. Click the Close button, the OK button, and the next OK button.

The MCI dialing rules

Secret

The default dialing rules for MCI that come with Windows 95 may be wrong. If you use MCI, you should check to make sure that they are correct for you. For example, the long-distance dialing rule for one of the MCI numbers is:

18006747000THTFG

These rules send your calling card number before the phone number. If this doesn't work for you, you might try rules that dial the MCI number, wait for the bong, dial 0, and then the area code and phone number, wait for a second bong, and then enter the calling card number. You would need to create a new MCI listing that would include a long-distance dialing rule like this:

18006747000$0TFG$TH

Format for the Numbers That You Dial Out

Windows 95-aware communications applications use certain styles to designate numbers that can be dialed out. The most flexible style is the international style as follows:

+CC (AC) LocalNumber

The plus sign, spaces, and parentheses are all required elements of this format. CC is the country code, which in the U.S. is 1. AC is the area code. There is a space between the country code and the area code and a space between the area code and the local number. The local number can have hyphens in it.

If a number is given in this format, it can be called from anywhere. If you are calling it from the same area code, in the same country, the area code and country code are not used (unless you specify to dial this number as a long-distance number — see the following section).

If you want to dial a number like 911 or an extension number within your company, you won't want to put the number in the international format. Just type it in as is.

You can type phone numbers in the Phone Dialer as shown in the section entitled *Setting up speed dial numbers* later in this chapter.

Undocumented

Phone numbers used by Dial-Up Networking and HyperTerminal connectoids (a word coined at Microsoft) are automatically formatted in the international format. You can change that by unchecking the Use country and area code box in any connection's Properties sheet. To get to this check box, right-click the appropriate connectoid in the Dial-Up Networking or the HyperTerminal folder window and click Properties.

If you uncheck the Use country and area code check box, only the phone number as you have entered it is sent. None of the location properties from the Dialing Properties sheet are used to format the sequence of numbers sent when you make this call.

Which local prefixes require long-distance dialing

Undocumented

It is assumed that all phone numbers with the same local area code as your location's area code are local numbers; that is, they can be reached without dialing a 1 followed by the area code. This may not be the case, so you need a way of telling the Windows 95-aware communications applications which numbers are not really local to a given location.

Windows 95 keeps track of which prefixes (the first three numbers of a local phone number) are long-distance numbers with respect to a given location. All local numbers that are entered with this prefix are assumed to require the long-distance dialing rules, that is, 1+area code+phone number.

Telling Windows 95 just which prefixes in the area code of a given location require long-distance dialing is not that straightforward. It can be done in the Phone Dialer, Dial-Up Networking, or HyperTerminal. To do this in the Phone Dialer, take the following steps:

STEPS

Identifying a Prefix that Requires Long-distance Dialing

Step 1. Click the Start button, then Programs, and then Accessories. Click the Phone Dialer icon.

Step 2. Click Tools, Dialing Properties in the menu bar of the Phone Dialer. Change the Location Name field to the desired location name. The prefixes for the phone numbers that require long-distance dialing will be associated with this location. Click OK.

Step 3. Type a local phone number in the Phone Dialer's "Number to phone" field that is a long-distance call from the location named in the Dialing Properties sheet but in the same area code.

Step 4. Click Tools, Dialing Properties in the menu bar of the Phone Dialer. The Dialing Properties sheet, as shown in Figure 26-6, will be displayed. Notice that near the bottom of the display is the number that you just typed in and a check box that states Dial as a long-distance call. Check this box. Click OK.

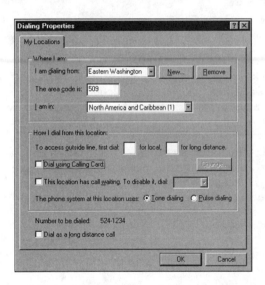

Figure 26-6: The Dialing Properties sheet with the number to be dialed. You can force this and all other numbers with this prefix to be dialed as long-distance numbers.

Phone numbers that have this prefix will now automatically be dialed as long-distance calls from the location given on the Dialing Properties sheet when the Dial as a long-distance call check box was checked. You can reverse this by calling up a number with the same prefix and unchecking this box.

It is possible to do this with phone numbers that are used by HyperTerminal and Dial-Up Networking. The Dialing Properties sheet displayed in these applications will have the designated connection phone number at the bottom if a connection is currently highlighted.

The list of prefixes that require long-distance calls is stored in the Telephon.ini file. See the section entitled *Telephon.ini* later in this chapter on how to read this file.

10-digit phone numbers

You may live in an area that requires that you dial the area code and the phone number even to make a local call. The prefix 1 is not used. Local calls may have different area codes.

Undocumented

The Dialing Properties sheet can be made to handle this situation for some limited cases, but Microsoft doesn't currently provide a general solution to this problem. We can give you a workaround.

When entering a phone number that you are going to call, use the international style to enter the area code in the area code field. In the local number field, enter the area code again as part of the local number, for example:

+1 (214) 214555-1234

If the area code for your location is 214, the full 10-digit number will be dialed. Unfortunately, if you are in another area code, the area code for this number will be dialed twice, unless you have unchecked Use country and area code. Even in this case, you will need to add the prefix 1 to get the number dialed correctly.

If your location is in a different area code, but the phone number is still local, you can enter your area code as its area code, and include its area code in the local phone number. For example, if your area code were 713, you would create the following number:

+1 (713) 214555-1234

Dialing from the location in the 713 area code would just dial a local 10-digit phone number. Again, this method is restricted to the 713 area code and would not work if you tried to call from another area code.

We await further developments from Microsoft concerning TAPI.

The Phone Dialer

If ever there was an application that was in fact an applet, it is the Phone Dialer, which uses your modem to dial your phone for you. You then pick up the phone and speak with the person whose number your modem dialed. Unless you have the Phone Dialer set up on your desktop to get at very conveniently, or you require a long string of numbers to place a call, you are not going to use it because it is more work than just dialing the number on your phone.

Microsoft doesn't intend the Phone Dialer to be a serious application. It is just an example to other developers of how they can use the facilities provided by Windows 95 to create full-fledged communications applications. Still, you can use it if you like.

The Phone Dialer will use the Dialing Properties sheet information to make the phone calls. Using a calling card cuts down quite a bit on the amount of numbers you have to key in.

The Phone Dialer can store up to 8 phone numbers on its speed dial buttons and keeps a record of the last 20 numbers called. It can prompt you to keep a record of the phone numbers of calls coming in and/or going out. The Phone Dialer is shown in Figure 26-7.

Figure 26-7: The Phone Dialer. Click a speed dial button and it will dial the number for you if your modem is hooked up to your phone line.

Setting Up Speed Dial Numbers

You can define the eight blank speed dial buttons to dial a number when you click the button, just like on a real phone. This is the productivity benefit of the Phone Dialer.

STEPS

Setting Up the Speed Dialer

Step 1. Click the Start button, then Programs, and then Accessories. Click the Phone Dialer icon.

Step 2. Click Edit, Speed Dial in the menu bar of the Phone Dialer.

Step 3. Click the button that you want to define in the Edit Speed Dial dialog box. Type in the person's name and phone number. Repeat this step for all the buttons that you wish to define.

Step 4. Click the OK button when you are done.

Step 5. You can define one blank button on the Phone Dialer just by clicking it.

When entering numbers in the speed dial buttons, use the international style if you want the numbers to be dialed correctly from any location.

Undocumented

The speed dial phone numbers and the last 20 phone numbers are stored in the Dialer.ini file in the \Windows folder. You can edit this file with Notepad if you like. It also stores the Phone Dialer desktop position and log book information.

Telephon.ini

The Telephon.ini file is stored in the \Windows folder. It stores data about the locations and calling cards, as well as pointers to applications that use the telephony services provided by Windows 95. Using an *ini* file is quite unusual as Windows 95 stores most of its data in the Registry files and Microsoft tries not to use Win.ini and System.ini files or any other *ini* files.

The sections in Telephon.ini of interest to us are [Locations] and [Cards].

Locations section

Here is an example of a line in the Locations section:

Location1=1, "Home," "9","","206",1,0,0,1,"357,847",0," "

Here is how to interpret the line:

Location*x*=ID, "location name", "# (number) for outside line", "# (number) for long-distance line", "area code", countrycode, card ID, previous card ID, use area codes, "LD prefixes"

Other variables are listed in Table 26-2.

Table 26-2	Location Variables
Variable	*Stands for*
x	Ordered sequence of location numbers.
ID	The location's identification number.
location name	Your name for the location.
# for outside line	The prefix you have to dial to get an outside line.
# for LD line	The number you have to dial to get a long-distance line.
area code	Area code.
countrycode	Country code.
card ID	If a calling card is used, this is its ID, otherwise it is 0 for direct dialing.
previous card ID	The previous calling card ID before its last modification.
use area codes	IF 1, the local phone numbers with prefixes listed in the LD prefixes (next variable) should be dialed using the area code. This is true only in North America, and if the country code and the area code for the number being dialed are the same as the current location and its prefix is listed in LD prefixes. IF 0, then don't include the area code before the local call number.
LD prefixes	List of prefixes that are long-distance calls from Location x.

Cards section

The Cards section stores the data about the calling card methods. These methods don't have to be calling cards exactly, but can include any alternative dialing methods that can utilize a special phone number and/or a user code number. You can define these calling methods yourself using the methods detailed previously. Here's an example:

```
Card12=1, "AT&T Direct Dial via 10ATT1","55041111938112",
"102881FG","102881FG","10288011EFG",1
```

The format of this line is as follows. Other variables are shown in Table 26-3.

```
Cardx=ID, "card name", "encrypted card", "local call", "long-distance",
"international", hidden
```

Table 26-3	Card Variables
Variable	*Stands for*
x	Ordered sequence of card numbers
ID	Card ID
card name	Your dialing method name
encrypted card	Your card number encrypted
local call	The dialing rules for making a local call
long-distance	The dialing rules for making a long-distance call
international	The dialing rules for making an international call
hidden 0,1,2,3	Whether or not this calling card method is displayed as an available dialing method
0	Not hidden
1	Not hidden — values can be set up only by an application
2	Hidden
3	Hidden — values can be set up only by an application

Summary

We focus on how to work with the Dialing Properties sheet to define the properties of each of the locations you dial out from. The Dialing Properties sheet is used by all Windows 95-aware communications applications.

▶ We show you how to describe each of your dialing locations.

▶ We describe how to use calling cards or alternative dialing methods with your modem or voice calls.

▶ We show you how to tell communications applications just which local phone prefixes require long-distance dialing.

▶ We show you how to use the Phone Dialer as a speed dialer.

Chapter 27

Disk Tools and File Systems

In This Chapter

Windows 95 provides new, powerful tools to give you lots of hard disk space while keeping your files safe and your disk fast. We discuss:

▶ Navigating through Windows to find all the tools

▶ Repairing your disks when trouble comes knocking

▶ Speeding up your disk drives

▶ Doubling the size of your hard disk and floppy drives

▶ Compressing very large drives to store much more data

▶ Letting weird programs have direct disk access

▶ Setting your disk cache parameters for optimum performance

▶ Choosing from new characters in long filenames

▶ Repartitioning your drives

▶ Creating super-high-density diskettes

The Real Changes

If you want to look for the changes that have been made to the fundamentals of an operating system, look for how it works with files that are stored on disk drives. They don't call it the Disk Operating System (DOS) for nothing.

The Microsoft personnel who handled the Disk Tools section of the Windows 95 beta forum on CompuServe (for the most part Brian Emanuels, William Keener, and Gregg Rivers) asked probing questions and provided detailed answers to beta tester queries and reports. They set a very professional tone. It was clear to those of us who followed this section that Microsoft was quite interested in getting its new disk tools thoroughly tested.

Most of the changes Microsoft has made to the "disk operating system" affect what is under the hood — speeding up access to your hard disk, diskettes, and CD-ROM drive. It also reduced the amount of user interaction required to set obscure performance parameters — like permanent swap files and disk cache size — while at the same time increasing the performance that tuning these parameters was supposed to provide.

Further, these improvements vastly increase the amount of available conventional memory and improve the responsiveness of your computer to multiple tasks. Improved compression drivers let you double (more or less) your hard disk (and diskette) space. In the following sections, we look at the major changes and additions.

VFAT

In Windows for Workgroups 3.11, the Virtual File Allocation Table (VFAT) is called *32-bit file access*. You get to it through the Control Panel, Enhanced icon. In Windows 95, it's called the 32-bit protected-mode VFAT file system. Microsoft released the prebeta version of this code when it produced Windows for Workgroups 3.11. It worked, except for numerous software and hardware incompatibilities. It sped up reading and writing files, when you didn't have to turn it off because of these incompatibilities.

The code has been much improved and now actually works reliably. It provides fast access to files. It improves multitasking by reducing the amount of time that it blocks other tasks. It is compatible with existing DOS partitions — the original FAT — on your disks. Because your processor doesn't have to switch to real-mode to read and write to the disk, everything gets faster.

Vcache

Windows 95 comes with a 32-bit protected-mode dynamic cache. It replaces 16-bit, real-mode SmartDrive (Smartdrv.exe). Vcache doesn't take up conventional or upper memory space. It does a much better job than SmartDrive of caching disk reads and writes. It also caches CD-ROMs and networked drives.

You don't have to specify how much memory should be set aside for Vcache (unlike SmartDrive). It sizes itself based on available free memory and disk read/write activity (that's the dynamic part of Vcache).

Direct CD-ROM support

No more messy ducks (Mscdex.exe) in your Config.sys file. Windows 95 provides another one of its 32-bit protected-mode drivers, CDFS (CD-ROM file system), to replace the 16-bit real-mode Mscdex.exe driver that comes with Windows 3.1x and MS-DOS to support CD-ROM drives.

You get a dynamic CD-ROM cache that works with Vcache. No conventional or upper memory is used by the driver. It isn't an add-on called by a line in Config.sys. CDFS is also quite a bit faster than Mscdex.exe.

Long filenames

You can type filenames up to 255 characters long. The names can include spaces. Windows 95 can read and write long filenames supported by other operating systems, such as Windows NT, NetWare, Unix, and OS/2.

Files with long filenames also have short filenames that are recognized by applications that can't handle long filenames (including DOS). These short names are automatically managed by Windows 95 so that only unique names are created.

The unique short filenames consists of the first six characters of the long filename plus "~1" or additional ordinals. See the section entitled *Long Filenames* later in this chapter for details.

Windows 95-based disk tools

Earlier versions of Windows and DOS required that you quit Windows and go to DOS if you needed to work directly with your disk drive at a low level. While this is still possible, it's a lot harder to "get out of" Windows 95.

Windows 95 comes with very powerful Windows-based disk tools that help you manage and protect your files. *ScanDisk* finds and repairs problems with your disks. *Defrag* makes your files contiguous. They are both Windows 95 programs, although you can also run ScanDisk from DOS and in batch files.

Compression disk drivers

Windows 95 comes with a 32-bit protected-mode compression disk driver that works with both DoubleSpace and DriveSpace disks. Instead of taking 50K of conventional memory, it is loaded in to extended memory.

You can approximately double your disk space with, in many cases, minimal or no impact on the speed of access to your files. You can also approximately double the room available on your diskettes.

Microsoft Plus! adds more disk compression (DriveSpace 3) for computers with 486 or faster processors. Files are further compressed (quite often at a ratio greater than 2.5-to-1) to free up more room on your hard disk. The file volumes can be up to 2 gigabytes in size. Compression, scanning for errors, and defragging can be scheduled to take place during idle times.

Built-in SCSI hard disk support

Earlier versions of DOS and Windows didn't support SCSI drives without special drivers from hardware manufacturers that were loaded in Config.sys. Windows 95 has built-in support for SCSI devices.

Installable File System Manager

Both the VFAT and the CDFS are installable file systems managed by the Windows 95 Installable File System Manager. You have the option of adding other file systems, and you will if you connect your computer to network servers. Windows 95 can manage multiple file systems, making it much easier to connect to many different networks at once.

Windows 95 doesn't support HPFS (*high performance file system*, which is native to OS/2) or NTFS (the Windows NT file system) file systems on local hard disks, but it does over a network. Third-party vendors are likely to provide solutions that can handle these file systems on local hard disks.

Dynamically sized swap file

Virtual memory no longer requires a permanent swap file for the fastest operation. Windows 95 can dynamically size the required swap file. This cuts down on the user decisions required to optimize Windows. The swap file can even be on a compressed drive without incurring a performance hit.

Support for enhanced IDE devices

Windows 95 supports the enhanced IDE (EIDE) specification, so drives larger than 1 gigabyte can be handled directly. In fact, Windows 95 supports EIDE hard disks as large as 137 gigabytes.

Windows 95 also supports IDE-based CD-ROMs. Without the need to buy a separate SCSI card to support the CD-ROM, you can hook these drives to the existing IDE card used by your hard disk.

Multitasked floppy drive formatting

No longer will everything grind to a halt while you format a floppy diskette. A Windows 95 32-bit driver now handles multitasked access to your floppy drives.

Finding Your Disks and the Disk Tools

You've got to be able to find the disk tools if you're going to use them. Fortunately, there are a lot of ways to go and still get to the same place.

The Start button

The easiest way is to click the Start button, Programs, Accessories, and finally System Tools. If you haven't edited your Start menus, you'll find the Disk Defragmenter, ScanDisk, and DriveSpace, as well as System Monitor and Net Watcher, if you installed them.

A disk icon

It is almost as easy to double-click My Computer on your desktop, right-click one of the hard disk icons, click Properties, and then click the Tools tab. These actions will cause Windows 95 to display the dialog box shown in Figure 27-1. You now have access to ScanDisk, Backup, and the Disk Defragmenter.

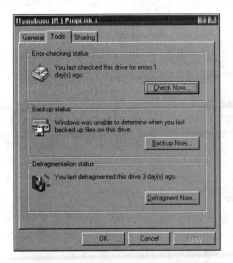

Figure 27-1: The Disk Tools Properties sheet. Click Check Now to launch ScanDisk, Backup Now to launch Backup, or Defragment Now to launch the Disk Defragmenter.

You can right-click any disk icon in any folder or Explorer window to get to this Tools dialog box.

Using help

The help system, because it contains its own shortcuts, can provide a path to all of the disk tools. While there are many ways through the help system to the disk tools, you should first click the Start button, and then Help, and then try any of the following:

■ Double-click the How To book in the Help Contents dialog box. Double-click Maintain Your Computer. You now have numerous options. Choosing "Detecting and repairing disk errors" leads you to a shortcut to ScanDisk.

■ Double-click Tips and Tricks in the Help Contents dialog box. Double-click For Maintaining Your Computer followed by "Defragmenting your hard disk regularly." You can now click the shortcut to Disk Defragmenter.

■ Click the Index tab in the Help Contents dialog box. Type **disk** and press Enter. Double-click "disk troubleshooter" and then click the button next to "Create more disk space by using DriveSpace disk compression." You now have a shortcut to DriveSpace, as well as some help in how to use it.

In a DOS window

You can type **Scandisk, Defrag,** or **Drvspace** in a DOS window. Each of these commands invokes the Windows 95 graphical version of these programs. You can run Windows programs from your DOS window.

Tip Type **Scandisk /?** in a DOS window and you will be referred to a specific section of the Windows 95 help system for how to use command line parameters with ScanDisk:

```
For information about the command-line parameters supported by
ScanDisk for Windows, look up 'checking for errors, in disks' in the
Windows Help index. Then view the topic 'Checking your disk for errors
every time your computer starts.'
```

ScanDisk can also be run from MS-DOS mode or from the DOS command prompt before Windows 95 starts. A DOS 7.0 version of ScanDisk will be run from this DOS prompt. Disk Defragmenter and DriveSpace can't be run in MS-DOS mode.

The Device Manager

The Device Manager lets you look at the basic resources used by your devices, including your disk drives and controller card(s). There are at least two ways to get to the Device Manager (one part of System Properties).

■ Right-click My Computer on the desktop, click Properties, and then click the Device Manager tab.

■ Click Start, Settings, Control Panel. Double-click the System icon and choose the Device Manager tab.

Once you're in the Device Manager, click the plus sign next to the icons labeled Disk drives, Floppy disk controllers, or Hard disk controllers. Highlight the controller or drive name that is displayed, click Properties, and then the Resources tab. The resources used by an IDE hard disk controller are shown in Figure 27-2.

File system performance

The File System Performance Properties sheets let you disable all sorts of 32-bit file access settings as well as optimize your disk caching scheme.

Use the same steps to get to the System Properties sheet as described in the preceding section, but click the Performance tab instead of the Device Manager tab. Click the File System button.

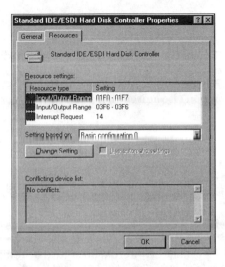

Figure 27-2: The Resources Properties sheet for a EDI/ESDI controller. You have the option of choosing between the two basic configurations.

Virtual memory performance

Windows can manage your swap file without any input from you. If you want to change its location and set a minimum or maximum size, you can do so.

Use the same steps to get to the System Properties sheet as described in the earlier section entitled *The Device Manager*, but click the Performance tab instead of the Device Manager tab. Click Virtual Memory.

The System Monitor

Using the System Monitor, you can track how your hard disks (or hard disks on other computers on your network) are being used. You'll find the System Monitor in the Start menu.

Click the Start button, Programs, Accessories, System Tools, and then System Monitor. It won't be there unless you did a custom installation and specifically chose to install it. You can use the Add/Remove Software icon in the Control Panel to add it. Look under the Memory Manager options.

The Disk Tools

You use ScanDisk and the Disk Defragmenter to fix your hard disks, diskettes, and other removable media (not CD-ROMs) when your files get corrupted or are stored in too many pieces. If parts of the surface of your hard disk are bad, ScanDisk will mark them so files won't be stored there. ScanDisk will move the data off those spots if it can.

ScanDisk

ScanDisk does an excellent job of analyzing your hard disk and repairing errors. Microsoft has taken great pains to make sure it works under all circumstances.

ScanDisk reviews and repairs errors on compressed drives as well as on physical drives. It repairs problems with long filenames, the FAT, the directory and file structure, the drive surface, and the internal structure of compressed volume files (CVF). It can find and fix errors on diskettes and hard drives, and, as if you really cared, RAM drives and memory cards that are treated as drives.

ScanDisk can find and repair problems found on both DriveSpace and DoubleSpace drives (but not Stacker or SuperStor drives). The CVFs don't have to be mounted (have a drive letter associated with them) for ScanDisk to work with them, although in most cases they will be.

ScanDisk won't be able to find or fix errors on CD-ROMs, networked drives, or pseudo drives created by using Assign, Subst, Join, or Interlnk (all of these are DOS commands).

If one of your applications reports disk problems when reading a file, run ScanDisk immediately to repair the file. If Windows 95 crashes while you are editing a file and the file is damaged, it is very likely that ScanDisk can fix it.

ScanDisk options

As stated earlier in this chapter, you can start ScanDisk by right-clicking a drive icon in a window, choosing Properties, clicking Tools tab, and then Check Now. If you do this, you are presented with a ScanDisk dialog box containing buttons labeled Options and Advanced, as shown in Figure 27-3.

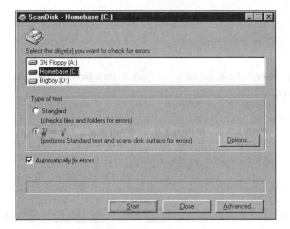

Figure 27-3: The ScanDisk dialog box.

It is easy to find out what all these options do. Take the following steps:

STEPS

Exploring ScanDisk Options

Step 1.   Start ScanDisk and click Thorough, and then Options.

Step 2.   Right-click any item in the Surface Scan Options dialog box. Click the What's This? button to see what the option really does.

Step 3.   Click the Cancel button in the Surface Scan Options dialog box and click Advanced.

Step 4.   Right-click any item in the ScanDisk Advanced Options dialog box to learn more about what it does.

ScanDisk command line parameters

ScanDisk can be run from a batch file or from the DOS prompt. You can create a shortcut to ScanDisk and include it in your Startup folder so it will check your hard disk every time you start your computer. You may want to add some of the following command line parameters to the command line of the shortcut.

ScanDisk can take the following parameters:

```
Scandisk {x:} {options}
```

or

```
        Scandisk x:\drvspace.nnn
or
        Scandisk x:\dblspace.nnn
```

x: is the drive letter for the drive to be checked. It can be the drive letter assigned to a compressed volume file.

ScanDisk can take the following options:

/all or /a	Checks all your local, nonremovable hard disks
/noninteractive or /n	Starts and finishes ScanDisk without user input
/preview or /p	Prevents ScanDisk from correcting errors that it finds
dblspace.*nnn*	Name of compressed volume file (CVF) to check
drvspace.*nnn*	Name of compressed volume file (CVF) to check

Hidden CVFs reside on host drives and are named by their type of compression (DoubleSpace or DriveSpace) and a number (*nnn*) as the file extension. If you want to scan an unmounted compressed drive, include dblspace.*nnn* or drvspace.*nnn* on the command line. The drive letter in this case would be the host drive letter.

Put ScanDisk in the Startup folder

Windows 95 help can tell you how to put ScanDisk into your Startup folder. There is no need to repeat these instructions here, but you might like to know how to find them. Here's how

STEPS

Learning How to Put ScanDisk in the Startup Folder

Step 1.   Click the Start button, Help, and then the Index tab.

Step 2.   Type **chec** to highlight the phrase *checking for errors*. Double-click *in disks*.

Step 3.   Click the Display button in the Topics Found dialog box while the first item is highlighted.

Step 4.   Click the Shortcut icon.

Follow the steps given in Windows 95 help for creating a shortcut to ScanDisk. You might want to add a command line parameter or two from the ones in the preceding section.

Running ScanDisk from DOS

Undocumented

There are really two ScanDisk programs, Scandskw.exe and Scandisk.exe. The Windows 95 version is Scandskw.exe, an executable stub, which calls code located in the dynamic link libraries Shell.dll and Dskmaint.dll.

Scandskw.exe is called when you click Check Now or ScanDisk in the System Tools menu. It is also called when you type **Scandisk** at a DOS prompt in a Windows DOS session. You could also type **Scandskw** at the command prompt in a Windows DOS session. There is one exception. If, in a Windows DOS session, you type a command of the form **Scandisk C:/dblspace.000,** the DOS version of ScanDisk is executed because the Windows version works only with mounted drives.

If you boot your computer to the DOS command prompt or start an MS-DOS mode session, type **Scandisk** at the DOS command prompt and the DOS version of ScanDisk will run. If you dual-boot into your previous version of DOS, you can still run the DOS 7.0 (Windows 95) version of ScanDisk. This comes in handy when you are setting up Windows 95.

Scandisk.ini

Undocumented

A ScanDisk configuration file, Scandisk.ini, is in your Windows 95 folder. This file works only with the DOS version of ScanDisk and is not used if you run ScanDisk from Windows or from a Windows DOS session.

This file is internally well documented and can be edited to change the way the DOS version of ScanDisk operates. Use Edit.com to edit this file. Open it and you will find plenty of documentation to tell you how to change ScanDisk's parameters.

ScanDisk and your FAT

Undocumented

The DOS version of ScanDisk always uses the primary copy of your FAT (unless it finds a physical disk error). The backup FAT is replaced by the primary FAT when errors are repaired.

The Windows 95 version of ScanDisk checks both of your file allocation tables and, if they are out of sync, determines the "better" one and uses it.

ScanDisk and Setup

The DOS version of ScanDisk is run when you run Windows 95 Setup. If you start Setup from the DOS prompt you can see ScanDisk; otherwise it is hidden behind a Windows face. If there are problems with your hard disk, you can fix them before proceeding with the setup process.

If you run Setup from Windows 3.1*x* and there are problems, exit Setup and run the DOS 7.0 version of ScanDisk from DOS.

Setup runs ScanDisk to put everything in order and cut down on the number of variables before you install this very complex operating system. This is discussed in more detail in Chapter 3.

Defrag, The disk defragmenter

As you probably know, neither DOS nor any version of Windows necessarily keeps the contents of your files stored in contiguous sectors of your hard disk. Your files become more fragmented as they are rewritten. Fragmented files take longer to read and write. You can speed up disk access by occasionally defragmenting the files on your hard disk.

Defrag is a Windows program. While you can run it from the DOS prompt in a Windows DOS session, it won't run in an MS-DOS mode session, unlike ScanDisk.

Defrag can be run while you are running other programs. It is running as one of the authors types these words. The defragmentation process is interrupted by disk reads and writes, but Defrag is always operating and continues to defragment where it left off, after the read or write is complete.

Defrag in details view

Defrag is a fun program to watch if you put it into details view. Here's how to do that.

STEPS

Running Defrag in Details View

Step 1.   Click the Start button, Programs, Accessories, System Tools, and then Disk Defragmenter.

Step 2.   Click the down arrow in the drop-down list to show the available drives. You can defrag your floppies if you want to (but why?). High-light the drive that you want to defragment and click OK. (Multiple drives can be defragmented by holding Ctrl and highlighting them as well).

Step 3.   Click the Start button, the Show details button, and then the Legend button. As shown in Figure 27-4, Defrag Legend will appear on top of rows and rows of little colored squares that represent disk clusters.

Showing details slows down the defragmentation process a little, but makes up for it in visual interest.

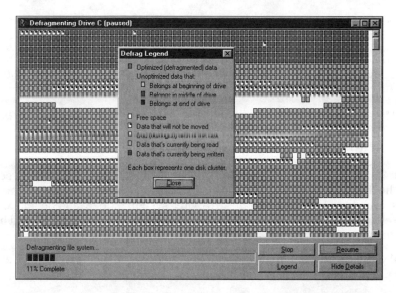

Figure 27-4: The disk defragmenter in details view with Defrag Legend showing.

Before you click the Start button in the Defrag window, you are given the choice of how extensive a defragmentation process to engage in. To see these options, click Advanced. To find out what each option does, right-click the text next to the buttons and click the popup What's This? button.

Data that will not be moved

Secret

You may notice that some or many sectors on your hard disk are marked "Data that will not be moved" in the details view of the Defrag screen. Defrag doesn't move files that are marked *both* hidden and system. Some copy protection schemes put a file or two in certain locations and mark them as both system and hidden. If they are moved, the copy protection scheme fails.

Defrag takes the conservative approach. In reality, almost all files that are marked both system and hidden are, in fact, not related to any copy protection schemes. Windows 95 marks many of its files as both system and hidden. Of course, they are easy enough to see in a folder or Explorer window, so they are not really all that hidden.

If you have a CVF on a host drive, it will probably appear as a large block of contiguous sectors and will be marked as "Data that will not be moved." If you view the compressed drive itself, you'll see that data in these clusters can indeed be moved. Both views are right.

The CVF shouldn't be moved, and you can defragment the files within it by defragmenting the compressed drive directly.

Your dynamically sized swap file will be also marked as unable to be moved, but it doesn't have the hidden or system attribute.

You can have Defrag move the files marked both system and hidden by changing their attributes. You (not Defrag) are taking the responsibility for the consequences.

To remove the system and hidden attributes from a file, type the following command at any DOS prompt:

attrib -s -h *drive:\pathname\filename*

It is unfortunate that the Windows 95 Find dialog box doesn't let you collect all the files that have a certain attribute turned on (or off). If it did, you could search for all the files with the attributes system hidden, and decide for yourself whether to turn these attributes off for each file displayed in the Find dialog box.

If you want to find out more about the attrib command, type **attrib/?** at the DOS prompt.

It's very important to reset any CVFs back to hidden and system so that they are not moved by Defrag. To do this, type the following command at the DOS prompt:

attrib +s +h c:\Drvspace.*nnn*

or

attrib +s +h c:\Dblspace.*nnn*

In the preceding command line, *nnn* is the number of the CVF volume.

DOS 6.*x* versions of Defrag would not move files if they were marked either hidden or system or both. The Windows 95 Defrag is a little less reluctant to move files.

Never use earlier versions of Defrag from MS-DOS 6.*x* because they will destroy long filenames.

The disk defragmenter will not work with Stacker or SuperStor compressed drives. If you have compressed drives, get a third-party disk compression program like the one included in Symantec's Norton Utilities for Windows 95. You also can't use Defrag over a network. It has real trouble with CD-ROMs, which are read-only. Don't try it on drives that are created by Assign, Subst, or Join.

You can run Defrag on the host drive and/or on the compressed drive if you have DoubleSpace or DriveSpace drives.

Defrag in the Startup folder

Like ScanDisk, you can run Defrag every time you start your computer. This can get pretty tedious if you start up your computer a lot.

If that's the case, you should create a shortcut to Defrag.exe (it's in the Windows 95 folder) and put it in your Startup folder. Edit the Target line of the shortcut to change the command line parameters as shown in the next section.

Defrag command line parameters

Defrag can be run from a DOS prompt, from the Run dialog box on the Start menu, from a batch file, and in the Startup folder with any of the following command line parameters:

```
Defrag {x: or /all} {options} {/noprompt} {/concise or /detailed}
```

The command line parameters are as follows:

x: Drive letter designator for drive to be defragmented

/all   Defragment all local, nonremovable drives

{*options*}

/f	Defragment files and free space
/u	Defragment files only
/q	Defragment free space only
/concise	Don't show the details view (this is the default)
/detailed	Display the show details view
/noprompt	Do not display confirmation message boxes

Disk-Related Functions

Numerous commands and functions affect the performance of disk drives and speed of file access.

Disk space

The Explorer displays the total size of the files stored in the folder you have highlighted in the Explorer's left pane in the status bar. You'll also find the amount of free space available on the drive partition that contains the highlighted folder.

Another way to find the size and available disk space on a particular drive is to take the following steps:

STEPS

Displaying Disk Size

Step 1.   Double-click My Computer on your desktop.

Step 2.   Right-click a disk drive icon and then click Properties.

These steps will display the General Properties sheet for the selected drive, as shown in Figure 27-5.

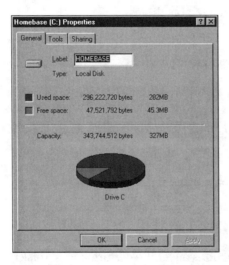

Figure 27-5: The General Properties sheet for a hard disk. You can change the disk's label by typing in a new one.

File size and attributes

The status bar of the Explorer (or any folder window) will tell you the size of the files you have highlighted in the Explorer or the number and total size of all the files in a folder if you highlight it in the left pane.

Right-click a file in an Explorer or folder window and click Properties to display its General Properties sheet, as shown in Figure 27-6. This sheet will also tell you the size of the file as well as its attributes (Read-only, System, Archive, Hidden).

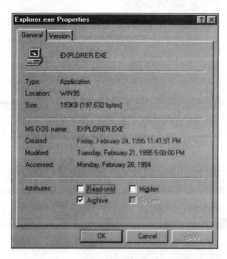

Figure 27-6: A file's General Properties sheet. You can change a file's attributes by clicking the boxes at the bottom of this Properties sheet.

If you have selected a group of files and then right-clicked the group and clicked Properties, the General Properties sheet displayed will show the total size of all the files. This is handy if you are dragging these files to your floppy disk drive. The total size of the selected files is also displayed in the status bar.

Want to know the total size of all the files on a hard disk? Take the following steps:

Undocumented

STEPS

Finding the Total Size of All Files on a Disk

Step 1.   Highlight a disk drive icon in the left pane of an Explorer window.

Step 2.   Highlight the top entry in the right pane on an Explorer window.

Step 3.   Scroll down the right pane of the Explorer Windows to the last entry. Shift+right-click the last entry.

Step 4.   Click Properties.

The total number of files and their accumulated size will be displayed. It may take a few seconds to count all the files.

Format

You can format a hard disk, diskette, or other removable media by right-clicking the icon representing the drive in either a folder or Explorer window and choosing Format from the right mouse button menu.

Undocumented

You won't be able to format a compressed diskette in this manner. If you try to format the compressed volume or the host drive, you'll receive error messages. If you want to format such a diskette, you'll need to uncompress it (which may require that you erase the files on it) first.

You can format a compressed drive using DriveSpace. See the *Other DriveSpace Options* section later in this chapter for details.

Thankfully, clicking Format in the right mouse button menu does not immediately begin the formatting process. You're given the opportunity to determine some format parameters. If you accidentally click Format after you right-click your boot drive, you will have an opportunity to back out.

Diskcopy

Tip

Want to make a copy of a diskette? Put the diskette in the diskette drive, double-click My Computer, right-click the diskette drive icon,and then click Copy Disk.

Sharing

If you are on a network (even if you just have Direct Cable Connection installed), you can give other computers access to files on your disk drives. To share access to all the files on a given drive, right-click the drive icon in a folder or Explorer window and click Sharing in the right mouse button menu to display the Sharing Properties sheet shown in Figure 27-7.

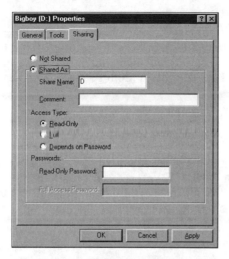

Figure 27-7: The Sharing Properties sheet. Check Shared As to share your disk with other computers on the network.

Recycle Bin size

Just because you delete a file doesn't mean it is gone. The files sit in your Recycle Bin, taking up disk space until you empty it. The free space on your disk doesn't increase until you empty the trash.

(An exception to this is when you click, Properties, the Recycle Bin on the desktop, and tell the program not to move deleted files to the Recycle Bin).

To set the Recycle Bin to warn you when it is getting full, set its maximum size. To do this, right-click the Recycle Bin on the desktop and click Properties. You can set the maximum Recycle Bin size as a percent of disk space for all hard disks at once or individually.

Chkdsk /f

Chkdsk (Check disk) is an outdated DOS command that deletes bad files when you specify the /f parameter. It doesn't work anymore and you should instead use ScanDisk to fix files or the DOS command Mem to give you a memory usage breakdown.

Troubleshooting disk access

Even though the 32-bit disk and file access provided by Windows 95 is much better than what came with Windows for Workgroups 3.11, there may still be incompatibilities. You can turn off various portions of the disk driver to track down problems with disk access. To access these troubleshooting options, take the following steps:

STEPS
Troubleshooting Disk Access

Step 1.   Right-click My Computer on your desktop. Click Properties. Click the Performance tab.

Step 2.   Click the Files System button.

Step 3.   Click the Troubleshooting tab.

Disk Compression

Windows 95 supports two versions of disk compression: DriveSpace and DoubleSpace. They are slightly different due to a legal settlement with Stac Electronics, the manufacturer of Stacker disk compression software. Windows 95 creates DriveSpace compressed drives.

Microsoft Plus! comes with DriveSpace 3, an upgrade to DriveSpace compression, and the Compression Agent, which gives you even higher levels of compression plus control over which files are compressed to what levels when. All the restrictions that we discuss later in this chapter regarding compressed volume size do not apply if you use DriveSpace 3.

Starting with Windows 95, Microsoft provides a unified driver that handles both DoubleSpace and DriveSpace. The files Dblspace.bin and Drvspace.bin, the disk compression drivers in the root directory of your host drive, are exactly the same.

Undocumented

You shouldn't erase either Drvspace.bin or Dblspace.bin. Only Drvspace.bin is needed for drives compressed while running Windows 95. Dblspace.bin (which is the same as Drvspace.bin but with a different name) is used when you mount old volume files compressed with DoubleSpace, such as when you place a DoubleSpace diskette in your diskette drive.

When you start your computer, either Dblspace.bin or Drvspace.bin is loaded in conventional memory if you have a mounted compressed drive. Once Windows 95 starts, the real-mode D??space.bin driver is unloaded, conventional memory reclaimed, and the 32-bit driver takes over.

Windows 95 can work with five disk compression schemes: DoubleSpace, DriveSpace, Stacker, SuperStor, and AddStor. Microsoft provides 32-bit drivers for DoubleSpace and DriveSpace compressed drives. You can use the existing Stacker or SuperStor real-mode drivers in conventional or upper memory to access drives compressed with these products. 32-bit drivers will become available for these disk compression schemes (but not from Microsoft). All the discussion in this chapter refers to the Microsoft-supplied disk compression schemes.

A compressed drive is not a physical drive or a volume (a DOS FAT partition) but rather a file stored on a disk drive. It is referred to as a compressed volume file (CVF) and is given a disk drive letter designator just as though it were a volume. Application software (and most of the operating system, including Defrag and ScanDisk) treats it as though it were a volume.

The CVF is stored in the root directory of an uncompressed drive referred to as the *host drive*. The CVF has the attributes read-only, hidden, and system. Defrag doesn't move it. If it is a Microsoft CVF, its name will be something like Drvspace.000 or Dblspace.002. CVFs created by Windows 95 use the Drvspace name.

Because the compressed drive is actually a file on a host drive, you can cause all sorts of mischief if you erase the file or in other ways fool with it. You might consider refraining from messing with this file.

Compressed disk size

You can divide a drive partition or volume into at least two drives, one the host drive and one the compressed drive. Compressed drives can't be larger than 512MB (unless you are using DriveSpace 3). The size of the CVF will depend on how compressible the files in the CVF are. If you create a compressed drive from free disk space the CVF will be half the reported size of the compressed drive.

The Explorer displays the uncompressed size of files stored on a compressed drive. Their actual file size can be (and most often is) less than that reported. If you were to compress a file on a physical drive, using WinZip, for example, the file size reported by the Explorer would be the compressed size. Because DriveSpace would not be able to further compress a WinZip file (at least not very much), its actual and reported size when stored on a compressed drive would be about the same. You don't get any benefit storing zipped files on a compressed drive.

A compressed drive isn't actually compressed, of course; it is the *files* on the drive (in the CVF) that are compressed. VFAT and FAT report their uncompressed size so it appears as though you have a bigger drive when you actually have smaller files.

When you create a new compressed drive from free disk space, VFAT doubles the amount of reported free disk space so that the reported drive size is twice the size of its CVF on the physical disk. The size of the compressed drive decreases if you start filling it with files that can't be compressed at a 2-to-1 ratio.

Secret

If you create a compressed drive from free disk space, the CVF won't be any larger than 256MB because the estimated compression ratio is 2 to 1 and the maximum size of a compressed drive is 512MB. If you fill the compressed drive with 512MB of highly compressible files, there will be unused (and unusable) space in your CVF. You can go back and reduce the size of the CVF.

Secret

If you have an existing physical disk with more than 512MB of files (in one partition) you won't be able to compress it (unless you are using DriveSpace 3 from Microsoft Plus!).

Undocumented

One way around this is to create a compressed drive from the free space (if any) on your physical drive. Move files from the host drive (your drive has now become a host drive) to the newly created compressed drive. Adjust the free space between the host and compressed drive, taking advantage of the newly released free space on the host drive to increase the size of the compressed drive (up to 512MB).

Continue moving files and increasing the size of the compressed drive until you have moved most (but not all) of the files from the host drive to the compressed drive.

Secret

If you have a drive partition (or a physical drive that isn't divided into multiple partitions) that is larger than 256MB and has no files on it, you won't be able to compress the volume into one compressed drive. You'll need to compress it into multiple compressed drives.

On a large disk you can create (from free disk space) multiple compressed drives, all up to 512MB in size. On a 1 gigabyte drive you could have up to four 512MB compressed drives.

So why does a compressed drive that reports, for example, 100MB free before you copy 40MB of files to it report only 40MB free afterward? Because, 100MB free is an estimate based on the anticipated compression ratio of the files yet to be copied to the compressed disk (defaulted at a 2-to-1 ratio). It turns out, in this example, that the files could be compressed only at a 1.5-to-1 ratio. They therefore took up 30MB of the CVF, or 60MB of the estimated space.

DriveSpace 3 can create CVFs that are as large as 2 gigabytes. You won't have to divide your large drive into multiple volumes if you purchase Microsoft Plus!.

Creating a compressed drive

It is quite easy to experiment with disk compression so there is no reason not to create a compressed drive out of some of the free space on your existing drive and play with it a bit. You can always uncompress the drive as long as the total file size isn't greater than will fit on your drive uncompressed.

You have the option of compressing an existing uncompressed volume or creating a compressed drive from the free space on an existing partition. Compressing an existing volume creates a CVF and stores the existing files and free space in the CVF. Creating a compressed drive from free disk space creates an empty CVF.

Compressing existing files and free space

There must be at least 2MB of free disk space on a boot hard drive to compress it. Nonbootable hard drive partitions (and diskettes) require at least 768K of free space.

To create a compressed drive with existing files take the following steps:

STEPS

Compressing a Drive

Step 1. Click the Start button, Programs, Accessories, System Tools, and Drive Space. The DriveSpace window, as shown in Figure 27-8, will be displayed on your desktop.

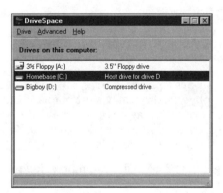

Figure 27-8: The DriveSpace dialog box. Highlight a drive you are going to examine: compress, uncompress, mount, or unmount.

(continued)

STEPS *(continued)*

Compressing a Drive

Step 2.   Highlight an existing physical drive.

Step 3.   To compress both the files and the free disk space on an existing drive, click Drive on the menu and then Compress. The Compress a Drive dialog box, as shown in Figure 27-9, will be displayed.

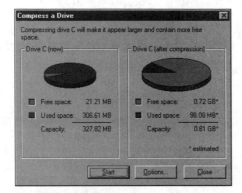

Figure 27-9: The Compress a Drive dialog box. Your only option is the letter designator for the host drive.

DriveSpace will figure out how to compress your drive based on its size and the total size of the files on your drive. If the drive is too big to compress into one CVF, it leaves the extra space on the host drive, which then can be compressed again into a new CVF.

While a host drive is always a physical drive, the host drive's letter designator can be changed. You physical drive may start out as C: but after you put on a bunch of compressed drives, it may be H:. You have the option of changing the host and compressed drive volume letter designators. You can't change the letter designator for the drive that contains the Windows 95 folder.

The CVF may be larger than 256MB if the compression ratio is less than 2 to 1 and the total reported size of the files in the CVF is less than or equal to 512MB.

Compressing free space

To create a compressed drive out of free disk space, follow these steps:

STEPS

Creating a Compressed Drive Out of Free Disk Space

Step 1. Click the Start button, Programs, Accessories, System Tools, and then DriveSpace.

Step 2. Highlight an existing physical drive.

Step 3. Click Advanced and then click Create Empty. The Create New Compressed Drive dialog box, as shown in Figure 27-10, will be displayed.

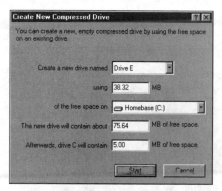

Figure 27-10: The Create New Compressed Drive dialog box. You can give the compressed drive a new drive designator but that is about it for this dialog box.

The new compressed drive will be as large as it can be (up to 512MB) taking all the free space that is available (up to 256MB). A CVF will be created on the physical drive that contains the free space and you can choose the letter designator for the new compressed drive.

Later, you can adjust the size of the compressed drive and the amount of free space left on the host drive (see the following section for details).

Changing the size of the compressed drive

You can increase the size of a compressed drive if there is free space available on the host drive. You are just increasing the size of the CVF that is stored on the host drive and thereby taking up more free space. You can't increase the size of the compressed drive beyond 512MB.

If there is free space on your compressed drive, you can increase the amount of free space on the host drive by decreasing the size of the compressed drive. You are decreasing the size of the CVF and freeing up space on the host drive.

To change the size of the compressed drive, take the following steps:

STEPS

Changing the Size of the Compressed Drive

Step 1. Click the Start button, Programs, Accessories, System Tools, and then DriveSpace.

Step 2. Highlight an existing drive.

Step 3. Click Drive and then Adjust Free Space. The Adjust Free Space dialog box, as shown in Figure 27-11, will be displayed.

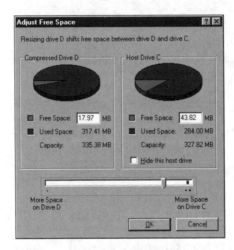

Figure 27-11: The Adjust Free Space dialog box. Move the slider to reapportion the free space between the compressed drive and the host drive. If you move the slider into the red area, Disk Defragmenter will be called to defragment the drive.

Step 4. Move the slider to adjust the free space.

Adjust the slider to move the free space from the host to the compressed drive and vice versa. The amount of used space on the compressed drive and the capacity of the host drive will not change.

The amount you can change the size of the compressed drive is determined by the sum of the free disk space on the compressed and host drive. If you need to make larger changes, you must first delete files.

Estimated compression ratio

The size of the compressed drive is determined by the size of the CVF and the actual compression ratio of the files in the CVF. When a CVF is created, the estimated compression ratio is automatically set to 2 to 1. This is before any file is compressed and put in the CVF.

After files are copied to the compressed drive, DriveSpace will report the actual compression ratio as well as the estimated compression ratio for the remaining free space on the compressed drive. The estimated compression ratio is, by default, set to 2 to 1.

Some files will compress to a greater extent than others. Just because the files that you have copied to your compressed drive have a certain average compression ratio doesn't mean that the next group of files will have a similar compression ratio.

The estimated compression ratio is used to report the size of the free space available on the compressed drive. If this ratio is higher than the average for files that you subsequently copy to the compressed drive, the actual amount of free space available will be less than was reported.

You can change the estimated compression ratio to match your actual compression ratio (as long as it doesn't make the compressed drive greater than 512MB) if you believe the actual compression ratio is a better estimate of the compression ratio of the files you will be adding to your compressed drive. This will give you a more realistic idea of the free space available on your compressed drive.

To change the estimated compression ratio take the following steps:

STEPS

Changing the Estimated Compression Ratio

Step 1. Click the Start button, Programs, Accessories, System Tools, and then DriveSpace.

Step 2. Highlight a compressed drive.

Step 3. Click Advanced and Change Ratio. The Compression Ratio dialog box, as shown in Figure 27-12, will be displayed.

Step 4. Move the slider to change the estimated compression ratio.

(continued)

STEPS *(continued)*

Changing the Estimated Compression Ratio

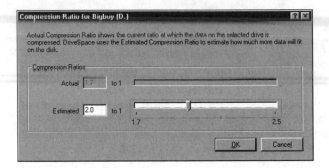

Figure 27-12: The Compression Ratio dialog box. Move the slider to change the estimated compression ratio.

Other DriveSpace options

DriveSpace gives you numerous other ways to manage your compressed drives.

You can format a compressed drive, thereby erasing all the files within the CVF using the Drive, Format command.

You can hide the host drive. Often the CVF will take up almost all of the host drive. There is no need for a extraneous letter designator for the host drive if there isn't any space to store files on it. You can hide the host drive if you like, no matter how much free space it has. To hide the host drive highlight it, click Drive, Properties, and "Hide this host drive."

Like physical drives, volumes, and drive partitions, compressed drives are automatically mounted when you start your computer. You don't even think about the process because the drives are always there. With compressed drives that weren't there when you booted your computer (a compressed diskette, for example), you have the option to mount them automatically or not.

You can turn off the auto mounting of new compressed drives by clicking Advanced, Options, and then the check box in the Disk Compression Settings dialog box. If you want to subsequently mount a compressed drive (or unmount one) click Advanced, Mount or Advanced, Unmount.

You can change the letter designator of a host drive and/or a compressed drive by clicking Advanced, Change Letter. You can't change the letter designator for the drive that contains the Windows 95 folder.

Tip

Your application configuration files and/or the Registry quite probably contain references to the drive letters that you are contemplating changing. You will have to make changes to these files and to the Registry if you want your applications to track the "new" location of their files.

Compressing a diskette

One of the great things about disk compression is that you can increase the capacity of your diskettes by compressing files as they are copied to them. Of course, if you want them to be read, DriveSpace must be on the computer that is going to read the diskettes you create on your computer.

Tip

Windows 95 computers can read diskettes with DoubleSpace and DriveSpace compression. Computers with DOS 6.x and Dblspace.bin in their root directories can read DoubleSpace diskettes. Computers with Drvspace.bin in their root directories can read DriveSpace diskettes.

Compressing a diskette is the same as compressing a hard disk. The diskette will contain the compressed drive and the host drive. The host drive will start off with zero free space. The letter designator for the compressed drive will be either A or B. The host drive letter designator will be a letter greater than the last drive on your computer.

You can't hide the letter designator for a host drive for removable media. The host drive will show up in your Explorer or My Computer window as soon as you click on the diskette drive icon (if the drive is automatically mounted).

If you haven't mounted a compressed diskette (auto mounting is turned off), you will find a file on it named Readthis.txt. Use the command dir/a in a Windows DOS session to find this file. This file explains how to mount the diskette. There will also be a CVF, Dblspace.000, that shows up with the dir/a command.

Secret

You cannot compress a diskette unless it has at least 512K of free space on it. Also, it cannot contain a single file that is greater than half the uncompressed size of the diskette.

The amount of file compression

You can see how much an individual file is compressed by using the directory command in a Windows DOS session. At the DOS command prompt type:

dir /c

This command will report the actual file compression ratio for each file in the current directory.

Compression safety

You can turn off your computer in the middle of compressing a physical drive and, when you turn it on again, compression will continue where it left off without any problems with the files being compressed. Microsoft made safety its number one design priority when developing disk compression.

Dblspace.ini

Undocumented

The parameters that define your DriveSpace or DoubleSpace drives are kept in a hidden, system, read-only file in the root directory of your host drive(s). If you change these file attributes by right-clicking the file in the Explorer, clicking Properties and then clicking the file attributes radio buttons, you can edit this file. Example parameters follow:

```
AutoMount=1
FirstDrive=D
LastDrive=E
MaxRemovableDrives=1
MaxFileFragments=241
ActivateDrive=D,C1
```

For example, to change the drive letter designator for the compressed drive from D to E, make the following changes:

```
ActivateDrive=E,C1
LastDrive=F
```

DriveSpace speed

This file compression is all fine and good, but doesn't it take longer to access your files from a CVF?

Secret

Small files should load faster because they are being loaded from a sector instead of from a cluster. Large files, like Windows 95 files or big applications, should load slightly slower because of the DriveSpace overhead as DriveSpace sorts out sectors and reports them as clusters.

If you are running a system with only 4MB of RAM, you'll see some slowdown as you have less disk cache space. But then, on a 4MB system, everything is slow.

DriveSpace command line parameters

DriveSpace is not a DOS program. You put the command line parameters in the Target field in a shortcut to DriveSpace. You can also use them in batch files. You can't run DriveSpace in MS-DOS mode. The options that follow match those provided in the more friendly DriveSpace menu.

```
Drvspace {options}

{options}
/compress e: {/reserve=n} {/new=f:}
     Compress an existing physical drive e:. Reserve a certain amount n
     uncompressed and give the host drive the letter designator f:.
/create e: {/size=n or /reserve=n} {/new=f:} {/cvf=nnn}
     Create a new compressed drive from the free space on physical
     drive e:, with drive letter f:, and report the CVF extension. Set
     the amount of uncompressed space on the host drive for the CVF, or
     reserve an amount of uncompressed space on the host drive.
/delete e:\d??space.nnn
     Delete the named CVF.
/format e:\d??space.nnn
     Format the named CVF.
{/info} e:
     How much free and used space there is on the compressed drive e:
     and other information.
/interactive
     Coupled with an operation switch (/ratio, /mount, etc.), tells
     DriveSpace to display the interactive path for the particular
     operation switch. If no drive letter or volume file is, DriveSpace
     will prompt you for additional input.
/mount {=nnn e: or e:\d??space.nnn} {/new=f:}
     Mount the named or extension numbered CVF.
/move e: /new=f:
     Change the letter designator of the e: compressed drive to f:.
/ratio{=n} e:
     Change the estimated compression ratio of the e: drive.
/noprompt
     Can be added to any other command but /info and /settings, and
     prevents the display of confirmation dialog boxes.
/size{=n or /reserve=n} e:
     Change the size of the compressed drive e:.
/uncompress e:
     Uncompress the compressed drive e:.
/unmount e:
     Unmount the compressed drive e:.
d??space.nnn
     The CVF filename, either Drvspace.nnn or Dblspace.nnn
```

As you can see, most of these command line settings mimic what is available from the menu of the DriveSpace Manager.

Compressing with DriveSpace 3

After you install Microsoft Plus! you'll want to upgrade your existing DriveSpace or DoubleSpace CVFs to DriveSpace 3 drives. You get an opportunity to do this as soon as you restart Windows 95 after you complete setting up the Plus! package. If you don't choose to upgrade immediately, you can do so later by clicking DriveSpace in the System Tools menu, clicking Drive, and then Upgrade on the menu bar.

To further compress files, run the Compression Agent that comes with Microsoft Plus!. You will find this agent on the System Tools menu in the Start menus.

The Compression Agent gives you two higher levels of compression (HiPack and UltraPack). The trade-off is a little slower time to read and write the files from your hard disk, and a lot longer time required to originally compress them. The System Agent (a scheduling program that comes with Plus!) has been preset to run the Compression Agent after 8 p.m., assuming that your computer is idle. It checks every 20 minutes after 8 p.m. to see if your computer is idle. It's convenient to have the Compression Agent run while you're asleep or away from work (assuming you leave your system on).

By default, DriveSpace 3 uses the same compression method (called standard compression) as DriveSpace. You can set DriveSpace 3 to use HiPack compression, which compresses your files an additional 10 to 20 percent. Click Advanced, Settings on the DriveSpace 3 menu bar, and then select HiPack from the choices shown in Figure 27-13.

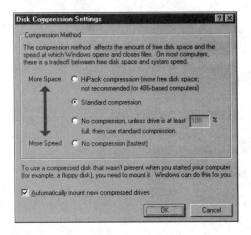

Figure 27-13: The DriveSpace 3 Disk Compression Settings dialog box.

Once a CVF is created, DriveSpace is continually used to compress files as you write them to the compressed drive. The DriveSpace window is just a front end for the behind-the-scenes, on-the-fly file compression that is always going on if you have a CVF.

You can turn off this on-the-fly file compression and just write the uncompressed file to your compressed drive, of course. But while this speeds up file writes, it also eats up disk space more quickly. To turn off compression, click "No compression" in the Disk Compression Settings dialog box.

Tip

If you combine No compression with the Compression Agent and a low disk space warning, as is standard in the System Agent setup, you can speed up your disk access to compressed drives and still have your files compressed at night. Your newly written files will be compressed to HiPack at night by the Compression Agent.

You can also turn off on-the-fly file compression by clicking No compression, unless drive is at least *nnn* percent full; then use standard compression. Compression isn't used until the drive starts to fill up. At night the Compression Agent will compress these files, giving you more room by morning.

When you read and write files during the course of a day, they are not stored in the UltraPack compression format, even if they had been previously compressed using that format by the Compression Agent. They are written back to the compressed drive either in Standard compression, HiPack compression, or No compression depending on which of the radio buttons in the Disk Compression Settings dialog box you have chosen. At night, the Compression Agent gets to work recompressing the files to HiPack or UltraPack.

The Compression Agent, as shown in Figure 27-14, can be configured to recompress some files to HiPack and others to UltraPack format. You can also have it reduce the compression of some files from UltraPack to HiPack. Click the Settings button in the Compression Agent to specify which files should be excluded from UltraPack compression, and which files should be recompressed to HiPack from UltraPack.

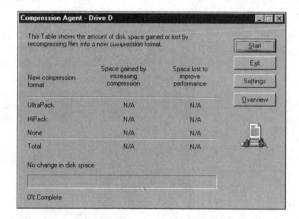

Figure 27-14: The Compression Agent.

To view the results on all these different levels of compression on a CVF, right-click the drive icon of a compressed drive in an Explorer or folder window, click Properties, and the Compression tab. You will see something similar to Figure 27-15.

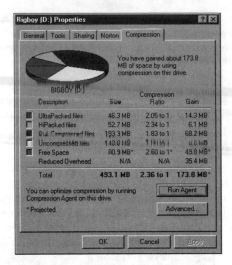

Figure 27-15: The Compressed Drive Compression Properties sheet.

Secret

Why would you create a CVF (a compressed drive) and then not compress any of the files that you store in it?

If you have a 1 gigabyte disk partition, the minimum cluster, and therefore file, size is 32K. Even a small file with only a letter to your aunt in it will be stored as though it contained 32,768 characters — a lot of slack space here.

If you store these small files in a CVF, they don't take up a cluster apiece. Files on compressed drives are doled out space one sector (512 bytes) at a time. The letter to your aunt may now take up only 1024 bytes — a 32-to-1 compression ratio without any "compressing" at all.

Why is there a 2 gigabyte limit to a DriveSpace 3 CVF? Let's not get greedy here. Plus! quadruples the size of any one compressed drive but, in order to know what comes next, it's good to know why.

Secret

Chad Petersen at Microsoft tells us that the 2 gigabyte limit is imposed by the maximum number of clusters and the largest cluster size supported by the FAT (and therefore VFAT) file system. The FAT file system is limited to 65,525 clusters. The size of a cluster must be a power of 2 and less than 65,536 bytes — this results in a maximum cluster size of 32,768 bytes (32K). Multiplying the maximum number of clusters (65,525) by the maximum cluster size (32,768) equals 2 gigabytes.

Windows NT allows a volume size up to 4 gigabytes.

Virtual File System

Starting with Windows for Workgroups 3.11, Windows significantly reduced its use of DOS for disk/file access. In WFWG 3.11 the file access subsystem was called 32-bit file access. In Windows 95 it is called the Virtual File Allocation Table (VFAT).

VFAT is compatible with the existing DOS File Allocation System. All DOS disks that were partitioned and formatted as FAT partitions can be read and written to by VFAT. This includes hard disks and removable media, including diskettes.

Both VFAT and CDFS (CD-ROM file system) are installable file systems that are automatically loaded by Windows 95. When the DOS portion of Windows 95 (Io.sys) loads, it calls a real-mode installable file system helper file (Ifshlp.sys) that gets the whole virtual file system going.

Lock and unlock

All disk access is directed through VFAT, and you don't normally access the disk directly, or through DOS or your BIOS. If you have programs, usually pre-Windows 95 disk utilities, that access the hard disk directly (using interrupts 25 and 26), Windows 95 will prevent them from accessing the disks.

It is possible to allow direct disk access by using the Lock command and, after you are done, the Unlock command. This can be done in batch files or directly at the DOS prompt. You can't access the disk directly even in MS-DOS mode unless you use Lock and Unlock. No access by other programs is allowed when a drive is locked.

If you have a DOS program that requires direct disk access, create a batch file that runs Lock and Unlock around the program. It is not a good idea to run pre-Windows 95 disk utilities because they can destroy long filenames. You should update your disk utilities to ones that are compatible with Windows 95.

Disk utilities provided with Windows 95 (including Defrag and ScanDisk) use the Microsoft-developed "volume locking" API. The commands in this application programming interface lock and unlock the disk drive. All third-party disk utilities should use this API.

Real-mode disk drivers

You may have a hard disk drive that requires a 16-bit driver. Microsoft has made a special effort to provide 32-bit protected-mode drivers for almost all disk drives available.

Some disk manufacturers shipped "fast" 16-bit drivers. These drivers are not as fast as the 32-bit drivers from Microsoft. Comment them out of your Config.sys file.

Compatible drives

Microsoft provides 32-bit protected mode VFAT drivers for the following
drive types:

- ESDI
- Hardcards
- IDE
- EIDE

And drive controllers of the following types:

- MFM
- PCI
- PCMCIA
- RLL
- SCSI
- SCSI 2

In addition, VFAT supports the following types of removable media:

- Floppy disk
- Iomega Bernoulli
- CD-ROM

Secret

Drivers for Floptical disks and Syquest drives were originally planned, but were
not included on the Windows 95 diskettes. Windows 95-compatible 32-bit
drivers should be available directly from the manufacturers of these devices.

IDE drives in the 1 gigabyte range were available at retail in early 1995 for
around $400. Windows 95 provides 32-bit protected-mode drivers for IDE drives
up to 137 gigabytes in size.

Up to two IDE controllers in one computer are supported by the Windows 95
drivers. You can add a CD-ROM to your IDE controller and Windows 95 will
support it.

Windows 95 provides 32-bit protected-mode drivers for Adaptec, Future
Domain, Trantor, and UltraStor SCSI adapters.

Disk Caching

You don't need SmartDrive for disk caching. Windows 95 dynamically sizes the
size in memory of your disk cache.

The Windows 95 Vcache is dynamic and caches on a per-file basis, unlike SmartDrive, which caches on a per-contiguous-sector basis. If your hard disk is fragmented, your files won't be stored together (in contiguous sectors); therefore, SmartDrive isn't as smart as Vcache when it comes to caching a complete file.

Vcache will read-cache removable media, although it won't read-cache their disk writes.

Setting Disk Cache Parameters

You can give Vcache a few suggestions about how to optimize caching your hard disk and, separately, your CD-ROM. The suggestions for caching the hard disk are rather broad.

Undocumented

These settings tell Vcache how to dynamically shrink and grow its cache according to the demands of a desktop, portable (mobile), or network server. If the computer is a network server, you probably want a larger cache and less RAM for applications than if it's a desktop (smaller cache and more RAM for applications). On a portable, you want a larger cache size, reducing the power requirements for hard drive access.

To modify a disk cache, take the following steps:

STEPS

Modifying Your Disk Cache

Step 1. Right-click My Computer on your desktop. Click Properties. Click the Performance tab.

Step 2. Click File System.

Step 3. Choose from among the options in the General File System Properties sheet.

To optimize caching the CD-ROM, you specify a cache memory size to use and the CD-ROM drive's speed. This cache should be sized like this:

Your Computer's RAM	CD-ROM Speed	Cache Size
8MB or less	Single	64K
8-12MB	Double	626K
12MB or more	Quad	1238K

Managing Your Swap Space

You don't need a permanent swap file because Windows 95 dynamically sizes your swap file space.

Windows 95 manages your dynamically sized swap space for you so you don't have to assign the volume or minimum and maximum size parameters. If you want to change these parameters, take the following steps:

STEPS

Managing Your Swap Space

Step 1. Right-click My Computer on your desktop. Click Properties. Click the Performance tab.

Step 2. Click Virtual Memory.

Step 3. Click the button next to Let me specify my own virtual memory settings.

Step 4. Choose volume and size parameters in the Virtual Memory dialog box, which is shown in Figure 27-16.

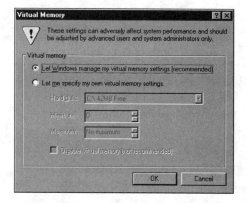

Figure 27-16: The Virtual Memory dialog box. You decide where to place your swap file and its minimum and maximum size.

Swap space on a compressed drive

Your swap drive can be on a compressed drive (in a CVF). It is stored in an uncompressed form on the compressed drive to ensure that writing to the swap space will never fail.

A swap file is not particularly compressible anyway so it doesn't hurt to write it out in an uncompressed form. There is an advantage to putting the swap space on a compressed drive. You don't have to set aside enough unused uncompressed disk space for the maximum size that the swap space might take. Much of the time this space will never be used.

Windows 3.x permanent swap file

Windows 95 and Windows 3.*x* can share the permanent swap file space. If you have both Windows 3.*x* and Windows 95 on your computer, and Windows 3.*x* has a permanent swap file, you may get the error message that the swap file has been corrupted when you start Windows 3.*x*.

Add MinPagingFileSize= to the [386enh] section of your System.ini file in your Windows 95 folder. Set the size to the size of your Windows 3.*x* swapfile.

If this doesn't help, do the following:

Undocumented

- Allow Windows 95 to manage Virtual Memory settings.

- While running Windows 95, delete the files 386spart.par (in a root directory), and Spart.par and/or Win386.swp from the Windows 3.*x* directory.

- Open the System.ini file in the Windows 3.1 directory and comment out the following lines in the [386enh] section:

```
PermSwapDOSDrive= {a drive letter}
PermSwapSizeK= {size in K}
```

- Add the following lines to the [386enh] section of the System.ini in the Windows 3.*x* directory:

```
MaxPagingFileSize={max swapfile size in K}
PagingFile={drive letter}:\{Windows 95 directory}\Win386.swp
```

Long Filenames

A major new feature provided by the VFAT file system is the ability to handle long filenames, up to 255 characters. Every file has two names, the new long filename and a short filename that is compatible with the FAT file system. The backwardly compatible short filename complies with the 8.3 filename rules.

In an Explorer or a folder window you will see the long filename. If you open a DOS window you'll see both names. VFAT creates a short filename using the long filename as a template. VFAT makes sure that the short filenames found in a folder are unique.

Valid filenames

A filename that obeys the 8.3 filename rules can have any alphanumeric character, any ASCII character greater than 127, and these special characters:

$ % ' @ ~ ! { } ( ) ^ # &

A long filename can have these same characters and additionally, a blank, and the following characters:

+ , ; = [ ] .

A null is included at the end of the long filename so its total length, including the null, can be 256 characters. With DOS 6.22 and previous versions, the maximum total length of a path and filename is 80 characters. It is now 260 characters, including the null. Filenames and folder names obey the same rules.

You can mix case throughout the filename. Filenames are not case sensitive, but the case is preserved. You can't have two files in the same folder with the same name except for the case of the letters. For example, ToDo.txt and TODO.txt are seen by VFAT as the same filename.

The double quote is not a valid character and can be used to designate long filenames. If you want to use the DOS prompt to copy a file that has blanks in the filename, use this format:

```
Copy "File with a long name" "A new name for the long name file"
```

Short filenames

The default method VFAT uses to create a short filename is to take the first six characters of the long filename (ignoring spaces), add "~1" (or later number), and then set the extension as the first three letters after the last period in the long filename. For example:

```
longfilename.txt -> longfi~1.txt
```

This is the default method and also the method that Windows NT uses for drives partitioned to use the NTFS (Windows NT file system).

There is another way to do this — the friendly short filename scheme. In this case the new filename would be longfile.txt, as long as there were no other files with this filename. Here's now to turn on the "friendly shortname scheme":

Undocumented

STEPS

Turning on Friendly Short Filenames

Step 1.   Using your Explorer, double-click Regedit.exe in your Windows 95 folder. This invokes the Registry editor.

Step 2.   Click the plus sign to the left of HKEY_LOCAL_MACHINE. Continue clicking the plus sign next to System, and then CurrentControlSet, and finally Control.

Step 3.   Highlight FileSystem.

Step 4.   Right-click the right pane of the Registry editor. Click New and then Binary value.

Step 5.   Type in the value name **NameNumericTail**. Press Enter.

Step 6.   Double-click NameNumericTail. Type **0** as the single entry for the binary value. Click OK.

Step 7.   Reboot your computer.

If you want VFAT to go back to the old scheme, set this binary value to 1.

Copy, rename, and more

Undocumented

The DOS commands that come with Windows 95 have been updated to handle long filenames (and the short filenames that must go with them). If you use DOS 6.22 or early versions of these commands, you will lose the long filenames. If the long filename and the short filename are the same, it doesn't matter.

If you copy files from a Windows 95 computer to a diskette, take that diskette to a computer running DOS 6.x or Windows 3.x and then edit those files on the diskette, the long filename is preserved when you copy those files back to the Windows 95 computer. If, on the other hand, you copy the files off the diskette onto the hard disk of the DOS computer, edit those files and then copy them back onto the diskette, there is no long filename associated with the file. Only the short filename is preserved.

Windows 3.x Norton Disk Editor

Undocumented

Pre-Windows 95 versions of Norton Disk Editor will work with Windows 95 files, but it is a better idea to use ScanDisk or Windows 95-specific disk utilities. Pre-Windows 95 versions of Norton Disk Doctor have an incompatibility with how Windows 95 uses the file size field and should not be used.

Long filenames across the network

If you use Windows 95 32-bit network clients, you will get long filename support over the network. The server must support long filenames. Earlier 16-bit real-mode network clients will provide only the short filenames. This includes

NetWare NETX and VLM drivers. You'll need to use Microsoft's Client for NetWare or a 32-bit client provided by Novell.

Other file systems on the servers create different short filenames from the long filenames. No big deal. They are still compatible with Windows 95.

NetWare servers must be configured to use the OS/2 namespace (which emulates the native OS/2 HPFS file system) in order for Windows 95 to see long filenames on them. Doesn't that seem a little weird that Windows 95 would rely on an OS/2 standard? Well, it is the past after all.

To configure the NetWare server to use the OS/2 namespace, take the following steps:

STEPS

Enabling Long Filenames to Be Seen on a NetWare Server

Step 1.   On the NetWare server, type the following commands at the prompt:

```
load os/2
add name space os2 to volume sys
```

Step 2.   To the file Startup.cnf, add the following line:

```
load os2
```

Step 3.   Shut down the NetWare server. Copy the file Os2.nam from your NetWare diskettes or CD-ROM to the disk and directory on the NetWare server that contains the file Server.exe.

Step 4.   Reboot the NetWare server.

Turning off long filename support

It is possible to turn off long filename support completely. You don't want to do this unless you have applications that do not work when long filenames are enabled. But if you need to do so, here's how:

Undocumented

STEPS

Turning Off Long Filename Support

Step 1.   Using your Explorer, double-click Regedit.exe in your Windows 95 folder to invoke the Registry editor.

Step 2. Click the plus sign to the left of HKEY_LOCAL_MACHINE. Continue clicking the plus sign next to System, and then CurrentControlSet, and finally Control.

Step 3. Highlight FileSystem.

Step 4. Double-click Win31FileSystem in the right pane.

Step 5. Press the Delete key and then press **1** to replace the 00 binary value with 01. Click OK.

Step 6. Close the Registry editor and reboot your computer.

You should remove all the long filenames from your hard disk before carrying out the above steps. The utility Lfnbk.exe lets you do this.

Disk Drive Partitioning

Physical drives must be partitioned before they can be formatted into FAT (or VFAT) volumes. A physical drive can have just one partition, a bootable partition, or multiple partitions with one bootable partition. Each partition is assigned a drive letter and is normally referred to as a *drive*.

Windows 95 works with third-party disk partitioning schemes, including Disk Manager, SuperStor, and Golden Bow. These schemes were originally created to partition hard drives that were larger than those handled by Fdisk, which Microsoft supplies.

Windows 95 also works with Fdisk-partitioned drives on removable media, including Iomega Bernoulli drives.

Windows 95 comes with Fdisk, which you can use to partition your drives. In most cases the computer manufacturer will have already set up disk partitions on your hard drive when you get a new computer. You can use Fdisk.exe to change these partitions, but you will lose any files stored on them unless you back them up first.

You won't want to use Fdisk if your hard disk is already partitioned with a third-party scheme. Use the third party's tools instead. You can determine if your hard disk was partitioned with a third-party product by examining Config.sys. You are using the third-party disk partitioner if you find references to the following files: Dmdrvr.bin, Sstor.sys, HarDrive.sys, or Evdisk.sys.

DMF Diskettes

If you purchased Windows 95 on diskettes, you now have diskettes that contain 1.7MB of compressed data. Since the data was already compressed before the files were copied to the diskette, it wouldn't have done any good to make these diskettes into compressed drives. Microsoft found a way to store more data (in whatever form) on 3½-inch diskettes.

These 1.7MB formatted diskettes are referred to as Distribution Media Format (DMF) diskettes.

Copy files from the DMF diskettes onto your hard disk using the extract command as follows:

```
extract /c a:*.cab d:\*.cab
```

If you want to format DMF diskettes and write files to them, you'll need to use the WinImage package featured on the shareware CD-ROM accompanying this book. To format a DMF diskette with WinImage, take the following steps:

STEPS

Running WinImage to Format a DMF Diskette

Step 1.   Double-click Winmaint.exe in a folder or Explorer Window.

Step 2.   Click Option and then Preference. Uncheck "Use only standard formats." Click OK.

Step 3.   Click File and then New. Drag and drop some files into the new image file.

Step 4.   Click File and then Save and give the image file a name.

Step 5.   Click Disk and then Format and Write Disk. Select the 1.7MB format when asked to choose and click OK.

The diskette in your diskette drive will now be formatted to store 1.7MB of data. You can write more data to it later using WinImage.

Future Domain Disk Controller

Secret

George Allan at Microsoft tells us that if you have a Future Domain disk controller, be sure to check the BIOS on the card. You need to update it to the most recent BIOS if it is version 3.2 or earlier.

Summary

The Microsoft support lines want to quit hearing from you about problems with your disk drives. They provide you with a set of tools to keep everything in working order.

▶ We show you how to find all the disk tools in all the little corners of Windows 95.

▶ We show you how to repair your disks when you experience a problem and to keep an eye on them before trouble arises.

▶ Microsoft includes a great little disk defragmenter that can speed up disk access. We show you how to get the most from it.

▶ Want to double your hard disk space at little or no cost in disk access speed? Try DriveSpace or DriveSpace 3.

▶ We show you how to create super-high-density diskettes.

Part V
Communications

Chapter 28

Calling Your Computer at Work from Your Computer at Home

In This Chapter

Windows 95 includes the capability to dial up another computer whether that computer is running Windows 95, Windows NT, LAN Manager, NetWare, or Unix. We discuss:

▶ Calling and connecting over a modem to a computer running Windows 95, Windows NT, Unix, or NetWare

▶ Setting up a Windows 95 computer to receive modem phone calls from another Windows 95, Windows 3.1, Windows NT, or other computer

▶ Setting up your Windows 95 computer as a guest and calling in to other computers

▶ Configuring the Windows 95 Dial-Up Adapter for the correct protocol

▶ Printing on a printer at work and faxing from a fax/modem at work while directing these operations from your computer at home

Networking? Over a Modem?

Many of you may have previously had the opportunity to use your computer and modem for communications purposes. In a typical scenario, you started some communications software, perhaps the Terminal emulator software that comes with Windows 3.1. You dialed into a bulletin board, a commercial online service like CompuServe, or an Internet service provider (using a dial-up shell account). Once connected you did whatever — downloaded files, sent e-mail, cruised the forums, looked at the news. This is what most of us have previously had in mind when we envisioned modem-to-modem communications. See Chapter 29 for more on this subject.

Many of you have also had the occasion to use software that allows you to connect two computers in close proximity, either through a serial or parallel cable. You run software like LapLink on both computers, which facilitates file transfer between the computers using a point and click interface. See Chapter 30 for more about this.

If your computer is connected to a local area network, you have experienced high-speed communications with other computers located in your general vicinity. Double-clicking the Network Neighborhood icon in Windows 95 gets you quickly to the shared resources available to you on the network. You can print your files on printers connected to other computers or servers on the network. You can quickly copy files, send e-mail, chat, and so on over the LAN (turn to Chapter 34 for more details).

Dial-Up Networking (DUN) is a mixture of all three of these communications modes. It allows you to connect your computer at home or on the road through a modem to the computer or network at work. It could be the computer on your desk at work. Or it could be to another computer at, for example, the business location of an Internet service provider.

Your computer at home can access the resources of the computer at work and/or the resources of the network connected to the computer at work. The resources available to your computer include shared disk drives, folders, printers, NetWare servers, NT servers, and much more.

DUN allows you to connect your computer to the network or to one computer on the network and have it communicate with that computer or network as though it were on the network directly and not connected to it through a modem and another computer on the network. The only difference is that the connection is slower than the direct network connection through a dedicated network card or port.

Undocumented

Using DUN, you can get your e-mail from work. You can print a file from your computer at home to a printer at work. You can send out fax files from your computer at home using the fax/modem on the computer at work. You can run programs that are stored on the computer at work on your computer at home. You can copy and update files between computers. You can copy programs from work. You can be a client of a client/server application running on a computer at work.

With DUN, you get what is known in the computer business as *remote access*. You don't have remote control, which is the ability to run your computer at the office as though you were sitting at the keyboard, while you are actually sitting in front of your computer at home. You do have access to the resources on the remote, or dialed-up, computer or network.

Once you get everything set up (which is somewhat tricky), DUN is actually easy to use. It's easy because it uses standard Windows 95 user interface objects such as Explorer and folder windows.

We use *computer at work* and *computer at home* to cut down on the level of abstraction that you have to deal with. By *computer at work*, we mean any computer that you dial in to, and by *computer at home* we mean the computer that does the dialing. You can, of course, substitute anything that makes more sense to you — computer A/computer B, computer connected to a network/remote computer, desktop computer/portable computer, guest/host, client/server, or mobile/remote.

Dial-Up Networking

You'll need to configure your Windows 95 computer at home as the Dial-Up Network client. We explain how in the section later in this chapter entitled *Setting Up Your Computer at Home as a Guest*. If you are calling into a Windows 95 computer at work, you'll need to configure that computer as a host. We show you how in the section later in this chapter entitled *Setting Up Your Windows 95 Computer at Work as a Host*.

To make the connection between the two computers you'll need:

1. Properly configured computers at home and work

2. A shared dial-up protocol (to allow creation of the connection)

3. A shared network protocol (to allow communication between the two computers)

Dial-up servers

You can connect your Windows 95 computer at home over the phone lines to another computer or server running:

1. Windows 95 dial-up server (if you have installed Microsoft Plus! on it, including the DUN server)

2. Windows NT 3.1 or 3.5*x* Remote Access Server (RAS)

3. Windows for Workgroups 3.11 RAS

4. Microsoft LAN Manager

5. NetWare Connect

6. Unix with SLIP or PPP protocols

7. TCP/IP with PPP protocol

You can also connect to a dedicated modem server like the Shiva LanRover or compatible devices, or to an Internet service provider (if you have a SLIP or PPP account).

Network protocols

Windows 95 supports the following network protocols:

1. NetBEUI (Microsoft's networking protocol)

2. IPX/SPX (Novell's NetWare protocol)

3. TCP/IP (the Unix and Internet standard protocol)

Dial-up protocols

To connect to the computer at work, the Windows 95 DUN client can use any one of the following dial-up protocols:

1. PPP (Point-to-Point Protocol)

2. NRN (Novell NetWare Connect)

3. RAS (Windows NT 3.1 and Windows for Workgroups 3.11 Remote Access Server using Asynchronous NetBEUI)

4. SLIP (Serial Line Internet Protocol)

5. CSLIP (SLIP with IP header compression)

Point-to-Point Protocol is the default dial-up protocol used by Windows 95 computers. It can be used to connect to a network or computer running any one of the three network protocols included with Windows 95. PPP is often the protocol used by Internet service providers.

Novell NetWare Connect allows you to dial into a NetWare Connect server.

RAS allows a Windows 95 computer to call into a Windows NT 3.1 computer running RAS or into a computer running Windows for Workgroups 3.11, and vice versa.

SLIP is an older dial-up protocol, but often used by Internet service providers and on some Unix servers.

Setting Up Your Windows 95 Computer at Work as a Host

If you have a significant network at work, then you will want to provide dial-up services through a Windows NT 3.5 server, LAN modem server, NetWare Connect server, or perhaps a Unix computer. If your network isn't so big (maybe it consists of just your desktop computer) and only a few people need dial-up access, then calling into a Windows 95 computer at work may fit the bill.

A Windows NT 3.5 server can handle up to 256 dial-up connections. The Shiva LanRover is built just for handling large scale dial-in communications in conjunction with your corporate-sized NetWare, NetBEUI, or TCP/IP local area network.

A Windows 95 dial-up server can take calls from and connect to Windows 95 clients, computers running RAS on Windows for Workgroups or Windows 3.1, and other computers running the PPP dial-up protocol. Window 95 servers can't act as an IP router. That is, you can't call into a Windows 95 computer using the TCP/IP networking protocol, and access a TCP/IP network through that Windows 95 server.

The Windows 95 server can handle NetBEUI and IPX/SPX network protocols and allow you to connect to network resources using these protocols.

The Windows 95 Dial-Up Networking Server software comes with Microsoft Plus! You have to get this software if you want to configure your Windows 95 system as a DUN server. Without Microsoft Plus! you can configure your system as a DUN client.

We are going to assume that you want to call in from home — or from a hotel when you are on the road — to your Windows 95 computer (and your network) at work. You must do four things to set up your Windows 95 computer at work as a host:

1. Install a modem driver (this may have occurred if you had your modem installed when you set up Windows 95).

2. Install the Microsoft Dial-Up Adapter and the accompanying network software/drivers (this may also have occurred during setup).

3. Install Microsoft Plus!

4. Set Dial-Up server to Allow caller access.

Undocumented

The Dial-Up Adapter will be automatically installed (if it is not already) the first time you select Connections, Dial-Up Server from the menu bar of the Dial-Up Networking folder. If you do this and you haven't yet installed your modem, you will be prompted to do so. You may separately install the Dial-Up Adapter (see the section below entitled *Dial-Up Adapter*) and the modem before you install the Dial-Up Server.

STEPS

Setting Up a Windows 95 Computer as a Host for Dial-Up Networking

Step 1.   If it is not already, set up your modem using the Modem icon in the Control Panel. Follow the steps in the Modem Wizard. See Chapter 25 if you need additional instructions. You will be prompted to do this if you take Step 4 below first.

Step 2.   If it is not already, set up the Dial-Up Adapter by double-clicking the Network icon in the Control Panel. Click the Add button, highlight Adapter in the Select Network Component Type dialog box, and click the Add button. Follow the steps in the *Dial-Up Adapter* section below. This is an optional step and will happen automatically if you take Step 4.

Step 3.   Install MIcrosoft Plus!, including the DUN server, on the computer at work.

Step 4.   On the computer at work, Double-click the Dial-Up Networking icon in the Explorer or click the Dial-Up Networking icon in the Start, Programs, Accessories menu on the Start button.

Step 5.   Click Connections, Dial-Up Server on the menu bar in the Dial-Up Networking folder window. The Dial-Up Server dialog box will pop up, as shown in Figure 28-1.

(continued)

STEPS *(continued)*

Setting Up a Windows 95 Computer as a Host for Dial-Up Networking

Figure 28-1: The dial-in options in the Dial-Up Server dialog box. You want to allow caller access if this Windows 95 computer is going to be the host and receive calls from the home computer.

Step 6. Click Allow caller access. You want people (perhaps just yourself) using other computers to be able to call into your host computer (the Windows 95 computer at work).

Step 7. To require a password to access your computer at work, click the Change Password button.

Step 8. Click the Server Type button if you want to change the dial-up protocol used when the server answers the phone. We suggest that you leave it on Default, which starts with PPP and switches to RAS if PPP fails. This makes it easy for Windows 95, Windows for Workgroups, Windows 3.1 RAS, Windows NT 3.5*x*, and Windows NT 3.1, as well as computers with other operating systems that support PPP, to call into your server.

Step 9. Click OK or Apply to begin monitoring for phone calls. The computer at the office will now pick up the phone line attached to its modem when that line is called. You don't have a way of telling it how many rings to wait until it picks up the line. Apply leaves the dialog box on the desktop. OK minimizes the dialog box.

You now have a computer at work (or a computer at a friend's house) that will respond to calls from your computer at home or on the road. You need to set the computer at work into this answer mode before you can call into it. You would normally want to leave it in this mode when you are away from the office.

Disallowing dial-in access

Your systems administrator (which may be you) can determine if a given Windows 95 computer should be available as a host. He or she can use the System Policy Editor to disable dial-in to Dial-Up Networking. The System Policy Editor is available only on the CD-ROM version of Windows 95.

If the "No caller access" box is checked in the Dial-Up Server dialog box, you won't be able to call into your computer at work

Security

Security is an issue because anyone with the right password (if even that is required) can gain access to the company's network by calling into a Windows 95 DUN server. Systems administrators are going to be wary of allowing users to configure their computers as servers when it leaves the whole network vulnerable.

If the Windows 95 server is on a network that includes NetWare or Windows NT servers, they can be used (and may already be used) to provide user-level (centrally controlled) password protection.

Setting Up Your Computer at Home as a Guest

You want to set up your computer at home to make the phone call and initiate the modem communications. You need to make sure that:

1. Your modem driver is configured.

2. You have set up your Dial-Up Adapter.

3. You have set up a specific dial-in connection (or connectoid) for your computer at work.

Undocumented

You don't have to set up the modem driver first. If it is not set up yet, you will be guided by a wizard through the setup process.

STEPS

Setting Up Your Computer at Home

Step 1. Double-click the Dial-Up Networking icon in the Explorer or click the Dial-Up Networking icon in the Start, Programs, Accessories menu on the Start button.

Step 2. Double-click the Make New Connection icon in the Dial-Up Networking folder window.

(continued)

STEPS *(continued)*

Setting Up Your Computer at Home

Step 3. The Make New Connection Wizard will start. If you have not set up the modem drivers, the Modem Wizard will pop up on top of the Make New Connection Wizard and ask that you set up the modem drivers first. Follow along with the Modem Wizard or turn to Chapter 25.

Step 4. Give the computer that you will be dialing into a name like **Computer at Work**. Click Next.

Step 5. Type the area code and number for the computer at work. Click Next.

Step 6. Click Finish.

Step 7. If you do not have a Dial-Up Adapter set up in your network configuration (or you have no network configured), you will be asked to install that now.

Step 8. The Dial-Up Adapter will now be installed along with the network protocols NetBEUI and IPX/SPX and network support software, if it has not already been installed.

A new icon for the new connectoid will now appear in the Dial-Up Networking folder window. It represents your connection to the computer at the office. If you want to see what your network configuration is like, double-click the network icon in the Control Panel.

To change the Server Type and other properties associated with this connectoid, right-click it in the Dial-Up Networking folder window, select Properties, and click the Server Type button. The Server Types Properties sheet, as shown in Figure 28-2, allows you to determine, among other things, whether you will log on to the network when you dial in to the server.

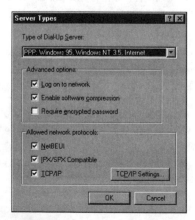

Figure 28-2: The Server Types dialog box.

Your Window 95 client computer uses your modem as a network interface card. The proper networking protocols must be bound to the Dial-Up Adapter. If you are calling into a Unix TCP/IP server, you will need to bind the TCP/IP protocol to the Dial-Up Adapter.

Dialing into another operating system

Dial-Up Networking lets you connect over the phone to a whole variety of networks, including the Internet. You can call into a computer running Windows NT 3.5 Advanced Server that allows up to 256 connections and supports IPX/SPX, NetBEUI, and TCP/IP protocols. You can call into computers running Unix and the SLIP or PPP protocols.

If you are calling into a Windows NT, NetWare, Shiva Netmodem/LanRover, Windows for Workgroups, LAN Manager, or Unix server instead of a Windows 95 computer, you will need to change the server type associated with the connection that you just created. Right-click the Computer at Work (or whatever the name of your new connection is) icon in the Dial-Up Networking folder window. Click Properties. Click the Server Type button.

You get to choose from PPP: Windows 95, Windows NT 3.5, Internet; NRN: NetWare Connect; SLIP Unix Connection; Windows for Workgroups and Windows NT 3.1, or CSLIP (Unix Connection with IP header Compression). Your Unix computer server (in some cases a remote Unix server at an Internet service provider) will use either PPP or SLIP. You need to find that out from your computer support staff.

Dial-Up Networking provides a connection to the Internet if you are calling into a dial-in Internet service provider. See Chapter 33 for more details.

SLIP Server Type

Tip

The SLIP and CSLIP server types won't be available unless you install SLIP support. To do so, take the following steps:

STEPS

Installing SLIP Support

Step 1. Click the Start button, Settings, and then Control Panel. Double-click the Add/Remove Programs icon and click the Windows Setup tab.

Step 2. Click Have Disk.

Step 3. Put your Windows 95 CD-ROM in the CD-ROM drive and point to E:\Admin\Apptools\Slip (using the appropriate drive letter for your CD-ROM).

Step 4. Click the Install button and then OK.

In order to connect to a server using SLIP dial-up protocol, you will need to bind the TCP/IP network protocol to your Dial-Up Adapter. To do so, take the following steps:

STEPS

Binding TCP/IP to Your Dial-Up Adapter

Step 1.   Click the Start button, Settings, and then Control Panel. Double-click the Network icon.

Step 2.   Click the Add button in the Network Properties sheet, highlight Protocol in the Select Network Component Type list, and then click the next Add button.

Step 3.   Highlight Microsoft in the Manufacturer's list in the Select Network Protocol dialog box, and click TCP/IP in the Network Protocols list box. Click the OK button.

Step 4.   Click OK buttons until the Network Control Panel is closed.

Step 5.   You will be asked to restart your computer by clicking the Yes button. Do so.

Now you need to create a SLIP connection. Here's how:

STEPS

Creating a SLIP Connectoid

Step 1.   Double-click the Dial-Up Networking icon in the Explorer or click the Dial-Up Networking icon in the Start, Programs, Accessories menu on the Start button.

Step 2.   Double-click the Make New Connection icon in the Dial-Up Networking folder window.

Step 3.   The Make New Connection Wizard will start. Give the computer that you will be dialing into a name, perhaps something like **Internet**. Click Next.

Step 4.   Type the area code and number for the SLIP computer. Click Next.

Step 5.   Click Finish.

Step 6.   Right-click the new connectoid, and select Properties. Click the Options tab.

Step 7. Click Bring Up Terminal Windows After Dialing. This will allow you to log onto your SLIP account. You will need to type in your name and password when you log on. (You can avoid having to type this in if you use DUNscript, as described in Chapter 33.) Click OK.

Step 8. Click Server Type, click the down arrow in the Type of Dial-Up Server drop-down list. Use the small arrows to scroll this list up and down.

Step 9. Highlight either SLIP or CSLIP depending on the capabilities of your Internet service provider or Unix server.

Step 10. If you want to change your IP address, click the TCP/IP button. See Chapter 33 for more details.

Step 11. Click the OK buttons until you are back to the Dial-Up Networking folder window.

Further details about the properties of TCP/IP and connectoids to the Internet can be found in Chapter 33. You will need to bind the protocol appropriate to the network that you are dialing into to the Dial-Up Adapter. If you are dialing into different networks you will want to bind all three protocols — IPX/SPX, NetBEUI, and TCP/IP — to the Dial-Up Adapter.

Setting up your basic telephone information

Windows 95 provides a means of keeping track of the basic telephone information for any number of locations. For example, it tracks whether you have to dial an access number to get an outside line, or whether your phone has call waiting. You can edit this location-specific telephone information as well as specifying whether a given connection is local or long distance.

Double-click the Computer at Work icon in your Dial-Up Networking folder window. Click the Edit Locations button. The Dialing Properties sheet will appear on your desktop. Turn to Chapter 26 for more details about the Dialing Properties sheet.

Your modem

Your modem was originally set up by the Modem Wizard. This most likely happened automatically when you first set up Windows 95, when you set up your computer at home as a guest, or when you double-clicked the Modem icon in the Control Panel, but if you need to, you can change the properties.

Right-click the Computer At Work icon in the Dial-Up Networking folder window. Click Properties. Click the Configure button. The Properties sheets for your modem will appear on the desktop. Details regarding what changes to make are found in Chapter 25.

The Dial-Up Adapter

To call into your computer at work over your modem, you need to have the Dial-Up Adapter set up on both computers. It is automatically set up on your home computer when you create a new connection. It will also be automatically set up when you configure your Windows 95 computer at work. You can directly set it up as follows:

STEPS

Setting Up the Dial-Up Adapter

Step 1.   Click the Start button, then Settings, then Control Panel. Double-click the Network icon in the Control Panel.

Step 2.   If Microsoft Dial-Up Adapter is not in the list of network components in the Network dialog box, click the Add button just below the list.

Step 3.   Click the Adapter icon and the Add button in the Select Network Component Type dialog box.

Step 4.   Scroll the manufacturer's list in the Select Device dialog box until you get to Microsoft. Highlight Microsoft.

Step 5.   Click Microsoft Dial-Up Adapter in the Models window on the right side of the Select Device dialog box. Click OK.

The Microsoft Dial-Up Adapter and the network software component necessary to carry out remote communications will now be installed. You will be asked to reboot your computer.

The default networking protocols that are bound to the Dial-Up Adapter are NetBEUI and IPX/SPX. If you need additional or different protocols, you will need to install them directly. If you are going to call into an Internet service provider, you will also need to bind the TCP/IP protocol to your Dial-Up Adapter.

After you have rebooted you computer, go back to the Control Panel and display the network components by double-clicking the Network icon. Highlight the Dial-Up Adapter and click the Properties button. You'll see the Dial-Up Adapter Properties sheet, as shown in Figure 28-3.

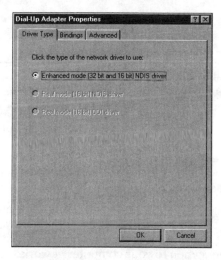

Figure 28-3: The Driver Type portion of the Dial-Up Adapter Properties sheet.

Undocumented

Microsoft has written an NDIS (Network Driver Interface Specification) 3.1 level driver for the modem/serial port. This is a low-level driver most often associated with network cards. The Dial-Up Adapter treats the modem as though it were a network card using this driver. NDIS 3.1 is a superset of NDIS 3.0, which allows for multiple protocols to be running on the network interface card (or, in this case, a modem) simultaneously.

The protocol of the Dial-Up Networking communication between two Windows 95 computers is either NetBEUI or IPX/SPX. These protocols were installed when you set up the Dial-Up Adapter and are bound to it. *Bound* means that they are used to carry out the communication between the two computers. You can find out whether one or both of the protocols are bound by clicking the Bindings tab, which you can see in Figure 28-3.

Dialing In to the Office

At home after you have connected your computer's modem to your phone line, you can dial in to the computer at work. Of course, the computer at work could actually be a networked modem server that acts like a Windows 95, Windows NT, or NetWare Connect server that is set up as a host. It answers your call and connects you to the network at work.

STEPS

Dialing In from Home

Step 1. Double-click the Dial-Up Networking icon in an Explorer window or click the Dial-Up Networking icon in the Programs, Accessories menu on the Start button.

Step 2. Double-click the Computer at Work icon in the Dial-Up Networking folder window. If you call work often, you might want to right-drag this icon onto the desktop or Start button and choose Create Short-cut from the right mouse button menu. That way you will have a convenient way of accessing the computer at work.

Step 3. The Connect To dialog box appears. Type in your name and password if you have set up a password on the computer at work. Click Save Password if you don't want to type in your password every time you make a connection to your computer at work.

Step 4. You have the option of editing your (at home) location information at this point. There are other entry points for editing this information, but this is as good as any. See the previous section entitled *Setting up your basic telephone information* for details.

Step 5. Click Connect.

Your computer will dial your modem and attempt to make a network connection across the phone lines to your computer at work. If all goes well, you will be networked to your computer at work.

If you have chosen Log on to network in the Server Types Properties sheet, you will also be logged onto the network that is connected to the server that you had dialed into.

Dialing In Manually

It is possible to dial into the host computer manually. You make the connection, perhaps through a operator or using your credit card. You then turn over the phone line to your computer.

Dialing In Manually

Step 1. Double-click the Dial-Up Networking Icon in the Explorer or click the Dial-Up Networking icon in the Start, Programs, Accessories menu on the Start button.

Step 2. Right-click the Computer at Work icon in the Dial-Up Networking folder window. Click Properties.

Step 3. Click the Configure button and then the Options tab.

Step 4. Click Operator assisted or Manual dial. Click OK.

Step 5. Double-click the icon for Computer at Work. You will be prompted to pick up the receiver and dial the number.

Step 6. When you hear the tone from the computer, click Connect, and then hang up the phone.

Networking over a Modem

Once you have made the connection, you are another node (albeit a slow one) on the network at work. If you are just hooking two computers together, then they are networking over the modem, and that is the only network.

Undocumented

If you are calling into a Windows 95 computer acting as the host, you won't see the shared resources in your Network Neighborhood. In order to reduce the overhead on a slow link such as a modem connection, the ability to browse the host computer is by default turned off. We show how to turn this back on in the section entitled *Seeing shared resources*.

Accessing shared resources

You access the shared resources of the computer at work (folder, printers and drives on the host computer) by explicitly naming the resource. Click the Start button, then the Run option. Type in the name of the computer at work followed by the shared resource name using the universal naming convention (UNC), for example, \\WorkComputer\C. (When users attempt to access these resources, they may be required to enter a password at this point — if it is not already in the user password cache stored on their computers or if this is the first time they have accessed a resource that is protected by a password.

The UNC allows you to access resources by their name without having to map them to a drive letter on your computer. It uses two back slashes before the server, host, or computer at work's name followed by a back slash separator to the resource name.

A folder window with this resource will open up on the desktop of your home computer. You can then browse the resource to find the files or programs that you are interested in.

Seeing shared resources

It is possible to configure the computer at work so that its shared resources are automatically available to the computer at home. That way, you don't have to use the Run command.

STEPS
Turning on the Browse Master

Step 1.   Click the Start button on the Taskbar, then Control Panel on the Settings menu. Double-click the Network icon.

Step 2.   Click File and Printer Sharing for Windows Networks in the network components window. Click the Properties button.

Step 3.   Browse Master should be the first item in the Properties window. Its default value in the Value window is Automatic. Click the drop-down Value list and highlight Enable.

Step 4.   Click the Accept button and then OK.

Step 5.   Restart Windows 95 on the host computer.

Step 6.   Double-click the connectoid for the computer at work on the computer at home.

Step 7.   When the connection is made, open the Network Neighborhood on the computer at home to see the shared resources from the computer at work.

Getting your e-mail when you're on the road

Using Microsoft Exchange to get your e-mail is the same whether you are away from the office or sitting at your desk. Your portable or home computer can be set up to automatically call in so you can check your inbox for new messages. The connection is made by Microsoft Exchange. You don't have to double-click the connectoid to your office computer.

You'll need to configure an Exchange Profile on your computer at home that uses Microsoft Mail as its transportation medium and connects to a Workgroup post office at work. See Chapter 32 for details.

Printing on the printer at work from home

It is quite possible to print a document on a printer at work while calling in from your computer at home or on the road. The printer at work must be shared and you need to have it in your Printers folder.

The first step is sharing the printer at work. If the printer at work is on a Windows 95 computer, you share it by clicking the Start button, then Settings, Printers. The Printers folder window will appear on your desktop. Right-click the printer that you want to share. Click Sharing. Click Shared As. (More details are found in Chapter 23.)

The printer at work also needs to be in the Printers folder on the computer at home. Double-click the Add Printer icon in the Printers folder on the computer at home. Tell the Add Printer Wizard that the printer is a networked printer and give it the path name to the printer using the universal naming convention such as \\server\HP. The printer drivers will automatically be downloaded from the computer at work if you are currently connected to that computer. More details are found in Chapter 23.

Once the printer at work is shared and you have it in your Printers folder on your computer at home, then you can simply print to it.

Faxing from work while on the road

It is possible, using Microsoft Exchange, to send a document from your computer at home over your modem to a shared fax/modem on your network (or computer) at work, and have that document faxed out from work. You might do this if your modem doesn't have a fax capability, or your fax/modem on your computer at home isn't compatible with Microsoft fax, or perhaps the company is paying the bills for the faxes sent from work.

The first requirement is for a shared fax/modem at work. The second is to configure an Exchange Profile on your computer at home that uses the shared fax/modem at work. For details on how to do this, turn to the section entitled *Shared Fax/Modems* in Chapter 32.

Summary

You can call into a server computer over your modem from your computer at home or on the road. The server can be either a Windows 95 computer, a Windows NT computer, LAN Manager server computer, a NetWare server, a Unix computer, or a dedicated networked modem server. We show you:

▶ How to set up a Windows 95 computer as a host at work so you can call into it from home.

▶ How to set up your computer at home so you can call into various servers, including your Windows 95 computer at work.

▶ How to access and use shared resources on the network with Dial-Up Networking.

▶ How to print on your printer at work and fax from your fax/modem at work, both under the direction of your computer at home.

Chapter 29

Calling the Bulletin Boards

In This Chapter

Windows 95 provides a way to communicate with bulletin boards and other computers over telephone lines. This terminal-to-computer style of communication, while going out of style, is still prevalent among bulletin board computers. We discuss:

▶ Setting up different bulletin board connections

▶ Dialing into a bulletin board

▶ Downloading a file

▶ Modifying the parameters of your bulletin board connection

▶ Capturing text to a file

▶ The differences between HyperTerminal in Windows 95 and Terminal in Windows 3.*x*

A Flash from the Past

This chapter is about using HyperTerminal, a wonderful little application that comes with Windows 95. Communication that takes place through computers comes in many different modes. Each type of communication has different applications that are best suited to its mode, and HyperTerminal is an excellent program for occasionally communicating with bulletin boards.

It wasn't too many years ago (perhaps for many readers, just a few months ago?) that communicating using a personal computer meant using a program like HyperTerminal. Now, there are lots of options for each little communications niche.

HyperTerminal has the word *terminal* in it because it is designed around the metaphor of a terminal calling into a multiuser computer. The *hyper* part of its name means that it can do more than act as a dumb terminal when it is connected to another computer. Downloading files using a binary file transfer protocol like Zmodem, for example, could not be done with a dumb terminal.

This type of terminal-computer communication has been around since the late '60s. It was created because computers then were expensive and needed to be shared to be cost-effective. This type of computer communication is still useful.

For example, your hardware vendor may provide on its computer certain files that you'll want to download. Or there may be a community bulletin board hosted on one computer that you need to call into if you wish to read the messages and post your own.

When bulletin board users call in, they typically are presented with a screen full of options. You, the user, basically only provide the computer running the bulletin board with keystrokes that determine how a program running on that computer presents information to you. The bulletin board computer doesn't care what kind of computer you are using. You might as well be using a terminal — that is, until you want to download or upload a file.

HyperTerminal lets you upload and download files to the bulletin board using one of five file transfer protocols. This is a handy feature that works well.

With HyperTerminal you can also call into a commercial service provider such as CompuServe — although using CompuServe's WinCIM navigation software is a much easier approach. After all, service providers such as CompuServe are just big bulletin boards. You can also call into your local Internet service provider (a company that provides commercial access to dial-up users to the Internet) if you have set up a shell (console or terminal) account. What this means is that HyperTerminal will let you run programs on the service provider's Unix computer. You can use its Unix e-mail program, for example, to send and receive mail on the Internet.

With HyperTerminal, you can connect your computer to another one through a cable on your serial or parallel port. Depending on what the other computer is, you can send files or use the computer's multiuser operating system.

Terminal, HyperTerminal's predecessor, was widely ignored — probably because it was too hard to use for a program that did so little and had so few file transfer protocols. Also, other communications packages did quite a bit more.

HyperTerminal is not the most powerful package of its type. The authors of HyperTerminal, Hilgrave, Inc., have more sophisticated communications software they would be happy to sell you. They assume that you will like the ease of use and features in HyperTerminal and hope that once you have gotten used to it you will want more.

HyperTerminal is easy to use and reliable. It is powerful enough for a significant percentage of the Windows user population. It doesn't have scripting, so you can't automate your sessions or your logon sequences. It won't store your passwords. It doesn't have built-in auto-answer. It doesn't have all the file transfer protocols that you might want. But it does have the basic features that make it easy to call into a bulletin board and upload or download a file occasionally.

Creating Connections (Connectoids)

One nifty feature of HyperTerminal is that it creates an icon and a file for each bulletin board or connection that you want to call. These icons are automatically collected and displayed in the HyperTerminal folder window — ready for easy access. You can create a shortcut to any of these connections and place them on the desktop.

Most communications packages of this type have a list of names and phone numbers for the bulletin boards. This list is normally accessed by first starting the communications package and using its menu bar to display the list. Terminal, the communications package that came with Windows 3.x, created a separate connection file for each bulletin board, but didn't present them in as straightforward a fashion as HyperTerminal does.

Putting the connection (referred to internally at Microsoft as connectoids) in a separate file means the data specific to that connection is kept within the file and each file can be customized. Each bulletin board can have its own icon that represents it in the HyperTerminal folder window. Just double-click the connectoid's icon and you're off and running.

Here's how to create a new connectoid.

STEPS

Creating a New Connection

Step 1. Click the Start button and then Programs, Accessories. In the Accessories menu click HyperTerminal.

Step 2. Double-click the icon labeled Hypertrm.exe in the HyperTerminal folder window. Fill in the name field for the bulletin board that you want to connect to and choose an icon. Unlike almost all other applications in Windows 95, icons for connectoids can be chosen only from the ones shown in this list. Click OK.

Step 3. The Phone Number dialog box, as shown in Figure 29-1, will appear on the desktop within a HyperTerminal window. Enter the area code and the phone number (country code if you need to) for the bulletin board.

If you are going to create a connection between two nearby computers using a serial cable, don't worry about the phone numbers.

Step 4. The default device for your connection is the modem that you have already installed and configured. You can change to another device, but if you are going to call into a bulletin board over the phone lines, there is no need to change this field. Click OK.

(continued)

STEPS *(continued)*

Creating a New Connection

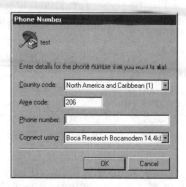

Figure 29-1: The Phone Number dialog box.

Undocumented

You also have the option of communicating through one of your serial ports. Click the down arrow in the "Connect using" drop-down list, and choose which serial port to use. You will need to have a null modem serial cable to connect the two computers.

Step 5. If you are using a modem and not a serial cable, you are presented with the Dial dialog box shown in Figure 29-2. You can click the Dial button if you want to make a connection immediately. If you just want to save the new connection information, click Cancel, and then File, Save from the menu bar.

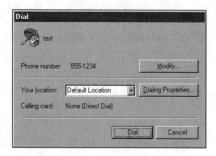

Figure 29-2: The Dial dialog box.

The Modify button in the Dial dialog box allows you to make changes in the phone number and settings for the connection, as well as changes to the modem settings. See the section entitled *Changing the Properties of the Connectoid* later in this chapter for information on changing the connection settings. Turn to Chapter 25 for information on modem settings.

The Dialing Properties button lets you choose a new originating location or edit the properties associated with the phone system at the location you are dialing from. Turn to Chapter 26 for more details about location settings.

Making a Connection

If you have already created a connectoid, dialing into a bulletin board is pretty easy.

STEPS

Making a Connection

Step 1. Click the Start button, then Programs, and Accessories. Click HyperTerminal.

Step 2. In the HyperTerminal folder window, double-click the icon for the bulletin board that you want to call. Click the Dial button in the Dial dialog box. If the Dial dialog box isn't showing, click the phone on the Toolbar. If the Toolbar isn't showing, click Call, Connect in the connectoid's menu bar.

Undocumented

If you are making a connection through a serial cable, you won't have to take step two. If you are connecting two Windows 95 computers, after you double-click the appropriate connectoids that use the serial ports, you are connected.

Downloading a File

The ability to download files is one of the main reasons people call bulletin boards. Downloading a file from a bulletin board is a two-step process, unfortunately. Downloading files off Internet file transfer protocol (FTP) servers if you use a World Wide Web browser such as Mosaic is quite a bit easier than the process we are going to outline here. When using Mosaic or Internet Explorer (part of Microsoft Plus!) to interface to an FTP server, all you have to do to download a file is click on the name of the file and then give the file a name and location on your computer.

STEPS

Downloading a File

Step 1. Call into a bulletin board as outlined earlier in this chapter in the section entitled *Making a Connection*.

Step 2. On the bulletin board, choose a file to download and the file transfer protocol. If the Zmodem file transfer protocol is available on the bulletin board, it is a good choice. The file transfer protocols supported by HyperTerminal are 1K Xmodem, Xmodem, Ymodem, Ymodem-G, Zmodem, and Kermit. (These protocols are described after these steps.) On the bulletin board computer, you'll have to choose from among those protocols. The CompuServe B protocol is missing so you will have to use another binary file format like Xmodem, Ymodem, or Kermit in the Transfer, Receive File dialog box of HyperTerminal if you want to use HyperTerminal to download or upload files on CompuServe.

Step 3. Issue whatever command is necessary on the bulletin board to begin sending the file from the bulletin board computer.

Step 4. Click the Receive file icon on the Toolbar, or Transfer, Receive File on the connectoid's menu. Choose the file transfer protocol that matches the one being used by the bulletin board and the location for the file on your computer. Click OK.

Step 5. If the file transfer protocol requires a filename on your computer for the downloaded file, you will be prompted for it. The file transfer will begin and be carried out automatically.

You can also send a file to a bulletin board using a slight variation on these steps. The send icon on the Toolbar is just to the left of the receive icon.

Among HyperTerminal's file transfer protocols, Xmodem is a basic, standard, but somewhat slow protocol that transfers files in 128-byte blocks while 1K Xmodem transfers files in 1024-byte blocks. Often this 1K protocol is referred to as Ymodem. Ymodem-G, a variation on Ymodem, can be used if your modem and modem driver support hardware error correction. Zmodem is the file transfer protocol of choice for most bulletin boards. It is relatively fast and reliable and uses a variable block size. Kermit is found at academic computer centers and on Digital Equipment Corp. VAX systems and some IBM mainframes. It is slow.

Changing the Properties of the Connectoid

The properties associated with a given connection include the phone number, the type of terminal that is emulated, how many lines of text of the communication are buffered (allowing you to scroll back to display them) and how text files are transferred between your computer and the bulletin board. You can get at these values a number of ways.

To change the properties of a connection, choose one of four methods:

1. Right-click the connectoid's icon in the HyperTerminal folder window and click Properties.

2. Double-click the connections icon, and then click File, Properties from the menu bar.

3. Click the telephone in the Toolbar of the connection's window and then click Modify.

4. Click the Properties icon on the right end of the Toolbar.

Changing the phone number and modem properties

The properties of a connection are maintained in two tabbed Properties sheets, as shown in Figure 29-3. The first sheet repeats much of what you saw in the Phone Number dialog box. The additions include the capability to change the connectoid's icon, and the Configure button, which gives you an entry point into changing the properties of the modem.

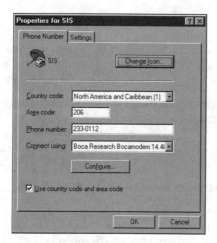

Figure 29-3: The Phone Number Properties sheet for a connection to a bulletin board.

Turn to Chapter 25 for a detailed discussion regarding Modem Properties sheets.

Setting terminal emulation and buffer size

The connection's Settings Properties sheet, shown in Figure 29-4, lets you change how the function keys are used in terminal emulation, which terminal you are going to emulate, how large a backwards scroll buffer to maintain, and the ASCII properties values.

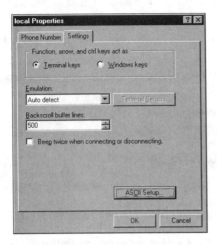

Figure 29-4: HyperTerminal's Settings Properties sheet. Choose whether the Ctrl, arrow, and function keys are sent to the bulletin board or used by Windows. Pick a terminal to emulate, how many lines back you can scroll, and whether your speaker beeps when the bulletin board sends a Ctrl+G.

Various terminal emulations can use the function, Ctrl, and arrow keys to control how text is displayed and manipulated on the bulletin board computer. If you want these keys to operate in this fashion, choose Terminal keys.

You can choose from seven terminal emulation types: ANSI, Auto detect, Minitel (common in France), TTY, Viewdata (common in the UK), VT100, and VT52. Within each terminal emulation mode, other than Auto detect, you can change some terminal settings. Click the Terminal Setup button after you choose a terminal emulation to allow further terminal-specific changes.

For most users, you will want to try the Auto detect, VT 100, or ANSI settings for terminal emulation.

The Backscroll buffer lines field determines how many lines of an ongoing communication you can review by scrolling back with the scrollbar on the right side of the HyperTerminal window, up arrow on the keyboard or the page up key on the keyboard. The maximum is 500.

If you want your computer to notify you when it successfully connects or disconnects from a bulletin board, click the "Beep twice when connecting or disconnecting" check box.

ASCII text handling

Click the ASCII Setup button to set the parameters for sending and displaying text information. The ASCII Setup dialog box is shown in Figure 29-5.

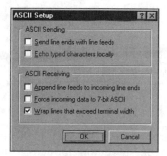

Figure 29-5: The ASCII Setup dialog box. Different bulletin boards send text to you in different ways. If the lines keep overwriting, click the third box from the top. Use this dialog box to make up for ASCII miscommunication.

Tip

If you are receiving text from a bulletin board and it is writing over itself, click Append line feeds to incoming line ends. If you want only ASCII text, just the printable lower 128 characters in the ANSI character set, to be displayed click Force incoming data to 7-bit ASCII. If the lines of text coming in are going off to the right, click Wrap lines that exceed terminal width.

If you are not seeing your text when you type it in, click Echo typed characters locally. If the text that you are sending to the bulletin board is writing over itself, click Send line ends with line feeds.

Capturing Incoming Text to a File

You might want to keep a record of your communications sessions or just capture text that is being sent from the bulletin board. To do that, start by clicking Transfer, Capture Text on the connectoid's menu bar. The default capture file is C:\Program Files\Accessories\HyperTerminal\Capture.txt. A Notepad icon will appear in the HyperTerminal folder window as soon as you click the Start button in the Capture to file dialog box.

You can close the Capture.txt file at any time by clicking Transfer, Capture Text, Stop in the connectoid's menu bar.

Your keystrokes are often echoed (that is, sent back to you) by the bulletin board computer. These echoed keystrokes will also be captured in the capture file.

HyperTerminal vs. Terminal

Microsoft shipped Terminal with Windows 3.1x. You would expect that HyperTerminal would be an upgrade of Terminal. It is, but it is also a newly designed product.

Terminal gave you three terminal emulations: TTY (very basic hard-copy terminal), VT100, and VT52 (Digital Equipment Corp. standards). HyperTerminal gives you six or seven (if you count Auto detect). Terminal supported three modem types as well as the ability to type in your own initialization strings. HyperTerminal supports hundreds of modems directly. Once you set up your modem, these settings can be used by any communications package that knows enough to take advantage of this capability built into the operating system.

Terminal gave you two binary file transfer protocols, Xmodem/CRC and Kermit. HyperTerminal comes with five: 1K Xmodem, Xmodem, Ymodem, Ymodem-G, Zmodem, and Kermit. Zmodem is the most widely used file transfer protocol between personal computers and bulletin boards.

The scrollback buffer size can be 500 lines in HyperTerminal. Its maximum in Terminal was 399 lines.

HyperTerminal creates separate files/icons for each connection. Double-click the icon for a given bulletin board and you are ready to connect. Terminal created a file for each different connection, but didn't make it easy to set up a folder of icons that allowed you ready and easy access to dialing the boards. You could create a Program Manager group and drag and drop the *.trm files that Terminal created for each connection into the group. Windows 95 makes this interface obvious.

With Terminal you could define function keys (buttons at the bottom of the Terminal window) to carry out a series of commands, such as logging in and sending your name and password. HyperTerminal doesn't provide for function keys. HyperTerminal has a Toolbar with one-click interface to the more often used menu bar options. Terminal gave you just a menu bar.

Terminal allowed you to send commands directly to your modem for troubleshooting. Windows 95 has a help-based modem troubleshooter. You can't type in commands to be sent to your modem with HyperTerminal.

Summary

Communicating with bulletin boards requires that, for the most part, you turn your computer into a terminal that can upload and download files.

▶ HyperTerminal, a little application that Microsoft bundles with Windows 95, is used to communicate with bulletin boards.

▶ We show you how to set up HyperTerminal for each bulletin board that you want to dial into.

▶ We also show you how to download files from the bulletin board.

▶ We compare HyperTerminal with its previous incarnation — Terminal.

Chapter 30

Laptop to Desktop

In This Chapter

▶ Easily connecting two computers using a serial or parallel cable

▶ Transferring files and how LapLink set the original standards

▶ Microsoft's first attempt at serial/parallel cable networking — DOS Interlnk

▶ Direct Cable Connection — Windows 95 parallel/serial cable networking

▶ What to expect in the way of speed and file transfer rates between Windows 95 computers

▶ Using a serial or parallel cable to give your laptop or other computer direct access to your network

▶ Setting up a parallel cable network that gives you much faster communication speeds

▶ Comparing LapLink for Windows with Direct Cable Connection

Connecting Two Computers

You can physically connect two computers using a serial or parallel cable, and even infrared transmitters/receivers. Depending on the software you use to drive the connection, the two computers may be limited to just transferring files. With more powerful software, one computer can use the resources (such as hard disk, files, and printers) of the other as though these resources were directly connected to it.

LapLink for DOS — a history

For years, Traveling Software has "owned" the file-transfer franchise with its DOS LapLink program. LapLink was the first popular software that allowed you to connect two computers using an inexpensive serial or parallel cable and easily transfer files back and forth.

All computers have a parallel port built in (some have two or three) and almost all have one or two serial ports. These ports are communication devices. Add a cable and file transfer software that's both quick and obvious to use, and you've got yourself a winner.

LapLink's competition in the file-transfer business is the floppy diskette. Traveling Software's first task was to make LapLink quicker and easier to use than a floppy diskette. That was a technical hurdle, but not a high one.

One of LapLink's strengths (in addition to its speed) was its intuitive user interface. You got to see your directories and files in full screen view. You could simply click a file to copy it from one computer to the other. No typing commands. No searching around with a one-line-high window (like a DOS command line) to find your file.

Traveling Software did not develop a serial- or parallel-port based network. Perhaps company officials felt that the speeds of these communications devices were too slow. Perhaps they didn't want to dilute their marketing message. But while the DOS version of LapLink competed against the floppy diskette, competing against Ethernet is a different story.

Interlnk — Microsoft's cable network

Operating systems like MS-DOS or Windows 95 already have built into them the ability to transfer files between the hard disk and floppy diskette, between directories, between hard disks, and between RAM and the hard disks. One might consider it an obvious extension of the operating system to allow file transfer between two computers — especially when the communications ports are already built into the computers.

Microsoft's first foray in this direction was the Interlnk program. (Interlnk is the DOS eight-character mode spelling for Interlink.)

Interlnk is a DOS program that allows you to connect two computers using a serial or parallel cable and then treat the host computer's hard disks as though they were additional local hard disks belonging to the guest computer. This allows the guest computer to treat the connected computers as though they were one system.

Unlike LapLink, which allows either computer to be in charge, Interlnk defines one computer as a *guest* and one as a *host*. The guest runs the show. The host simply provides the guest with its hard disks to be used as the guest determines. It sits there passively responding to the guest's commands. All commands are typed on the guest computer.

Treating two computers as one is a much more powerful metaphor then the file-transfer metaphor. You can do anything with two computers that you can with one. The only problem is that the hard disks of the host computer are available only through a relatively slow connection. Microsoft apparently felt the speed penalty was not enough to offset the benefit of the networking model.

Unlike LapLink, Interlnk can run programs on the guest that are stored as executable files on the host. You can also transfer files. There isn't a nice user interface built in, just DOS, but you can use any DOS shell, even DOSSHELL, which comes free with DOS 6.*x*. This gives you a front end for file transfers that is similar to LapLink, and at no additional cost.

Interlnk is a network, specifically a *zero slot network*, that is, a network without a network card. And because it doesn't have a dedicated network card, it is a relatively slow network. Here are some of Interlnk's downsides:

- You have to install Interlnk.exe in the guest's computer Config.sys file — where it stays in memory.

- It doesn't work with Windows (it doesn't even come with Windows 95, only DOS 6.*x*).

- There is no security, other than the physical security of being in the same room with the computers.

- Interlnk is quite a bit slower than LapLink when using the serial ports and a serial cable.

Microsoft never heavily promoted Interlnk and brought it out after the company's emphasis had shifted to Windows. Still, it's a useful and very inexpensive product. Too bad you never heard about it. You might call it a DOS 6.*x* secret.

Direct Cable Connection

Windows 95 makes it easy to directly connect two computers using a serial or parallel cable. That's because Windows 95 comes with Direct Cable Connection (DCC), which is a serial and parallel port network. DCC is Interlnk taken to the next level. Like Interlnk, there is a guest (presumably a laptop computer that you've brought into the office) and a host computer. DCC adds the ability to connect not only to the host but to the other computers or servers on the network to which the host is attached.

DCC is a network. DCC uses the built-in Windows 95 network protocols to provide the communications link between the guest and the host and the network connected to the host computer. You have the choice of NetBEUI (Microsoft's peer-to-peer networking protocol), IPX/SPX (Novell's NetWare protocol), and/or TCP/IP (the protocol used in Unix networks and/or with dial-up Internet connections). Both IPX/SPX and TCP/IP are routeable, so you can network across network routing systems to connect to the much wider network.

DCC's user interface is a folder window that displays the shared resources (drives or folders) on the host. You don't have to learn how to use a different set of conventions. The beauty of integrating this kind of capability into the operating system. is that you already know how to use it. When you use DCC, Windows 95 treats other computers and servers networked to your computer like close friends. You can see the files and folders on hard drives that are shared. On your guest computer, you can run programs that reside as executable files on other computers. Those programs are loaded into your computer's memory.

Your computer can easily find information or documents that are stored on other computers. And, of course, you can easily transfer files back and forth, updating older files to the latest versions.

Speed

DCC's speed varies depending on whether you are using serial or parallel port communications. Serial communications can be quite slow, to say the least. If your computer has the older or less expensive serial ports that use 8250 or 16450 universal asynchronous transmitter/receivers (UARTs), (the chip that drives the serial port), you are limited to speeds of up to 57,600 bits per second (bps). Most new computers come with 16550 UARTs or better, which can be driven at up to 115,200 bps.

Unfortunately, DCC is not able to give you the 14 kilobytes per second (KBps) of file transfer speed that the 115,200 bps rate would imply 115,200/1024*8. DCC is much slower on a serial cable than LapLink for Windows. Once you've used LapLink, DCC is essentially unusable.

Undocumented

Parallel ports come in a number of varieties. New computers have incorporated enhanced standards for parallel ports, known as EPP or ECP (see the section later in this chapter entitled *Parallel ports and cables* for a full explanation). EPP/ECP ports can facilitate very high speed communications between computers — approaching the speed that is available from dedicated networking cards. It is possible to reach speeds of 120 KB/sec. (or approximately 70 times faster than DCC using a serial cable) with the appropriate cable and automatic data compression that is built into Windows 95 for parallel ports. At these speeds, networking over parallel cables is about a third as fast as dedicated 10 megabit (Mb) Ethernet cards, without the cost of an Ethernet card.

Although they don't have a reputation for speed, the older parallel ports still have better speed performance then serial ports. Windows 95 has enhanced parallel port software drivers that allow computers with standard parallel ports (4-bit unidirectional and 8-bit bidirectional), using a standard bidirectional parallel cable to connect them, to network at speeds that are often quite acceptable — not just for file transfer, but for data and program sharing, too.

Setup

Direct Cable Connection is not installed unless you use Custom installation or go back after you have set up Windows 95 and choose Add/Remove Programs in the Control Panel. During Custom installation you must choose the Communications icon in the Components dialog box and then specifically click the Direct Cable Connection check box to install it.

If you didn't install Direct Cable Connection when you set up Windows 95, you can take the following steps to do so:

STEPS

Installing Direct Cable Connection

Step 1.   Click the Start button, then Settings, then Control Panel.

Step 2.   Double-click the Add/remove Programs icon, and then the Windows Setup tab.

Step 3.   Click the Communications icon, and then the Details button.

Step 4.   Click the Direct Cable Connection check box.

Step 5.   Click the OK button in the Communications dialog box, and in the Windows Setup dialog box.

If you install Direct Cable Connection, you will also automatically install Dial-Up Networking (DUN) and networking in general. Direct Cable Connection is really just a variant of Dial-Up Networking. It is a dial up network that doesn't require that you dial-up (or have a network card).

DUN is discussed in Chapter 28. The Windows 95 setup program, or installing DUN later from the Add/Remove Programs icon, automatically configures the network protocols necessary to run DCC. You have the option of changing these protocols and reconfiguring DUN and therefore DCC.

The Network Neighborhood is placed on your desktop when you install DCC. If you remove this icon using either Tweak UI, the Policy Editor, or directly by editing the Registry, you can no longer use DCC.

Configuration

To access the Direct Cable Connection, click your Start button, then Programs, then Accessories, and finally Direct Cable Connection.

The first time you try to use DCC, the Direct Cable Connection Wizard pops up, as shown in Figure 30-1, and helps you configure DCC.

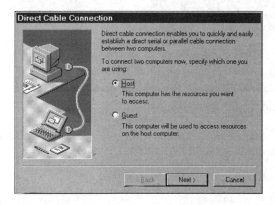

Figure 30-1: The Direct Cable Connection Wizard. Run the Wizard on both your host and guest computer.

The DCC Wizard identifies the serial and parallel ports that are not already in use and can be used for communication, as shown in Figure 30-2. You can pick from among the available ports. If you add ports later, you can rerun the Wizard and ask it to check for new ports.

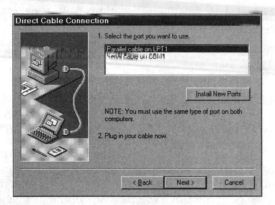

Figure 30-2: The Direct Cable Connection Wizard, page 2. Click the Install New Ports button if you have installed new serial or parallel ports since the last time you ran the DCC Wizard.

If you wish, you can set a password that is required to connect the guest to the host computer, as shown in the third page of the DCC Wizard in Figure 30-3. You can also click Cancel at any time during the process to forget the whole thing.

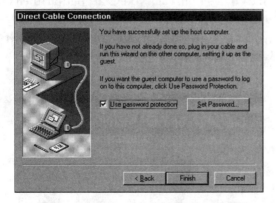

Figure 30-3: The Direct Cable Connection Wizard, page 3. Click the Use password protection check box to require a password to get access to the host computer.

Network configuration

When DCC is installed, the Dial-Up Network is also installed. The default installation is shown in Figure 30-4. If your host computer isn't connected to a network, you will not need to add other protocols or change this configuration.

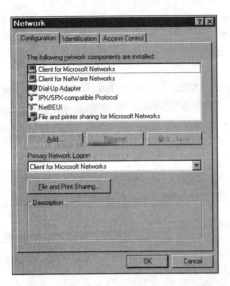

Figure 30-4: The Dial-Up Networking network configuration. All the components for the Dial-Up Network have been installed. The network configuration must be the same on both the guest and the host computer. By default, it will be.

If you want your guest computer to be a full-fledged member of the network to which your host is attached, you may need to add protocols to the Dial-Up adapter. Turn to the Network Installation section of Chapter 38 for instructions on how to add protocols to your Dial-Up adapter.

Installing all the right protocols

If you are trying to use DCC to connect from a Windows 95 guest computer to a Windows 95 host computer that is connected to a network, you may experience problems if you haven't bound the IPX/SPX protocol to your dial-up adapter on both the host and guest computer. If on the guest computer you see the messages: "Verifying Username and Password," and then "Disconnect," it may be because NetBIOS has not been able to find the computer names on the host. To correct this problem, install and bind the IPX/SPX protocol to the Dial-Up adapter on both the host and guest computer.

Sharing comes first

If you want your guest computer to see anything on the Windows 95 host computer or on other computers on the network, their resources must be shared. When the connection is made to the host, the window that appears on the Desktop is a window that displays the shared resources of the host.

To enable the host to share its resources, File and Print Sharing for Microsoft or for NetWare networks must be installed. File and Print Sharing for Microsoft Network is installed by default when you install DCC.

Further, you must actually share some resources on your host computer. You can do this by right-clicking a folder, disk icon, or printer icon and then clicking the Sharing menu item in the right mouse button and choosing Shared As in the Sharing dialog box.

Once resource-sharing has been established, the resources can be seen by the guest computer.

If the host computer has user-level security (there is a Windows NT or NetWare server on a network that the host is connected to that keeps a user database), you will need to add the guest user to the user list. To do this, take the following steps:

STEPS

Sharing with User-Level Security

Step 1.   On the host computer, open up a folder or Explorer view of your disks, printers, and/or folder.

Step 2.   Right-click the resource you want to share and then click Sharing in the Context button menu.

Step 3.   Click Shared As in the Sharing Properties sheet for that resource, type in a name (if different) for the resource, and then the Add button.

Step 4.   In the Add Users dialog box, click the name of the guest (or guests) that will be allowed to access the resources on the host computer.

Step 5.   Click the access type desired.

Step 6.   Click OK buttons until you are out of the Properties sheets.

Browsing the host

Secret

The Windows 95 host computer, by default, won't show up in your Network Neighborhood if you double-click the Network Neighborhood icon on your Desktop. You also won't be able to see other computers on the network in the Network Neighborhood. If you want to get to them (and their shared resources) you will have to type in their UNC names in the Find Computer dialog box (click the Start button, Find, and then Computer).

Microsoft turned off the capability for DCC (and Dial-Up Networking) to see the host or the network because they felt this would slow DCC down too much. Seeing the host and the network is called, by Microsoft, *browsing* (not to be confused with browsing the Internet) and it requires updating lots of information about disk, folders, and files that are on the host computer and on the network connected to the host computer.

You can turn the browsing feature back on and see for yourself if it is too slow for you. To do this, take the following steps on your host computer:

STEPS

Forcing Browsing with DCC

Step 1.   On your Windows 95 host computer, click the Start button, then Settings, then Control Panel.

Step 2.   Highlight File and printer sharing for Microsoft networks, and then click the Properties button. This will bring up the dialog box shown in Figure 30-5.

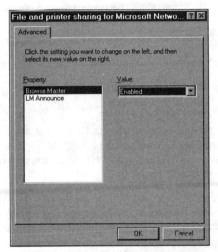

Figure 30-5: The File and printer sharing for Microsoft Network dialog box. Highlight Browse Master and then choose Enabled in the Value field.

Step 3.   Click the arrow in the Value drop down list and click Enable.

Step 4.   Click the OK button in this dialog box and the Network dialog box.

Step 5.   Restart your computer for the change to take effect.

Now you will be able to "browse" the Windows 95 host and the network from your guest computer. There is one problem. If the Windows 95 host is also configured as a Dial-Up Network server that will in fact pick up the phone when a Dial-Up network client calls, the Browse Master function will still be enabled, and now it's enabled for a Dail-Up connection which is a much slower connection. If you are using a serial DCC connection, the connection is also slow, but this really doesn't seem to cause a problem with browsing, at least when the Windows 95 host is not connected to another network.

You can't see the guest from the host, even if you enable the Browse Master on the guest. The host will find only the network it is attached to and won't recognize the fact that there is a guest computer networked to it.

Connected to what?

The fact that DCC is a network has manifold implications. While you might be interested in just hooking your laptop to your desktop computer, much more than that can be accomplished.

You also can use DCC to connect directly to a computer running Windows 95. You can connect indirectly through the network to a NetWare server computer, to a Windows NT server, to other computers running Windows 95, or to other computers on the network.

If you want to connect through the network to the NetWare server, be sure to bind the IPX/SPX protocol to the Dial-Up Adapter on your guest computer — your laptop perhaps. IPX/SPX and NetBEUI are the protocols that are initially bound to the Dial-Up Adapter when you install DCC.

You can hook your cable up to a computer that is running Windows 95 and is running DCC in host mode. To connect to a NetWare server while directly connected to this Windows 95 computer, the Windows 95 host has to be on a network with a NetWare server.

You can also connect indirectly to a Windows NT server through a Windows 95 computer if the Windows 95 computer is connected to the Windows NT computer on a network. Just use DCC and whatever protocol your Windows 95 host computer is using to talk to the Windows NT computer — probably NetBEUI, but it could be IPX/SPX.

Running Direct Cable Connection

You run DCC by clicking the Start button, then Programs, Accessories, and Direct Cable Connection. If you use DCC a lot, you can easily put a shortcut to it on your desktop. You can configure (or reconfigure) DCC at this point, which really means that you can change it from guest to host and change which port it is using. Clicking Connect, as shown in Figure 30-6, sends a request on the cable to connect to the computer at the other end. You need to run DCC on both the guest and the host computer.

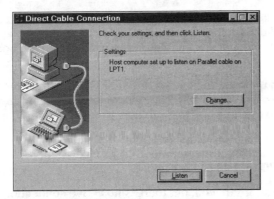

Figure 30-6: The Direct Cable Connection dialog box. On the host computer screen, you have a Listen button. On the guest, you have a Connect button. If you wish to invoke the DCC Wizard, click the Change button.

Click the Listen button on the host computer to begin polling for the guest. Click the Connect button on the guest to begin trying to connect to the host. Once the connection is made, the host's shared drivers and folders plus the shared resources of whatever other network the host is connected to are available to the guest in the shared resources window. Double-click the Network Neighborhood icon on the guest's desktop and you will be able to see the resources available to you if you have set the Browse Master to Enabled on the host computer.

The guest is treated as any other node on the network (except for the fact that the host can't see it). The security provisions of the network are enforced, and the guest may be required to provide a password to connect with the host Windows 95 computer.

Accessing the host

As soon as you make a successful connection with DCC, you will see the host's shared resources in a window on the guest computer. You can double-click on any of the shared folders (or disks) to open a folder view of the contents of that folder.

You won't see disk icons in the shared resource window even if you have shared the whole disk drive on the host. A folder icon is used instead. This is true even if you browse the host with the Network Neighborhood.

You can map a networked resource (which may be a complete drive or perhaps just a folder) to a local drive letter. A networked drive icon will then appear in the Network Neighborhood if you enabled Browse Master on the host computer.

If you disconnect from the host, the folders or folder views of the host that are displayed on your guest are not closed. They just aren't connected to anything anymore. Reconnect to the host and these folders become active again.

You can drag a shortcut to a file, folder, or application from the host to your desktop or any folder on the guest computer that you like. Double-click the shortcut icon and the file or folder is opened.

If you double-click the shortcut icon, but there is no active connection to the host, you won't force DCC to be activated and connect to the host. Instead, you will get the message shown in Figure 30-7. Click No and you'll be reminded that you need to make the network resource available by the message shown in Figure 30-8.

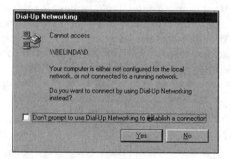

Figure 30-7: The Dial-Up Networking error message. You see the connection between Dial-Up Networking and DCC again. DCC doesn't automatically make a connection, and neither does Dial-Up Networking.

Figure 30-8: The Problem with Shortcut message box. The shortcut can't find the connection to the host.

Serial ports

You can use DCC with a null modem serial cable or a LapLink serial cable. (See Chapter 25 for a discussion of null modem cables.)

The LapLink serial cable is blue and comes with a yellow parallel cable. Both of the LapLink cables are about 8 feet long. Traveling Software sells these cables both with and separately from its LapLink software. They can be used with DCC and Interlnk without any problem. You might want to get some longer cables, but they will be heavier to carry around.

Parallel ports and cables — one-third the speed of 10Mb Ethernet

There are five types of parallel ports: 4-bit, 8-bit, semi 8-bit, EPP, and ECP. Most PCs have 4-bit or 8-bit parallel ports. Many portables with the Intel 386 SL chipset have EPP ports. Computers that support the full IEEE 1284 parallel port specification have ECP parallel ports.

- **Standard parallel ports: 4-bit, 8-bit, semi 8-bit.** Almost every PC since the IBM PC-1 has come with an ordinary, 25-pin D-connector parallel port. These low-speed ports are fine for sending output to a printer (which is usually the slowest device in a computer system). But when transferring data between two PC parallel ports — using a LapLink cable or similar — the speed of data transfer varies. While 4-bit ports can output data 8 bits at a time, they can input data only 4 bits at a time (about 40 kilobytes per second or KB/sec.). Eight-bit ports can output and input 8 bits (80 KB/sec. or more). Semi 8-bit ports can too, but only with more sophisticated software and peripherals.

- **EPP ports.** The *enhanced parallel port* (EPP) was developed by Intel, Xircom, Zenith, and other companies that planned to exploit two-way communication with external devices. Many laptops built since mid-1991 have EPP ports. One source estimates that 80 percent of Intel 386SL and 486SL portables support EPP version 1.7, the first widely used version.

- **ECP ports.** At the same time that Intel and others developed the EPP port, Microsoft and Hewlett-Packard were developing a spec called ECP — the *extended capabilities port.* It has about the same high-speed, two-way throughput as an EPP port but can use DMA (direct memory access) and a small buffer to provide smoother performance in a multitasking environment, which is why Microsoft supports ECP over EPP.

Both the EPP and the ECP specs were defined by the IEEE 1284 committee in 1993. Chipsets that support 1284 (and therefore can operate in ECP mode or a new EPP 1284 mode) started appearing in PCs in 1994.

Four-bit ports are capable of effective transfer rates of 40-80 KB/sec., while 8-bit ports can handle between 80-150 KB/sec. ECP/EPP ports can sustain rates of 300 KB/sec. Unfortunately, just because a port can sustain this speed doesn't necessarily mean you will get file transfer rates at these speeds.

If your computers have ECP or EPP parallel ports, they can sustain about one-third of Ethernet link speeds when networked together with DCC. (Standard 10Megabit per second Ethernet networks commonly deliver an actual through-put of 350-400 KB/sec.) This means that with a proper cable, you may not need to buy Ethernet cards to link together these two computers.

If you have the LapLink cable package (about $15.95), you already have an 8-foot basic bidirectional parallel cable. This cable is fine for 4-bit ports found on most computers.

Another type of cable, known as a *universal cable module* (UCM), contains active electronics that speed two-way communications through the ECP/EPP enhanced parallel ports. Because there are several incompatible enhanced parallel ports in the market, the universal cable is key. It detects your port hardware and software and automatically transfers data at the highest available rate.

Microsoft has chosen to license software code to support the UCM technology from a small firm called Parallel Technologies Inc., 10603 170th Ct. NE, Redmond, WA, 98052, 206-869-1136. This code is incorporated in Windows 95. You can obtain UCM cables from Parallel Technologies.

More on speed

Undocumented

We have made an effort to quantify the file-transfer speeds that you can obtain using the various cables and ports and to compare them with LapLink for Windows. The file transfer speeds that you measure will depend greatly on the compressibility of the files and the speed of the computers to which you connect. The results are shown in Table 30-1. We transferred only already zipped files in order to eliminate efficiency of compression as a variable. The speeds are in KB/sec. The file transfer tests used one 486-66 computer with 16MB of RAM and IDE drive and one Pentium 166 Mhz computer with 32 MB of RAM and SCSI drives.

The serial port settings were set at 115,200 bits per second, both in the port settings and in the modem settings using the Device Manager. Serial ports default to 9600 bits per second and you have to change these defaults in order to spped up DCC using a serial cable. Laplink defaults to setting the ports to 115,200 bits per second.

Table 30-1	File Transfer Speeds	
Port	**LapLink for Windows**	**DCC**
Serial	22 KB/sec.	11.5 KB/sec.
4-bit parallel	46 KB/sec.	76 KB/sec.
ECP/UCM	N/A	120 KB/sec.

Notice that LapLink for Windows is quite a bit faster than Direct Cable Connection over a serial cable. It is our understanding (from Microsoft support personnel) that Traveling Software has a patent for a particularly fast method of transferring data for a serial cable utilizing more than the normal data lines. Microsoft does not use this technology. No wonder Microsoft strongly encourages you to use the parallel port for DCC.

The ECP ports with the UCM cable are quite a bit faster than the other means of file transfer, but only a third as fast as the potential speed of the ECP ports. This makes file transfer over ECP port and a UCM cable not as fast as dedicated Ethernet cards.

Watch the interrupts

Secret

DCC over parallel ports utilizes the interrupts assigned to those ports. LPT1 most often uses interrupt 7, and LPT2 most often interrupt 5. Parallel printers really don't utilize these interrupts, so it usually doesn't matter if something else in your computer grabs them first.

Sound cards and CD-ROMs often use these interrupts. Because the parallel ports really don't use them, Windows 95 doesn't report a conflict between the ports and the sound card or CD-ROM.

If you use DCC over a parallel port and there is a conflict with that port's interrupt, DCC will be slowed down by a factor of three. To prevent this from happening (if you can), you need to be sure that interrupt 7 is not used by some other card if you are using LPT1 for DCC. The same holds for interrupt 5 and LPT2.

To find out if there is a conflict, take the following steps:

STEPS

Determining if an Interrupt Conflict Exists

Step 1. Click the Start button, Settings, and the Control Panel.

Step 2. Double-click the System icon and then the Device Manager tab.

STEPS *(continued)*

Determining if an Interrupt Conflict Exists

Step 3. While the computer is highlighted in the Device Manager, click Properties.

Step 4. From the list of utilized interrupt requests, you can determine if 7 or 5 is used.

You may be able to change the interrupt used by the card(s) that conflict with DCC. If your card is plug and play compatible, you can do this using the Device Manager. If not, you may need to change some jumpers on the card or run a piece of setup software from the card's manufacturer.

Troubleshooting DCC

If you experience problems getting DCC to work, a troubleshooter dialog box will appear that gives you some guidance in how to proceed. Answer the questions and carry out the actions it suggests based on your answers.

You can invoke the DCC troubleshooter manually by taking the following steps:

STEPS

Getting to the DCC Troubleshooter

Step 1. Click the Start button, then Help, then Contents tab.

Step 2. Double-click the Troubleshooting icon in the Help Contents window.

Step 3. Double-click the Direct Cable Connection troubleshooter.

Step 4. Answer the questions in the DCC troubleshooter help window by clicking the gray button next to the questions.

DCC to Windows NT

Undocumented

You can use DCC to connect a Windows 95 computer to a Windows NT computer. The Windows NT computer will run NT Remote Access Server (RAS) and the Windows 95 computer will run DCC.

On the Windows NT computer, use the Null Modem 19200 driver since DCC defaults to 19200 speed. Either computer can be the guest or the host (referred to as the server in Windows NT-speak). Windows NT won't let DCC go any faster than 19,200 bits per second over serial lines. Windows 95 computers can communicate with each other using DCC at 115,200 bits per second over serial lines.

Windows NT uses user-level security. Your Windows 95 computer needs to log into the NT domain if the Windows NT computer is the host. You can set the NT domain by double-clicking the Network Icon in the Control Panel, highlighting Client for Microsoft Networks, clicking the Properties button, clicking "Log on to Windows NT domain," and then typing in the domain's name.

To connect the Windows 95 computer to the Windows NT computer, you need to install a Null Modem driver. For information on this, look at http://www.vt.edu:10021/k/kewells/net/index.html.

Administering the Host Computer's Print Queue

Tip

Let's say you are connecting your laptop to your Desktop computer using DCC. Let's assume that the Desktop computer has a printer connected to it. You might want to be able to delete or pause print files that you are printing from your laptop onto the Desktop's printer. Unfortunately, the Desktop's print queue isn't automatically available to you unless you move over to the Desktop computer and administer it there.

To administer the Desktop's print queue from the laptop you'll need to set your Desktop computer to allow for remote administration. To do this, double-click the Passwords icon in the Control Panel of the Desktop computer, click the Remote Administration tab, then click the "Enable Remote Administration on this server" check box.

So What about LapLink for Windows 95?

LapLink for Windows is not a network on a serial or parallel cable. It doesn't give you full remote access. It does give you easy-to-use file transfer and file synchronization capabilities across a cable, network, modem, or radio modems. It also provides chat and remote control facilities. Remote control lets you run the other computer from your computer.

Traveling Software has incorporated a Windows 95 Explorer-like front end to its file transfer software. This cuts down on the cognitive dissonance that you would experience if they had stayed with their old File Manager-like front end.

LapLink's serial cable file-transfer speeds are much higher than what is available under DCC on a serial port.

Windows 95 provides file synchronization in the Briefcase applet, which we describe in Chapter 31. LapLink for Windows' file synchronization is automatic. When you copy the files back over the originals, only the changes are copied, and the original is updated. This is much faster.

Traveling Software can be reached at 18702 Northcreek Parkway, Bothell, Washington, 98011. The phone number is 800-343-8080.

Summary

▶ Windows 95 comes with a built-in network to allow you to connect two computers with a parallel or serial cable, or through infrared devices.

▶ We show you how to configure this network connection, the Direct Cable Connection.

▶ We discuss what kinds of network connection speeds you can expect from different serial and parallel ports.

▶ We show how Windows 95 has taken the next step to make the parallel port connection a true networking connection with almost network standard speeds.

▶ We compare the file transfer standard — LapLink for Windows — with the offerings built directly into Windows 95.

Chapter 31
Synchronized Filing — The Briefcase

In This Chapter

▶ Windows 95 provides a facility, the Briefcase, to help you keep the same files on two computers up to date on both.

▶ You can use the Briefcase to move files between a computer at the office and one at home, between a portable and a desktop computer, or across a network.

▶ We describe how to create and move a Briefcase.

▶ We show how to move files and folders into and out of the Briefcase, and how to update files on different computers.

Why a Briefcase?

Let's take a look at the metaphor of a briefcase before we incorporate its Windows 95 version into our mental framework.

The idea of a briefcase is that you have some documents you want to take with you so you can work on them outside the office. The documents in a briefcase may be copies or they may be the original set. All changes that you make to these documents are written into the documents as you work on them.

Having two computers with local storage capacity presents a problem. Which document is the most up to date — the one on your computer at the office or the one on your portable? Changes made to documents stored on computers are not as easily recognizable as changes made to documents on paper. You can quickly lose track.

The Windows 95 Briefcase helps you keep track of files you are working on using two computers. Like a real briefcase, it moves from place to place. Unlike a real one, you carry only copies of your original documents. The Briefcase can exist on a floppy disk or can be moved from computer to computer over a network. Copies in the Briefcase that have been updated can be used to overwrite the originals.

Tip

The Briefcase relies on the date and time stamp of the file to determine whether it is the latest copy, so be sure to match the date and time on both computers.

The following scenarios describe three common ways you might use the Windows 95 Briefcase.

Scenario 1

You have a desktop computer at work and a desktop computer at home. You want to work at home on some documents that you normally work on at work.

You have a Briefcase on the desktop of your computer at work. You copy files from folders on your work computer into the Briefcase. You move the Briefcase to a floppy disk.

You take the floppy disk with the Briefcase on it home, perhaps in your actual briefcase. At home, you view the floppy disk using the Explorer or My Computer. You copy files from the Briefcase on the floppy disk into folders on your hard disk. You open the documents in their folders on the computer at home and edit them.

Before returning to work, you click Update All in the Briefcase on your floppy disk, which copies the edited files from their folders on the hard disk in your home computer into the Briefcase on your floppy disk.

At work, you put your floppy disk in your computer and open the Briefcase using My Computer or the Explorer. You then click Update All to update the documents in their original folders on your computer at work. The most recent version of the files in the Briefcase are copied over their original files in their folders on the hard disk of the computer at work.

Both your computer at home and the computer at work now have the latest versions of the documents. Your Briefcase on the floppy disk also has the latest versions.

Scenario 2

You have a laptop and a desktop computer at work. You want to work on documents on your laptop while you are away from the office.

You have a Briefcase on the desktop of your desktop computer. Copy documents that you are working on into the Briefcase on your desktop computer. Continue working on those documents in their original folders.

When you are finished working on your documents at the office, click Update All in the Briefcase to update all the copies of your documents in the Briefcase based on the originals on your desktop computer.

Connect your laptop to your desktop computer with Direct Cable Connection (DCC) or over the office network. Move the Briefcase from the desktop of your desktop computer to the desktop of your laptop computer.

The files in the Briefcase remember their relationship with the original files in the folders on the hard disk of the office computer. Edit the documents in the Briefcase on your laptop *without copying or moving them out of the Briefcase*.

The next day at work, connect the two computers with DCC. Move the Briefcase from the laptop to the desktop computer. Click Update All in the Briefcase to update the original documents on the desktop computer.

Scenario 3

You want someone whose computer is on your network to work on your files. They will return the files to you when they are done.

Copy your files into your Briefcase on your desktop. Move the Briefcase to the desktop of the other person across the network.

They can work on your files, *never copying them out of the Briefcase*. Later, when they are done, they can move your Briefcase back to the desktop of your computer.

Update all your original files by clicking Update All in the Briefcase on your desktop.

What Does a Briefcase Do?

After you create a Briefcase and copy a file into it, a synchronization relationship, a *sync link*, is maintained between the original file and its copy in the Briefcase. After you have established this sync link, you can edit either the copy in the Briefcase or the original file. If you want to ensure that both the original and the copy are the latest version, choose Update from inside the Briefcase. The later version is copied over the earlier version so both the original and the Briefcase copy are the latest version.

The idea is that you edit either the Briefcase copy or the original copy, but not both, before you perform an update. If both files are edited without an update, you will need to manually edit a combination of the files to create a latest version. See the section later in this chapter entitled *Both the original and the Briefcase copy have been modified* for details on how to do this.

The Briefcase can travel. If it couldn't, it wouldn't be of much use. It is presumed you will edit or work on files in different places sequentially — that you will edit files in one place, carry the Briefcase with the files in it to another location, edit the files in this new location, and later return the Briefcase to the original location. Updates and edits happen sequentially.

Creating a Briefcase

If you chose to install a Briefcase when you set up Windows 95, the Briefcase icon is on your desktop. You can set up this feature using the Custom or Portable setup. If you choose Custom, you'll need to choose to install the Briefcase when given the option.

To create a Briefcase on the desktop, right-click on the desktop, click New, and then Briefcase. You can create Briefcases in any folder by right-clicking in the folder window, clicking New, and then Briefcase.

Putting the Briefcase on the desktop makes it easy to drag files from the Explorer or other folder windows to the Briefcase as long as you can see the Briefcase icon on the desktop. The Briefcase appears in the left pane of the Explorer window connected by a dotted line to the desktop at the top of the pane, as shown in Figure 31-1. This makes it easy to drag files from folders into the Briefcase.

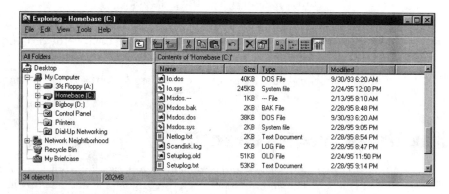

Figure 31-1: An Explorer view that includes a Briefcase. You can drag and drop files from the right pane into the Briefcase in the left pane of the Explorer window.

The dialog box shown in Figure 31-2 is the introduction that Windows 95 provides to the Briefcase. It appears shortly after you create the Briefcase. The Windows 95 help files contain additional help.

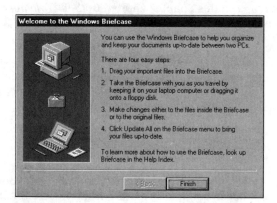

Figure 31-2: This quick overview of the Windows 95 Briefcase appears the first time you create one or when you open the Briefcase for the first time during a session.

Undocumented

You can create a Briefcase on a floppy disk or in a folder other than the desktop folder. After they are created, Briefcases can be moved into any other folder that you like. For additional information, see the section entitled *Moving the Briefcase* later in this chapter.

You can create as many Briefcases as you like. You can name the Briefcases anything you like. You can change the names of any of your Briefcases. This has the possibility of getting out of hand. You have to remember which Briefcase contains the copies of which file.

Copying Files or Folders into a Briefcase

You can use the Explorer, My Computer, or any folder window to copy files and folders to the Briefcase. If the Briefcase is on the desktop you can drag and drop a file or folder from a folder window onto the Briefcase icon.

When you copy files or folders to the Briefcase, they are copied with a *sync link*. The copy in the Briefcase is connected to the original file or folder. If there is a change in the copy or the original, the status of the copy in the Briefcase is changed from Up-to-date to Needs Updating.

You copy every document that you want to work with on another computer into your Briefcase. The originals stay put but you carry the copies in the Briefcase that you take with you.

Moving the Briefcase

Once you copy all the files and folders that you want into the Briefcase, you can move the Briefcase to another computer. You won't want to do this until you have finished editing the original documents for the day. You'll want to move only a fully updated Briefcase to the new computer.

Be sure to close the Briefcase before you try to move it. Otherwise, you will get an error message saying that you have to close it before you move it. It may not be obvious that you have the Briefcase open if you are viewing it in the Explorer. The Briefcase is open if you can see its contents in the Explorer view or in a folder window.

Moving a Briefcase to a floppy disk

One option is to move the Briefcase to a floppy disk. You can drag and drop the Briefcase icon from the desktop to the floppy disk drive icon in your Explorer. If none of the files in the Briefcase is larger than the capacity of the floppy disk, the Briefcase and the files that it contains will be moved to the floppy disk. You won't be able to copy any files that are too big to fit on the floppy disk.

Secret

If there are more files than will fit on one floppy disk, you will be asked to put in additional floppy disks. Unfortunately, the files on the second and later floppy disks will be marked as *orphans*, which means there will be no sync link between these copies and the original files. Because of this feature, a Briefcase that is copied to a floppy disk cannot be any bigger than one floppy disk and still operate as a Briefcase.

The whole point of a Briefcase is to maintain the sync link. While Briefcases can contain orphans, these are no better than regular copies of the original files. This limits Briefcases transported on floppy disks to floppy disk size, which is one reason for multiple Briefcases.

Secret

You should not move the Briefcase off the floppy disk onto the computer at home. If you want to work on the files in the Briefcase at home, copy the files out of the Briefcase on the floppy disk into folders on your home computer's hard disk. This allows you to edit them faster because they are now stored on the hard disk. Just don't copy the Briefcase itself.

When you copy the files from the Briefcase on the floppy disk into folders on the hard disk, a new and additional sync link is developed between the files in the Briefcase and the new files on the computer at home. The files in the Briefcase now have two sync links: one with the original files on the computer at work and one the copies on your hard disk at home.

If you move the Briefcase from the floppy disk to the desktop of the home computer, you will not be able to create the second sync link. If you copy files out of the Briefcase after it is moved to the desktop of the home computer, there will be no connection between these copies and the copies in the Briefcase. The files in the Briefcase will still maintain a sync link with the original files on the computer at work.

You can move the Briefcase from the floppy disk to a folder other than the desktop folder of the home computer. Again, you will not be able to create a second sync link.

So the point here is: don't move the Briefcase off the floppy if you want to maintain the proper sync links. Updating the Briefcase will be easiest if you just leave it on the floppy disk.

You can also move the Briefcase from one computer to another over a network. You can do this over Dial-Up Networking, DCC, or a LAN connection. You won't run into the same size limitations over these connections that you would using a floppy disk.

Moving a Briefcase to a portable computer

Secret

When you move the Briefcase from the desktop of the desktop computer to the desktop of the portable computer, only one sync link is maintained — that between the files in the Briefcase and the files in the folders of the desktop computer. You need to keep the files in the Briefcase on the portable computer and edit them within the Briefcase in order to maintain the sync link.

Moving the Briefcase to the desktop of the portable is the same as moving the Briefcase from a floppy disk to the desktop of the home computer. Once you do that, you need to work with the files on the portable or on the home computer only while they are in the Briefcase.

The Briefcase gives you the ability to copy files back and forth without explicitly copying them or to having to remember which is the latest version. You can still copy files yourself without using the Briefcase if you so desire or if it is easier.

Opening the Briefcase

In some ways, the Briefcase is like any other folder. Double-click its icon on the desktop and it will open into a folder window. Click its icon in the Explorer and its contents will appear in the right pane. Right-click the Briefcase icon on the desktop and choose Explore to open an Explorer view of the Briefcase.

Secret

Say you have moved the Briefcase from the desktop of your desktop computer to the desktop of your portable computer. When you open the Briefcase on the portable, a message window may appear asking if you want to reconnect with the desktop computer. Just click No. This message window appears because Windows 95 is automatically trying to reestablish the link in the Briefcase with the original files across a network that is no longer connected.

Copying Files or Folders from the Briefcase

You have copied your Briefcase from your desktop computer to your portable computer. You should leave your documents in the Briefcase on the desktop of your portable computer. If you copy them out of the Briefcase, then the copies in the folders on the hard disk of the portable have no relationship to the files in the Briefcase.

On the other hand, it is a good idea to copy the files from the Briefcase on a floppy disk to the hard disk of your computer at home. The second sync link is created and you can edit your files on the hard disk.

Secret

Update the Briefcase on the floppy disk before you take it back to the office. Update the files on the office computer from the Briefcase on the floppy disk. The Briefcase on the floppy disk can be left on the floppy disk or moved back onto the desktop on the office computer.

Determining the Status of Files or Folders in Your Briefcase

Copying files and folders to the Briefcase establishes a sync link between the original files and the copies in the Briefcase. If any of the files (either the originals or copies) are modified, then the Briefcase is aware that the files are out of sync and need to be updated.

If you have just finished placing files or folders into a Briefcase, their status is shown as Up-to-date. The files in the Briefcase haven't yet been modified. If you now edit the original files or the files in the Briefcase, you will need to perform an update to get both the original and the copy to be the latest version, that is, to get them in sync.

STEPS

Determining Briefcase File Status

Step 1. Double-click the Briefcase icon on your desktop. If the Briefcase isn't showing the details view, click View on the Briefcase menu bar and then Details.

Step 2. The status of each file and folder is displayed in the third column of the Details view and the possibilities are Up-to-date, Needs Updating, Orphan, or Unavailable.

Step 3. The second column is labeled Sync Copy In. Here is where you find the location of the original file or folder. An open Briefcase displaying these columns is shown in Figure 31-3.

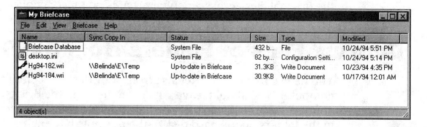

Figure 31-3: An open Briefcase. The first column is the file name, the second column shows the folder name of the folder where the synched file is sorted, and the third column gives the current status of the link between the two files.

Step 4. Further details about a particular file or folder are obtained by right-clicking it, selecting Properties, and clicking the Update Status tab. The Update Status Properties sheet for an example file is shown in Figure 31-4.

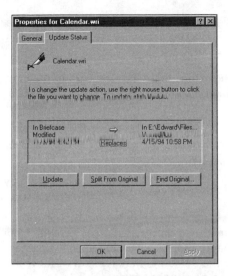

Figure 31-4: The Update Status Properties sheet for a file in the Briefcase. By right-clicking a file in the Briefcase and picking Properties, you can determine its status by clicking the Update Status tab.

Updating Files and Folders

If you edit your original files after you have placed them in the Briefcase, you will want to update them before you move your Briefcase.

When you bring your Briefcase back from home to your computer at work with the original files, you will want to update your original files based on their new modified versions in the Briefcase.

If you have copied your files or folders from the Briefcase on the floppy disk onto your portable, you will want to update the files in the Briefcase after you made changes to them in their new folders.

The files are marked Needs Updating if you have edited or modified either the file/folder outside the Briefcase or the copies inside. Updating the files/folders will ensure that both the original and the copy in the Briefcase are the latest version.

The default action of the Briefcase is to replace the file that has an earlier date with the file that has a later date. You can override this action if you so desire.

STEPS

Updating Files and Folders

Step 1. Click those files in the Briefcase that you want to update. Use Ctrl+click or Shift+click if you have more than one file. If you are going to update all the files in the Briefcase, you don't need to high light any of them.

Step 2. Click Briefcase in the menu bar of the Briefcase.

Step 3. Click either Update All (to update all the files and folders in the Briefcase) or Update Selection (to update only the highlighted files and folder).

Step 4. The dialog box shown in Figure 31-5 will pop up and allow you to continue the update as indicated or make some changes. Right-click near the horizontal arrow between file names to see how you can change the default action. A small window/menu will pop up to allow you to choose which action to take.

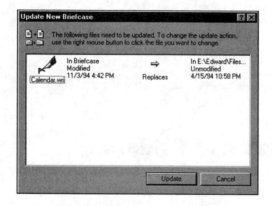

Figure 31-5: The Update New Briefcase dialog box. This box appears when you click either Briefcase, Update All or Briefcase, Update Selection.

Step 5. Change the arrow's direction if you like or skip this particular update. Merge is not an option in most cases, unless an application has been modified to handle merges.

Step 6. Click Update.

You have now synched the files and their copies in the Briefcase. You may not have synched the files in the Briefcase with the originals or, conversely, with the files on the portable or home computer. You will need to move the newly updated Briefcase to the other computer and then update the files once again. The default action will be to update the older files on the computer from the newly updated Briefcase.

Multiple syncs

Undocumented

The Briefcase can keep a sync between the original files on the computer at the office and the copies in the Briefcase as well as between the copies on the home computer and the Briefcase. It is this ability to keep multiple sync links for each file, depending on where the Briefcase is stored, that allows you to copy files out of the Briefcase on the floppy disk into other folders on the home computer.

You can see this feature in action when you open the Briefcase. The Sync Copy In column in the Briefcase shows the relationship of the copies inside the Briefcase to the files outside the Briefcase. If you move the Briefcase on a floppy disk to another computer and copy the files inside the Briefcase on floppy disk to folders outside the Briefcase, the Sync Copy In column will change to the new file folders. Moving the Briefcase back to the original computer causes the Sync Copy In column to change back to the original folders.

Both the original and the Briefcase copy have been modified

The Briefcase doesn't really solve all the problems of keeping all your files up to date. For example, the merge feature has to be implemented by third-party developers so that their applications can, with some action from you, intelligently update their files.

It is quite easy to modify the original files on your computer at work and forget to update their copies in the Briefcase. Later, you modify these non-updated copies in the Briefcase on the computer at home. You now have two files with different modifications to them and no easy way to sort out those modifications.

The Briefcase does give you fair warning. If you modify your file outside the Briefcase, the file is marked as Needs Updating in the Briefcase. If you edit both the copy in the Briefcase and the file outside, then the Briefcase keeps track of the fact that both have changed. When you go to update, you are informed of this sad fact.

If you now try to update your original files you may be wiping out important modifications that you made to them.

STEPS

Dealing with Multiple Modifications

Step 1. Click the files in the Briefcase that you want to update. Use Ctrl+click or Shift-click if you have more than one file. If you are going to update all the files in the Briefcase, you don't need to high-light any of them.

Step 2. Click Briefcase in the menu bar of the Briefcase.

Step 3. Click either Update All (to update all the files and folders in the Briefcase) or Update Selection (to update only the highlighted files and folder).

Step 4. When you try to update the files, Skip (both changed) will appear in the Update Briefcase dialog box.

Step 5. Right-click the file in the Briefcase that has been updated on both computers. If the application that you used to created these files has the ability to merge files, click the Merge menu option on the right button menu.

Step 6. If Merge is not an option on the menu, it is possible to capture both sets of changes and merge the files manually.

Step 7. Create a third file and copy in the original file and the Briefcase file. You can these edit or modify this third file to get rid of the redun-dant information, but manually choose which updates to keep.

Step 8. Copy this third file over the original or over the Briefcase copy and then perform an update.

Breaking the Sync Link

It is possible to break up the sync relationship between the original file and its Briefcase copy. You might want to do this in order to create a new document and leave the older version as a backup.

STEPS

Orphaning a Briefcase File or Folder

Step 1. Right-click the file in the Briefcase folder and click Properties.

Step 2. Click the Update Status tab.

Step 3. Click Split From Original.

If you change the name of the file outside the Briefcase, you will orphan the file inside the Briefcase. To find the copy of the file outside the Briefcase, click Find Original.

Data Files

One of the possible scenarios for the use of the Briefcase involves salespeople keeping track of and updating customer files while out in the field. Back at the office, the customer files are also being changed. When the salesperson comes back to the office, it is time to update the customer files on the office computer, but data files on both computers have been modified.

The Briefcase doesn't solve this problem, but rather provides a standard means for others to solve the problem. Database developers are encouraged to use the Briefcase facility and combine it with a means of merging data files. This would include highlighting changed records in the data and allowing the salesperson (or someone else) to manually decide which modifications to accept.

The Briefcase doesn't provide any means of copying a file over multiple floppy disks. This means that large data files in the Briefcase will need to be moved over networks, including DCC, Dial-Up Network, a LAN, or others.

Summary

▶ In this chapter, we describe how to create and use the Briefcase to "carry" files and folders between computers.

▶ If you want to make sure that the files on your desktop computer at the office and your home computer are the same, the Briefcase is for you.

▶ If you use a portable and a desktop computer, the Briefcase can help you make sure that your computers are in sync.

▶ If you have someone else work on your files, you can send them a Briefcase full of them to work on.

▶ We describe how to avoid losing the sync relationship between your master files and your copies.

Chapter 32

E-mail (and Faxes) Everywhere

In This Chapter

If you want to send e-mail or a fax, Microsoft provides a heavy-duty application that takes these functions to the next level. We discuss:

▶ Quickly configuring Microsoft Exchange to send and receive a fax

▶ Sending and receiving e-mail over the Internet, CompuServe, and the Microsoft Network

▶ Dealing with the funny ways Exchange behaves, which are different from the rest of Windows 95

▶ Using command-line switches to view message headers and begin composition of new messages

▶ Using message stores to manage your documents

▶ Renaming message stores and address books

▶ Composing mail from many different sources

▶ Creating a Microsoft Mail Postoffice for your workgroup

▶ Monitoring your phone line for incoming faxes without having to exit Exchange to send e-mail

But, I Just Want to Send a Fax

You may have imagined Microsoft as a bunch of wildly individualistic nerds being overseen by a boy genius. Nice image, but Microsoft Exchange demonstrates that Microsoft is also a corporation — ponderous (it takes its own sweet time loading up in memory), thick (you really have to drill down to find what you want), and reliant on hidden human experts (postoffice managers).

Microsoft Exchange (which Microsoft calls its "universal messaging client") was built assuming you are connected to a vast empire of corporate mail (just like at Microsoft). Microsoft felt that what you needed most was a means to control and view this sea of memos. The ability to quickly and easily send and receive a bit of e-mail (or fax) got lost in the design process (requiring one Wizard to bring back some ease of use and another to ease installation).

Microsoft Exchange is an e-mail and fax tool. You use it to send, receive, and store e-mail and faxes from numerous different sources (mail delivery services). We'll use this chapter to blast through all the armor surrounding Microsoft Exchange and get you up and running quickly with this tank of a product. Once the steady stream of messages begins pouring in, you'll learn to appreciate its gift for mail (and document) management.

In June, 1995, Microsoft stripped out a good chunk of the functionality of the Windows 95 Microsoft Exchange client. Their plans as of this writing were to ship a special Exchange client when they shipped the Exchange server later in 1995. This Exchange client was not to be made available to Windows 95 users who did not purchase Microsoft Exchange server (the vast majority of us). We consider this an unfortunate decision because Microsoft took out some very useful features such as signature lines (Auto Text), shared folders (found in Microsoft Mail 3.2), message filters, mark all messages as read, message threading, and form composition. This reduces significantly Microsoft's claim for Exchange client as a "universal messaging client."

At the end of the Windows 95 custom setup, the Microsoft Exchange Setup Wizard takes over and steps you through the setup process. It sets up a default "profile" with the information and mail delivery services that you desire. You'll most likely need to change the properties of your profile and information services after you go through the Windows 95 setup to get things working right, so we'll show you how to do that.

Yes, But, I *Still* Just Want to Send a Fax

Here's how to install, set up, and run Exchange so you can send a fax.

STEPS

Installing, Setting Up and Running Microsoft Exchange
to Send a Fax

Step 1. If you haven't yet installed Windows 95, be sure to choose the Custom option in Windows 95 Setup. When you are presented with the Select Components dialog box, click the Microsoft Exchange and Microsoft Fax check boxes. This will install the software that you need to send faxes. Jump to Step 5.

Step 2. If you have already installed Windows 95, but you didn't install Microsoft Exchange and Microsoft Fax, click the Start button, then Settings, and then Control Panel. Double-click the Add/Remove Programs icon.

Step 3. Click the Windows Setup tab and then click the Microsoft Exchange and Microsoft Fax check boxes. Click OK. You'll need to restart Windows 95 when prompted to do so.

Step 4. Click the Start button, then Settings, and then Control Panel. Double-click the Mail and Fax icon in the Control Panel. This starts the Microsoft Exchange Setup Wizard if the previous steps haven't already done so.

Step 5. If you have a fax modem that has been detected correctly by Windows 95 Setup, it will be acknowledged by the Microsoft Exchange Setup Wizard. Otherwise, this Wizard will run the Modem Detection Wizard. You'll to need to step through the modem detection process to be sure that your modem can deliver faxes (for details turn to Chapter 25).

Step 6. You will be asked by the Exchange Setup Wizard to help configure a "profile" that can include the Microsoft Fax as a mail delivery service. Since you just want to send a fax, go ahead and add Microsoft Fax to the profile when given the opportunity. Step through the Exchange Setup Wizard and accept the default values. You will need to type in your phone number at one point. Click Finish.

If you have previously created a profile, you can add Microsoft Fax to it by double-clicking the Mail and Fax icon in the Control Panel, clicking the Add button, and then highlighting Microsoft Fax.

Step 7. Click the Start button, and then Programs, Accessories, Fax, Compose New Fax. This starts the Compose New Fax Wizard.

Step 8. Click Next in the first dialog box of the Compose New Fax Wizard. Enter a known fax number in the first field on the second dialog box in the following format:

[fax:*nnn-nnnn*]

Click the Next button, and the following Next button as well.

Step 9. Enter a subject and a message in the next dialog box. This dialog box isn't much of a fax editor, and in fact, there are much better ways to compose a fax, which we cover later in this chapter in the section entitled *Microsoft Fax*. You can attach a file (document) to your fax using the next dialog box. Click the Next button, the next Next button, and the Finish button.

A fax with your message will now be sent to the number that you typed in during Step 8.

If you want to receive a fax, carry out the previous steps and then double-click the Inbox icon on your desktop. If your current profile includes the Microsoft Fax, a small yellow phone will appear on your Taskbar. You have the option of editing just how the phone is answered by double-clicking the Mail and Fax icon in your Control Panel. See the rest of this chapter for more details.

Microsoft Exchange Features

Here are some of the features included with Microsoft Exchange:

- Send, receive, store, view, and store e-mail, faxes and other documents using a variety of mail delivery services including Microsoft Mail (over your local area network), CompuServe, the Internet (if you purchase Microsoft Plus!), Microsoft Fax, and the Microsoft Network

- Include files, documents, and OLE 2 objects in your messages

- A complete workgroup version of the Microsoft Mail Server (the Microsoft Mail postoffice that is identical to the one created by WFWG 3.11, so that WFWG 3.11 users and Windows 95 users can share the same postoffice)

- The workgroup version of Microsoft Mail Server, which is upgradable to the enterprise-wide version of Microsoft Mail Server or (when it exists) the Microsoft Exchange Server

- Create and store multiple Exchange configurations (profiles)

- Universal address book (that is, an address book that can be used by and incorporated into many different applications)

- Customizable Exchange Toolbar

- Remote access and remote message header preview (call your Microsoft Mail postoffice at work from your computer at home)

- Send formatted documents over the Internet transparently using MIME or UUENCODE

- Send editable files through MS Fax with binary file transfer (attach a Word for Windows file to a fax message and ship it to someone with MS Fax running on their computer)

- Send e-mail or faxes from Windows applications

- Print faxes from Windows applications

- Exchange public key encrypted faxes

- Send faxes over a shared fax modem on your local area network

- Create fax cover pages with a cover page designer/editor

- Send a note on the fax cover page without having to send another fax page

- Use a really cool fax viewer

- Retrieve, without having to use a touch tone phone, faxes (and files) from fax-on-demand systems

- A general OLE 2 data store that can be used to store, organize, find, and view any of your documents — a much more powerful version of a file management system than the FAT or VFAT

Or Lack Thereof

So what features are missing from Microsoft Exchange?

- Inability to transparently store messages that come from the Microsoft Network bulletin boards, CompuServe forums, and Internet newsgroups

- No online conferences, forums, or conference message threading

- No optical character recognition (Exchange can't turn a Group 3 type fax into an editable document)

- No fax annotations

- Only one e-mail address per address-book entry

- No automated distribution of faxes received by a shared fax across a local area network to the intended recipients

- No ">>" symbols around quotes in replies

- No shared folders (Microsoft has stated that this feature *may* go back into the product before it is released to manufacturing)

- No automated signatures (AutoText)

- No message filtering

- Limited message organizing

- No spelling checker (If you have installed a 32-bit word processor with a spelling checker, such as Office for Windows 95, that spelling checker *will* be used by Exchange. You'll find it under the Tools, Options menu item.)

Tip Exchange can eat up resources and swap space. If you experience trouble running Exchange, be sure that you have 20MB of free disk space on the hard disk that includes the Windows 95 dynamic swap file. Also, Microsoft recommends a minimum of 8 megabytes of RAM.

Microsoft Exchange Is Its Own Product

The people who wrote Microsoft Exchange are not the same ones who wrote the rest of Windows 95, or if they are, they aren't talking to themselves. Throughout the Windows 95 beta cycle, Microsoft Exchange and the Microsoft Network were considered to be the most problematic (and furthest from finished) parts of Windows 95. Just before the "final" beta (near the end of March, 1995) that was to be distributed as the Windows 95 Preview product, the Internet mail client was pulled and put into Microsoft Plus!.

In May, the CompuServe mail client was pulled as Microsoft negotiated with CompuServe to determine which company would support the product. In addition, some of the mail document-management capability was cut from Exchange. Microsoft said they would add this capability back into the Exchange client that would be included with its Exchange server. Unfortunately, because the Exchange server will not be purchased by many Microsoft Windows 95 users, we lose significant functionality.

Undocumented

As just one example of the Exchange's own personality, check out the column buttons in the right pane of an Exchange window. Clicking any of the column buttons orders the message headers within the current folder in your message store by that column. This is similar to how the details view works in a folder or Explorer window when it orders files by name, date, and so on.

Microsoft Exchange has a little triangle that appears in the button in the column that orders the messages. There is no such triangle in the details view of a folder or Explorer window. Also, in the details view, if you want to switch the file order from descending to ascending (and vice versa), left-click the column button once more. In Exchange, you right-click the column buttom and choose Sort Ascending or Sort Descending. The triangle points up or down depending on which sort order you use.

Hold Ctrl and click the column button to order the messages in ascending order. Click the column button again (without holding Ctrl) to order them in descending order.

Undocumented

There are other examples of the systemic differences between Exchange and Windows 95. Compare the Message Find feature in Exchange (Tools, Find on the Exchange menu bar) with the Find feature in the Explorer. Notice that you can customize the Exchange Toolbar, but not the Toolbar found in a folder or Explorer window.

Microsoft Exchange creates a configuration (*ini*) file, Exchng32.ini. Don't these guys know about the Registry? It also will use Msmail.ini for backward compatibility if you previously used Microsoft Mail 3.2.

Microsoft Exchange is a large and complex application, even in its stripped-down form. It includes a complete workgroup edition of Microsoft Mail Server and e-mail clients for MSN and CompuServe. Microsoft Exchange includes Microsoft Fax as just a part of the product. If you purchased Microsoft Plus!, Exchange serves as a client of Internet mail as well as a sophisticated mail management system and universal address book.

Any of these capabilities are worthy of separate Windows software products. In fact, they are available in separate products from other vendors.

Microsoft Exchange is almost as complicated and deep as the Windows 95 operating system itself. Detailing every aspect of Microsoft Exchange would require a book almost as thick as the rest of this book. We'll show you where the interesting stuff is hiding and what to watch out for.

Installing Microsoft Exchange

You can install Microsoft Exchange during your Windows 95 Setup, or later using the Add/Remove Programs icon in your Control Panel.

Installing Exchange is not particularly difficult. You just need to click the Microsoft Exchange (and Microsoft Fax) check boxes during Windows 95 Setup. You'll click the Microsoft Exchange and Microsoft Fax check boxes in the Windows Setup dialog box if you use the Add/Remove Program icon in your Control Panel. Turn to Chapter 3 for more details about setting up Windows 95.

Tip

The Microsoft Network and Microsoft Fax can't be installed unless Microsoft Exchange is already installed, or installed at the same time. If you want to uninstall Microsoft Exchange, you will be warned that MSN and MS Fax can't operate without it and will be uninstalled also.

Microsoft Exchange command line switches

The Inbox icon on the desktop starts Microsoft Exchange and puts the focus on the Inbox. The focus is on the Inbox (the Exchange default) when the program Exchng32.exe is invoked (as long as there isn't a %1 parameter on the command line that invokes Microsoft Exchange).

You can't change what double-clicking the Inbox icon does, but you can add a Microsoft Exchange icon to your desktop that opens Exchange with the focus on something other than the Inbox (see Chapter 10 for instructions on creating Shortcuts).

Undocumented

You can also change what clicking the Microsoft Exchange menu item on the Start menu does by adding a command line parameter after Exchng32.exe. If you add /b, you will now open the New Message composition portion of Exchange (see *Creating and Sending Mail* later in this chapter). If you add /i, you open View message headers (see *Remote Access to Microsoft Mail* later in this chapter).

Other legitimate command line parameters for Exchng32.exe are /f and /p, but they work (for opening and printing a file, respectively) only if a message file (a file with the *msg* extension) is specified in the command line or by double-clicking a message file in a folder or Explorer window. For example: Exchange32 *filename*.msg /f.

The Microsoft Exchange Setup Wizard

Installing Exchange invokes the Microsoft Exchange Setup Wizard. This Wizard creates a "profile." We get into profiles in the next section. You choose which mail delivery services will be part of your default profile (named MS Exchange Settings). Unless you've done this a bunch already, go ahead and let the Wizard configure a profile for you as much as possible and don't click "Manually configure information services" in the Wizard's first dialog box.

The Exchange Setup Wizard doesn't let you configure all the properties that you'll want to, and you'll need to go back later and review the numerous properties associated with each profile and each mail delivery service. The Wizard will prompt you for different information depending on which mail delivery services you choose to attach to a profile.

Exchange Profiles

Windows 95 presents you with hardware profiles, user profiles, and Exchange profiles. They are not related to each other in any way and do not interact. You can set up user profiles (for different users) on the same computer and also different Exchange profiles for each of these users. Logging on as a given user (user profiles) does not connect you to the Exchange profile that you might want to associate with that user.

The Exchange Setup Wizard steps you through the configuration of a default profile named MS Exchange Settings. This may be the only profile you ever need. You can edit this profile at any time to reflect the way you wish to send and receive e-mail and faxes. You can kind of ignore profiles if you only use this one.

You'll want additional profiles if:

- More than one person uses the same computer, so each user can have his or her own message store

- Your computer is sometimes locally connected to a network, and sometimes calls into a network from a remote location using a modem and connects to a Microsoft Mail postoffice on the network

- You want different profiles for different information or mail delivery services

Tip

You can't change the name of the default profile during the Windows 95 Setup or when you run the Exchange Setup Wizard for the first time (unless you click the "Manually configure information services" button). Later, you can make a copy of this profile, change its name, and erase the original profile.

Many Windows 95 beta testers experienced problems if they had more than one mail delivery service associated with a given Exchange profile. If you find Exchange attempting to connect to more than one mail delivery service, create separate profiles for each mail delivery service you use. Create a profile with two services and see if they get along, and then try a profile with three, and so on.

An Exchange profile is just a specific set of information services. These services include:

- Message store(s)

- Your personal address book and perhaps other address books

- E-mail (and fax) delivery service(s)

- The location of your postoffice (which Microsoft insists on spelling as one word) if you are connected to Microsoft Mail

If you configure your MS Exchange Settings profile with the information services that work for you, you don't have to do anything else. You can forget about Exchange profiles and just double-click the Inbox on your desktop to use Exchange.

Personal Information Store

A *message store* is a database of messages (stored in one file). It includes your message inbox and outbox, as well as other subdivisions (folders). The default filename for the message store is Mailbox.pst and it is found by default in the Exchange folder (directory).

The message store starts with the default name Personal Information Store and is referred to in Exchange Properties sheets as Personal Folders. You have the option of renaming this message store and creating additional stores. You need only one message store and can store all your messages from all information services in this single store.

You might create other special-purpose message stores. For instance, you might create different message stores for:

- Archival messages
- Messages from different information services
- Messages for different users
- Documents unrelated to messages

Different message stores can have different filenames and can be stored in different Windows 95 folders (directories).

Address books

Your *address book* is a database and, like your message store, it is stored in one file. Your default address book is the file Mailbox.pab in the Exchange folder. Its default name is Personal Address Book. You can name your address book anything you like and store it wherever you want.

If you are connected to a local area network, you will find address books tied to your postoffice(s). If you are using Microsoft Mail, you will find a postoffice address list on the computer that houses your workgroup postoffice.

You will no doubt want to store the addresses of your regular e-mail correspondents in your personal address book. A system or workgroup administrator may maintain the postoffice address list. You can send mail to correspondents on that list by choosing names from it.

Other mailing lists are maintained by other information services to which you connect. The Microsoft Network maintains a list of all the people who have accounts on it. You can keep a separate CompuServe mailing list on your computer if you like.

A profile can have only one personal address book attached to it.

Mail delivery services

Using Microsoft Exchange, you can connect to the following e-mail and fax delivery services:

- Microsoft Mail
- The Microsoft Network (MSN)
- CompuServe
- Internet mail
- Microsoft Fax
- Other third-party e-mail delivery services compliant with Messaging Application Programming Interface (MAPI)

The MAPI drivers that these mail delivery services use to connect to Microsoft Exchange are considered by Microsoft to be personal gateways — gateways that connect Microsoft Exchange (the client) to another mail system. Microsoft sells other gateways that link Microsoft Mail Server to other e-mail systems.

Microsoft Mail

Windows 95 (like Windows for Workgroups 3.11) comes with a workgroup version of Microsoft Mail. You can create and administer a workgroup postoffice that can be shared by all the members of a workgroup whether they are running Windows 95 or WFWG 3.11. In most cases you will want to have only one postoffice for your workgroup.

If you want to exchange mail using the Microsoft Mail connection with postoffices outside your workgroup, you'll need to upgrade the computer with the postoffice to the Microsoft Mail Server by installing the Microsoft Mail Postoffice upgrade, or, when it is available, Microsoft Exchange Server. Gateways to other mail systems are available and work with Microsoft Mail Server or Microsoft Exchange Server.

The Microsoft Network

The Microsoft Network (MSN) is Microsoft's online (over the telephone lines) information service. You can send and receive e-mail to and from other Microsoft Network subscribers or over MSN's Internet connection to and from anyone with an Internet e-mail address. MSN will provide full Internet access as well as its own interest areas.

Note that Microsoft Exchange is not used for messages on the MSN bulletin boards.

CompuServe

If you have a CompuServe account, you can have Microsoft Exchange call your account (using its TAPI-compatible dialer) and see if you have any mail. Of course, you can also send out mail through CompuServe.

You can send and receive mail to and from CompuServe subscribers, or to and from anyone with an Internet e-mail address.

Secret

Unfortunately, you can't send and receive messages that are posted on CompuServe forums, even if the messages are addressed to you. You'll still need to use WinCIM or some other CompuServe interface program to manage your forum message traffic.

Internet

If you have an account with an Internet service provider, you can use Microsoft Exchange as your e-mail client. You can send and receive regular ASCII Internet e-mail, as well as e-mail formatted as MIME (Multipurpose Internet Mail Extensions) or UUENCODE.

The Internet delivery service capability is available only if you purchase the separate Microsoft Plus! software package. The Internet client will connect to SMTP (Simple Mail Transport Protocol) and POP3 (Postoffice Protocol version 3) mail boxes. You'll need to bind TCP/IP to your Dial-Up Adapter if you call into an Internet Service provider, or to your network card if you access the Internet through a server on your local area network. You'll find details about TCP/IP and Dial-Up Networking in Chapter 33.

Microsoft Fax

You can send and receive faxes if you install the MS Fax delivery service in one of your profiles. Faxes can be sent through the fax/modem card in your computer or over a shared fax modem in your workgroup on a computer running Windows 95.

Third-party MAPI mail delivery systems

Other companies can (and may already) provide MAPI interfaces to their mail systems. For example, Novell may provide a MAPI interface to its HMS mail. If so, you can configure an Exchange profile to use this mail delivery service just as you would any other.

Tip

You can't use Exchange to receive e-mail from or deliver e-mail to services that don't have MAPI drivers. This includes almost all the bulletin boards without Internet services that are run by small companies and individuals. Neither AOL nor Prodigy had announced support for MAPI before the release of Windows 95.

Creating Exchange profiles

You don't have to create Exchange profiles, because you already created a profile when you installed Microsoft Exchange. You can edit that profile, if you like, so it matches your needs. See *Editing Exchange Profiles* later in this chapter.

If you want to create a new Exchange profile, you have two entry points. To add a new profile when you only have one, take the following steps:

STEPS

Creating a New Exchange Profile

Step 1.   Click the Start button, then Settings, and then Control Panel.

Step 2.   Double-click the Mail and Fax icon.

Step 3.   Click Show Profiles.

Step 4.   Your current profiles are displayed in the list box of the Microsoft Exchange Profiles dialog box, as shown in Figure 32-1. Click Add to start the Microsoft Exchange Setup Wizard or click Copy to make a copy of the highlighted profile. You can edit it later.

Figure 32-1: The Microsoft Exchange Profiles dialog box.

Undocumented

If you have more than one Exchange profile and you chose the option to pick the profile you will use when you start Microsoft Exchange, you can start the Microsoft Exchange Setup Wizard by double-clicking the Inbox icon on your desktop and then clicking the New button. You are given the opportunity to choose a profile when you double-click the Inbox icon if you have previously edited one of your profiles as detailed in the following section.

Editing Exchange profiles

You can edit your Exchange profile(s), not just to change the properties of a given profile, but also to change the properties of an address book, a message store, or a mail delivery service.

You start editing an Exchange profile in one of two ways. You can double-click the Mail and Fax icon in the Control Panel, click Show Profiles (if you have more than one), highlight a particular profile, if you have more than one, in the Microsoft Exchange Profiles dialog box, and then click the Properties button.

Or you can double-click the Inbox icon on your desktop, and then click Tools, Options from the Exchange menu bar.

The second method gives you access to more properties to edit than the first. Just click Tools, Options in the Exchange menu bar. The first method allows you to pick which profile you are going to edit before you do so. The second method also lets you select a profile to edit, but only if you have previously configured a profile to allow for this choice. The following section shows you how to do that.

Picking among profiles at Exchange startup

In order to configure Exchange to allow you to pick which profile to use when you start Exchange (assuming you have already created more than one profile), take the following steps:

STEPS

Picking Your Own Startup Profile

Step 1. Double-click the Inbox icon on your desktop.

Step 2. Click Tools, Options on the Exchange menu bar. The Microsoft Exchange General Properties sheet will be displayed on your desktop, as shown in Figure 32-2.

Step 3. Click the "Prompt for a profile to be used" radio button underneath "When starting Microsoft Exchange."

Step 4. Click OK.

(continued)

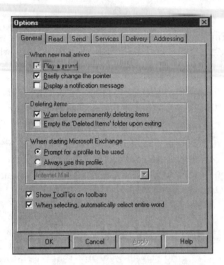

Figure 32-2: The Microsoft Exchange General Properties sheet. Click Pick the profile that will be used to allow you to choose which profile to use when you start up Microsoft Exchange.

The next time you double-click the Inbox icon on your desktop, a dialog box will be displayed that lets you choose among different profiles.

Adding or removing information services

When you originally create a profile, you have the option to choose which mail delivery services will be included in it. You can later go back and remove or add additional mail delivery services and message stores or change to another personal address book.

To add or remove information services, you have two options.

STEPS

Adding or Removing Information Services

Step 1. Click the Start button, then Settings, and then Control Panel.

Step 2. Double-click the Mail and Fax icon.

Step 3. If you want to add or remove information services in the profile that would normally be started when you double-click the Inbox icon on your desktop, click the Add or Remove button. If, you want to add or remove information services from another profile, click the Show Profiles button first, highlight the desired profile, and then click the Properties button. The profile's Services Properties sheet will be displayed, as shown in Figure 32-3.

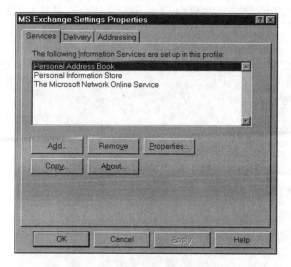

Figure 32-3: The Services Properties sheet of an Exchange profile. Click Add or Remove to add or remove an information service.

Step 4. Click the Add button to add a new information service or the Remove button to remove the highlighted service.

You can also get to a profile's Services Properties sheet by double-clicking the Inbox icon on your desktop, clicking Tools, Options on the Exchange menu bar, and then the Services tab. The Properties sheet shown in Figure 32-3 appears, allowing you to add or remove information services.

When adding a mail delivery or other information service, you may be prompted to configure the service. To do this, edit the Properties sheets associated with that service. We discuss editing the properties of individual mail delivery services in the *Mail Delivery Services* section later in this chapter.

Editing Information services

Each information service — personal address book, message stores, and mail delivery services — has associated Properties sheets. To edit these Properties sheets, you only have to highlight the information service in the profile's Services Properties sheet and click the Properties button.

Each mail delivery service has its own unique set of Properties sheets as determined by the characteristics of the mail delivery system. The first of eight tabbed Properties sheets for Microsoft Mail (the Connection Properties sheet) is shown in Figure 32-4. We discuss editing the individual properties of the different mail delivery services in the section later in this chapter entitled *Choosing Mail Delivery Services*.

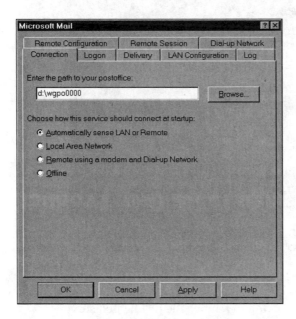

Figure 32-4: The Microsoft Mail Connection Properties sheet.
Enter the path for your postoffice in the first field.

Properties for the message store can be set by highlighting the name of the message store in a profile's Services Properties sheet, and then clicking the Properties button. We discuss these additional properties in the *Message stores* section later in this chapter.

Not only can you change the properties of your address book, but you can change the properties of each address (or individual) in the address book. On the Exchange Toolbar click the address book icon, then double-click a name in your address book. We discuss address books further in the *Address books* section later in this chapter.

Choosing Mail Delivery Services

The first step in creating a profile is choosing the mail delivery service(s) that will be included in the profile. Each mail delivery service has a specific set of dialog boxes which get included in the Exchange Setup Wizard if that mail delivery service is chosen for inclusion in the profile being created.

Each mail delivery service will have its own set of Properties sheets. Figure 32-4 shows the first of eight Properties sheets for Microsoft Mail delivery service. Most of the values in these Properties sheets are not accessible during profile creation. To change these values, you need to edit these sheets after you create a profile.

Internet Mail Properties sheets

In the Internet Mail Server field of the Internet Mail General Properties sheet (as shown in Figure 32-5), you can enter either the IP address or the name of your Internet mail server. You get the name of your POP3 and your SMTP mail server from your Internet Service Provider when you contact them to establish an account. Type the name of your POP3 mail server in this field.

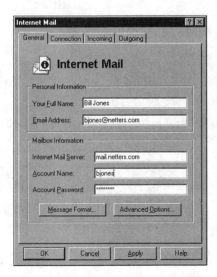

Figure 32-5: The Internet Mail General Properties sheet.

If your SMTP mail server has a different name, click Advanced and type in the name of your SMTP mail server. You can type in friendly names if your service provider has a DNS (Domain Name Server) server. Otherwise, type in IP addresses.

The SMTP server will handle outgoing mail, and the POP3 server will handle incoming mail. Internet mail is available only if you have Microsoft Plus!.

You have the option of sending outgoing messages in either MIME or UUENCODE format. If the person that you are writing to has an e-mail reader that can handle the MIME format, you'll want to use this higher level format. You can send messages that include files that have been inserted into the messages as Attachments if you use the MIME format.

The UUENCODE format is a tagged ASCII format. Your recipient will need an UUDECODE program to translate your message into a formatted text message. Click the Message Format button on the Internet General Properties sheet to choose between MIME and UUENCODE.

Unfortunately, you can't just send a text message without MIME and without UUENCODE. If you send a MIME message you'll find an "=" at the end of each of your sentences. Not real pretty. If you send UUENCODE, there will be an unreadable section at the end of your e-mail message.

CompuServe Properties sheets

The CompuServe mail delivery service comes with its own unique set of Properties sheets. You can get to them by taking the following steps:

STEPS

CompuServe Properties sheets

Step 1. Click the Start button, then Settings, and then Control Panel.

Step 2. Double-click the Mail and Fax icon.

Step 3. Highlight a profile that contains the CompuServe mail delivery service. Click the Properties button. Highlight CompuServe Mail. Click Properties.

Message Stores

Microsoft Exchange refers to message stores as Personal Information Stores or Personal Folders. Messages that you receive and messages that you create are stored in a message store file, which is also a database. Messages are stored in folders in the message store.

You can have multiple message stores, although one is plenty. The default message store (Exchange\Mailbox.pst) is created for you when you set up Microsoft Exchange.

A message store comes with a standard set of folders: Inbox, Outbox, Sent Items, and Deleted Items. You can add additional folders to conveniently order your messages.

Adding a message store to a profile

As a message store is one of the Exchange information services, you can follow the steps detailed in the section earlier in this chapter entitled *Adding or removing information services* to add a new message store to a profile. Then, take the following steps:

STEPS

Adding a Message Store to a Profile

Step 1. When the Add Service to Profile dialog box (as shown in Figure 32-6) is displayed on your desktop, double-click Personal Folders in the list box.

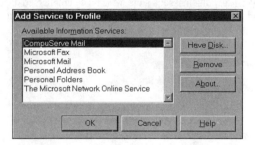

Figure 32-6: The Add Service to Profile dialog box. Double-click the information service you want to add to the profile. In this case, double-click Personal Folders.

(continued)

STEPS *(continued)*

Adding a Message Store to a Profile

Step 2.   You'll be asked to provide a name and location for the message store file. You can put a message store file wherever you like. You can name it whatever you like, but make sure that its extension is *pst*.

Step 3.   You now have the option of renaming this particular message store as shown in Figure 32-7. You can also protect this message store with a password.

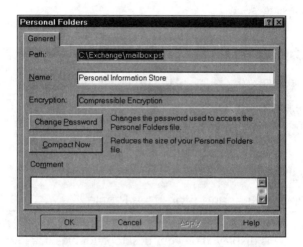

Figure 32-7: The dialog box that appears when you're creating Personal Folders. You can give the message store a password if you like. If the message store file is on a compressed drive and you want to encrypt it, choose Compressible Encryption.

Step 4.   Click OK.

Changing a message store's name

You can change the long descriptive name of an existing message store by taking the following steps:

STEPS

Changing a Message Store's Name

Step 1. Double-click the Inbox icon on your desktop.

Step 2. Click Tools, Services on the Exchange menu bar. Highlight the name of the message store you want to change.

Step 3. Type a new name in the name field and click OK.

Which message store?

If you have only one message store, all the messages go there. If you have more than one, you can specify which one to use by taking the following steps:

STEPS

Specifying the Active Message Store

Step 1. Double-click the Inbox icon on your desktop.

Step 2. Click Tools, Options on the Exchange menu bar.

Step 3. Click the Delivery tab.

Step 4. Choose from among the message stores listed in the first field on the Microsoft Exchange Delivery Properties sheet.

Step 5. Click OK.

You can switch back and forth between message stores, making first one then another the active store. You can also drag and drop messages between folders in a given message store and between message stores. This works well if one of the message stores is for archival storage.

Sorting message headers

Undocumented

Each message in your message store has a header. There are 37 fields—Subject, From (sender), Received (date), Conversation Topic, and so on—in the message header. The Exchange window displays the message headers in a type of details view in the right pane of your Exchange client area. As can be seen in Figure 32-8, the Exchange looks like an Explorer window in details view.

Unfortunately, in the May, 1995, beta of the Exchange client, Microsoft pulled Exchange's capability to let you filter and group your message headers to give you different message header views. Before this beta, you could define which fields and in what order the message headers would be displayed in the right pane of your Exchange window. You could define custom header views, store these views, and apply them to any of the folders. We can only hope Microsoft makes these features generally available in the future.

Tip

A message store doesn't have to store just messages. It is a general document storage, sorting, viewing, and retrieval system. If you store OLE documents in a message store, summary and other information about the documents is available to you as fields that can be used to sort document headers.

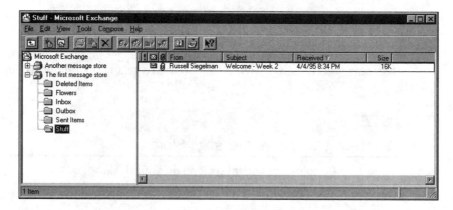

Figure 32-8: Microsoft Exchange. The message store and its folders are in the left pane. The message headers in a given folder are in the right pane.

Messages outside message stores

You can store messages outside your message stores by saving them as separate files with the *msg* extension. Simply double-clicking a message header in Microsoft Exchange and then clicking File, Save As will do it.

If you double-click a message file in an Explorer window, the message-composition portion of Exchange will be invoked. Your message will be loaded, ready to be edited or sent.

Address Books

The really cool thing about the Microsoft Exchange address books is that they are (almost) full featured. For example, you can assign up to eight phone numbers to each person in a book, as shown in Figure 32-9, and dial them by clicking any one of eight Dial buttons. Funny thing though, there is only one e-mail address or fax number per entry. This last issue causes a lot of problems.

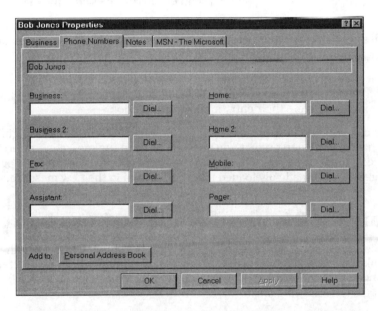

Figure 32-9: The Phone Numbers Properties sheet for Bob Jones. Click the Dial button to call any of the numbers.

It's not like you can start printing labels from an address book (which is why the shareware CD-ROM accompanying this book features the program Address Manager), but it does provide a name, address, and phone number database upon which other applications can be built by third parties.

Undocumented

You can have only one personal address book used by any one profile at any one time. You can have, in addition, a CompuServe address book attached to a profile that includes the CompuServe mail delivery service. A Microsoft Network address book (maintained in Redmond, not on your computer) can be associated with a profile that uses MSN. Address books on various mail servers can be associated with Microsoft Mail delivery services, but you can have only one personal address book per profile at a time. The same personal address book can be used by numerous different profiles.

You must remove a personal address book from a profile before you can add another. Removing an address book does not delete the address book file. In fact you can add a new address book to a profile, but have it actually be the same address book file perhaps with a new long descriptive name. You could have a number of address book files that aren't attached to any profile and therefore not able to be viewed, edited, or added to.

Undocumented

You can create "personal distribution lists" made up of selected members of your address book. You can then send e-mail (or faxes) to any one of these lists.

Undocumented

You can copy names from the MSN, CompuServe, or Microsoft Mail server address books into your personal address book. You can create personal distribution lists from names stored in these other address books.

Right-click anywhere in the client area of your personal address book, and a small menu pops up allowing you to bring up the properties of the highlighted individual or delete their entry in the address book.

You can compose a message starting from your address book by highlighting the name of the person that you are want to send the message to, and then clicking the New Message button on the address book Toolbar. The person's address is automatically loaded into the To: field in the new message.

Changing the name of the address book

Undocumented

While the personal address book will always be named Personal Address Book (unlike the Personal Information Store, whose name you can completely change), you can add another name to identify a particular address book. To do so, take the following steps:

STEPS

Changing the Name of Your Personal Address Book

Step 1.   Double-click the Inbox icon on the desktop.

Step 2.   Click Tools, Services, highlight Personal Address Book, and then click the Properties button.

Step 3.   Type a new name in the name field. This new name will be added to the name Personal Address Book. For example, type in **Brian's Address Book** and the new name becomes "Personal Address Book (Brian's Address Book)."

The Address Book's big problem

Each entry (record) in the address book can have only one e-mail address or one fax number (despite what is displayed in Figure 32-9). This means you must have two entries for a given individual if you wish to reach them both by fax and by e-mail using Exchange—two entries that repeat all the same information except the e-mail or fax number.

This is nuts. Microsoft apparently hasn't been able to figure out how to solve this problem. It is the fax number or the e-mail address (as well as the Display name) that is the "live" portion of the record, that is, that part of the record that connects to the rest of Exchange. You could easily end up with three or four records for the same person with display names as follows:

Bill Smith - Internet

Bill Smith - Fax

Bill Smith - MSN

Bill Smith - CompuServe

Creating and Sending Mail

You create and send e-mail and faxes from within Microsoft Exchange using the Compose feature. You can print faxes from other Windows applications. Microsoft Fax has the ability to act like a printer driver. If you print to it from a Windows application, it can take whatever it is you are printing and send it out as a fax.

If you have MAPI-enabled applications (like Word for Windows), you can compose e-mail and faxes from within these applications. To send e-mail or faxes, click File, Send on the application's menu bar. The current document is sent as an attachment to a message over your active mail delivery service. If Exchange isn't running when you click Send, it will be invoked.

To compose a Message while using Microsoft Exchange, click the New Message icon in the Exchange Toolbar, or click Compose, New Message on the Exchange menu bar. This will bring up what feels like a whole new application, your e-mail message composition application. New Message should remind you a lot of WordPad, as can be seen in Figure 32-10.

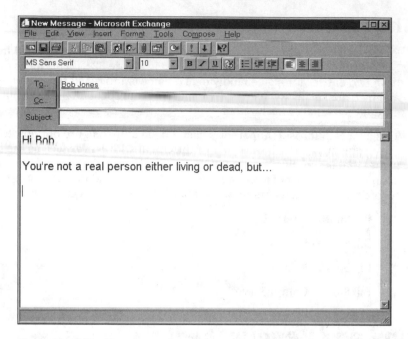

Figure 32-10: The New Message window in Microsoft Exchange. Create and send messages from here. Click the envelope on the left end of the Toolbar to send a message.

Sending mail

To send a message after you have composed it, click the envelope on the left end of the New Message Toolbar, the send icon. Your message will be placed in the outbox of your message store. If you are not currently connected to your mail delivery service, your message will sit right there until you do get connected.

Undocumented

If you are connected to a LAN, *and* your active Exchange profile is configured to use Microsoft Mail, *and* you are sending a message to another person on your Microsoft Mail mailing list, your message will automatically be delivered from your message store's outbox to your Microsoft Mail postoffice. At the same time, it will be moved to the Sent Items folder of your message store.

Undocumented

If you are using the Internet mail delivery service, you can configure the service to call up your Internet service provider when you double-click the Inbox icon and immediately transfer the mail waiting for you there, or it can be configured to use remote preview. If you choose automatic, you won't be able to compose an e-mail message and send it (to the outbox) while you are off line. If you click the Send icon, you'll get an error message stating that the transport medium wasn't available, but your message is now stored in the Sent messages folder, and not in the Outbox. If you want to send it, you'll have to connect to your Internet service provider and then forward the sent message to the original recipient.

If you have chosen remote preview, your e-mail messages are sent to the Outbox when you click the Send icon on the Taskbar. They aren't really sent, and your Internet service provider is not called when you click the Send icon. This is not intuitive.

You need to click Tools, Remote Mail on the Exchange menu bar. The Remote Mail window will appear on your desktop. You need to click Tools, Connect, or you can click Tools, Connect and Transfer Mail in the Remote Mail menu bar to actually send the e-mail message that you just composed.

To configure your Internet mail service for one or the other of these connection options, take the following steps:

STEPS

Configuring the Internet mail delivery service

Step 1. Click the Start button, Settings, Control Panel. Double-click the Fax and Mail icon in the Control Panel.

Step 2. Click the Show Profiles button first if the Internet mail delivery service is not included in the default profile. Otherwise, highlight Internet Mail and click the Properties button.

Step 3. Click the Connection tab. In the Message Transfer Information section click the "Select the mode for transferring messages" field. You have the choice of Automatic or Selective - using the Remote Preview. Make a choice.

Step 4. Click OK.

If you are sending e-mail via the Microsoft Network, mail will be sent to the Outbox until you connect to MSN. You can use Tools, Remote Mail in the Exchange menu bar to bring up the Remote Mail window and then Tools, Connect and Transfer Mail on the Remote Mail application's menu bar to connect to MSN and send and receive e-mail.

If you are sending a fax and you have configured your fax mail delivery service to send faxes immediately, Exchange will initialize your fax modem and send the fax as soon as you click the Send icon.

Undocumented

When you compose a message, you must provide an address to send the message to. This address identifies the mail delivery service that will transport the mail. Even if you have multiple mail delivery services attached to your active Exchange profile, each message will be sent through the correct mail delivery service.

Sending mail without using an address book

Undocumented

You don't have to put someone in your address book before you can send them mail. You just have to identify the mail delivery service that you are going to use and properly write an address into the To: field. Table 32-1 contains examples of what you could type in the To: field·

Table 32-1	Sample Addresses
Address	**Mail Delivery Service**
[FAX:{ +1 (*nnn*) *nnn-nnnn*}]	fax
[MSN:{*msn alias*}]	Microsoft Network
[MSNINET:{*internet address*}]	Internet address through MSN
[SMFT:{*address*}]	Microsoft Mail (local area network)
[CompuServe:{*nnnnn,nnnn*}]	CompuServe
[SMFT:{*Internet address*}]	Internet service provider

It's more than e-mail

When you think of e-mail you normally think of ASCII text notes — a short note with little or no formatting. With Exchange, Microsoft is attempting to change that whole perception.

Exchange can be used to create and send fully formatted documents. Documents can be inserted into messages as attachments (click Insert, File). When received, the attachment symbol for the document can be double-clicked and the document opened by an associated application (if the recipient has an application that is associated with the document type — see Chapter 13 for details on document types). OLE 2 objects can be created in place in the New Message window. Exchange is a full OLE 2 application. You can insert OLE 2 objects in a message and mail or fax them.

To see how OLE 2 objects are edited in Exchange, take the following steps:

STEPS

Editing OLE 2 Objects

Step 1. Click the New Message icon on the Exchange Toolbar.

Step 2. Click Insert, Object in the New Message menu bar.

Step 3. Scroll through the Object Type list box and highlight the type of object that you want to create. Click OK.

Step 4. The New Message window will be transformed to incorporate the tools needed to edit the new object. Figure 32-11 shows the window created for a bitmapped object.

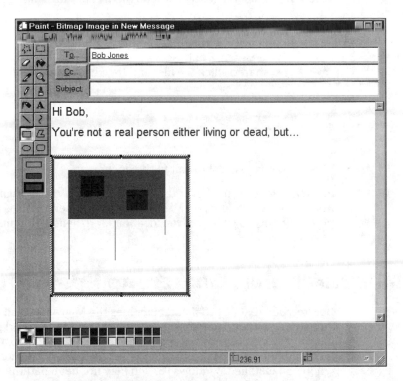

Figure 32-11: The New Message window is now a hybrid of its former self and MS Paint.

Step 5. You can send the message with the enclosed object(s).

Sending pointers to attachments

If you send mail over your LAN using Microsoft Mail, it is possible to send pointers to attachments (files) instead of the attachments themselves. This is just a fancy way of sending someone (or a bunch of someones) a file without actually sending it. By sending a pointer to the file (which is itself stored in a shared folder) you cut down on the amount of space used in your postoffice, especially if you are sending out a document to a number of other people.

STEPS

Sending a Pointer to a File

Step 1.   Click the New message icon on the Exchange Toolbar.

Step 2.   Click the Insert File icon on the New Message Toolbar.

Step 3.   Click Link attachment to original file .

Step 4.   Browse to the file (in a shared folder) that is to be linked to the message. Double-click a shared folder (or if the volume is already shared, click the file) and then click the filename.

Step 5.   Click OK.

The pointer is just a shortcut to the document.

If you are sending mail over the Microsoft Network, you can send shortcuts to documents and folders on MSN to other MSN users. This is a handy way to point out how to get to a given location, or to send a document without making a copy.

Microsoft Mail Workgroup Postoffice

Before you create a profile that includes the Microsoft Mail delivery service, you should either have the name and location of your workgroup's shared Microsoft Mail postoffice, or you need to create such a postoffice. If you included Microsoft Mail as a mail delivery service in the default profile created when you installed Windows 95, you may not have had the opportunity to create a postoffice first. You can go back and do that and then edit your Exchange profile.

If your computer is connected to a LAN and you are using Microsoft Mail, all the users in your workgroup should use the same postoffice. When you set up Exchange, you need to tell it only the name and location of the shared postoffice.

To create a Microsoft Mail postoffice, double-click the Microsoft Mail Postoffice icon in your Control Panel. This will create a workgroup postoffice. You'll need to decide on whose computer you are going to store the postoffice, and who is going to look after it. You'll need to mark the postoffice folder as shared among the members of your workgroup. You'll want only one postoffice for your workgroup so that everyone will be able to send mail to everyone else in the workgroup.

If you want to send mail (using Exchange) to people in other workgroups, you'll need to have Microsoft Mail Server, Microsoft Exchange Server, or some other company's Microsoft Mail-compatible server.

Clicking the Microsoft Mail Postoffice icon in your Control Panel will start the Microsoft Workgroup Postoffice Administration Wizard, which will guide you through setting up a postoffice.

Upgrading your Microsoft Mail message store

Microsoft Exchange comes with its own form of a message store. If you install Windows 95 over your existing Windows 3.x directory, your existing message stores (files with the extension *mmf*) will be converted to Personal Information Store (files with *pst* extension) format. If you have additional older message stores that weren't converted, you can do it manually.

STEPS

Converting Older Message Stores

Step 1. Double-click the Inbox icon on your desktop.

Step 2. If you need to create a message store to store these converted messages, follow the steps detailed in the *Adding a message store to a profile* section earlier in this chapter.

Step 3. If you have more than one message store and you want to store the converted messages in a secondary message store, click Tools, Options, the Delivery tab, and then choose the appropriate message store. Click OK.

Step 4. Click File, Import on the Exchange menu bar.

Step 5. Browse to find the older message store and then double-click it.

Your older messages will be added to the new message store you chose.

Remote Access to a Microsoft Mail Postoffice

If you use CompuServe, MSN, and/or the Internet as mail delivery services, you are already familiar with remotely accessing your mail delivery service. You need to access them through a modem. This is not the case if your LAN has server access to the Internet.

If you have Microsoft Mail running on your office network, you can also set up your portable computer or computer at home to access your e-mail account at the office over the phone. You can call either your computer at work or your company's network, depending on how these computers are set up.

Any of the remote mail delivery connections give you a number of options. One option is to review just the message headers and decide which messages to download. Outgoing messages are queued in your portable's outbox until the next time you connect with the office. You can create a schedule that tells your computer (if it is turned on) when to call into the office (or other mail delivery service) and check for e-mail.

If you have a portable computer that you use at the office and on the road, you will most likely want to set up two different profiles, both of which use the Microsoft Mail delivery service, but one that uses it over the phone lines. To configure a new profile for remote access to your Microsoft Mail postoffice, take the following steps:

STEPS

Creating a Profile for Remote Access to a Microsoft Mail Postoffice

Step 1. Click the Start button, Settings, then Control Panel.

Step 2. Double-click the Mail and Fax icon in the Control Panel, and then the Show Profiles button.

Step 3. Highlight a profile that contains your Microsoft Mail delivery service. If you don't have such a profile, click the Add button to create a new profile using the Microsoft Exchange Setup Wizard.

Step 4. Once you have a profile that uses Microsoft Mail, highlight that profile and click the Properties button. Highlight the Microsoft Mail information service and click the Properties button in the Services Properties sheet.

Step 5. Click the Connection tab and then Automatically sense LAN or Remote, as shown in Figure 32-12. If you want to force a remote connection, click Remote using a modem and Dial-Up Network.

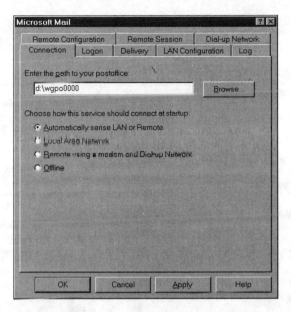

Figure 32-12: The Microsoft Mail Connection Properties sheet. Enter the server name and folder name for your Microsoft Mail postoffice. Click one of the two radio buttons that allows for a remote connection.

Step 6. Click the Remote Configuration tab and choose the options that you want.

Step 7. Click the Remote Session tab. If you want to dial up your Microsoft Mail postoffice as soon as you double-click the Inbox icon, click When this provider is started, as shown in Figure 32-13.

Step 8. To create a schedule for regular connections with the office Microsoft Mail postoffice, click Schedule item delivery. You'll need to already have a Dial-Up Network (DUN) connection defined, so you might want to wait for the next step first.

Step 9. Click the Dial-up Network tab to define how to make a connection with your office. If you don't already have a DUN connection for your office you can create one by clicking the Add Entry button in the Microsoft Mail Dial-up Network Properties sheet, as shown in Figure 32-14.

It is not a simple one-step operation to create a new Dial-Up Networking connection. You should review Chapter 28 if you are unfamiliar with how to do it.

Step 10. Click OK when you are done.

(continued)

STEPS *(continued)*

Creating a Profile for Remote Access
to a Microsoft Mail Postoffice

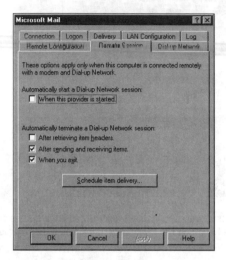

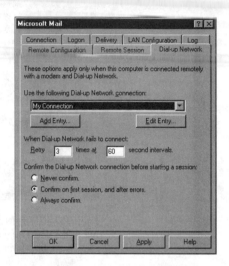

Figure 32-13: The Microsoft Mail Remote Session Properties sheet. You determine when the computer at the office will be called up and when it will be terminated.

Figure 32-14: The Microsoft Mail Dial-up Network Properties sheet. Click Add Entry to create a new connection to your office.

You can create a DUN connection to a computer running Windows 95 (if you have installed the DUN server on it), a Windows NT server, a Novell NetWare server, Shiva LanRover, or other servers. Check Chapter 28 for more details.

Troubleshooting Microsoft Exchange

Secret

Terri Bronson at Microsoft gives the following advice when you have big general problems with Microsoft Exchange:

STEPS

Troubleshooting Microsoft Exchange

Step 1. Delete the Exchange profile you are having problems with (perhaps your *only* one). Double-click the Mail and Fax icon in the Control Panel, click Show Profiles, highlight the bad profile, and click Delete.

Step 2. Create a new profile (Click Add).

Step 3. Click the Start button, then Run, type in **AWADPR32.EXE,** and then press Enter.

Step 4. Make sure there are no files left in your \Windows\Spool\Fax director due to prior crashes that are "stuck."

Step 5. Make sure there are no "stuck" messages in your Outbox.

Step 6. If you also run MSMail, make sure it is not the first mail delivery service in your profile.

Microsoft Fax

Microsoft Exchange treats faxes printed from other applications as attachments to messages. The messages are stored in your Exchange message store, and you can view the stored faxes by double-clicking the attachment symbols in their messages. The fax message header contains the pertinent information identifying the fax.

A message store is an OLE 2 container. It can store all sorts of different kinds of files and objects. Faxes printed from other applications just happen to be another kind of document.

With MS Fax you can send editable documents as faxes to recipients, who can then open them using compatible applications. MS Fax utilizes the Microsoft-developed *binary file transfer* (BFT) capability to fool the fax transport into sending documents instead of dots to Class 1 fax/modems . Of course, you can't send these editable documents to a fax machine or Class 2 fax/modems. MS Fax sends documents as faxes to Group 3-compatible fax machines.

Faxing from the Start button

Click the Start button, then Programs, Accessories, and Fax. You'll find four options in the Fax menu: Compose New Fax, Cover Page Editor, Fax Viewer, and Retrieve File.

Compose New Fax

This starts the Microsoft Fax Wizard and Microsoft Exchange. The Wizard lets you compose a little fax or send a file. Exchange has a much better composition window then the little dialog box that the Wizard gives you. To compose and send a fax from Exchange, take the following steps:

STEPS

Composing and Sending a Fax

Step 1.   Double-click the Inbox icon on your desktop and choose a profile with a Microsoft Fax mail delivery service if you have more than one profile.

Step 2.   Click Compose, New Message on the Exchange menu bar (or click the New Message icon on the Toolbar).

Step 3.   Click the To: field to choose someone to send the fax to.

Step 4.   Compose the fax and then click the envelope on the left end of the New Message Toolbar to send the fax.

Undocumented

Faxes composed within Exchange or by using the Fax Wizard are messages and not attachments to messages, as is the case of faxes printed from Windows applications.

Cover Page Editor

The Cover Page Editor is a standalone application that you use to create and edit fax cover pages. Cover pages can be fairly complex and rich documents in and of themselves. The editor allows you to place fax information fields as well as graphics. It is an OLE 2 application, so you can use MS Paint to create graphical items.

You don't need to send cover pages with your faxes or have edited any cover pages before you send your first fax. Cover pages are a frill, and the Cover Page Editor is quite a powerful utility that shows off the capability of OLE 2 and reusable code and objects (from WordPad), but it's still just an accessory.

Fax Viewer

The Fax Viewer is found inside Microsoft Exchange. Double-click a fax attachment in a message to invoke the Fax Viewer and view the fax.

Once you are in the Fax Viewer and viewing a fax, it is possible to save the fax in a file outside of the message store. You can then use the Fax Viewer in standalone mode to view the fax file (a file with the *awd* extension). Double-click a file with an *awd* extension to invoke the Fax Viewer.

Undocumented

You can't save a fax to a file from Microsoft Exchange itself (using File, Save as on the Exchange menu bar) — only from the Fax Viewer, invoked while you are using Exchange.

Request a Fax

Do you want to call a fax-on-demand service and download a fax or two? This is what the Request a Fax menu item is for (Start button, Programs, Accessories, Fax). It invokes a Wizard that makes the call and retrieves the fax (or a document, file, or software update from a fax server that supports BFT).

The first fax should be the names of the other faxes that are available on the service. You can then call again and ask for specific faxes (or files).

Request a Fax is also available from the Exchange menu bar. Double-click the Inbox icon on your desktop and choose a profile that includes Microsoft Fax if you have multiple profiles. Click Tools, Microsoft Fax Tools, and Request a Fax to start the same Wizard that Request a Fax menu item on the Start menu does.

Receiving faxes

You can set your computer to answer the phone when a call comes in and receive incoming faxes. You first need to double-click your Inbox icon and then choose a profile (if you have multiple profiles) that includes MS Fax as a mail delivery service.

A little icon that looks like a fax phone combination will appear next to your clock on the Taskbar. You can click the fax phone to see its status. Click Options, Modem Properties to determine how Exchange will answer the phone (and display the Fax modem Properties sheet, as shown in Figure 32-15). If you choose Answer after 4 (or more) rings, Exchange will automatically answer the phone and begin to make the fax connection if you don't pick up the phone before four rings. You can't set the automatic answer for fewer than two rings.

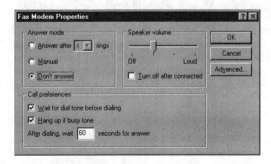

Figure 32-15: The Fax Modem Properties sheet.
Choose how Exchange will answer incoming phone calls.

If you want to use your phone primarily for voice communication, set the Answer mode to Manual. The phone status box does appear when a phone call comes in and you can click Answer Now if you think a fax is coming in.

Tip

You can't use Windows 3.x or DOS communications packages while Exchange is waiting for a fax phone call unless you click Don't answer in the Fax Modem Properties sheet. These other packages will report being unable to use the serial port that is connected to your modem.

Other Windows 95 TAPI-aware communications packages (including HyperTerminal) can use the modem at the same time Exchange is waiting for a fax phone call. Of course, only one communication can be going on at a time so you can't use HyperTerminal while you are sending or receiving a fax.

Tip

Fax machines are on all the time. Computers often aren't. If you want your computer to operate as a fax machine and to be always ready to receive faxes, you'll need to run Exchange with a profile that includes MS Fax at all times and leave your computer on.

Fax type

Faxes can be sent as editable files, as regular Group 3 faxes, or as either—depending on the capabilities of the recipient hardware. You can determine how a particular fax is sent by taking the following steps:

STEPS

Determining in What Format a Fax is Sent

Step 1. Double-click the Inbox on your desktop.

Step 2. Choose a profile that has Microsoft Fax as a mail delivery service if you have more than one profile.

Step 3. Click Compose, New Message in the Exchange menu bar.

Step 4. Click File, Send Options in the New Message menu bar. The Message Options Properties sheet, as shown in Figure 32-16, will be displayed on your desktop.

Step 5. Choose Editable, if possible; Editable only; or Not editable.

Figure 32-16: The Message Options Properties sheet. Choose the type of fax that you are going to send. Click Paper to set image quality.

You can set numerous other Send Options. These same properties can be set in general for all faxes by clicking Tools, Microsoft Fax Tools, Options in the Exchange menu bar.

Sharing a fax/modem on a network

A fax/modem board in a sufficiently powerful Windows 95 computer at work can be shared with dial-up networking guests, as well as other computers on the network. If you are calling into the Windows 95 computer at work using a modem in your computer at home, the fax/modem that is shared at work must be different than the modem that is answering your call and also be on a different phone line.

If the fax-server computer is dedicated to that task, it needs 8MB of RAM; if it's used for other tasks as well, it needs 12MB. In addition, at least a 486 processor is required.

Share the fax/modem on the network by taking the following steps:

STEPS

Sharing a Fax/Modem

Step 1. Double-click the Inbox icon on the desktop of a Windows 95 fax-server computer. If you have multiple Exchange profiles set for a choice, choose a profile that includes Microsoft Fax. If you haven't previously set up a profile that contains Microsoft Fax as a mail delivery method, step back a few sections in this chapter and do so.

Step 2. Click Tools, Microsoft Fax Tools, Options in the Microsoft Exchange menu bar. Click the Modem tab.

Step 3. In the Microsoft Fax Modem Properties sheet, as shown in Figure 32-17, click "Let other people on the network use my modem to send faxes."

Figure 32-17: The Microsoft Fax Properties sheet. Clicking "Let other people on the network use my modem to send faxes" enables fax/modem sharing.

Step 4. Type in a shared fax name in the Share name field, choose a volume on which the NetFax folder will be stored, and click the Properties button.

Step 5. Define the characteristics of the shared folder (NetFax) that will store the faxes. Enter a password if you want to password-protect this folder and you are using share-level protection.

Step 6. Click the next two OK buttons.

Connecting to a shared fax/modem server

Whether you are calling in from your computer at home or accessing the networking fax/server from another computer on the network, you need to create an Exchange profile on your computer that will let you use the shared fax/modem on the Windows 95 fax server.

If you are going to connect to the fax server at work from a computer at home, be sure to create a Dial-Up Networking connectoid first before you begin these steps. For details on crating connectoids, see Chapter 28.

To create a connection to a shared fax server, take the following steps:

STEPS

Creating an Exchange Profile to Use a Shared Fax Server

Step 1. Double-click the Mail and Fax icon in the Control Panel of your computer. Click Show Profiles.

Step 2. Click the Add button. Choose only the Microsoft Fax services in the Exchange Setup Wizard. Click Next.

Step 3. Type a name for this profile such as **Shared fax.** Click Next.

Step 4. Click Network fax service or other type of device and then Next.

Step 5. Click the Add button (if necessary). Highlight Network fax server and click OK.

Step 6. Type in the name of the shared fax-server computer preceded by two back slashes followed by the name of the shared fax/modem (given to the shared fax in Step 4 of the previous Steps) preceded by a single back slash. Click Next.

If the shared fax is on a remote computer (perhaps, your computer at work and you are setting this up on your computer at home) and you enter the name of the computer at work and the name of the shared fax when you are not presently connected to the computer at work over the phone lines, you will asked if you want to connect to the fax server using Dial-Up Networking. Click Yes. Go to Step 8.

Step 7. Enter your phone number and click Next. Continue clicking Next until you have completed the Exchange Setup Wizard. You're done.

Step 8. It is assumed that you have previously created a connectoid to connect to the fax server computer. Choose the name of the connectoid after completing Step 7.

Step 9. Enter a password for connecting to the shared fax/modem if needed. Click Cancel unless you want to connect to the fax server at work now.

If you are sending a fax to a Group 3 fax machine, use 14-point Arial (if you have only the basic fonts that come with Windows 95) for the text in your fax. This will significantly improve the readability of your fax as fax printers are often of poor quality and low resolution (200 x 100 or 200 x 200). If you have additional fonts (like Lucida Fax from the Microsoft True Type Font Pack), you can use them instead of Arial.

Troubleshooting Microsoft Fax

Terri Bronson at Microsoft once again provides help. If you have received a fax successfully, but it never appeared in your Inbox, take the following steps:

STEPS

Faxes Don't Appear

Step 1.   Exit Microsoft Exchange.

Step 2.   Locate the received files in the fax spool directory. This directory is typically \Windows\Spool\Fax. The files have the following form:

     `RCVxxxxx.MG3`

     or

     `RCVxxxxx.EFX`

where *xxxxx* is a 5-digit hex number. Each of the files contain one fax message.

Step 3.   Copy these files to another directory, just as a backup.

Step 4.   Open the following key in the Registry:

`HKEY_Local_MACHINE\SOFTWARE\Microsoft\At Work\Fax\LocalModems\Received`

This key may have several values all of type "string" (REG_SZ)), with the format: R*nn* and F*nn,* where *nn* is a two-digit decimal number starting with 00. The F*nn* entries contain filenames (the RCV*xxxx*.mg3/.efx files referred to in 1). The R*nn* entry contains the result code for the transmission. A value of 001 indicates a successful receive.

Example: F00 = RCV3edd0.MG3

     F01 = 001

     R00 = 001

     R01 = 001

Step 5. Add entries for all the files identified in 1. above to this list if they are not already on this list, making sure that (a) each F*nn* has a corresponding R*nn* (you can set all R00 values to 001); and (b) the *nn* numbers are consecutive, starting from 00 (so we have F00, F01, F02 . . . R00, R01, R02 . . .)

Step 6. Restart Exchange. If all went well, the messages should soon show up in the Inbox, and the "Received" key above will get cleared.

Summary

Microsoft Exchange provides full e-mail and fax connectivity.

▶ You can send and receive e-mail using the Internet, CompuServe, the Microsoft Network, or Microsoft Mail servers.

▶ Windows 95 comes with a complete workgroup version of Microsoft Mail for local e-mail and document exchange.

▶ You can send a fax or e-mail message without putting someone in your address book.

▶ With Microsoft Exchange, e-mail is not just an ASCII text message, but can include all types of attached files and OLE 2 objects.

▶ You can edit OLE 2 objects within Microsoft Exchange.

▶ If you are sending e-mail over the phone lines, you have to tell Exchange to connect to the remote e-mail service; you can't just send the mail.

Chapter 33

Connecting to the Internet

Microsoft and the Internet

Millions of Windows 3.x users have been accessing the Internet for the last two years without any help from Microsoft. Numerous companies, individuals, universities, government agencies, and loose associations have created a solid body of Internet applications that take advantage of the Windows 3.x interface.

These applications started becoming available in 1993, both as retail packages and as shareware distributed over the Internet, or sometimes a combination of both. The academic culture (and sometimes government-financed research) encouraged the authors to make their applications freely or cheaply available.

Microsoft has not been a pioneer in cyberspace, but with Windows 95 it is catching up. Even when general Internet awareness was rising in 1993 and 1994, Microsoft's presence was limited to e-mail and later a file transfer protocol (FTP) site. In late 1994, the company cobbled together a Web server.

Why was Microsoft so late? The Internet used to be a strictly Unix kind of thing. Microsoft's culture is not a Unix culture, nor is it an academic culture. Microsoft is doing what it can to defeat Unix in the marketplace and is not interested in developing software to give away.

Windows software for the Internet didn't really get going strong until 1994, so Windows machines weren't seen as Internet clients. The Internet gets a lot better with faster modems, and the mass market didn't have a critical mass of 14.4Kbps modems until 1993-94. Microsoft just didn't see a demand for Internet-based services.

Before 1994, few Internet service providers allowed ordinary businesses and individuals to purchase access to the Internet at competitive rates.

The Internet's killer app was a program named Mosaic. Written by a group of college students at the University of Illinois at Champaign-Urbana's National Center for Supercomputing Applications, Mosaic is a browser that is used to view files on the Internet's World Wide Web (WWW). Mosaic was created in 1993. Windows versions of the browser followed the initial versions written in Unix in late 1993. The Unix version was developed first because it was written at a university (universities are Unix strongholds). Academic sites also have access to fast Internet connections, which puts them ahead of the general public in demanding high-level Web tools. In 1994, the original authors of Mosaic formed their own company to create Netscape, which as of mid-1995 had captured 80% of the WWW browser "market."

At the same time, Microsoft was providing its product support and receiving its e-mail from customers electronically through CompuServe. Since CompuServe pays a royalty of 8 to 10 percent of connect-time charges on their service to software vendors, Microsoft and other software vendors found CompuServe to be an attractive addition to their support programs. There was no way to charge on the Internet in 1994. This explains in part why Microsoft and other software vendors have been slow to use the Internet for this purpose.

Microsoft now has a strategy of connecting everyone to the Microsoft Network (MSN), as well as to the Internet. It wants to provide on MSN the electronic services found on the Internet, and a lot more. They also want to capture a very large client base (potentially, all Windows users). So MSN is a competitor to the Internet. At the same time, Microsoft wants to be the Internet service provider of choice.

This strategy means Microsoft is choosing to use its resources to make it easy for Windows 95 users to access the Microsoft Network and, through it, the Internet. Fewer Microsoft resources go toward making it easier for everyone to go to their local service provider for Internet access. It wasn't until very late in the beta test cycle (June of '95) that Microsoft finally acknowledged the need for a scripting utility that would allow easy access to many Internet service providers. In this chapter, we show you how to access the Internet from Windows 95, whether or not you use MSN to do so.

Your First Point of Internet Attachment

There are two fundamentally different ways to gain access to the Internet from your computer — retail and wholesale. First, you can call through the modem connected to your computer to a local or national Internet service provider. Or, second, you can communicate over a Local Area Network (LAN) to a server that is connected by a phone line to an Internet service provider. The connection can vary from a dial-up 28.8Kbps service to a fast, dedicated leased-T1 line.

Service providers that offer call-in modem access to the general public are a relatively new phenomenon. Before 1994, most Internet users had access through their Unix workstations on campus or on the job at defense contractors. They didn't have to worry about how to get access. The systems administrator took care of those details. Once the rest of us were allowed to join the party, *we* became the systems administrators for our own computers.

CompuServe, America Online, Prodigy, and other online services are turning themselves into Internet service providers. These national online services have offered Internet mail service since 1993, and in 1995 began providing full Internet access, just like their Internet service provider competitors. If you have an account with these online services, you will soon have a full Internet connection.

Microsoft offers MSN with Windows 95 and has purchased partial interest in a nationwide service provider named UUNET. MSN provides an Internet mail connection and access to Internet news groups. Soon after the release of Windows 95, MSN plans to provide full Internet access. You'll be able to use Internet Explorer and your MSN access to surf the Internet. Its nationwide service provider will provide both Internet and MSN access.

Tip

You'll want to find a service provider that has enough phone lines so you won't get a busy signal too often. The Internet works best at the highest speed you can afford. If the service provider has 28.8Kbps (V.34) modems and so do you, great. Some service providers are very small and may not have adequate technical support to keep their lines up and functioning. Move on to another one if this is the case.

Some service providers let you connect with ISDN. This will give you 56Kbps transfer rates. See if your telephone company will install an ISDN line to your home or business. If so, purchase an ISDN card with a Windows 95-compatible driver for your computer, and you are ready to really cruise the Internet.

Microsoft's TCP/IP Stack

Windows 95 comes with tools that allow you to access the Internet either over a modem or through a network. At the lowest level, Microsoft provides a TCP/IP stack. TCP/IP (transfer control protocol/Internet protocol) is the Internet language or protocol. It can be spoken over your modem, network card, or Windows 95's Direct Cable Connection (see Chapter 30 for more on DCC).

The TCP/IP stack can be associated with (bound to) your Dial-Up Adapter and/or your network card. If it is bound to your Dial-Up Adapter, you can use Windows 95's Dial-Up Networking to call your service provider and connect to the Internet using TCP/IP.

If the TCP/IP stack is bound to your network card, and your network is connected to a Unix server or Windows NT 3.5 server, you can communicate with that server using applications compatible with Winsock 1.1 (Windows Socket). The server can provide the gateway to the Internet.

Installing an Internet Dial-Up Connection

To gain Internet access through your modem, you need to carry out the following tasks:

- Install and configure your modem
- Sign up for an Internet account with your service provider or online service
- Obtain from the service provider the information needed to successfully connect your computer to their computer
- Install Dial-Up Networking on your Windows 95 computer
- Install and bind the Windows 95 TCP/IP stack to the Dial-Up Adapter
- Configure your Windows 95 TCP/IP Properties sheets using the information provided by your service provider
- If you have a SLIP (Serial Line/Internet Protocol) account at your service provider, install the SLIP connection software, and the connection scripting utility
- Define and configure a Dial-Up Networking connection for your service provider
- Write a connection script if your Internet service provider doesn't provide PPP with CHAP or PAP

Installing and configuring your modem

We discuss how to install and configure your modem in Chapter 25. The Windows 95 Setup program's hardware detection routines may already have correctly identified your modem and installed the appropriate driver for it. If you installed your modem after you installed Windows 95, these same routines may have correctly detected it and similarly installed the right drivers.

You can check your modem by double-clicking the Modems icon in your Control Panel to display the Modems Properties sheets. This is also where you will find the Properties that characterize your calling location (click the Dialing Properties button on the General Properties sheet). You can install a modem driver at this point, if it hasn't been done for you already.

An Internet service provider account

You need an account with a service provider, which will provide you with access to the Internet through its computer and fast, dedicated telephone lines. The service provider will maintain a bundle of incoming dial-in lines attached to racks of modems that in turn are attached to the service provider's computer(s).

Tip

If this is a new account, you will want to obtain a PPP (Point-to-Point Protocol) type account with the service provider. If you already have an account, you will want to change it to a PPP account. In addition, you will want the service provider to provide either PAP (Password Authentication Protocol) or CHAP (Challenge-Handshake Authentication Protocol), if possible.

If you don't have a PPP account with one of these types of authentication, you will need to create a script file that will type in your user or logon name and password.

If you have a SLIP (Serial Line/Internet Protocol) account instead of a PPP account and a dynamically assigned IP address, your script will need to capture the address and send it back to the service provider.

Some service providers don't offer PPP or SLIP accounts directly, but require that you send a message to switch to this type of connection from what is known as a *shell account.* A shell account is the most basic account type available from a service provider. It treats your expensive computer as a dumb terminal and requires that you run Unix software on the service provider's computer in order to do anything on the Internet. You can use the scripting utility to send a command to switch from the shell to SLIP or PPP.

Tip

If you just want to maintain a low level shell account, you can use the HyperTerminal feature (see Chapter 29) to call into your service provider. HyperTerminal doesn't come with scripting to automate the logon process, but otherwise it will work fine with a Unix computer.

Tip

Your service provider may offer a TIA (The Internet Adapter) account that allows you to switch to a SLIP-type account after you log on in your shell account. The scripting utility works with TIA accounts to switch to SLIP.

Service provider account information

Of course, you are going to need to find a service provider to begin with. If you live in a metropolitan area, there should be available at computer stores a free local computer newspaper that lists service providers. They will no doubt also advertise in the local paper.

A local service provider can provide a local number and perhaps an 800 number. A national service provider may provide local numbers, an 800 number, or a number in the closest town. You can find ads for national service providers in national computer magazines or national newspapers like the *New York Times* (especially the Tuesday *Science Times* section). Online services provide Internet access throughout the U.S. and often throughout the rest of the world.

You need some specific information from your service provider. The staff at service providers much prefer to talk to other people (sometimes known as customers) by way of their computers. This can be quite difficult when you haven't got an electronic mail account yet (which is one of the reasons that you're calling the service provider to begin with). If you have an electronic mail account with an online service, you might be able to send the service provider some e-mail, if you have any idea of the e-mail address of someone at the service provider.

You can always just call them up (on a voice line), but it is often difficult to reach anyone. You can fax them your questions, and hope that they fax you back the answers.

This poor "out-of-the-box" experience with service providers has been a major bottleneck in their growth. Many are very small companies run by one or two technically minded people. No glad-handing sales types are allowed.

The major online services and the Microsoft Network are attempting to break through this barrier. Microsoft is very smart to make it so easy to connect to MSN. A journey of a thousand miles begins with a single step.

You need the following information from your service provider:

- Dial-in phone number connected to the service provider's modems
- Account type
- If a SLIP account, whether it is "compressed SLIP" or not
- If a PPP account, whether it has either PAP or CHAP
- If a PPP account and not PAP or CHAP, whether software compression and encrypted passwords are supported
- User name or logon name (for example, something like *billsmith* or *georgef*)
- Password
- Your host name (which can be the same as your user name)

  This is often thought of as your computer's name, or as your name on the Internet. It will be appended to the service provider's domain name to become your address on the Internet. Since this will become your address, you should tell the service provider what you want as a host name, and see if they can swing it without any conflicts.

- The service provider's domain name (for example, let's make up a company's domain name, like *netters.com*)

  Your host name and the service provider's domain name are combined, as in *billsmith.netters.com,* to become your address (your e-mail address will be *billsmith@netters.com*). You can have as many different e-mail addresses on the Internet as you have accounts.

■ Domain Name System (DNS) server's Internet Protocol (IP) address

DNS servers translate (from a lookup table) the somewhat-user friendly domain names into the underlying IP addresses. Get the IP address of the DNS server that you'll be automatically accessing when you use your service provider's services.

In some cases your service provider will be assigning you a different IP address every time you log on. The service provider will translate your Internet address to this dynamic IP address. To do this, the service provider requires a dynamic host configuration protocol (DHCP) server.

If your service provider doesn't have a DHCP server, it will assign you a fixed address. In this case, you'll need to get:

■ Your own IP address

■ An IP subnet mask

■ A gateway IP address

The above information is all you need to be able to connect to the service provider. To be able to access e-mail and news groups, you'll need the following information:

■ Your e-mail address (most likely the combination of your host name and the service provider's domain name, as shown above)

■ POP mail server's address

■ SMTP mail server's address

■ News server's address

■ Mail gateway's address (needed only for some mail readers)

All these information needs are pretty standard, and your service provider should have no problem meeting them (if you can actually talk to someone). You'll use this information to configure your Windows 95 TCP/IP stack.

Of course, what the staff at the service provider is going to want to know is your credit card number. Alternately, they may just take your check once every three months or so and cut off your account if you don't get around to paying it on time.

Dial-Up Networking

If you installed the Direct Cable Connection (DCC) during Windows 95 Setup, Dial-Up Networking (DUN) is already installed. You may have installed DUN when you ran the custom setup.

To find out if DUN is installed, click the Start button, click Settings, and then click Control Panel. Double-click the Network icon in the Control Panel and see whether you have a Dial-Up Adapter driver installed in the Network Configuration Properties sheet.

If not, you can install DUN by taking the following steps:

STEPS

Installing Dial-Up Networking

Step 1.   Click the Start button, Settings, then Control Panel.

Step 2.   Double-click the Add/Remove Programs icon. Click the Windows Setup tab.

Step 3.   Click the Communications check box and the Details button.

Step 4.   Click the Dial-Up Networking check box and the OK button in the Communications dialog box.

Step 5.   Click the OK button in the Add/Remove Software dialog box. DUN will now be installed. You may be asked to insert your Windows 95 source diskettes or CD-ROM.

Bind TCP/IP to your Dial-Up Adapter

Adding Dial-Up Networking to your Windows 95 configuration doesn't automatically add the TCP/IP stack to the list of protocols bound to the Dial-Up Adapter. You need to do this separately.

STEPS

Binding Your TCP/IP Stack to Dial-Up Adapter

Step 1.   Click the Start button, Settings, then Control Panel.

Step 2.   Double-click the Network icon. Click the Add button.

Step 3.   Highlight Protocol in the Select Network Component Type dialog box and click Add.

Step 4.   In the Select Network Protocol dialog box, highlight Microsoft in the list of manufacturers and click TCP/IP in the list of network protocols. Click the OK button.

Step 5.   Click OK in the Network Properties sheet. You may be asked to insert your Windows 95 source diskettes or CD-ROM.

You now have a TCP/IP stack and a dialer. After you configure these items for your service provider account you will be able to make an Internet connection.

Tip

You will notice that other protocols are bound to the Dial-Up Adapter. In addition, you'll find other network components installed by default. You can remove the other protocols, such as NetBUEI, if you like. If you are going to use the Direct Cable Connection or connect to a local area network, you shouldn't remove these other network components.

Configuring the TCP/IP stack

You need to configure your TCP/IP stack (dialer and protocol) based on the information you received from your service provider. To do so take the following steps:

STEPS

Setting TCP/IP Properties

Step 1.   Click the Start button, Settings, then Control Panel.

Step 2.   Double-click the Network icon. Highlight TCP/IP in the Configurations Properties sheet and click the Properties button.

Step 3.   Click the DNS Configuration tab. In the DNS Configuration Properties sheet, which is shown in Figure 33-1, fill in your host name, domain name, and IP address of the DNS server you will use. Click the Add button to put the DNS server's IP address on the list. The DNS server's addresses will be added in that order. If you have multiple DNS servers' addresses to search, type them in the order that you want them searched. Be sure to click the Add button after you type in each one.

If you didn't get an IP address for a DNS server you might try these DNS addresses: 128.95.1.4, or 192.135.191.3, or 198.137.231.1.

Undocumented

If you have multiple Internet service providers, you'll want to provide a DNS IP address appropriate for each connection. Disable DNS in the DNS Configuration Properties sheet, and set the DNS IP address for each connection as in Step 8 in the *Dial-Up connection to your service provider* section below.

Step 4.   Click the OK button and then the IP Address tab.

Step 5.   In the IP Address Properties sheet, as shown in Figure 33-2, click the Obtain an IP address from a DHCP server radio button if your service provider provides you with a dynamic IP address at logon time. If you have a fixed IP address, enter it and the Subnet mask. If you have a TIA account it doesn't matter what you enter here. Click OK.

(continued)

STEPS *(continued)*

Setting TCP/IP Properties

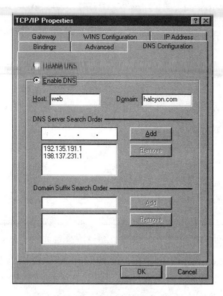

Figure 33-1: The DNS Configuration Properties sheet. Fill in the fields for your host name, service provider's domain name, and DNS server's IP address.

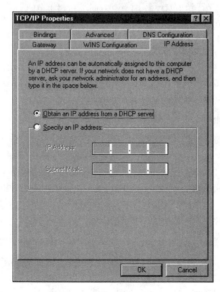

Figure 33-2: The IP Address Properties sheet. Click Obtain an IP address from a DHCP server if your service provider gives you a new IP address every time that you log on to their computer.

Step 6.   If you have a fixed IP address, click the Gateway tab, enter your Gateway IP address, click the Add button, and finally the OK button.

Step 7. Click the WINS Configuration tab and be sure that the Disable WINS Resolution radio button is checked.

Step 8. Click OK .

Step 9. Restart your computer.

Undocumented

Just to make this clear, you create one configuration for your TCP/IP stack for your Dial-Up Adapter. You can configure another for your LAN card. Therefore, you provide the settings for one service provider and one primary DNS server.

Multiple TCP/IP settings for multiple connections

You can provide different TCP/IP settings for different connections if you have multiple Internet service providers.

The TCP/IP settings that can be specific to a given connection to an Internet service provider include:

- Your IP address (fixed or dynamically assigned)
- IP address for DNS or WINS server (fixed or dynamically assigned)
- Use IP header compression or not
- Use default gateway at Internet service provider or not

Follow the steps in the *Dial-Up connection to your Internet service provider* section below to set these TCP/IP settings.

Dial-Up connection to your service provider

Now that you have installed DUN and bound the TCP/IP stack to the Dial-Up Adapter, you are ready to create a DUN connection (a connectoid) that will call your service provider and establish the connection to your account. To do this, take the following steps:

STEPS

Creating a Service Provider Connection

Step 1. Click the Start button, Programs, Accessories, and then Dial-Up Networking. (You can place a shortcut to DUN on your desktop or in any other folder if you like. For details on creating and using shortcuts, see Chapter 10.)

(continued)

STEPS *(continued)*

Creating a Service Provider Connection

Step 2. If this is your first connection, Step 1 will initiate the Make New Connection Wizard; otherwise click the Make New Connection Icon in the Dial-Up Networking window.

Step 3. Enter the name and phone number of your service provider when prompted by the Make New Connection Wizard. You also have the opportunity to change the modem-specific characteristics for this connection if you like by clicking the Configure button on the first page of the Wizard. Click the Finish button when you finish defining the service provider connection.

Step 4. Right-click the service provider connection icon in the Dial-Up Networking window. Click Properties.

Step 5. Click the Server Type button in the General Properties sheet of the service provider connection. The Server Types Properties sheet, as shown in Figure 33-3, will be displayed.

Figure 33-3: The Server Types Properties sheet. If you have a PPP account, leave Server type at the default, which is PPP: Windows 95, Windows NT 3.5, Internet. If you have a SLIP account, change server type to CSLIP (for com-pressed SLIP) or SLIP: Unix Connection.

Step 6. Choose the Server type (by clicking the down arrow in the drop-down list at the top of the Properties sheet) that describes your account at the service provider. If you have a SLIP account you will need to change the Server Type to either CSLIP: Unix Connection with IP header compression or SLIP: Unix Connection, depending on which type of SLIP account you have.

Step 7. Uncheck NetBEUI and IPX/SPX protocols in the Allowed network protocols box. You will be using TCP/IP only to connect with your service provider, and this will speed things up a bit at connect time.

If you choose SLIP or CSLIP, these check boxes will be grayed out. You are only going to be using the TCP/IP protocol to communicate to a Unix server.

Step 8.   If you want to set specific TCP/IP settings for this connection and disable DNS above in the *Configuring the TCP/IP stack*, then click the TCP/IP Settings button. You can set your IP address, the DNS or WIN IP address and other settings as shown in Figure 33-4. Click OK.

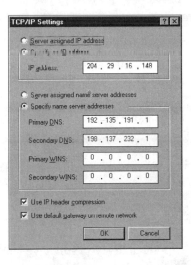

Figure 33-4: The TCP/IP Settings Properties sheet. These settings are specific to this connection to an individual Internet service provider. The default settings are those that were set earlier.

Step 9.   If you have a PPP account and your service provider enables password encryption (instead of PAP or CHAP) and software compression, you can click these check boxes. Click the OK button in the Server Types Properties sheet.

Step 10.   Click the Configure button in your service provider connection's General Properties sheet. Click the Options tab to display the Options Properties sheet as shown in Figure 33-5.

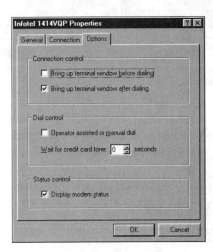

Figure 33-5: The Options Properties sheet. Click "Bring up terminal window after dialing" if you have a SLIP account or a PPP account without PAP or CHAP and you are not using the scripting utility.

(continued)

STEPS *(continued)*

Creating a Service Provider Connection

Step 11. If your service provider requires that you manually log in before you start your session, you will need to check Bring up terminal window after dialing on the Options Properties sheet. This will be the case with a SLIP account or a PPP account without PAP or CHAP.

Don't do this if you are going to use the connection scripting utility The scripting utility doesn't need the terminal window opened by this setting.

Step 12. Make any other changes you think are necessary in the other Properties sheets associated with the modem and this connection. Click the OK button in the Option Properties sheet and in the General Properties sheet for the service provider connection.

You are now ready to connect to your service provider. If you want to automate the connection with the scripting utility, you still have a little bit of work to do. See the section entitled *Automating your logon* below.

Calling Your Service Provider

Now that you have created a connection to your service provider, you are ready to make the connection.

STEPS

Connecting to Your Service Provider

Step 1. Double-click the new service provider connection icon in your DUN window. The Connect To dialog box will be displayed on your desktop, as shown in Figure 33-6.

Step 2. Type in your user or login name and your account password and click the Save password check box if you would rather not type your password every time. User names and passwords are case-sensitive. Be sure you type them correctly.

Step 3. Click the Connect button to direct your modem to dial into your service provider and make a connection. Once the connection is made, you are on the Internet and ready to run Winsock 1.1-compatible Internet applications. If your account requires that you manually log in, a terminal window will be displayed first, as shown in Figure 33-7.

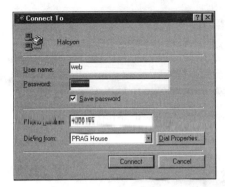

Figure 33-6: The Connect To dialog box. The User name and Password fields won't be used unless you have a PPP account with PAP or CHAP. Click the Connect button to start the modem dialing up your service provider.

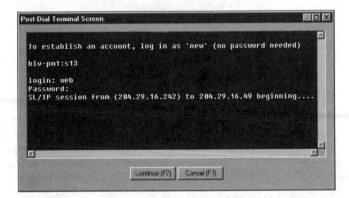

Figure 33-7: The Post-Dial Terminal Screen. Type in **PPP or SLIP** and press Enter if your service provider requires that you first specify your account type. Type in your logon name and password when prompted. If you have a SLIP account wait for your dynamically assigned IP address to be displayed and write it down so that you can remember it for a few seconds.

Step 4. If you need to specify your account type to your service provider, type in PPP or SLIP. When prompted by your service provider's computer, type in your logon name and password. Again, logon name and password are case-sensitive. If you have a TIA account, you will log on first and then type **TIA** at the shell prompt.

Step 5. If you have a SLIP account with dynamically assigned IP addresses, your IP address will be displayed. Write it down; you will need it in the next step and this terminal window is going to disappear. Click the Continue button or press F7.

If you configured your TCP/IP stack for a fixed IP address that matches the first two or three numbers of your dynamically assigned one, you will only have to worry about typing in the last number or two in the next step.

(continued)

STEPS *(continued)*

Connecting to Your Service Provider

Step 6.   If you have a SLIP account, you will need to type in your IP address. The dialog box shown in Figure 33-8 will be displayed after Step 5. Be sure to type in your IP address exactly as the terminal window displayed it. If you get it wrong, your Winsock 1.1-compatible Internet applications will not work.

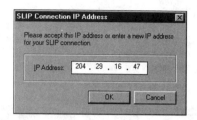

Figure 33-8: The SLIP Connection IP Address dialog box. Type in your dynamically assigned IP address exactly as displayed in your terminal window.

Step 7.   If you have a TIA account, you will be presented with the dialog box shown in Figure 33-8. If you earlier specified a fixed IP address in the IP address Properties sheet for your TCP/IP stack, this address will be displayed in the IP address dialog box. You may need to change your IP address if requested in the terminal window after you typed **TIA.** You would enter the new IP address now.

If you are using the scripting utility, steps 4 through 7 can be automated.

If you are using the Internet mail client that comes with Microsoft Plus!, you can make the connection with your service provider just by double-clicking the Inbox icon on your desktop (if you have configured the mode for transferring Internet messages as Automatic — see Chapter 32). If you have configured Internet mail for selective message transfer, you need to double-click the Inbox icon, click Tools, Remote mail on the Exchange menu bar, then click Tools, Connect on the Remote mail menu bar.

Installing SLIP and Automating your logon

The scripting utility will run a script that you create for a specific connection. This script will send your logon name, password, and account type. It will also capture a dynamically assigned IP address and send it back to your Internet service provider.

You can install SLIP and the scripting utility during Windows 95 Setup by clicking the SLIP and Scripting for Dial-Up Networking check box. If you didn't set it up then, you can do so later using the Add/Remove Programs icon in the Control Panel, clicking the Windows Setup tab, and then clicking the aforementioned check box.

The installation of SLIP and Scripting for Dial-Up Networking will add access to SLIP accounts on Unix computers to your Server Type drop-down list found by right-clicking any Dial-Up Networking connectoid and clicking Properties A script interpreter and sample scripts file can be found in your \Program Files\Accessories folder. You can edit a copy of one of these script files to meet the requirements of your Internet service provider. Double-clicking a file ending in *scp* brings up NotePad.

Undocumented

Notice that Microsoft didn't use the *scr* extension for its script files, like everybody else in the world does. This is because they already used this extension for their screen saver files. Windows 95 creates an association with the *scr* extension and the screen saver tester. Double-click a file with an *scr* extension, and Windows 95 will try to play it as a screen saver. (In Chapter 13 we show you how to solve this problem for any script files that you have that end in *scr*.)

To associate the edited script with your Internet service provider's connectoid, you need to click the Start button, Programs, Accessories, Dial-Up Scripting Tool. You can place your script files anywhere you like and you can erase the example script file from the \Program Files\Accessories folder. Just highlight the name of your service provider's connectoid in the Connections window of the Dial-Up Scripting Tool; then browse for the actual script file.

Making sure you have a good connection

You can check out your connection to your service provider. If you are having connection problems, disable software compression using the Server Types Properties sheet. If you have a SLIP account, switch from CSLIP to SLIP or vice versa in the Server Types Properties sheet.

Make sure you have the correct account type specified in the Server Types Properties sheet of your TCP/IP stack.

After you have dialed up your server provider, open a Windows DOS session. Type **ping 198.105.232.1.** This is the IP address for ftp.microsoft.com (the file transfer protocol server at Microsoft). If ping works, your TCP/IP stack and connection to the Internet is working.

Tip

To test your DNS server connection, try to ping to an IP address and then the name that goes with that IP address. For example, type **ping 198.105.232.1** and, if that works, type **ping ftp.microsoft.com.**

If the first case works but the second doesn't, then your DNS is set up wrong. If the first fails, either you are not talking to the network or the network doesn't know "who" you are.

Creating a connection log file

You can generate a log file that will record the progress of your attempt to connect to your service provider. This file can help pinpoint problems. To generate this log file, take the following steps:

STEPS

Creating a Connection Log File

Step 1.   Click the Start button, Settings, then Control Panel.

Step 2.   Double-click the Network icon. Highlight the Dial-Up Adapter and click the Properties button.

Step 3.   Click the Advanced tab, highlight Record a log file in the Property field, and Yes in the Value field.

Step 4.   Click OK in both the Dial-Up Adapter Advanced Properties sheet and the Network Properties sheet.

Step 5.   Double-click the service provider connection icon in your Dial-Up Networking window.

A file, Ppplog.txt, will be created in your Windows folder when you take Step 5. You can review this file after you attempt to make your connection.

Disabling IP header compression

If you have a PPP account, you may experience connection problems that can be cured by disabling IP header compression. To do this take the following steps:

STEPS

Disabling IP Header Compression

Step 1.   Click the Start button, Settings, then Control Panel.

Step 2.   Double-click the Network icon. Highlight the Dial-Up Adapter and click the Properties button.

Step 3.   Highlight "Use IP header compression" in the Property field. Highlight No in the Value field.

Step 4.   Click both OK buttons.

TCP/IP Utilities

Microsoft ships some low-level TCP/IP utilities with Windows 95. Most of these utilities are DOS based — which is kinda weird. Well, Unix and DOS are text based and TCP/IP is down there below the user interface, so it makes some sense. Microsoft also provides one Windows-based TCP/IP utility.

Table 33-1 lists the TCP/IP utilities you get with Windows 95:

Table 33-1	TCP/PI Utilities
Command	*What It Does*
DOS Utilities	
Arp	Displays and modifies the IP-to-Physical address translation tables used by address resolution protocol (ARP).
Ftp	File Transfer Protocol. Allows you to log on to other computers on the Internet (perhaps as anonymous) and download files. We feature a much better Windows-based FTP program on the shareware CD-ROM and suggest that you use it instead.
Nbtstat	Displays protocol statistics and current TCP/IP connections using NBT (NetBIOS over TCP/IP).
Netstat	Displays protocol statistics and current TCP/IP connections.
Ping	Checks for a connection to a remote computer. Use our featured shareware, Ws_ping, instead.
Route	Manually controls network routing tables.
Tracert	Displays the route taken to a remote computer. Use Ws_ping instead.
Windows Utility	
Winipcfg	Displays current TCP/IP network configurations. You don't use it to change these configuration; for that you go to the Properties sheet of your TCP/IP stack.

To find out how to use the DOS-based TCP/IP applications, open a DOS Windows session and type the command name followed by **-?.** Winipcfg is found in the Windows 95 folder. You can create a shortcut to it and put it in an Internet folder. (You can also do this for the DOS-based utilities).

Shareware Internet Utilities

Among the Windows-based utilities featured on the *Windows 95 Secrets* shareware CD-ROM are Winsock Finger and WS_ping. You use WS_ping to see if you can connect to a certain remote computer. It will also trace the route taken to the remote — very instructive.

Winsock Finger gives you information about the person at a certain address. Type in the address and this information is displayed.

Internet Applications

The whole point of having a TCP/IP stack and a dial-in connection to a service provider is to be able to run Winsock 1.1-compatible Internet applications, such as those that let you download files from remote computers, send e-mail, participate in news groups or mailing-list discussions, search databases, or browse World Wide Web sites.

Many Internet applications are available as shareware over the Internet. Microsoft has a hard time justifying to itself spending time and resources on the development of many different Internet applications. Microsoft ships three Internet applications with Windows 95 — Telnet, Internet mail, and (with MIcrosoft Plus!) the Internet Explorer. We feature WS_FTP on the shareware CD-ROM that accompanies this book.

Telnet

Windows 95 comes with a reasonably good Telnet client. Telnet lets you log on to a remote computer (or even your service provider's computer) as a terminal (like HyperTerminal). You can then run the Unix software running on that remote computer.

This might seem like a step backwards, but it is handy at times to be able to get the Internet out of the way of talking to a specific computer. Telnet.exe is found in the Windows folder. Create a shortcut to it and place it in an Internet folder.

Internet mail

Microsoft Plus! includes an Internet mail client that works with Microsoft Exchange. Microsoft Exchange is an integrated mail system that allows you to access CompuServe mail, Microsoft mail, Internet mail, and mail from the Microsoft Network and also send or receive faxes.

Most Windows mail tools for the Internet are not as strong as we would like, especially given the fact that the Internet is for the most part used to exchange e-mail. The mail tools on CompuServe or America Online are stronger than such Internet mail tools as the shareware version of Eudora, or Air Mail, which comes with Spry's Internet-in-a-Box. Microsoft is doing everyone (except its competitors) a big favor by including a very strong Internet mail client with Microsoft Plus!.

We discuss the features of the Microsoft Plus! Internet mail client in Chapter 32.

What's missing

Tip

Windows 95 doesn't have a network file system (NFS) or installable file system for Unix or something like Spry's Air FTP. The directories and file systems on non-Windows or DOS-based computers don't look like the file systems on Windows 95 computers. It's nice to have a translation layer that makes them look like VFAT, the Windows 95 file system — perhaps adding drag and drop between file systems. That way you can just drag a file from a remote Unix computer and drop it in your local folder.

NFS lets you put your data or your programs on a Unix computer and run or access them from your Windows computer. The Unix computer looks like a hard disk, and all the naming conventions for the files are the Windows 95 naming conventions.

A no-cost program called Samba that runs on a Sun server allows Windows 95 computers to access the files on the Sun as though they were FAT type files. You can get information about Samba from the World Wide Web at the following address:

    http://lake.canberra.edu.au/pub/samba/samba.html.

Air FTP from Spry gives you a program that looks like the File Manager and allows you to drag and drop files between your computer and remote computers. AirFTP, however, does not turn the Explorer into a real explorer that can transparently connect to Unix computers.

You won't be able to find the Unix or Windows NT servers on the Internet by double clicking the Network Neighborhood icon on your desktop. If you are logged onto a Windows NT server on your local area network, you will be able to see it.

You'll probably want to download a news reader. You can use Mosaic or Netscape to read newsgroups, but that isn't their main focus. MSN carries the newsgroups, so you can access them that way.

We haven't included a mailing-list manager, so if you're on an Internet mailing list (a small news group) you might want to download one of these from the Internet.

Internet Through Your LAN

As we mentioned at the beginning of this chapter, you can also access the Internet through your local area network. In fact, you can have Unix and Windows NT servers on your LAN and access them through your TCP/IP stack — no need to dial them up. Your LAN becomes a little Internet.

Tip

You can place a World Wide Web server on a local server and publish your own home pages internally. Computer users throughout your business can surf the local net, using copies of Internet Explorer, Mosaic, or Netscape to access local home pages that are updated to provide corporate information. E-mail can be handled as though it were any other Internet mail.

Of course, the system administrator can provide access to the Internet through a server over any level of telephone access to some type of Internet service provider. There may be a firewall in place that keeps overly inquisitive outsiders from accessing internal corporate information.

Your computer is configured in a manner similar to that described earlier in this chapter in the section entitled *Installing an Internet Dial-Up Connection*. The TCP/IP stack is bound to your local area network card instead of to your Dial-Up Adapter (local modem). Your system administrator can set up a local DHCP server to resolve addresses. You won't need a Dial-Up Adapter, except for the Direct Cable Connection.

If you have TCP/IP bound to your Dial-Up Adapter and your network card and there is no DHCP server in your local area, your computer will pause every now and then while trying to find something or somebody. If this gets annoying, you will need to unbind TCP/IP from your network card (or get a DHCP server locally).

Tip

A Windows 95 computer set up as a Dial-Up Networking server can't route TCP/IP. So you can't call in from home (to this computer) by using the TCP/IP protocol bound to your Dial-Up Adapter at your home computer and expect to be able to connect to the Unix or Windows NT server on your LAN at work and have that server get you out on the Internet. You'll have to go directly to an Internet service provider from your computer at home.

Windows NT servers set up as RAS (or DUN) servers can take your TCP/IP call and connect you to the internal (LAN) Web pages (or URLs) or to your service provider.

Undocumented

If you have two Internet connections — a LAN and an Internet service provider and if you have a DNS server on your local area network, you should list your DNS server second in your TCP/IP DNS Configuration Properties sheet under Network Control Panel. The local DNS server won't have the IP address of your Internet service provider. If you are dialing out to the Internet, the Internet DNS server can resolve your IP addresses if it is first on the list. If you are connecting locally, the Internet DNS server won't reply and the local DNS server will be contacted next.

Microsoft Plus! Internet Explorer

Now that you've taken care of getting connected to the Internet, you get to do something fun. The Internet Explorer that comes with Microsoft Plus! is a full-featured Windows 95-compatible World Wide Web browser. Unlike other browsers, it takes advantage of Windows 95 interface elements, such as shortcuts.

Internet Explorer is Microsoft's claim to be "with it" regarding the dramatic increase in interest in the Internet. You can use Internet Explorer with any service provider, including Microsoft Network. Microsoft lets you download Internet Explorer from CompuServe, MSN, and other online services without having to purchase Microsoft Plus!. Just like other Web browser vendors, they want to get their browser in everybody's hands.

Internet Explorer is accompanied by the Internet Setup Wizard, which automates many of the processes that we have gone through in this chapter to create an Internet connection. You can use the Wizard to create a connection and then go back and manually check it out by using the steps that we have detailed here. The connectoid you create is associated with the Internet Explorer and is called everytime you double-click the Internet icon on your desktop.

An Internet Control Panel is installed and configured when you install Microsoft Plus!. The Internet service provider connectoid that you created with the Internet Setup Wizard is specified in the Internet AutoDial Properties sheet that appears when you double-click the Internet Control Panel. If you have another connectoid that you wish to call instead of the one you originally created using the Wizard, you can change it by using this properties sheet.

Connecting to CompuServe

Undocumented

You can use Internet Explorer and your CompuServe account to connect to the Internet. H&R Block, CompuServe's corporate owners, paid $100 million to purchase Spry, the makers of Internet-in-a-Box, and used their technology to quickly get a Web browser front end and a TCP/IP stack. You can completely ignore their expenditure of this vast amount and use the better 32-bit TCP/IP stack that comes with Windows 95, and the more advanced web browser Internet Explorer.

Compuserve's version of Air Mosaic comes with its own Winsock.dll file. You want to make sure if you install Air Mosaic (a course that we argue you shouldn't take) that its accompanying Winsock.dll hasn't overwritten the one that comes with Windows 95. You can look in the \Windows\System folder and check the file dates to be sure you have the right one. You can copy the Windows 95 Winsock.dll to your \Windows\Sysbckup folder before you install Air Mosaic, and copy it back to \Windows\System later.

The problem of incompatible-Winsock.dll's is quite common and you want to be sure your Winsock compatible Internet applications are not using the wrong Winsock.dll. You'll want only one Winsock.dll (plus the backup copy in \Windows\Sysbckup) on your computer, and you can search your hard disks with Find to make sure this is the case.

To make a connection to your CompuServe account, take the following steps:

STEPS

Connecting to CompuServe with Internet Explorer

Step 1.   Click the Start button, Programs, Accessories, and then Dial-Up Networking.

Step 2.   Double-click Make New Connectoid to start the Make New Connection wizard and to start the process of creating a connectoid to your CompuServe account.

Step 3.   Enter CompuServe as the name of the connectoid and click the Next button.

Step 4.   Type in your regular local CompuServe connection number. CompuServe has added 28.8Kbps lines, so if you have a 28.8Kbps modem you might try that number. Our experience in the Seattle area is that it is always busy, but this may change. Click Next. Click Finish.

Step 5.   Right-click your new CompuServe icon in the Dial-Up Networking folder window and click Properties.

Step 6.   Click the Configure button and then the Connections tab. Be sure the communications parameters are the default choices — 8, n, 1.

Step 7.   Click the Server Type button, then TCP/IP Settings.

Step 8.   Be sure to click the following parameters in the TCP/IP Settings Properties sheet:

   Server assigned IP address

   Server assigned name server address

   Use header IP compression

   Use default gateway on remote network

   Click OK.

Step 9.   In the Server Type Properties sheet, be sure the server type is PPP (the default). Also check "Log on to network," and "Enable software compression." Uncheck "Require encrypted password." Check TCP/IP and uncheck NetBEUI and IPX/SPX compatible. Click OK.

Step 10.   Edit the sample script file Cis.scp found in the \Program Files\Accessories folder to make any changes necessary for your connection to CompuServe.

Step 11.   Click the Start button, Programs Accessories, Dial-Up Scripting Tool. Highlight your CompuServe connectoid and browse for Cis.ini. Click OK.

Step 12.   Double-click the Internet icon in the Control Panel. Click the down arrow in the drop-down list and highlight CompuServe. Click OK. This connects the Internet Explorer to the CompuServe connectoid.

Step 13.   Double-click your CompuServe connectoid in the Dial-Up Networking folder. Enter your CompuServe account number in the User Name field, and your CompuServe password in the Password field. Click the Save password check box.

You have created a connectoid that logs you into CompuServe as an Internet service provider. You can just double-click the connectoid to make the connection or you can double-click the Internet icon on your desktop to make the connection and start the Internet Explorer.

The CompuServe connection is just like any other Internet service provider connection, although—in our experience— quite a bit slower. You can run other Internet application software on it using the Windows 95 Winsock.dll. You could run Netscape if you like, or whatever. You don't have to run Internet Explorer, or Air Mosaic. Microsoft gave you in Windows 95 what CompuServe paid $100 million for.

Internet Explorer features

You can start the Internet Explorer just by typing in the address of where you want to go in the Run box. Click the Start button, and then click Run. Type in a location like the following:

ftp://ftp.microsoft.com

or

http://www.windows95.com

Want to send e-mail while you're using the Internet Explorer? Click the Address field just below the Internet Explorer's menu bar or click the Start button and then Run. Type in the following:

mailto:brian_livingston@infoworld.com

Then press Enter.

If you want to see the source code of the home page you are currently viewing, right-click the Internet Explorer border and then click View Source.

Internet Explorer Shortcuts

You can place a shortcut on the desktop to your current location on the Web (URL). Either right-click the border of the Internet Explorer, an area in the Internet Explorer client window without a graphic, or a link to another location, or click File in the menu bar. Then click Create Shortcut.

To create a shortcut to a link (a jump to another URL) in a Web page, drag the link to the desktop. You can later double-click this shortcut to start the Internet Explorer and go to the indicated location on the Web.

Images take a long time to download if you are connected to the Internet through a 14.4 or 28.8Kbps phone line. Internet Explorer will load the graphics in the background and let you read the text if you click the scrollbar down to read the text below a graphic.

Versions of Netscape available in June, 1995, wouldn't frame the graphic and display the following text if the height and width of the graphic wasn't provided in the HTML source.

Want to save a graphic file you are viewing in Internet Explorer? Right-click it, click Save As, and then give it a path and a name. The graphic file is saved automatically anyway in the \Program Files\Plus!\microsft inter\cache folder. You can determine how many previously viewed or visited graphics files and web pages are stored locally on your hard disk by clicking View, Options, Advanced in the Internet Explorer menu bar. Slide the Cache size slider to a percentage of the hard disk that you are willing to use for caching these files.

If you want to turn the graphic into wallpaper, right-click the graphic, and click Use As Wallpaper.

Internet Explorer will cache quite a bit of the material that you gather off the Internet, making it quite a bit quicker to review this material. Graphics and web pages may have been updated since you last visited. To get the latest information of a given site, click View, Refresh on the menu bar or press the F5 key.

The Microsoft Network won't be an Internet service provider until the end of 1995, although you can use it to get to Usenet newsgroups and to send and receive Internet e-mail. Until then you'll need to have an account with a full service Internet service provider to use the Internet Explorer.

When MSN is a service provider, Web site authors will be able to mix material from MSN and from the Web putting in links to areas in MSN and locations on the Web.

Microsoft has licensed the Lycos database to be put on MSN. You can visit the Lycos Web site with Internet Explorer just by clicking File, Open in the Internet Explorer menu bar and typing in **http: //lycos.cs.cmu.edu/**. This database will also be available on the Microsoft network. The Lycos database is a full text database of all the Web sites that the Lycos Web crawlers have been able to find.

Favorites

The Internet Explorer tracks a list of favorite Web sites. Favorites is a folder, and you'll find it in the \Windows folder. You can place it wherever you like (say, off the drive that contains the Windows folder), and the Internet Explorer tracks its location. You can divide the Favorites folder up into subfolders organized around common topics and place shortcuts to your favorite sites in these subfolders.

To create subfolders, click Favorites and then Open Favorites on the Internet Explorer menu bar. Right-click the Favorites folder window and click New, Folder — just the way you do in the Explorer.

All favorite sites are shortcuts, and you can put copies of these shortcuts on your desktop and start Internet Explorer by double-clicking them. You'll find the reference to the current location of your favorites folder in the Registry in the following location:

HKEY_CURRENT_USER\ Software\Microsoft\Windows\CurrentVersion\Explorer\Shell Folders

Tip

Want to send e-mail while you're using the Internet Explorer? Click the Address field just below the Internet Explorer's menu bar. Type in the following:

mailto:{*person's name*}

This will start Microsoft Exchange and, if you have properly configured Exchange to use the Internet mail client, you will be able to compose a message.

You can send a friend a document that contains the shortcuts to your favorite places. Shortcuts (any shortcut, actually) can be placed in Word or WordPad documents. These documents can be sent as e-mail MIME documents. Shortcuts can also be placed in Exchange e-mail messages. Just cut and paste them from your Favorites folder.

Undocumented

Thomas Reardon at Microsoft points out a little secret about Internet Explorer fonts. You can change the fonts for different HTML tags. The settings are available in the registry under:

H_Key_Local_Machine\Software\Microsoft\Internet Explorer\Styles

Windows 95 Home Pages

What follows are some interesting Windows 95 related sites that you can visit on the Web:

Table 33-2: Windows 95-Related Web Sites	
Site	*Address*
Windows 95 Secrets	http://www.halcyon.com/davis/secrets.htm
IDG Books	http://www.idgbooks.com
Brian's InfoWorld Column	http://www.infoworld.com/cgi-bin/displayNew.pl?/livingst/livingst.htm
Windows Sources	http://www.zdnet.com/~wsources/
Windows95.com	http://www.windows95.com
Windows 95 Annoyances	http://www.creativelement.com/win95ann/index.html
Pop's Windows 95-NT Report	http://www.clearlight.com/~visanu/report.html
Andrew Schulman	http://www.ora.com/windows/
The Microsoft Exchange Center	http://www.slipstick.com/exchange/
Bob Cerelli's Windows Page	http://www.halcyon.com.cerelli/
Gordon Carter's Exchange help site	http://www.ourworld.compuserve.com/homepages/G_Carter/default.htm
The Internet Starting Point for Windows 95	http://www.total.net/~bklein/win/
Animated Cursor Schemes	http://www.islandnet.com/~wwseb/cursors.htm
The Windows 95 Answer Center	http://www.lpdsoft.com/jturner/
Stroud's Windows 95 Applications	http://www.cwsapps.com//win95.html
Ed Tiley's Windows 95 Home Page	http://www.supernet.net/~edtiley/win95/

Site	*Address*
Internet Mail and News Tips	http://www.home.sprynet.com/sprynet/edm/
Dale's Windows 95 Themes Page	http://www.bitshop.com/~dale/
Windows 95 Startup Logos	http://www.nucleus.com/~kmcmurdo/win95logo.html
The One Stop Windows 95 Site	http://www.win95.com/
#Windows 95	http://www.windows95.org/
Software for the Internet	http://www.tucows.com/window95.html
Microsoft Windows 95	http://www.microsoft.com/windows/
Internet Explorer	http://www.microsoft.com/ie
Windows 95 Tip Sheet	http://www.cs.umb.edu/~alilley/win.html
ClubWin WebMeister's	http://www.cris.com/~randybrg/other.sites.html
Club Internet Explorer	http://www.clubie.com/
How to Search for Operating System Articles	http://www.microsoft.com/kb/peropsys/windows/q96132.htm
Windows 95 FAQ	http://www.primenet.com/~markd/wind95faq.html
Costa's Tips for Windows 95	http://www-na.biznet.com.gr/sail/isa/tipfrm.html
Window Watch Magazine	http://www.windowatch.com/
Dylan Greene's	http://www.wam.umd.edu/~dylan/windows95.html
The Windows 95 Page!	Http://bilogy.queensu.ca/~jonesp/
The Unofficial Windows 95 Software Archive	http://www.netex.net/w95/
The (Unofficial) Windows 95 Home Page	http://www.southwind.net/~leeb/win95.html
The Computer Paper	http://www.tcp.ca/
Windows 95 TCP/IP	http://www.aa.net/~pcd/slp95faq.html95

Summary

Windows 95 comes with the basic tools that you need to get onto the Internet.

▶ Windows 95 supports three networking protocol stacks, one of which is TCP/IP (the protocol used by the Internet).

▶ Combine TCP/IP support with a dial-up networking capability, and Windows 95 gives you the tools you need to connect to the Internet.

▶ We help you secure the right kind of account with an Internet service provider.

▶ You also need to get the right information from your service provider; we show you what you need to get.

▶ Each of the steps in setting up your Windows 95 computer for Dial-Up Networking and TCP/IP support is detailed.

▶ We show you how to connect to your service provider and make sure that you've got a good connection.

▶ Want to surf the Net? Here's where you start.

Chapter 34

Networking

In This Chapter

Microsoft has made Windows 95 a very strong networking client as well as a peer server.

▶ Connecting to Microsoft and Novell NetWare networks

▶ Working with 16-bit networks

▶ Setting up a $60 network

▶ Dealing with interrupts and I/O addresses in preplug and play network adapters

▶ Turning your Windows 95 computer into a NetWare file and print server

▶ Setting up a peer server on a share- or user-level network

▶ Connecting to multiple networks simultaneously

▶ Understanding network security so you can use the resources you need

▶ Connecting to folders and printers with the Universal Naming Convention

▶ Cleaning up network problems with Net Watcher, System Monitor, System Policy Editor, Registry Editor, and Password List Editor

▶ Using Windows networking applications

Basic Network Support

Windows 95 comes with all of the necessary networking software required to set up a 32-bit protected-mode Microsoft Windows network between computers running Windows 95, or to a network with computers running Windows NT, LAN Manager, and Windows for Workgroups 3.11. Additionally, Windows 95 includes a 32-bit protected-mode client for Novell NetWare networks so your Windows 95 computer can be a compatible client on a NetWare network.

Microsoft has finally agreed that, for the time being at least, Novell has almost as strong a monopoly in the networking operating system market as Microsoft has in the desktop operating system market. To honor that market position (as well as to undermine it), Microsoft has written a very strong 32-bit protected-mode Client for NetWare Networks product and an IPX/SPX-compatible protocol.

A Windows 95 computer can be configured as a NetWare print and file server on a NetWare network. Three networking protocols are provided: NetBEUI, IPX/SPX, and TCP/IP. Windows NT and NetWare servers can be directly accessed by Windows 95 workstations. Multiple (up to 10) 32-bit network clients can be running on your computer at the same time, allowing access to multiple networks and network services simultaneously, for example, using TCP/IP to access a Unix server using the Internet Explorer and Client for NetWare Networks to access a NetWare server. Because they run in protected mode, these network clients don't take up conventional memory.

All the networking components developed by Microsoft are 32-bit protected-mode Virtual Device Drivers (Vx Ds). Because Windows 95 uses protected-mode network components, it doesn't have to switch your processor (386, 486 or Pentium) from protected mode to real mode (a process that wastes too many processor cycles), and therefore networking speeds get much faster (50–200 percent).

Real-mode drivers, especially for NetWare, have a nasty habit of causing some programs to lock up your computer — the dreaded "black screen of death." There isn't any way to completely eliminate this problem without using protected-mode drivers. The real-mode drivers create memory conflicts as well as pose unresolved contention for control of interrupts.

Real-mode network drivers are loaded in conventional memory. Memory managers allow you to partially load these drivers between the 640K and 1MB memory addresses. Network components are particularly large, and this size causes a reduction of the memory resources available to DOS programs, sometimes to the point that some DOS programs can't be run on networked computers. The new protected-mode network components are loaded above the lower 640K area, leaving this memory available for Doom and other mission-critical DOS programs.

Apart from its 32-bit network drivers, Windows 95 can still be a good client for the 16-bit real-mode versions of all of the major networks that are available for PCs. These include:

- Artisoft LANtastic version 5.0 or later
- Banyan VINES version 5.52 or later
- Beame and Whiteside Network File System 3.0c or later
- DEC Pathworks version 5.0 or later
- IBM OS/2 LAN Server
- Microsoft Windows Network (version 3.11)
- MS-Net compatibles
- Novell NetWare 3.11 or later
- Sunselect PC-NFS version 5.0 or later
- TCS 10Net version 4.1 or later

What Windows 95 Networking Buys You

The whole point of networking is to be able to access resources that are beyond your computer. These resources are shared because they are too expensive to be given exclusively to one user, or because they are a managed resource (for example, a corporate transaction processing database) that needs to be always available to many different users simultaneously.

Windows 95 has been designed to be a particularly good networking client (and peer-to-peer server). Microsoft put more programmer resources into this aspect of Windows 95 than any other.

Windows 95 supports:

- User profiles and system policies that make it possible (with appropriate network administration) for users to log on to any networked Windows 95 computer and have their own desktop and applications available to them

- Protected-mode networking clients, protocols, and adapter drivers that don't take any conventional memory

- User-level security enforced by either Windows NT or NetWare servers and centrally administered

- A single logon dialog box that allows you to log on to your Windows 95 computer (and bring up your user-specific desktop) as well as on to all the network resources and servers available to you

- Backup agents, so backup software running Windows NT or NetWare servers can back up Windows 95 computers

- Direct Cable Connection (DCC) and Dial-Up Networking (DUN)

- Diskless (or floppy disk-only) workstations connected to shared copies of Windows 95 on Windows NT or NetWare servers

- Browsing of shared network resources or resources on network servers through the Explorer, folder windows, or the new common dialog boxes (Network Neighborhood)

- Remote printing and printer administration

- Network management through Simple Network Management Protocols (SNMP) using third-party software and a supplied agent

- Simultaneous access to multiple networks and multiple networking protocols

- 32-bit protected-mode multiple networking protocols: NetBEUI, IPX/SPX, and TCP/IP

- Remote administration and network resource monitoring

Quick and Dirty Networking

If you want to hook up a couple of computers to share resources (like a printer and some folders), here's what you need to do:

Setting up a Quick and Dirty Network

Step 1. Buy (at about $25.95 each) two NE2000 compatible network cards. These don't need to be plug-and-play compatible (which will cost you a little more, most likely), but they should be software configurable (using a DOS-based configuration program that comes on a diskette) from the card manufacturer.

Step 2. Get 25 feet or so of RG58 Thinnet Ethernet cable with BNC connectors on each end for less than $10.

Step 3. Install the cards in available slots in both of the computers. If one or both of the computers are portables, this is going to get a lot more expensive because you will need either a parallel port adapter or a docking station. (Too bad most portables don't have built-in Ethernet ports).

Step 4. T-connectors and terminators come with the cards; you'll use them to connect the cable to the T-connectors, the T-connectors to the cards, and the terminators to the other end of the T-connectors.

Step 5. If the cards aren't plug and play-compatible cards, run the DOS-based configuration software first to set up its interrupts and I/O addresses. The default values for the cards may be OK, depending on what hardware you have installed in your computers.

To find out which interrupts and I/O addresses are available on your computers, you can boot them, double-click the System icon in the Control Panel, click the Device Manager tab, and then click the Properties button while Computer is highlighted. Used interrupts are shown first; click the I/O radio button and see which addresses are already used.

Reboot your computers and go to the DOS prompt by pressing the F8 key at boot-up time and then run the DOS-based configuration software, or just open up a windowed DOS box and run the configuration software in it.

Step 6. Double-click the Add New Hardware icon in the Control Panel on both computers. You can have the Add Hardware Wizard search for your new adapters or you can specify what you have. The Wizard will load and configure the 32-bit protected-mode NDIS 3.1 driver for your adapters.

Step 7. Double-click the Network icon in the Control Panel. Highlight your adapter in the list of networking components and see which networking protocols are bound to the adapter (in Step 6) by clicking the Properties button and the Bindings tab. For a small computer network, you'll most likely want to bind either NetBEUI or IPX/SPX. If you need to bind a protocol, click the Add button, highlight the protocol, and click the next Add button.

Step 8. Be sure to allow sharing of your resources so either or both of the computers can be peer servers to the other. Make sure that Client for Microsoft Networks and File and Print Sharing for Microsoft Networks are implemented in the Network Control Panel. Add them if they aren't with the Add button.

Step 9. Click the Identification tab in the Network Control Panel. Be sure that both computers have different names, but the same workgroup name. Click OK.

Step 10. Click the OK button in the Network Control Panel and then reboot your computers for all of this to take effect.

Step 11. Open Explorer or folder windows on the desktops of both computers. Right-click resources (disk drives and/or folders) that you want to share, click Sharing in the right mouse button menu, and configure the sharing Properties sheets. Do the same in the Printers folder for printers that you are going to share.

Step 12. Double-click the Network Neighborhood icon on the desktop of one of the computers. You should be able to see the name of the workgroup in the Network Neighborhood folder window. Double-click the workgroup name to see the name of the other computer. Double-click its name to see the shared resources.

Further elaboration and hand-holding for these steps are provided in the next section.

Network Installation

Windows 95 Setup will install Microsoft Network or Microsoft's NetWare client software. It can also install the Windows 95 client software to work with the other networks, but the 16-bit real-mode network software from these other vendors should be installed before the Windows 95 setup process.

If you are, at this moment, setting up Windows 95 and you haven't previously installed the 16-bit network software from your other networking vendor (if you have one), click Cancel when you reach the Network Configuration dialog box, and restart the Windows 95 setup process after you install this software. Otherwise you will have to configure the Windows 95 network components yourself as well as install this third-party software.

If you need to work with a 16-bit network, you can configure Windows 95 networking using the Network icon in the Control Panel after you have installed the third-party networking software.

When you are setting up Windows 95, the Network Configuration dialog box will be displayed, if you choose Custom Setup, as is our recommendation. The Network Configuration dialog box, as shown in Figure 34-1, allows you to choose which network client to install, which network adapter to support, which networking protocol to bind to the adapter, and which networking services (for example, peer file and printer sharing) to offer.

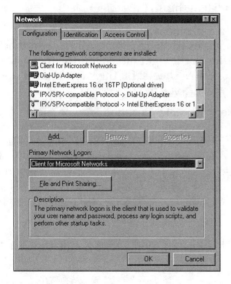

Figure 34-1: The Network Configuration dialog box. Click the Add button to install additional networking components.

If Windows 95 Setup has successfully detected your existing hardware and software network components, you don't need to make any changes in the Network Configuration dialog box. This is true, even if the only network adapter you had installed is a serial or parallel port that can be used for Direct Cable Connection (DCC), or a modem, to be used for Dial-Up Networking (DUN). There are exceptions, however, as we discuss later in this chapter.

If you add a network card or install networking software for networks other than Microsoft Network or NetWare after you have installed Windows 95, you'll need to go to the Network Control Panel to install networking support. The Configuration Properties sheet in the Network Control Panel looks a lot like the Network Configuration dialog box. Double-click the Network icon in the Control Panel to display it.

A network configuration consists of networking client software, software drivers for a given network adapter, a networking protocol, and networking services. To install any of these components, click the Add button in the Network Configuration dialog box to display the Select Network Component Type dialog box, as shown in Figure 34-2.

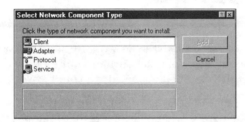

Figure 34-2: The Select Network Component Type dialog box.

Choosing a client

Highlight Client in the network components list box and click the Add button to display the Select Network Client dialog box, as shown in Figure 34-3. The 32-bit protected-mode clients for Microsoft networks and NetWare networks are provided by Microsoft on the Windows 95 source diskettes or CD-ROM.

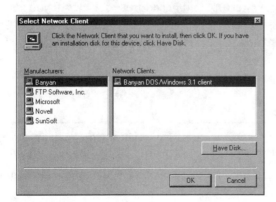

Figure 34-3: The Select Network Client dialog box. You have the option of selecting a networking client from those provided on the Windows 95 source diskettes or CD-ROM, or finding a client on another network vendor's diskette.

You can install one 16-bit real-mode networking client and up to 10 protected-mode clients. Only two 32-bit protected-mode clients are available from Microsoft — Microsoft Networks and NetWare Networks clients. If you install LANtastic, you can't install a protected-mode client.

If you install a 16-bit networking client only, you won't need to deal with the other networking components in this dialog box, because you will use the client software to specify how these items are configured.

If you install the Client of Microsoft Networks or NetWare Networks, you have the option to add or change the network adapter, protocol, and network services.

Choosing an adapter and configuring its resources

Your computer is physically connected to the network through either your network adapter (card), your serial or parallel port, or your modem. Windows 95 installs adapter driver software specific to your network adapter.

Microsoft provides a broad range of adapter drivers that support the Network Device Interface Specification (NDIS) 3.1 standard. It is this standard that allows for multiple protected-mode networking protocols. Microsoft worked with all the major network adapter manufacturers to make sure that adapter drivers were available for their cards.

The NDIS 3.1 specification supports Ethernet, Token Ring, and ArcNet networking cards and hot docking with plug and play adapters.

Real-mode NDIS 2.*xx* and ODI (Open Datalink Interface) drivers that come (on diskettes) with preplug and play adapters can also be used if Microsoft hasn't provided a new NDIS 3.1 driver for your specific adapter.

The Windows 95 Setup hardware detection routines should have correctly determined which network adapter card you have installed in your computer and its range of possible interrupt and I/O address settings. If you install a card later, or Setup didn't get it right, you can configure the adapter driver settings yourself. If you need to add an adapter driver, first take the following steps:

STEPS

Adding an Adapter Driver

Step 1. Click the Add button in the Network Control Panel or, during Windows 95 Setup, in the Network Configuration dialog box.

Step 2. In the Select Network Component Type dialog box, highlight Adapter and click Add.

Step 3. In the Select Network Adapter dialog box, select an adapter manufacturer in the left-hand list and an adapter model in the right-hand list. Click OK.

If you use Direct Cable Connection (DCC) or Dial-Up Networking (DUN), you'll use the Dial-Up Adapter driver. The Dial-Up Adapter is the NDIS 3.1 driver for your serial or parallel port, or modem. DCC and DUN are real networking options and require full network configuration based on the Dial-Up Adapter.

See Chapters 28 and 30 for more details about these networking options.

Configuring resources for the adapter driver

Once you have told Windows 95 which network adapter you have physically installed, it will load the correct driver and determine the current hardware settings for your card. This is where it gets sticky, as Windows 95 may not correctly determine your network adapter's interrupt and I/O address settings. To determine which values Windows 95 has chosen, take the following steps:

STEPS

Determining Network Adapter Resource Values

Step 1. Highlight the network adapter in the Network Control Panel or, during Windows 95 Setup, in the Network Configuration dialog box.

Step 2. Click the Properties button, and then the Resources tab. The Network Adapter Resources Properties sheet for your adapter will be displayed, as shown in Figure 34-4.

Step 3. Compare the values given in the Resources Properties sheet with the known values for the adapter card. If you don't know what those values are, you are going to have to accept for now what this Properties sheet says they are.

(continued)

STEPS *(continued)*

Determining Network Adapter Resource Values

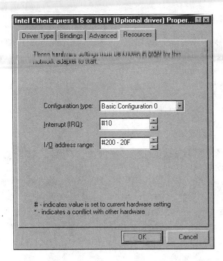

Figure 34-4: The Network Adapter Resources Properties sheet. During Windows 95 Setup, you won't be able to change these values.

If you are going to be installing Windows 95 over Windows for Workgroups 3.11, you can find the previous values for your network card by double-clicking the Network Setup icon in the Windows 3.*x* Program Manager. In addition, Windows 95 Setup will find those values (in the file Protocol.ini) and correctly configure the adapter driver to conform to the current card settings.

If you have a plug and play adapter, Windows 95 will configure it correctly. If you have a preplug and play adapter, your adapter's settings can be changed either by changing jumpers on the adapter or by running configuration software provided by the adapter's manufacturer. For these preplug and play adapters (except for the Intel EtherExpress adapters), the Resources Properties sheet will at first display only possible settings for this adapter, not necessarily the actual current settings for the card. It is up to you to get the actual and the possible settings to match.

The possible adapter resource settings are set by Windows 95 to avoid conflicts with other devices — if this is possible, given the set of possible settings for the given adapter. If a conflict is determined to exist (because all the possible settings of the adapter card conflict with other devices in your computer), this will be indicated by an asterisk in the appropriate field in the Resource Properties sheet next to the conflicting setting.

Secret

You can't change the resource settings during Windows 95 Setup, and this can be a source of some difficulty — especially if you are setting up Windows 95 over a network and through the adapter to which Windows 95 has now assigned the incorrect address or interrupt, for example, if your CD-ROM is connected to another computer on the network. To complete the setup, Windows 95 will need to copy files over the network after the computer upon which you are installing Windows 95 has been rebooted and is running under Windows 95. This means the network is no longer available to this computer because the network adapter has been incorrectly configured — a little Catch-22.

The source files that may no longer be available include files needed to configure your modem, printer, and Microsoft Exchange. You will have to go back after you have correctly configured your network adapter and install these items separately using the Modems Control Panel, the Printers folder, and the Add/Remove Programs Control Panel (to configure Exchange).

To get the adapter's settings to match the settings specified in the Network Adapter Resources Properties sheet, you'll need to first complete the Windows 95 setup process as far as possible, and then go back and change either the adapter or the resources settings.

To change an adapter that uses jumpers: Turn off your computer, pull the card, move the jumpers to match the settings given in the Resources Properties sheet, reinstall the card, and restart Windows 95.

To change an adapter using the manufacturer's configuration software: Open a DOS window when Windows 95 restarts after setup and run the manufacturer's configuration software for the adapter. You'll need to restart Windows 95 after making these changes.

To change the resources settings to match the adapter's current settings: Restart Windows 95, follow the steps earlier in this chapter entitled *Determining Network Adapter Resource Values,* and change the values to match your adapter's value. Restart Windows 95.

Choosing a networking protocol

Individual computers have to speak the same language if you want them to talk to each other. The language they speak is the *networking protocol*. Microsoft provides 32-bit protected-mode implementations for three networking protocols: NetBEUI, IPX/SPX, and TCP/IP. A networking protocol must be bound to the network adapter (or to multiple adapters) for the adapter and the protocol to work together to get the messages across the wire.

■ NetBEUI (*NetBIOS extended user interface*) is Microsoft's fast, efficient, workgroup (non-routeable) protocol. It works great between other Windows 95, Windows for Workgroup 3.11, LAN Manager, and Windows NT workstations and servers.

■ IPX/SPX (*Internetwork Packet Exchange*) is Novell NetWare's protocol, and therefore a standard for small- to medium-sized businesses and department-level networks. Both NetWare and Windows NT 3.5 servers (as well as Windows 95 computers) can be accessed using this protocol. Windows 95 computers can be configured as NetWare file and print servers and addressed through IP/SPX. Microsoft's IPX/SPX-compatible protocol is the default for Windows 95.

■ TCP/IP (*Transmission Control Protocol/Internet Protocol*) is the Unix and Internet standard protocol. It provides networking support to a broad range of different computer operating systems, indeed, to all computers that can communicate over the Internet. Windows 95 includes a set of TCP/IP utilities, as described in Chapter 33. Internet addresses (which are assigned to each computer on the network) can be dynamically allocated because this version of TCP/IP can be configured to use the Dynamic Host Configuration Protocol (DCHP) or Windows Internet Naming Service (WINS). Microsoft also supplies a Winsock version 1.1 DLL so Winsock-compliant Internet programs like Mosaic and Internet mailers can work with TCP/IP.

In addition to these protocols, protocols from other manufacturers are supported.

To choose a protocol, take the following steps:

STEPS

Choosing a Protocol

Step 1.   Click the Add button in the Network Control Panel or, during Windows 95 Setup, in the Network Configuration dialog box.

Step 2.   In the Select Network Component Type dialog box, highlight Protocol and click Add.

Step 3.   In the Select Network Protocol dialog box, select a manufacturer in the left-hand list and a protocol in the right-hand list. Click OK.

Choosing network services

Most network services, such as the ability to connect to remote computers and browse their disk drives, are available once you've configured your client, adapter, and protocol. Microsoft and other manufacturers provide additional network services. If you use Microsoft's clients for Microsoft or NetWare Networks, you can configure your computer to share its folders, drives, and/or printers with other users on the network. You can have your files backed up with tape-backup software running on a Windows NT or NetWare server. You can administer HP printers running on NetWare networks.

To add these services take the following steps:

STEPS

Adding Network Services

Step 1.   Click the Add button in the Network Control Panel or, during Windows 95 Setup, in the Network Configuration dialog box

Step 2.   In the Select Network Component Type dialog box, highlight Service and click Add.

Step 3.   In the Select Network Service dialog box, select a manufacturer in the left-hand list and the Service in the right-hand list. Click OK.

Sharing your resources

You make your hard disk drives, folders, and printers available to others on the network by sharing them. Although sharing isn't always easy, in this case it is.

To share your folders or disk drives and printers using the network services provided on the Windows 95 source diskettes or CD-ROM, you need to install either Client for Microsoft Networks or Client for NetWare Networks. In addition, you need to choose Microsoft as the manufacturer in Step 3 above, and either File and printer sharing for Microsoft Networks, or File and printer sharing for NetWare Networks as the network service.

You can share your disk drives as Read-Only, Full, or Depends on Password (if your computer is set for share-level security). Full access allows users at other computers on the network to create files and folders on your computer. They can also delete or edit new or existing files and folders on your computer. If you are using user-level security you can name the users who have access to your resources. (If you are a network administrator with remote administration privileges, you can determine who has access to which resources on a client computer.)

If you allow only Read-Only access to your disk drives, other nonadministrative users cannot delete your files and folders. If you don't share disk drives and folders, other users cannot see what you have on your computer.

Once you have chosen to turn on the ability to share, you'll still need to specify which resources you are going to share. Chapter 23 provides details on making your printer available across your network.

To share a folder or disk drive take the following steps:

STEPS

Sharing a Folder or Drive

Step 1. In an Explorer window, right-click the icon for the drive or folder that you wish to share.

Step 2. Click Sharing in the right mouse button menu. (Note that the Sharing option will appear in the right mouse-button menu only if you are on a network, have DCC configured, or have Dial-Up Networking (DUN), which gives you the ability to have connectoids to the Internet, MSN, and so on.) The Sharing Properties sheet, as shown in Figure 34-5, is displayed.

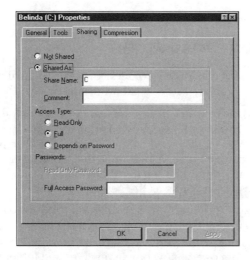

Figure 34-5: The share-level security Sharing Properties sheet. Click either Not Shared or Shared As. If you have configured your computer for user-level security, you will be able to specify which users will have access to your computer.

Step 3. To share your drive or folder, click Share As.

Step 4. You can enter a new name for the resource as well as a comment to help others understand which resource is being shared.

If you add a dollar sign to the end of the resource's share name, it is hidden from users who are using Network Neighborhood for network browsing. You might want to do this for your Microsoft Mail postoffice, which needs to be shared but not browsed.

Step 5. If your computer is configured for share-level security (most likely on a peer-to-peer network), you'll be able to set access type (Read-Only or Full) and the password required to access your resource.

If your computer is configured for user-level security (you have a Windows NT or NetWare server on your network), you can specify who has access to your resources.

Step 6. Click OK.

We discuss user-level and share-level security in the *Network Security* section later in this chapter.

Primary Network Logon

If you click the down arrow in the Primary Network Logon field in the Network Configuration dialog box, or the Network Control Panel, you'll have the following choices:

- Windows Logon
- Client for Microsoft Networks
- Client for NetWare Networks

Choose Windows Logon if you are not logging on to a network or are logging on to a peer-to-peer network. Choose one of the two clients if you are logging on to a network with either a Windows NT server or a NetWare server and have installed one or both of these clients.

File and Print Sharing

You can decide if you are going to share your printer(s), your folders and drives, or both. Click File and Print Sharing in the Network Configuration dialog box or the Network Control Panel to make this choice.

Name that computer

During the Windows 95 setup process, you will be asked to give your computer a name. You will also need to enter the name of your local workgroup, as shown in Figure 34-6. The *workgroup name* is a name that a group of computers will share, and it defines them as an entity. Your computer name must be unique on your LAN.

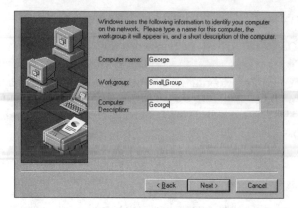

Figure 34-6: The identification dialog box. A similar Properties sheet is displayed when you double-click the Network icon in the Control Panel and then click the Identification tab.

You must give your computer a name and specify a workgroup no matter which networking software you are using. Your computer name can be as long as 15 characters, must contain no spaces, and may use only alphanumeric characters and these special characters:

$$! @ \# \$ \% \char`\^ \& () - \_ ` \{ \} . \sim$$

You also can enter a description of your computer up to 48 characters in length (no commas) to help other users on your network identify your computer.

You can change all of these values by double-clicking the Network icon in the Control Panel, and then clicking the Identification tab.

Microsoft Networks

You can install Client for Microsoft Networks to connect your Windows 95 computer with computers running Windows 95, Windows NT (both versions 3.1 and 3.5x), LAN Manager, Windows for Workgroups 3.11, Workgroup Add-On for MS-DOS, as well as other Microsoft Network-compatible networks. If you configure it as the Primary Network Logon client, you have the option to:

■ Use a Windows NT server as a password server, allowing for user-level security and control from the server (as opposed to share-level security, which is standard on peer-to-peer networks)

■ Share your files and printer(s) with other network users

■ Use user profiles to allow for different network connections and configurations for different users

■ Allow for the remote administration of the Registry on your computer

If you are installing Windows 95 on a computer that is running Windows for Workgroups 3.11 networking, Client for Microsoft Networks will be installed automatically by Setup. Otherwise, you can install Client for Microsoft Networks using the procedure detailed in the *Network Installation* section earlier in this chapter, choosing Microsoft as the manufacturer in the Select Network Client dialog box.

If you install DCC and/or DUN (either during Windows 95 Setup or later using the Add/Remove Programs Control Panel), Client for Microsoft Networks and the Dial-Up Adapter are automatically installed.

Configuring your computer as Client for Microsoft Networks

If you are connecting your Windows 95 computer to other computers using Windows 95, Windows for Workgroups 3.11, or Workgroup Add-On for MS-DOS, you don't need to worry about logging on to a Windows NT domain for user-level security. All security on this peer-to-peer networking scheme is handled with passwords assigned to resources (share-level security). You can choose to reconnect to the resources that are shared on your network at startup time, or later when you actually browse the shared folders on another computer or print to a printer connected to another computer.

If you have a Windows NT computer on your Microsoft network, you may need to log on to it if you want to have access to network resources. If the Windows NT server has been configured to provide user-level security, shared resources on other peer servers (Windows 95 computers that are running File and Print Sharing for Microsoft Networks) are available to you after you enter your user password.

To configure your Windows 95 computer to Client for Microsoft Networks, take the following steps:

STEPS

Configuring Client for Microsoft Networks

Step 1. Highlight Client for Microsoft Networks, either in the Network Configuration dialog box during Windows 95 Setup or in the Configuration Properties sheet of the Network Control Panel. Click the Properties button. The General Properties sheet for Client for Microsoft Networks will be displayed, as shown in Figure 34-7.

(continued)

STEPS *(continued)*

Configuring Client for Microsoft Networks

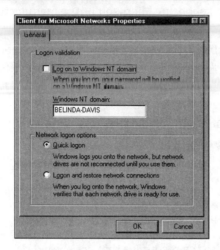

Figure 34-7: The Client for Microsoft Networks General Properties sheet.

Step 2.   To use a networked Windows NT server for logon validation, click "Log on to Windows NT domain."

Step 3.   To log on to your Microsoft network and delay connecting to network resources until you need them (if you have previously established a persistent network connection), click Quick logon.

A persistent network connection is established for shared folders and disk drives by checking the Reconnect at Logon check box in the Map Network Drive dialog box. For printers, check Reconnect at Logon in the Capture Printer Port dialog box.

Step 4.   To establish a connection at startup with all the shared network resources with which you have previously specified a persistent connection, click Logon and restore network connections.

Step 5.   Click OK.

Configuring a Microsoft networking protocol

Client for Microsoft Networks can work with any of the three protocols provided by Microsoft. NetBEUI is the default protocol for communication among Windows 95, Windows for Workgroups 3.11, Windows NT, LAN Manager, and Microsoft Workgroup Add-On for MS-DOS. Still, IPX/SPX and TCP/IP can be used to communicate with other Windows 95 and Windows NT computers.

Highlight the protocol used with Client for Microsoft Networks in the Network Control Panel or in the Network Configuration dialog box and then click the Properties button. Click the Bindings tab to see if the Client for Microsoft Networks uses this protocol, as shown in Figure 34-8.

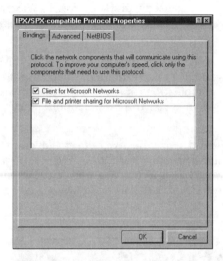

Figure 34-8: The Protocol Bindings Properties sheet. Click the check box next to the network components that you want bound to this protocol.

Novell NetWare Networks

Microsoft doesn't supply the NetWare network operating system software. That is, it doesn't provide the operating system for the NetWare server. That's Novell's job. Microsoft does provide 32-bit protected-mode versions of NetWare-compatible client software, IPX/SPX-compatible protocol, and NDIS 3.1 adapter drivers. These drivers allow your Windows 95 computer to connect to a NetWare server. The server can be running Novell NetWare versions 2.15 or later, 3.*x*, or 4.*x*. You won't need to run any of the real-mode software from Novell to turn your computer into a NetWare-compatible client (or NetWare-compatible file and print server).

Novell makes available two NetWare clients — NETX (for NetWare 3.*x*) and VLM (for NetWare 4.*x*). Windows 95 supports these two 16-bit real-mode clients, and you can use them instead of the Microsoft Client for NetWare Networks. There is no benefit to using the NETX client. VLM (Virtual Load Module) provides access to NetWare Directory Services (NDS), an enterprise-wide naming service that simplifies the management of user access to a wide range of network resources. After Windows 95 is released, Microsoft will provide NDS access in an updated Client for NetWare Networks.

Client for NetWare Networks goes naturally with Microsoft's 32-bit protected-mode IPX/SPX-compatible protocol and NDIS 3.1 adapter driver. If you choose to install it, these components are automatically configured and installed with it. Your existing real-mode ODI adapter drivers and Novell-supplied IPX/SPX protocol stack can be used with Client for NetWare Networks if you want to run TSRs that absolutely require Novell's implementation of IPX/SPX.

Because Windows 95 computers can connect to NetWare networks using so many different configurations, you have the option of trying different combinations to see what difference the combinations make. It is particularly easy to go from one to the other, so there's no need for trepidation about starting with something and changing it later.

To install Client for NetWare Networks, use the procedure detailed in the *Network Installation* section earlier in this chapter. Choose Microsoft as the manufacturer in the Select Network Client dialog box, and select Client for NetWare Networks in the Network Client list box.

Configuring your computer as Client for NetWare Networks

Client for NetWare Networks will be automatically installed and configured if you install Windows 95 in the Windows directory of a computer configured correctly as a Novell NetWare client. Log onto a NetWare server before you install Windows 95 to make sure that everything is correctly configured.

STEPS

Configuring Client for NetWare Networks

Step 1.   Highlight Client for NetWare Networks, either in the Network Configuration dialog box during Windows 95 Setup, or in the Configuration Properties sheet of the Network Control Panel. Click the Properties button. The General Properties sheet for Client for NetWare Networks will be displayed, as shown in Figure 34-9.

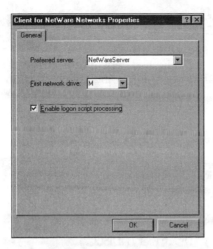

Figure 34-9: The Client for NetWare Networks General Properties sheet. Type in the UNC name of the NetWare server that you will first log onto.

Step 2. Enter the UNC name of your preferred NetWare server. (See the section *The Universal Naming Convention (UNC)* later in this chapter for information on the UNC naming convention.)

Step 3. Enter the volume designation letter for your first network connection.

Step 4. If you want to process a NetWare logon script, click Enable logon script processing.

Step 5. Click OK.

Using a Windows 95 computer as a NetWare print and file server

The Microsoft file and printer sharing for NetWare Networks software allows your Windows 95 computer to become a NetWare file and print server on a NetWare network. A Windows 95 computer can perform file and print services as if it were a NetWare server. You can add Windows 95 peer servers to your network without purchasing additional NetWare licenses. It does require that you have at least one NetWare server on your NetWare network.

Configuring the IPX/SPX-compatible protocol

If you are using Microsoft's IPX/SPX-compatible protocol, you can configure it (or any of the Microsoft-supplied networking protocols) using the Network Control Panel or the Network Configuration dialog box. Just highlight the protocol and click the Properties button.

Configuring the adapter driver

Highlight your network adapter in the Network Control Panel or the Network Configuration dialog box and click the Properties button. You have the choice of three adapter driver types:

- Enhanced-mode (32-bit and 16-bit) NDIS driver (NDIS 3.1)
- Real-mode (16-bit) NDIS driver (NDIS 2.*x*)
- Real-mode (16-bit) ODI driver

The default adapter driver chosen automatically when you choose Client for NetWare Networks or Client for Microsoft Networks is the NDIS 3.1 driver. The IPX/SPX-compatible networking protocol will be bound to this adapter. Click the Bindings tab to see which protocols are bound to your adapter.

The adapter's interrupt and I/O address are found in the Resources Settings Properties sheet. Click the Resources tab. For additional information, see the section earlier in this chapter entitled *Configuring resources for the adapter driver.*

The properties displayed in the Advanced Properties sheet depend on the specific adapter.

Logging Onto the Network

If you are connected to a network using a 16-bit real-mode driver, a network logon prompt will appear on your screen in text mode before the Windows 95 desktop is displayed. You'll need to log on before Windows 95 starts.

If you have installed Client for Microsoft Networks or Client for NetWare Networks, separate logon dialog boxes will appear the first time that you restart Windows 95. There will also be a logon dialog box for logging on to your own computer — pretty rude, actually.

If you use the same password in all the logon dialog boxes, the next time you start Windows 95, you will be presented with one "unified" logon dialog box. The only way this is going to work is if your password for your logon to your primary NetWare server is the same as your logon password to your Windows NT server and the same as the password for your own computer.

If you are logging on to a Microsoft Network without a Windows NT server (for example, connecting to other Windows 95 and WFWG 3.11 computers), you won't be faced with a Microsoft Network logon dialog box. Resources on peer-to-peer networks are protected (if protected at all) with passwords that are unique to the resources, not to the users. You will need to configure your logon correctly using the steps outlined earlier in this chapter in the section entitled *Configuring your computer as Client for Microsoft Networks.*

Passwords for resources that are protected by share-level (peer-to peer) security are encrypted and remembered in the *password cache,* a file stored on your Windows 95 computer. They are retrieved from the password cache after the first time you successfully log on to a shared network resource, so you don't have to enter the password for a resource again. You (or your network administrator) can configure your computer so passwords aren't cached and you have to enter them anew each time you access a resource or server that requires a password.

If you have configured your Windows 95 computer to enable user profiles, you will always have to (at least) negotiate with the Windows 95 logon dialog box. To enable user profiles, double-click the Passwords icon in the Control Panel, click the User Profile tab, and then click "Users can customize their own." Your password can be blank.

You would be able to log on to the network without seeing a logon dialog box if you have disabled user profiles, selected Windows Logon as the Primary Network Logon in the Network Control Panel, used a blank password, and your passwords for logging on to your NetWare or Windows NT server are also blank. This would also be the case if you were logging on to a Microsoft peer-to-peer network under these conditions.

The great Windows 95 innovation is to cache the various passwords so only one password dialog box is required to log onto a network (if you do it right), no matter whether it is a peer-to-peer network, a NetWare network, or a Microsoft network with a Windows NT server.

The passwords that you have acquired are stored in an encrypted file, Share.pwl, referred to as a *password cache*. Delete this file and you lose access to password-protected resources and servers.

You can change some passwords by double-clicking the Passwords icon in the Control Panel. The Password List Editor doesn't let you change passwords, but does let you delete passwords from your password cache. You might want to use the Password List Editor to get rid of passwords that are no longer in use or, if you are a network administrator, to disallow access to some resources or servers whose passwords were previously cached.

You'll find the Password List Editor on the Windows 95 source CD-ROM in the \Admin\Apptools\Pwledit folder. You can use the Add/Remove Programs icon in the Control Panel and the Windows Setup tab to install it. Click the Have Disk button and give the dialog box the above path name.

The Network Neighborhood

The servers and shared resources on the network are made visible through the Network Neighborhood, either by double-clicking this icon on the desktop or clicking it in an Explorer view. You'll also find the Network Neighborhood icon in common dialog boxes (like the File, Open dialog box) used by 32-bit Windows 95-aware applications (like WordPad and MS Paint).

You can use the Map Network Drive icon found on an Explorer or folder-window Toolbar to give a volume drive letter designation to a server and shared directory or disk drive. You can likewise map a networked printer to an LPT port, using the Capture Printer Port dialog box found in the Details Properties sheet of a networked printer. (Right-click a printer icon in the Printers folder, click Properties, and then click the Details tab.)

The Network Neighborhood bridges the chasm between your computer and the network. You browse the network in the same manner that you browse your own computer. There isn't a different interface.

Tip

This is not the case if you browse the Internet. To see files on the Internet, you need a tool like the Internet Explorer (which comes with Microsoft Plus!). The Internet Explorer may have the Explorer name, but it doesn't look like the Windows 95 Explorer. Files on other computers on the Internet aren't displayed in the same fashion as they are in the Explorer.

Microsoft hasn't written extensions to the Explorer that allow it to display file listings from Unix computers (which are prevalent on the Internet) in a manner consistent with the display of file listings on Windows 95 computers. Spry, the company that wrote Internet-in-a-Box, wrote a File Manager-like Internet (Winsock-compatible client) application that let you display files on other systems in a manner that mimicked the Windows 3.*x* File Manager.

Windows 95 integrates your computer and the network by making files and printers on other computers look and feel the same as local resources.

Unlike the case with Windows 3.*x*, you do not have to map a network drive to be able to see and use the files on that drive. As long as the file is displayed in your folder window, it is available to you. You can run programs (you may need to make other adjustments in the program's configuration) and edit documents that reside on other computers without mapping that computer disk drive to a logical drive letter.

The Universal Naming Convention (UNC)

Every computer and server on your network has a name. You provided a name for your computer when you installed Windows 95.

You refer to other computers and resources on the network by their names. For example, \\Billscomputer\Cdrive\Mystuff refers to another computer (Billscomputer) that is sharing its resources, the folder — Mystuff — on the hard disk drive name Cdrive (most likely the C:\ drive on Bill's computer).

This way of referring to servers or computers that are sharing their resources is referred to as the *universal naming convention* (UNC). Notice that there are two back slashes before the computer's name. There are single back slashes between the name of the computer and the name of the shared resource (a hard disk drive, Drive). There is a single back slash between the name of the shared resource and a folder.

This same convention is also used to refer to networked printers. You assign a name to a networked printer so it can use this convention.

Resource Sharing

The resources on your computer (printers, folders, drives, CD-ROMs) are accessible to other users over your network if you enable file and print sharing through the Network Control Panel or Network Configuration dialog box. This peer-to-peer resource sharing requires that you use Client for Microsoft Networks, Client for NetWare Networks, or both. Other users on your network who want to access your resources must be running the matching client as well as the same network protocol.

It is not necessary that resources found connected to individual computers on the network be shared with others. Network servers may be the only computers that have resources available to other users.

If your network is a peer-to-peer network — one without a server — then individual users are able to access network resources only by sharing resources. Not every computer needs to share its resources, and every computer that does becomes a peer server.

Network Security

As a user, you don't want others — whatever authority they hold over you — messing about with your files and programs. If you are a network administrator, on the other hand, you want to be able to allow others to use resources that are available on the network, no matter whose computer they are connected to. You also want to be able to install software on client computers from your computer. No one wants just anyone calling in from anywhere to be able to download private information from their computer or network.

Network security is maintained by restricting access to network resources, either through the use of passwords or through lists of authorized users. Your computer is quite secure if you:

■ Don't share any resources

■ Don't enable Remote Administration

■ Don't enable the Dial-Up Networking server (found in Microsoft Plus!)

■ Require a logon password to your computer

■ Don't allow others physical access to your computer

When you allow some access to your computer, however, you will need to provide some security measures to restrict who has access.

Windows 95 computers are not completely secure. Even if a password is required to access Windows 95, anyone can boot your computer in Safe mode by pressing F8 at bootup time and making a choice from the menu.

You can disallow the use of F8 by putting the statement BootKeys=0 in your Msdos.sys file.

Choosing between two kinds of security

Windows 95 provides two different kinds of security. The first is *share-level security,* which was also available in Windows for Workgroups 3.1 *x* and other peer-to-peer Microsoft Network-compatible networks. The second is *user-level security,* which requires a Windows NT or NetWare server.

Share-level security is enforced by the use of passwords attached to each shared folder or disk drive, and printer. User-level security is enforced through the use of user lists maintained on a server.

Each Windows 95 computer stores, for that computer, the list of resources and their accompanying passwords or users allowed to access them. The list of users on the network is maintained on the Windows NT or NetWare server.

A network administrator with the remote administration password can set up the list of users and passwords for resources on any of the client Windows 95 computers on the network, as long as they are configured for remote administration.

Share-level security

Armed with a remote administration password for each computer and for each shared resource, a network administrator in a share-level security system (for example, a peer-to-peer Microsoft Network with no Windows NT server) has some administrative control over the computers on the network. It is the peer servers (that is, Windows 95 computers with shared resources), that are accessed by the network administrator.

Share-level security is enforced by a remote administration password for your computer. If someone (an officially designated network administrator or not) has that password, he or she can create, add, or delete shared resources on your computer. Change the remote administration password and he/she loses administrative access until you give them the new password. A network administrator would normally have all the remote administration passwords for all the computers that he/she administers stored in a cached file on his/hers computer.

If your network does not have a Windows NT or NetWare server, the choice is easy — you use share-level security. Share-level security is not available on computers running File and Print Sharing for NetWare.

User-level security

You (and/or the network administrators) have control over which users will have access to your resources. The list of users is kept on your Windows 95 computer.

A network administrator who has been given remote administration authority can grant access to the resources on your computer to other users and administrative access to other system administrators. The names of the users and administrators are kept on the Windows NT or NetWare server.

Administrators who have remote administration authority over your computer can carry out any of the administrative-access actions detailed later in this chapter in the section entitled *Network Administration*. They can edit your Registry, customize your computer's configuration and desktop, edit your password list, and monitor system performance. They can also add or remove other remote administrators.

User-level security is required in order to use the network management tools (other than Net Watcher) that come with Windows 95, and those available from third parties. The tools that come with Windows 95 are described in the *Network Administration* section later in this chapter.

Setting the type of security

It is not a good idea to switch back and forth between these two different kinds of security. Choose one, or follow the guidelines of your network administrator, and stay with it.

STEPS

Setting the Type of Security

Step 1. Double-click the Network icon in the Control Panel. Click the Access Control tab. The Network Access Control Properties sheet is displayed, as shown in Figure 34-10.

(continued)

STEPS *(continued)*

Setting the Type of Security

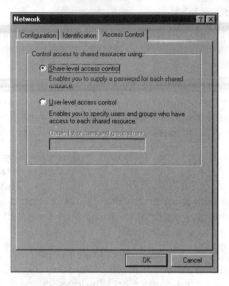

Figure 34-10: The Network Access Control Properties sheet. Choose between share-level and user-level security. If you choose user-level, enter the name of the server that stores the list of users that will have access to your resources.

Step 2.   Click either Share-level access control or User-level access control.

Step 3.   If you choose User-level access control, enter the name of the server that stores the list of users.

Step 4.   Click OK. Restart your computer.

Network Administration

Windows 95 comes with four network management tools: System Policy Editor, Registry Editor, System Monitor, and Net Watcher. Only the Net Watcher can be used on a peer-to-peer network to remotely administer shared resources on a peer server. The other tools require a Windows NT or NetWare server, the designation of user-level security on the computers to be administered, and the installation of Microsoft Remote Registry service on Windows 95 client computers as well as on the network administrator's computer.

Using Net Watcher, a network administrator can:

- Determine which clients are connected to any peer server on the network
- Disconnect any clients from any peer server
- View which resources any peer server is sharing
- Change the share attributes of any resource on a peer server
- Start/stop sharing any peer server resource
- Determine which files are open on a peer server
- Close those open files

Because a network administrator, using Net Watcher, can create, add, or change the properties of a shared resource, he or she can also edit and delete files as well as create new ones on any disk drive on your computer, even on drives that you have specified as read-only. He or she can install new software on your computer while sitting at his/her computer.

Just as you have the ability to determine which disk drives, folders, and printers are shared on your computer, now the network administrator with the remote administration password also has that capability.

Using the System Policy Editor, network administrators can change many of the Registry settings and customize the desktop on remote Windows 95 computers. Of course, the System Policy Editor can also be used locally to customize your Windows 95 computer without having to go through the network.

The Registry Editor can be used locally and remotely to edit other people's Registries. It is covered in detail in Chapter 15. Many of the changes that are made to a computer's Registry are not reflected until that computer is rebooted. Click Registry, Connect Network Registry to connect to a Registry on a remote Windows 95 computer.

The System Monitor can be used both locally and remotely to provide computer performance information.

Enable remote administration

If you have implemented user-level security on your Windows 95 computer as per the steps earlier in this chapter, remote administration is automatically enabled.

To enable remote administration of a Windows 95 computer with share-level security, take the following steps:

STEPS

Configuring Your Computer for Remote Administration

Step 1. Double-click the Passwords icon in the Control Panel. Click the Remote Administration tab. The Remote Administration Properties sheet for Passwords is displayed, as shown in Figure 34-11.

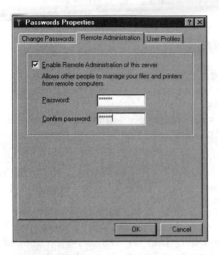

Figure 34-11: The share-level Passwords Remote Administration Properties sheet. Click the check box and type in a password to allow a network administrator to remotely administer your computer.

Step 2. Click Enable Remote Administration of this server.

Step 3. If the computer is configured for share-level security, enter a password.

If, instead, the computer is configured for user-level security, click the Add button and enter the names of the administrators.

Step 4. Click OK.

Install Remote Registry services

If you are going to allow a network administrator to edit your Registry using the System Policy Editor and/or the Registry Editor, or allow him or her to monitor the performance of your computer with System Monitor, you need to install

Microsoft Remote Registry services. Of course, if the administrator has your remote administration password, he or she can take these steps. There is no need to do this (because none of these packages work with share-level security) unless you have enabled user-level security on your computer. To install Remote Registry services, take the following steps:

STEPS

Installing Microsoft Remote Registry Services

Step 1. Double-click the Network icon in the Control Panel. Click the Add button and in the Select Network Component Type dialog box, click Service, and then the Add button.

Step 2. Click Have Disk.

Step 3. Click the Browse button, and browse to the \Admin\Nettools\Remotreg folder on the Windows 95 source CD-ROM. Regsrv.inf will be highlighted. Click OK.

Step 4. Highlight Microsoft Remote Registry and click OK. Restart your computer.

Do this on the network administrator's computer also. There must be a common networking protocol between the administrator's computer and the client computer — and it must be one of the three from Microsoft.

Net Watcher

If you have multiple peer servers on the network, you can run multiple copies of Net Watcher and continuously keep track of them all. All peer servers that have been configured for remote administration can be administered by Net Watcher. You can use Net Watcher to administer your own computer if it is a peer server (that is, if you are running File and Print Sharing for Microsoft or NetWare Networks).

If your computer is using share-level security and File and Print Sharing for Microsoft Networks, you can use Net Watcher to administer only other computers of the same configuration. If your computer is configured for user-level security and File and Print Sharing for Microsoft Networks, you can use Net Watcher to administer other computers running File and Print Sharing for Microsoft Networks irrespective of their security scheme. If you are running File and Print Sharing for NetWare Networks, you can administer only peer servers also running it.

Net Watcher provides three different views of a peer server. The default view is the User view, which displays the user connections to the peer server. The Share view displays the resources that are shared on the server. The Files view displays the files that are open on the server.

Net Watcher can be installed during Windows 95 Setup if you choose Custom Setup and click the Net Watcher check box under Accessories in the Select Components dialog box. You can also install it later using the Add/Remove Programs Control Panel and the Windows Setup tab.

To run Net Watcher after it is installed, click the Start button and descend through the Programs, Accessories, and System Tools menus. When Net Watcher first starts, it is focused on your computer. To administer another peer server, click the Select Server button on the left end of the Net Watcher Toolbar, as shown in Figure 34-12.

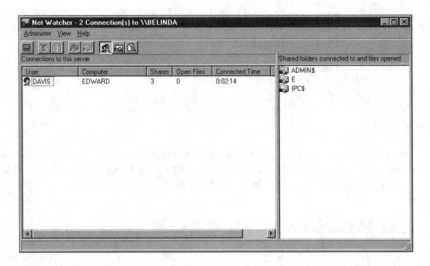

Figure 34-12: The Net Watcher seen by connections in details view.

Disconnecting users from a peer server

To disconnect a user from a peer server, highlight the user and click Disconnect (second button from the left) on the Toolbar in Net Watcher.

Changing or adding sharing on a peer server

You can share resources that aren't currently being shared on a peer server, change the share properties of an existing shared resource, or quit sharing.

STEPS

Changing Sharing on a Peer Server

Step 1.   Click the Show shared folders icon (second from the right) in the Net Watcher Toolbar. Net Watcher is switched to the by Shared folders view. Both shared printers and folders are displayed, as shown in Figure 34-13, despite the name of this view.

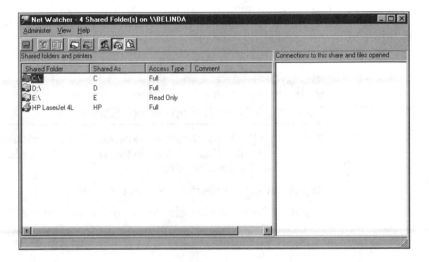

Figure 34-13: Net Watcher in the Shared folders and printers view.

Step 2.   Highlight the name of the resource whose sharing properties you want to modify.

Step 3.   Press Alt+Enter. The Share Properties sheet appears on your desktop. You can quit sharing the resource, change sharing to Full, Read-Only, or Depends on Password, and change the passwords required to access the resources.

If the peer server is using user-level security, you can change the names of the users who can access that resource if you are also using user-level security.

Step 4.   Click OK.

You can also stop sharing a resource by highlighting it in the Shared folder view, and clicking Administer, Stop Sharing Folder on the Net Watcher menu bar.

You can turn the peer server into a shared resource by clicking Administer, Add Shared Folder on the Net Watcher menu bar. Click the Browse button in the Enter path dialog box to display the resources on the peer server.

Tip

If you want to share a folder, click the *disk* icon in the Browse for Folder dialog box that contains the folder, not the *folder* icon that represents the shared disk drive.

Dealing with open files

You can determine which files are open and close them if you need to. You might want to do this if a client computer is hung with an open file on the peer server.

STEPS

Closing an Open File on a Peer Server

Step 1.   In the Net Watcher window, click View, and then Open Files. You can also click the icon in the Toolbar that looks like a manila folder and a magnifying glass.

Step 2.   Click the file that you want to close.

Step 3.   Click Administrator in the menu bar, and then Close File.

Watching a particular peer server

You can set up multiple Net Watcher icons, one for each server.

STEPS

Watching Multiple Peer Servers

Step 1.   In an Explorer window, click Network Neighborhood.

Step 2.   Click Entire Network icon, one of your workgroups, or the icon for the computer that you want to administer.

Step 3.   Right-click the computer icon for the peer server that you want to track with Net Watcher. Click Properties in the right mouse button menu. Click the Tools tab. The Adminstration Tools dialog box, as shown in Figure 34-14, will appear.

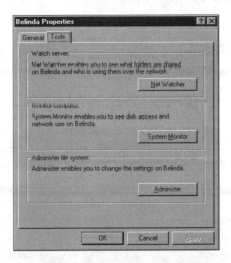

Figure 34-14: The Administration Tools dialog box.

Step 4.   Click the Net Watcher button.

Step 5.   Continue doing this for as many peer servers as you want to track.

You can also browse for a peer server by clicking Administer, Select Server in the Net Watcher menu bar.

System Policy Editor

The System Policy Editor is a friendly front end to a number of user and computer configuration values stored in the Registry. Using it you can, for example, remove users' Settings and Run menu items from the Start button menu; get the Network Neighborhood icon off the desktop; disable the Shut Down menu item; remove a number of Control Panel icons including System, Display, and Network; require validation from a network server for access to the local computer; disable password caching; disable dial-in from Dial-Up Networking; disallow print and/or file sharing; and so on.

You can define system policies for a given user and computer, or for similar groups of users. These policies can be stored on a Windows NT or NetWare server, downloaded at logon time to an individual computer, and used to modify the Registry settings on the fly. If the system policies are on a server, they can be protected from tampering.

You install the System Policy Editor (on your computer or on the network administrator's computer) from the Windows 95 source CD-ROM. Take the following steps:

STEPS

Installing the System Policy Editor

Step 1. Double-click the Add/Remove Programs icon in the Control Panel and then click the Windows Setup tab.

Step 2. Click the Have Disk button and then Browse. Browse to your Windows 95 source CD-ROM and the folder \Admin\Apptools\Poledit.

Step 3. Click the OK button and then the check boxes next to Group policies and System Policy Editor in the Have Disk dialog box. Click the Install button.

Step 4. Click OK.

The System Policy Editor is installed and its shortcut put in the System Tools menu (under Start, Accessories).

To allow the System Policy Editor to create group policies, each client Windows 95 computer needs to have the Grouppol.dll file in its \Windows\System folder. Take the steps above on each client computer, but install just Group policies.

Registry Editor

To edit the Registry resident on another Windows 95 computer, click Registry, Connect Network Registry in the Registry Editor menu bar. You can then browse to find the computer whose Registry you wish to edit. The Registry Editor is dealt with in detail in Chapter 15.

System Monitor

The source files for the System Monitor are not stuck in some obscure folder on the Windows 95 CD-ROM. You do need to click its check box in the Accessories dialog box during Windows 95 Setup if you want it installed (assuming you specified Custom Setup). You can also add it later using the Add/Remove Programs Control Panel and the Windows Setup tab.

You'll find the System monitor in the Start menus, under System Tools from the Accessories menu. To connect System Monitor to another computer (or multiple copies of System Monitor to monitor multiple computers) click File, Connect in the System Monitor menu bar.

Network Applications

Microsoft still supplies network applications that let you do more than just share resources and administer the network. Microsoft Exchange (see Chapter 32) lets you send e-mail (and attachments) to anyone on your network. It is possible to share a fax over a network using Microsoft Exchange.

WinPopup, which can be used to broadcast or send messages and pops up when a job that you have sent to the networked printer is complete, can be installed during Windows 95 Setup. WinChat is found in the \Admin\Other\Chat folder on the Windows 95 source CD-ROM. Hearts and Clipbook (for network sharing of the Clipboard) are also in the \Admin\Other folder.

Summary

▶ We show you how to turn your Windows 95 computer into a networking client or peer server, sharing resources with other computer users on your network.

▶ You can build a great little two-computer network for $60.

▶ Windows 95 will work with your existing 16-bit real-mode network.

▶ Windows 95 comes with 32-bit protected-mode networking client, protocols, and adapter drivers, allowing for a much reduced load on conventional memory.

▶ It is a lot easier to configure pre-plug and play network adapters using built-in Windows 95 hardware detection and the Device Manager.

▶ You can turn Windows 95 computer into a full- or part-time (shared) NetWare file and print server.

▶ You can configure Windows 95 as a protected-mode peer server on either a Microsoft network (with or without a Windows NT server) or a NetWare network.

▶ You can connect to multiple networks simultaneously using different networking protocols.

▶ Windows 95 comes with a raft of network management tools and the ability to interact with third-party network management SNMP tools.

▶ You can configure your computer to allow for remote administration.

▶ You don't have to map networked printers or drives to local logical ports or drive letters in order to access them using the universal naming convention.

Part VI
Windows 95 Shareware

Chapter 35: The Best in Windows Shareware

Chapter 35

The Best in Windows Shareware

Windows 95 Secrets includes a CD-ROM disk containing hundreds of freeware and shareware programs — more software than we have ever been able to feature in previous *Windows Secrets* books. We are pleased to bring you this huge sampling of the best Windows shareware programs.

What Is Shareware?

Shareware refers to "try before you buy" software that is distributed electronically, or on disks, by software authors. You get a trial period to use the software, usually 30 days. After this period, you are required to register with the software author if you continue to use the software. Each program has its own accompanying file that explains how to register. Note that you did not purchase a license to the software when you purchased this book—you purchased the book and an included CD-ROM that contains a number of shareware and freeware programs.With your purchase of the book and CD-ROM, you did *not* purchase a license for individual shareware programs. In essence, your purchase of this book and its included CD-ROM is the same as if you had purchased a trial shareware diskette from a shareware catalog. If you plan to use the shareware after the trial period, you should register those programs with their respective authors.

Shareware is copyrighted software that is owned by the software author. We, the authors of this book, are authorized vendors of the Association of Shareware Professionals (ASP), and have permission from the ASP and from individual shareware authors to distribute their shareware to the public.

The two of us, as co-authors, have registered scores of separate shareware programs over the years, paying whatever registration fees were required. The benefits of registration have far outweighed the small registration fees. The upgraded versions, free additional software, and other offers continually amaze us. Shareware programs are truly the biggest bargain in the software industry today.

What Is Freeware?

Freeware refers to programs that require no registration fee. Some freeware programs are also called *public domain* software. This means that the software author has released the copyright to the program, and anyone may use the software for any purpose. Most freeware, however, is not in the public domain, and you should not assume you can use a freeware program for a commercial purpose (bundling it with retail software, for example) without contacting the software author for permission.

Freeware programs come with no technical support. If certain programs do not work on your system, try other programs on the CD-ROM that will work.

The CD-ROM and Software Are Copyrighted

The software on the CD-ROM is copyrighted by the various shareware authors, and the CD-ROM and its installation routines are copyrighted by the co-authors of this book. You may copy the contents of the CD-ROM to your personal computer system, but you may not distribute or sell the contents of the CD-ROM or bundle it with any product that is for sale without permission from the copyright holders.

Quick Installation Instructions

To install any of the programs on the *Windows 95 Secrets* CD-ROM, follow these instructions:

STEPS

Installing the *Windows 95 Secrets* CD-ROM

Step 1.   Insert the *Windows 95 Secrets* CD-ROM into a CD-ROM drive, such as drive D.

Step 2.   In Windows 95, click the Start button, then Programs, and then click Windows Explorer. In the left-hand Explorer window, select the CD-ROM drive, such as D. In the right-hand Explorer window, double-click the file Setup.exe. This allows you to install any program. You can also print or search the entire database.

Step 3.   Click a button, such as Applications, on the left side of the File Installer window (see Figure 35-1). Then click any button in the Program Category window (shown at lower right).

This step takes you to a list of programs in that category.

Step 4.   Simply click the name of any program, and it begins to install for you automatically. You can cancel the install process before it begins copying files, if you wish.

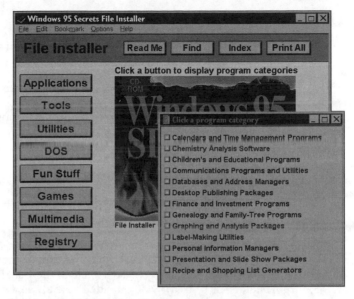

Figure 35-1: The *Windows 95 Secrets* CD-ROM File Installer.

Following are some other features of the File Installer.

- Click the Read Me button for important information about this CD-ROM, including "uninstall" instructions.

- Click Find or Index to perform a full-text search or to see an index of all programs described in the Installer.

- Click Print All to print a complete description of all programs in the Installer to your current printer.

That's it! Be aware that some programs may require that you run a separate setup routine to configure the software after you have installed it. In this case, you should simply run the software once to configure it.

If you are a new Windows user (less than a few month's experience), turn to the end of this chapter and read the section entitled *Tips for New Windows Users* before installing the programs.

How Do I Get Technical Support?

All Windows programs have bugs. This includes all retail Windows software and all shareware featured in *Windows 95 Secrets.* Every program, no matter how simple, has some unexpected behavior. This is the nature of software and is usually fixed with the release of a newer version.

Most shareware authors, but not all, provide technical support to users after they register. Some shareware authors provide limited technical support to unregistered users if they have problems installing the software. In either case, the best way to get technical support is to look in the text file or help file that accompanies each program and send electronic mail to the e-mail address listed there. Some shareware authors also provide technical support by fax or by U.S. mail. Shareware authors do not usually have a technical support telephone line, although some do for registered users.

Many shareware authors list CompuServe addresses for e-mail and technical support purposes. If you do not already have an e-mail account, you can obtain a CompuServe account by calling 800-848-8990 in the U.S., Puerto Rico, and the U.S. Virgin Islands, or 614-457-8650 outside these areas. Or you can write to: CompuServe, Customer Service, P.O. Box 20212, 5000 Arlington Centre Blvd., Columbus, OH 43220.

Once you log on to CompuServe, type **GO MAIL** at any prompt to get to the electronic mail service. At that point, type your message and send it to the CompuServe I.D. number listed in the shareware author's documentation. Most shareware authors check and respond to their electronic messages once or more each business day.

If a program is freeware, it probably has no technical support. In this case, if a program does not work on your particular PC configuration, you probably will not be able to obtain technical support for it.

The co-authors of this book, and IDG Books Worldwide, Inc., are not familiar with the details of every program and do not provide any technical support for the programs on the CD-ROM. The programs are supplied as is. Brian Livingston, Davis Straub, and IDG Books individually and together disclaim all warranties, expressed or implied, including, without limitation, the warranties of merchantability and of fitness for any particular purpose; and assume no liability for damages, direct or consequential, which may result from the use of the programs or reliance on the documentation.

See the *IDG Books Worldwide License Agreement* at the back of the book for a complete description of the uses and limitations of the CD-ROM disc and the programs it contains.

IDG BOOKS WORLDWIDE REGISTRATION CARD

RETURN THIS REGISTRATION CARD FOR FREE CATALOG

Title of this book: Windows 95 SECRETS

My overall rating of this book: ❏ Very good [1] ❏ Good [2] ❏ Satisfactory [3] ❏ Fair [4] ❏ Poor [5]

How I first heard about this book:

❏ Found in bookstore; name: [6]   ❏ Book review: [7]

❏ Advertisement: [8]   ❏ Catalog: [9]

❏ Word of mouth; heard about book from friend, co-worker, etc.: [10]   ❏ Other: [11]

What I liked most about this book:

What I would change, add, delete, etc., in future editions of this book:

Other comments:

Number of computer books I purchase in a year: ❏ 1 [12] ❏ 2-5 [13] ❏ 6-10 [14] ❏ More than 10 [15]

I would characterize my computer skills as: ❏ Beginner [16] ❏ Intermediate [17] ❏ Advanced [18] ❏ Professional [19]

I use ❏ DOS [20] ❏ Windows [21] ❏ OS/2 [22] ❏ Unix [23] ❏ Macintosh [24] ❏ Other: [25]_____
(please specify)

I would be interested in new books on the following subjects:
(please check all that apply, and use the spaces provided to identify specific software)

❏ Word processing: [26]   ❏ Spreadsheets: [27]

❏ Data bases: [28]   ❏ Desktop publishing: [29]

❏ File Utilities: [30]   ❏ Money management: [31]

❏ Networking: [32]   ❏ Programming languages: [33]

❏ Other: [34]

I use a PC at (please check all that apply): ❏ home [35] ❏ work [36] ❏ school [37] ❏ other: [38] _____

The disks I prefer to use are ❏ 5.25 [39] ❏ 3.5 [40] ❏ other: [41]_____

I have a CD ROM: ❏ yes [42] ❏ no [43]

I plan to buy or upgrade computer hardware this year: ❏ yes [44] ❏ no [45]

I plan to buy or upgrade computer software this year: ❏ yes [46] ❏ no [47]

Name: _____ Business title: [48] _____ Type of Business: [49] _____

Address (❏ home [50] ❏ work [51]/Company name: _____)

Street/Suite# _____

City [52]/State [53]/Zipcode [54]: _____ Country [55] _____

❏ **I liked this book!** You may quote me by name in future
IDG Books Worldwide promotional materials.

My daytime phone number is _____

IDG BOOKS

THE WORLD OF
COMPUTER
KNOWLEDGE

 **YES!**
Please keep me informed about IDG's World of Computer Knowledge.
Send me the latest IDG Books catalog.

What Do I Get If I Register?

We strongly encourage you to register any shareware you use past the initial "try before you buy" free evaluation period. Registration brings you a variety of benefits. Each program has its own set of registration benefits, which are described in the accompanying text or help files. Depending on the specific program, you may receive one or more of the following:

■ At the very least, you receive a permanent license to use the program on your PC.

■ In most cases, you receive the capability to upgrade to a future version of the program, with features that may significantly enhance the version you have.

■ In most cases, you are entitled to receive technical support to configure the software for optimum performance on your particular type of PC. This technical support is usually provided by electronic mail, in which case you receive a response directly from the software authors in a matter of hours. In other cases, technical support is also provided by fax, by mail, or by telephone.

■ Sometimes you receive a printed manual with more detail or better illustrations than can be provided in the shareware version. If you register multiple copies for a company installation, you may be able to receive a copy of the printed materials for each of the users in your company.

■ In a few cases, you may receive a diskette that contains "bonus" shareware programs along with the registered version of the program you licensed. Some shareware authors include a whole mini-library of shareware programs along with your registered diskette.

■ In *all* cases, when you register shareware, you help finance the development of new Windows shareware programs. This helps to bring new "killer apps" to the shareware marketplace — which you can, again, try out in advance, like all shareware.

Shareware Registration from Outside the U.S.

Most of the shareware authors in the U.S. require payment "in U.S. funds, drawn on a U.S. bank." The reason for this requirement is that U.S. banks charge large fees — sometimes more than the entire registration fee for a shareware package — to accept non-U.S. checks.

If you wish to register a shareware package with a shareware author who lives in a different country, you can send payment in the form of a Postal International Money Order with a U.S. dollar amount. These money orders are available at most post offices around the world and are accepted without a fee by all U.S. post offices and many U.S. banks. If you are in Europe, do not send Eurochecks to U.S. shareware authors, since Eurochecks are not accepted by U.S. banks.

Why Have Shareware Registration Notices?

All shareware programs have some kind of popup window that lets you know how to contact the author and register the program. Some programs display this window after you click Help About or another menu choice, while others display it automatically when you start or exit the program.

The ASP specifically allows this type of reminder notice. It does not cripple a program in any way, but provides the user with the address of the shareware author and an incentive to register.

We view these incentives like the membership appeals you sometimes hear on listener-supported radio stations. The appeals are slightly annoying, but the stations could not continue to broadcast without the memberships they receive. Similarly, the shareware authors cannot continue to distribute their programs without the registrations they receive. Reminder notices — which disappear totally after you register a package — are a slight irritation but are well justified by the full functionality (no crippling) you get in a true shareware package.

What Is the Association of Shareware Professionals?

As shareware grew into an accepted means of distributing serious software over the last several years, authors of shareware felt a need for a nonprofit organization to promote this new form of distribution. The Association of Shareware Professionals (ASP) was formed in 1987 to "strengthen the future of 'shareware' (user-supported software) as an alternative to software distributed under normal retail marketing methods."

The ASP certifies programs as meeting its criteria for shareware and also sponsors events at computer industry shows. If you are a software author, the ASP may help you find distribution channels for your program. For more information, write the Executive Director, Association of Shareware Professionals, 545 Grover Road, Muskegon, MI 49442-9427, or send a message to 72050.1422@compuserve.com.

The ASP Ombudsman program

To resolve any questions about the role of shareware — registrations, licenses, and so on — the ASP established an ombudsman program to hear all parties.

Not every shareware author represented on the *Windows 95 Secrets* CD-ROM is a member of the ASP, but a good number of shareware authors *are* members. ASP members usually list this fact in the text or help files that accompany their programs.

If you have a problem with a software author who is an ASP member, and you have tried unsuccessfully to resolve the problem directly with that author, the ASP ombudsman may find a remedy. Remember that you cannot expect technical support from the author of a program unless you are a registered user of that program.

As the ASP's literature describes it, "The ASP wants to make sure that the shareware concept works for you. If you are unable to resolve a shareware-related problem with an ASP member by contacting the member directly, the ASP may be able to help. The ASP Ombudsman can help you resolve a dispute or problem with an ASP member, but does not provide technical support for members' products. Please write to the ASP Ombudsman at P.O. Box 5786, Bellevue, WA 98006, or send a CompuServe message to 70007,3536."

General ASP license agreement

Each of the shareware programs on the accompanying disk has its own license agreement and terms. These may be found in a text or help file accompanying each program. In general, you should assume that any shareware program adheres to at least the following license terms suggested by the ASP, where *Program* is the specific shareware program, and *Company* is the program's author or publisher:

The Program is supplied as is. The author disclaims all warranties, expressed or implied, including, without limitation, the warranties of merchantability and of fitness for any purpose. The author assumes no liability for damages, direct or consequential, which may result from the use of the Program.

The Program is a "shareware program," and is provided at no charge to the user for evaluation. Feel free to share it with your friends, but please do not give it away altered or as part of another system. The essence of "user-supported" software is to provide personal computer users with quality software without high prices, and yet to provide incentives for programmers to continue to develop new products. If you find this Program useful, and find that you continue to use the Program after a reasonable trial period, you must make a registration payment to the Company. The registration fee will license one copy for one use on any one computer at any one time. You must treat this software just like a copyrighted book. An example is that this software may be used by any number of people and may be freely moved from one computer location to another, as long as there is no possibility of it being used at one location while it's being used at another — just as a book cannot be read by two different persons at the same time.

Commercial users of the Program must register and pay for their copies of the Program within 30 days of first use or their license is withdrawn. Site-license arrangements may be made by contacting the Company.

Anyone distributing the Program for any kind of remuneration must first contact the Company at the address provided for authorization. This authorization will be automatically granted to distributors recognized by the ASP as adhering to its guidelines for shareware distributors, and such distributors may begin offering the Program immediately. (However, the Company must still be advised so that the distributor can be kept up-to-date with the latest version of the Program.)

You are encouraged to pass a copy of the Program along to your friends for evaluation. Please encourage them to register their copy, if they find that they can use it. All registered users will receive a copy of the latest version of the Program.

Tips For New Windows Users

If you are a relatively new user of Windows or PCs in general, the following tips can help you get the most out of your system.

How to add a program to a new directory or folder

Always install a new program into its own "directory" or "folder." Do not install a program into your Windows directory (such as C:\Windows) unless you are specifically instructed to do so by a program's documentation or installation instructions. Also, do not install a program into the root directory of your C: drive (C:\) or a directory that already contains another program. It would be a bad idea, for example, to create a directory called C:\Games and then install all game programs into that directory. Some files may have the same name, which would cause problems with other programs and would also make it hard to remove a particular program at a later date.

When you run an Install program and you are given a choice of which directory to install the program into, type in a new directory name, such as **C:\Blue** for a program named Blue, or **C:\Red** for a program named Red.

How to add an application to your path

Windows programs do not need to be on the path (a listing of directories Windows will search in for programs) as much as they used to in the early days of Windows. However, if the documentation for a program asks that you "place it on the path," here's how to do it.

In Windows 95, click the Start button on the Taskbar, and then click Run. In the dialog box that appears, type the command **NOTEPAD C:\Autoexec.bat** and click OK. In the Autoexec.bat file, you should see a line that reads like the following:

```
path=c:\win95;c:\win95\command;c:\bat
```

This line indicates that three directories are on the path: the Windows 95 directory, the DOS 7 directory (called Win95\Command), and a directory containing batch files.

To add a directory, add a semicolon (;) to the end of the line, and then type the full name of the directory. To add the directory C:\Calendar, for example, your path statement would look like this:

```
path=c:\win95;c:\win95\command;c:\bat;c:\calendar
```

You must save the file, exit Windows 95, and restart your PC for this change to take effect.

If you are at a plain DOS prompt, you can type **Edit C:\Autoexec.bat** to run a character-based editor to make changes in your Autoexec.bat file.

You must make sure that your path statement does not exceed 127 characters (including the word "path" and the equal sign). The characters after the 127th are ignored as part of the path, but can cause strange behavior. If your path gets too long, you must take some directories out of the path or change their directory names to shorter alternatives.

How to make an application run when you start Windows 95

To make an application load automatically every time you run Windows 95, you must place a "shortcut" for that program into the Startup folder. One way to do this is with the Windows 95 Explorer. Find a copy of the program you want to start up every time. Use your *right* mouse button to drag the program's icon to the C:\Win95\Start Menu\Programs\Startup folder. When you drop the icon on this folder, click Create Shortcut Here on the popup menu that appears. (Do *not* click Copy Here or Move Here, which can create problems running your application.)

The Best Is Yet To Come

On the CD-ROM that accompanies *Windows 95 Secrets,* we have featured some of the best and most popular Windows shareware and freeware available today. Some of the software is specific for Windows 95 (with support for long filenames, for example), while some software is still available only in a Windows 3.1 version (supports only 8-character filenames). We have tried to eliminate Windows 3.1 programs that are not appropriate for Windows 95, such as utilities and shells that work poorly or not at all under Windows 95. Some programs that are buggy under Windows 95 may have slipped through. In almost all cases, shareware authors are preparing upgrades, including Windows 95-specific versions or improvements that will take better advantage of Windows 95 features.

These upgraded programs will become available several months to a year after the release of *Windows 95 Secrets.* The way to find out about these upgrades is to contact the shareware authors at their e-mail addresses or, even better, register the programs you like and encourage the authors to invest in the development of even more powerful Windows 95 versions of their products.

We hope you enjoy using the programs on the *Windows 95 Secrets* CD-ROM.

Index

F

G

V

W

X

Y

Z

IDG BOOKS WORLDWIDE
LICENSE AGREEMENT

disc. IDG's entire liability and your exclusive remedy shall be limited to replacement of the Software, which is returned to IDG with a copy of your receipt. This Limited Warranty is void if failure of the Software has resulted from accident, abuse, or misapplication. Any replacement Software will be warranted for the remainder of the original warranty period or thirty (30) days, whichever is longer.

5. No Other Warranties. To the maximum extent permitted by applicable law, IDG and the authors disclaim all other warranties, express or implied, including but not limited to implied warranties of merchantability and fitness for a particular purpose, with respect to the Software, the programs, the source code contained therein and/or the techniques described in this Book. This limited warranty gives you specific legal rights. You may have others which vary from state/jurisdiction to state/jurisdiction.

6. No Liability For Consequential Damages. To the extent permitted by applicable law, in no event shall IDG or the authors be liable for any damages whatsoever (including without limitation, damages for loss of business profits, business interruption, loss of business information, or any other pecuniary loss) arising out of the use of or inability to use the Book or the Software, even if IDG has been advised of the possibility of such damages. Because some states/jurisdictions do not allow the exclusion or limitation of liability for consequential or incidental damages, the above limitation may not apply to you.

7. U.S.Government Restricted Rights. Use, duplication, or disclosure of the Software by the U.S. Government is subject to restrictions stated in paragraph (c) (1) (ii) of the Rights in Technical Data and Computer Software clause of DFARS 252.227-7013, and in subparagraphs (a) through (d) of the Commercial Computer—Restricted Rights clause at FAR 52.227-19, and in similar clauses in the NASA FAR supplement, when applicable.

Windows 95 Secrets CD-ROM
Complete Installation Instructions

Step 1. Insert the *Windows 95 Secrets CD-ROM* into a CD-ROM drive, such as drive D.

Step 2. In Windows 95, click the Start button, then Programs, and then Windows Explorer. In the left-hand Explorer window, select the CD-ROM drive, such as D. In the right-hand Explorer window, double-click the file Setup.exe. This allows you to install any program. You can also print or search the entire database.

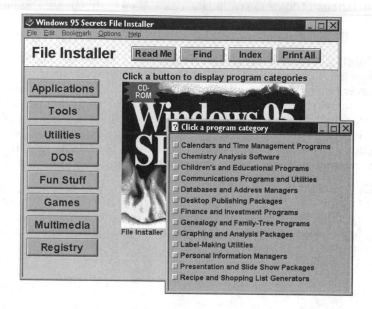

Step 3. Click a button, such as Applications, on the left side of the File Installer window. Then click any button in the Program Category window (shown at lower right).

This step takes you to a list of programs in that category. Simply click the name of any program, and it begins to install for you automatically. You can cancel the install process before it begins copying files, if you wish.

Click the Read Me button for important information about this CD-ROM, including "uninstall" instructions.

Click Find or Index to perform a full-text search or see an index of all programs described in the Installer.

Click Print All to print a complete description of all programs in the Installer to your current printer.

Over 120 MB of the best freeware and shareware.

We hope you enjoy the *Windows 95 Secrets CD-ROM*!

Brian Livingston and Davis Straub